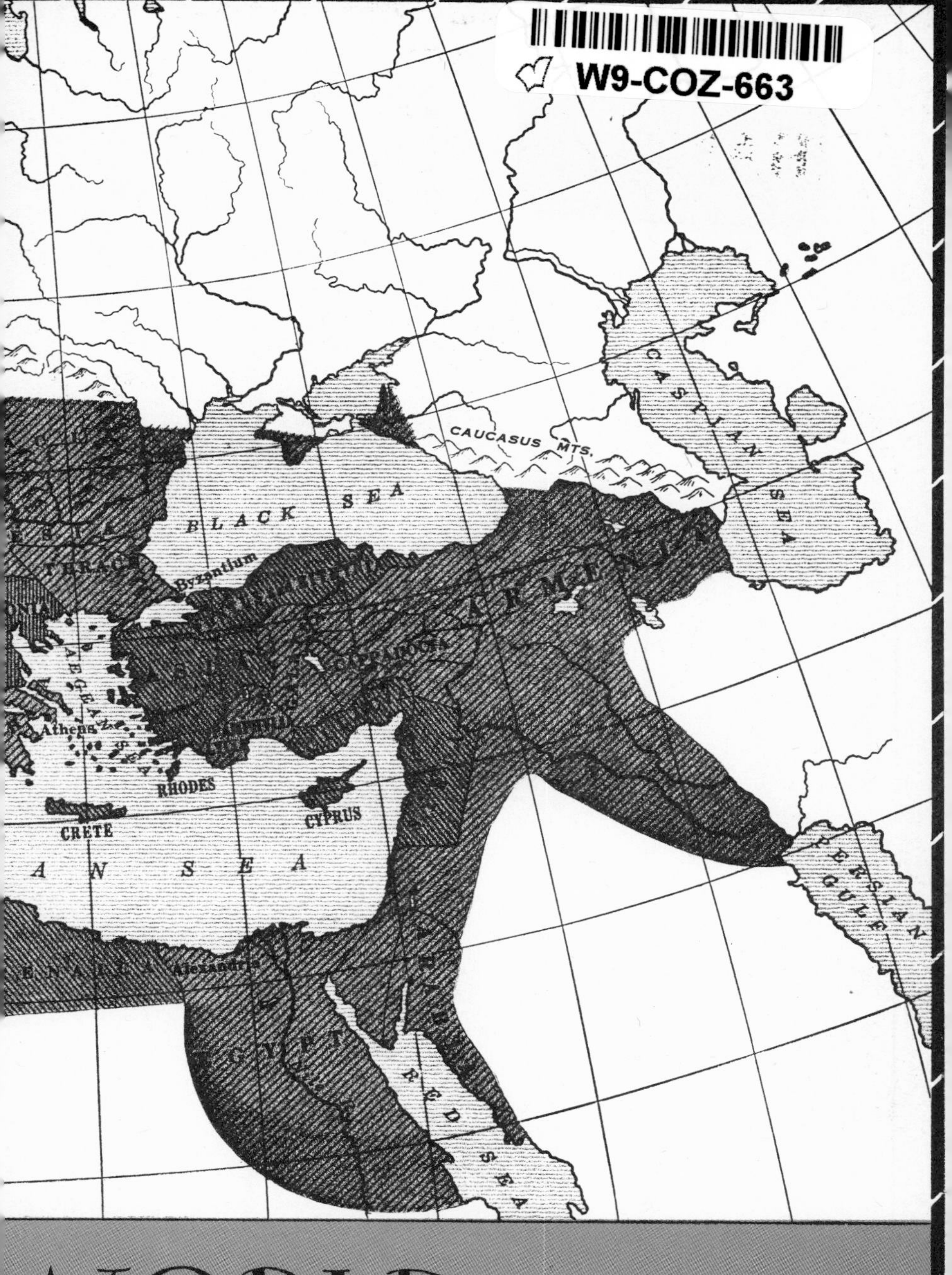


WORLD *about 117 A.D.*

VOLUME TWO

# THE HELLENISTIC WORLD AND ROME TO THE DISSOLUTION OF THE WESTERN EMPIRE

*Under the Editorship of*
WILLIAM SCOTT FERGUSON
AND THOMAS A. BRADY

# *A Political and Cultural*

# ANCIENT

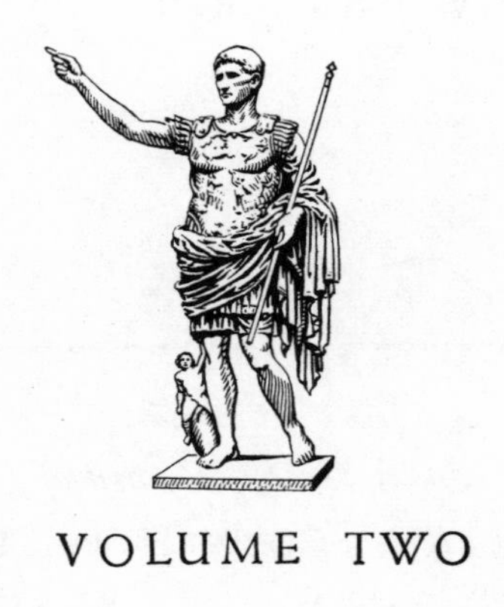

VOLUME TWO

# *History of the* WORLD

## *From Prehistoric Times to the Dissolution of the Roman Empire in the West* ❖ ❖

C. E. VAN SICKLE
ASSOCIATE PROFESSOR OF HISTORY
OHIO WESLEYAN UNIVERSITY

GREENWOOD PRESS, PUBLISHERS
WESTPORT, CONNECTICUT

Reprinted by permission
of Houghton Mifflin Co.

First Greenwood Reprinting 1970

SBN 8371-2961-3 (SET)
SBN 8371-2960-5 (VOL. 2)

PRINTED IN UNITED STATES OF AMERICA

TO PRESCOTT WINSON TOWNSEND

*Who first awakened in the author of this book an abiding interest in the history and cultures of the ancient world*

# EDITOR'S INTRODUCTION

THE SECOND VOLUME of Doctor Van Sickle's book *A Political and Cultural History of the Ancient World*, begins with early Rome and ends with the triumph of the Church and the barbarian invasions in the West. It thus covers the standard material treated in our courses in Roman History and in the second half of courses in Ancient History. As in the first volume, the division of material into chapters is made on a basis that insures the ease and convenience of the teacher in the assignment of reading.

Any good textbook of Roman History today must deal wisely and critically with the vexed problem of the sources for early Roman History. This task is accomplished succinctly and adequately in this volume. The treatment of constitutional problems is full and, on the whole, conservative and traditional. Throughout the early chapters, the author, by clear and concise explanation, makes the student feel at home in this maze of disputed problems and conflicting explanations.

I wish to call attention to three features which are expected today, I believe, in an up-to-date treatment of this period. In the first place, the significance of the Etruscans in Roman History must be made clear. Some authors would emphasize the rôle of the Etruscans more than others, but I think we all agree that their influence on early Roman institutions was very pronounced. The Etruscan archaeological material is here brought together with a critical evaluation of tradition and legend. Doctor Van Sickle's interpretation of the rôle of the Etruscans in shaping Rome's institutional organization is convincing and intelligible to the student.

Another feature of this book which is in line with the best modern practice is the consideration of the Hellenistic Monarchies and their culture as a part of Roman History, closely linked with Rome's expansion in the East. From the early third century on, the history of the Mediterranean world is treated as one large, interlocking international system. Thus the cultural integration which Rome gave to the Mediterranean world is explained and referred to repeatedly as a frame of reference in which, alone, later events in Rome's history can adequately be explained.

Again, we find considerable attention given here to the social and economic aspects of the Roman Empire, although the political and constitutional history is not neglected. Throughout the entire work, in fact, special chapters deal with these aspects and additional chapters summarize the cultural developments of each period. The latter, of course, have long been regarded as significant in their influence.

One further word. As H. G. Wells once pointed out, one cannot write Rome's history without giving great attention to war as an important agent of causation in human history. The author of this work has done full justice to the importance of military history without giving it undue stress as one might easily do in writing a history of Rome.

The student will find incorporated here the important critical studies and scientific research of modern scholarship, presented with the clarity and human interest which characterized the first volume.

THOMAS A. BRADY
*Vice President in Charge of*
*Extra Divisional Educational Activities*
*University of Missouri*

# PREFACE

THE BEGINNING of the second volume of this history would seem to be a convenient point at which to present the reasons that led the author to divide the subject between the two volumes as he did. Since each volume is designed to serve as a textbook for a college survey course in which classes will meet approximately fifty-five times, it is desirable to divide the treatment of ancient history, as nearly as possible, evenly between the texts which will serve these courses. However, in making the division, the material must be arranged so that the story can be told clearly and logically. The division point between these volumes represents the judgment of the present writer as to how the task should be performed. In his first volume he has treated prehistoric man, the ancient Oriental peoples, and the Greeks to the break-up of Alexander's Empire, and in the second, the Hellenistic States and Rome to the dissolution of the Western Empire.

There seems to be a general agreement among teachers and authors of textbooks that Greek and Roman history should each be studied as a complete and uninterrupted sequence. Apparently, for this reason, it has been customary to continue textbooks dealing with Greek history, through the Hellenistic Age to the Roman conquest of the Greek Peninsula. This custom, however, is open to serious objections. To treat the Hellenistic Age as a mere appendage to Classical Greek history is to distort historical perspective in several ways. Too often, coming as it does at the end of a course for which the instructor feels that he has insufficient time, it is either omitted entirely or hurriedly summed up in one or two hours of lecture or discussion. Even if sufficient attention is given to it, the student who has just learned to admire the institutions and cultural achievements of the Classical Greeks finds it impossible to readjust his viewpoint so as to look objectively at societies living under absolute monarchies as dominant castes in the midst of servile alien populations. The Hellenistic Age occupies an important place in the cultural history of mankind, and should receive the kind of attention which will fix this fact in the mind of the student. We must remember that it produced scientists who discovered the circulation of the blood, framed the heliocentric theory of planetary motion, systematized the study of mathematics, and made important discoveries in physics. In geographical exploration it achieved more than any other age prior to the fifteenth and sixteenth centuries A.D., and in philosophy it produced work which has been of lasting value to mankind. Its relative importance in human history can, the present writer believes, be better portrayed by describing its polished urban life and brilliant achievements in connection with the world to which it was contemporary, than by studying it in connection with the culture of Classical Greece. Moreover, it was this Hellenistic culture, and not that of Classical Greece, with which the Romans came into contact when they emerged from isolation to play a part in Mediterranean politics, and from it they derived the stimuli which were so influential in the molding of their subsequent cultural activities. For these reasons, the three chapters dealing with Hellenistic civilization have been placed in the second volume rather than in the first. Yet this brilliant culture belongs to the third and second centuries B.C., and at that time, the Romans already possessed a long history. To clear the record up to the time when Rome and the Hellenistic peoples began to have close contacts, the opening chapters of the second volume have been devoted to a study of prehistoric Italy, the origin of Rome, and her early history and civilization. Only in Chapter 8 do we resume the study of the states which arose from the ruins of the empire of Alexander the Great, which we left at the close of Volume I.

After devoting Chapters 8 to 10, inclusive, to the study of the Hellenistic world and the barbarian background of ancient civilization, we return to the study of Rome's conquest of the Mediterranean world. Chapters 11 to 13 tell the story of the conquest, Chapters 15 to 17 trace the decline of the Republic, Chapter 19 describes the Principate of Augustus, Chapters 21 to 23 carry us through the events of the period between the death of Augustus and the accession of Diocletian, while Chapters 26 to 27 continue the record to the dissolution of the Western Roman Empire and the partial regeneration of the Eastern Empire. Chapters 6 to 7, 14, 18, 20, 24 to 25, and 28 treat various phases of Roman civilization.

As in Volume I, the story told in the pages which follow is based upon all the available sources, interpretations gleaned from secondary works, and the author's own conclusions. Controversial judgments have been avoided wherever possible, but in a few instances he has included his own personal opinions, which have been previously stated and explained in articles published in learned journals of the United States, Great Britain, and Belgium. Instructors who do not agree with these theories are always at liberty to present divergent views.

A problem which always faces writers on Roman history is that of treating the causes of the decline of the Western Roman Empire and the disappearance of the ancient classical civilization. Many hypotheses, varying from the temperate and well-reasoned to the bizarre and doctrinaire, have been presented to account for these phenomena. No one can doubt that the problem is a fascinating one, and that in the present disordered state of the world, the attention given to it is very timely. But the author of a textbook must confine himself as nearly as possible to accepted facts, and the very multiplicity of the theories presented on this subject by thoughtful and reputable scholars proves that we are not much nearer to a definite solution of the problem than the scholars of the nineteenth century were. If anything, our greater knowledge of the human mind and the laws which govern individual and group activities has served to deepen the mystery rather than to dispel it. We can describe phenomena, but in historical as in physical science, ultimate causes continue to elude us. It is better to confine one's self to a statement of known facts and of finite causation where its presence can be proved, and to await the time when greater knowledge will enable the historians of the future to speak with certainty on the riddle which still baffles us. Hence the subject has been avoided in this volume, except in so far as the facts speak for themselves, and from them every reader is at liberty to draw his own conclusions.

C. E. Van Sickle

# CONTENTS

# ILLUSTRATIONS

# MAPS

# I

**************************************************************************************************

# *The Sources for the Study of Early Roman History*

## Archeology and Oral Tradition

For over five centuries after the traditional date of the founding of Rome in 753 B.C., we have no record of any attempt on the part of her people to write her history in literary form. This fact is not surprising, for even the Greeks did not begin to use writing extensively until the middle of the seventh century B.C., and their oldest surviving history was not written until two centuries later. In the latter part of the fifth century and throughout the fourth when Herodotus, Thucydides, and other Greek historians were recording their country's history in matchless prose, the Romans and their Italian neighbors were still without connected literary accounts of their past, and it was not until the last half of the third century B.C. that Fabius Pictor, the oldest known Roman historian, attempted to tell the story of Rome's origin and growth.

The scarcity of conventional historical records of primitive Rome is not relieved by the existence of any great national epic poetry comparable to that of Homer, in which early legends could be preserved. Extant traditions may tell us a few garbled facts from the eighth century, and furnish somewhat more copious and reliable information for the seventh and sixth, but such evidence, recorded only after long oral circulation, is at best uncertain. Thus the early history of Rome and her Italian neighbors has to be gleaned largely from archeological sources. The limitations of such evidence are many and baffling, but the historian must always be willing to admit ignorance when it exists.

### *Roman Tradition and Its Historical Value*

To the later Romans, of course, the problem of their country's origin seemed much simpler than it does to us. They had an elaborate body of traditions which carried the story of Rome and Latium back to the Trojan War (twelfth century B.C.), and traced the pedigrees of their principal families from the fugitive Trojan prince Aeneas and his followers. These traditions described with minute detail the founding of Rome by *Romulus*, and gave a fairly full account of her subsequent history under a series of kings prior to the foundation of the Republic. But such stories do not stand the test of criticism. Although they contain some facts which modern historians have carefully sifted out, the amount which can be used is small. The deeper we delve into the Roman past, the smaller the proportion of truth and the larger that of fiction which we encounter. Many of these traditions are not genuine folk-memories at all, but transparent literary devices invented by writers who either had not the courage to admit their ignorance of the past, or wished to gratify family pride and patriotism with fictitious stories of heroic ancestors. Age-old wonder tales, such as that of the she-wolf which suckled Romulus and Remus, were borrowed from Greek writers and given a local setting. Other stories were invented out of whole cloth to account for the existence of monuments, holidays, and customs whose real histories had been forgotten. Obviously, as some of the more educated and sceptical Romans clearly saw, such stories were unreliable, but since the general public accepted them, they continued to find their way into the works of Roman historians until the end of the ancient world.

## Written Sources

### *Early Records*

Probably about 500 B.C. the Romans began to keep some written records, but for a long time they were quite meager. Occasional inscriptions commemorated important events or acts of government, while laws, such as the famous *Twelve Tables*, preserved data on social and economic conditions. The *pontifex maximus*, who was the titular head of all the Roman priesthoods, began to record each year the chief events and the names of the magistrates on boards which he fastened to the walls of his residence for public inspection. These *annales pontificum* were kept until 121 B.C., when the prevalence of private historiography made it unnecessary to continue them longer. At that time the existing records were put together to form a connected Roman chronicle, the *Annales Maximi* or "Greatest of Chronicles," in eighty books. This work has perished, and we can only judge its character by the use later historians made of it. Its chronological scope is not known with certainty. In 387 B.C. the Gauls occupied the city of Rome except the Capitoline Hill, and most of the area in their possession was reduced to ashes. Some later Roman writers state that all the pontifical records in existence at the time of this catastrophe were destroyed, but of this we cannot be entirely certain. The same uncertainty rests upon the *fasti*, or lists of priests and magistrates, of which the pontiffs were also the custodians. If the records were destroyed by the Gauls, then our knowledge of the earlier history of Rome rests only upon official traditions which are not very reliable for the fifth century B.C., and which are quite nebulous for any time prior to that.

Family traditions were carefully preserved among the Romans and were at an early date reduced to writing, but they help us less than might be expected. Every family of high rank preserved, it is true, wax death-masks of its male ancestors, and with each one a *titulus* or biographical sketch recounting the honors and offices held by the deceased. Funeral orations, which contained similar data, were also often written down and preserved. If authentic, these records would have been of great value to the historian, but even the Roman historians doubted their authenticity, although they used them. Family pride and other influences often led to such reckless falsification as to render the documents almost worthless, and where their influence can be detected in a Roman historical narrative, the facts must always be checked with extreme care. Like the *Annales Maximi*, these family records have long since perished, and our knowledge of them depends upon statements in the works of writers who used them.

### *Sources for Social, Economic, and Cultural History*

For social, economic, and intellectual history our footing is much more certain. In this field we are aided by the tremendous conservatism of the Romans, especially in religious matters, which made them extremely tenacious of old customs, institutions, and religious rites. Thus the rules governing the lives of the pontiffs, vestal virgins, and other priests and priestesses often clearly reflect the customs prevalent among all the Roman people at the time when these priesthoods were instituted. The rule that no iron implement might be used in repairing the *Pons Sublicius* (the oldest bridge across the Tiber River) points to its origin in the Bronze Age, and the use of a cake made of spelt (a grain not used for human food in historic times) at weddings reminds us that at one time it had probably been the ordinary bread-stuff. As previously indicated, the *Laws of the Twelve Tables* are a mine of information on Roman customs in the fifth century B.C., and their antique Latin allows us to trace the evolution of the language. Etruscan influence upon Roman civilization — which the Romans never denied — can be deduced from the similarity of manners and customs between the two peoples.[1] When all has been said, enough material is available to enable us to draw a far more reliable picture of early Roman civilization than of the first three centuries of Roman political history.

*Early Roman Literary Sources; Greek Historians*

Lastly, if we are to evaluate correctly the existing literary sources which tell the story of Rome's early development, we must remember that they were not the first of their kind. Every one of them is based wholly or in part upon older chronicles or histories now lost. The work of Fabius Pictor, who wrote in the third century B.C., has been mentioned. Like several other Roman historians of the same period, he wrote his country's history in Greek. Ennius, a native of southern Italy who had fought in the Roman armies during the Second Punic War (218–201 B.C.), wrote in Latin a long epic poem in which he described the struggle. A little later Cato the Censor, himself a prominent actor upon the stage of Roman history, composed a dry but on the whole reliable history of Rome from the earliest times to his own day. A later school of rhetorical historians, who aimed at striking literary effects rather than accuracy, told the same story in a more interesting but less dependable manner. The outstanding member of this school was the notorious Valerius Antias (late second century B.C.) whose faults of omission, commission, and distortion rendered his work quite untrustworthy. Still a third type of historical writing, practiced by the Romans of the second and first centuries B.C., is typified by the *Roman Antiquities* of Marcus Terentius Varro, a contemporary of Julius Caesar. This was merely an interesting collection of facts and alleged facts about men and gods, gathered uncritically from all sources, with little effort at arrangement or organization.

Meanwhile, the Greeks had been inspired by the growing importance of

[1] Anthropologists aid us in this field by gathering data on the customs of present-day peoples in a state of civilization analogous to that of the early Romans, but their findings must be used with caution. Differences of racial temperament, physical environment, and other pertinent matters often render such parallels treacherous and misleading.

Rome to write their own version of her early history. Not long after 400 B.C. one of them, whose identity is not certain, originated the story that Rome had been founded by fugitives from Troy. As time went on, the Greeks took an ever increasing interest in the affairs of the great Italian city, especially after 264 when she began to dispute with Carthage the mastery of Sicily. Thus Polybius, one of the greatest historians whom the Greeks ever produced, wrote the history of Rome's wars with Carthage and of her contacts with the Greeks down to 146 B.C. While much that the earlier Greek historians wrote about Roman affairs has been lost, we do have a large section of the work of Polybius. Some fragments also of the lost portion of his history, together with excerpts from the works of other Hellenistic writers, have been preserved in miscellaneous collections pieced together by later editors. The most important of these historical scrapbooks now extant is that made by Diodorus of Sicily.

*Livy: His Sources and Historical Method*

From the foregoing discussion it is evident that the oldest history of early Rome now extant — that of Titus Livius (Livy, 59 B.C. to A.D. 17) — had behind it a long tradition which largely determined its character. As a stylist, Livy has had few equals in any age, but he was not a scientific historian. In addition to such sources as the *Annales Maximi* and the *Fasti Consulares*, he had at his disposal many secondary histories of varying value, some in Greek and others in Latin. He consulted but one inscription during all the years spent in collecting material for his work, and probably seldom employed a source of any kind to clarify a point covered by a secondary work, whether good or bad. Nor did he have the objectivity and love of truth for its own sake which the modern world has been led to expect of a historian. He was not entirely credulous, for he sometimes expressed a mild distrust for the extravagant statements and fantastic traditions which he encountered in his researches, but he never went so far as to repudiate them completely. His Roman patriotism and his desire to impress his readers with stories of noble and heroic deeds often betrayed him into unconscious distortions of fact. These failings are especially prominent in his account of Roman history in the eighth, seventh, and sixth centuries. For the fifth century, since he had more copious and reliable materials at his disposal, he probably told a much more accurate story; and with the opening of the fourth century he begins to place his readers upon reasonably firm ground. The parts of his history which deal with the third and second centuries need not concern us here. So great was the popularity of his work that it set the standard for later histories of Rome's infancy, and those traditions which varied from it were relegated to obscurity or lost.

*Summary*

In short, our knowledge of early Roman history becomes progressively more scanty and inaccurate as we attempt to trace it back through the fifth, sixth, seventh, and eighth centuries B.C., except where archeology comes to our aid. This statement does not warrant a wholesale rejection of the literary tradition represented by Livy's works, but it means that we must realize the limitations of this tradition and the many errors which it contains. For early Roman cultural history we must rely upon the vestigial remnants of an earlier age which lingered in later Roman institutions, supplemented by archeological evidence.

# 2

# *Italy and Her Early Inhabitants*

## The Country

To Italy belongs the unique distinction of having been the cradle of the Roman people — probably the most successful group of conquerors and rulers in the history of the world. As the geographical environment of a people is always a potent factor in shaping its destiny, we may well begin our study of the history of the Romans with a brief survey of their country.

### *Location and Physical Characteristics*

Somewhat west of the halfway point between the Straits of Gibraltar and the coast of Syria, the Mediterranean narrows to a width of less than a hundred miles, being bounded by the coast of Tunis on the southwest, and by Sicily on the northeast. Across the narrow sea are scattered the islands of Malta, Pantelleria, and Lampedousa, like the ruins of a broken bridge. In prehistoric times such a land bridge actually existed and connected Africa with Europe; but before the dawn of history, geological convulsions had caused the southern portion of it to sink below sea level, and the Mediterranean coasts and islands had assumed substantially their present form. Even so, these island stepping stones make the passage between Africa and Sicily practicable for small and primitive craft. Between Sicily and Italy, the Straits of Messina are at one point only two miles wide. Hence the course of the prehistoric land bridge has always been a relatively easy route for human migration. As it cuts across the Mediterranean sea route from east to west, Sicily is aptly said to lie at the "Cross roads of the Mediterranean World." Italy, which formed the northern part of the land bridge, is still connected with the European continent, and is in easy communication with the countries to the north of her, while the Straits of

Otranto, which separate her from the Balkan peninsula on the southeast, are but fifty miles wide and easily passable. These facts are of primary importance in Italian history, for in both ancient and modern times they have exposed the peninsula to invasion and cultural penetration from all three directions.

The Italian peninsula joins the European continent at about 44° north latitude and extends from thence in a southeasterly direction for some 600 miles to about 38°. Its width varies from 80 to 125 miles. It is, as everyone knows, shaped like a boot, the "heel" being in ancient times known as Calabria, and the "toe" as Bruttium.[1] Its total area is slightly less than 60,000 square miles.

### *Surface and Coastline*

The most striking physical features of the Italian peninsula are the Apennine Mountains. Separating from the Alps in the extreme northwest, they extend eastward and then southeastward, forming a rough dividing line between the lands of the peninsula and those of the Po Valley. Farther south they lie close to the Adriatic coast which, like most mountainous districts, has always been poor and backward, and has had little influence upon the course of Italian history. In the southern part of the peninsula they swing toward the southwest, pass through the "toe," cross the Straits of Messina, and reappear in the mountains of Sicily. In a few places they attain an altitude of nearly 10,000 feet, and their highest summits are covered with snow until July in an average summer. A low and broken offshoot extends to the southeast, forming the "heel" of the peninsula, and other spurs project westward nearly to the coast of the Tyrrhenian Sea. Thus, except in the northeast and at one spot along the southeastern coast (the plain of Apulia), the most attractive lands of Italy are found between the western coast and the base of the Apennines, and it is here that the economic, political, and cultural life have usually reached their highest levels.

Along the west coast, between the tumbled masses of hills which form the western projections from the central ridge, spread several fairly extensive and fertile plains — Etruria (Tuscany), Latium, and Campania. The first of these lies between the Tiber and the Arno Rivers. Latium is situated to the south of Etruria, between the Tiber and the Liris, and still farther south, along the Bay of Naples, is Campania. The rivers men-

[1] By a curious reversal, the name of Calabria came in medieval times to be applied to the "toe," while the "heel" was called Apulia. These names are still in use.

*Sawders-Combine*

LANDSCAPE OF EASTERN ETRURIA

tioned above are the largest in peninsular Italy, but none of them are navigable for any great distance, even for small boats. The whole western coast of Italy is geologically active — subject to earthquakes and sprinkled with extinct or quiescent volcanoes. Mt. Vesuvius on the Bay of Naples and Mt. Etna in Sicily are now the only active craters in this immediate region except those in the Lipari Islands. Much of western Italy is underlaid with igneous rock, and some of its most productive soil is composed of weathered volcanic ash. The lowlands of Etruria and Latium have poor natural drainage, and when neglected become pestilence-ridden swamps, like the Pontine Marshes or the Tuscan *Maremma*. In Campania the fertile soil and mild climate combine to produce one of the richest farming districts in the world.

Nature does not encourage seafaring habits among the people of peninsular Italy. The Adriatic coast has no good harbors except Bari and Brindisi at the southeast corner, and the coast of the Ionian Sea has only the Bay of Tarentum. On the western coast the Bay of Naples furnishes several safe and commodious ports, but Latium and Etruria have, for the most part, only shelving beaches on which the shallow draft vessels of the ancient Mediterranean sailor might be drawn up. Even artificial harbors have always been maintained with difficulty, for the Mediterranean is almost tideless, and the silt brought down by the streams is deposited close to shore instead of being carried out into deep water, as in the oceans. Except in the direction of Sicily, there are no continuous island chains, like those of the Aegean world, to tempt primitive man to try his skill as a sailor, and the land is rich enough to make this almost unnecessary. Hence the ancient Italians were a race of landsmen, except when foreign immigrants, like the Greeks or Etruscans, brought with them nautical skills acquired in other environments. After the earlier centuries of the Greek colonization movement, contacts with foreigners were almost always made in the north or on the western coast, whence the saying, "Italy turns her back upon Greece and the East."

### *Climate and Resources*

Except in the mountains, the climate of peninsular Italy is that of the warm Temperate Zone. Winter temperatures do not sink below 20° Fahrenheit, and seldom fall even that low. Snow does not often fall, and soon melts. Winter is the rainy season, and the summers are dry. Rain rarely falls between May and September, and, especially in southern Italy, irrigation is often necessary to ripen the crops. Summer temperatures are frequently oppressively high, and the blazing noonday heat lends to the phrase "Sunny Italy" a meaning which is not always favorable.

In ancient times the land was covered with thick forests of oak, pine, fir, and beech, which reckless lumbering and too-close pasturage by sheep and goats have since largely destroyed. Both then and now, the climate and soil have been propitious for the farmer and the herdsman. The fruits of the Temperate Zone, including the vine and the olive, flourish, while wheat, millet, spelt, barley, and garden vegetables yield well. Animal husbandry has always been easy and profitable in a land where livestock can be pastured all winter, and cattle, sheep, goats, pigs, and donkeys thrive. The ox is the common draft animal. Horses, introduced into the country by northern invaders, have never been used for heavy work, but draw carriages or serve as mounts for wealthy men.

Herding is subject by nature to strict conditions, which have played an important part in Italian history. In winter the coastal plains, wet with seasonal rains, produce plenty of grass, while the mountains are covered with snow. In summer the drought dries up the grass of the plains, while the mountains afford good pasture. Each autumn the herdsman will if possible drive his charges from the mountain pastures to the plains, and each summer he will return to the moist mountain pastures. Therefore a class of nomadic herdsmen has always existed. At first the whole population lived primarily by stockraising, and the passage of the flocks and herds through the land occasioned little or no inconvenience. Later, when the men of the plains took up agriculture, their efforts to protect their crops from damage were an important factor in the beginning of the bitter and prolonged struggle between mountaineers and plainsmen which was only decided when Rome subjected both groups to her suzerainty.

In mineral resources Italy is but little better off than Greece. Building stone of various kinds is plentiful — tufa, travertine, limestone, sandstone, and in a few places marble. There is plenty of clay suitable for brick and pottery. But in metals Italy has always been poor. From early times Etruria produced some copper, and enough tin to supply a flourishing small-scale bronze industry. Iron occurs both there and in the island of Elba, with small deposits elsewhere in the peninsula. Silver is not found anywhere in Italy, and gold was obtained in ancient times only on the north side of the Po Valley, outside the peninsula.

The Po Valley and the Venetian plain, though not part of the Italian peninsula, are joined to it by bonds so close that the whole region is frequently termed "Continental Italy." This district is about 320 miles long from east to west, and about 90 miles wide from the Apennines to the Alps. Its heart is the triangular alluvial plain drained by the Po, which in prehistoric times was a vast expanse of forest and swamp. When reclaimed by the hand of man its soil has been phenomenally rich, and today this district is the most progressive part of Italy. The climate is colder than that of the peninsula, with four distinct seasons as in central Europe, and winter temperatures which fall as low as 5° F. above zero.

*The Influence of Italian Geography on History*

The western, northern, and eastern boundaries of continental Italy are formed by the various ranges of the Alps mountains. They are highest on the western and northern sides, and lowest on the eastern side. The highest peaks have altitudes of nearly 16,000 feet, and at first glance it would appear that they form an effective barrier between Italy and the lands to the north of her. Such ~~has never~~ been the case. A number of easy passes exist, of which the most famous, the Brenner Pass, is only 4500 feet high. Thus passage from Gaul, the Danube Valley, and the Balkan peninsula

*Sawders-Combine*

LANDSCAPE OF THE ITALIAN ALPS

into the Po Valley has never been insuperably difficult, and once there, the immigrant or invader can easily cross the Apennines into the peninsula. Throughout the ages, in peace and in war, a stream of northerners has been flowing southward across the mountains, bringing new blood and customs into the land.

But in spite of a multitude of invasions and conquests by outsiders, Italy shapes the destinies of her children with a sure hand, largely in disregard of conquerors and statesmen. She has made them farmers and herdsmen by inclination, rather than manufacturers, merchants, or sailors. Except in the Apennines, there were no serious handicaps to communication between districts such as existed in Greece. Political union was therefore not impossible of attainment, as in the sister-peninsula. The age-old feud between the mountaineers and their brethren of the plains helped the

Romans to weld the latter together into a strong federation for self-defense, and once such a union was achieved, the mountaineers themselves soon had to submit to it. Thus ancient Italy gained by her own efforts a political unity which in Greece was brought about only by an alien conqueror.

The islands near Italy did not, in the early historic period, greatly influence her destiny. Sicily (area about 10,000 square miles) formed part of the route over which some of the earlier Italians crossed from Africa, but in later ages the relationship between the Sicilian and Italian cultures was not very close. In the third century B.C., its presence at the very door of Italy, and the necessity of controlling it, tempted the Romans to undertake their first imperialistic venture overseas. Corsica (3386 square miles) and Sardinia (9300 square miles) were never in ancient times considered parts of Italy, and their influence upon Roman history was negligible.

## Prehistoric Man in Italy

### *Paleolithic and Neolithic Man*

Italy was inhabited in the Old Stone Age, but the fact is of little or no importance to the student of her later history. Very few of these early hunters and fishermen seem to have survived long enough to mingle their blood with the other strains who were to form the Italian people of later days, and their cultural influence must have been very slight. Our study may well begin with the dawn of the Neolithic Age.

In the New Stone Age an overwhelming majority of the people belonged to the short-statured, long-headed, brunette Mediterranean race. Their progenitors seem to have come from Africa, probably by two routes. One group crossed the "Narrows" from Tunis to Sicily, whence they spread northward into the Italian peninsula. The other entered Spain by way of the Straits of Gibraltar, and from there spread northeastward through Gaul into northwestern Italy. No great difference can now be discerned between the cultures of the two groups, but this may be due to the archeological character of our evidence, which does not cover their intellectual life, or their political and social organization. Both groups entered the country well before 3000 B.C.

Neolithic Italian culture may be described as an advanced stage of barbarism. Axes, knives, and weapons were made from carefully selected flints, nephrite, jadeite, and obsidian — hard stones which took and kept an edge and a fine polish. Where these were not to be had from local quarries, they were obtained by trade from distant localities. They were carefully shaped by repeated chipping and the final touches were given by the "pressure" method, except in the finest work which was polished on a whetstone. Bone and wood were used for implements which could not be fashioned from stone. The Neolithic Italians wore clothing, probably made from skins. They shaped their pottery by hand and baked it in an open fire, but it was well made and serviceable. They lived either in caves or in round huts with walls of plaited branches covered with mud, and with thatched roofs. Such huts were placed over holes in the earth, often two or three feet deep, and the accumulation of debris in these excavations shows that the huts built over them must have been unspeakably filthy. The people lived in villages of a few families each, and there is no evidence of any larger political or social groupings. The dead were buried in the earth or in caves, with offerings which indicate a belief in a future life. Hunting was still an important means of livelihood, but it was supplemented by herding. It is possible that they practiced a little agriculture, but this is not certain.

In this barbaric condition the inhabitants of Italy lived, undisturbed by any important outside influences, until shortly before 2000 B.C. Meanwhile Egypt, Babylonia, Crete, and the other lands in the eastern Mediterranean had developed complex and splendid civilizations, and in the Danube Valley there were evidences of the beginning of another progressive culture. In these regions the Age of Metals had long since begun, and in several localities the arts of painting, architecture, and sculpture were highly developed. The Egyptians and Babylonians had discovered the art of writing. All the while the Italians continued in their stagnan neolithic culture. When at last they came to share in the great discoveries which had transformed other lands, it was through the agency of foreign immigrants and traders.

### *The Chalcolithic Age*

Not long after 2500 B.C., metal-workers from Crete or Asia Minor made their way into the regions now called Bohemia and Hungary, where they began to work the local deposits of copper and tin. A flourishing trade in objects of copper and bronze was the result, and native workmen not only learned the arts of the metallurgist, but developed it along independent lines. Pottery-making and other practical skills took root and developed in the same region, and traders carried the products of these Danubian workshops to regions as far off as western Gaul and the Baltic coast, where they secured amber in payment for their wares. From this center Italy was to learn her first lessons in the arts of civilized life.

About 2000 B.C., a new people appeared on the shores of the lakes which lie between the Po and the Alps. They were probably emigrants from the Swiss lake region, and in their new homes they built villages on piles over the water, just as they had done on the lakes of their Alpine homes. No skeletons have survived to show us to what physical type these immigrants belonged, but it is probable that they were members of the stocky, broad-headed Alpine race then prevalent in central Europe. The newcomers brought with them an early phase of the Danubian bronze-age culture, which we may call chalcolithic. Stone was still used extensively, especially for the cheaper tools, but bronze was known, and was gradually becoming more plentiful. These people practiced agriculture, producing crops of wheat, millet, spelt, vegetables, and fruit. They wore clothing made of linen or wool which they wove themselves. They probably cremated their dead. This interesting and progressive people appear to have settled almost entirely north of the Po, for there is no indisputable evidence of their presence farther south.

During this same period the merchants of Minoan Crete began to introduce the more elementary arts of civilization into Sicily. In course of time the natives developed a culture of their own into which they incorporated the lessons taught by their Cretan instructors. It included the use of copper and bronze tools, pottery which displayed a strong Minoan influence, the excavation of elaborate tombs for the dead, and, no doubt, the art of weaving.

It is hard to say which of these centers affected peninsular Italy more profoundly, but the fact remains that under the stimulus of one, or both, her people slowly learned the use of metal and the arts which generally accompanied it. The habits of neolithic life were not given up, but from them evolved a higher and more serviceable culture, into which the new discoveries were incorporated.

### *The Terramare People*

While peninsular Italy was adopting the chalcolithic culture (probably about 1700 B.C.) a new wave of migrations began in central Europe. The Achaeans spread down into the Greek peninsula, and other violent repercussions were felt along the eastern shore of the Mediterranean, while a new people and a more advanced culture were brought into the Po Valley. We do not know by what name the newcomers were known to contemporaries, but the modern Italians, who use the earth from the ruins of their settlements for fertilizer, call these sites *terre mare*: hence they are known as the "Terramare people." Probably they were of the Alpine race, like the earlier lake dwellers, for the two cultures display striking similarities. However, since the Terramare people were in direct and constant contact with the Danubian bronze-age culture, they enjoyed a higher state of civilization than their predecessors. They spread over much of the Po Valley and the adjoining Venetian plain, always confining themselves to the fertile lowlands.

Terramare villages were usually located in swampy regions, but they were not actually built over water. Like the lake-villages, they were set on platforms supported by piles. These village platforms were laid out on various plans, but the most popular one was shaped like a trapezoid, the long sides being parallel. The two principal streets crossed each other at right angles dividing the settlement into four parts, and the other streets were parallel to them forming a "checker-board" pattern like that of many modern American cities. On the west side was a space devoted to religious purposes. The whole village was surrounded by an embankment, a palisade, and a moat. The dead were cremated, and the ashes were collected in urns which were placed on another platform just outside the moat. Bronze weapons and implements were either imported from the Danube Valley or manufactured on the spot. Two-edged swords, daggers, spears, and arrowheads show that they understood the arts of war; while axes, sickles, pins, safety-pins, and jewelry prove that they also practiced those of peace. Amber beads found among the ruins indicate that they were in contact with the great European trade routes. Although they remained to some extent hunters and herdsmen, the Terramare people had become primarily farmers. Everything that we know about them indicates that they had abandoned the ways of barbarism for an orderly and civilized life, and although their material civilization was still crude, it held great promise for the future.

While the Terramare people seem not to have crossed the Apennines in any great numbers, their influence upon the people of the peninsula was profound. Largely through contact with them the peninsular Italians learned the use of bronze, and while the latter clung tenaciously to such customs as the burial of the dead (as opposed to cremation), they made great advances in both material culture and institutions. It is uncertain whether or not the Terramare folk introduced the Indo-European languages into Italy, for our evidence is purely archeological, and languages leave no material remains. It seems at least possible that they did so. Few if any of Italy's many invaders have left so deep and permanent a stamp upon her life.

*The Iron-Age Culture of Villanova*

Some six centuries after the coming of the Bronze Age civilization into Italy, a new disturbance in the northern lands once more set hordes of invaders in motion. The distinguishing feature of the age was the rapid spread of the use of iron — at first as a metal supplementary to bronze, and later to replace it. This series of migrations no doubt drove the Dorian tribes into Greece, and it probably caused the entry of a group of iron-using Alpine peoples into the Po Valley.[1] The Terramare settlements were abandoned, and their occupants must have been pushed southward. It is probable that they finally settled in Latium and its vicinity, where they mixed with the aboriginal population to become the Latins of later times. Some of the displaced Mediterranean tribes settled in the upper Po Valley and the Maritime Alps, where their descendants in later centuries were known as Ligurians. Part of the newcomers may have penetrated as far south as the district later called Samnium, since the later Sabellian dialects show a marked similarity to the speech of the Umbrians. Northern Italy, from the Alps southward across the Po Valley, the Apennines, Umbria, and Etruria, was occupied by the invaders. From the Tiber to the Alps a single culture prevailed, and because some of its finest remains come from a village named Villanova (near Bologna) we call it the "Villanovan civilization."

The Villanovan civilization was characterized by the plentiful use of bronze and by a rather sparing use of iron. The former metal continued to be used for edged tools for a century or two along with iron, but gradually the cheaper and more serviceable iron replaced it. Bronze vessels, often tastefully ornamented, were made in great numbers. Wheeled vehicles — wagons, carts, and chariots — were plentiful, and the harness was often reinforced with bronze and iron. Cremation remained the prevalent funeral rite among the Villanovans, and the dead were provided with elaborate tomb furniture for their use in the world to come.

*Italy in the Iron Age*

Villanovan culture, at least in its material aspects, spread through most of Italy, and although both Greeks and Etruscans settled her shores in the eighth century, it remained as the basis of the later Italian civilization.

We may well close with an attempt to get a bird's-eye view of the whole scene just before the eastern invaders arrived. Apparently all of the peo-

[1] It is supposed that this group is represented by the Umbrians of historic times.

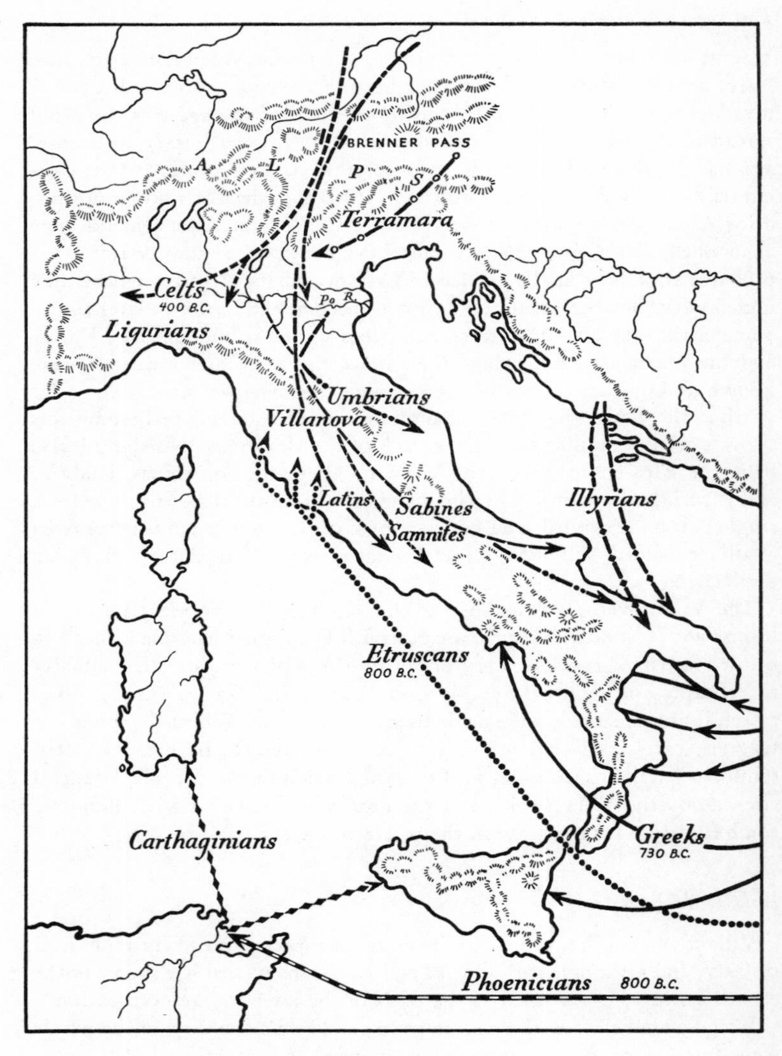


EARLY INVASIONS OF ITALY

ples of Italy by this time spoke Indo-European dialects, and had adopted such other Indo-European institutions as the monogamous, patriarchal family, with the system of clans and tribes which grew out of it. But with these and a few other customs of equally general character, the uniformity of Italian civilization ended. Three great cultural groups existed — the Umbrians, who spoke a series of closely related dialects and cremated their dead, the Latins who practiced both cremation and burial and

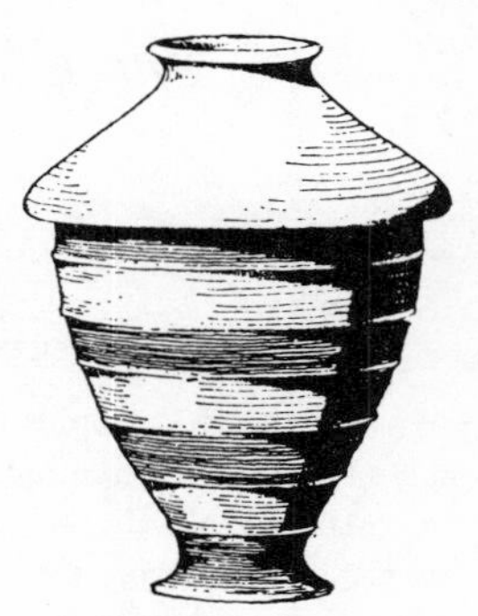

*By R. A. Cordingley*

VILLANOVAN BRONZE AND IRONWARE

spoke a language which later developed into classical Latin, and the Sabellians, who buried their dead and spoke a dialect of their own. In Venetia at the northeast corner, and in Apulia just above the "heel" of the peninsula, tribes from the Balkan peninsula had established Indo-European cultures differing somewhat from the rest, but these never assumed great historical importance. Only in the north had agriculture begun to displace herding as a means of livelihood. Elsewhere the older occupation was dominant. There were few cities in peninsular Italy, and they seem to have been in the north. The center and south were sparsely populated and forests and swamps were predominant. The only governments were those of tribes and clans. Italy was a land of great possibilities, but it required long contact with the civilized lands of the eastern Mediterranean to bring them into the realm of reality, and the closest of these contacts were yet to come.

# 3

## *Civilizing Contacts:*

## *The Etruscans and Greeks*

### The Coming of the Etruscans

About 800 B.C. the peoples of Italy entered upon a new stage of development. Up to that time practically all of the impetus toward progress had come to them from the lands north of the Alps. By the end of the ninth century B.C., however, they had learned all that these northern teachers could impart, and from that time on the influences from that quarter were to retard rather than to help them. The road to further progress lay in contacts with the more advanced peoples of the eastern Mediterranean.

In the Aegean region and in western Asia there were several groups who were by this time competent to assume the role of instructors. After three centuries of barbarism a new Greece was beginning to arise from the wreckage of the Mycenean world — crude as yet, but with considerable attainment in the mechanical arts and in some branches of literature, and with enormous possibilities of further advancement. In Asia Minor and on some of the near-by islands of the Aegean Sea lived the Lycians, Lydians, Carians, and related peoples who had inherited the traditions of the old Hittite and Minoan cultures, and had enriched their knowledge by direct and indirect contacts with Egypt and Babylonia. From Greece, Italy was to receive many colonists and to learn a great deal, and she was to be almost as deeply indebted to the Asiatic immigrants and conquerors whom we call Etruscans.

#### *The Etruscans: Early Home and Language*

With one exception, all ancient writers who mention the Etruscans agree that they were not natives of Italy, but came thither from Asia

*Metropolitan Museum*

ETRUSCAN WARRIOR

*Terracotta. About 500 B.C.*

Minor. Modern scholars, after considerable discussion, have arrived at the same general conclusion, but are still uncertain about the exact location of the Etruscan homeland. It may have been either Lydia, or perhaps some of the northern Aegean islands. Their language did not belong to the Indo-European family; but it appears to have been closely related to some of the tongues spoken in the eastern Aegean region before the coming of the Greeks. Their customs and institutions, which will be treated later, resembled those of other near-eastern peoples.

Our knowledge of Etruscan history and culture is gained from archeological remains, and from statements in the works of Greek and Roman writers. While the Etruscans themselves understood the art of writing, and used an alphabet the sound-values of which are known, their language has never been translated. More than eight thousand inscriptions of various lengths have been discovered, but the meanings of few of the words are known. Indeed, it is quite probable that the known documents would tell us little, even if we knew how to read them. Either the Etruscans had no histories of themselves, or the documents have vanished without leaving a trace of their existence. Since their later history was contemporary with that of the western Greeks and the Romans, these peoples have accordingly preserved a sufficient quantity and quality of isolated facts about them to provide useful clues for the sixth, fifth, and fourth centuries. The rest must be left to archeology.

### *The Conquest and Development of Etruria*

The Etruscan invaders seem to have landed first on the western coast of Italy, about half-way between the Tiber and Arno rivers. Seizing a series of easily defensible hill-tops, they founded fortified cities upon them. Unlike their Italic neighbors, they understood the art of building in stone, and their strongholds were soon surrounded with massive walls. Iron was scarce among the natives of the region, but the invaders had iron weapons and armor, and probably understood the rudiments of military discipline and tactics. With these advantages, the newcomers were able gradually to reduce the natives to subjection. A series of city-states grew up, each one being ruled by a small clique of Etruscan aristocrats with a king at its head, while the masses of the people in town and country were of Italian descent. We can only guess to what extent the language and customs of the masters were adopted by their subjects. Probably the situation differed noticeably from city to city, with the Etruscan influence strongest in seaport towns such as Tarquinii, Vulci, Caere, and Vetulonia, and progressively weaker as it spread inland. Apparently within a century of the first landing they had overrun the country up to the base of the Apennines.

In any case, the Etruscans rapidly transformed the land. They were able teachers of the practical arts, and their Italian subjects were apt pupils. Forests were cut down, swamps were drained, and the vine and olive were introduced into the country. The local deposits of iron, copper, and tin were worked energetically, and soon both iron and bronze were plentiful. Skilled craftsmen from Asia taught the common people the arts of the smith, the stone-cutter, the weaver, and the carpenter, while agriculture made great progress. Houses of stone or sun-dried brick largely replaced wooden or plaited-and-daubed huts. As the immigrants

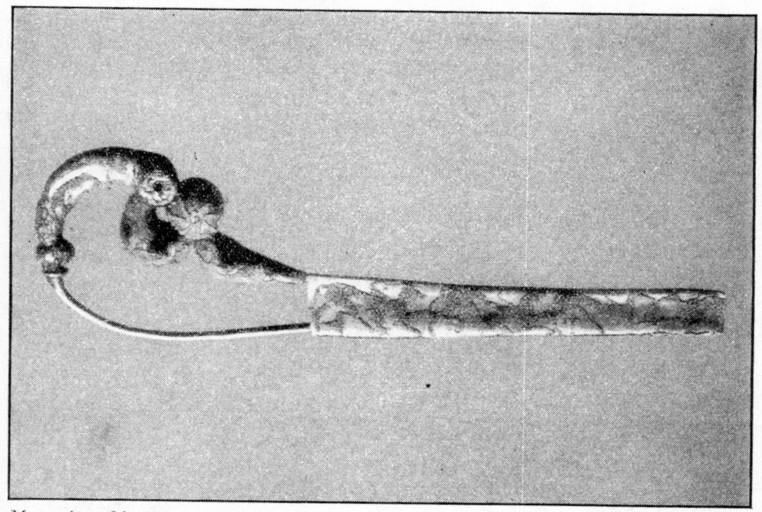

*Metropolitan Museum*

ETRUSCAN PIN

had in their old homes mastered the art of shipbuilding, they soon put the indifferent ports of the Etruscan seacoast to use. From Italian wood they built ships, and with crews formed largely from their Italic subjects they began to practice a combination of piracy and commerce. Soon they were disputing the mastery of the sea between Italy, Sicily, Sardinia, and Corsica with the equally predatory Greeks. Either piracy or trade brought in manufactured goods from the eastern Mediterranean area — at first Phoenician, and later Greek wares. Their own pottery continued to imitate the black *bucchero* ware of their Italic subjects, but with cleaner clay, better shapes, the potter's wheel, and closed furnace.

With this advance in material culture came both political organization and intellectual progress. More than a score of important cities and numerous smaller towns had been founded. On or near the coast were Tarquinii, Caere, Vetulonia, Vulci, Populonia, and Rusellae, while farther inland were Clusium, Perusia, Cortona, Arretium, Volaterrae, and Volsinii. Veii — immortalized by her stubborn struggles with Rome — was a place of only secondary importance. The mixture of aristocracy and monarchy mentioned above long continued to be the prevailing form of government in each of these cities, but in later times the monarchies were superseded by simple aristocracies. The twelve principal ones formed a league, whose purpose must have been religious rather than political, for seldom if ever was united military action secured against external enemies. Aside from this shadowy bond of unity, each state was an independent sovereignty. With plenty of metal to use in the construction of arms and armor, the Etruscan lords were able to equip and discipline large forces of foot-soldiers; they themselves served as cavalry. Theirs was the most formidable military force in Italy. Nor had intellectual culture lagged. Early in the seventh century they had adopted — probably from the western Greeks — an alphabet of twenty-six letters. The fine arts had kept pace with other activities. Compared with other civilizations of the early seventh century B.C., that of the Etruscans does not suffer.

## The Etruscan Empire

### *The Conquest and Loss of Latium and Campania*

With their position on the plains of northwestern Italy thoroughly consolidated, the Etruscan aristocrats were now ready to make conquests in other lands. The details of their early struggles for the mastery of Latium, Campania, and the Po Valley are lost in the haze of legend, but (thanks largely to archeological researches) the extent of their conquests and their approximate dates have been accurately established. This was not the work of a united Etruscan nation, for in a political sense such a nation did not exist. Instead, there is reason to think that each conquest was the work of an independent band of adventurers, led by a chief of proved ability. When such a band had conquered a district, it settled down to rule it, with the chief as king. One such group seized the most convenient ford of the lower Tiber, collected the scattered inhabitants of the Latin and Sabine villages in the neighborhood into a single city, and thus in a sense became the founder of Rome. Others took possession of the remaining cities of Latium and pressed on into Campania. There, although they found the Greeks already in possession of Cumae and Naples, they subjugated the Campanian back-country up to the Apennines and founded or rebuilt Capua, Nola, Herculaneum, and Pompeii. A new Etruria came into existence south of the Tiber, and the conquerors developed and exploited it just as their ancestors had the older Etruria.

The Etruscan occupation of Campania was a standing challenge to the Italian Greeks, who were already in possession of the Sicilian and Italian coasts and were still expanding. After the middle of the sixth century

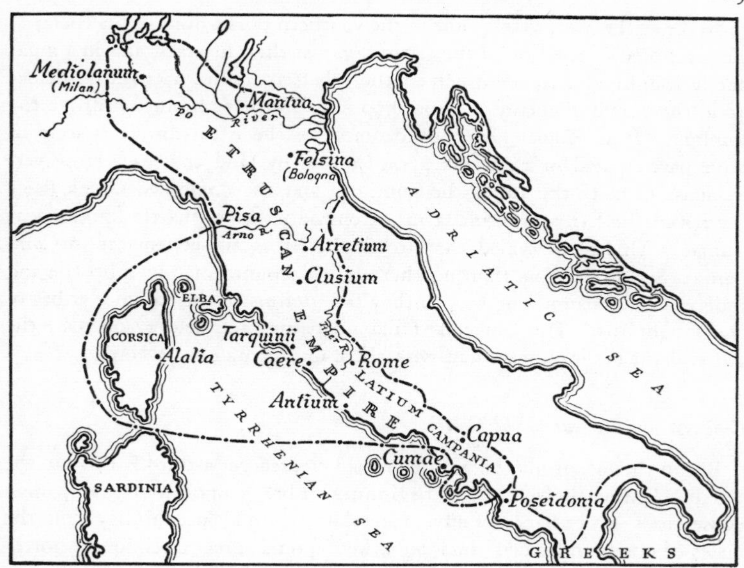


ETRUSCAN EMPIRE[1]

B.C., war between these aggressive peoples, while broken by intervals of peace, was the normal condition. The first phase of the struggle ended in favor of the Etruscans. The Sicilian Greeks were already engaged in an intermittent contest with the Phoenician city of Carthage for western Sicily. The existence of a common enemy naturally led the Etruscans and Carthaginians to form an alliance, and about 535 B.C., these allies expelled the Greek colonists from Corsica. The Etruscans occupied it. Thenceforth the sea between Italy, Sicily, Sardinia, and Corsica was recognized as an Etruscan "sphere of influence," and as the Greeks called the Etruscans *Tyrrhenoi*, it was known as the Tyrrhenian Sea. This alliance with Carthage became permanent.

By 500 B.C., however, the fortunes of war had changed. About 524 B.C., the men of Cumae repulsed an Etruscan attack, and a few years later took the offensive. Aristodemus, the tyrant of Cumae, shrewdly decided

[1] The Etruscans did not occupy all of the area designated as their "empire" at any one time. Latium and parts of Campania had been lost before the Po Valley lands were conquered.

to strike at the most vital point in the southern possessions of his enemies. He promoted a rebellion of the Latins against their masters, and in a great battle fought at Aricia he helped the rebels to inflict a crushing defeat upon the common enemy. About 500 B.C., another revolution drove the foreigners from Rome. In 474 B.C., most of the Etruscan cities seem to have participated in an attack upon Cumae, by land and sea. However, Syracuse came to the aid of the Cumeans, and the combined Greek fleets destroyed the Etruscan armada in a tremendous naval battle fought near Cumae. This blow sealed the fate of the Etruscan settlements in Campania. Separated from their northern fellow-countrymen by a hostile and independent Latium, one by one they fell victims to the Samnite tribes of the mountains. The Cumeans fared no better, for before 400 B.C., the triumphant mountaineers had won all of Campania except Naples.

### *Conquest and Retreat in the North*

But in the meantime the Etruscans had created yet a third Etruria in the north. Just as the storm was beginning to break upon their Campanian possessions, other bands of adventurers, drawn in all probability from the cities of northern Etruria, had embarked upon a career of conquest northeast of the Apennines. Probably before 500 B.C., they had succeeded in conquering the Umbrians of the Po Valley, and had extended their dominions to the foothills of the Alps. The Ligurians of the upper valley and the Venetians of the plain which was afterward to bear their name successfully resisted the invaders. In the north, as elsewhere, the conquerors established their civilization. To them Bologna, Milan, Parma, Piacenza, and Verona probably owe their foundation. Forests were felled, dikes and canals built, and the fertile soil of the valley was for the first time brought under systematic cultivation. For a century or more northern Etruria prospered, and Bologna in particular attained a high level of elegance and prosperity.

About 400 B.C., however, the Etruscans in the Po Valley were also overtaken by disaster. Bands of Celtic warriors from Gaul began to move eastward in search of lands to plunder and settle. Some followed the Danube Valley route to the Balkan peninsula, while others crossed the western Alps and descended onto the plain of the Po. The Etruscan lords of the plains made only brief resistance. In a few decades the choicest part of their possessions in that region was lost, and only a few years more sufficed to carry the Gauls down the eastern coast of the peninsula to the borders of Picenum. By 350, there were no free Etruscans in Italy except

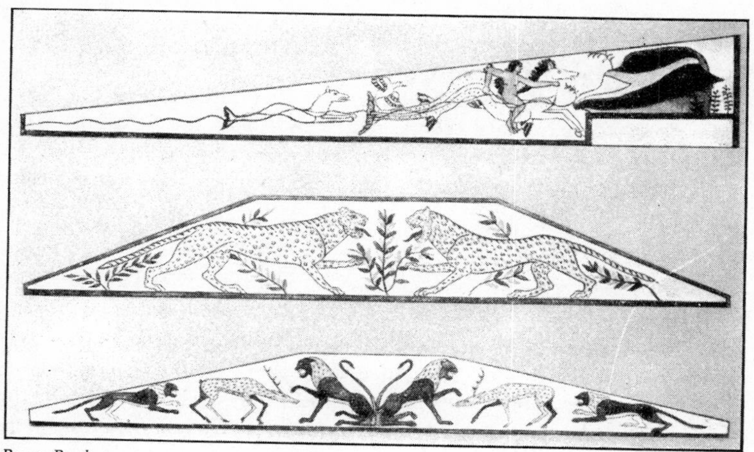

*Brown Brothers*

ETRUSCAN WALL PAINTING

in the region between the Tiber, the Arno, and the Apennines. Less than a century later that too was to fall before the growing power of Rome. The Etruscan "empire," which at its greatest extent had included a third of Italy, was a thing of the past.

The reasons for the fall of their splendid creation are fairly obvious. Only in their oldest settlements did the conquering people assimilate their Italic subjects. Elsewhere they could never have been more than a dominant minority, exposed to the threat of revolution within, and of attack by the Greeks, Gauls, and free Italians without. Even if they had been united in their opposition to these dangers, it is doubtful whether they could have held their own. Probably the whole Etruscan people never did unite and act together, for in most cases each city stood and fell alone before more numerous and better organized enemies.

## The Etruscan Civilization

The Etruscans were the schoolmasters from whom a large portion of the Italian peoples learned the more advanced arts of civilization, and for this reason their cultural achievements are of unusual interest to the historian. They had themselves learned from many schools. In their earlier homes they had acquired the practical arts at second and third hand from the Egyptians and Babylonians. During the first century or so of their residence in Italy they seem to have been in close touch with the Phoenicians, and this contact was later continued through their alliance with Carthage. From about 700 B.C., until their conquest by Rome, the Etruscans alternately fought and traded with the Greeks. Lastly, their relations with the Italic people led them to take over some features of the indigenous culture of their adopted country.

*Religion*

Above all else the Etruscans were a religious people. The gods seem to have dominated their lives in both public and private affairs. Every city which they founded was consecrated to a set of patron deities, whose property both land and people became. Before the site was laid out, the will of the gods was ascertained by divination. The city's limits were marked by the plowing of a sacred furrow, which no one could ever cross thereafter. Before repairing the walls the consent of the patron god had

*Brown Brothers*

ETRUSCAN TOMB PAINTING

first to be obtained. Etruscan gods were *anthropomorphic* (i.e., conceived of as having human forms and qualities), and images of them were placed in temples to receive the homage of their worshippers. Each city adored a "holy trinity," consisting of the god Jupiter and the goddesses Juno and Minerva, who were usually all housed in a single temple. They believed in an after-life of rewards and punishments, but on what basis these were apportioned is unknown. Hideous demons often appear in the paintings on the walls of their tombs, but on the other hand the dead were frequently represented as enjoying feasts in company with the gods of the underworld. Divination of several kinds flourished. From Babylonia they had gotten the practice of foretelling the future by inspecting the livers of sacrificed animals. The organ was marked off into squares according to a chart, and discolorations or malformations in any given square were interpreted according to a prearranged table. Thunder, the flight of birds, or the alleged birth of deformed or unusual creatures — all were looked upon as tokens from the gods. From the Etruscans the Romans took over this whole body of divination-lore, which became an important affair of state. At a later date Greek mythology became so popular in Etruria that Greek religious ideas made serious inroads upon the older religion.

Human sacrifices were a part of the cult of the dead, and to them can be traced the cruel custom of gladiatorial combats. At every well-appointed funeral a pair of slaves would be compelled to fight each other until one of them was killed, and probably the soul of the slain man was looked upon as a sacrifice to the spirit of the departed. Later, however, the custom seems to have become a mere means of amusement for the living, and we even hear of such combats being held to entertain the guests at a dinner party.

### *The Fine Arts and Literature*

In the fine arts Greek influence was strong, but not entirely dominant. Thus the Etruscan temple was built upon a peculiar floor-plan of its own, the proportions of length to width being about 6 to 5. The length was divided into two equal parts, the front a portico supported by a triple colonnade; and the cella, which was divided into three rooms, occupied the rear half. The roof, which resembled that of a Greek temple, covered both portico and cella. Instead of a stylobate, the Etruscan temple had a high platform of earth, which was confined and supported by a stone wall. Sculptors did excellent work in terra cotta and bronze, but seldom attempted stone. In fresco-painting and pottery-painting the Etruscans de-

*University Prints*

HUELSEN'S RECONSTRUCTION OF AN ETRUSCAN TEMPLE

veloped considerable skill, but the finest pottery was still imported from Greece. Indeed, much of the local product was made in imitation of Athenian styles. Sculptors and painters alike displayed a vivid realism which appeared at its best in portraiture, and which was later imparted to the Romans. An Oriental love of finery led to the development of the jeweler's art, and many of its products have been found in the tombs of Etruscan nobles.

Among the most impressive mementoes of the Etruscan civilization are the tombs of the aristocrats. Wherever possible they were hewn in the solid rock; but when this was impossible, they were constructed of masonry and covered with mounds of earth. The largest were veritable subterranean houses, the bodies being deposited in niches cut into the walls, or on stone platforms built above floor-level. Grave furniture for the use of the deceased in the world to come was rich and varied, and the free spaces on the walls were frequently adorned with scenes depicting life in the spirit-world, episodes from Greek mythology and legend, or everyday activities.

In literature, science, and philosophy the Etruscans seem to have done little or nothing. Their only use for the art of writing seems to have been for personal inscriptions, manuals of religious ritual and divination, and (possibly) epic poetry. Their knowledge of Greek mythology and legend seems to pre-suppose an acquaintance with Greek literature, but it may also have been gained from pottery-paintings or from sailors' yarns. If anything, the latter alternative seems the more probable.

### *Society and Cultural Influence*

Our knowledge of the everyday life of the Etruscans is gained mainly from artistic and archeological sources. Apparently the descendants of the conquerors were great landlords, who fought, hunted, governed their dependents, and feasted. Women occupied a respected place in the family, and appeared at social gatherings in the company of men. All of this was in strong contrast with their subordinate position in the patriarchal families of the Italic peoples, and it helps to account for the paradox of legal

*Brown Brothers*

ETRUSCAN SARCOPHAGUS

subordination and social equality with men which we find Roman women possessing. If we may trust our sources, the Etruscan aristocracy lived a gay, luxurious existence, with plenty of the good things of life but no very serious vices.

Italy owes much to these Asiatic intruders. Their language, it is true, was later replaced by Latin, and many of their habits and customs failed to find favor among the Italic peoples. But they established a settled economic, social, and political order in areas where none had existed before, and by so doing they greatly accelerated the march of progress. City life in Etruria, Latium, Campania, and parts of continental Italy was their creation, and it was from them that the men of these regions learned the advanced methods of soil reclamation and cultivation which made them the masters of their physical environment in a sense never possible before. With their coming there arose in Italy the clear-cut distinction between the agricultural lowlanders, with private property in land, and governments based upon sovereignty; and the highlanders, with tribal governments and primitive pastoral economies. The inevitable struggle between the two was a large factor, if not the decisive one, in the rise of Rome to the mastery of Italy. Of their contributions to the education of the Italians in the material arts and in religion nothing need be said here. The whole subsequent history of Italy is a commentary upon it.

## The Cultural Role of the Italian Greeks

### *Policies and Methods of Colonization*

As the political history of the Greek colonies in Italy has already been sketched in Volume One, it need not be repeated here. Suffice it to say that in the two centuries following 750 B.C., the whole southeastern coast of the peninsula, together with the western coast as far north as the Bay of Naples, had been sprinkled with Greek city-states. The larger ones, such as Tarentum, Heraclea, Sybaris, Croton, Rhegium, and Cumae, were important centers of commerce, industry, wealth, art, and learning, but there were also many smaller places which in their own way played a part analogous to that of their more important neighbors. Every one of them embodied to some degree the strife, turbulence, intellectual curiosity, sturdy individualism, and artistic creativeness of the mother-country.

Greek colonization differed radically in both method and objective from that of the Etruscans. The Greeks were a maritime people, who seldom if ever ventured to settle far from the coast. Occasionally they cultivated a fertile plain near the shore, but their chief interest was the sea. Among

*Bettmann*

THE CHIMERA

*Probably Etruscan Bronze. About 500 B.C.*

their cities there was even less union and co-operation than among the Etruscans. City fought against city, and within the walls of each there was rancorous factional strife which might slumber, but never died. The colonies were points of contact between the men of continental Greece, the Etruscans, and the Italic natives. To them came textiles, pottery, arms, jewelry, household furniture, and scores of other articles from the homeland, and their own workmen supplemented the output. These goods were passed on to the inland tribes, who paid for them with raw materials.

Through commerce, war, and diplomacy, communication with the natives was constant. To gain personal, party, or civic objectives, the men of one city often allied themselves with near-by Italian tribes against neighboring cities or against political enemies in their own. Dionysius I of Syracuse (404–367 B.C.) hired thousands of Italic mercenaries for his army. In the fifth and fourth centuries a number of Greek cities were captured by the natives, who thereafter formed an aristocratic class with Greek servants and dependents. By these means, and by ordinary peaceful trading, the natives of southern Italy became acquainted with Greek civilization.

### *Greek Influence Upon Italian Life*

The influence of the Greeks upon the Etruscans and upon the Italian natives was not equally strong in all lines. Politically the Greek had little to teach the others, for that was the point at which, in practice, he was weakest. In general the Italians were abler organizers and rulers than the Greeks, and learned but little from them in the field of government. However, a few Greek city-states continued to preserve traces of their Hellenic institutions after being conquered by the Samnites or Lucanians. In material culture the influence of the Greeks largely paralleled that of the Etruscans. It was in intellectual progress that the Greeks made their unique contribution to Italian civilization. There can be but little doubt that they introduced alphabetic writing into the peninsula, and that both the Etruscans and the Italic natives learned it from them, either directly or indirectly. Greek religious influence heavily supplemented that of the Etruscans in Rome. Some Roman gods were adopted without change from Cumae, while others, still bearing Roman names, were given Greek attributes and appearance. When in the fourth century Rome and her Italic neighbors began to feel the need of a higher intellectual culture than they possessed, it was to the Greeks of southern Italy that they turned for their first lessons. From this source they learned to coin money, carve statues, and build ships; but from it they also received the literary models from which they later built their drama, histories, poetry, and philosophical treatises. Rome's debt to Greece began with her borrowing from the Greeks of her native peninsula, but it continued to increase as long as both existed.

# 4

## *The Origin of Rome and the Etruscan Domination*

### Latium and the Latins

Considered as a separate people, the Romans arose rather late in Italian history. When we speak of their language as *Latin*, we commemorate the fact that originally they were no more than a single branch of the Latin tribe, and that only gradually did they come to overshadow the other Latins in importance. To see the early history of Rome in its proper light, therefore, we must begin by considering Latium and the early Latins.

#### *Latium*

Latium was, at the dawn of history, a district lying between the Tiber River, the Tyrrhenian Sea, and the western edge of the Apennines. Its southeastern frontier was rather vague, but in later times it reached the Liris River. In shape this early Latium was roughly a square, measuring somewhat less than forty miles on a side. The corners almost exactly faced the cardinal points of the compass. The Tiber itself was worth little as a highway for seaborne commerce, and of the whole seacoast, Antium possessed the only harbor fit for ancient ships. It seems, indeed, that Nature took more than ordinary pains to make the Latins landsmen rather than sailors.

The soil of Latium is of volcanic origin, and while the volcanoes have long been quiescent, the signs of their former activity are everywhere. Along the coast, and for some distance up the Tiber Valley, the surface is a low plain underlaid with igneous rock which has weathered on top to form a thin layer of earth. Like most disintegrated volcanic rock, it is very rich, but in a natural state the fertility of the Latin plain was of little use to man. Drainage was very poor. In the rainy seasons the hollows filled with water which in warm weather became the breeding places for disease-bearing mosquitoes. Along the Tiber disastrous floods are fairly common. In view of these disadvantages, it is not surprising that for a long time it was used exclusively for pasturage, and even for this purpose it was subject to severe limitations. Profuse as was the growth of grass during the rainy season, it was almost completely dried up by the summer drought, and herdsmen found it necessary to drive their charges to the green mountain pastures for several months each year.

Apart from the foothills of the Apennines, which form her northeastern boundary, the high ground in Latium includes the Lepine and Alban Hills. They are for the most part remnants of the old volcanic cones, and the principal peaks attain altitudes of over 3100 feet. The soil of their sides is as fertile as that of the plain, and they are watered both by rain and by springs which issue from the rock. They are free from the taint of malaria, and from the stifling summer heat of the plains. Hence they have always been densely populated and well cultivated, and it is here that the political, economic, religious, and social activities of Latium were centered.

### *The Early Latins*

Prior to about 1000 B.C., Latium was sparsely populated by Mediterranean Italians, who had progressed from the Neolithic Age through the Chalcolithic and Bronze Ages. Then, just as the Iron Age was beginning in central Italy, the people whom we shall henceforth call Latins made their appearance. It seems possible that a tribe from the Terramare settlements in the Po Valley, pushed out by the incoming Umbrians, entered Latium, where they subdued the earlier inhabitants, and mingled with them. From this mixture sprang the Latins of historic times. They spoke an Indo-European language, and their customs were predominantly those of their northern ancestors, but they made use of both cremation and burial as means of disposing of the dead.

The Latins were a pastoral and agricultural people. Politically they were grouped into a large number of *pagi* (a word usually translated "cantons"). Each of these consisted of a series of clans whose members were related by blood, and occupied a tract of land, with a fortified stronghold or *oppidum* as a refuge in time of invasion. Apparently each *pagus* was governed by the traditional Indo-European king, council of elders, and assembly, but according to modern standards there was little government worthy of the name. Its chief functions were to defend the community against external enemies, and to attend to the worship of the divine powers; more personal matters would naturally be handled by the clans of the interested parties. Occasionally *pagi* having common interests formed leagues or alliances, and at an early date most if not all of the Latin communities were grouped into the loosely organized Latin League. The functions of this League were chiefly religious, and the shrine of *Jupiter Latiaris* ("Latin Jupiter") on the Alban Mountain was its headquarters.

From a cultural viewpoint the Latins were, if anything, even more backward than their neighbors. They still lived in round or elliptical huts of wattle-and-daub, like those of their remote northern ancestors. They were just beginning to use iron, and it was still less plentiful among them than bronze. The fine metal-work of the Villanovan craftsmen was imported in small quantities, but Latin artisans seem not to have imitated it to any extent, for local influence was still predominant. Agriculture and herding formed almost the exclusive means of livelihood, and long association with plants and animals left indelible traces upon the thought processes of the people and the language which represented them. Thus *egregius* originally meant "set apart from the herd," and by derivation, "distinguished," or "excellent." *Pecus* meant "flock," and its derivative *pecunia* at first signified "wealth," but later "money." *Puto* meant at first "to trim or prune," and later "to think." In all fields of craftsmanship the older designs long persisted, even where more useful and artistic objects of foreign manufacture were available. In this we may, even at this early stage in their national life, distinguish the working of that conservatism which was to be an outstanding feature of the Latin character.

Yet the Latins had, to an unusual degree, the personal qualities which we associate with civilized life. They were naturally orderly and self-controlled, and had a well-developed legalistic sense which enabled them to build strong and efficient governments when the need arose. Their family life was unusually wholesome and stable, and they were truthful and honest in their dealings. While they were brave and persistent fighters, they were not militaristic by inclination. Their religion was simple and unimaginative, and although it lacked the beauty and charm which characterized that of their Greek cousins, it was free from the cruel and immoral features found in many oriental cults, and was neither priest-ridden nor oppressive. Upon such human material a sound and stable civilization might be reared.

## The Origins of Rome

### *The Site*

About fifteen miles above its present mouth, the course of the Tiber is interrupted by a large island, some 300 yards long and 75 yards wide. Up to that point the river is too deep to ford, and too wide to be bridged by the primitive methods known to the Italians of the early Iron Age. Here, however, nature came to man's aid, for each of the channels which flowed by the island was only about half as wide as the entire stream. Long before the dawn of history the river was crossed at this point by a crude wooden bridge, over which ran the road from Etruria to Campania. As this was the only practicable crossing place for the road over the Tiber, the land on either bank had a high strategic value, and its owners were certain to play an important part in the affairs of lowland Italy.

On the eastern bank of the river, in a position to command the crossing, rises the rugged Capitoline Hill — an isolated knob surrounded by a swampy plain. South of it, and about the same distance from the river, are two other knobs of similar appearance — the Palatine and Aventine Hills. From the upland on the eastern side of the Tiber Valley, and opposite the three hills just mentioned, a series of "fingers" of high ground project toward the river. Four of them are worthy of notice. They are (from north to south) the Quirinal, Viminal, Esquiline, and Caelian Hills. Thus we have the "Seven Hills of Rome." The Janiculum and the Vatican Hills, situated on the western side of the Tiber, were not included in early Rome. North of the hills, surrounded on two sides by the river, lies the low plain called the *Campus Martius*, and it, like the ground between the hills, is by nature a swamp. In addition to its strategic value, the site had in early times a certain economic importance, but it had never been a pleasant place in which to live. Occasionally the Tiber floods the low ground to a depth of nearly twenty-five feet. Malaria is endemic, and the summer temperatures are almost unbearable. Only on the hills can one breathe a fresher air, and only there can one be safe from the floods and disease-bearing mosquitoes. Hence the upper classes have always lived on them, leaving the low ground to public buildings and the hovels of the poor.

### *The Traditional and Historical Accounts of Rome's Origin*

As previously indicated (Chapter 1) the Romans believed that their city had been founded about 753 B.C. by a hero named Romulus, as a colony of

*University Prints*

THE SHE-WOLF OF THE CAPITOL

the Latin city of Alba Longa. The naïve story of Romulus and Remus, the twins who were rescued by a she-wolf and reared by a kindly shepherd, and who returned to found the city of Rome on the spot where the wolf had discovered them, is familiar to every educated person. Its literary charm cannot be denied, but it is not history. The true story of Rome's origin is a complex one, and we know little of it except what archeology can teach us.

The first part of Rome to be inhabited was the Aventine Hill, where a village of primitive Mediterranean Italians had existed from time immemorial. Later, about the tenth century B.C., a colony of Latins settled on the western spur of the Palatine Hill. Within the next two centuries, six other Latin villages were founded on these hills, together with two Sabine villages. Thus about 700 B.C., there were within what was later to be the city limits of Rome, ten villages, but the city itself did not as yet exist. The seven Latin hamlets, having a common religion and common customs, formed a confederacy known as the *Septimontium*, or "League of the Seven Hills," but it was as weak a bond as the Etruscan or Latin confederacies — a mere rope of sand, devoted almost entirely to religious matters. Such was the population on the site of Rome when, in the last half of the seventh century B.C., a band of Etruscan freebooters seized the land around the Tiber crossing. With their coming a new age dawned.

## Etruscan Rome

### *The Birth of the Roman City-State*

The conquerors ruled Rome for more than a century. Of the political history of the period we have a few confused hints, but no connected account. Tradition has preserved for us the names of three kings — Tarquin I, Servius Tullius, and Tarquin the Proud, but there must have been others whose names have been lost. Indeed, it is not impossible that Rome underwent several Etruscan conquests, one band conquering it from another. However, all that can be stated with certainty is that for at least a century the Etruscans held both sides of the Tiber crossing, and that the natives were in contact with their superior civilization.

The first tangible effect of the foreign occupation was that Rome became a city. All of the villages on the Seven Hills were united under a strong government, based upon territorial sovereignty. The whole tract of land which the invaders occupied, including the seven hills and the valleys between them and the Tiber, was dedicated to the gods with Etruscan rites, and became a single indivisible unity. Along the designated limit of the new city the founder plowed a sacred furrow, using a plow with a bronze share, drawn by a white bull and a white cow. Where the gates were to be he picked up the plow and carried it, for no one must cross the furrow. The land within it became the *pomoerium*, or consecrated area. As no dead body could be burned or buried within it the village cemeteries were abandoned. On the Capitoline Hill the conquerors built a temple in honor of the Etruscan triad — Jupiter, Juno, and Minerva. In this sense it may be said that the Etruscan kings were the true founders of Rome, and that their work was a lasting one, for never again were the constituent parts to be separated. At the same time, the Etruscans created for her a governmental machine which furnished the foundation for the whole political system of the later Roman Republic.

Under Etruscan rule Rome became the most important city in Latium. Her kings conquered the Tiber Valley from the sea to the edge of the Sabine Mountains, and pushed their boundaries far back into the Alban Hills. In all, they may have had direct control over some 350–400 square miles of land—a petty domain if judged by American standards, but very large for the time and place. Yet their influence did not end with this. Most if not all of Latium was ruled by Etruscan lords, and over these too, the influence of the King of Rome was paramount. Probably the Latin League was reorganized at this time, and the King of Rome was placed at its head.

### *Material Improvements in Rome and Latium*

At home the new rulers treated the land as they had previously treated the older Etruria to the north. In the city itself they dug the first drains to carry off the water from the swampy land between the hills. Some of the soil thus reclaimed became the *Forum*, or marketplace. Apparently they planned and built the first wall.

Economic progress in the city was rapid. Etruscan craftsmen flocked to Rome, where they later settled in such numbers as to give their name to a street — the *Vicus Tuscus*. There they introduced both practical and fine arts. Commerce kept pace with the crafts. From other parts of the Etruscan world and from Greece the Romans received both useful articles and luxury goods. With material goods came intellectual wares which strongly influenced the future of Roman civilization, including the alphabet and a number of Greek religious customs.

In the country districts revolutionary changes were made. Probably with local labor, but certainly under the guidance of an Etruscan king and his nobles, the swampy plains of Latium were drained. A carefully integrated system of tunnels was cut into the tufa rock for many miles, to tap all the larger veins of water. This practice, in valleys otherwise without drainage, carried off the surplus water, dried up the swamps, and made the land both habitable and cultivable. Thus the Latian lowlands ceased to be used exclusively for winter pasture, and farmers took the place of herdsmen. A new era had dawned under the leadership of these foreign masters.

### *Government and Society in Etruscan Rome*

Having made Rome a city-state, the Etruscan kings gave her a set of institutions adapted to her new status. In doing so, they did not sweep away the social structure which had previously existed among the Latins, but merely accommodated it to the new circumstances imposed by city-state life and their own supremacy. Like other city-states of the period, Etruscan Rome had a government which was quite clearly based upon a system of family, clan, and class relationships, and which must be understood before her political institutions can be made intelligible.

The first important feature of Roman society under the monarchy was the existence of two distinct social classes, the *patricians* and *plebeians*. The origin of the distinction is unknown, but the line of cleavage between them was clear and profound. The members of the one class were unable to contract marriages with the members of the other, and no individual could pass from one class to the other. Political, social, and religious power was concentrated in the hands of the patricians. In all of these respects the plebeians were in a state of complete and apparently permanent inferiority.

The patricians were organized into patriarchal clans (*gentes*) and families. Relationship was traced entirely through the male line, and the oldest living male ancestor had complete and unlimited authority over all his male descendants and their wives and children, with one exception. When a girl married she passed from her father's family into that of her husband and was under his authority or that of his eldest living male ancestor. This method of family government was called *patria potestas* ("paternal authority"). The central part of the patrician marriage ceremony was the eating by both bride and groom of pieces of a cake made of spelt (*far*). Hence it was called *confarreatio*, and only patrician couples were permitted to use it. Families descended from a common male ancestor formed a clan, all of whose male members bore a common clan-name, preceded by a personal one. Thus the members of a clan were easily able to identify each other, and their loyalty was stimulated by a common worship of the deified ancestors and other patron spirits of the group. By virtue of their clan organization, superior wealth, and efficiency in war, the patricians monopolized the government of the state except in so far as it was dominated by the king.

The plebeians as a class bore the earmarks of an irregular origin, and their status was correspondingly low. They seem at first to have had very flimsy family bonds, and their oldest form of marriage ceremony was little more impressive than a common law marriage (*usus matrimonii*). Hence for a long time they had no clan organization, and they lacked the solidarity which this institution gave to the patricians. In the rude society of the time and country this was certain to put them at great disadvantage. Equally detrimental was their poverty, which deprived them of the means to purchase arms and the leisure to practice their use. Only by attaching themselves to some of the great patrician class could they secure legal protection or be sure of a means of livelihood. To do this many of them became *clients*.

A *client* was a plebeian who had voluntarily placed himself under the protection of a patrician *patron*. The latter undertook to assist his client in legal business, to protect him against unjust aggression, and to aid him financially if he were in need. In return the client followed his patron to war, swelled his train of followers when he went to the law courts or the assembly, and performed any other honorable service which the patron demanded. If the patron had to raise a sum of money, his clients were expected to assist him in doing so. As a patrician's standing in the eyes of the world was somewhat in proportion to the number of his clients, he naturally tried to secure as many as possible. A client would, in time, come to be loosely identified with the clan of his patron, and no doubt in some instances he would even be looked upon as a member of it. This may account for the fact that in later times there were in some clans both patrician and plebeian branches which bore the same name.

Having considered the patrician clans and their plebeian dependents, we must next take up the larger social and political units. A varying number of clans made up a *curia*, of which there were thirty in the Roman state. The adult male members of these groups collectively formed the *Comitia Curiata*, or popular assembly of the state. In this body the vote was taken by *curiae*, the majority in each one deciding the will of the group. At least sixteen *curiae* had to agree in order to reach a decision.

Far more important than the assembly was the *Senate*, or "Council of Elders." It was composed of the heads of three hundred patrician families, who were men of mature age and approved character. It was the advisory body to whom the king applied for opinions on all questions of policy before submitting them to the assembly. Neither Senate nor assembly was primarily a legislative body, for like other primitive peoples, the Romans seem to have considered the law sacred and unchangeable under all ordinary circumstances. Questions of war and peace, alliances, the interpretation of signs sent from the gods, and other matters of this kind must have formed the bulk of the business of government.

The royal office seems to have been elective, the choice being made by the assembly. Although by no means an absolute monarch, the king had important duties and powers. He was the commander-in-chief of the army, which consisted of all able-bodied men who could buy their own arms and armor. He was the judge of all law-suits which were not settled by the clans or by private arbitration. Not the least of his functions were those of a priest who represented the state in its dealings with the gods. He officiated at sacrifices offered on behalf of the people, undertook to determine the will of the gods in matters of public concern ("take the auspices" was the term), and supervised the activities of the other priests.

*University Prints*

THE ORATOR

*Bronze. About 200 B.C.*

Given a strong personality and statesmanlike ability, the king would usually secure willing obedience from his people. But he was expected to lead his subjects, not to drive them, and hence was a father rather than a master.

Both the social and the political organization of Rome under the kings are important, for the patterns established at that time were never violently destroyed, and subsequent political and social growth were merely in the nature of evolution. Class distinctions, while they came to be much less glaring, continued for more than three centuries. The monarchy was abolished, and two annually elected consuls succeeded to the royal prerogative. Their purple-bordered robes, the *curule* chairs upon which they sat in public places, and most of their powers, were relics of the Etruscan kingship. The Senate and assembly continued to function for many centuries very much as in the early stages of their existence. Indeed to the end of her independent career, Rome bore the stamp which her Etruscan rulers had given her.

### *The Fall of the Etruscan Power*

We have seen under what conditions the Etruscans lost control of Latium and of Rome. The immediate circumstances of the revolution which drove the last Etruscan king from Rome are told, with much detail and immortal charm, by Livy; but most if not all of his story is probably fiction. In view of our present knowledge it is safer to adhere to a few known generalities rather than to attempt to sift the grains of truth out of the chaff-bin of Roman legend. It would seem that the expulsion of the kings was due to a conjunction of three contributing causes.

The first was a general reaction of the Italian natives against both Greeks and Etruscans. In Latium it seems to have taken two forms. The Latins themselves, as we have seen, revolted against their masters, and several mountain tribes — Sabines, Aequians, and Volscians — invaded the lowlands. It is even thought by some scholars that the Sabines captured Rome, and that they were the true founders of the Roman Republic. Certainly there were a goodly number of families of Sabine descent among the later Roman aristocracy, but the theory of a Sabine conquest cannot be proved.

These invasions were aided by an aristocratic reaction against monarchy within the Roman kingdom. The Roman revolution resulted in the supremacy of the landed aristocracy, and must have been largely its work. Such movements seem to have occurred in other Etruscan cities as well as in Rome, and the later Roman aristocracy included some families of Etruscan origin, as well as Latin and Sabine families. Hence the expulsion of the kings cannot have been a purely national effort against Etruscans as such.

A third important factor in the expulsion of the kings from Rome was the weakening of the Etruscan power in general by conflicts with the Greeks of Cumae and Syracuse. We have seen how Aristodemus helped to defeat the Etruscans at Aricia — a feat which almost certainly hastened the fall of their kingdoms in the Latin cities. The disaster which befell the Etruscan fleet before Cumae in 474 undoubtedly helped to relieve the pressure upon the infant Roman Republic from the north. It must be remembered, however, that the immediate effects of these events upon the Roman situation must be inferred, since we have no information on them.

Whatever the relative importance and interrelation of these causes may have been, the fact remains that about 500 B.C., Rome had ceased to be ruled by Etruscan kings, and had become an aristocratic republic with a predominately Latin culture.

# 5

# *Rome Unifies Italy (500–265 B.C.)*

## The Fifth-Century Struggle for Existence

### *Rome and Latium after the Expulsion of the Etruscans*

When the Etruscan power in Latium collapsed, chaos descended upon the land. To understand the peril which both Rome and the other Latin cities faced, we must remember that in the fifth century B.C. the Sabellian tribes of the Apennine Mountains were engaged in a large-scale expansion movement into the more fertile lowland areas of the peninsula. The civilized plainsmen, whether Etruscans, Latins, Campanians, Apulians, or Greeks, were subjected to constant pressure from these barbarian neighbors. Masses of Sabines, Aequians, and Volscians battered the weakened Latin communities incessantly and threatened to deprive them of their hard-won freedom. Moreover, for many years the Etruscans attempted to regain their lost Latin possessions. Hence it is not surprising that the fifth century saw both Rome and her Latin sisters engaged in a desperate struggle for survival.

Threatening as were conditions without, they were not ideal within. The Etruscan kings had bequeathed to Rome a taste for mastery over the Latins which the latter refused to indulge, but for some years the Romans were engaged in a fruitless struggle to substantiate their claims. While Rome still grasped at the fragments of her old-time pre-eminence, her own immediate territory was slipping away. Most of the land on the eastern side of the Tiber Valley north of the city was lost, as was almost all of the land on the western side of the river. In the struggle which resulted in the expulsion of the Etruscans, the city had lost her earlier walls and was in constant danger of surprise attacks. Marauders from three sides raided and wasted the Roman territory. Thus the early history of the Roman Republic is the story of a grim and constant struggle for life — a struggle similar to that which a little later engulfed Campania — and it lasted for two and a half centuries. Eight generations passed in succession across the stage of history without ever knowing a state of peace. But the significant fact is that in this time of trial Rome did not succumb as did so many other lowland communities. Instead she survived and became the mistress of the whole peninsula.

### *The Roman Character*

The causes of this phenomenal success have been variously stated, and to some extent many of them contributed to it. But the principal cause must be sought in the character of her people. Like the other Latins, they were unemotional, practical, and matter-of-fact. They had a strongly developed sense of law, and a love of orderly procedure which enabled them to pass through two centuries of intense political strife without ever once experiencing a civil war. Respect for law went hand in hand with an intense conservatism in other lines, but the Romans never carried love of the past to the point of rejecting advantageous new ideas when once their benefits had been proved. Throughout their history they lagged behind the Greeks in art, literature, science, and philosophy, but in such practical arts as road-building, fortifications, and aqueducts they excelled. As a people they were wedded to the soil — farmers by preference and imbued with the stubborn persistence indispensable to success in their calling. They were fierce fighters when compelled to defend their homes. In the early centuries of their history as an independent people, they produced but few good strategists, and they often lost battles; yet their indomitable perseverance in the face of disaster, together with their shrewd diplomacy, always succeeded in bringing them victory. In dealing with conquered peoples they displayed a fairness, moderation, and good faith which frequently caused the enemy in one war to become a devoted ally in the next. Whenever conditions permitted, they did not hesitate to receive the vanquished into their own ranks as full citizens. In a land as disorderly as Italy of the fifth century B.C., such a people could hardly fail to forge to the front.

## The Struggle for Survival

Under the conditions just described, the first century of Rome's career as a republic was completely dominated by the struggle to maintain her independence. She was no longer the suzerain of the other Latin cities, as she had been under the Etruscan kings. Her commerce declined to the vanishing point, her urban population suffered from lack of employment, and poverty dogged her steps. Aside from the labor necessary to win a bare livelihood, the energies of the Roman people were entirely absorbed in war. Many years were to elapse before the clouds began to lift.

### *The Latin Alliance: Defensive Wars*

The first landmark in the history of republican Rome was the readjustment of her relations with the Latins. After the expulsion of the Etruscans, the Latin League was reorganized, and for nearly two decades Rome struggled against it in an effort to restore her hegemony over it. Neither party to the strife could afford the conflict, and it was probably while it was in progress, that the Volscians from the near-by spurs of the Apennines conquered a wide strip of land across the Latin plain southeast of the Alban Hills, culminating in the capture of Antium, Latium's most important seaport. Farther to the northwest the Aequians, another Sabellian tribe, occupied Tusculum. The Sabines raided the Tiber Valley, and across the Tiber the Etruscan city of Veii wrested from the Romans all of their lands to the water's edge. Under such conditions both Romans and Latins were willing to reconcile their differences. In either 493 or 486 B.C., the Roman consul Spurius Cassius concluded a treaty with the Latins which was to remain in force, with some interruptions, for about a century and a half. Rome on the one side, and the Latin League as a collective unit on the other, were the parties to the pact, and they negotiated as equals. Each was to aid the other in war, and both were to share alike in the spoils. Latins domiciled in Rome, and Romans in Latin cities, were to enjoy the personal rights possessed by citizens of their adopted cities. The first of these was the *ius commercii*, or right to carry on trade and make valid contracts with the inhabitants of the city which granted it. The second was the *ius connubii*, or right to contract a valid marriage with a person of the granting city. A short time later the Romans concluded a similar agreement with the Hernici, a tribe living on the eastern border of Latium and likewise threatened by the advance of the Sabellians.

There was need for all the combined strength of the triple alliance. Throughout the fifth century it was constantly at grips with its foes, and it did not always have the upper hand. Indeed, we have seen that Veii had, for a time, superiority over Rome, while with the others the fortunes of war swayed back and forth for decades. We must not, of course, attribute to these wars of early Italy anything resembling the tragic intensity and fierce destructiveness of those with which we are unfortunately familiar. They were fought by citizen-soldiers, usually in the season when their farms demanded least care, and consisted for the most part of raids and skirmishes, with few large-scale operations of any kind. A typical incident is preserved in the story of Cincinnatus, who left his plow to accept the command offered him by the Senate, rescued a Roman army blockaded in the enemy's country, and in sixteen days was back at his plow.

Before the end of the fifth century the tide had begun to turn. The invaders of Latium had been either subdued or driven back to the mountains. On the lands reconquered from them the League formed a series of Latin cities which were admitted to membership in it. About the middle of the century the Sabines ceased raiding the Tiber Valley. In her dealings with Veii, Rome had shrewdly taken advantage of the chronic dissensions of the Etruscan cities to form an alliance with Caere which, although a member of the Etruscan League, was threatened by the imperialistic ambitions of the people of Veii.

### *The Capture of Veii*

About 405 the Romans, freed for the moment from dangers on other fronts, closed in a death struggle with their enemies of Veii. Of the war which followed, few authentic details have been preserved, and these are overlaid with a mass of fictitious legends. It would appear that the Romans, led by the able Marcus Furius Camillus, drove their enemies from the open field, and then besieged Veii herself. The siege lasted several years — tradition says ten. Several near-by towns tried unsuccessfully to relieve the besieged, but the Etruscan League as a whole did nothing. By paying her soldiers Rome was able to keep them continuously in the field, and in 396 her efforts were rewarded. Veii was sacked, her citizens were sold into slavery, and her territory was annexed to the Roman domain. Not long afterward much of it was divided into small lots and given as farms to the poorer citizens. East of the Tiber, Fidenae, the ally of Veii, shared her fate, and in a few years Rome either owned or dominated by means of alliances most of southern Etruria. The indomitable pluck, energy, and cleverness of the Roman people had begun to bear fruit.

## The Gallic Crisis

If the Etruscans had shown little interest in the affairs of Veii, it was to be explained in part by the fact that they were threatened with danger from another quarter. We have seen how the Gauls wrested the Po Valley from Etruscan control. This movement was in progress at the same time that the Romans were besieging Veii, and it did not cease until long afterwards. The newcomers swept eastward along the north-Italian plain until stopped by the Veneti, and then turned southward along the eastern side of the Apennines. Some of them crossed the mountains to raid Etruria, and about 390 a large band of them descended the Tiber Valley toward Rome.

### *The Gauls Capture Rome*

The Romans were ill-prepared to meet the Gallic threat. The Capitoline Hill had defensible fortifications on its summit, but the city as a whole was still unwalled, its limits being marked with an earthen embankment and ditch. The army was still organized as a stiff and unmanageable phalanx of spearmen, with an insufficient number of either officers or cavalry. It could not maneuver on broken ground, and when once its line had been broken, there was little chance for recovery. The Gauls were strangers in Italy, and the Italian peoples were so terrified by their ferocious appearance that they did not immediately perceive their weak points. It was the custom of the barbarians to rush into battle uttering blood-curdling yells, wielding huge broadswords of soft iron; but if their first onset was repulsed, they usually became discouraged and retreated. They were divided into tribes, of which the Boii, Senones, Cenomani, Insubrians, and Lingones seem to have been represented among the invaders of the Po Valley, but these groups seldom co-operated with each other. Later the Romans, even with inferior numbers, repeatedly defeated them, but in the fourth century B.C., the Gauls swept all before them.

At the River Allia, eleven miles from the city, the Roman army faced the invaders, but it suffered a disgraceful and calamitous defeat. Except for a small detachment left to defend the Capitol, the Romans fled across the Tiber to Veii, and the barbarians entered Rome unopposed. For seven months they besieged the garrison of the Capitol; but the latter, under the leadership of the heroic Marcus Manlius, beat off all assaults. The Gauls were anxious to be gone, for they had seized all the spoils within reach, the climate was unhealthy, and the Veneti were attacking their new homes in the Po Valley. When the fugitives at Veii offered them a thousand pounds of gold as a ransom for the city, they accepted it and departed. Later Roman writers, ashamed of the unheroic part played by their ancestors in the affair, invented a series of legends to redeem the reputation of their city; but the falsity of such stories is quite apparent. Rome had had a very narrow escape. Her prestige in Central Italy suffered heavily, and for a generation afterward she had to resist a series of attacks by jealous neighbors, as well as to prepare for renewed Gallic invasions.

*The Recovery of Roman Prestige*

But however ingloriously the Romans may have acted in redeeming their city from its invaders, the event proved that they made a wise decision, and their subsequent conduct was marked by uncommon courage, wisdom, and energy. All of the jealousy which recent Roman successes had inspired in the Etruscans, Latins, Hernici, Volscians, and Aequians now found vent in hostile demonstrations. At home the destruction caused by the invasion precipitated an economic crisis. The citizens had to rebuild their homes and fortify their city in the brief intervals between foreign war and domestic political strife. Yet they resolutely faced all of these perils and hardships, and gradually made headway against them. The leading spirit for many years after the Gallic crisis was still the heroic Camillus, who merits the title of "the Second Founder of Rome." A stone wall, 24 feet high, 12 feet thick, and 5½ miles in length, was built along the lines of the Etruscan rampart. Later historians, supposing that it was the original structure, called it the "Servian Wall," after the great Etruscan king, Servius Tullius, its reputed builder. Behind it the Romans could well defy their enemies. On the north the division of the land of Veii into small farms rendered many of the poorer citizens, who had until that time been too poor to buy arms, eligible for military service. Farther west, the small Etruscan towns of Nepete and Sutrium were reorganized as Latin colonies, and thenceforth served as bulwarks against invasion from that quarter.

The Latins had done nothing for Rome when she had to face the Gallic peril; and afterwards they took advantage of her misfortunes to try to check her further growth. A number of Latin cities allied themselves with the Volscians, who now renewed their attacks upon her. On at least one occasion she came to blows with her former allies the Hernici, and the Etruscans seem also to have joined in the onslaught against the too-prosperous upstart. Gallic raids continued at intervals. In short, the generation following the Gallic catastrophe saw the Romans at war with most of their neighbors all of the time.

From these stern trials Rome gradually emerged in triumph. The hostile Latin cities, together with the Hernici and Volscians, were subdued, and the Latin League was once more reorganized, this time with Rome as its avowed head. The cities of southern Etruria were vanquished, and forced to sign treaties of alliance. When the Gauls returned, they found their erstwhile victim secure behind new walls, and in 351 the Senones, who before had sacked Rome, signed a truce with her. Rome had not only survived but even prospered in the face of what seemed to be impossible odds. She had annexed some territory, and had broadened and strengthened her circle of alliances. Alone among the states of peninsular Italy she had successfully resisted the barbarians, and the fact gave her credit as a champion of civilization. It was a very respectable record of achievement for a city which had so recently seemed on the verge of collapse.

## Latins and Campanians (343–336)

### *Rome's Broadening Horizon*

In a land as completely devoid of unity as was Italy in the fourth century B.C., policies such as those which Rome pursued were certain to bring her into contact with an ever-widening circle of neighbors until the whole peninsula had fallen into her power. In spite of her never-ending wars and conquests, she cannot be called consciously imperialistic. But war or alliance were the normal alternatives in interstate relations in the peninsula, and Rcme always fought on doggedly until she won. Victory brought an alliance between victor and vanquished, with the mutual obligation to defend each other's interests. That meant wars with new peoples, new victories, and new alliances. The Gallic inroads had themselves helped to bring the Romans into contact with a broader circle of neighbors. In 354 they had formed an alliance against the barbarians with the Samnites, a Sabellian people who lived to the southeast of Latium. This agreement strengthened them against enemies nearer home — the Latins, Hernici, and Volscians, and it continued in force for more than twenty years.[1]

Before long, however, an event took place which soon involved the Romans in a bitter struggle with their former allies, the Samnites. The Samnite bands who had conquered Campania had settled down to a life of ease in the rich lowland cities, and had absorbed much of the civilization of their Greek, Etruscan, and Italic subjects. In the process of readjustment to the new conditions, they had lost much of their early military

[1] Later Roman tradition told of a war between Romans and Samnites in the years 343–341, but this probably never occurred.

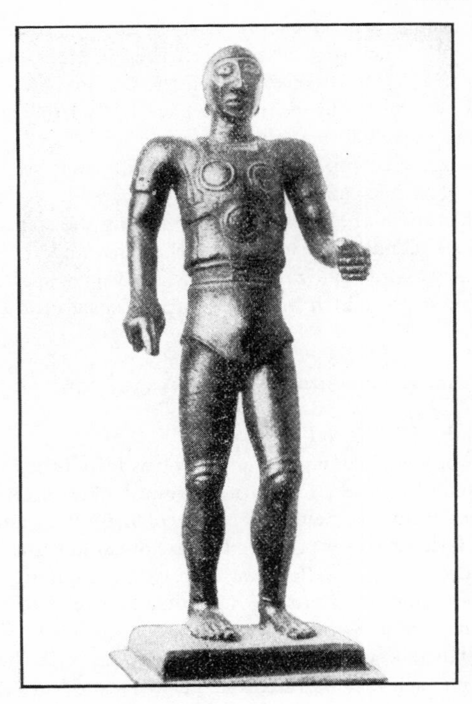

SAMNITE WARRIOR

zeal, while their wealth exposed them to the envy of their Sabellian brethren in the mountains. Politically Campania was not united, but its cities were organized into several leagues, of which that headed by Capua was the most important. In 343 the Capuan League incurred the displeasure of the Sabellian mountain tribes, who subsequently attacked it. Unable to beat off the enemy unaided, the Capuan confederacy sought help from Rome, and asked for a permanent alliance with her. The Romans accepted the offer, for Campania would afford them a supply of food in times of need and a base of operations against their discontented Latin and Volscian neighbors. However, the other Campanian Leagues did not join the Roman alliance at this time, and later, some of them aided the enemies of Rome. Although the pact was intended to check the expansion of the Samnites into Campania, the latter were too busy in other quarters to take up the challenge for seventeen years after it was made (343–326 B.C.)

*The Latin War and the Organization of Latium*

The wisdom of the new arrangements was soon brought to the test, for in 340 B.C. the Latins revolted. They had long viewed with alarm the huge expansion of Rome in both territory and population, inasmuch as she, a single city, had now become a match for their united strength. When the Gauls ceased to menace Latium, the last visible reason for their alliance with this formidable neighbor vanished. Already she had annexed some land in southern Latium, and had organized it as part of her permanent domain. Lastly, the alliance with the Campanians caught Latium as though in a vise, and placed at the disposal of Rome forces which would render her might all the more overwhelming. The Latins countered by demanding either full independence or complete incorporation into the Roman state, and in the latter case they wished to have a guarantee that one consul and half of the Senate would always be Latins. The demand was refused, and the Latins, aided by the Volscians and some of the Campanians, rushed to arms. The outcome of such a war was scarcely in doubt. The rebels mismanaged everything, while Rome fought with adequate forces and perfect strategy, and in two years the war had ended decisively in her favor. She could now settle the Latin problem once and for all.

It was at this point that the Romans made a decision the effects of which were to be seen in their entire subsequent history. They were not the first people to find themselves in the position of victors with defeated enemies at their mercy. The Oriental Empires, Athens, Sparta, Thebes, Syracuse, and Macedonia had all faced the same problem. With few exceptions, none of which had lasted long enough to harden into well-defined policies, they had reduced the conquered peoples to subjection, making them pay tribute and service with no hope of ever having equality with their conquerors. Such a course was certain to breed discontent, and in each of the cases mentioned, it had proved to be an important factor in the overthrow of the dominant state. It is hardly likely that the Roman Senate was acquainted with these cases; but native good sense and fairness made it repudiate entirely the policies of the exploitation and permanent degradation of conquered peoples. Instead it undertook to give each of the Latin communities opportunity for participation in all the civil rights and political privileges of Roman citizenship as soon as it was ready to receive them. In the meantime, those communities which did not desire or were not ready for complete assimilation were to have temporary governments suited to their needs. Care was taken in all cases to avoid humiliating the vanquished peoples, and no tribute of any kind was to be collected from them. Even the least-favored were enrolled as allies of the Roman Republic, enjoying its protection and sharing the burdens of the common defense according to well-defined stipulations. At the same time, every effort was made to place all Latium under effective Roman control.

In accordance with these maxims, the Latin League was deprived of all its political functions, but retained the right to hold meetings for religious purposes. About half of Latium was annexed outright to the Roman domain, its people receiving full Roman citizenship. To care for local affairs, however, they retained their local governments. Such communities were called *municipia*. Other groups, whose loyalty was still doubtful, were put upon a sort of political probation. Their local governments were destroyed, and they were governed instead by *prefects* sent out from Rome; on the other hand, they received all of the rights of Roman citizenship except those of voting and holding office at Rome. They were called *cives sine suffragio* — "non-voting citizens," and they could easily gain the rights which they lacked by continued loyalty and good behavior. A few Latin cities, such as Tibur and Praeneste, were too firmly rooted in their traditions of independence to be annexed at all. They, together with the fortress-colonies founded by the Latin League on conquered lands, retained the name and status of "Latin Allies." As such they had the rights of trade and marriage with Roman citizens as before, but they did not have these rights with each other. Latins who settled in Rome became Roman citizens. Each community was bound to Rome by a separate treaty which provided that it should have "the same friends and the same enemies as the Roman people" — in other words, that Rome should control completely the foreign relations of herself and her allies. The obligation to furnish military aid also formed a part of the new treaties. Antium, the greatest seaport of Latium and a stronghold of piracy, received special treatment. A part of her land was confiscated, and on it three hundred Roman citizen families were settled. Their heads were relieved of the obligation to do military service, on condition that they guard the harbor against possible invaders from overseas.

The complicated character of this system is in itself proof that an effort was made to treat each case on its merits, and as a whole it worked remarkably well. The discontent which had agitated the Latin cities for nearly sixty years vanished. A few years later, when Rome was engaged in her wars with the Samnites, and afterward when Pyrrhus of Epirus strove to stir up revolt among her allies in Central Italy, not one Latin colony displayed the slightest disloyalty. No greater tribute could have been paid to the wisdom and fairness of the statesmen who worked out this settlement.

## The Wars of Italian Independence (326–265 b.c.)

### *Rome the Champion of the Lowland Italians*

By 330 b.c., Rome was the largest and most powerful state in Italy, owning or controlling a territory with an area of about 4250 square miles, and a population of citizens and allies which was not far short of 1,000,000 persons. Her lands lay almost entirely on the western coastal plain, stretching from central Etruria to southern Campania. By this very fact she had become the champion of the civilized lowland peoples against the backward and predatory mountain tribes. Indeed, the union of so large a part of the Italian plains under a single head was in itself enough to handicap the Samnite mountain tribes severely, both in their winter drives of livestock from the mountains to the plains, and their outpouring of surplus population.

### *The Samnite Wars: The First Stage (326–310).*

The Samnite Confederacy in particular must have viewed with jealous aversion the closing of Campania to its further inroads. From the moment that Rome formed her alliance with the Capuan League, it was only a question of time until the two powers would be driven into a decisive struggle for the mastery of the Campanian plain and the adjoining portions of southern Latium. The outbreak of hostilities was delayed, however, by the fact that the mountaineers were for some years engaged in a war with Tarentum. But in 326 their bad feeling toward the Romans was aggravated by a series of "incidents." The Roman historian Livy, writing centuries later, attributes the breaking of the peace to the formation of an alliance between Rome and the Greek city of Neapolis (Naples), and to her foundation of the Latin colony of Fregellae on the Samnite frontier. Whatever the occasion, the real cause of the Samnite wars was the fact that Rome stood for peace and order on the Italian plains, while the Samnites were intent on continued plunder and colonization in the same area. The dispute could only be decided by the sword.

There were three wars between Rome and the Samnite Confederacy, or four if the aid given by the latter to the Epirote king Pyrrhus be counted. Their dates were respectively 326–321, 315–304, and 298–280. While they were in progress their character changed radically. They began as a simple war between two peoples over disputed territory; but after 310 their scope broadened until they came to include almost all of Italy, and so became veritable "wars of Italian independence." These wars were the supreme test of Roman strength, courage, and leadership, and at their conclusion the fate of Italy was decided.

The first Samnite War ended in disaster for the Romans. The Roman army was still organized on the lines of the Graeco-Etruscan phalanx, which was good enough for fighting on the plains, but not nearly flexible enough for work in the mountains of Samnium, and the cavalry was poorly armed and disciplined. In 321 practically the entire Roman field-army was attempting to invade Samnium by way of the pass known as the "Caudine Forks," when the enemy closed in on both front and rear and compelled the whole army to surrender. It was first humiliated by being made to "pass under the yoke" (two spears stuck into the ground with a third laid across their tops); then a treaty was drawn up which settled every question in dispute in favor of the Samnites. The Latin colony of Fregellae, and with it the southern extremity of Latium, became Samnite property. Probably most of the Campanian allies fell away from a suzerain who could no longer protect them. Six hundred Roman knights were given as hostages for the fulfillment of the terms, and for six years the fighting was suspended.

In this dark hour the Romans once more displayed the same dogged persistence, adaptability to new conditions, and diplomatic skill, which they had shown in previous crises. The army was reorganized along lines suitable to mountain fighting. Old alliances were strengthened, and new ones were made with peoples, like the Lucanians and Apulians, whose lands lay in the path of Samnite expansion. Within six years the Samnites found themselves almost completely surrounded by Roman allies, and faced with a reorganized and strengthened Roman army. In desperation they declared war.

The renewed war lasted eleven years from 315 to 304. Almost at its beginning the Samnites won a great victory at Lantulae in 315, but the relentless hammering directed against them by the Romans, who could strike from any side when they saw fit, began at last to show results. By 310 the Samnites had been again reduced to the defensive, and had suffered at least one great defeat. The Roman hold on Campania had been restored and strengthened, and a chain of Latin colonies had been established all along the borders of Samnium to hold the mountaineers in check. In 312 the progressive censor, Appius Claudius, had begun the construction of the Appian Way from Rome to Capua — the first of a long series of such strategic highways which were later to cover the soil of three continents. At this time the Samnites adopted a new policy, and the war entered its final stage.

*The Second Stage (310–280)*

The growing strength of Rome had again aroused the apprehensions of her northern and eastern neighbors; and the Samnites, taking a leaf from the book of their enemies, formed an anti-Roman coalition. Its members included the Hernici, Aequians, Paelignians, and several of the Etruscan cities. The move prolonged the war, but did not essentially alter the outcome. One by one all of Samnium's northern and eastern allies were defeated, and according to her custom, Rome would grant them peace only on condition of their becoming her allies. In 304 the war ended when the Samnites themselves agreed to accept the same status. It was a Roman victory, but by no means a decisive one, and for this reason it proved but the prelude to further hostilities.

It would seem that by 300 B.C., the steady advance of the Roman power was arousing general apprehension among the other peoples of Italy. No doubt this was in a large measure due to the methodical and efficient manner in which the gains made in the previous war had been consolidated. In the Apennines, to the north of Samnium, two Latin colonies (Alba Fucens and Carsioli) were founded, and a new road — the Valerian Way — was built through them toward the eastern coast. In Apulia, to the southeast of Samnium, the foundation of the Latin colony of Luceria shut off the Samnites from further expansion in that direction. It was plain that Rome meant to hold all that she had won. The Samnites, under the leadership of the able Gellius Egnatius, made capital of the alarm which these steps occasioned. Taking advantage of Rome's preoccupation with a new Gallic invasion, Egnatius formed a coalition consisting of the Samnites, Lucanians, free Etruscans, some of the Gallic tribes, and possibly some communities of Umbrians and Sabines (298). The Romans soon gained the upper hand in Samnium and Lucania, but in 296 a large force of Samnites slipped away northward and effected a junction with the northern allies at Sentinum in Umbria.

In this crisis the Romans displayed a brilliant mastery of that large-scale strategy by which campaigns are won. Leaving a small force to guard the frontiers of Samnium, they concentrated their chief strength in the north. A Roman detachment made a daring raid into Etruria and Umbria, and the contingents from these regions deserted the allied army in order to defend their homes. Then the principal Roman force, led by the consuls Fabius Rullianus and P. Decius Mus, fell upon the remainder of the hostile army at Sentinum. After a ferocious struggle, in which both Egnatius and Decius Mus were killed, the Romans won a decisive victory. The allied army was all but destroyed, and the back of the coalition was broken. After six more years of desultory warfare the Samnites submitted, and returned to their alliance with Rome on harder terms than before.

During the 280's the Romans were for the most part occupied in stamping out the remnants of the war in the north. At Arretium the allied Etruscans and Gauls annihilated a Roman army (284), but the next year the consul Manius Curius Dentatus avenged the defeat by entering the territory of the Gallic Senones and driving them from their homes. Their land, situated on the Adriatic coast northeast of Umbria, became Roman public domain, and colonies were founded on parts of it at Ariminum and Sena Gallica. The Etruscan malcontents were let off with treaties of alliance which bound them closely to Rome. Other extensions of Roman territory were made. In 290 the redoubtable Dentatus had entered the Sabine country and annexed it, making the people citizens without suffrage. Picenum and Umbria were brought into the Roman alliance about the same time. In the South the Lucanians were again subjugated. In short, Rome now controlled all of Italy except the Greek cities and native tribes of Calabria and Bruttium — the "heel" and "toe" of the peninsula. Her hold over Samnium and Lucania was not yet firmly established; but the fault was soon destined to be remedied.

*The War with Pyrrhus (280–272)*

Rome was now brought into direct relations with the Italian Greek cities. The latter had long been in a decline, because of internal political strife, intercity wars, attacks by the Italian natives, and the aggressive policies of the tyrants of Syracuse. Many of them had already fallen into the hands of the Bruttians, a Sabellian people who in the early fourth century had occupied the "toe" of the peninsula, and of those which remained, only Tarentum was still prosperous. Even she could not have defended herself against the hostile Italic tribes if she had not had constant recourse to the expedient of calling in help from the Greek homeland. The Spartan king Archidamus (346), Alexander the Molossian (338), and another Spartan named Cleonymus (314) had successively fought in her behalf, but each in turn had quarreled with his employer. The Tarentines would neither fight for themselves, nor give loyal support

THE ROMAN FEDERATION IN 265 B.C.[1]

to outsiders who fought for them. The last of these foreign auxiliaries was Agathocles of Syracuse, who died in 289. Yet even before his death circumstances had changed so radically that the Tarentines no longer looked upon the Sabellian Samnites and Lucanians as their most dangerous enemies. The chief threat to their independence was now Rome.

It is at least probable that Tarentum had had a hand in stirring up the Samnite war of 298–290, and the Roman victory which ended the struggle left her more alarmed than ever. The smaller Greek cities of Italy, which had hitherto looked upon Tarentum as their protectress, now began to

[1] The Latin colony of Brundisium, shown on the above map, was not founded until 244 B.C.

look toward Rome, the champion of law and order who had already demonstrated her ability to defeat their Sabellian persecutors. About 285 Thurii obtained an alliance with her, and others soon followed the example. Naturally the Tarentines resented this interference in their "sphere of influence." A Roman fleet was attacked and partly destroyed by them, and when they refused to make reparations, war ensued. This time Tarentum appealed to Pyrrhus, the king of Epirus, to do the fighting for her.

The Epirote king was one of the greatest living masters of the art of war as developed by Alexander the Great and his successors. His army numbered about 20,000 men, including a phalanx, cavalry, and twenty war elephants — the ancient precursor of the tank. Pyrrhus was an affable and chivalrous enemy, and a very popular ruler among his people. His chief fault was a lack of steadiness of purpose which constantly led him into new enterprises, only to desert them when the difficulties which they involved became apparent. Hence his life was spent in a series of impractical undertakings. He had already made an unsuccessful bid for the throne of Macedonia, and he did not come to Italy merely as an employee of Tarentum. Instead he seems to have intended to build up an empire which would include southern Italy, Sicily, and as much land as possible east of the Adriatic Sea. When, in 280, he arrived at Tarentum, he at once assumed full control of the city — much to the disgust of the people. His plan of campaign was to march into central Italy, to stir up a revolt among the allies of Rome, and to break up the Roman Federation. More than this he could hardly hope to achieve, but to one who reasoned from analogous cases in the Greek world, this objective seemed thoroughly feasible.

The Romans met the threat with their usual promptness and efficiency. Armies were posted at points in northern and central Italy where danger seemed to threaten, and a force under P. Valerius Laevinus advanced to meet the enemy. At Heraclea the two armies met. The Roman soldiers, as well as their cavalry horses, were terrified by the unaccustomed sight of the elephants, and this fact, together with the tactical skill of Pyrrhus, won him a victory. But his losses had been extremely heavy, and the Roman army was not yet destroyed. Many Samnites and Lucanians now joined him, and he advanced into Campania and Latium in an effort to stimulate revolts against the Romans in these districts. The effort was a failure. City after city shut its gates and manned its walls. After coming within forty miles of Rome without achieving a single success, he retreated to Tarentum. In 279 he won a similar barren victory at Ausculum in Apulia, and followed it up with an equally fruitless march up the eastern coast. It was now obvious that Rome's allies intended to stand fast.

Baffled in the principal objective of his campaign, Pyrrhus began negotiations for peace through his agent, the orator Cineas. His terms were merely that Rome should respect the independence of the Italian Greek cities, and of the Italic peoples who had joined him. A portion of the Senate favored the acceptance of the offer, but the ex-censor Appius Claudius, now old and blind, had himself led to the Senate-house and there delivered an impassioned plea against the making of any treaty with a victorious enemy still located on Italian soil. It is probable that in this he was supported by the vigorous group of plebeian senators who had in recent years been the backers of the policy of expansion, and it is certain that Carthage took a hand in the negotiations. Fearing that the Epirote king might attack her Sicilian possessions if freed from his Italian commitments, she sent a fleet to the mouth of the Tiber with an offer of aid for the Romans. The peace movement broke down.

With a characteristic lack of steadiness, Pyrrhus now abandoned his unprofitable Italian venture for more promising prospects in Sicily. The death of Agathocles in 289 had left the Syracusans without any leader capable of coping with Carthage; and they were now in a desperate plight. In answer to their appeal for help, Pyrrhus in 278 crossed over to Sicily. He was gone nearly three years, and the Romans utilized the opportunity to the full. The rebellious Samnites and Lucanians were brought into line, and some of the Greek cities were won back. When in 276 Pyrrhus returned, they had the situation well in hand. He had fared but little better in the new venture than in the old. At first he had carried everything before him, but his success was short-lived. The Syracusans soon became afraid that he would attempt to make himself their master, and ceased to support him.

His second Italian venture fared worse than the first. Near the Samnite town of Beneventum he came to blows with the veteran Manius Curius Dentatus, and was badly defeated (275). Plainly the west was no place for him to found an empire, and at that moment the prospects in Greece began to look attractive. Leaving a garrison in Tarentum, he sailed away, and a little later he withdrew most of his garrison to strengthen his army in Greece. Tarentum, left to shift for herself, surrendered (272). In the next few years the Romans subjugated the few remaining independent districts of southern Italy. By 265 she controlled all of peninsular Italy.

Less than two centuries and a half elapsed between the expulsion of the kings from Rome and the completion of her mastery of Italy. From a small community with a land area of less than 400 square miles, she had come to control nearly 60,000 square miles, and most of the people of this area were sincerely loyal to her. Few states in the history of the world can claim such a record of achievement.

# 6

******************************************************************************************

# *Roman Civilization Under the Early Republic: Political Evolution*

## Lines of Cultural Development

While the Romans were fighting the wars which assured their freedom and made them the masters of Italy, they were also evolving a new civilization. True to their national character, they made it practical rather than ideal or aesthetic. War, government, law, and religion were highly developed, as were the arts of building camps, roads, and aqueducts. Although the Romans had an alphabet and written documents, they had little that could be called literature. In the fine arts they still relied upon Greek or Etruscan workmen, and had few if any beautiful buildings, statues, or paintings. Homes were small, crude, and comfortless, and economic life remained on primitive levels. In short, Roman civilization was still during this period essentially a native product, suited to the hard conditions of life in war-torn Italy, and nearly isolated from the cultural currents which flowed from older lands. It is fitting to begin our discussion with a survey of the political and social progress of the Roman people during this period, for in these fields the Romans first showed their creative power, and made their greatest contributions to the development of the world at large.

## Political and Social Evolution

The nature of Roman government and social organization under the monarchy has been treated already in Chapter 4. It would seem that the expulsion of the kings at first resulted merely in the substitution for the kingship of two annually elected consuls and several priesthoods.

Its subsequent evolution was marked by four important innovations. The first of these was to break the power of the clans and other kinship-groups over the people, and to make them dependent directly upon the state. A second major change occurred when the state granted to the plebeians complete political and social equality with the patricians. The third important change was gradually consummated as the government assumed a large number of functions not exercised by the monarchy, and created new offices to perform them. Lastly, it worked out a system of government for dependencies which enabled it to unite the peoples of Italy under its suzerainty, and to win their loyal co-operation.

*Patricians and Plebeians in the Early Republic*

It would seem that the revolution which made Rome a republic was the work of the patrician aristocracy, and to it, in the first instance, went the fruits of victory. Its members had wealth, political and military experience, and clan solidarity, and an unusually large proportion of them were persons of great ability. The plebeians were generally poor, lacked the closely-knit clan relations of the patricians, and had had little or no experience in either government or war. Many of them were the clients of the great patrician aristocrats, and were accustomed to a position of dependency. All consuls and senators were drawn from the patrician order, and the Assembly of the Curiae was completely dominated by them. The laws were unwritten, and could be manipulated by a magistrate to favor his own class or friends. To do business with the courts at all, or to practice the religious cults of the state, one had to know an elaborate set of verbal forms and ceremonies, and the aristocracy guarded these secrets as jealously as any modern lodge does its ritual. All in all, its position seemed impregnable.

The plebeian class was divided into two groups — urban and rural. The former owed its existence in Rome largely to the stimulation of industry and commerce by the Etruscans. Some of its members were well-to-do shopowners and merchants, but the majority were working men who suffered severely in the economic depression that followed the departure of the kings. The rural plebeians were small landholders, or tenants on the estates of patrician landlords. In any case their holdings were small, and they were harassed by crop failures and the devastation caused by the inroads of enemies. Frequently they fell into debt to their landlords or other rich patricians, and in the ancient world debt was a short-cut to slavery. Since they were barred from personal appearance in the courts and from all political power, they found their only protection from oppression in the aid rendered by their patrons, and this was probably both insecure and humiliating.

### *First Steps Toward Equality of the Classes*

The first step toward the equalization of the patricians and plebeians was taken so early that later tradition assigned it to the Etruscan king Servius Tullius. The real date is unknown. To increase the size of the army all men, whether patricians or plebeians, who had sufficient property in land to enable them to equip themselves for service, were called upon to enter the armed forces; and the kind of service which each had to perform was determined by his wealth. For this purpose a survey (*census*) was made, and the population was divided into six property classes, each of which had its own type of armament. This census was revised periodically. But military service brought with it political privilege, and the net result of the military reform was the beginning of a new assembly — the "Assembly of the Centuries." Each class was divided into an arbitrary number of *centuries*, or voting-groups, which served the same purpose that the *curiae* did in the *Comitia Curiata*. Such a plan could hardly be expected to favor the poor. Of a total of 193 *centuries* in the new assembly, the relatively few members of the highest class had 98, a clear majority. Worse yet, the voting stopped as soon as a majority had been counted for or against a proposition, and so the votes of the lower classes were probably seldom called for. But by breaking down the rule that birth alone determined man's standing in political life, the reform helped the plebeians somewhat. The new assembly rapidly superseded the old *Comitia Curiata* as a legislative and elective body, although purely formal meetings of the latter were still held, to give legal validity to measures adopted by the Assembly of the Centuries.

But the Republic had not been many years in existence when other and more drastic measures were taken by the plebeians to defend themselves against official oppression and the injustice of the laws. Probably sometime before 490 B.C. (again the date is uncertain), the whole body of plebeians renounced their connection with a state in whose government they had no part, and began a new settlement on a hill some miles from the city. To induce them to return, the patricians made sweeping concessions. These, with other privileges won within the next fifty years, made the organized body of plebeians a veritable "state within a state." They were to have an assembly and officials of their own, the latter with ample powers to protect the plebeians against the regular magistrates. Such was the origin of plebeian tribunes, who finally came to be ten in number. They had four distinguishing characteristics. The first was *personal inviolability*. Any person injuring or insulting one of them was subject to death and confiscation of property. Their second prerogative was the "*right of aid*." This enabled them to free from arrest and protect from official oppression any plebeian who appealed to them. A third tribunician power was that of the *veto*, by virtue of which they could annul any official act, or prohibit in advance any legislative proposal injurious to the interests of the plebeians. As a climax to their powers they had the right to summon and preside over meetings of the new plebeian assembly — *Comitia Tributa* or "Assembly of the Tribes." Their only important limitation was that they had to be unanimous in order to act. Armed with such powers, the tribunes could, when agreed among themselves, override all the other agencies of government. They were soon admitted to the Senate, and it was conceded that they might arrest and punish any magistrate who disobeyed them. As clerks and assistants they had two *plebeian aediles* of whom more shall be said later.

Whereas the Assembly of the Curiae was organized on the basis of blood kinship, and that of the Centuries on the basis of wealth, the Assembly of the Tribes had voting-groups based upon residence. The territory of the Roman state was divided into twenty-one (later thirty-five) districts, called *tribus* — a word incorrectly translated "tribe." The plebeians from each district formed a voting unit in the plebeian assembly. Later on, patricians were admitted to vote upon legislation which was brought before it, but not upon the election of plebeian officials.

Thus for about two centuries there were in Rome two governments, one created in direct opposition to the other. In a Greek city-state this condition would have meant conspiracies, revolutions, massacres, confiscations, and foreign conquest, but in Rome nothing of the sort happened. The struggle between the classes was carried on in an orderly, legal manner, and however bitterly domestic issues might be contested, it was always a united Roman people who faced foreign enemies. The patricians had the wisdom to yield gradually and gracefully rather than to fight to the bitter end, and concessions once granted were never again brought into question. Thus this critical situation was finally resolved by a complete reconciliation, which left no heritage of bitterness from the struggle that had gone on so long.

*The Twelve Tables: Political and Social Significance*

While the plebeians were winning for themselves and their tribunes a recognized place in the state, they were also struggling toward legal and social equality with the patricians. As we have seen, the patricians used their monopoly of knowledge of the laws and of legal procedure to manipulate them against their unprivileged fellow-citizens. About 450 the plebeians won their point, and a commission of ten men (*Decem viri*) was chosen to take charge of the state for a year in place of the ordinary magistrates, and during that time to reduce the laws to writing. Since the task was not completed at the end of the first year, a second board was chosen for the following year. Later tradition accused the second commission — particularly the aristocrat Appius Claudius — of tyranny, and related that it was forced to resign; but like so many Roman legends, this one is gravely suspect. At any rate, the two commissions produced Rome's first law-code, the Twelve Tables.

This code was a mixture of primitive crudity, cruelty, and superstition with more enlightened principles. The law of retaliation governed the punishment of personal injuries unless the offender paid damages. Debtors might be sold into slavery, and persons who damaged standing grain were hanged. For a number of offenses the penalty was "Let him be accursed" — a probable declaration of religious boycott against the criminal, which would deprive him of all contact with his fellowmen. But against these primitive survivals we must place other provisions which safeguarded the property rights of married women, permitted freedom of contract and testamentary disposition, and regulated interest rates. The intermarriage of patricians and plebeians was forbidden, but in the courts both classes were to have equal standing. Characteristically, the code contained a list of days which were unlucky (*nefasti*), when courts could not sit or assemblies meet. The Twelve Tables, while modified in some details, remained the foundation upon which all subsequent Roman law was built; and Cicero, writing four centuries after their compilation, tells us that even in his day Roman schoolboys learned the whole code by heart.

With the laws clearly expressed, the plebeians could effectively attack those which were hostile to their class, or plead for supplementary legislation to benefit them. Within a year the tribunes Valerius and Horatius secured the passage of a series of laws which reaffirmed the rights of tribunes, provided for appeals from the sentences of magistrates to the Assembly of the Centuries, and (probably) compelled the same assembly to act upon legislation proposed by the Assembly of the Tribes. A few years later the intermarriage of patricians and plebeians was legalized. In 445 a characteristically Roman device opened even the higher magistracies to plebeians: the Senate might thereafter at any time decree that for the next year there would be no consuls, but that instead there should be a board of from three to six "military tribunes with consular power." In the next seventy-three years military tribunes were chosen fifty times. This office was open to plebeians, and they frequently attained it. In 421, when the office of *quaestor* was created to care for the finances of the state, plebeians were made eligible to it. Then came a lull in the strife, which continued for about thirty years.

### *The Sexto-Licinian Laws and the Final Plebeian Victory*

The recurrence of civil strife in the years following 390 seems to have been largely due to the economic distress which followed the Gallic invasion. The poor, reduced to want by the ravages of the enemy, clamored for relief; and the richer plebeians renewed their demand for full political rights. The struggle came to a head in the later 370's, when the tribunes Sextius and Licinius sponsored a series of laws to satisfy the demands of both groups. After a spirited contest which lasted several years they succeeded. In 367 the Sexto-Licinian Laws were passed, and another stage was reached in the solution of the class problem.

As may be surmised from the varied interests which prompted their passage, the Sexto-Licinian Laws dealt with several subjects. The plebeian leaders secured the re-establishment of the consulship, with the proviso that one consul each year might be a plebeian. (A few years later it was enacted that one consul *must be* a plebeian, and that both of them *might be*.) As a concession to the patricians, and to meet the pressure of increased government business, the consulship was shorn of some of its powers. These were thenceforth to be exercised by an official called a *praetor*, who had to be a patrician. The poor secured some relief from their debts by the passage of a law providing that interest already paid on a debt should be deducted from the principal, and giving the debtors four years more in which to discharge the remainder of their obligations. Perhaps with a view to compelling the state to keep control of its public lands so that there would always be some available for distribution as small farms, Sextius and Licinius carried a law providing that no man without sons could rent more than 500 *jugera* of the public domain, with a maximum of 1000 for men with two or more sons. The same law forbade the pasturing of more than 100 oxen or 500 sheep on a tract rented from the state.

Although eighty more years were to elapse before the final termination of the class struggle, the Sexto-Licinian Laws broke the back of patrician resistance to the demands of the plebeians. Within a few years all of the important magistracies and priesthoods of the state were open to men of plebeian rank, and with them went membership in the Senate. The poor, to whom such prizes were unattainable under any conditions, gained others more to their liking. Probably in 326 imprisonment and slavery for debt were forbidden, and as new colonies were founded on conquered lands, a constant stream of settlers was provided with farms. Only those who were too unenterprising or too well-off to leave the city were passed over, and these were not likely to cause trouble.

In 312 the patrician censor Appius Claudius undertook to ameliorate the condition of Rome's urban population at the expense of the rural element. He caused the first aqueduct to be built to improve the city's water-supply. Because the population of the capital had grown out of all proportion to that of the rural districts, the old arrangement by which they had been enrolled in only four of the twenty-one tribes gave the country people an unfair preponderance in the Assembly of the Tribes. Appius Claudius enrolled the urban populace indiscriminately in all the tribes, and as they were better able to attend meetings than were their country brethren, this move gave them a great advantage. Up to that time the urban middle class had suffered from the rule that only real property counted in assigning a voter to his proper class in the *Comitia Centuriata*. Appius Claudius counted money and merchandise as well as land, and thus at a stroke greatly increased both the number of voters in the higher classes and the man-power available for military service. He even enrolled the sons of freedmen in the Senate — a revolutionary step in that aristocratic society. A few years later he sponsored the publication of a lawbook in which all of the jealously guarded mysteries of court procedure were clearly explained. His policies as censor were too radical for the time and country, and few of his innovations were allowed to stand, but they remained as precedents for future reformers.

The last act in the struggle between the classes came in 287 B.C. Under circumstances of which we have only vague and contradictory reports, the urban populace renewed its agitation, and as a result the Hortensian Law was enacted. The Assembly of the Tribes had long been in the habit of passing resolutions (*plebiscita*), which thereafter might either be re-enacted by the Assembly of the Centuries or brought before the Senate for confirmation. The Hortensian Law provided that these resolutions should have the force of law without the necessity of confirmation by the Senate or the assembly. It may have been at this time that the patricians were given a limited membership in the Assembly of the Tribes.

Thus the Roman class struggle had ended, and the plebeians were the victors. In the beginning the patricians had been the only true Roman citizens, and had monopolized the machinery of government. Then the plebeians had organized a second state inside of and in a sense opposed to the first; and now the two had coalesced to form one. Every office of note was open to plebeians. Every adult male Roman citizen was a voter, and the will of a majority of the voting groups in the assemblies was law. Plebeians made up a majority of the Senate, and a new nobility, of mixed patrician and plebeian stock, based upon office-holding, had taken the place of the old patrician order. Did these developments make Rome a democracy? To answer this question, we must survey the structure and workings of her government as it emerged from this class strife.

## Roman Government in the Third Century B.C.

### *Religious Functions of the State*

The functions of the Roman state (and hence of the officials who represented it) were of three kinds — religious, civil, and military. The first, religion, was woven into the fabric of Roman life to an extent which a member of a modern Christian community can hardly appreciate. Its part in private life will be discussed in the following chapter. But it was also one of the most important fields of activity of the state, and not infrequently it shaped public policies with a strong hand. The religious functions of the state and its officials fell into two classes: divination and worship.

A Roman official could not undertake any important business until the will of the gods regarding it had been determined. To found a colony, hold an assembly, or fight a battle without first taking this important step was unthinkable. The practice was called "taking the auspices," and it was the prerogative of the highest-ranking official if done in Rome, or of the commander-in-chief of the army if taken during a campaign. The divine will was supposed to be made known to men by thunder, the flight of birds, the birth of deformed animals and children, or unusual appearances in the entrails of sacrificed animals. In performing this function the official in charge was assisted by professional diviners, called *augurs* or *haruspices*. The former were Romans of good social standing; but the latter, who confined themselves to the inspection of entrails, were almost always Etruscans, and were held in low esteem.

*Metropolitan Museum*

SACRIFICIAL PROCESSION
*Glass Relief*

In addition to knowing the will of the gods, one had to keep them on good terms with the Roman people by appropriate acts of worship. Some sacrifices and prayers were mere matters of routine administration, to be performed at stated times. Such were the services which opened a session of the Senate or of one of the assemblies. There were also festivals to be held at fixed times each year. But officials had to be constantly on the alert for signs that the gods were angry. Especially in times of crisis, reports would reach them that animals had spoken, that swarms of bees had settled upon an altar, or that a mule had borne a colt. Such happenings meant that the gods were angry, and the Senate, after solemnly debating the matter and taking the advice of some of the priesthoods, would order expiatory sacrifices.

Roman priests were officials of the state; and like other officials, they were laymen chosen without preliminary training to fill a specified post, either for a term of years or for life. They were not confined to their priestly duties, and frequently the same man would at the same time hold one or more priesthoods along with an important secular office. Chief among them were the nine *Pontifices*, whose chairman, the *Pontifex Maximus*, was the highest ranking priest in Rome, and had extensive powers over the other priesthoods. Next in rank were the *Flamines*, each of whom was devoted to the worship of a different god. The worship of the fire-spirit was in the hands of six Vestal Virgins, who had to be women of unspotted character and who were forbidden to marry. If one of them allowed the sacred fire of Vesta to go out, she was beaten by the *Pontifex Maximus;* and if guilty of unchastity, she was buried alive. In other respects, however, they suffered few or no deprivations. The Board of Ten for the Celebration of Sacred Rites had charge of the famous *Sibylline Books*, a collection of prophecies written in Greek, and said to have been brought to Rome from Cumae.

While each individual was free to worship in private any god that pleased his fancy, no deity could have a temple or be worshiped publicly within the *pomoerium* without the consent of the Senate. So important a matter was the "naturalization" of foreign gods that this consent was given very slowly and grudgingly. Usually a new cult had to be conducted for some years outside the city before being admitted to it.

### *Civil Administration and Imperium*

The civil powers of the magistrates (*potestas*) covered ordinary judicial and administrative business. In exercising them they were strictly controlled by the laws and by the right of appeal to the Assembly of the Centuries or to the tribunes, which every citizen enjoyed. Except in the most severe crises, when it was deemed necessary to proclaim martial law and appoint a dictator, this was the only kind of authority enjoyed by magistrates within the city of Rome.

But when vested with the command of an army, or when appointed dictator in a time of crisis, a Roman magistrate had the power of life and death without appeal over all persons committed to his care by the terms of his appointment. This power was called *imperium* Through his possession of it he was enabled to enforce a type of military discipline far stricter than any known to the armies of the Greek states. It also applied to the civilian population of districts under military occupation. But the possession of *imperium* did not free the holder from the necessity of obeying the Senate and the assemblies in matters of policy, and it could only be used to carry out the orders which had been received from them.

### *The Magistrates*

Having seen the nature of the powers with which the state was vested, we must now observe the agencies through which these powers were exercised. In the earliest days of the Republic, the executive and judicial powers of the state were united in the two consuls. They were chosen by the assembly, held office for a year, and could not normally be chosen for two successive terms. They wore togas bordered with broad purple stripes, and one of the prerogatives of the office was to use the *sella curulis* — a chair with legs shaped somewhat like those of a campstool. When on duty each of them was preceded as he traveled by twelve attendants called *lictors*, each of whom bore, while in the city, a bundle of rods to signify that his master could chastise culprits. When outside the *pomoerium*, each lictor bound an axe with his rods, to signify that the magistrate might inflict capital punishment. These rods (with or without the axe) were called *fasces*.

The consuls had inherited collectively the powers formerly held by the king; but they held them in a much-diminished form. Each of them tended to act as a check upon the other; and the Senate kept a close watch upon both. The Senate and the great majority of the Roman people were determined that no man should ever revive the hated kingship, and so every device was used to keep the consuls properly subordinated to the Senate and the assemblies. Moreover, the men who were chosen for the position were themselves, it would seem, thoroughly in sympathy with the republican form of government, and we hear of no well-authenticated instances of their usurping powers which did not belong to them. The Romans, after all, did not in the early ages of their history produce leaders cursed with that selfish individualism which was the bane of Greek political life.

At an early date the growing volume of state business forced the Romans to devise a more elaborate set of executive agencies. About 450 the introduction of a system of military service based upon property holding necessitated the taking of a census, and for this purpose the office of censor was created. Every five years two were chosen, to hold office for eighteen months. They counted the citizens, assigned each to his appropriate property class, and compiled a list of senators. In the cases of both senators and ordinary citizens they had the right to make inquiries into personal conduct, and to remove the former from the Senate list, or to brand the latter with public infamy, for improper conduct. They also acted as auditors and comptrollers of finance, in which capacity they let contracts for public works, and even levied taxes. Each census was closed with solemn religious rites intended to purify the Roman people of all religious guilt incurred since the last census.

About 421 the control of the treasury was withdrawn from the consuls and vested in a board of four *quaestors*, elected annually. Two of them served as quartermasters for the consuls when the latter were in command of the armies, while the others assumed charge of the treasury and record office located under the temple of Saturn, and hence called the *aerarium Saturni*. The quaestors were usually young men just entering upon a political career.

We have seen (Chapter 6) under what circumstances the office of *praetor* was created. In powers and functions the praetor was a small-scale replica of a consul, for he could, on occasion, do practically anything that a consul could do. But the consuls ranked above him, and where they were present he was under their orders. In practice, although he might, in emergencies, lead armies or summon meetings of the Senate, his routine duties were judicial. The consuls surrendered to him the administration of justice, leaving them free for the more pressing military duties entailed by the never-ending wars of the time. In the first century of the praetorship's existence there was only one praetor, but in 244 B.C., the number was raised to two. Thereafter one of them (the *praetor urbanus* or "city praetor") administered justice in cases involving Roman citizens; while the other (the *praetor peregrinus* or "foreign praetor") took charge of those in which both parties were foreigners. They had the same insignia as the consuls, except that the number of lictors attending them varied from two to six.

In the period of the Samnite Wars it was frequently found necessary to keep a capable consul or praetor at his post after his term of office had expired. To do this a new custom was developed. A successor would be elected to care for the ordinary duties of the office, but his predecessor would be continued in charge of the task for which he was needed, sometimes for several years. In such cases his title was *proconsul* or *propraetor*. By this means the disadvantages of annual election were partly overcome.

For miscellaneous duties connected with the government of the city of Rome there was a board of four *aediles*, who acted as police commissioners, judges of petty jurisdiction, and inspectors of markets and buildings. To them also fell the task of repairing the streets, and of providing a food-supply for the citizens.

Occasionally, in times of severe crisis, all of the ordinary magistrates were for a time superseded by a single chief executive, the *dictator*. He was appointed by one of the consuls on authorization by the Senate. The name, in view of its present-day connotation, is misleading. The Roman dictator did, it is true, have complete control of the government for a period not to exceed six months, but he was bound by the laws and by the instructions issued to him when he was chosen. As soon as the purpose for which he had been appointed was accomplished, the dictator was required to resign; and never during this period of Roman history did he fail to do so. The dictator had the right to appoint an assistant whose title was "Master of the Cavalry" (*magister equitum*). To denote his exalted position, the dictator had the ordinary insignia of high office, but in addition, his *lictors* numbered twenty-four.

The plebeian tribunes and their functions have been fully discussed. Their office continued to be an important one, even after the class struggle which produced it had ended.

Theoretically any freeborn Roman of good character was eligible for office, but the fact was far different. No public office paid any salary, and the state did not even furnish the incumbent with clerical help. Clan and family feelings were so strong that only occasionally did an interloper (a "new man") break into the charmed circle and then the clique whose prerogatives he had usurped were sullen and cool toward him.

With this bewildering variety of officials there was a strong chance that chaos would settle upon the government, and the chance was greatly strengthened by the obstructive powers of the tribunes. From this danger the state was saved by two safeguards. The first was the paramount authority enjoyed by the consuls. Except when a dictator was in office, they could annul the acts of all officials except the plebeian tribunes. Thus, when necessary, they could secure unity of policy and action. The second co-ordinating factor was the Senate, which now demands our consideration.

### *The Senate and the Assemblies*

Throughout the first four centuries of the Roman Republic, the Senate consisted of three hundred members, chosen every five years by the censors. To be eligible for membership, one had to be a freeborn Roman citizen of mature age and good character. Such, at least, was the theory; but in practice the matter was not so simple. In making up their lists the censors first included ex-magistrates, and then the persons who had achieved glory in war, or who came of good families. Thus, while men of the middle class might gain membership, the great majority of the senators belonged to a small aristocratic clique of patrician and plebeian families, closely intermarried, thoroughly class-conscious, and steeped from infancy in the mysteries of government. From this senatorial aristocracy the magistrates were almost always taken (including even the plebeian tribunes). They shared its opinions and its prejudices, and wished to stand well with it. Furthermore, from it they could get valuable advice on all sorts of problems, based upon the collective experience of men who had become minutely acquainted with these problems. Hence the magistrates were almost always in sympathy with the aristocracy. Even the tribunes, who were by tradition the champions of popular rights, succumbed to its spell, for not only did they largely cease to make trouble, but on occasion they even vetoed radical proposals.

As Rome had no written constitution, the powers of the Senate were ill defined. Its decrees had the force of law unless annulled by an act of the Assembly of the Tribes. By tacit consent, it controlled finance, assigned military commands, declared war, and ratified treaties. The Assembly might interfere in any of these spheres, but seldom did. When directed by competent and aggressive leaders, the Senate was likely to invade almost any department of government.

Theoretically the last word in matters of government lay with the popular assemblies, whose organization we have studied. A *plebiscitum* passed by the Assembly of the Tribes had the force of law, while a *lex* enacted by the Assembly of the Centuries required only a formal senatorial confirmation stating that it was properly drawn up. Hence we must now consider the respective parts played by these bodies in the Roman government, and how well they expressed the popular will.

Both were composed of any full citizens who could be personally present. Thus the same voters sat in both, but they were differently organized and had different procedures. As a rule the Assembly of the Tribes was summoned to legislate, and the Assembly of the Centuries to elect the higher officials except plebeian tribunes. The tribunes presided over the former, and a praetor or consul over the latter. Neither was dominated by a simple majority vote. A majority of the voters present from eighteen tribes or from ninety-seven centuries carried the decision. Thus in either case less than a third of the total number of voters could if properly distributed dominate the assembly.[1] In order to vote, one must be personally present in Rome, and as many citizens lived far from the capital, only a minority of the total number could attend a given session. Technicalities abounded. A simple tribunician veto or a declaration that the omens were unfavorable would stop action on any measure. Occasionally a disgruntled minority in the Senate would carry a pet project to the assemblies. This was very likely to be true of aggressive foreign policies, which the Senate generally opposed, and it involved Rome in several of her severest

[1] If 100 voters were present in each of the thirty-five tribes, 51 voters from each of eighteen tribes, or a total of 918 voters out of 3500, could theoretically win a decision.

wars. But on the whole the Senate was the mainspring of government. Most important of all, the people trusted their aristocratic leaders, and the trust was seldom misplaced.

### *The Army*

In a state which was constantly at war the army was certain to occupy an important place, and the Roman army was no exception to the rule. In the early Republic it was a citizen army. Every male possessing a small property qualification had, between the ages of seventeen and forty-six, to serve at least sixteen years. In times of stress even boys, old men, and the very poor were pressed into service. Originally the men of each property class had been differently armed, but the introduction of pay for military service tended to standardize equipment. In the third century the state even furnished a cavalryman the money with which to purchase his horse. Army discipline was strict. From the time that a recruit took the military oath until he was mustered out of service, he was governed by martial law, and could be put to death for cowardice in battle, desertion, sleeping while on guard, and other serious offenses.

In the third century B.C. the Roman army had abandoned the phalanx formation for a flexible grouping which permitted the greatest possible efficiency either of mass action or of maneuvering with isolated detachments. The basic unit of organization was the legion (*legio*), a brigade consisting of from 4000 to 5200 infantry and 300 cavalry. The infantry of a legion was divided into forty-five [1] companies called *maniples*, each of which had as officers two centurions (who combined the functions of a second lieutenant with those of a company first sergeant), two rear-guard officers, and two standard-bearers. The older of the centurions commanded the maniple, but if he were absent, dead, or disabled, the command passed from one officer to another in a fixed sequence. In like manner the legionary cavalry was divided into ten squadrons (*turmae*), each of which was officered by three *decurions*. At the head of the legion were from three to six *military tribunes*, some of whom were elected by the people, while others were appointed by the commander-in-chief. Thus each maniple of infantry and each squadron of cavalry was a complete unit in itself, capable of maneuvering independently if accidentally separated from the rest, or of executing orders demanding the use of small detachments. This feature of the new legionary organization was especially valuable for fighting on mountainous terrain, and had repeatedly proved

[1] Later, thirty.

its worth in the later phases of the Samnite wars and in the struggle with Pyrrhus. At the same time, the whole force of a legion could be effectively concentrated when necessary.

Roman infantry included both light-armed skirmishers and heavy-armed infantry of the line, the latter about three times as numerous as the former. The skirmishers (*velites*) had helmets and shields, but wore no body-armor, and were armed with spears and light javelins. Infantry of the line had as standard defensive equipment helmets, oblong shields, corselets to protect their bodies, and greaves to cover the lower parts of their legs. Their offensive armament consisted of two heavy javelins and a short, double-edged sword for each man.

Troops furnished by the Latin and Italian allies were armed and disciplined like Roman-citizen soldiers, except that in place of the legion they were organized into smaller bodies called *cohortes* (infantry), or *alae* (cavalry). Each numbered about 600 men. They were under the immediate command of their own officers, but had to obey the orders of the Roman commanders in whose armies they were serving. Usually an army consisted of equal numbers of citizens and allies, except that the allies furnished a double quota of cavalry. The ordinary consular army consisted of two legions and a proportionate quota of allied troops, with a total strength of from 17,000 to 22,000 men.

There is no finer tribute to the discipline of the Roman soldier or to the organization of the army in which he served than the camp in which he spent his nights. When an army was on the march, a detachment of engineers was usually sent ahead to select a campsite, and to lay it out before the main body of the soldiers arrived. The plan was practically invariable — a square which for an army of 20,000 men would measure 2000 feet on a side. When the army arrived, often after a march of twenty miles, carrying heavy packs, the soldiers fell to work fortifying it. Each centurion knew exactly what part of the work his maniple was to perform. A deep ditch was dug, and the earth was thrown up on the inside to form an embankment, in the top of which palisades were set. Four spaces were left for gates, which were carefully fortified. Inside this enclosure each maniple of infantry, each squadron of cavalry, and each body of allies, had a fixed place for its tents. Streets traversed the camp, crossing each other at right angles. Only when this essential task was completed and details of guards were on duty to prevent surprise attacks did the soldiers unpack their hand-mills, grind the wheat or barley which constituted their rations, and bake cakes or cook porridge for their suppers. The advantage which the possession of such a camp gave to a Roman army would be hard

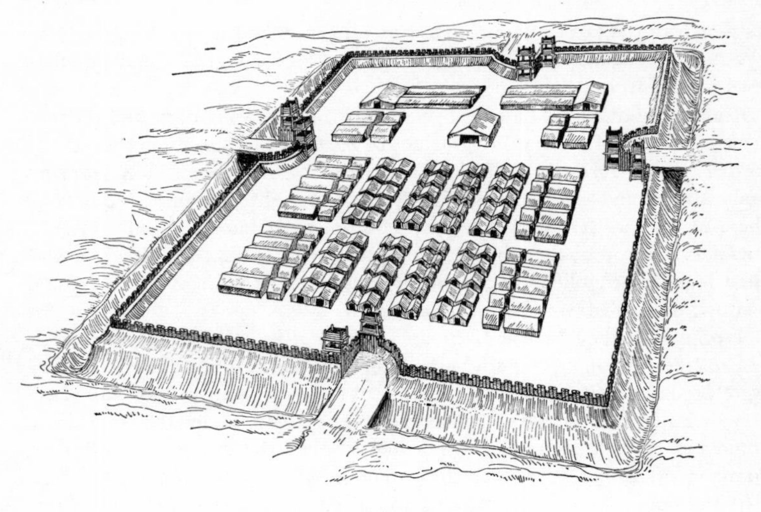

PLAN OF A ROMAN CAMP

to exaggerate. Not only could it pass its nights in relative security, but the commander could await favorable moments to attack the enemy, and if beaten in the field, had always a rallying point in which to reorganize his forces. Camps intended for continuous occupation over a long period of time had much more elaborate fortifications than those which were to be used but a short time by armies on the march. The experience gained by the soldiers in the use of the spade proved very valuable in sieges, where relieving forces often found that the Roman besiegers were surrounded by a double line of entrenchments — one to hold back the besieged, and the other to repel attacks from without.

The battle tactics of this formidable fighting force, while reasonably effective and generally adequate to the exigencies of Italian warfare, were as yet far from a complete realization of the possibilities which the legionary formation afforded. Cavalry was usually employed to cover the flanks of an army, for scouting or foraging, or to pursue a beaten enemy. Cavalry charges such as those which won battles for Alexander the Great or Pyrrhus were unknown. The infantry was drawn up in three lines, the openings between the maniples of the front line being covered by the maniples of the second line. A battle usually began with a volley of javelins hurled by the front line, after which the soldiers used their swords and their remaining javelins for close fighting. When the first line could maintain the conflict no longer, the men sifted back through the openings in the second line, which then renewed the attack. In cases of emergency the maneuver would be repeated, and the third line would then be brought into action. In this way the enemy had for a long time to deal with fresh and unwearied troops. Except in the rare instances when the Romans were opposed by a tactician of a high order, this sustained pounding would usually bring them ultimate victory.

On the other hand, the Roman generals of the fourth and early third centuries made little if any effort to concentrate masses of men at critical points, or to vary the order of fighting to meet new conditions which might develop during a battle. Since experience was later to prove that the manipular organization of the legion was splendidly adapted to such maneuvers, we can only conclude that at this time Rome's commanders were entirely ignorant of the science of winning battles at minimum cost in human life. The law required that even a military tribune must have served a minimum of five campaigns, and a consul at least ten. Hence all the officers were veteran soldiers, and the consuls in particular were certain to be well acquainted with their routine duties. Occasionally, as in the campaign which destroyed the army of the Samnites and their allies at Sentinum, they displayed a profound understanding of large-scale strategy. But the practice of changing commanders every year tended to prevent a Roman from gaining the long and continuous experience in command which would enable him to make instantaneous and correct decisions upon the battlefield. Moreover, even when defeated he had advantages which made it possible for him to retrieve his mistakes. He had an inexhaustible supply of manpower from which to fashion new armies, while the roads and Latin colonies scattered over the surface of Italy were insuperable obstacles to invaders such as Pyrrhus. Most important of all, Rome had won the loyalty of her allies. The farsighted wisdom which had built these bulwarks of Roman rule, together with indomitable courage and fortitude, gave to Rome the power to win wars when battles had been lost.

## The Roman Confederation

The Roman Republic stood, as we have seen, at the head of a confederation which included all of peninsular Italy. This body, whose organization was the finest monument to senatorial statesmanship, included three chief classes of members: Roman citizens, Latins, and Italian allies. But it was a fundamental maxim of Roman policy that every case should be treated as nearly as possible on its individual merits, and as no two were exactly alike, each class had numerous subdivisions. While we have already seen something of the nature of this confederacy, it will be well to consider it in the elaborate form in which it existed about 265 B.C.

*Grades of Membership*

We have learned that Roman citizens were divided into two classes: full and non-voting. The full citizens living in Rome or its neighborhood needed no local organization other than that provided by the assemblies and magistrates. Others to whom the state had given land at a distance from the city were governed by deputies of the praetors, and had little or no local organization. But a citizen-colony like Antium, or a Latin or Italian city to which full citizenship had been granted, enjoyed complete local self-government, and its citizens had only to go to Rome to vote in the assemblies. Such colonies were called *municipia*. Non-voting citizens, while enjoying the private rights of Roman citizens, were subject to all the burdens of citizenship, but had neither local self-government nor the right to vote and hold office in Rome. All told, the land occupied by Roman citizens may have had an area of some 10,000 square miles, and the citizen population of both sexes and all ages would be about 1,000,000 in number.

The Latins, who enjoyed the rights of *commercium* and *connubium* with Roman citizens and could gain Roman citizenship by settling in Rome, were scattered throughout Italy in thirty-five colonies, which could have no direct relations with each other. Each of these Latin colonies had local self-government and was an ally of Rome with the obligation to furnish a fixed quota of soldiers for her armies. The combined territorial area of these communities was perhaps 5000 square miles, and the inhabitants numbered about 500,000 persons.

The remainder of Italy, some 37,000 square miles, was occupied by a group of persons numbering about 1,500,000, called collectively "Italian Allies." Each community of this class, whether tribe or city, had a separate treaty of alliance with Rome, but these treaties were by no means uniform. Most of them provided that the Italian ally must furnish a fixed quota of ships or soldiers for Rome's use; however, in the case of impoverished and senile Greek cities with a brilliant past but no present or future prospects, this obligation was sometimes waived. When allied troops were in Roman service, the Roman state furnished them with food. All Italian communities had the right of *commercium* with Rome, and most of them had also that of *connubium*; yet they did not enjoy these rights in other allied states. Except in the case of Tarentum, Rome maintained no garrisons among them. They might have no foreign relations of any kind except with Rome; but they did have complete freedom in local government, with one condition. Rome insisted that each state be governed by an aristocracy, for she did not trust the masses. Neither Latins nor Italians paid any tribute, but they sometimes rented Roman public land, for which they paid the same rent that a Roman would have given.

### *Bonds of Loyalty and of Fear*

Such a system was in the main fair and just, and its benefits for both parties were obvious. The wars which for centuries had convulsed Italy ceased, and the suzerain would not tolerate revolutions. Strong and predatory communities no longer tyrannized over weak neighbors. Merchants found in the Roman state a sure protector against pirates and robbers, and in the Roman roads which were beginning to span so much of Italy they saw a means for penetrating into hitherto inaccessible localities. On the other hand, the Romans had little or no commercial ambition, and did not try to throttle Italian commerce through fear of competition. There was no domineering interference in local affairs, such as modern imperialists so frequently attempt. Lastly, if one were not satisfied, there was always the hope of improvement. Every few years some allied city was rewarded for loyal service with some form of Roman citizenship or with a lightening of its burdens. It was easy to develop a sense of loyalty to a suzerain from whom one received so many benefits.

But the confederacy was held together by fear as well as by love. Every Latin colony was in effect a Roman fortress, and they were so located as to control all the strategic mountain passes, river crossings, and harbors. The real purpose of the Roman roads and bridges was to facilitate the transport of troops, and over them an army could reach any rebellious people in a few days at the most. Thus an uprising was easily nipped in the bud, and Rome punished rebels with a heavy hand. In each allied city the aristocracy was securely bound to the cause of Roman supremacy, which relieved it from the threat of social revolution. By this combination of positive and negative elements the confederacy was so securely cemented together that no foreign invader was able to break it apart.

# 7

## *Roman Civilization Under the Early Republic: Private Life and Culture*

### Dominant Influences: Agriculture and Religion

In the third century b.c. the weakening of class distinctions and the absence of glaring inequalities of wealth resulted in the evolution of a homogeneous culture, which can, with some exceptions, be described as a unit. Life was simple and somewhat crude, wedded to agriculture as a means of livelihood, and governed by rigid traditions inherited from a hoary past. Clan and family bonds were strong, and they were fortified by a religion which emphasized ancestor worship. Aesthetic interests were few, and the Romans had done little to satisfy them.

#### *Agriculture and Farm Life*

It is safe to say that about 265 b.c., the average Roman family either was engaged directly in agriculture, or had an immediate farm background. No doubt there were among Roman citizens a few professional craftsmen, and some laborers who lived by working for wages, but these were somewhat exceptional cases. Farms and fortunes alike were small. A tract of seven *jugera* (less than 4½ acres) was sufficient to support an average family, and one of twenty-five *jugera* was ample for a family of senatorial rank. Even holdings of two *jugera* or less were common.

The small size of the holdings and the scarcity and crudity of agricultural implements tended strongly to place Roman farming on a subsistence basis. Instead of growing crops primarily for market and considering land as a form of capital, the Romans of the third century b.c. produced food and the raw materials for clothing principally for their own use, and marketed very little. Hence if we are to understand their way of life, we must learn to think in terms quite unfamiliar to us.

While the Roman farmer raised livestock as well as field crops, he pastured his animals most of the time upon state-owned common land, and needed little pasture or meadow land of his own for their support. On the other hand, he could maintain the fertility of the soil only by leaving between a third and a half of his holding fallow each year — a practice which the smaller proprietors could hardly afford to follow. For this reason, and also because of ignorance of fertilizers and of leguminous crops, soil exhaustion was an ever-present danger. Implements were few and crude. On the smaller holdings the spade and the mattock were probably used to break up the soil, for the owners could hardly afford to support ox-teams or to own plows for this purpose. The plows were primitive affairs, which did not turn a furrow, and the land had to be plowed three or four times before grain could be sown. This tedious process required from three to four days for a single *jugerum* (5/8 of an acre). On soil equally good a modern American farmer, even if he uses a two-horse team and a single plow, can break up two acres in a day, and do far better work than the Roman would have done. Grain was sown by hand, cut with a sickle, threshed with a flail or trodden out by animals, and separated from the chaff by throwing it into the air and allowing the wind to blow the chaff away.

Like the Greeks, the Romans were principally interested in the production of grain-crops; but whereas the poor alkaline soil of continental Greece made barley the popular crop, in Latium the richer volcanic lands gave wheat a decided advantage. Spelt, barley, and millet were also grown, along with beans, onions, garlic, peas, and turnips. Grapes and olives had probably been introduced by the Etruscans, and some wine was made, but such crops were the exception rather than the rule. The usual farm animals were cattle, sheep, goats, pigs, and donkeys, and the horse, as elsewhere in the Mediterranean world, was an animal aristocrat used for riding or driving but not for farm-work.

Under such conditions life was simple and laborious. As we have seen, Latium was not an easy land to cultivate. The plains had to be drained, and the hillsides required terracing, before they could be farmed effectively. Military service took weeks or months each year. When not busy in the fields, the farmer and his family made their own clothing, shoes, household furniture, farm implements, pottery, and nearly everything else that they used. They sold little, and had correspondingly small means with which to buy foreign manufactured goods. Thus everyone in the family worked hard and lived simply. Yet life was not without its distractions. Religious holidays were numerous, and citizens were called upon rather frequently to attend meetings of the assemblies or law-courts in Rome. Markets were held in the capital and at various points throughout the rural areas, usually every ninth day. There was little distinction in living standards between rich and poor. Consuls and dictators worked like common men. In later ages conservative Romans loved to tell how the generals who smashed the Samnite Confederacy and defeated Pyrrhus cultivated their lands with their own hands and cooked their own dinners of turnips.

### *The Religious Factor in Roman Life*

Intimately connected with every phase of the Roman's life was his religion. It served to reassure and strengthen him in his battle for a livelihood and in his struggles with his neighbors, and it also expressed and reinforced his natural conservatism. We have seen something of the part which it played in the government of the state, and we must remember that the state only copied, in the beginning, the practices of clans and families. Like the Greeks, the Romans saw little or no order in nature; and they made no attempt to picture any order among the powers that governed it. No prophets or theologians had reduced their beliefs to the form of creeds or dogmas; and so it was a chaos of haphazard ideas, gathered from Italic, Greek, and Etruscan sources to meet very material everyday needs.

The primitive Latins, lacking the imagination of the Greeks, did not think of the powers that ruled the universe as concrete personalities. Their religion was what we call animism — the belief that each material object, force of nature, and customary activity of men or animals has or is presided over by a spirit. The primitive Romans regarded these spirits (*numina*) as impersonal, sexless forces, which manipulated the world about them for either good or ill. Thus the spirit of the fire that blazed on the hearth was *Vesta*, that of the door was *Janus* (from *janua* "door"), and that of the hinges was *Cardea* (from *cardo*, "a hinge"). The family storeroom was presided over by a group of spirits, the *Penates;* and another group, the *Lares*, also held a place as protectors of the household. Associated with each man was a spirit which gave him strength — the *genius*, and similarly, each woman had her *juno*. Perhaps the most important of all were the *di manes*, or spirits of the ancestors. To the Roman, his departed forebears did not become malignant ghosts, but kindly protectors,

*Metropolitan Museum*

LAR: REPRESENTED AS A YOUTH HOLDING A HORN OF PLENTY AND A PATERA

to whom offerings of food were made at meal-times, and who came back each year to attend the family reunion. But not all departed spirits were propitious. There were some — the *Lemures* — who found no peace in the hereafter, and wandered about the world tormenting the living. On a certain night in May of each year the head of a household had to rise at midnight, make an offering of black beans to these fearsome visitors, and repeat a prayer in which he tactfully urged them to leave the house.

In addition to the old Italic animism, which always remained dear to the people, there was also the worship of the so-called "New Gods" — anthropomorphic deities borrowed from the Etruscans or Greeks, or old spirits which had taken on anthropomorphic characteristics. Such were Jupiter the king of the gods, Juno his wife, Minerva the patroness of the arts, and Mars the war-god. Their worship remained largely an affair of state; and although no one doubted either their existence or the propriety of worshiping them, they never gained a strong hold upon the popular mind except in a few cases.

Such a religion was a businesslike, unemotional affair at best, as devoid of fear as of love. But it was free from the taint of human sacrifice and the other abominations which so often disgraced the Semitic religions. The spirits could always be placated if one knew the proper prayers and ritualistic acts. Prayers were usually accompanied by sacrifices, and the words read like legal documents. They informed the spirit what the worshiper expected in return for his gift so exactly that he had no loophole through which to escape the fulfillment of his obligations. Every word had to be repeated correctly, for otherwise the rite lost all value. But if the rites were properly performed, even the most malevolent spirit could be induced to let one alone. There was no obvious connection between religion and morality, but its very legalistic character gave to men a sense of obligation and responsibility which was easily carried over into human relationships. The cult of the ancestral spirits was another aid to moral living, for it strengthened the family bond, and inculcated the habit of carefully scrutinizing one's conduct so as to avoid giving offense to the deified dead. For all that, it must be admitted that morality was primarily a secular matter, which was regulated according to the dictates of prudence and utility.

Mention has already been made of the cult of the deified ancestors, but we must now consider it as a factor in the organization of the family. The Roman family, as we have seen, was strictly patriarchal, and the cult of the ancestors had, accordingly, to be carried on by the sons. When a daughter married, she passed into the family of her husband, and it was from his family that her spirit would receive worship. A son, on the other hand, was responsible for the prescribed sacrifices of salt, flour, and wine, to his ancestors in the male line, and from his own male descendants he would himself receive the same services. Without them the soul could never be happy in the hereafter. Hence the greatest of all misfortunes was to die without sons, for not only the childless man himself, but all of his ancestors, were thus reduced to misery for all time to come. This misfortune could, however, be averted by the adoption of a son, for adopted children had exactly the same duties and standing as real ones. From ancestor worship came the sharp division of relatives into two classes of *agnates* (who were descended from the same ancestors in unbroken male succession), and *cognates* (relatives in general). Only agnates could inherit property and have a place in the family cult.

## The Family and Its Daily Life

### *Patria Potestas*

Over his wife, unmarried female descendants, and his sons and their families, the oldest living male ancestor exercised absolute power. He could punish, sell, or kill them at will. None of them could own property, marry, or undertake legal proceedings without his consent. This was the famous *patria potestas* or "paternal authority." Originally it had been confined to patrician families, but the better class of plebeians had evolved a form of marriage which established it among them as well. Unless the holder voluntarily renounced it, such authority lasted until his death, but it was suspended in the case of a son elected to a state office, and abolished with respect to a daughter when she became a vestal virgin. A married daughter merely passed from the authority of her father into that of her husband or some of his family. In theory the *patria potestas* enabled the holder to play the tyrant, but in fact this seldom if ever happened. Although a Roman woman was legally always a ward of some man, actually she enjoyed a great deal of freedom. She was treated with respect, appeared at all sorts of social functions at which men were present, acted as the mistress of her home, and went visiting if she chose. No doubt sons and daughters were governed firmly, but they were not oppressed. A married son was allowed the use of such property as came into his possession, and public opinion protected him against the danger of being deprived of it. Before taking any action affecting the interests of those under his authority, the head of the household was expected to secure the advice of the older members of the household, and if he grossly abused his

*University Prints*

ALDOBRANDINI MARRIAGE

power, he might be publicly disgraced by the censors. The average father was at the greatest pains to bring his children up well, and to start them on successful careers. Indeed, so strong were family loyalty and affection that they became a formidable force in Roman political life.

### *The Family and Nomenclature*

A number of families descended from a common male ancestor made up a clan (*gens*), whose members were distinguished by a common clan name. Each clan worshiped a common set of ancestral spirits and other divinities, and often had a common burial place for its members. At one time the clan bond had been much stronger than it was in the third century B.C., but the social and political reforms which accompanied the rise of the plebeians had deprived it of practically all legal significance, and left it merely sentimental in character.

Clan and family relationships were clearly expressed in the names of both men and women. Normally a man had three names — a given name, clan name, and family name. The Romans had in all about thirty given names for men, but some of them became obsolete at an early date, and as a rule each clan had from three to ten of them which its members used. Some of the more common ones were Lucius, Gaius, Manius, Marcus, Spurius, Titus, and Tiberius, together with several like Quintus and Sextus, which originally denoted one's position in the family but later were used indiscriminately. Clan names were numerous, but a few of them, like Cornelius, Claudius, Tullius, Julius, Aemilius, and Pompeius, appear with disproportionate frequency in Roman history. The scarcity of given names and their repeated use by members of certain clans led to confusion; and to obviate this difficulty a third name came into use. Let us suppose, for example, that the clan of the Curii had several members named Manius. One of them, however, was remarkable for the size and prominence of his teeth. To distinguish him from the others of the same name-combination, he was given the nickname of *Dentatus* ("Toothy"). This *cognomen* descended to his sons, regardless of their appearance, and in time it became a family name. Other family names of this description were Caepio ("Onion"), Naso ("Big Nose"), Agrippa ("Born-feet-foremost"), and Brutus ("Stupid"). Again, a family name might commemorate a famous deed of the founder of the family, like Torquatus, the bearer of which had slain a Gallic chief in single combat and taken his gold collar (*torques*). When a man's name was written officially, it was customary to place first his given name, then his clan name, then his father's given name, followed by the name of his tribe, and finally his family name. Thus the name of the orator Cicero was written Marcus Tullius Marci filius Cornelia tribu Cicero (Marcus Tullius Cicero, the son of Marcus, of the Cornelian Tribe). Women used the feminine form of the father's clan name, with such other names as their parents chose to give them, and without any discernible general rule.

Slaves in early Rome were usually war-captives taken from the neighboring Italian peoples. In this simple society they were generally used as agricultural laborers, and they lived with the families of their masters. So small was their number that the only names necessary for them were such as *Marcipor* and *Lucipor* ("Marcus' or Lucius' slave"). The only difference of status between them and free men under paternal authority was that they did not become free at the death of the owner, as did a son when his father died. As a rule they were treated kindly, and easily gained their freedom. Once free, they became the clients of their former masters, and in some cases the sons of freedmen rose to high offices. Not until much later did the introduction of large numbers of Asiatic and Greek slaves, and their harsh exploitation by capitalistic farmers and industrialists or use for purposes of luxury and vice, make the institution a menace to the integrity of the Roman people.

### *Houses and Home Life*

With our description of social institutions completed, we must next see what sort of everyday life the Romans led. Let us first consider their houses. The round huts of primitive times had everywhere given place to square or oblong structures, which might be made of wood, sun-dried brick, or even of stone. Of these, sun-dried brick was the easiest to secure, and when covered with stucco to resist the rains it was both durable and comfortable. The roofs had originally been made of poles covered with thatch, and in the country this custom was continued. But in the better houses of Rome and other Italian cities tile roofs were becoming common.

In early years rich and poor alike lived in one-room houses which probably had no windows. In the center of the floor was a hearth, where a fire blazed to cook the family's food and to temper the chill of winter days. Above the hearth was a hole in the roof, through which the smoke might escape on windless days, and into which the rain came so copiously that it was called the *impluvium*, or "rain-inlet." No doubt more rain than smoke passed through it, for the rafters were so blackened with smoke that the whole structure bore the name of *atrium* (probably "black-room"). The floor was of hard-packed earth. Furniture was scanty — a few chairs or benches, a table, jars for the storage of food, a loom on which the mother wove the family's clothing, and a chest for the master's most treasured possessions. Clothing, arms, and agricultural implements hung on the walls. At night hard cots were spread for the family and its dependents to sleep on. In this restricted space, with no possibility of privacy, the family spent the small portion of its existence which was passed indoors.

In the country, and among the urban poor, this simple type of dwelling continued in use for many years, but among the wealthier classes in Rome more elaborate houses gradually came to be popular. The size of the building was considerably enlarged, and along each side-wall a series of small windowless rooms were partitioned off to serve as sleeping quarters and storage space. At the rear a lean-to addition was built (the *tablinum*) in which were stored the family records and the wax death-masks of the ancestors. But even in these more commodious dwellings furniture was scanty and simple, and housekeeping was severely plain.

### *Food and Clothing*

The clothing worn by the Roman partook of the same simplicity as his house and furniture. Wool was the material worn in both summer and winter. In almost every case it was provided by the family's sheep, and carded, spun, and woven by the womenfolk. Men wore a *tunic* — a short-sleeved shirt which reached, when at full length, to the ankles, but which was usually belted up and bloused so as to fall about to the knee. When at work, or when living informally at home, this was the only garment needed, but in cold weather or on formal occasions it was covered with an outer wrap, the *toga*. The latter was a voluminous woolen robe, roughly semicircular in shape, which varied considerably from age to age, in both style and shape. One end was thrown forward over the left shoulder so as to reach the feet. Then the remainder was brought around under the right arm and thrown back over the left shoulder until it reached the feet behind. As no pins or buttons seem to have been used to keep it in position, it imposed upon the wearer a slow, dignified pace, and in warm weather the weight of so much wool must have been well-nigh unbearable. Underwear was unknown, and in cold weather one had only to put on one or more additional tunics. The Roman wore neither socks nor stockings, but he had sandals and shoes to protect his feet when walking. It is probable that the poor went barefoot at all times. Women wore a feminine version of the tunic (the *stola*), and when walking covered it with an oblong strip of cloth (the *palla*), which was wound around the body and held in one hand. Boys and girls alike wore small *togas* bordered with red, and not until they were considered grown-up did they assume the garb of their elders.

Food was plain with little variety. The staple dish of all classes was a kind of wheat-porridge, made by cracking the grain and boiling it with salt and water. This grain ration was supplemented by onions, garlic, turnips, beans, peas, and fruit. Meat was rarely eaten except on religious holidays, when the larger part of each sacrificed animal was distributed among the worshipers. Butter was unknown, the milk being made into cheese, and honey furnished the only sweetening. Some wine was made, but it was not sufficiently plentiful to be in common use.

Like ourselves, the Romans ate three meals a day. In the third century B.C. they still followed the same rule as our grandfathers and as rural America today — a light breakfast and supper, and a heavy dinner served at noon. Table equipment and dining-room furniture were plain and scanty. It is probable that the majority of the people had not yet learned the habit of reclining on couches as they ate, although this practice was known to the Etruscans. Neither individual plates nor forks were used, and the diners took their food directly from the platters with their fingers. The women ate with the men and the latter had apparently not yet begun to hold drinking-parties after the main meal. As late as 241 B.C. there seems to have been only one silver table service in Rome, which was borrowed by all families who had guests of distinction to entertain.

### *Funeral Rites*

Nothing better illustrates the strength of the family bond in Roman society than the rites performed over the dead. Only if these rites had been properly celebrated could the souls of the departed be at peace, and if they were not contented in the world to come, they would certainly punish the relatives whose negligence had caused their misfortunes. But the loving care accorded them was not due to fear alone. The Romans, unlike ourselves, felt that their power to benefit their loved ones did not terminate with death, and their funeral customs must accordingly have been a potent source of comfort to the bereaved survivors. The ritual was, in its essential points, rigidly prescribed. As soon as life was extinct, the eldest son of the deceased bent over the body and thrice called the departed by

*Metropolitan Museum*

ROMAN GRAVE MONUMENT

name. Having done so, he announced, "He has been called." The body was then washed and dressed. When a man of aristocratic family died, a sheet of wax was laid over his face, and a death-mask was made. The family would preserve these masks in its *tablinum*, each with a short note giving the name of the departed and the honors which he had gained. The actual funeral was held at night. When the procession formed, the death-masks were taken down and worn by family servants. Each one dressed like, and imitated, the person whose mask he wore. Even the deceased himself was thus symbolically present. It was therefore a weird and uncanny procession which moved through the streets by torchlight to the place outside the city where the body was to be buried or cremated. Before the remains were disposed of, a member of the family might be called upon to deliver a funeral oration praising the deceased. Thereafter the corpse was either burned upon a pile of wood, buried in the ground, or laid in the family tomb. If cremation was practiced, the ashes were carefully collected and were later placed in an urn and either buried or deposited in the family tomb. A pig was sacrificed. Then the family and other mourners purified themselves with water from the contamination incurred by contact with the dead body. The house in which the death had taken place was likewise purified with a solemn sacrifice to the *Lares*. Nine days later a sacrifice was offered to the departed spirit, and a dinner was given in his honor by the family. Thereafter he was the recipient of the attentions regularly accorded to departed ancestors. The poor naturally had to curtail the funeral rites of their dead to fit their purses, but even slaves were usually given some sort of obsequies by their masters.

Thus the private life of the Roman like his public career was completely dominated by religion. It made him cautious, conservative, and scrupulous, but not timid or cowardly. His was a virile faith, fit for warriors and statesmen.

## Economic Organization

The promising beginnings made by the Romans in commerce and manufacturing under the monarchy largely came to naught as soon as the foreigners had been driven out. Traces of Etruscan craftsmanship still lingered on under the early Republic, but did not regain their original importance. As fast as a large class of urban poor grew up who might have become traders and craftsmen, new conquests and the resulting colonies were certain to reinstate the more worthy members in the possession of land. This fact, together with the large losses of life in battle and the unproductive expenditure of time in military service, drained off the energies which might have made Rome able to profit by the economic opportunities which conquest opened up for her. As it was, these opportunities usually worked for the benefit of her allies rather than herself, and in time, these conditions led to the growth of an aristocratic and agrarian prejudice against commerce and industry from which the Romans never freed themselves.

### *Commerce and Industry*

Another influence which tended to keep the Romans economically backward was the prevalence of a domestic economy — the necessary supplement to the subsistence farm. Only those articles whose production required too much skill for the home-worker, and those services which had to be rendered by highly trained professionals, could withstand his competition. The first list of industrial guilds, which dates from the earliest days of the Republic, is interesting because it shows us which tradesmen could meet this condition successfully. They were musicians (who played an important part in religious rites), goldsmiths, carpenters and builders, dyers, shoemakers, bronze-workers, and potters. There were no textile-workers, millers, bakers, or butchers, for such trades were carried on in the home, and the same could be said for the makers of many other types of consumers' goods. There can be no doubt that industry expanded somewhat in Rome during the fifth and fourth centuries, but few if any articles were produced for export. The manufacturing centers of Italy were still to be found in Etruria, Campania, and the extreme south, where Greek and Etruscan influence was still strong.

Even more pronounced was Rome's backwardness in commerce. Tradition asserted that there had been a seaport established at the mouth of the Tiber under the kings, but Ostia, the earliest historic settlement on the site, was not founded until 348 B.C., and then probably as a military colony. When treaties were made with Carthage, she was allowed to exclude the Romans entirely from several lucrative fields of trade without a protest from them. To a people as warlike and as jealous of their honor as the Romans, this could only mean that they had no commerce of sufficient importance to quarrel over. A treaty of alliance likewise existed between the Romans and the Greek city of Massilia in Gaul, but its commercial provisions and economic consequences are unknown.

Yet a certain amount of business had to be carried on even in this unprogressive community. In early times the marketplace of Rome was the Forum — a piece of reclaimed swamp land between the Capitoline and Palatine hills. Cattle and other livestock were, however, sold in a separate marketplace, the *Forum Boarium*, on the bank of the Tiber. But these were not the only places in the immediate neighborhood of Rome where buying and selling were done. No doubt many of the people took advantage of their right of *commercium* with Latin cities like Praeneste or Tusculum to attend their markets, and there were fairs held at regular intervals in some of the Etruscan towns. For local trade there were markets held in a number of country villages in the Roman territory — a fact which accounts for the presence of the word *forum* in the names of so many Roman villages. In these places the farmer might pick up those articles which he needed but could not easily make for himself — metal implements, pottery, and an occasional article of luxury. In general, it may be said that the bulk of Rome's commerce was distinctly local, and such wares as were imported from abroad were brought by foreign merchants who reaped the middleman's profit to the detriment of the native merchant.

In the later fourth century B.C., however, the government itself began to provide new opportunities for the profitable investment of funds. The equipment and provisioning of the armies led to the letting of large contracts, and the local businessmen had almost a monopoly in this field. When the censor Appius Claudius undertook the construction of the road and aqueduct which bear his name, his enterprises were done by contract, and as both were subdivided into a large number of units, many men of moderate means were able to participate and profit. When the censors began to collect rents on government-owned pasture lands, they also found it advantageous to put this work on a contract basis and let it out to private firms. Hence the Roman businessman at a very early date found his best source of profit in the operations of government, and this tendency became more evident in succeeding ages.

### *Coinage*

It is significant of the prevailing indifference to economic interests that the Romans did not adopt a regular system of coinage until three centuries after the Greek cities had done so. In the Laws of the Twelve Tables (about 450 B.C.) fines were set in terms of sheep and cattle, and these, together with uncoined lumps of copper, continued to be the media of exchange until just before 300 B.C. The first effort in the direction of true coinage resulted in the production of a bulky block of copper weighing one pound — the *as*.[1] Fractional coinage may have been made in the same medium, but of this we cannot be certain. For dealings with their

[1] The Roman pound (*as* or *libra*) was equal to 11⅘ ounces avoirdupois. It was divided into twelve *unciae* (usually translated "ounces").

*Numismatic Society*

AS. LATE THIRD CENTURY B.C. ROME.

*Obverse: Head of Janus. Reverse: Prow of Ship*

neighbors in Campania and Etruria the Romans secured silver coins from Capua and other Campanian mints. In 269, however, a more advanced system came into use. The *as* was reduced in size so that it weighed only two Roman ounces, and a new silver coin was struck in the Roman mint. As it was worth ten of the new copper coins, it was called a *denarius*. Halves and quarters of a denarius were also struck in silver. Rome now had a system of coinage fit to compare with those of other civilized states in the Mediterranean world.

## Art and Literature

As might be expected of an eminently practical people engaged in coping with a hostile human and physical environment, the Romans did little in the fine arts during their early history. The Etruscans had taught them how to build temples, and to adorn them with terra cotta sculptures and fresco paintings. To them Rome owed the temple of Jupiter on the Capitoline Hill, and the red terra cotta statue of the god which it contained. Other temples were built by the Roman government during the first two centuries of the Republic, but they were constructed of the local tufa rock — an ugly material at best — with no sculptures or paintings worthy of comparison with contemporary Greek work. After all, Roman religion, with its formless, disembodied spirits, did not encourage the talents of the sculptor or the painter.

### *Painting and Engraving*

Yet the Romans were not entirely devoid of artistic appreciation, and the lessons which they had learned from Etruscan artists were never entirely forgotten. The latter had often adorned the walls of tombs and temples with fresco paintings, designed to tell stories by means of a series of scenes, on much the same principle as the modern "comic strip." A fourth-century Roman tomb on the Esquiline Hill was adorned with just such a series of frescoes, representing incidents in the Samnite wars. The painter may have been a Roman, but the treatment is thoroughly Etruscan. About 304, Fabius Pictor, a member of one of Rome's most aristocratic clans, executed a similar series of frescoes on the walls of a temple erected in honor of the Goddess of Health, but of course none of them have survived.

Both in Rome and in the near-by Latin cities there were skillful engravers who worked in bronze. A fine example of this type of work, the so-called "Ficorini Casket," is decorated with a scene from the legend of the Argonauts, probably a copy of a Greek painting, which may indicate that the artist had gotten his training in a Greek city. Both the drawing and the composition are excellent. The casket bears the inscription in archaic Latin: "Dindia Macolnia gave me to her daughter. Novius Plautius made me at Rome." Another specimen (probably from Praeneste) bears a spirited scene showing servants preparing a dinner.

*Roads and Aqueducts*

But it is in the practical arts of road and aqueduct building that the fourth-century Romans excelled. Although they probably learned the rudiments of these arts from the Greeks and Etruscans, they easily surpassed their teachers. Their success was probably due in part to the use of a kind of concrete made of lime or other stone, which when pulverized and mixed with water resumed its original hardness. An architectural device which proved useful first in these works of utility and later in the fine arts was the arch, with its derivatives, the vault and the dome. But the finished products were true expressions of the Roman spirit, of its appreciation of practical values, its grandeur of conception, and its indomitable will.

The quality of Roman roads is proverbial. They swept straight to their goals, across swamp, river, and mountain, and they were so well paved that some of them continued in use without any repairs for a thousand years after the Roman Empire was no more. To construct such a road the builders began on ordinary ground by removing the topsoil until a firm base had been secured. They then hammered the surface of the roadbed with wooden rammers to render it still more substantial. The first coat of paving material consisted of loose stones no larger than a man could hold in his hand. Over it was poured a nine-inch layer of coarse concrete. Another layer of fine concrete about six inches thick was placed over the first, and into this, while still wet, were fitted paving stones cut to an exact joint. The resulting pavement was two or more feet in thickness, and varied from eight to twenty-four feet in width. Like a modern road, it had a convex surface to drain the water off. Along the side ran a paved footpath, for the Romans, unlike modern road-builders, recognized the existence of pedestrians. Swamps were crossed on earthen embankments built between stone or concrete retaining-walls, and rivers were bridged with masonry arches. To avoid steep grades, the hills were sometimes tunneled. The Appian Way was about the only road begun in the period

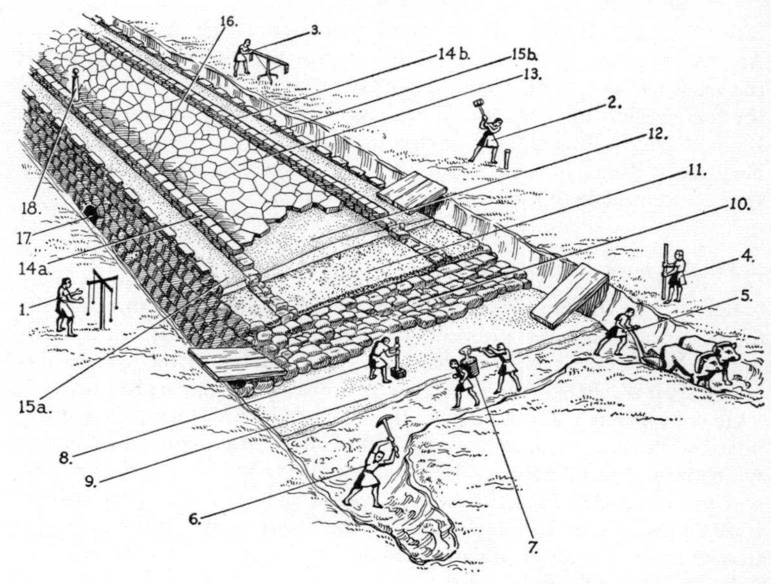


*United States Department of Agriculture*

SECTION OF A ROMAN ROAD

*Showing methods of construction and appearance when completed.*

1. Field engineer aligning road with a *groma.*
2. Stake man placing stake in position according to directions of the field engineer.
3. Field engineer running levels for the road with a *chorobates.*
4. *Chorobates* rodman assisting field engineer.
5. Loosening earth and marking the margins of the road with a plow.
6. Excavator digging the marginal trenches to the depth of the solid foundations.
7. Laborers shoveling loose earth and removing it in a basket.
8. Workman consolidating roadbed with a tamper.
9. *Pavimentum.* A bedding of lime mortar or sand to form a level base for the statumen.
10. *Statumen.* The first course, consisting of stones small enough to be held in a man's hand, cemented together with lime mortar or clay. Thickness, from 10 inches to 2 feet.
11. *Rudus.* The second course, consisting of lime concrete, grouted with broken stone and broken fragments of pottery, 9 inches thick.
12. *Nucleus.* The third course, consisting of concrete made from gravel or coarse sand mixed with hot lime, placed in successive layers, and compacted with a roller. 1 foot thick at the sides and 18 inches thick under the center of the road.
13. *Summum dorsum.* The top course, consisting of polygonal blocks of hard stone, carefully fitted and set in the concrete of the *nucleus* while it was still soft. Thickness, about 6 inches.
14. *a* and *b.* Side curbs, about 2 feet wide and 18 inches high.
15. *a.* and *b.* Paved footpaths.
16. Inlet to surface-water drain.
17. Outlet to surface-water drain.
18. *Miliarium.* Milestone.

*Note*: The road shown here had a width of approximately 15½ English feet between curbs, the crown being about 6 inches higher than the road surface at the bottoms of the curbs.

*Sawders-Combine*

ROMAN ROAD
*The Street of Tombs, Ostia*

under discussion, but in it were to be found all the essential features of the later highways.

By 265 B.C., Rome had acquired a public water system served by two aqueducts called respectively the *Aqua Appia* and *Anio vetus*, of which the first had been built in 312 and the second in 272. A Roman aqueduct was a conduit of stone and concrete, which carried water at low pressure. The definition goes far toward explaining its structure. A high-pressure water-line built of cast-iron pipes can be carried uphill and downhill, the pressure of the water behind forcing that ahead over the low spots. Greek and Roman engineers could (and occasionally did) build such aqueducts of heavy masonry or lead pipes, but they were not practical in the region around Rome, where the water was so full of calcium that the conduits had frequently to be emptied and cleaned. Hence Roman aqueducts carried their water on a nearly uniform grade, under low pressure. The earlier aqueducts were almost entirely subterranean, with only short stretches near the city elevated on arches to preserve the grade. At intervals the vaulted tops of the conduits were pierced by ventilating shafts through which workmen could enter to remove the accumulated lime. Both the *Aqua Appia* and the *Anio vetus* were engineering feats of quite respectable magnitude. The channel of the former was ten miles long, five feet high, and two feet six inches wide, while the latter was forty-two miles long, and its channel measured seven feet ten inches by three feet seven inches. By means of her aqueducts, Rome was assured of a plentiful supply of water, and as a rule it was of fairly good quality.

### *Literature*

Up to the middle of the third century B.C., Rome had produced nothing which could truly be called literature. Books of any kind written in Latin were few, and they were entirely in the fields of law, oratory, and religion.

*Galloway*

ROMAN AQUEDUCT
*Pont du Gard, Nîmes*

But here, as in many other fields, the name of Appius Claudius, the censor of 312 B.C., is very important. To him the Romans owed the publication of the book entitled *Legal Procedure* (written by him or at his order) which broke the patrician monopoly of the law-courts. At the same time he reformed the spelling of the Latin language to make it more phonetic, introducing the letter *g* into it, substituting *u* for *o* before *s* and *m*, changing *s* to *r* between two vowels, and making other changes. In his old age he delivered an impassioned plea in the Senate against a proposed compromise peace with Pyrrhus. It was published, and was extant two centuries later. Manuals of religious ritual for the use of priests must have existed, but they have all perished, and are mere "echoes of echoes" to us. In the fields of drama, poetry, and conventional history, wherein the Greeks had already done so much, the Romans had as yet no accomplishments to their credit. Not until later, when their genius had been stimulated by foreign contacts, and increasing wealth and security had given them leisure, were they to do anything along these lines.

# 8

# *The Mediterranean World of the Third Century B.C.: Political History*

## General Survey

When Rome completed her conquest of Italy, she emerged from the narrow confines of peninsular affairs into the position of one of the world's great powers. From that time on, she was in constant contact, whether friendly or hostile, with the other civilized states of the Mediterranean area, and with the barbarian tribes who surrounded it in the north, west, and south. As Rome left an indelible mark upon so many of the peoples with whom she came into contact, and was in turn profoundly affected by them, we can best understand her subsequent history by studying the history and civilization of her neighbors. In addition, it should of course be said that such a study is, at least with regard to the Hellenistic east, amply worth while for its own sake.

### *The Civilized World and Its Barbarian Background*

To understand the ancient civilizations, one must always keep in mind the fact that, unlike those of the modern world, they covered but a small part of the earth's known surface. Collectively they formed, as it were, an island in the sea of barbarism, which surrounded them on all sides and constantly threatened to overwhelm and destroy them. Except in western Asia and Egypt, where they covered a fairly large and compact area, the civilized peoples occupied a relatively narrow strip of land on either side of the Mediterranean Sea, which was not at all continuous. Within this civilized world great differences of cultural level might have been observed; but between the rudest back-country town in Macedonia or Italy and the great cities of Antioch or Alexandria there were essential resemblances which set them off sharply from their barbarian neighbors. In the barbarian world similar variations were to be found, yet as a whole they did not destroy the essential validity of the distinction. In the one group was to be found a high development of the arts, the use of writing, a settled manner of life based upon agriculture, manufacturing and commerce, relatively advanced means of communication, and orderly governments based upon territorial sovereignty. In the other were rudimentary political groups based upon clan and family relationship, a poor development of the means of livelihood which made frequent migrations necessary, a tendency to supplement ordinary sources of income by plundering neighbors, a complete ignorance of the art of writing, and a very low level of achievement in both applied and fine arts. While one naturally tends to focus his attention upon the civilized world, he cannot understand either one without studying the other.

## The Western Mediterranean Area: Carthage, Syracuse, and Massilia

In that portion of the Mediterranean Sea which lies west of the "Narrows" there were, in the third century B.C., three states besides Rome which were of first-rate importance: — Carthage, Syracuse, and Massilia. A century earlier the Etruscans would have deserved a place on the list, but not long after 300 B.C., as we have seen, they lost their independence and became part of the Roman Confederation. All of these states were sea-powers, and Carthage, the most powerful of them all, was engaged in intermittent hostilities with the others for the control of the whole region.

### *The Carthaginian Empire*

Carthage had been founded by Phoenicians from Tyre shortly before the end of the ninth century B.C. The city stood on the northern coast of Africa on what is today called the Bay of Tunis, some miles from the modern city of that name. Like the other Phoenician cities, it was a trading center from which commerce was carried on with the African back-country, and with the lands to the north and west of her. At first she was only the most prominent among many Phoenician colonies in that region, and like them was politically subject to her mother-city in Phoenicia. However, in the sixth century B.C., the conquest of the Phoenician coast, first by the Chaldeans and later by the Persians, freed all the Phoenician colonies abroad to shift for themselves. Carthage then established a republic, subjected her sister cities and the neighboring African tribes, and came to control the whole northern coast of Africa from the western boundary of the Greek colony at Cyrene as far as the Straits of Gibraltar, and even a section of the Atlantic coast to the south of these.

Throughout its history the government of Carthage was an oligarchic republic. At the head of the state were two judges (*shophetim* or *suffetes*) elected annually. There was a fairly complicated system of councils, with a popular assembly to represent the will of the people. It was unusually stable and free from the threat of revolution, and for this reason won favorable mention from Aristotle. But in her government of dependencies Carthage was not successful in that she never succeeded in winning the good-will of her subjects. Our sources are fairly unanimous in their testimony that her attitude toward them was one of brutal arrogance when they obeyed, and of inhuman ferocity when they revolted. Nor was this type of treatment reserved for them alone. Unsuccessful military and naval commanders were in danger of crucifixion when they returned home. Religion demanded that the eldest child of each family be sacrificed, and at least in some instances, this took the form of roasting alive on the arms of the image of the god Moloch. Such practices explain the implacable hatred with which the subject populations viewed their oppressor, and show why, whenever a foreign invader appeared in Africa, or a mercenary captain revolted, they were willing to join him. We shall presently see several examples of this tendency. In the immediate territory of Carthage the natives were apparently reduced to slavery or serfdom, and worked the estates of their lords. Foreigners were struck with the advanced state of cultivation which prevailed in this region, and Carthaginian agricultural methods were widely copied by the Romans of later times. Unfortunately their callous brutality in the treatment of slaves was also imitated by Roman masters.

In general the Carthaginians, in keeping with the Phoenician tradition, were seafarers, with a large merchant marine and a navy which dominated the western Mediterranean. In the fourth century their warships were the largest and most efficient in use anywhere, and their crews, which were apparently Carthaginian citizens, were excellently trained. The armies, on the other hand, were for the most part composed of mercenaries. To a small nucleus of citizen-troops and a somewhat larger number of African subjects were added cavalry from the vassal-state of Numidia and hordes of Greek, Spanish, Gallic, and Italian infantry. As the blood of these hirelings could be spent without great damage to their employer, they were very effective in sieges, where wave after wave would assault a town without regard to losses until the defenders were worn out. Yet they were prone to mutiny if discontented, and on more than one occasion their uprisings brought the state to the brink of ruin. Moreover, they had not the self-sacrificing heroism which leads a soldier to fight on, even when his cause is apparently lost. Hence Carthage was dangerous to her neighbors when on the offensive, but showed unexpected weakness when attacked. Only when her citizens had to fight for their own homes and families did they rally for a last desperate stand, displaying a furious courage which defeated more than one invader.

By the end of the sixth century B.C., Carthage had become the dominant power in the western Mediterranean. Her alliance with the Etruscans had enabled her to drive the Greeks from Sardinia and Corsica, and she had acquired strongholds in western Sicily which enabled her to dominate the "Narrows." In Spain she destroyed a flourishing native state — the so-called "Empire of Tartessus" — and thereafter ruled the southern coast of the peninsula from the city of Gades (Cadiz). The commerce of the Atlantic coast was completely in her hands. It was no idle boast, when one of her admirals said, "that no one could wash his hands in the sea without the consent of Carthage."

*Massilia and Syracuse*

At two points the Carthaginians were unable to make good their claims. The Greek city of Massilia (Marseilles) situated on the coast of Gaul near the mouth of the Rhone, had become a great naval power, with colonies which dotted the coast-line from the border of Italy to a point on the coast of Spain halfway between the Pyrenees and the Straits of Gibraltar. Her government was an efficient oligarchy, and we hear nothing of internal strife among her citizens. Massilian society was noted for its high moral tone, and the people for their courage, thrift, and enterprise. As Massilia retained her colonies and commerce in the face of the advancing power of Carthage, she must have done so by force of arms, but no mention of war between the two cities has come down to us. At an early date the Massilians became faithful allies of Rome.

Far better known is the stormy and eventful history of Syracuse. At all times she was the largest and the strongest of the Greek cities which dotted the shores of Sicily, and to her fell the task of heading the opposition of the Sicilian Greeks to Carthaginian expansion in the island. Her earlier history, with its bloody wars, frequent revolutions, and unscrupulous tyrants, is told in connection with Greek affairs. About 337, thanks to the disinterested magnanimity and heroism of the liberator Timoleon, the Sicilian Greeks found themselves free for a time from Carthaginian invaders, tyrants, and civil wars. This happy state of affairs lasted for some twenty years, until about 317 they reverted to their normal condition of disorder, oppression, and misery. In that year there arose in Syracuse yet another tyrant, Agathocles, who was to be the worst and bloodiest of them all.

After gaining his position by the wholesale massacre of his opponents, he entered upon a war of aggression against the other Sicilian Greek cities, which soon resulted in the entry of Carthage into the strife. In 311 the Carthaginians drove Agathocles into Syracuse and besieged the city. His cause seemed hopeless, but he retrieved it by a brilliant stroke of aggressive strategy. Gathering a small army and a few ships, he stole out of the harbor at night and made straight for Africa, where he launched an attack upon the enemy's capital. The African subjects of Carthage joined him in large numbers, and he received aid from the Macedonian governor of Cyrene, whom he rewarded by murdering him. In a campaign lasting three years he almost captured Carthage herself, forcing her to lift her siege of Syracuse in Sicily, and gravely undermining her power in Africa. When fortune at last turned against him, he deserted his army and his two sons in Africa, and returned to Sicily. Carthage made peace, and Agathocles soon brought all but the western tip of the island under his power. When he died, in 289, Syracuse regained her liberty.

After his death the Sicilian Greeks were again in a desperate plight, at odds among themselves and at the mercy of Carthage. A new feature was introduced into the situation when some of Agathocles' discharged Italian mercenaries (the *Mamertini*, or "Sons of Mars") seized the city of Messana. There they set up a robber-state, from which they plundered all of their neighbors, and especially Syracuse. By 277 Carthage again owned three-fourths of the island, and was besieging Syracuse once more. This time the prize was torn from her grasp by King Pyrrhus of Epirus. Finding his prospects of success against the Romans fading away, the Epirote king crossed to Sicily to aid the distressed Greeks, and in a victorious campaign lasting two years he deprived the Carthaginians of all but one of their strongholds on the island. But his protégés with characteristic fickleness quarreled with him, and in disgust he abandoned their cause. Pyrrhus had saved Syracuse, but the enemy had recovered almost all of the remainder of Sicily.

Again a tyrant arose in Syracuse, and this time his character was a welcome exception to the rule. Hiero II (269–215) was a humane and able ruler, who without bloodshed restored order in the city. He then gained a victory over the Mamertini, and besieged Messana. In 264 the city was reduced to such severe straits that it appealed for aid to both Carthage and Rome. With this development the contest for the mastery of the blood-stained island entered a new phase, which will be treated in another place.[1] The conduct of the Sicilian Greeks can hardly at any time be called admirable or wise, but in spite of their treachery, fickleness, murderous quarrels, and short-sightedness, they had halted the march of the Carthaginian imperialism at a crucial point. It was thanks to them that she failed to conquer their island; and if she had been able to do so, Rome might never have had the opportunity to unify Italy.

## The Heirs of Alexander the Great

### *Alexander's Empire*

In the third century B.C. the eastern part of the Mediterranean Basin and western Asia were dominated by a series of states which had arisen on the ruins of the empire founded by Alexander the Great. When the Conqueror died in 323 he ruled a domain which included most of the Balkan peninsula, most of Asia Minor, Syria, Egypt, the Tigris-Euphrates Valley, the whole Iranian Plateau, and a strip of land in northwestern India. Alexander himself was a Hellenized Macedonian, and his conquests had been achieved by a mixed force of Macedonians and Greeks. As he proceeded on his expedition, he founded large numbers of cities, in each of which a nucleus of Greeks and Macedonians formed the governing class. Greek was the official language throughout most of the empire, and when Alexander died the majority of the high officials were either Macedonians or Greeks. At one time he had made strenuous efforts to give the Iranian peoples a place in the governing class and in the army, but in this project he had encountered difficulties which had not been solved, and at his death it was abandoned.

Only a transcendent genius, acting under the most favorable circumstances and gifted with a long life, could have rendered permanent the union of so many peoples of widely divergent cultural background. Alexander died at thirty-three, and after his death no leader of his calibre appeared. His successors were a half-witted brother and a son born after Alexander's death. His Macedonian officers were men of great ability,

[1] Chapter 11.

*British Museum*

MACEDONIAN COIN
*Obverse: Head of Alexander the Great*
*Reverse: Pallas Nicephoros*

and two of them — Antipater and Perdiccas — were apparently loyal to the new kings. But the others wished to make their own fortunes, and no one of them was sufficiently pre-eminent to control the rest. The dissolution of the state was only a question of time.

*The Division of the Empire*

A little more than twenty years (323–301) sufficed to divide Alexander's empire permanently into a series of states, large and small, ruled either by Macedonian kings or by native princes who had profited by the discord among the conquerors. The process had been a bloody one. The two legitimate kings were ruthlessly murdered, as were also Alexander's mother and wife. Four of his generals, Cassander, Lysimachus, Seleucus, and Ptolemy, each seized a convenient portion of their departed master's lands, while a fifth, Antigonus "the One-Eyed," attempted to unite the empire once more under his own rule. To safeguard their mutual interests the four formed a coalition, which in 301 brought Antigonus to bay at Ipsus in Phrygia where he was slain. Their victory made permanent the dissolution of the Empire.

The political map which grew out of the wars of the "Successors" was to remain relatively stable for more than a century. Macedonia (with a claim to the suzerainty of Greece) went to Cassander. Lysimachus ruled Thrace and western Asia Minor. To Ptolemy went Egypt, Cyrene, Palestine, southern Syria, Cyprus, and a series of small districts on the southwestern coast of Asia Minor. Seleucus held northern Syria, part of Asia Minor, the Tigris-Euphrates Valley, and the Iranian Plateau. Alexander's

Indian possessions had already been lost. In northeastern Asia Minor there already existed or soon grew up a series of small states under native or Persian dynasties — Bithynia, Cappadocia, Armenia, and later Pontus.

With the conquests of Alexander, Greek civilization entered its final phase. In the states that arose on the ruins of his empire it was dominant, but it dominated peoples who were not Greek. Likewise, it was itself different from the Hellenism of the classical period. It was no longer closely integrated with the independent city-state, and hence was more cosmopolitan and less provincial than before. For this reason a special name has been coined for it. It is termed the Hellenistic culture, and the period in which it flourished is called the Hellenistic Age.

## The Hellenistic State-System: Political History

Although the broad outlines of the new state-system were blocked out in the settlement which followed the Battle of Ipsus, a certain amount of re-shuffling took place in both dynasties and territories within the next generation. Thus the Kingdom of Lysimachus, which had a heterogeneous population of Thracians, Greeks, and Asiatics, and whose only bond of unity was the authority of the king, lasted about twenty years. Lysimachus was an able ruler, who succeeded in adding much territory to his dominions. In 285 he took advantage of a dynastic quarrel in Macedonia to become its king, and for the next few years his military and financial strength were the greatest of any of the "Successors." His fall was sudden and complete. For his third wife he had married Arsinoë, the daughter of Ptolemy, who, although quite young, was ambitious, unscrupulous, and bloodthirsty. To clear the way for the succession of her own children, she induced her husband to murder the son whom he had by a former marriage. As the slain prince had been very popular, this crime precipitated his father's ruin. When, in 281, Seleucus attacked Lysimachus, the latter was deserted by his army and fell upon the battlefield. Seleucus appropriated western Asia Minor, but was himself murdered before he could claim Macedonia. Thrace lapsed into anarchy.

### *Macedonia and Greece*

A different scene presents itself in Macedonia. There we see a well-integrated national group surviving a series of wars, revolutions, and changes of dynasty merely because of its internal cohesiveness. After the death of Cassander in 297, his two sons divided his dominions, but they soon quarreled and their strife led to the ruin of both. Between 294 and

279 B.C., Macedonia had four kings: Demetrius, the son of Antigonus "the One-Eyed," Pyrrhus of Epirus, Lysimachus, and Ptolemy Ceraunus, a disinherited son of Ptolemy of Egypt. The first two were soon driven out, while Lysimachus' reign was terminated by his overthrow. Then a calamity nearly wrecked the country. A horde of Celts called Galatians (near relatives of the Gauls) invaded Macedonia from the north, killed Ptolemy Ceraunus, and devastated the countryside. Luckily, however, a deliverer was at hand. In 277 Antigonus Gonatas, the son of the dethroned Demetrius, defeated the Galatians, put down all opposition to his rule, and was crowned king. He and his descendants held the Macedonian crown until the Roman conquest, over a century later.

Some of the Galatians driven from Macedonia and Greece, founded a kingdom at Tylis in Thrace; others crossed into Asia Minor, where they took service as mercenaries with various kings and pretenders, or plundered the country on their own account. Eventually they settled upon the uplands of Phrygia, where their descendants perpetuated their language and customs until at least the fourth century A.D.

Under Antigonus Gonatas and his descendants Macedonia was one of the three most important states in the Hellenistic world. She was the smallest and poorest, and had suffered cruelly from the drain made upon her man-power by Alexander and the "Successors," and from the disorders mentioned above. Her kings had a virile and effective army, but their financial resources were small, and they were surrounded on all sides by enemies. On the north were the Illyrians, who had plundered the land whenever possible for centuries. On the east they had to cope with the Thracians and the Galatians of Tylis, and on the south there was Greece.

To control peninsular Greece and the Aegean islands had been the aim of Macedonian policy since the days of Philip II (358–336 B.C.). With this purpose before him, Philip had organized a Hellenic League which was designed to put an end to interstate wars and revolutions and to wage war upon the Persians. But this league did not survive the death of Alexander the Great, and thereafter the country became a battleground for Alexander's would-be successors. Usually its control was divided between the kings of Macedonia and whatever power they happened to be fighting at the moment: hence no one was in a position to revive Philip's Hellenic League effectively. Some cities were garrisoned by the Macedonian kings or their Ptolemaic rivals, while others were ruled by tyrants set up by these war-lords, and a few preserved at least the appearance of free allies of one or the other of the contestants. All of these outsiders made unscrupulous and cynical bids for support among the factions into which the population of Greece was divided; and their incitement, together with the concentration of wealth and the economic distress which prevailed, caused class-warfare and party strife, the twin evils of the old free Greece, to rage anew.

Even before Antigonus Gonatas became king of Macedonia, he had controlled part of the peninsula, and he spent most of the latter part of his career trying to subjugate the rest. However, there were two obstacles which stood in the way of his success. He was frequently at war with Ptolemy II, who, seeing in the Greek situation a convenient means of embarrassing Antigonus with little trouble to himself, constantly aided the Greek malcontents with his fleet and with niggardly subsidies which were just enough to keep them from capitulating. The second difficulty lay in the tendency of the Greek states to combine of their own volition in order to resist foreign domination — a tardy recognition of the cause of their national misfortunes.

The first attempt at union was made shortly after the death of Alexander the Great. About 320 the backward tribal state of Aetolia, in northwestern Greece, began to transform its cantonal strongholds into cities, which formed a close confederation. The government of the Aetolian League was a fair compromise between centralized control and local autonomy. Each city had complete freedom to govern its local affairs. For business of general interest there was an assembly, in which every citizen of an allied city had a vote, and a senate composed of members chosen by the cities in their corporate capacity. After being for many years a purely local institution, the Aetolian League sprang into prominence in 278 when the Gauls invaded Greece. By skillful guerrilla warfare it contributed heavily to the repulse of the invaders, and thereafter it won adherents rapidly. Where persuasion failed, the Aetolians used force, until by the middle of the third century they had overrun all of central Greece north of the Gulf of Corinth except Athens. At the same time they had won control of Elis in the Peloponnesus. But their tendency to plunder both enemies and neutrals largely nullified their efforts to uphold Greek independence.

The second important Greek confederacy was an outgrowth of the older Achaean League of the northern Peloponnesus. In the more advanced sections of the Greek peninsula the threat of social revolution made the lot of the propertied classes increasingly insecure, and up to about 251 they had fared badly in many places. In that year Aratus of Sicyon overthrew the tyrant who ruled his native city, and soon succeeded in gaining for it membership in the Achaean League. Thereafter Aratus was the leading

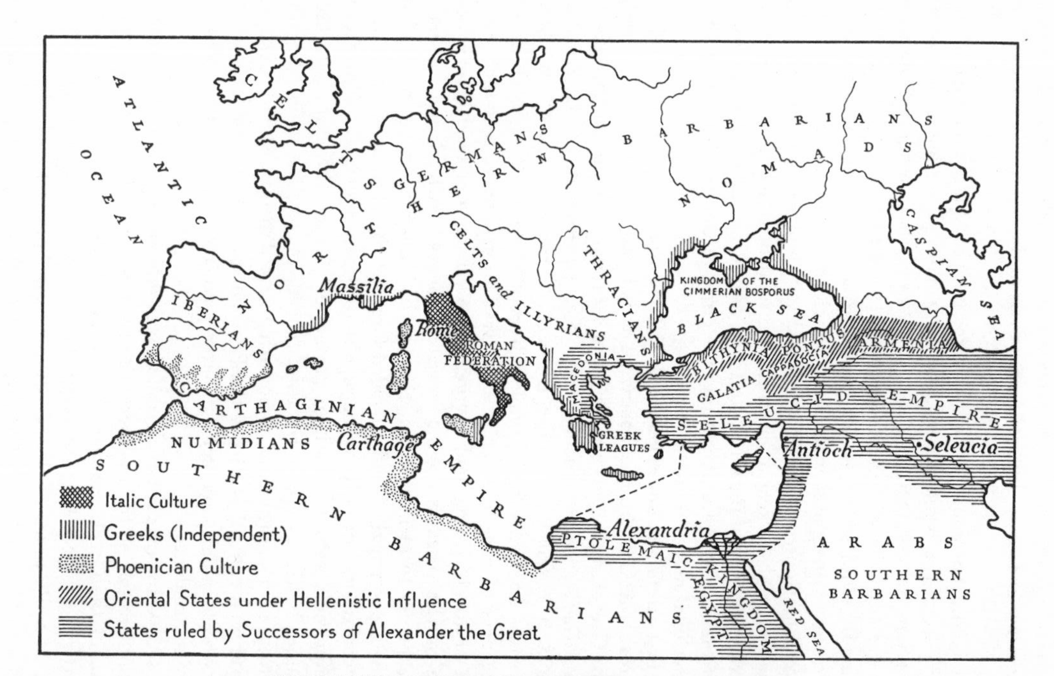


THE CIVILIZED WORLD AND ITS BARBARIAN BACKGROUND

*About 265 B.C.*

spirit of the league until his death in 213. Under his leadership it wrested Corinth from Antigonus Gonatas, and gained the voluntary adhesion of Argos. As the champion of the propertied classes it attracted many adherents in Arcadia, and became the dominant power in the Peloponnesus. The constitution of the Achaean League resembled that of the Aetolian League in providing for local autonomy, and for both an assembly of individual citizens and a senate of city-representatives. As a military power, however, it never equaled its northern neighbor. Both Sparta and Athens remained outside the leagues, although the latter recovered her independence from Macedonia in 229 B.C.

The growth of the leagues, wars on the northern frontiers, and changes of kings had all contributed to wreck Macedonian control of Greece, so that by 229 it was almost a thing of the past. But Macedonia was destined soon to recover her power. In 229 her crown fell to Antigonus III (*Doson*), an able and far-sighted statesman. A new revolutionary movement had broken out, this time in Sparta, where King Cleomenes was attempting to redistribute the land in order to increase the number of men available for military service. For some time this movement was successful, and Sparta became the most powerful state in the Peloponnesus. Aratus, unable to check the upstart, appealed to Antigonus. In 222 the latter invaded Greece, where he began by organizing a new Hellenic League on the model of that formed by Philip II over a century earlier. It included all of peninsular Greece not controlled by the Aetolian League. Then the Macedonian king and his Greek allies attacked Cleomenes, defeated him at Sellasia, and captured Sparta. It was a great triumph for Antigonus, but in 221 he died, leaving the crown to Philip V (221–178), a boy of seventeen.

Philip was one of Macedonia's ablest kings, but the times were against him. Even before his accession, the Romans had crossed the Adriatic Sea to punish the Illyrian pirates. Ten years later a second expedition was sent to the same region. Although neither one touched Greece or Macedonia directly, they were affronts to Macedonian dignity and stirred up hard feelings. In 215 Rome's first war with Macedonia began, and from that time on she was to exert an ever-increasing influence in Greek affairs. However, that phase of the story must be told in another chapter.

### *The Seleucid Empire*

Of all the states which arose on the ruins of Alexander's Empire, the largest and most populous was the kingdom of Seleucus. From their capitals, Antioch in Syria and Seleucia in Babylonia, he and his successors dominated for a time a territory many times larger than either Macedonia or the Kingdom of the Ptolemies. As we have seen, it was Seleucus who overthrew Lysimachus, and from that victory he gained western Asia Minor. His dominions now stretched from the Mediterranean and Aegean Seas to the borders of India and the steppes of central Asia.

To hold together so extensive a domain was difficult by reason of its very size, and the trouble was intensified by the heterogeneous character of the population and the diversity of its institutions and culture. In Asia Minor alone there were probably twenty different peoples, many with traditions of former independence and greatness to render them intractable. No doubt the problem was as baffling in other parts of the Seleucid realm. Except for the Greeks and Macedonians, none of these peoples were actively loyal to a dynasty which ruled solely by right of conquest. Therefore Alexander the Great and his Seleucid successors had planted Greek and Macedonian colonies all over the kingdom to act as a unifying force and as a source of recruits for the army. Only as long as the older Greek and Macedonian colonists were protected and new ones attracted to the kingdom could the widely divergent oriental peoples who formed the bulk of the population be held together. This fact accounts for the outstanding policies of the Seleucid kings, their constant foundation of new Greek cities, and their struggle to keep possession of Asia Minor and the Syrian coast, from which they could maintain contact with the Greek world.

Three strong influences, however, worked constantly for the overthrow of this unwieldy, sprawling state — the discontent of the oriental subjects (which led to efforts to set up native kings and states), quarrels within the royal house, and wars with the Ptolemies of Egypt. It was largely because of the continued action of these forces that the history of the Seleucid Empire is principally the story of its decline.

Under Seleucus I (*Nicator*, "the Conqueror," 312–280 B.C.), the founder of the dynasty, the forces of disruption were held in check, and as we have seen, western Asia Minor was annexed to his other holdings. But under Antiochus I (280–261 B.C.), Asia Minor began to fall into other hands. We have seen under what circumstances the Galatians entered the peninsula. Although Antiochus defeated them, they forced him to pay tribute, and intermittently ravaged the lands of their neighbors. Southeastward from Galatia lay Cappadocia, a region conquered only after Alexander's death. There about the year 260, Ariarathes, a noble of Persian descent, assumed the title of king and made good his independence. North of Cappadocia another Persian family secured possession of the Black Sea coast and founded the kingdom of Pontus. Bithynia, on the Asiatic side of the Bosporus, which had never been conquered by the Macedonians, continued to be free. In the northwestern part of the peninsula a Greek named Philetairus assumed control of the city of Pergamum and its surroundings, and his successors Eumenes I and Attalus I became completely independent. Ptolemy II controlled the southwestern coast.

In the east the same process was at work. To secure Bactria, on the frontier which faced the steppes, Alexander the Great and the first Seleucid kings had planted numerous colonies of Greeks. About 250 Diodotus, the Greek governor of the province, repudiated the authority of his Seleucid master and founded the Greek kingdom of Bactria, in which his countrymen were the ruling caste, and which lasted from about 250 to 128. An offshoot of this Graeco-Oriental state later arose in the Indus Valley, where it stood until near the beginning of the Christian Era. Farther west, near the southern end of the Caspian Sea, a tribe of Indo-European nomads from the steppes conquered the province of Parthia, which they made the seat of a kingdom.

The process of disintegration was greatly stimulated by dissensions within the Seleucid family. Of these the most dangerous were the work of Laodice, the queen of Antiochus II (261–246 B.C.). Like so many other Macedonian princesses, she was headstrong, ambitious, passionate, and cruel, but in the beginning she suffered a wrong which may partially explain if not justify some of her crimes. Divorced by Antiochus so that he might marry Berenice, the daughter of Ptolemy II, she undertook to secure her own position and that of her children by a series of intrigues which culminated in the murder of her rival and the latter's infant son — an act which involved the kingdom in a disastrous war with the victim's brother Ptolemy III. When Laodice's elder son Seleucus II (246–223) at last secured the crown, she set up against him his younger brother Antiochus the Hawk. Seleucus finally secured peace by ceding to Antiochus all the family possessions in Asia Minor, which the latter promptly lost to the Galatians and the kings of Pergamum. A little later Achaeus, a cousin of Seleucus, raised a revolt in the same region, but was put down.

Wars with the Ptolemies conclude the list of subversive tendencies. Beginning in the reigns of Ptolemy II and Antiochus I, the two kingdoms clashed at least five times during the third century B.C. Antigonus Gonatas of Macedonia was usually to be found on the Seleucid side. Southern Syria changed hands several times in the course of the century, and Ptolemy III on one occasion penetrated the Seleucid dominions as far as Babylon. From 246 to 218 even the Syrian Seleucia, a few miles from the capital

*British Museum*

SELEUCID ROYALTY

*Antiochus I* *Antiochus III* *Berenice II*

city of Antioch, was in the hands of the Ptolemies. It was during these struggles, and indeed largely because of them, that so many parts of the Seleucid state were able to break away.

Accordingly, when Antiochus III (223–187) became king, he succeeded to only a fraction of the territory which had once belonged to his ancestors. His holdings in Asia Minor had been reduced to a few scattered districts, while in addition he controlled Syria, the Tigris-Euphrates Valley, and the western edge of the Iranian Plateau. This was not much more than half of the area which Seleucus I had ruled sixty years earlier. With him began a short-lived revival of the Seleucid power. His reign opened unfortunately with a smashing defeat by Ptolemy IV at Raphia (217), but fortune soon began to favor him. Rebellions in Asia Minor and Babylonia were put down, and between 212 and 204 Antiochus led a great expedition eastward to reclaim the lost provinces. Parthia, Bactria, and other regions of eastern Iran were reduced to vassalage and nominally restored to their place in the Seleucid state; in fact, however, they were left under the control of their local rulers, and their autonomy was not interfered with. The prestige of Antiochus was greatly increased by this showy feat, and his ambition kept pace with it. On his return he formed an alliance with Philip V of Macedonia to despoil the infant Ptolemy V of his non-Egyptian possessions. But the time for such grandiose international banditry was already past. The Roman Republic was beginning to take an interest in affairs east of the Adriatic, and both parties to the alliance were soon to feel the weight of its hand.

*The Ptolemaic State*

The kingdom of the Ptolemies had its center in Egypt, and its capital was the Egyptian Alexandria. There, between 306 and 30 B.C., fourteen kings named Ptolemy reigned, with the notorious Cleopatra as the last ruler of the line.[1] In its most prosperous period, under Ptolemy I and Ptolemy II (306–246), it included, besides the Nile Valley, Cyrene, Palestine, southern Syria, Phoenicia, Cyprus, the southwestern coast of Asia Minor, and at times the islands of the Aegean Sea. Plainly only military and naval superiority enabled a single ruler to unite under his sceptre lands and peoples so diverse as these. In Egypt, as in the Seleucid lands, the population consisted of a small minority of Macedonians, Greeks, and other foreigners, and an overwhelming majority of subject Egyptian natives. Due to the efficient exploitation of these lands, the Ptolemies were enormously rich, and for the first century of their rule the Egyptian population gave them no trouble. Ptolemy I established his rule firmly in the land, and attempted little more than that.

It was with the accession of Ptolemy II (283) that the family entered upon a period of intensive internal development and ambitious imperialism. The new king was an able diplomat and a great financier, but in his private life he was pleasure-loving and self-indulgent. During the first part of his reign the moving spirit in the government was his sister and wife, the headstrong, passionate, and ambitious Arsinoë, formerly the queen of Lysimachus. Largely under her influence he began the long series of wars with the Seleucid kings which were to convulse the whole Hellenistic world for most of the third century. His wars ended disastrously, however, and at his death the Aegean region and southern Syria had slipped from Ptolemaic control. His son Ptolemy III, as we have seen, retrieved the fortunes of his house for a time in a whirlwind campaign against Seleucus II. Meanwhile every effort had been made to develop Egypt. Land was reclaimed and irrigated, commerce was encouraged, and a tax-system was devised which left the Egyptian natives with only enough of their earnings to feed and clothe themselves and rear families to pay more taxes when the parents were gone.

Under Ptolemy IV (221–203) the decline of the Graeco-Egyptian state began. When Antiochus III attacked, he was beaten, largely with the aid of native Egyptian troops. But this step was fraught with the seeds of future trouble, for it encouraged the natives to hope for a more tolerable lot, and gave them confidence in their abilities. Ptolemy was a compound

[1] The latter part of this period lies outside of the scope of the present chapter.

of the debauchee and the religious mystic, who left all serious business to his ministers. As a result of these conditions, native revolts broke out, the efficiency and honesty of the government declined, and when the throne passed to the infant Ptolemy V, the dominions of the once-powerful family seemed an easy prey to ambitious neighbors. The native revolts continued throughout the second century B.C. Hardly had Ptolemy IV died when Antiochus III and Philip V of Macedonia formed the alliance (of which we have already heard) to despoil his heir, and the former soon conquered most of the Ptolemaic lands in Asia. From the danger of further spoliation Rome was to rescue the Ptolemies, but their salvation had to be purchased at the heavy price of vassalage.

Meanwhile the Kingdom of Pergamum had slowly but steadily grown stronger while its larger neighbors fought with one another. Its Greek kings were men of middle-class outlook and sympathies, who ruled a mixed population of Greeks and Asiatics. It was as protectors of the civilized peoples against the barbarous Galatians that they first gained prominence, and they discharged this function well. In addition they made Pergamum the center of a culture which was less showy, but more purely Greek, than that of Egyptian Alexandria. Their natural field of expansion lay in the crumbling dominions of the Seleucids, and every crisis in that much-harassed family resulted in accessions of territory for Pergamum. At the end of the third century B.C., King Attalus I still ruled a small kingdom, including only the northwestern corner of Asia Minor, and he was beset by the larger states of the ambitious and unscrupulous Philip V and Antiochus III, while the Galatian menace still hung over his eastern frontier. It is not surprising that in 200 B.C. he was one of the group of suppliants who appealed to Rome to stop the onward march of these two potentates. In this respect he may be said to have played a large part in bringing the Aegean world under alien control.

## The Barbarian World

Of the vast areas which lay outside the pale of this troubled Mediterranean civilization relatively little can be said, because little is known. Already in the third century B.C. the Greeks had been in contact for centuries with the Celts, Thracians, and the nomadic tribes of the Russian Steppes. In Spain and northern Africa both the Greeks and Phoenicians had long had colonies and trade connections. A Greek explorer, Pytheas of Massilia, had ventured out into the ocean and explored the Atlantic coast of Europe as far north as Scandinavia. But much of the data accumulated by traders and travelers was never committed to writing, and of that which was written, a great deal has perished. Hence any description of the ancient barbarian world must rely upon archeology, deal in general terms, and abound in uncertainties.

### *The Celts*

In the third century the Celtic speech and culture prevailed over a broad domain, which stretched from the northern part of Scotland and the western coast of Ireland to the Mediterranean coast of Gaul, and far down the Danube Valley. Small groups of Celts had pushed over into northern Italy and Spain, and others were to be found as far east as the Black Sea coast, Thrace, and Asia Minor. In southwestern Gaul and in most of Spain their progress had been checked by an older indigenous people, who are known in history as Iberians and Basques, while in northwestern Italy the Ligurians had also successfully resisted Gallic influences. Elsewhere within this wide area the Celtic culture was dominant.

Naturally no stereotyped description will fit so extensive a people, with so many foreign contacts. Politically they seem to have preferred a tribal form of organization, each tribe being an agglomeration of related clans and families, completely independent of all outside influences. Feuds and intertribal wars were frequent and destructive. Although many of the tribes were ruled by kings, the aristocracies were numerous and strong, and may already in some cases have overthrown the monarchies under which they lived. The Celts of Britain, Gaul, and northern Italy had begun to practice agriculture, but stock-raising was still as popular among them as it was in the mountains of Italy three centuries earlier. They wove cloth, worked iron, copper, gold, and silver, and they made fairly good pottery. Their houses were mere huts of wood, or wattles daubed with mud. In religion the Celts of Gaul and Britain practiced a crude polytheism, and their priests, called Druids, were numerous, powerful, and closely organized. Human sacrifices and other cruel rites were a part of their worship. Very few of them had taken up the art of writing, but even then the Gallic Druids may have begun to use the Greek alphabet employed by the people of Massilia. While not a nomadic people in ordinary times, the Celts could easily make up their minds to move, and throughout the fourth and third centuries B.C., Gaul sent forth swarms of armed emigrants in all directions to plunder and conquer, or to serve as mercenaries in the armies of Carthage, Syracuse, and the Hellenistic states.

### *The Germans*

Along the Baltic shore from the Vistula to the Rhine, in the valleys of the intervening rivers, and in southern Scandinavia, were the German tribes. In the third century B.C., very few travelers had found their way into the maze of forests and swamps which formed their home, and the civilized world hardly knew of their existence. In material civilization they rated somewhat below the Celts, and apparently their numbers were too few to make migration beyond the bounds of their northern forests necessary. Only in the second century B.C. did some of their tribes wander far enough south to attract the notice of geographers and historians.

### *The Thracians and Illyrians*

In the lower Danube Valley and the Balkan peninsula, mixed with invading Celts, was a complex of very similar peoples known, according to locality, as Thracians or Illyrians. They were barbarians of a rather high order who had settled habitations and had made marked progress in agriculture and the practical arts. Their religion was marked by a vein of orgiastic excitability; and it had impressed the Greeks so much that they had taken from it the cults of Dionysus and Orpheus. Tribal states of considerable extent and stability had developed among them, but further growth in this line was hindered by the continual inroads of the Celts and of the nomads from the Russian Steppes. The Thracians shocked the Greeks by their bloodthirsty customs, and their habits of raiding the lands of settled neighbors made them a menace to the Greeks and Macedonians, which only the finely organized Macedonian army could hold in check. Celts, Germans, and Thraco-Illyrians all belonged to the great Indo-European family of peoples, and they showed their cultural relationship in similarities of language, religion, and social organization.

### *Northern and Southern Nomads*

Lastly, we must consider two areas which were occupied by nomadic herdsmen, the northern steppes and the southern desert. The steppe region extends eastward from the Carpathian Mountains and the Danube River to the deserts of central Asia. Where it skirts the Black Sea coast, there dwelt in the third century a few sedentary agricultural tribes who raised wheat and barley for the Greek market. Elsewhere its sparse population of mixed Caucasian and Mongolian blood lived a nomadic life, making their homes in tents and subsisting on the meat and milk of their flocks and herds. In the Arabian Desert, and in the wide belt of sterile waste which extends across northern Africa, a very similar state of affairs existed, except that in Arabia the people were of the same Semitic stock as the Jews and Babylonians, while the North African nomads made use of Hamitic languages and institutions similar to those of the Egyptians.

The essential character of nomadic life was the same in both regions. The nomad had to be constantly on the move in order to find pasturage for his animals, and if a series of dry or inclement years came, then his only resource was to move into regions where a better living could be found. Even under normal conditions this pastoral economy will support only a sparse population, and any growth in numbers was certain to send a stream of emigrants abroad in search of new homes. Such migrations were never peaceful unless the adjoining lands were held by governments too strong to be attacked successfully. Otherwise the nomad went forth to plunder and to conquer. Most of the political revolutions of the past five thousand years in western Asia and northern Africa may be traced to this cause, either directly or indirectly.

### *The Conflict Between Civilization and Barbarism*

But to a lesser extent the whole barbarian world constituted a similar menace to the world of civilization. To the Celt, the Thracian, or the North African Moor, the lands of his civilized neighbors were regions of fabulous wealth, and he longed to help himself to the good things which they contained. Hence only a slight stimulus was needed — a bad season, or a raid by a neighboring tribe — to send a wave of desperate plunderers rolling in upon the frontier of Italy, Macedonia, or Egypt. The ancient civilized peoples enjoyed no such advantages over these predatory neighbors as we have over the primitive peoples of the world. They had no guns, tanks, or planes, and their swords, spears, and bows, while perhaps superior to those of the barbarian, were still of the same general kind. Only better discipline and tactical knowledge gave civilized man any marked advantage, and this was partly neutralized by the barbarian's animal courage and ability to attack unexpectedly at points of his own choosing. Let a government become inefficient, or a people softened by peace, and hordes of naked robbers from the forests or steppes would find them easy prey. This ever-present menace must be kept in mind by all who would understand the history of Rome or of any other ancient state.

# 9

## *Hellenistic Civilization: Government, Society, and Economic Organization*

### Greece and Macedonia

*Old Greece in a New World Order*

In the Hellenistic Age, as we have seen, peninsular Greece ceased to be the political and social center of the Hellenistic world, and sank to a subordinate position. After the time of the Macedonian conquest (338 B.C.) her people were never again entirely free from foreign interference, and the system of independent city-states lost, once and for all, its exclusive importance in men's thinking. Outside of it, dwarfing it by reason of their colossal size and vast resources, were the great Hellenistic monarchies, and even the most fanatical champions of Greek liberty could defend it only by playing one of these giants off against another. Hence political life became hollow and insincere, its most vital issue being that rancorous and savage class strife which was a heritage from the days of independence.

Linked with the change in political conditions was an equally profound alteration in economic affairs. Alexander's conquests had made revolutionary changes in trade-routes, and had brought the Greek manufacturing centers into direct competition with the equally skillful and lower-paid labor of the Orient. Egyptian grain captured the market formerly supplied by the Black Sea region. Of at least equal importance was Alexander's seizure and release of the Persian royal treasure, which may have amounted to 300,000 silver talents.[1] The effects of this measure were pro-

[1] About $87,000,000 at the current price of silver, but with vastly greater purchasing power at that time.

found and immediate. During the last twenty years of the fourth century, prices rose by leaps and bounds. Thus between 330 and 300 B.C. the price of wheat rose from five drachmas a *medimnus* to ten drachmas. Oil (the only common source of fats in Greece) rose from twelve drachmas a *metretes* to forty-two, and wine, from four drachmas to ten and a half or eleven. Rents went up accordingly. Only one commodity, labor, failed to respond to the trend. Its money wages not only did not rise, but actually fell. In the same period skilled labor which had commanded two and one-half drachmas a day fell to two drachmas. Unskilled labor suffered most, for the surviving records show that, even when fully employed, a laborer could sometimes afford only a scanty ration of barley bread (the cheapest food), with no allowance for any other kind of food and nothing for clothing. After 300 B.C. prices gradually fell, but with little benefit to the workers. Their lot had become permanently and vastly worse than before the days of Alexander. Agriculture was no better off. The small farmer was being squeezed out, and tenants faced eviction for failure to pay rent.

### *Social, Political, and Intellectual Trends*

The social consequences of the new economic trends were far-reaching and disastrous. To the outward view the Greeks were prosperous, with business good and fortunes growing larger all the time. But beneath this pleasing exterior was a mass of poverty and want, and many moderately well-to-do persons were ruined by their failure to adjust themselves to the changing times. Hence the class struggle — always the bane of Greek political life — broke out again with a savagery long unknown. The two old war-cries of the "have-nots" were heard again — cancellation of debts and redivision of the land. The rich lived in daily fear of the poor, and the middle class, which had acted as a shock-absorber in former ages, had largely disappeared.

Fear bred hatred, and this, joined with the constant intervention of various Hellenistic kings, poisoned political life to a degree never heard of before. The upper classes, as always, favored an oligarchic form of government in which the rabble would be deprived of the suffrage. This was natural, for in old Greece, as in other lands and times, the right to vote too often meant only an opportunity to vote other people's property into one's pocket in the form of taxes, confiscations, and cancellation of debts on the one hand, and of unearned donations, free entertainments, and free land on the other. To make up for the smallness of their numbers the oligarchs sought outside aid, and this usually meant Macedonian aid. Each of the successive Pan-Hellenic leagues sponsored by Macedonia was to people of property a guarantee against social revolution, and as the guardian of law and order it could usually count on the support of the wealthy class. After the formation of the Achaean League, however, the oligarchs tended rather to rely on it for protection, until about the end of the third century Philip V reversed the traditional policy of his country by supporting the submerged class.

One safety-valve remained for the discontented. The Hellenistic kings were in constant need of mercenary soldiers, to whom they paid high wages and gave grants of land. Moreover, the Seleucids were founding new cities in their dominions, where the citizens were generously provided for. In lands like Egypt and Asia Minor, which were rich in resources but inhabited by ignorant and thriftless peasants, business opportunities were dazzling. Hence any man who cared to migrate to the new lands opened up by Alexander's conquests had an excellent chance to better his condition, and in the course of the third century hundreds of thousands must have seized the opportunity. Among them would be both the best and the worst — the energetic and progressive, and the worthless riff-raff.

Another sign of the times, which like the foregoing tended toward a decline in population, was the voluntary limitation of the size of families in old Greece. This phenomenon, as is well known, is always likely to occur in times when the standard of living is rising faster than the wealth of the people is increasing. Infanticide and the exposure of infants became more common than ever, with girl-babies the usual victims. In one list of 78 families there were 118 sons, but only 28 daughters. Celibacy among the upper classes had long been a problem, and it now became more common than ever. Instead of marrying, young men often took slave-mistresses, whose children could be easily disposed of. However, it was not until the end of the third century that depopulation became an acute problem.

At the same time a pacifist and humanitarian sentiment was developing, in direct opposition to the trends of class strife and revolution then prevailing in the Greek world. The spread of the Achaean and Aetolian Leagues seems to mark a decline in the hostility between states. The arbitration of disputes became a popular practice, and there grew up a sentiment against the sacking of captured cities and the sale of free captives as slaves. Even the lot of the slave came to be bettered somewhat, although no one seems to have protested seriously against the injustice of the institution of slavery.

In the midst of this turmoil and unrest the prosperous classes were seeking new means of enjoying life. Comforts and luxuries were becoming increasingly common. Social clubs, supported by subscriptions and much like our own clubs, were started in large numbers. Cities multiplied the number of their public festivals, and added to the splendor of those already in existence. Of the serious interests, only philosophy flourished. Otherwise, what one might be tempted to call "good society" was, if we may believe the dramatists, incredibly vain, empty, and frivolous. Moral looseness, unhampered by the scruples of conscience and invested with a halo of romance, was almost the rule among young men of good family. In short, Greek society, while not entirely devoid of virile elements and serious interests, showed distinct signs of decadence, and it was elsewhere that Hellenistic culture was to reach its richest development.

### *Macedonia*

Macedonia, on the other hand, was largely untouched by this unrest. The conquests of Alexander and the subsequent civil wars had cost her heavily in man-power and had not brought her great wealth. In the third century she was actually weaker than she had been in the fourth. Her people were still, for the most part, either free, landed proprietors or tenants on large estates — a sturdy, virile, and independent race. The social problem which was convulsing Greece hardly affected her. Her kings still ruled by the will of the people, and they never succeeded in transforming their position into a despotism like those of the Seleucids and Ptolemies. Although the land suffered cruelly from the ravages of the Galatians, after the rise of Antigonus Gonatas it recovered quickly. In contrast with the feverish unrest of peninsular Greece, her people lived a simple, wholesome national life, and her kings could form their armies from hardy peasants and herdsmen animated by national patriotism, rather than from foreign mercenaries.

## Hellenism in the Asiatic States

### *The Old Hellenism and the New*

On the eastern shore of the Aegean Sea, Greek civilization had flourished from prehistoric times, but until the days of Alexander the Great it had not penetrated far inland. It continued to thrive in this region, and the old cities, such as Smyrna, Ephesus, Miletus, and Halicarnassus, enjoyed an enormous increase in prosperity in the late fourth and third cen-

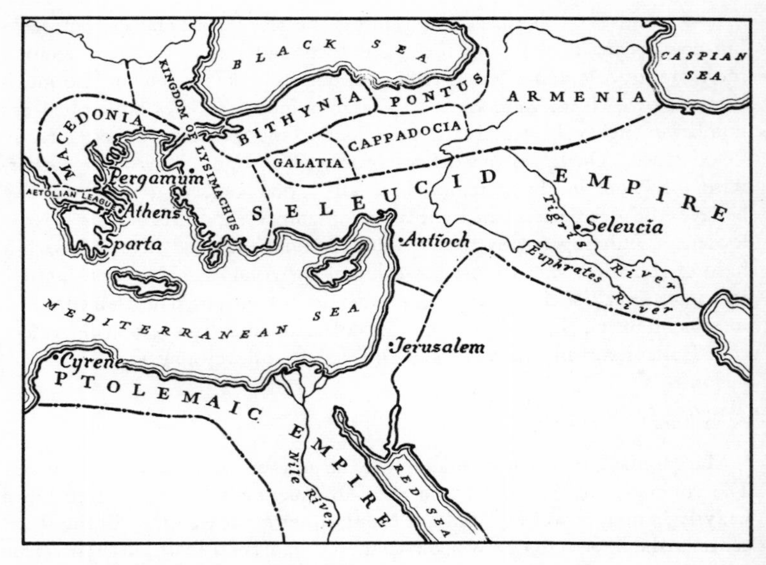


DIVISION OF THE EMPIRE OF ALEXANDER THE GREAT [1]

turies, due principally to the new economic opportunities which the age afforded. Just off the coast, the island of Rhodes took over the position which Athens had formerly enjoyed as an international shipping center, with a corresponding increase in wealth and influence. For a time in the third century the cities of the Asiatic coast suffered severely from the ravages of the Galatians, who plundered the open country up to the city walls, but after 230 Attalus I of Pergamum effectively checked the menace by his victories over the marauders. On the northern coast Heraclea long maintained her independence, and Sinope did not fall into the hands of the kings of Pontus until 183 B.C. Both of these centers, while remote from the more lucrative trade-routes, drew great wealth from the Black Sea commerce and from the back country of Asia Minor.

[1] The boundaries shown on this map are roughly those of 281 B.C., but in western Asia Minor, the state of Pergamum and the Galatian Confederacy did not arise until after the fall of Lysimachus, which occurred in that year. In Continental Greece the boundaries of the spheres of influence controlled by the various Hellenistic rulers fluctuated so frequently and violently that no attempt has been made to delineate them.

In the interior of Asia Minor, Syria, and the eastern provinces of the Seleucid Kingdom, Hellenism was a new and exotic growth, which owed its existence largely to the colonizing activities of Alexander the Great and his successors. In these regions a series of cities, named for old places in Greece, or called Alexandria, Antioch, Seleucia, Laodicea, Apamea, or Stratonicea after members of the reigning dynasty, were either new foundations or old centers refounded and colonized with Greeks. Similar cities were established by the kings of Pergamum and Bithynia. In these regions the Greeks were intruders, settled in the midst of non-Hellenic Asiatic peoples, and they occupied a highly privileged position, with large holdings in land, local self-government, and preferential treatment in taxation.

*Greeks and Asiatics in the Hellenistic Kingdoms*

In these new or reconstructed cities there grew up a type of urban life never before known in the Greek world. They had never experienced the stormy independence of Athens, Thebes, Corinth, and Sparta. Having been founded by kings, they had none of the Greek prejudice against monarchy, and the kings in general gave them little cause for complaint. Following a practice already old in Asiatic Greece, they worshiped their living sovereigns as gods, and the kings in turn showered the cities with favors. From them came officers, soldiers, and administrators for the royal service, and they served as fortresses against foreign invaders and native revolts. By placing the adjoining country districts under their jurisdiction the kings were relieved of the wearisome details of local administration in regions where their direct supervision could hardly have been effective had they attempted to maintain it.

When the Macedonians came to Asia they found the land studded with great feudal baronies ruled by nobles, and with temple-states governed by priests. Most of the former were confiscated and either retained as part of the royal domain or granted to Macedonians or Greeks. The temple-states were found all over western Asia, and were peculiar to that region. Indeed, such was the government of Judea which in 200 B.C. was taken over from the Ptolemaic Kingdom by Antiochus III. It was ruled by the high-priest of the temple of Yahweh at Jerusalem. There we find a double government, the land paying a tax of about a third to a half of the crop to the king, and in addition, a ten per cent tax to the high-priest, as well as various indirect taxes. Judicial administration was in the hands of the high-priest or his subordinates, who enforced the so-called "Law of Moses." Even though a Jew might live abroad, he was compelled by religious pressure to pay dues to the temple treasury. The kings, however, interfered at will in the choice of a new high-priest, and apparently at times sold the office to the highest bidder. As a rule the priests were not very zealous in the observance of their religion, for at times they were willing to compromise seriously with paganism, in spite of the jealous exclusiveness of the Yahweh cult. Some of the temple-states maintained hordes of religious prostitutes, and waxed rich from the proceeds of this traffic. Whenever possible the kings suppressed these religious principalities, and reorganized them as Greek cities, to which the administration of the temples was entrusted.

Thus over large areas of western Asia there were two populations — a small minority of privileged Greeks living either in self-governing cities or as feudal barons, and a large majority of Asiatic natives, who were for the most part tenants on lands owned by the king, the priests, or the lay aristocracy, and in any case were in a species of serfdom. When an Asiatic became a resident of a Greek city, he usually had no share in its government, although the non-Greek population of such a city might have its own organization to settle law-suits arising among the members according to their own laws.

To preserve this cultural line of demarcation in its entirety was, naturally, impossible. The peasants and petty craftsmen, who formed a large majority of the native population, were, it is true, scarcely touched by Hellenism. But the Greeks on their side soon began to worship the gods of their Asiatic neighbors, and this fact in particular provided a common ground on which the two groups could meet. Because Greek was the language of the royal administration, many natives learned at least a smattering of it, and since it was spoken more widely than any other tongue then in use, the knowledge of it was necessary for persons having wide commercial connections. The well-deserved prestige of Greek literature also attracted many educated Asiatics to its study. Most of the Greek cities had no objections to granting the privileges of citizenship to natives who were exceptionally well versed in their language and manners, and these Hellenized natives intermarried with their Greek neighbors. But the converts to Hellenism always brought with them something of their old cultures, and thus Asiatic Hellenism became constantly less Greek and more Asiatic in character.

Out of this wide extension of the Greek language grew a new dialect — the so-called *koine* or "common tongue." The Greeks of Asia usually tried to speak the Attic dialect, but its use by half-Hellenized Asiatics led to the discarding of many of its complicated inflections, and to a radical simplification of sentence structure. It was this dialect which, in the first century of the Christian Era, was used by the authors of the New Testament.

### *The Uneven Spread of Asiatic Hellenism*

A significant example of the reaction of an Asiatic people to Hellenism is to be found in the case of the Jews. Their home land was surrounded on three sides by Greek cities, and in Jerusalem itself there were many who adopted Greek ways and Greek names. Thousands of Jews settled in Alexandria, Antioch, and other Hellenistic centers, where they discarded the Aramaic tongue spoken in Palestine and took up "common" Greek. Their scriptures were translated into it, and the services in their synagogues were conducted in it. Yet they clung stubbornly to their national faith and manner of life, and when in the second century B.C., a Seleucid king tried to force the Jews of Palestine to adopt the Greek culture and religion, he provoked a rebellion which was never entirely put down.

In Babylonia Hellenism encountered another old and thoroughly self-conscious civilization. In order to weaken the great native capital of Babylon, the Seleucid kings founded a city at Seleucia-on-the-Tigris, to which they forcibly transferred many of the inhabitants of Babylon. The new city became one of the two capitals of the kingdom, and had 600,000 inhabitants. Other similar examples of Greek colonization in the same region might be cited. Yet the area in which the Babylonian culture had prevailed was not Hellenized. In spite of the hardships which they had to suffer by reason of the favors shown to Seleucia, the Babylonians continued to use their Semitic language, their cuneiform system of writing, their traditional religious cults, and other features of their venerable culture. Early in the second century B.C. we find the Greek settlers in Babylonia beginning to adopt Babylonian names and ways, and although Seleucia prospered and kept its Greek character, it remained an island of Hellenism in a sea of Oriental civilization. In fact, it was through the Greeks of the Tigris-Euphrates Valley that such Babylonian contributions as the pseudo-science of astrology reached the western world.

On the western edge of the Iranian Plateau, particularly in Media, a number of Greek cities were founded, but here again, Hellenism made little progress. The sense of national solidarity among these peoples was strong, and it was fortified by the Zoroastrian religion. Although in the latter half of the third century Persia was a Seleucid province, in which a few Greek cities had been founded, its people still clung to their own ways

*British Museum*

KINGS OF BACTRIA

*Euthydemus I* *Euthydemus II* *Antimachus I*

and scorned Hellenism. In Bactria, Sogdiana, and the other eastern provinces of the kingdom, Hellenism seemed for a time to have made a stronger impression. Alexander and the early Seleucids had founded so many Greek cities in this area, and had settled so many thousands of Greek colonists there, that even after they became separated from the Seleucid state, they were able to dominate an extensive kingdom until near the end of the second century B.C. A similar condition existed in the Indus Valley, which was reconquered for Hellenism by the Bactrian kings and held far into the first century B.C. But since our literary sources have little to say about these regions, and very little excavation has been done in them, we do not know much about the state of Greek civilization there, or its influence upon the natives. Only the fact that the Bactrian kings issued a beautiful coinage of purely Greek type leads to the conclusion that other phases of Hellenistic culture may also have been fostered. At any rate, the Greeks can have been no more than a small, exclusive caste in the midst of an overwhelming majority of Asiatics, and constant civil and foreign wars so diminished their numbers that they fell easy victims to the new invasions from the steppes.

After all, the center of the Seleucid power was in northern Syria, a district colonized so thickly with Macedonians and Greeks that it had become almost a "second Macedonia." There lay Antioch-on-the-Orontes, their principal place of residence. It was perhaps more purely Greek and less Oriental than Seleucia-on-the-Tigris, but it too had a polyglot population of Syrians, Jews, and other Asiatics in addition to the Macedonians and Greeks. At Apamea, not far away, was the military depot of the government, and at the mouth of the Orontes was yet another Seleucia, the seaport of the capital. Other centers of Hellenism numbered at least a score. Nowhere else except in Asia Minor did Hellenism take such deep root, and here, for nearly a thousand years, the Greek language and Greek culture held their own beside the native Syrian civilization, until in the seventh century A.D. the Mohammedan invaders submerged both.

### *The Seleucid Administrative System*

With its vast area and its diverse cultures and peoples, the Seleucid state could be governed only by a system which made large concessions to local autonomy and at the same time maintained an efficient central authority. In attacking this problem Seleucus I and his successors borrowed heavily from the experience of the Persian kings who had previously ruled the same land. Let us first survey their provincial system. The kingdom was divided into *satrapies*, or provinces, which were generally smaller than the Persian divisions of the same name. Over each one was a *strategos* (literally "general," actually "governor") appointed by the king. The satrapy was divided into districts, each with its governor. It was the duty of the governor to carry out the king's commands in every field except finance. Hence we find each satrapy provided with an independent tax collector, while the royal domain lands were under the control of a steward, probably also independent of the governor. There was no attempt at uniformity in laws or taxation. Each group retained its own legal system, and frequently had its own officials to apply and interpret them. Thus in a typical satrapy one might find "allied" Greek cities which paid only lump sums of tribute to the king and had their own law courts, military colonies of Greeks or Asiatics under a somewhat stricter central control, temple-states like Judea, feudal baronies whose lords enjoyed varying degrees of independence, and royal estates whose tenants paid the king both rent and taxes and were under unlimited royal control. As time passed, Greek law to some extent displaced the native customary laws in some localities, but this was more by accident than design.

Not all of the kingdom, however, was included in the provincial system. At all times there were vassal tribes and kingdoms whose only obligations to the king were tribute and the furnishing of contingents under their own command for the army. Such states had a tendency to drift away into complete independence unless carefully watched, but sometimes this was the best arrangement possible under the circumstances. When Antiochus III reorganized the kingdom, he allowed the Greek and native rulers of the eastern provinces to continue in office as vassals, and his successors were forced more and more to tolerate them as their own authority weakened.

Over this chaos of diverse authorities the royal government strove to retain such control as circumstances permitted. The king was, in theory, an absolute monarch, some of whose subjects worshiped him as a god. He claimed the right to make laws valid throughout his immediate domains, but in practice he did not interfere much with the existing laws of his subjects. He had an army composed of Greeks, Macedonians, and the more warlike of the Asiatics. Some of these were settled in military colonies; others were mercenaries. In times of crisis additional Asiatic troops were probably raised from among the tenants on the royal domain. Superficially the Seleucid army was still organized and disciplined on the Macedonian model, but the Asiatic levies were probably allowed to use their own types of armament. A special feature of the Seleucid army was its corps of five hundred trained Indian elephants, which proved effective on more than one battlefield. From their predecessors the Seleucids inherited a system of roads and a postal service, by means of which they were enabled to keep in close touch with the more critical parts of their dominions. Another symbol of the unity of the kingdom was the royal coinage, which was legal tender everywhere, although the cities and vassal kings were in some cases allowed to issue coins of their own.

In short, the Seleucid Kingdom was only nominally centralized. Within its bulky structure were cracks which with very little strain might cause it to fall apart, and it was, as we have seen, subjected to constant shocks both from foreign foes and domestic rebels. It speaks well for the individual ability of the kings who ruled it that they held it together so long, and that it finally collapsed only beneath the impact of Rome's irresistible might. But there is another side to the story. It is doubtful if strict centralization would ever have been feasible under the circumstances, and the Seleucid kings, facing the situation realistically, worked out a valuable combination of monarchical centralization with local self-government, which was later to influence the structure of the Roman provincial system.

## The Ptolemaic State

Compared with the Seleucid state, the Kingdom of the Ptolemies was small in both area and population, but at least in so far as Egypt was concerned, its government was closely centralized. Egypt was its core, a land whose habitable area was less than 10,000 square miles. It also had outlying dominions — Cyprus, Cyrene, Palestine, Phoenicia, southern

Syria, parts of the coast of southern and western Asia Minor, and at times the Aegean Islands — with an area several times as large as Egypt itself.

*The Ptolemaic Government*

In Egypt the new rulers had to deal with a civilization and a system of government already over three thousand years old. The conditions of life were rigidly prescribed by nature. With its deep, black soil and never-failing river, Egypt was principally agricultural, but agriculture was only possible with an adequate system of irrigation, rigidly controlled by government. Largely on this basis the native kings had built up a despotic "planned economy," with the result that most of the national income went into the treasury of the king or the coffers of the priests. Long before Ptolemy I came to Egypt, the theory had been established that all land belonged to the king, to whom one paid rent rather than a real estate tax. Yet the system, so repugnant to the citizens of a modern democracy, had proved workable. Agriculture had prospered, and manufactures had sprung up: wood and metal working, weaving, glass-blowing, paper-making, pottery manufacturing, and a host of other trades. Religion, of a crass, superstitious kind, dominated government and governed alike. Men bore the despotism of the king because they believed him to be a god and son of a god, and they submitted to the exactions of the priests because they claimed to be the earthly regents of the gods. But for all their cheerful submissiveness, they had a stubborn will of their own, and would fight to the death against a government whose policies they disliked. Under Persian rule the prosperity of the country had received a serious set-back from long-continued neglect of the irrigation system and from the ravages of war, but these could be easily repaired. It was a land of great opportunities for an enterprising but tactful ruler who could fit himself into the rigid framework of Egyptian institutions; Ptolemy I was such a man.

Ptolemy and his successors constructed a skillful compound of Greek and Egyptian institutions which for a time served the interests of the rulers without exciting the hatred of their subjects. More and more they arrogated to themselves the position of god-kings, and as such they exercised the rights of absolute monarchs. They took over the traditional system of landholding, and with it government control of agriculture and irrigation. The Egyptian peasants were not legally slaves, but they had little more freedom than slaves, and their nominal freedom did not interfere with the government's complete control of their activities. Thus they could be compelled to take leases on state-owned land whenever it suited the purposes of the ruler, but the government was not bound by any contract which it made with them. Officials could beat them, or force them to labor on public works, at will. All this was in line with the age-old tradition of the land, and they did not object.

Yet the Ptolemies revolutionized the system while professing to preserve it. From the beginning they, like their predecessors the native Pharaohs, used mercenary soldiers almost exclusively, and at first these mercenaries were mostly Macedonians and Greeks. Every effort was made to induce these foreigners to settle permanently on the land. Farms varying in size from twenty-five to one hundred acres were granted to those who would pay a moderate rent, so long as they would do military service when called upon. Naturally, these military colonists did not personally cultivate their farms, but left such work to the natives. The land needed for this purpose was secured by reclaiming extensive tracts along the edge of the valley which had been uncultivated during the Persian regime because of the neglect of the irrigation system. Where these reclaimed lands were not needed for military colonies, enterprising Greek civilians — especially of the royal civil service — were invited to take charge of them. All the higher civil officials, and most of the lower ones, were Greek. Greek businessmen settled in the villages throughout the country, where they acted as tax-farmers and carried on various types of petty commerce. The government, recognizing the importance of these immigrants as its potential soldiers, civil officials, and partisans in time of crisis, granted them extensive privileges. They were organized into associations based upon their places of origin, and each group tried all law cases arising among its members. Jews, Phoenicians, Persians, and other foreigners were also found in great numbers, and they, like the Greeks, were organized and enjoyed legal privileges. Thus the Egyptian countryside was completely penetrated by foreigners for the first time in its history.

But the Ptolemies, unlike the Seleucids, did not found many Greek cities. In Egypt the old Milesian colony of Naucratis still continued to exist, and Alexandria had recently been founded by Alexander the Great. Ptolemy I added to the list Ptolemais, a small place in upper Egypt. But of these only Alexandria became outstanding. Her commercial advantages, added to the fact that she was the royal capital, combined to make her one of the world's largest and richest cities. She soon lost her predominantly Greek character, and became a polyglot metropolis, with Egyptians, Jews, Phoenicians, and many other nationalities among her 600,000 people. However, the kings deprived Alexandria of her rights of self-government, and placed her under the direct control of their officials.

This negative attitude toward the self-governing Greek city-state on the part of the Ptolemies is not surprising, for plainly such an organism did not readily fit into the scheme of things in the Nile Valley.

*Graeco-Egyptian Cultural Relations*

To preserve the Greek character of their citizens, neither Naucratis nor Ptolemais allowed intermarriage between the Greeks and the Egyptian natives, but in the countryside no such restrictions existed. As in Seleucid Asia, the dilution of the Greek element in Egypt arose from two sources. Greek men married Egyptian women, and Egyptians gained the legal status of Greeks either wholly or in part by adopting the language and customs of the ruling class. Thus there grew up along with the Egyptian natives a group with mixed blood and a veneer of Greek culture, but with a fundamentally Egyptian temperament and viewpoint. As Greek was the language of the government, many natives learned just enough of it to enable them to do business with the officials. Although the old Egyptian tongue was undoubtedly still the common language, and for some purposes continued to be written, Greek acquired a strong position as a secondary language, and maintained it until centuries after the Mohammedan conquest of the seventh century A.D.

*The Ptolemaic Economic Policy*

With a genuine Greek business sense the Ptolemies set out to exploit the resources of the people of Egypt to the uttermost. They encouraged the introduction of new crops and of improved agricultural methods. Tenants on royal land — by far the largest part of the kingdom — paid a rent of one-third of their crops. While the tax on land granted to soldiers and officials was light if it was planted to grain, it ran as high as $15.00 an acre (with a purchasing power several times as great as at present) on vineyards and olive groves. To this was added in all cases an interminable list of levies which included poll taxes, house taxes, and taxes on various trades. The manufacture of oil, beer, paper, salt, and many other commodities was a royal monopoly. The local offices of the royal treasury served as banks, whose profits all went to the king. Cargo boats operating on the Nile were government owned, and were merely leased to the operators. The king's officials could buy all surplus grain at a price fixed by themselves, and the profits from its sale in foreign markets went to the treasury. Mines of all kinds belonged to the king. In short, seldom if ever in the history of the world has a people been so ingeniously and ruthlessly deprived of everything but a bare subsistence for the benefit of its government. Even the priesthoods, which the native Pharaohs had treated with marked consideration, were brought under the yoke. The landed endowments of the temples were now administered by the king's agents, and the taxes levied for the support of religion passed through their hands. No doubt also much of the income nominally accruing to these religious corporations actually found its way into the bottomless pit of the royal treasury. To the income from Egypt was added the tribute from outlying parts of their empire, and although the evidence on this point is scanty, it seems to show that these provinces fared proportionately no better than did the Nile Valley.

Egypt is a natural point of exchange for the products of the Mediterranean world, Africa, and India, and the Ptolemies did not neglect this source of income. Their fleet long dominated the eastern Mediterranean and the Red Sea. Goods from Africa and India were landed on the Red Sea coast, hauled overland to the Nile, shipped by boat to Alexandria, and there exchanged for the products of Greece, Carthage, and Italy. Customs duties as high as fifty percent and royal monopolies put most of the profits of this commerce into the king's hands. It is no wonder that Ptolemy II was the wealthiest sovereign in the civilized world.

It is only fair to say that this all-pervasive despotism conferred some benefits upon Egypt. The old economy of barter was largely replaced by a money economy, while the productivity of the land was increased by improvements in the irrigation system and in methods of cultivation. For instance, the introduction of the "Archimedean Screw," an improved type of pump, made the raising of water from the river to the fields much easier and more efficient than before. During the first century of Ptolemaic rule the country was more prosperous than it had been for some time previously. Yet it is not surprising that the Egyptian natives came to hate this foreign domination with an intensity that neither material prosperity nor the conciliatory gestures of the government could lessen. They were used to exploitation, but never before had it been so inhumanly thorough. The foreigners were everywhere. Even the house of the Egyptian was not exempt from their presence, for the Greek landholder often had a part of a native dwelling assigned to him as permanent quarters. The strangers were armed and trained for war, while the natives were disarmed and without organization. Hence for a long time they sullenly endured their lot; but in 217, when Ptolemy IV used an army largely composed of natives to defeat Antiochus III, the storm broke. The remainder of the history of Ptolemaic Egypt is shot through with the lurid light of savage native rebellions and equally savage repressions.

## Hellenistic Society and Economics

### *A New World of Opportunity*

In the third century B.C., the Greeks who migrated to Asia and Egypt found themselves part of the dominant caste in a Hellenistic empire far richer and more extensive than any Greek had dared to dream of before. It was a land in which opportunities to gain wealth and power seemed limitless, and, as in frontier America, men were little hampered by the social distinctions of the homeland. Personal worth of a very positive kind — the ability to dare, to do, and to command — counted for everything. For nearly a century after the death of Alexander, the opportunity for enormous personal advancement was open to any Greek who could meet the severe requirements of the new environment, and it evoked a tremendous outburst of energy and enterprise. Slight evidence of its extent is the fact that Greek explorers in the services of the Ptolemies visited East Africa, that Greek mercenaries made and unmade kings in India, and that a small minority of Greeks founded and long upheld a kingdom in faraway Bactria. The idea formerly held by classical scholars, that the Greeks of the third century B.C. were as a whole a decadent people, is absurd when one considers these facts.

Commerce flourished as never before, and Greek enterprise tapped areas not previously brought into connection with the Mediterranean world. India was reached by land through the eastern provinces of the Seleucid Kingdom, and by sea through Egypt, the Red Sea, and the Indian Ocean. The spice trade, which has never since entirely died out, was first placed on a regular footing at this time. Chinese silk, African ostrich plumes, ivory, and hosts of other articles either appeared for the first time in the Greek market or became available in commercial quantities. From the workshops of Egypt, Phoenicia, and Babylonia a constant stream of manufactured goods was sent to the most distant corners of the Mediterranean and Black Seas, whence raw materials were sent back in exchange.

Navigation improved. Although piracy continued to be a problem, the great naval powers — the Ptolemies, Carthage, Rhodes, and Syracuse — dealt resolutely with it. Larger and more seaworthy ships were built. Lighthouses were erected at critical points, and one, the famous Pharos of Alexandria, was visible for thirty miles at sea. Guide books for the use of shipmasters were published, describing the harbors of the Mediterranean and Red Seas.

Another feature characteristic of the age was a great expansion of banking and an increased use of money. Whereas in the fourth century only the larger cities had banks, there was now hardly a town of medium size without one. The Ptolemaic state banks have been mentioned. Cities deposited their surplus funds and drew interest from them, or borrowed money, much as in modern times. We even hear of insurance against the escape of slaves, based upon the same general principle as modern insurance. These innovations, added to the increased circulation of coined money, gave the Hellenistic business world a distinctly modern appearance.

### *Greek Society in Asia and Egypt*

As might be expected, the society of the Greek colonies in the Orient, recruited as it was from all quarters, for a long time developed no hard-and-fast class distinctions. The only indices to social position were wealth and official rank, and these usually depended upon the ability and good fortune of the holder. There was little stability in these new societies. He who was rich and honored today might be dead or in beggary tomorrow, and often no reason could be assigned for the change except pure luck. Hence men came to talk more than ever of the capriciousness of Fortune, whom they personified as a goddess and worshiped more assiduously than they did any other deity except the king under whose authority they lived.

The lot of women was greatly improved. Among the Macedonians they had always enjoyed great freedom and influence, and this tradition was continued by the Hellenistic royal families. Beginning with Olympias, the mother of Alexander the Great, we find a series of strong-willed, unscrupulous, domineering, and often bloodthirsty Cleopatras, Laodices, Berenices, and Arsinoës taking leading parts at the Hellenistic courts. They played the game of politics for high stakes, and shrank from no crime necessary to achieve their ends. When they won they not infrequently controlled governments, and when they lost they met death without flinching. Among the Egyptians and Babylonians also women enjoyed much the same privileges as men. The cumulative influence of these foreign examples among the Hellenistic Greeks was great, and it was heightened in the new Greek cities by the relative scarcity of women in a predominantly masculine society. Greek law still regarded them as inferiors, but for practical purposes their condition improved noticeably. Both in Greece and in the Greek colonies abroad they were allowed to move about freely, and provision was made for their education. A few even attended the philosophical schools at Athens, the most conservative spot in the educational world of the day.

Public education everywhere received more attention than formerly. At Athens the course of training which had formerly fitted young men for the army was now remodeled along literary lines. In many (perhaps most) Greek cities, public schools were established, at which teachers hired by the state presided. Endowed schools assumed an even greater importance. Hence the percentage of literacy must have risen considerably, although unfortunately we are without statistics by which this assertion might be proved. For higher education there were, before 250 B.C., five philosophical schools at Athens — Cynic, Platonic, Aristotelian, Epicurean, and Stoic — while at Alexandria the Ptolemies had established the Museum and the Serapeum, famous for their libraries and scientific studies.

City life attained attractive qualities unknown in classical Greece. In the new Greece that sprang up in the multitude of cities founded by the Hellenistic kings the talents of the municipal architect were called into use. Streets were wider than in the old cities of the homeland, and were laid out on a rectangular pattern like that in the American Middle West. Municipal aqueducts, some of which were provided with filters to purify the water, largely replaced the wells and cisterns of former times. Paving was still far from common, but the main streets had sewers to carry off the waste products, and an attempt was made to keep them clean. Although houses were packed closely together, they were much larger and more commodious than before. Fine basilicas (a combination of market building and courthouse), theaters, baths, fountains, and temples satisfied both the material needs and the artistic taste of the inhabitants. From the Hellenistic world Rome was to learn much in the art of municipal engineering.

In all, the Hellenistic Age was a bustling and progressive one, in which a modern man would have felt more at home than during any other period of the ancient world. In no era previous to the nineteenth century A.D. was so much mental activity discernible, nor so much material progress made. But its bloom was all too brief, for after a single century of brilliance came decline.

# 10

***

## *The Hellenistic Age: Art and Intellect*

### Importance in Cultural History

#### *A Respectable Record of Achievement*

In spite of their preoccupation with war, government, commerce, and colonization, the Hellenistic Greeks did not neglect aesthetic and intellectual interests. In these fields they have too often received scant justice from critics, both ancient and modern. Reverence for the art of classical Greece has tended to blind the observer to the real merits of much Hellenistic sculpture and painting, and intolerance of any literature which developed a style and content different from that popular in fifth-century Athens has consigned the great bulk of Hellenistic writing to oblivion. Yet we are now coming to realize that this attitude is a mistaken one. Not only did Hellenistic artists, poets, and prose writers produce a great deal which was worthy of the attention of later ages, but in science the record of achievement was more brilliant than that of any previous period, and in philosophy the creative power of the Greek mind was shown in the appearance of two of the world's most influential approaches to the problem of human conduct — Stoicism and Epicureanism. It was from the Hellenistic Greeks rather than from their classical predecessors that the Romans received their training in the higher aspects of civilized life, and the modern world is also deeply indebted to them.

### Art

#### *The Classical Heritage*

To appreciate both the strength and the weakness of Hellenistic art, we must remember that it began where the art of classical Greece ended, without any sharp line of division between the two. Thus the architects, sculptors, and painters of the third century B.C. inherited the technical knowledge, manual skill, and artistic mannerisms of their immediate predecessors in the fourth century. In some respects this continuity of tradition was an aid to them, but in others it was a millstone about their necks. The themes which the great masters of sculpture and painting had treated were all but worn out. No one could hope to surpass or even equal them in depicting gods, heroes, or athletes, and the religious faith which had lingered to inspire Praxiteles, Scopas, and their fellows was vanishing. On the other hand, portraiture was a branch of art which kings and great men were certain to encourage, and which always offered new material, while the interest of the people in everyday life afforded an opportunity for the development of creative power.

*Architecture*

In one respect the architects were better off than either the painters or the sculptors. While they were still bound by the old traditions in the planning of temples, the conditions of life in the new Greek world of Asia and Egypt gave them abundant opportunities for creative work. Basilicas, fortifications, palaces, and similar structures were in demand there, and for such buildings classical traditions afforded few precedents. Thus Sosistratus, the designer of the four-hundred-foot Pharos of Alexandria, solved the unprecedented problem which it presented by a very free adaptation of a Babylonian temple-tower. So great was his success that his influence may still be seen in modern lighthouse construction and in the towers of Christian churches. The colonnade, which in classical times had been principally associated with temples, now came to be widely used for secular purposes. A marketplace was commonly surrounded on three sides by a wall, with a colonnade running along the inside. In this manner the shoppers and the loafers who frequented Greek markets could find protection from the sun, wind, or rain. Sosistratus, always an innovator, designed for the people of Cnidus a colonnaded sidewalk several stories high, with walks on the upper floors. These structures (on a somewhat simpler scale than the one at Cnidus) became very popular in Roman times. Gymnasia were built larger, more elaborately, and with better equipment than in classical times.

*Sculpture*

The same mixture of old and new tendencies is to be seen in sculpture. The weakened religious feeling was reflected in the statues of the Olympian gods which were far below the fifth and fourth century standard of excellence. But these were exceptions. At Rhodes there flourished in the late fourth and third centuries a school of sculptors which worked in both bronze and marble. In 305 one of its members, Chares of Lindus, celebrated the deliverance of Rhodes when besieged by King Demetrius Poliorcetes, by making the celebrated "Colossus." It was a bronze statue of the sun god, one hundred feet in height. Its artistic quality we can only judge from descriptions, and contemporaries were more impressed by its size than by its beauty. Half a century after its completion it was overthrown by an earthquake, and lay for 1300 years prostrate on the ground. Then the Mohammedan invaders of Rhodes sold it to a Jewish junk dealer, who demolished it.

A second masterpiece from the Rhodian school was the "Victory of Samothrace," a marble statue set up to commemorate the naval victory of Antigonus Gonatas over Ptolemy II. Its mutilated remains are now in the Louvre. The goddess is represented as having just alighted on the prow of a ship. Her wings are still spread, and the breeze caused by the movement of the vessel blows her clothing backward, so that her limbs are outlined through it. This statue is a splendid study of life and motion, embodying perfect technical skill as well as true artistic feeling.

The school of Lysippus continued to be active until far into the third century, and many of its productions are extant in the form of Roman copies. One of its outstanding products was the bronze "Fortune of Antioch," executed about 300 B.C., for Seleucus I. The goddess was seated on a rock, her head crowned with walls and towers. Her robes, instead of falling in heavy folds as the fourth-century style would have dictated, were tightly stretched, and their creases formed a rather intricate pattern. At her feet a swimming youth represented the River Orontes. That statues of the elusive goddess of Fortune were so common is an index to her importance in an age of rapidly changing conditions, when spectacular alternations of good and ill luck were prevalent. Another product of the school of Lysippus was the seated statue of Hermes, the messenger of the gods, found in Herculaneum. Aside from his winged heels and *caduceus*, there is nothing divine about him. His figure is that of a mortal athlete — lithe, muscular, and lifelike, but not at all divine.

Athens in this period still clung to the tradition established by Praxiteles, but without his genius. Some of the best Athenian work was in the field of portraiture, which now became thoroughly realistic. Examples of the work of the Athenian portrait sculptors are the statues of the comedian Menander and the statesman and orator Demosthenes. The latter, made

*Galloway*

NIKE OF SAMOTHRACE

*Galloway*

FORTUNE OF ANTIOCH

about forty years after the death of the subject, is a perfect expression of the fiery enthusiasm and intense seriousness of the last great Athenian patriot. Other schools followed the same lead in realistic portraiture. Instead of idealized faces with the conventional straight noses, we have convincing and strongly individualized faces and figures which preserve the likenesses of kings and other great men from all parts of the Hellenistic world. An eclectic work showing strongly the influence of this school is the famous "Venus of Milo," which combines a Praxitelean treatment of the head and torso with a heavy folded drapery of the fifth-century type. The ensemble forms one of the most beautiful artistic remains of the ancient world.

The influence of Athenian ideas in sculpture was also to be seen in a colossal statue symbolic of the River Nile, set up in Alexandria. Here the river was represented as a majestic bearded god, reclining on one elbow. Beside him was the Sphinx, and behind him on a high pedestal were grapes and other fruits found in Egypt. Around him were the typical Egyptian animals, while among them and clambering over the body of the deity, were sixteen pygmy human figures representing the sixteen cubits which the river rose in its annual flood.

In the later third century Pergamum became the seat of a productive school of sculptors best known for a series of statues celebrating the victories of Attalus I (241–197) over the Galatians. This group (called the first Pergamene School) produced a number of fine bronzes, of which the "Dying Gaul" and the "Gaul Stabbing Himself" are known to us through copies. The former was a masterpiece of restrained pathos, and has been widely copied in modern times. The second represented a Galatian warrior who, with his pursuers in sight, had just stabbed his wife, and supported her dying form in one hand as, with a frenzied glance at the approaching enemy, he plunged the sword into his own heart. Both were characterized by a fine realism, and by a true appreciation of the barbarians. To the same school belonged the group which showed the punishment inflicted by Apollo upon the satyr Marsyas for presuming to challenge the god to a musical contest. The artist had the good taste to choose the moment before the flaying, when Apollo's Scythian slave was whetting the knife for the horrible task, the satyr hung helplessly by his hands, and the god looked languidly on. As studies in character the stupid countenance of the slave and the brutal, terror-stricken face of the victim rank very high.

Thirty years later a second school of Pergamene sculptors celebrated the victories of Eumenes II and the Romans over Antiochus III and the Gauls by carving a frieze for the great altar of Zeus in Pergamum. Large fragments of this composition have been recovered by modern excavators. The theme was a hackneyed one — the victory of the Olympian gods over the snake-legged giants. To the Greek imagination this always typified the victory of civilization and order over the forces of chaos. Technically the work is excellent, but in conception and spirit it is not above criticism. In its original form it was a mass of colossal figures, contorted and unreal, whose tense muscles and flying draperies failed to create any illusion of reality. It was just this tendency to exaggerate emotional stress and muscular strain which resulted, not long before the beginning of the Christian Era, in the production, by a Rhodian sculptor, of the famous "Laocoön Group," which at one time evoked a high degree of admiration from art critics.

In the field of realistic sculpture the Hellenistic artists left classical tradition behind, and catered to the taste of their own day. Hence, we need not be surprised that in this field they achieved some of their finest work. The penchant for realism, already apparent in the work of the First Pergamene School, led them to portray children, old men, and old women with a faithfulness and attention to detail never seen before. It touched religious sculpture, and resulted in the production of a charming series of figures of snub-nosed satyrs, and of the juvenile god of love. Boethos of Chalcedon discarded even the pretense of religion and dealt with strictly human scenes. His bronze "Boy Struggling with a Goose," which exists in a marble copy, is a charming domestic scene, in which the anatomy of the childish body is rendered with careful observation and sure touch. In the same vein are the seated figures of the drunken old woman holding a wine jar, by Myron of Thebes, and that of the old marketwoman, by an unknown sculptor.

### *Painting, Mosaic, and Jewelry*

In painting, the Hellenistic artists were less hampered by tradition than in sculpture, for this art had, in the days of Alexander the Great, only recently "come of age." Hence it produced, as a whole, better work than its sister art, sculpture. But this judgment has to be reached on a very slender body of evidence. None of the masterpieces of this period exist in the originals, and there are no first-rate copies. We are driven to form our estimates of Hellenistic painting from literary descriptions, from a few personal portraits found in Egypt, and from copies of the great masterpieces in fresco or mosaic used as house decorations in the Italian cities of Herculaneum and Pompeii. Yet even so we are made aware of the existence of works which combined technical perfection with psychological insight to a degree which compares favorably with the greatest paintings of Renaissance Italy. The studies in light and shadow made by earlier Greek artists had not been forgotten, and the drawing was masterly. Facial expressions, the fall of draperies, and the play of skin and muscle in action were thoroughly understood. Best of all was the ability to sum up a whole story in a single striking scene.

A splendid example of this highly developed art is the "Achilles among the Daughters of Lycomedes" by an unknown third-century artist. Thetis, the divine mother of Achilles, was unwilling to see him enter the Trojan War, in which she knew he was doomed to die, and therefore hid him, disguised as a girl, among the many daughters of King Lycomedes of

*University Prints*

THE DYING GAUL

Scyros. Ulysses and Diomed came in search of him, disguised as merchants selling arms and armor. As they displayed their wares, a bugler blew the alarm call, and Achilles, forgetting his rôle, seized sword and shield. It was this tense moment which the artist chose to illustrate. With little or no background, and in subdued colors, he shows us the dramatic scene. Achilles, his feminine apparel in wild disorder and his face distorted with excitement, grasps the telltale weapons. Ulysses, open-mouthed with surprise, clutches Achilles' arm while Lycomedes and his queen helplessly view the betrayal of their secret.

Another, of which the meaning is not so obvious, is the "Hercules in Bondage," of which our surviving copy is also from Pompeii. The mental agony of a strong man in bondage, the unpleasant leer of triumph on the face of Hercules' mistress Queen Omphale, and the sensitive, downcast countenance of one of Omphale's attendants who pities the captive — these and many other details bring the old legend to reality.

But everyday life also claimed its share of the painter's attention. Mendicant musicians performing on the street, actors rehearsing a play, and similar scenes were reproduced with fidelity and humor. A series of

Pompeian sketches showing various trades being carried on by cupids, probably goes back to Hellenistic origins.

In mosaic the Hellenistic artists found an old Egyptian art which could be adapted to their purpose. By making skillful use of bits of colored glass set in soft plaster or cement they could adorn floors and walls with scenes almost as lifelike as paintings, and far more durable. It was not, however, until the Roman and Byzantine periods that mosaic achieved its greatest popularity.

The chief remains of Hellenistic jewelry come from an out-of-the-way corner of the Greek world — the Crimea and its neighborhood. In that region both the Scythian chiefs and the Greek kings of the Cimmerian Bosporus had splendid gold and silver ornaments buried with them, some

*University Prints*

GAUL STABBING HIMSELF

of which escaped the hands of tomb-robbers. Not only do they display the skillful craftsmanship and good taste of other Greek art, but the engraved figures show a faithful study of barbarian life and manners rare among the Greeks of any age.

When we consider the drawbacks under which the Hellenistic artists labored, we may well concede that their achievements were by no means contemptible. It was this living art, not the obsolete art of the classical period, from which the Romans received their artistic education, and of which Roman art was an immediate descendant.

## Literature and Scholarship

### *Libraries, Erudition, and Literary Criticism*

Following the trend established by Aristotle, Greek education in the third century began to concern itself with pure erudition, in addition to the sciences and philosophy. In this field as well as in the physical sciences, much encouragement was afforded by the Ptolemies and the kings of Pergamum. Both of these learned dynasties established libraries. The Ptolemies set up in Alexandria the Museum, a literary and scientific institute, on a plan which they may have gotten from the exiled Athenian oligarch, Demetrius of Phalerum. In it a number of scholars were provided with ample endowments, so that they could pursue their studies without interruption. It housed a library of about 500,000 "books," or inscribed papyrus rolls, equal perhaps to about 50,000 fair-sized modern volumes. A smaller library was located in the Serapeum, or Temple of Serapis.

These libraries were operated on a system which contained at least the germs of modern library science. For the official copy of each book the literary critics of the Museum established a correct text by comparing all of the known manuscripts — a necessary task in an age when all copies were handmade and each copyist added new errors to those of his original. But the task of the literary critics did not end with correct texts. Serious efforts were made to furnish the reader with critical and explanatory notes for each work. The geographical data in Homer and other old poems were checked and examined in the light of the new knowledge. Monographs were written to explain obscure points. Now for the first time the older classical works were divided into "books" as at present. Theories regarding literary styles and methods of composition were closely studied and hotly debated. Thus Hellenistic literature as a whole tended toward self-consciousness and sophistication.

### *Volume and Variety of Output*

In volume and variety of output, the Hellenistic age far surpassed any preceding period of Greek history. The three leading Athenian comedians produced about one hundred plays each, while three prominent prose writers are credited with four hundred and fifty-three, seven hundred, and eight hundred "books" each. Every possible type of subject was treated, from mathematics and philosophy to fiction. Of this enormous mass of literature, only a little has survived, although some has won vicarious immortality by being quoted or paraphrased in surviving works. The disappearance of so much writing is probably due to the prevailing inferiority of style, which in many cases no amount of theorizing could improve. The reading public of the Roman Empire, which cared more for style than for content, allowed such works to perish through neglect.

### *History and Travel Books*

It is not surprising that an age characterized by so many stirring events produced many historians. At the beginning of the period Ptolemy and Aristobulus, two of Alexander's generals, composed memoirs in which they told the story of his campaigns from the viewpoint of eye-witnesses. At the same time Nearchus, his Cretan admiral, wrote an account of his voyage from the mouth of the Indus River through the Indian Ocean to the Persian Gulf. These memoirs and journals never achieved the popularity which they deserved, and soon after they were written they were superseded in popular favor by a sensational historical romance about Alexander composed by Cleitarchus, who overlaid the sober facts with wild legends and fabrications. So few copies of the works of Ptolemy, Aristobulus, and Nearchus were made that they were eventually lost, but in the second century A.D., Arrian, an Asiatic Greek, used them extensively for his *Anabasis of Alexander* and his *Indica.* His citations show that all three authors wrote clearly and truthfully. At a later time Cleitarchus' work was also lost.

In the histories dealing with the last decades of the fourth century and the first half of the third, the same uneven quality is apparent. A Greek officer in the service of the Successors, Hieronymus of Cardia, wrote a history of the wars which ended in the breakup of the Empire, and although the original has been lost, there is evidence that it was an excellent piece of work. But to balance this reliable production there were many others which were either shallow and sensational, or mere vehicles for propa-

*Galloway*

ATHENA SLAYING A GIANT

*From the Frieze of the Altar of Zeus, Pergamum*

ganda. A new type of historical research, characterized by the scientific method prevalent in the Alexandrian Museum, was undertaken by Eratosthenes of Cyrene. Beginning with the fall of Troy (which he placed in 1184–1183 B.C.), he attempted to fix the dates of the principal events in Greek history, designating them by the regnal years of the Spartan kings, the years of the Olympic Games, and other well-known chronological systems. In the Greek peninsula Aratus of Sicyon, the reorganizer of the Achaean League, wrote memoirs in which he explained and defended his political career. In western Greece, Timaeus of Tauromenium (*ca.* 300–250 B.C.) told the story of the Sicilian and Italian Greeks in a very extensive work, which was crammed with information. Unfortunately none of these histories survive.

For the second century we are better off. In it lived Polybius of Megalopolis (*ca.* 200–120 B.C.), whose character as a historian is second only to

*University Prints*

LAOCOÖN

that of Thucydides in the ancient world. In his youth he held high offices in the Achaean League, but in 167, was taken to Italy as a political prisoner, and remained there for seventeen years. He became a friend of the Scipios and other Roman aristocrats, studied the secret of Rome's astounding successes, and when he had found it, wrote his history with a view to explaining his conclusions to the Greeks. It covered the period between 264 and 146 B.C. in forty books, of which six survive in their entirety, and fragments of others exist as quotations. His industry was immense. He read everything that was written on a disputed question, balancing the partisan statements on both sides against each other. To be sure that his topographical data were correct, he visited the sites of important battles in person, and traveled all over the Mediterranean world in his quest for knowledge. He insisted that no one could write history competently unless he had had personal experience in political life; the arm chair historian could never understand the motives of men, nor the difficulties which they had to surmount in real life. His own history was a monumental work, and although the style in places is very bad, he succeeds in making the period of Rome's first conquests crystal clear.

A large number of local histories were also written, usually at the order of the governments of the cities concerned. Their standards of style and accuracy were alike poor. In fact, the royal founders of the colonies in Asia sometimes hired unscrupulous hacks to compile for their upstart foundations fictitious chronicles connecting them with places famous in Homeric legend.

Travel books began to appear, and of these two stood out above the rest, the *Treatise on the Ocean* by Pytheas of Massilia, and the *Indica* of Megasthenes. The former explored the Atlantic coast of Europe as far north as the British Isles and Scandinavia, and wrote an interesting and accurate account of what he had seen. Megasthenes was an ambassador of Seleucus I at the court of an Indian king. His *Indica* was a mixture of accurate personal observations and of weird fables of wonders and monsters which he had heard and believed. Neither of these men gained the credit he deserved, for the scholars at home, with few exceptions, merely branded them both as shameless liars.

### *Prose Fiction and Poetry*

Prose fiction gained a recognized place in literature during the Hellenistic era. About 300 B.C. Euhemerus anticipated More, Bacon, Campanella, and Swift by using a fictitious travel story as a means of expressing his views on current questions. He claimed to have visited an island in the Indian Ocean, and to have seen there a true history of the gods. They were, he said, nothing but dead kings or heroes whom men had been taught to worship. This statement of philosophical atheism enjoyed a wide popularity among rationalists until the coming of Christianity. Others used similar stories to paint pictures of imaginary utopias where social justice and righteousness prevailed. Again we must record the sad fact that real and imaginary travel books alike have sunk into oblivion.

In spite of the increasing popularity of prose and the general lack of emotional fervor, the output of verse in the Hellenistic world was large, and some of it approaches the dignity of true poetry. In fact, verse was still so popular a means of expression that it was at times used even in popular treatises on mathematics and physical science. Kings supported court poets, while many others either depended upon less-distinguished patrons or lived from their own means. But with little or no religious faith or fine feeling, most of them could produce no more than polished verses, often crammed with obscure learning.

The Museum of Alexandria naturally took a leading place in this type of literature. There Callimachus acted by turn as library catalogue maker, literary critic, and poet. He wrote hymns to the gods which contained every element necessary to religious poetry except emotion. His *Aitiai* ("Causes") is an unassimilated jumble of information on many subjects. In treating Greek legend he sometimes painted charming word pictures, like the visit of Theseus to the hut of the old peasant woman Hecale. To these must be added occasional poems composed for wealthy clients and for the royal court. His rival Apollonius Rhodius essayed to write epic poetry. In his *Argonautica* we have the story of Jason's quest for the golden fleece, but aside from a fine analysis of the feelings of the lovelorn Medea and some pleasing descriptions of natural scenery, it does not merit much attention. In fact, its chief claim to distinction is to be found in its having influenced the Roman poet Virgil.

In Theocritus (*ca.* 305–250 B.C.) we may see a poet with some claim to greatness. He was born in Sicily, later traveled to Alexandria, and finally settled in Cos. He composed works of several kinds, but is best known for two types of poetry — the *idyll* and the *mime*. The former is a somewhat idealized description of the life led by shepherds and peasants of the Mediterranean countryside. Lovesick swains engage in singing matches celebrating the objects of their affections in woodland pastures, which the poet describes with a fine realism and true feeling. Pastoral poetry was not new in Theocritus' time. It is the natural reaction of an urbanized people who are tired of their stuffy and artificial surroundings, and who long for the freedom and beauty of the country. In the hands of others it was often so conventionalized as to be almost caricature, but Theocritus drew for his readers a series of pictures which were essentially true to life. From Theocritus, Virgil was later to draw the inspiration and much of the material for his *Eclogues*.

### *Drama and Farce*

The *mime*, a realistic description of everyday life in dramatic form, was an old Sicilian product, having originated shortly after 500 B.C. Several of Theocritus' extant works (included in the collection called *Idylls*) are really mimes. For example, in *The Syracusan Women* he describes the visit of Gorgo and Praxinoë to an Alexandrian festival. It is an exquisite reproduction of feminine small talk, complete even to the exasperated man sitting behind them at the concert, with his "Stop that Dorian chatter; I can't hear the singer." But Theocritus' feminine characters are not all as empty-headed as this precious pair. Simaetha, the heroine of *The Sorceresses*, is the victim of a fickle lover, and the poet portrays her passion, anger, and final resignation with a masterly touch. Another writer of mimes, whose works have been recovered in Egypt, was Herodas. Very frequently he represented low life with coarse, broad realism.

In legitimate drama this was the age of the "New Comedy," or comedy of manners, which flourished principally at Athens. The chief writer in

*Metropolitan Museum*

OLD MARKETWOMAN

*Second Century B.C.*

this field was Menander (born about 340). We have none of his plays complete, but large portions have been found on Egyptian papyri, and we are further helped in our understanding of him by literary notices and by quotations from his lost works. The New Comedy as represented by Menander had few traces of the boisterous fun, local color, and plentiful vulgarity of Aristophanes. The stage technique was different, for the chorus had been dropped entirely. Although the characters bore imaginary names, this mattered little. All of them conform to a few types: the stingy, heavy-handed father, the shrewish mother, the young man in love, the rascally but likeable slave, the bragging soldier, the sponger who lives by his wits, and the dancing girl or courtesan who has a noble character and is really the daughter of an aristocratic family. The atmosphere is highly romantic, but the plots (in so far as we know them) have a monotonous sameness only relieved by a series of comic incidents. The society which Menander and his fellow comedians portrayed was an empty, frivolous one, with accommodating morals and no serious purposes. Ancient critics praised Menander for "holding the mirror up to nature." If their verdict is correct, it is sufficient condemnation of the society of post-Alexandrian Athens. From the writers of the "New Comedy" the Roman comedians of the second century B.C. not only learned dramatic technique, but borrowed so copiously that in some cases their work is perilously near to what the modern world calls plagiarism. Comedy never flourished in Alexandria or in Asiatic Greece, where apparently the mime was the only form of the comic drama to win popularity, but tragedy achieved a short-lived and artificial vogue. Of the tragedies of the period only a few of the names have survived, and we have little reason to regret the loss of the remainder.

## Science

In the Hellenistic world the physical sciences and mathematics did not suffer from the disadvantages which beset literature. Sovereigns like the Ptolemies and Hiero of Syracuse furnished financial support to investigators, and the more tolerant attitude of the general public freed them from the danger of religious persecution. For the first time in Greek history, the sciences began to offer serious competition to philosophy for the attention of the keener minds, and more progress was made in them than during any other period of comparable length prior to the eighteenth century.

It was natural that the endowed scholars of the Alexandrian Museum should forge to the front in scientific studies, for their opportunities for achievement were greater than elsewhere. During the third century and part of the second, Alexandria was the scientific capital of the known world, but it did not monopolize the field. Syracuse was the home of the physicist and mathematician Archimedes, while Seleucia in Babylonia and Nicea in Bithynia each produced a famous astronomer.

### *Astronomy and Mathematics*

Astronomy made enormous advances. The fanciful speculations regarding the heavenly bodies which had, with few exceptions, satisfied the thinkers of the fifth and fourth centuries, gave way to a truly scientific method. The results which the astronomers of the third and second centuries achieved were not surpassed until the invention of the telescope in the seventeenth century A.D. Beginning in the late fourth century, Heracleides Ponticus initiated a movement to survey carefully the courses of the heavenly bodies. He decided that at least Mercury and Venus revolved around the sun as a center. But it remained for Aristarchus of Samos (about 280 B.C.) to anticipate by about 1800 years the "Copernican" theory that the earth and other planets all revolved around the sun and that the earth rotates daily on its axis. Without a telescope he could not prove this theory conclusively, and it failed to gain general acceptance. He also attempted to measure the distance of the sun and moon from the earth, but owing to the inaccuracy of his data he calculated the distance of the sun as only about 4,500,000 miles, about one-twentieth of the real figure.

In the second century Seleucus, a Greek from Seleucia, not only accepted Aristarchus' heliocentric theory, but established the existence of a connection between the movements of the moon and the rise and fall of the tides. This was the nearest approach made in the ancient world to the theory of gravitation. Hipparchus of Nicea in Bithynia (*ca.* 185–120 B.C.), the greatest of the Greek astronomers and a creative mathematician, although he did not accept the heliocentric theory, otherwise brought Greek astronomy to the highest point that it ever attained. He calculated the length of the solar year within six minutes and fourteen seconds of the actual figure. Finding from observations taken by an earlier astronomer that a star had changed its position about two degrees from the autumn equinoctial point in about two hundred and fifty years, he discovered the precession of the equinoxes, and calculated the amount of change within five seconds of the correct figure. He catalogued some eight hundred and fifty fixed stars, determined their locations, and classified them in order of brightness. In fact, there was hardly a phase of astronomy in which he did not make important discoveries. His generosity in making observations for which he himself had no particular use, but which he left as the raw material for later astronomers to work upon, shows his far-sighted altruism. After his time the pseudo-science of astrology diverted the attention of many observers from legitimate astronomy, and did much to check its progress.

Mathematics made progress comparable to that of astronomy. For us the most interesting figure in this field is Euclid (about 300 B.C.), who compiled the *Elements*, a textbook of plane and solid geometry which summarized all that was known about these subjects. The first six books of this monumental treatise, which dealt with plane geometry, continued in use as a textbook in modern schools until about a generation ago. Archimedes of Syracuse (287–212 B.C.) did distinctive work in both mathematics and physics. In the former he determined the value of $\pi$ (the ratio between the diameter and the circumference of a circle) very nearly as it is estimated today. He also worked out the ratio between the volume of a cylinder and that of an inscribed sphere. In physics he is best known for his discovery of a method for determining specific gravities, and for studies in the use of levers and pulleys. To him is also attributed the invention of a screw-pump (still used in Egypt) and other mechanical devices.

In one respect, however, Hellenistic mathematics failed to progress very greatly. No system of algebraic notation was used, and no convenient set of numerals was adopted. Some advance was made when the letters of the Greek alphabet, including two that had been dropped from use in writing, were given numerical values, but since no symbol for zero was adopted, little use could be made of it for purposes of calculation. Fractions were expressed as series, each of which had one as a numerator. Thus $13/16$ would be written as $1/2 + 1/4 + 1/16$. Beyond this point mathematics made little progress until the later Middle Ages.

### *Geography*

Geography ceased to be a series of travelers' tales and became a science. Most of the credit for this change is due to the versatile Eratosthenes of Cyrene. In a monograph entitled *The Measurements of the Earth*, he undertook to compute the circumference of our globe by means of observations of the noonday sun taken at Alexandria and Syene. Finding the difference of the latitudes between the two points to be $7° 12'$, or one-fiftieth of the earth's circumference, and the actual distance to be 5000 *stadia*, he reckoned the circumference at 250,000 *stadia*. This would be either 24,485 miles or about 28,300 miles, according to the length of the *stadion* used. In either case it is a close approximation of the real distance. In his *Geography* he boldly discarded the authority of Homer, and attempted to use only trustworthy sources of information. Following the example of Pytheas of Massilia, he used a crude system of latitude and longitude for the purpose of locating places, but the lack of accurate timepieces robbed this device of much of its usefulness. It was he who first advanced the theory that India could be reached by sailing westward — a theory which was later to inspire Christopher Columbus.

### *Medicine and Botany*

In medicine, men built upon the foundation laid by Hippocrates and his school. At Alexandria the dissection of the human cadaver was permitted, and (so their enemies said) the professors of the Museum even vivisected condemned criminals. The charge of vivisection may not be true, but it is certain that these physicians were able to gain a good knowledge of anatomy, and to verify their diagnoses by post-mortem examinations. About 300 B.C. Herophilus, the greatest of the Alexandrian anatomists, discovered the true functions of the brain and nerves (neither of which had been known to Aristotle), and distinguished between sensory and motor nerves. He also studied the circulatory system, and came very near to making an accurate description of the circulation of the blood 1900 years before Harvey. In ordinary practice Herophilus advocated the extensive use of drugs. Anatomical research was carried further by Erasistratus, the personal physician of Seleucus I, but he repudiated drug-therapy and returned to the mild remedies and hygienic regimen advocated by Hippocrates.

After 250 B.C. anatomical studies made but little progress. Dissection of human cadavers was still frowned upon in some places. Soon a new school of physicians, the Empirics, arose to claim that the cause and true nature of a disease need not be known. Physicians, they said, should be interested in discovering the cure for a certain set of symptoms. The new school made some useful discoveries in pharmacy, such as the stupefying properties of opium and mandragora, but they discouraged anatomical studies. In fact, these were not revived on a scientific basis until the days of Vesalius, in the sixteenth century A.D.

The biological studies of Aristotle were carried on by his pupil Theophrastus, who did for botany what his master had done for zoology. His

*History of Plants* and *Causes of Plants*, which are still extant, contain descriptions of about five hundred different species of vegetable life. In his hands botany became a pure science, independent of utilitarian considerations, but his influence upon his successors was small. The study of plant life soon degenerated once more into the search for useful species, and not until modern times did it again reach the heights to which Theophrastus had raised it.

Mechanical inventions were more numerous in the Hellenistic Age than during any other period of the ancient world. The screw-pump of Archimedes, a predecessor of the modern turbine, has been mentioned. His contemporary Ctesibius devised a water-organ, an air-gun, and probably a turbine steam engine. Other inventors continued to produce useful or curious mechanical appliances up to the first century of the Christian Era.

But all the splendid work done by both scientists and inventors seems, when we consider the history of the later Graeco-Roman world, to have been nearly barren of results. The greatest scientific discoveries failed, as we have seen, to gain general recognition, and apparently did not usually stimulate others to test their validity by careful research. It may have been in part due to the lack of precision instruments, without which conclusive proof was impossible, but this fact alone cannot explain it. The intellectual tradition of the Greeks somehow predisposed them to philosophical speculation rather than to scientific truth. The masses, and even the educated classes, took little interest in science and few besides the professional scholars ever heard of the discoveries of Aristarchus or Herophilus. Therefore, it was not until the echoes of their research reached the scholars of sixteenth-century Europe that they bore fruit. The same may, with few exceptions, be said of mechanical inventions. In general they neither increased the production of goods nor lightened the labor of the workers, and soon only vague traditions recalled the existence of many of these devices.

## Religion and Philosophy

### *New Needs in a New World*

After all, the need which the Hellenistic Greeks felt most keenly was not for more knowledge of the physical world so much as for solutions to the ethical and spiritual problems which beset them. These problems were all the more pressing because the Hellenistic Greeks were living in an environment radically different from that of their ancestors, who had still, for the most part, been able to explain the universe in terms of religion and mythology, and had based their morality upon considerations of family loyalty and patriotism. But religion had been growing steadily weaker and less vital since the fifth century, and although the old gods still received their sacrifices from the Greek states and enjoyed the perfunctory homage of the masses, mythology no longer offered explanations of the world that would satisfy the thinking minds. Furthermore, the progressive weakening of city-state bonds everywhere, and the removal of many thousands of Greeks to new homes where their old patriotism no longer played any part in life, destroyed the old sanctions for ethical conduct, and left them only self-interest as a guide to action.

### *Religion*

One new religious movement has been mentioned previously.[1] Each of the Hellenistic kings (except the king of Macedonia) was worshiped as a god by his Greek subjects either during life or after death. Such a cult was, however, by its very nature purely official, and could have no hold upon the affections of the people; nor could it furnish them with a new intellectual or moral background. The unsettled condition of men's thinking was intensified by the rapid and unpredictable changes of fortune produced by the wars of the Successors, and by the wills of powerful and despotic kings. A man might be poor today, rich and honored tomorrow, and dead or reduced to poverty or even slavery the day after, all through the operation of forces over which he had little or no control. These freaks of fate were attributed to *Tyche* (Fortune), a blind and wayward goddess who seemed to have complete power over the affairs of this world. Her cult was the only one of Greek origin which enjoyed increased popularity in this period, and its popular appeal accounts for the number of statues of her that have been found.

In Egypt and Asia the Greek colonists came into contact with mystical and emotional cults like those of Isis and Serapis (which had been partly Hellenized by Ptolemy I), or that of the Great Mother and Atys. In these Oriental religions the worshiper was promised purification from the stains of his past life, the watchful care of the deities while he lived, and happiness in the hereafter. The popularity of these cults among the lower classes of Greeks was great, and they gradually made their way into Delos, Athens, Corinth, and other Greek centers. They had however, little ethical content, and were the very negation of that reasoning faculty which the Greek world prized so highly. Hence they failed to satisfy the keener

[1] Chapters 8 and 9.

minds. The way was open for the formation of new philosophies, better suited to the needs of the new age.

*The Philosophies of Resignation — Minor Sects*

To meet these needs, thinking Greeks turned to an old philosophy, Cynicism, and to three new ones, Skepticism, Epicureanism, and Stoicism. The problem which all of these faced was this: If Fortune rules the world, and rules it quite unintelligently, how can we escape from her grasp, and recover our independence? On one fundamental point all were agreed: It is useless, they said, to try to improve the present world. It is permanently enslaved to Fortune, and will never be any better or more intelligible to thinking people than it is now. To achieve freedom from Fortune's tyrannical whims, a man must retire within himself, and give up the ambitions and desires through which she can hurt him. Whatever his external circumstances may be, every man is the master of his own soul. By freeing it from the desires, passions, and strivings generated by his wish for earthly goods, he can retire within himself and there gain freedom. But so long as he is alive, he must have some motive for going through the necessary actions of life, and must therefore retain some interest in the world without. What shall this interest be? On this point all four schools presented different solutions.

Students of Greek history have already heard of the Cynics, a school founded in the fourth century by Antisthenes, the pupil of Socrates. His answer was that if one voluntarily abandons all worldly ambitions and discards all the comforts and decencies of civilized life, then Fortune has lost her power to hurt him. Of what can she deprive him if he has already renounced everything? The more radical Cynics carried this doctrine so far that they ceased bathing, dressed in rags, went unshaven and unshorn, and ate only the meanest food. They were militant missionaries, who went from city to city, preaching pointed sermons ("diatribes") to street-corner audiences. But although they advocated kindliness toward others, it had no logical place in a scheme of life based upon a selfish desire for individual happiness, and the antics of these unwashed champions of the good life disgusted sensible people. In the end Cynicism became a mere caricature of a philosophy. None of the other schools went so far toward flight from the world as this.

The Skeptics may be quickly dismissed. Pyrrhon, their founder, taught that man can never know anything with certainty. He must not, therefore, quibble over good and evil. He should act as though he believed in conventional standards, and take all of the pleasures which gratuitously come his way, but remember that he does not really know good from evil, and never become attached to any of the pleasures which Fortune may at any moment snatch away from him. This is not a doctrine likely to appeal to a strong character in search of spiritual freedom, and the thinking portion of the Greek world tended to gravitate to either the Epicurean or Stoic school.

### *The Epicureans*

Epicurus (341–270 B.C.) was born at Samos, but spent most of his life in Athens. There he owned a garden in which he taught his disciples. Later the name "Garden" was occasionally applied to the philosophical school which he founded. He tried to give his followers the inner freedom which they craved by first furnishing them with a convincing explanation of the universe which would free them from imaginary terrors. He then provided them with a rule of life that would free them from the whims of Fortune. From Democritus, a fifth-century thinker, he borrowed the

*Bettmann*

EPICURUS

*Keystone*

ZENO

theory that the universe is a mass of atoms which, in falling through space, accidentally formed the combinations that we know as the world, plants, animals, and men. The human soul, like the body, is composed of atoms, and when death occurs both dissolve into their component parts. Thus there can be no hereafter, and therefore we should cease to fear death. Epicurus did not deny the existence of the gods, but he taught that they lived in a far-off heaven where they had no interest in human or mundane affairs.

His definition of the good life was that it is that way of living which produces a maximum of pleasure with a minimum of pain. Thus defined, his doctrine left no room for loose living. Drunkenness, sexual indulgence, and other forms of sensuality are ruled out by reason of the misery which results from them. A simple, quiet life, enlivened by those pleasures which leave no after-sting and brightened by friendships with congenial people, makes one more independent of Fortune's whims than any other. Hence, one should withdraw from public life, where disappointments are so likely to occur, and give up all the other soul-disturbing ambitions. "Live unobtrusively" was his motto. The first Epicureans practiced a simple and democratic way of life, ignoring class distinctions and furnishing a refuge to the victims of misfortune. Epicurus himself was a generous and affectionate friend of his many disciples, who regarded him with utmost veneration.

Such was true Epicureanism. A character molded by this doctrine was not likely to be vicious or even unduly self-indulgent, but it would never be heroic. The worst fault which can be attributed to it is timidity, which makes one leave the battles of life to others and shirk his rightful duties. But the true Epicurean doctrine was often misunderstood or corrupted by brutal and stupid disciples who made it a cloak for their misdeeds. We must not lay the blame for this perversion upon Epicurus.

### *The Stoics*

While Epicurus was formulating his views, Zeno (*ca.* 330–260 B.C.), a Greek or Graeco-Phoenician from Cyprus, began to teach philosophy on the "Painted Porch" (*Stoa Poikile*) in Athens. Because of this, his disciples received the name of Stoics, which clung to them after Zeno had founded a conventional school of philosophy like those of his rivals.

Zeno like Epicurus provided his disciples with a cosmology as well as a way of life. He taught that there is but one god, whom men have worshiped under many forms. Hence his followers accepted the official pagan cults, but with interpretations of their own. Zeno taught that God is not a person, but a force — a cosmic reason which is infused through the physical world, and gives form and meaning to it. By cultivating reason, man identifies himself more and more closely with God, conforms to the divine purpose, and gains his freedom. Zeno likewise systematized education, which he divided into physics, ethics, and logic. His test of truth was not objective reality so much as intensity of feeling, and hence was subjective and undependable.

Accepting, as did his contemporaries, the helplessness of man before the vagaries of Fortune, Zeno, also like them, advised his followers to withdraw within the sovereign limits of their own personalities. But instead of seeking happiness as the only good, they were to seek virtue, for he asserted that it is the only good, and vice the only evil. These are matters in which the human will has free choice, and the wise man will choose virtue. If an external circumstance does not affect moral character, it is neither good nor bad, but "indifferent." Such are wealth and poverty, sickness and health, and a host of other factors affecting the temporal well-being of man. He need not shun pleasant things in this category, but must never let his heart be set upon them so that they distract his attention from his real objective, the pursuit of wisdom and virtue. It is not enough to act well; in addition it is necessary to have good intentions. Every act behind which there lurks an improper motive is immoral. So with a pure mind, unenslaved by worldly desires, the Stoic attains "freedom from suffering" (*apatheia*). Then Fortune has no hold upon him, and can no longer hurt him. Pain, poverty, or the loss of family and friends, all leave the "wise man" unmoved or even happy, for they cannot reach the inner self.

Stoicism was an aristocratic creed, for there were few who could conform even measurably to its ideals. But it was not a formula for selfish egotism. Zeno taught his disciples to regard the world and the human race as unities, and the "world-city" (*cosmopolis*) was one of his favorite phrases. He insisted that all men, whether wise or unwise, from the slave to the king, are to be regarded as brothers, and that their welfare must be the object of the wise man's efforts. He may even, within limits, work for his own welfare and material comfort. He need not, like the Cynics, abandon his family, friends, and property, eschew baths, and dress in rags. He may engage in war, business, or politics like other men, and may throw into them his best efforts, but he must always regard these activities as matters of no consequence, and himself merely an actor upon the stage of life. His proper aim is not to achieve success in his undertaking but rather to play well the part for which life has cast him. With this ideal to guide his conduct, he will feel no pain or disappointment if Fortune dooms his efforts to failure or strips him of his possessions. If he has played well his allotted part his real success is far greater than that of persons who enjoy the smiles of Fortune but who are still her slaves.

Of all the Hellenistic philosophies, Stoicism was the most dynamic and socially useful. It produced a long series of noble characters, such as Antigonus Gonatas of Macedonia, Cato the Younger, and the Roman emperor Marcus Aurelius. It lent courage to many a Greek or Roman who dared brave certain destruction at the hands of a tyrant rather than to betray his principles, and it breathed a spirit of humanity into the society of imperial Rome.

But from our modern point of view all these philosophies had one common fault. They began with an attitude of despair toward the world and the destiny of man, and they never rose above it. They assumed that the present state of the world was irrevocably fixed, and that efforts at permanent improvement of it were certain to be futile. One who holds such views may be good or even noble, but he can hardly be a great force toward the uplift of mankind.

# 11

********************************************************************************************

# *Rome Dominates the Western Mediterranean World (265-201 B.C.)*

### *New Neighbors and Further Wars*

ALTHOUGH AFTER 265 B.C. the Romans controlled all of peninsular Italy, they were not by that fact relieved from the necessity of fighting further wars. The same inexorable fate which had led them to master their native peninsula now compelled them to fight and conquer an ever-widening circle of non-Italian peoples. At least in the earlier stages of their career as builders of an extra-Italian empire, they seem to have been chiefly actuated by the same motives as in their Italian wars. These, as we have seen, were primarily defensive. As before, the need for defense brought wars; wars ended in conquests; while conquests gave them new frontiers to defend by further wars. In the course of these conflicts they occasionally committed acts of aggression, but there is no evidence that they had a conscious policy of imperial expansion.

The conquest of Italy had brought them into touch with a new group of neighbors. On the south their alliance with Rhegium gave them a frontage on the Straits of Messina, within two miles of the coast of strife-torn Sicily. This meant closer relations than before with both Syracuse and Carthage, the contestants for the mastery of the island. With the former they had, until that time, had few dealings, and since their commercial interests were as yet negligible, they had previously permitted the Carthaginians to exclude them completely from contact with the more lucrative foreign markets. But now political considerations forced them to take a stronger tone toward Carthage, who controlled so much of the western Mediterranean area, and out of the clash which resulted came the two ferocious *Punic* wars (so called from the Roman word for *Phoenicians*, who formed the citizen body of Carthage). As usual, Rome fought doggedly until she won, and victory made her the predominant power in the region once swayed by Carthage.

In the north lay her old enemies, the Gauls of the Po Valley, with whom no permanent peace short of conquest was possible. To the east was the pirate-infested Adriatic Sea, whence issued Illyrian marauders to harass the commerce of the Italo-Greek allies. Here again, peace could be secured only by their complete subjugation, but in accomplishing this Rome was certain to become embroiled with Macedonia, who controlled the back country to the east of Illyria. Thus each new contact brought with it the certainty of strife and the probability of conquest.

## The First Punic War (264–241 B.C.)

### *The Opening of the War*

The first foreign entanglement arose in Sicily, where the Mamertini [1] found themselves hard pressed by Hiero II of Syracuse. In 264, these international outlaws had been in possession of Messana for twenty-five years, and their status had been recognized by Carthage and by various Greek cities. Accordingly, when one faction in Messana appealed for help to Carthage, she sent a garrison to protect them from Hiero, and, incidentally, to control their city and the straits on which it lay. However, another faction appealed to Rome. The Senate, always averse to foreign entanglements, refused the alliance which the Mamertini offered, but a tribune induced the popular assembly to reverse the decision and to vote to send them aid. In view of the situation, this meant war with Carthage, but the popular leaders probably saw that Carthaginian control of Messana would end by closing the strait to the Romans, and constituted a threat to their control of southern Italy. This calamity could only be averted by Rome assuming control of Messana, and it was at least arguable that the probable benefits of the step were worth the risk. At any rate, the possession of Sicily was sure to be the prize of the victor.

### *The Roman Offensive by Land and Sea (264–255 B.C.)*

In the first stage of the struggle which followed, the Romans conducted a vigorous and well-planned offensive. They lost no time in securing Messana, which they occupied after the Mamertini had induced the Carthaginian garrison to withdraw. The severity of the blow to Carthage

[1] See Chapter 8.

may be measured by the fact that she crucified the faint-hearted commander to whose weakness it was due. The Carthaginian government now took energetic steps to retrieve the lost advantage. An alliance was patched up with Hiero of Syracuse, whom the Romans had offended by aiding his enemies, and the allies besieged Messana and its Roman garrison. At this time, however, the consul Appius Claudius Caudex slipped an army across the strait at night, broke up the siege of Messana, and drove Hiero's forces back toward Syracuse. Probably the Syracusan king was only half-hearted in his support of the city's age-old enemy, and the next year he made peace with the Romans, paid an indemnity, and became their ally. For the remainder of his long life he never broke faith with them, but supported them loyally. Strengthened by his support, the Romans pushed on into Sicily, where in 262, they captured the enemy stronghold of Agrigentum (Acragas). The Carthaginians were now confined to their fortified cities of Lilybaeum, Drepanum and Panormus in the extreme west. From these points they could not be driven so long as Carthage controlled the sea. Yet peace could not be gained until they were completely expelled from Sicily. To accomplish this purpose the Romans, whose navy had hitherto been insignificant, decided to wrest from Carthage her naval supremacy.

### *Naval Victories and the Invasion of Africa*

The task seemed impossible, but in 260, with sublime self-confidence, the Romans undertook it. Carthage had a fleet of about a hundred and fifty quinqueremes, or battleships of the highest class; within two months the Romans had turned out one hundred of the same class, together with twenty smaller ones. The Greek historian Polybius, writing more than a century later, states that the Romans used a captured Carthaginian ship as a model, and that the Roman crews were taught to row in wooden frames set up on land. The consul Duilius, who may never have been on board a ship before, was put in command of this mushroom navy. However, his apparently foolhardy enterprise succeeded beyond all reasonable expectations. Up to that time customary naval tactics had been based upon the ramming of enemy vessels, and an ordinary war vessel carried as few as ten marines. Realizing that his raw crews could not hope to outdo the expert Carthaginians in such tactics, Duilius placed a full maniple of infantry (120 men) aboard each vessel. From the mast he suspended a light drawbridge, from the bottom of which a pointed iron spike protruded. The plan was that when a Carthaginian ship came within range, the bridge

*Bettmann*

ROMAN BIREME

*Relief from Temple of Fortuna, Praeneste*

would be dropped so that the spike would stick in her deck, holding her fast. Then the marines would charge across the drawbridge and sweep all before them. When Duilius met the Carthaginian fleet near Mylae, he astonished the civilized world by capturing fifty ships. For this success he was honored with a column bearing a laudatory inscription.

Other successes followed. In 259, a Carthaginian fleet was attacked by the Romans off the coast of Sardinia and driven ashore. In 257, a minor naval battle cost Carthage eighteen ships, and her possessions in Malta were raided. Plainly the Romans had the upper hand at sea, but the war was proving costly. For the fleet and army together, about 120,000 men had to be kept under arms all the time. It seemed that the time had come to end the deadlock with a smashing victory under the walls of Carthage.

In preparation for the invasion of Africa, huge forces were collected. In 256, a fleet of warships and transports sailed southward carrying nearly 150,000 men on 330 ships with the consuls of the year in command. Off Cape Ecnomus in Sicily it fell in with the Carthaginian fleet of 250 ships, of which it sank or captured eighty, losing only twenty-four ships itself. Proceeding to Africa, it landed the army, under the consul Marcus Atilius

Regulus, and returned home. At first Regulus carried all before him. He defeated a Carthaginian army, ravaged the country around the capital, and reduced the enemy to dire distress. The African natives rose in revolt against Carthage, and she sued for peace. But Regulus was only a mediocre general and not at all a diplomat. He failed to make use of the Africans, and his terms of peace were so severe that Carthage broke off negotiations. Then Fortune deserted him. A Spartan mercenary captain reorganized the Carthaginian army, which also acquired one hundred war-elephants. In 255, the Romans were defeated, Regulus was captured, and only two thousand men escaped. To make matters worse, the fleet which had been sent to rescue the fugitives was caught in a storm off Sicily while returning, and 170 ships with all aboard were lost. Rome's first African expedition had ended in a crushing disaster.

### *Stalemate and Disaster: The Mission of Regulus*

Rome now entered upon a long period of deadlock in Sicily and disaster at sea. In 253, a storm destroyed a hundred and fifty of her ships. In 249, the Carthaginians defeated a Roman fleet off Drepanum, the only naval victory which Carthage won during the war. Shortly afterward another Roman fleet of a hundred warships and hundreds of transports was wrecked in a storm. For the next seven years Rome was without a navy. During this time she clung tenaciously to Sicily, besieging the great stronghold of Lilybaeum, but without command of the sea she could not hope to take it. In 247, Carthage sent Hamilcar Barca to take command of her forces in the island. He was able and energetic, and not content with upholding her cause in the Sicilian war, also organized raids on the coast of Italy. But Carthage gave him little support, and neither side was able to gain a decisive advantage. It was plain that only by winning the supremacy at sea could Rome bring the war to a victorious close, and that Carthage could not win even when her fleet had undisputed sway in the middle Mediterranean.

Later Roman historians told how, during this dreary time, the Carthaginians sent a peace-mission to Rome. With it came the captive Regulus, who was expected to plead for peace in order to gain his liberty. However, when the embassy arrived at Rome, Regulus addressed the Senate with a stirring appeal not to make peace or exchange prisoners with the enemy, and showed how great was the misery and exhaustion of Carthage and how near she was to defeat. Then, according to the story, he voluntarily returned with the embassy, and was tortured to death by his captors. How much, if any, of this story is true is a matter of dispute, but it later served as the theme of one of the most stirring odes of the Augustan poet Horace.

### *Victory and Peace*

From the disastrous impasse which began with the defeat of Regulus, Rome was at last rescued by the patriotic self-sacrifice of her richer citizens. The treasury was empty, and the rate of taxation could not be safely increased. But these men, by private subscription repayable only in the event of victory, raised the necessary funds to build a fleet of two hundred warships. In 241, under the command of the consul Quintus Lutatius Catulus, it met a Carthaginian fleet off the Aegates Islands, sank fifty of the enemy ships, and captured seventy more. By this stroke Rome recovered control of the seas, and Carthage had to acknowledge defeat. Hamilcar and Catulus negotiated a treaty, which was accepted with some reservations. By it Carthage agreed to evacuate Sicily, to cede to Rome the Lipari Islands, to pay an indemnity of 3200 talents in ten installments, not to sail her ships in the Tyrrhenian Sea, and not to recruit mercenaries in Italy.

Rome had paid a tremendous price for her victory. Hundreds of thousands of men had been drowned or slain in battle, and hundreds of ships had gone down. For twenty-three years her energies had been entirely devoted to the struggle. Although Carthage had lost the war, her losses in men, ships, and money had not been great in comparison to her resources. In fact, such losses as she sustained had fallen principally upon her mercenaries, and more of these hirelings were always to be had. Even the indemnity which she had promised to pay the Romans was small considering the circumstances. Yet the war had exposed once more the weakness in her imperial structure. The unpopularity of her rule in Africa had long been known, and it had been demonstrated anew. The inefficiency of her citizen-troops in battle, which Agathocles had previously discovered, had again been brought out by the campaign of Regulus, but it was not due to inherent inferiority so much as to dislike for military service. The real surprise of the war had been the series of defeats administered to the veteran Carthaginian navy by the upstart fleet of the Romans. Thenceforth Carthage was never again able to control the western seas, and the fact was to be of profound importance when for the second time she fought the Romans. Rome's victory had been due to her superb army, the unswerving loyalty of her allies, her combination of skill and good fortune at sea, and her unconquerable will. In the years which followed the defeat of Regulus she several times suffered blows as severe as that which finally drove Carthage to admit defeat, but she fought on without thought of surrender. That same spirit which led her to victory in the Samnite War caused her to win the first round of her struggle with Carthage. But the peace which Catulus and Hamilcar negotiated could not be lasting, for it settled nothing. Carthage had been defeated, but she was still able to renew hostilities, and sooner or later she would surely do so. It was only a series of accidents which made her keep the peace during the next twenty-three years (241–218).

## Rome and Carthage Between the First and Second Punic Wars

### *Domestic Policies in Rome and Italy*

The end of the First Punic War found Rome with a number of political, social, and military problems awaiting solution. Some of these were consequences of the war, while others had arisen independently of it. The Italians had supported her loyally, and some of them deserved rewards. Their claims were recognized when, in 241, the Picentines and the few Sabines, not already full citizens, were promoted to citizen status. In the same year the half-Etruscan city of Falerii revolted, and was severely punished. Perhaps in recognition of the services of the Roman commons in the war, the Assembly of the Centuries was reorganized, so that the number of voting units was raised to 373, and the glaring inequality between the voting strength of the richer and poorer citizens was abolished. In the north the barbarous Ligurians, who had begun to encroach upon northern Etruria, were driven back into the mountains. Having driven the Carthaginians from most of Sicily, the Romans now had to provide it with a government; to do so they organized, in 227, the first tribute-paying province. Of this momentous step and its consequences more will be said in another place. When, as a result of the revolt of the Carthaginian mercenaries, Sardinia came into her possession, it was joined with Corsica and formed into a similar province. Of Rome's conduct toward Carthage on this occasion a fuller discussion will be given presently. By 235, Rome was at peace with all her neighbors, and the Temple of Janus was solemnly closed for the first time in her recorded history.

At home, however, political strife soon broke out with a bitterness unknown for over fifty years. Far up in northeastern Italy, near the Gallic frontier, lay the *Ager Gallicus*, from which the Romans had once driven the Gallic Senones, and which had since been public land, rented out to wealthy landowners as pasture for their sheep and cattle. A tribune,

Gaius Flaminius, brought in a bill providing for its division into small tracts, to be given as freeholds to needy citizens. The Senate resisted the passage of the bill to the limit of its power, but in vain. The bill was passed. The motives of the contestants in this struggle are by no means clear, and it is useless to speculate on them. The incident raised Flaminius to a position of great influence, and also initiated an era of class strife which was forgotten only years later under the stress of the Second Punic War.

### *Rome's Illyrian and Gallic Wars*

To political strife at home there was soon added renewed foreign wars. By the terms of her alliance with the Greeks of southern Italy, Rome was obligated to protect their commerce against pirates, and in 229, they called upon her to redeem the pledge. The Illyrians, who occupied the island-studded eastern shore of the Adriatic Sea, had been united under the rule of a chief named Agron, and after his death his place was taken by his widow, Queen Teuta. By 230, she had conquered the eastern shore of the Ionian Sea as far south as the Gulf of Corinth, and had taken Corcyra. Her subjects now habitually preyed upon Greek ships from Italy, and even raided the Italian coast. Demands for redress were refused, and a Roman ambassador was killed. This was too much. A Roman fleet and army reduced Teuta to submission, forced her to pay tribute, and took from her Corcyra and the other Greek cities which she had seized. At this point the Romans made the acquaintance of a Greek soldier of fortune, Demetrius of Pharos, who, although an official of Teuta, betrayed Corcyra to them. He was rewarded with the gift of his native island of Pharos and other territories, which he held as a Roman vassal. The liberated cities became Roman allies. For the next ten years peace of a sort reigned in this troubled region.

It was well that the Illyrian question could be temporarily shelved, for another and more serious danger had appeared on the northern horizon. For over fifty years the Gauls of the Po Valley had been quiet, but shortly after the First Punic War new tribes from across the Alps disturbed the peace in that quarter. It would seem that the Po Valley Gauls tried to save themselves from conquest by joining these newcomers and inciting them to attack Roman Italy. A first attack upon the frontier post of Ariminum failed because of dissensions among the attackers, but in 226, the Gauls again raided Roman possessions. Seventy thousand barbarians moved southward into Etruria. Great alarm prevailed at Rome, where memories of the attack of 390 were still fresh, and energetic measures were taken to meet the peril. A census of citizens and allies showed that the Roman federation controlled nearly seven hundred thousand men of military age and from this great reservoir of man-power four legions and an equal number of allied troops were drawn to meet the invaders. As the Gauls, loaded with spoil, moved northward through Etruria, they found a Roman army planted across their path and another coming up behind them. In the ensuing battle of Telamon the Romans slaughtered or captured all but ten thousand of their enemies. Italy was safe, but this was not enough. To prevent further depredations, the Romans now undertook the systematic conquest of the Po Valley. One Gallic tribe — the Cenomani — which had taken no part in the war, readily came to terms with the Romans, as did also the non-Celtic Veneti in the extreme northeast. The remainder were subjugated in a war which lasted several years. Latin colonies were planted at Placentia and Cremona, and a citizen colony at Mutina (Modena). The conquered lands were reduced to the form of a province, just as the lands taken from Carthage had been.

Hardly had the Gallic peril been dissipated when the Illyrian question again flared up. This time it was the Roman protégé Demetrius of Pharos who caused the trouble. Apparently he was a man with neither principles nor prudence, for having formed an alliance with Philip V of Macedonia, he took to large-scale piracy, in addition to conquering his neighbors and annexing their lands. In 219, the Romans undertook to chastise him. His towns were taken by storm, and he escaped capture only by fleeing to Macedonia. Rome now controlled a strip of the Illyrian coast about two hundred miles long and in some places forty miles wide, whose inhabitants were either her allies or her subjects. In crossing the Adriatic Sea, Rome had trespassed upon the "sphere of influence" of Macedonia. Philip V, who at that moment was engaged in a struggle with the Aetolians, could not aid Demetrius, but he was deeply offended. A few years later we find the Macedonian king among the allies of the Carthaginian Hannibal.

### *The Revolt of the Carthaginian Mercenaries*

We have seen how light had been the losses of Carthage in the First Punic War. But it had hardly ended before a worse disaster struck her. When Hamilcar Barca disbanded his mercenaries in Sicily, he was aware that his home government did not intend to pay them in full for their services. Hence he sent them to Carthage in small detachments, with an intimation that each group should be paid off and sent away before the next arrived. His political opponents, who happened to be in power at the time, disregarded his advice, and allowed all of them to congregate near the city before attempting to defraud them of their pay. As a result they mutinied, and for the next three years Carthage was engaged in a life-and-death struggle, with her African subjects on the side of her enemies.

The "Truceless War," as the revolt came to be called, was fought on both sides with a ferocity rare even in the bloody annals of Carthage. Tunis and the other Phoenician cities in Africa either joined the rebels or were captured by them. Hamilcar was put in command of one Carthaginian army, and his rival Hanno of another, but party enmity made co-operation between them impossible during the first two years of the war. A rebel leader tortured seven hundred Carthaginian captives to death, only to suffer crucifixion at Hamilcar's hands when he himself was captured. At length the quarrels of the Carthaginian leaders were patched up, new troops were raised, and the revolt was stamped out in blood. By 238, Carthage was again mistress in her own house, but she was nearly exhausted, and her troubles were not over.

During most of the "Truceless War" Rome had shown herself unusually friendly toward her former enemy, and had even allowed Carthage to raise mercenaries in Italy. Then abruptly her attitude changed. The most important Carthaginian province beyond the sea after the loss of Sicily was Sardinia, whose mercenary garrison mutinied in sympathy with their comrades in Africa and for two years retained their independence. When Carthage seemed likely to attack them, they appealed to Rome, promising to surrender the island to her. The offer was refused. In 238, they repeated it, and this time Rome accepted. Carthage protested, but a sudden and drastic change had taken place in Rome's foreign policy. In flat defiance of right and justice she alleged that by attempting to reoccupy Sardinia, Carthage had broken the peace, and declared war. For the moment Carthage was too weak to resist. As the price of peace, she ceded Sardinia to Rome (who at the same time occupied Corsica), and consented to pay an additional indemnity of twelve hundred talents. Peace was restored, but the Carthaginian victims harbored a bitter grudge, and only awaited a suitable opportunity to satisfy it.

### *The Barca Family in Spain*

With Sicily and Sardinia gone, the Carthaginians turned to Spain as a suitable field for the rebuilding of their fortunes. Before the First Punic

War they had had extensive holdings there, but during the struggle (perhaps through the agency of Rome's allies at Massilia) these had largely slipped away. The task of restoring and extending the Spanish province was committed to the able Hamilcar Barca. He nursed a fierce hatred of Rome, and apparently looked upon Spain as an advantageous spot in which to build up his country's strength for a renewal of the struggle with her enemy. In 237, he sailed for Spain, taking with him his young son Hannibal and his son-in-law Hasdrubal.

The enterprise was a brilliant success. By force and conciliation Hamilcar added one district after another to his country's possessions. From tribute and from the produce of the silver mines he secured for her an enormous income, which restored her shattered finances. By recruiting the natives as mercenaries and drilling them in continuous campaigns he built up a large and effective army. When he was killed in 229, he had secured the success of his venture. His son-in-law Hasdrubal continued the work, relying more upon diplomacy than upon war. To him was due the founding of New Carthage as a capital for the province, and he advanced its northern boundary to the Ebro and Tagus rivers.

Rome had meanwhile been watching the career of the Barca family in Spain with an anxious eye. The new province gave the Carthaginian state a fabulously large income, which could be used to finance a new war. In it was stationed an army of fifty-six thousand veteran soldiers and two hundred war elephants, and from it this formidable force might advance by land to attack the possessions of Rome's ally Massilia or even Italy, without effective hindrance from Roman sea power. Hence the Senate soon attempted to meet the incipient danger by diplomatic means. In 231, a Roman embassy met Hamilcar and asked for a statement of his future intentions, but he evaded the issue. In 226, another embassy negotiated a treaty with Hasdrubal by which he agreed to make no conquests north of the Ebro River. Whether Rome conceded to Carthage the territory south of the Ebro is not known, but a few years later the native Spanish city of Saguntum, located a long way to the south of the line of demarcation, appears as a Roman ally. Obviously Saguntum's position was a perilous one, surrounded as she was by Carthaginian territory, and the danger was increased when, in 221, Hasdrubal was assassinated. His successor was Hannibal the son of Hamilcar, a fiery-tempered and aggressive leader, and a bitter enemy of Rome. Hannibal soon found a pretext for war against Saguntum, and besieged her.

Hannibal's war with Saguntum immediately involved both Carthage and Rome. Roman embassies interceded with Hannibal, but in vain. The

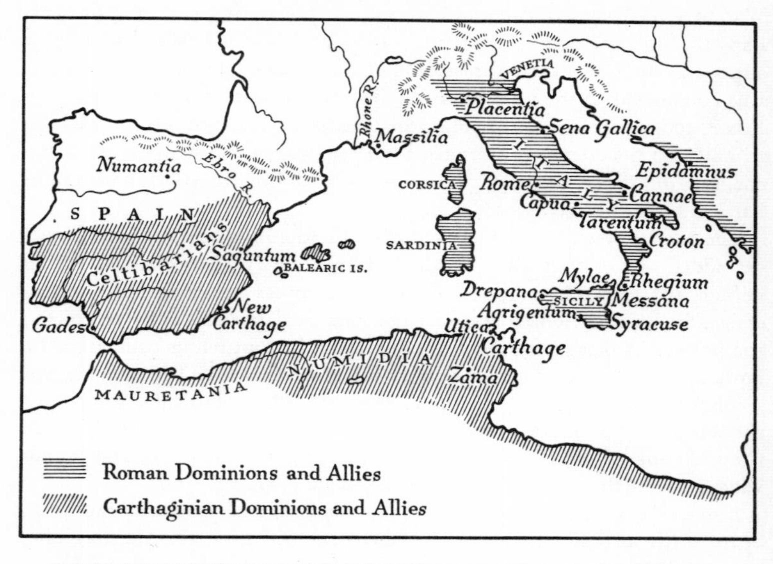


ROME AND CARTHAGE AT THE BEGINNING OF THE SECOND PUNIC WAR

siege continued, and Saguntum fell, after holding out for eight months. As an ally of the stricken city, Rome could not abandon her cause with honor, and Hannibal had openly flouted her protests. Another embassy was sent to Carthage to demand the surrender of Hannibal and his staff. The demand was rejected. Marcus Fabius, the leader of the Roman ambassadors, held out two folds of his toga with the words,[1] "I bring you here peace and war, Men of Carthage. Choose whichever you wish." "Give whichever you will!" the Carthaginian senators shouted. "Then it is war," replied Fabius, dropping one of the folds. The final struggle between the two great powers of the western Mediterranean world was on.

## The Second Punic War (218–201)

### *The Strength of the Contestants*

When Rome and Carthage again resorted to arms, the advantages seemed at first glance to be heavily in favor of the former. Rome was the mistress of the greatest reservoir of dependable man-power in the civilized world,

[1] Polybius, III, 33.

and from it she had fashioned an army whose fighting powers, except in cavalry, were unsurpassed. Italy, with its Latin colonies, its splendid roads, and its loyal Italian allies, was almost a single fortress, unassailable by land except on the north. Rome also controlled the sea, and Carthage, in spite of her century-old naval tradition, never seriously challenged that control during the Second Punic War. On the other side, experience had shown that Carthage could not depend upon her African subjects, who were always ready to revolt when an invader appeared. The weak points and dangers of her reliance upon her mercenaries had been shown in the First Punic War and the Truceless War. In fact, aside from the resources which she could draw from Spain, her strength, in 218, was much less than it had been in 264. But at the beginning of the war she had what Rome lacked — a military genius in command of her forces, backed by the very respectable talents of his brothers Hasdrubal and Mago, and by several other first-rate officers.

### *Hannibal and the Invasion of Italy*

Hannibal was by far the most important figure in the war on either side, and not without reason has it been called the Hannibalic War. Up to the end of the Second Punic War he seems to have been actuated by one sole purpose, to which all other motives were subordinated — hatred of Rome and a wish to cripple her. The story is that when he was nine years old his father Hamilcar took him to an altar and made him swear eternal enmity to his country's chief foe, and whether true or not, the story is consistent with his subsequent conduct. Both in planning campaigns and in fighting battles, he seldom made a mistake, while he knew with uncanny accuracy both how to tempt his opponent to commit blunders, and how to profit by them after they were made. Over his men he exercised an influence such as few generals have ever enjoyed. With a heterogeneous collection of mercenaries, bound by no tie save that of self-interest, he fought for fourteen years in a hostile country without once suffering a serious reverse, and without a single mutiny. When at last the able Scipio Africanus brought him to bay at Zama, his devoted mercenaries stood fast and died at their posts without flinching. In his tragic later life he also showed great abilities as a statesman. Only once was his judgment at fault, and that was when he supposed that the Roman allies in Italy would welcome his coming. Even there he was more successful than his predecessor Pyrrhus had been, and at one time seemed measurably near to breaking up the Roman Federation. His Roman enemies accused him of cruelty and treachery, but while both traits were common among the Carthaginians, no outstanding examples can be cited from Hannibal's career. Measured by any standards, he was the greatest man of his time, and one of the greatest men of the ancient world. We may say with confidence that except for him the war would have been of short duration.

Both sides began the struggle with a strategy of offense. The Romans expected to send an army to Spain under the consul Publius Cornelius Scipio to hold Hannibal in check, while an army and fleet under the other consul, Tiberius Sempronius Gracchus, attacked the Carthaginians in Africa. Hannibal's plan was a far more daring one. He had no adequate fleet with which to contest Rome's control of the sea, and yet to remain in Spain meant, in the end, certain defeat. He supposed that Rome's Italian and Latin allies, like the African subjects of Carthage, awaited only an opportunity to regain their independence, and that to break up the Roman Federation he had only to appear in Italy at the head of a strong army. Hence he determined to lead his army across the Pyrenees and the Alps into the Po Valley, and to strike from there at the heart of the Roman power.

In May, 218 B.C., Hannibal began his march from New Carthage at the head of an army of between forty and fifty thousand men and a corps of elephants. His most effective troops were his Spanish and African infantry and his Numidian cavalry. Progress was slow, however, for many of the tribes of southern Gaul resisted his passage. It was not until near the middle of August that he succeeded in crossing the Rhone River and approaching the Alps, but the Romans had not discovered that he had left Spain until it was too late to interfere with his plans.

The passage of the Alps nearly wrecked Hannibal's army. In midsummer the crossing of the mountains would have been relatively easy, but by this time the first snows of autumn had begun to make the footing treacherous. Roads had to be widened to get the elephants through. All the while the Alpine tribes, believing that their homes were being invaded, inflicted heavy losses upon the Carthaginians by attacking them from above with rocks and weapons. When, about the middle of September, the Carthaginians finally descended into the Po Valley, only about twenty-six thousand men and a few elephants had survived.

### *Roman Disasters and Recovery*

Hannibal's arrival in Italy changed the whole character of the war. The African expedition was hastily recalled. Scipio, learning at Massilia that Hannibal had crossed the Rhone, sent his brother ahead to Spain with the army, and himself returned to Italy. The Gauls of the Po Valley, recently conquered and still disgruntled, welcomed the Carthaginians as liberators. A Roman army, led by both consuls, met the enemy, but only to suffer disaster. A preliminary cavalry skirmish at the Ticinus River was a Carthaginian victory, while in December of 218, at the River Trebia, a Roman army of thirty-three thousand men was defeated with the loss of two thirds of its number in killed, wounded, and prisoners. When the year closed, Cisalpine Gaul was lost to the Romans, and Hannibal could winter there in security, enlisting Gauls to fill up his depleted ranks.

During the winter the Romans gathered new armies, totaling nearly a hundred thousand men. The populace, bent upon ending the war quickly by destroying Hannibal's army, elected to the consulship the author of the recent land-law, Gaius Flaminius, who had made a good military record in the Gallic war. He was assigned to the northern front, but he fared even worse than his predecessors. Hannibal with his reorganized army crossed the Apennines into Etruria. Once in peninsular Italy, he set out to annihilate his Roman pursuers. Flaminius was decoyed into a narrow pass between Lake Trasimenus and the surrounding mountains, where he was attacked from three sides at once. The consul himself and nearly his entire army were destroyed. True to his belief that the Italians were eager to be freed from the Roman yoke, and anxious to show himself their friend, Hannibal at once released without ransom all of the Roman allies who fell into his hands, and sent them home with kind words. But he was chagrined to discover that not one town in northern Italy opened its gates to him. In anger he ravaged the country in his path, passing back eastward over the Apennines and southward into Apulia.

In Rome the accumulation of disasters caused great alarm, but the indomitable Roman spirit soon regained its accustomed sway. A dictator was appointed, the aristocratic Quintus Fabius Maximus. Realizing that he could not hope to beat Hannibal in the open field, Fabius adopted a new policy. He followed the Carthaginians closely, refusing to fight pitched battles, but harassing them with skirmishes, cutting off stragglers and foraging parties, and keeping them in a constant state of alarm. It was an inglorious strategy, which lowered Rome's standing among the allies as more and more of their land was ravaged by the armies. At Rome it provoked a reaction. When the consular elections for 216 were held, one of the new consuls was the aristocratic L. Aemilius Paullus; the other was the popular leader Marcus Terentius Varro. Both seem to have been pledged to a strategy of action.

True to their policy and instructions, the new consuls gathered an army said to number eighty thousand, and set out in pursuit of Hannibal. Their cavalry, however, were few in numbers and far inferior in quality to Hannibal's Numidian, Spanish, and Gallic horsemen. Neither of the consuls was an able general, and no Roman commander of the time had as yet conceived the idea of shifting his men about during a battle to meet unforeseen circumstances. It was precisely here that Hannibal held the advantage. Early in August, 216, near Cannae in Apulia, Paullus and Varro came in touch with the enemy, and drew up their forces for battle. Trusting to the fighting quality of their infantry, they massed it in the center, with the cavalry as usual on the wings. Hannibal arranged his heterogeneous army so as to make allowance for its strong and weak points. Its front formed a crescent, with the convex side toward the enemy. On the wings were his cavalry, and next to them on either side were his Spanish and African infantry. In the center were the Gauls, the least dependable part of his force. At the beginning of the battle the Carthaginian cavalry attacked the Roman cavalry and drove it back, uncovering the wings which it had been protecting. The Roman infantry at the same time attacked the Gauls, who retreated in good order, keeping the Romans engaged. The Spanish and African infantry held firm. Thus the Romans were gradually drawn into a narrow space with Carthaginians on three sides of them, when Hannibal's cavalry came up and attacked them in the rear. Crowded together and incapable of movement, the hapless legionaries were slaughtered where they stood. It was alleged that seventy thousand men, including the consul Paullus, were killed, while from ten to fifteen thousand were taken prisoner. Varro, with perhaps ten thousand more, cut his way through and escaped. When Hannibal's brother Mago, reported the news of the victory at Carthage, he poured out on the floor of the Senate-house a peck of gold rings taken from the fingers of slain Roman cavalrymen. Later Roman tradition, which was framed by the aristocratic party, attributed the disaster to the rashness of the popular leader Varro, but with what justice cannot be determined.

The effects of this terrific blow were immediate and far-reaching. Many of the Samnites, and all of Lucania and Bruttium except the Greek cities of the coast, joined the invader. Some of the Apulians did likewise, and worst of all, when Hannibal appeared in Campania, the important city of Capua along with several lesser cities espoused his cause. Almost the whole south was lost for the time, but there the defections stopped. Latium, the Sabines, Umbria, Picenum, and Etruria held fast to their Roman allegiance, as did many of the Greek cities of southern Italy.

In this dark hour, the Romans displayed their best qualities. There was no thought of yielding. No reproaches were leveled at the defeated Varro, but the fugitives from Cannae were disgraced and sent to Sicily for the remainder of the war. The popular leaders whose flair for aggressive campaigns had cost Rome such a series of disasters, tacitly surrendered the control of affairs to the Senate, which supported the cautious Fabius.[1] For some years thereafter the Roman strategy was one of attrition. Roman armies occupied the walled towns, attacked Hannibal's new Italian allies, cut off detachments of his troops, and prevented reinforcements from reaching him, but fought few pitched battles.

The tide of misfortune did not immediately turn. In 215, two more blows fell upon Rome. The Gauls in the Po Valley cut to pieces the Roman army which occupied their lands and killed its commander. The same year Philip V of Macedonia, who was eager to drive the Romans from Illyria, formed an alliance with Hannibal and attacked the Roman allies east of the Adriatic Sea. During the ten years between 215 and 205, the Romans with slender forces and with the aid of the Aetolian League kept Philip occupied at home, so that he never succeeded in coming to the aid of Hannibal or doing much harm to their allies in Illyria. Also in 215, King Hiero of Syracuse died, leaving his throne to a grandson who was still a child. A year later the boy was killed and the Syracusans deserted the Roman alliance and sought a treaty with Carthage, while a strong Carthaginian army landed in the island.

### *First Steps Toward Recovery*

Amid these dangers the Romans continued their Fabian policy. A Roman army under Marcus Claudius Marcellus besieged Syracuse, which was defended by war-engines constructed by the great physicist and mathematician Archimedes. In 211 the city was taken and sacked, and by the end of 210 Sicily was completely pacified. In 212, three Roman armies also converged upon Capua and besieged it. A double line of entrenchments was constructed around it, facing both inward against the Capuans and outward against a possible relieving force. The next year Hannibal tried to force these lines and relieve the besieged, but failing to do this he sought to draw off the besiegers by making a dash against Rome. This caused great alarm in the city, but failed of its purpose, and Hannibal

[1] The change in sentiment is illustrated by the altered significance of his surname *Cunctator* ("the Delayer"). Originally it had been coined by his enemies as a token of derision. Later generations of Romans remembered it as a title of honor for him.

abandoned Capua to her fate. The rebel senate of the city committed mass suicide, and the commons surrendered to Marcellus. Capua's lands were confiscated and her city government was destroyed, but the lives of the people were spared. Tarentum, which had revolted in 213, did not fare so well. In 209, Fabius took the town and sold the inhabitants as slaves. Meanwhile Samnium and the remainder of Campania had been retaken. Hannibal was now confined to Lucania and Bruttium — the extreme southern part of the peninsula. Slowly but none the less surely, the tide had begun to turn.

### *The War in Sardinia and Spain*

The years of Rome's crucial struggle in Italy had also found her engaged in Sardinia and Spain. A Carthaginian expedition to Sardinia in 215 failed ignominiously. In Spain the brothers Publius and Gnaeus Scipio began by establishing a base north of the Ebro, and for seven years held the Carthaginians at bay, inflicting numerous defeats upon them, and preventing them from sending reinforcements to Hannibal. But calamity at last overtook the Scipios. In 211, while their army was divided, both brothers were surprised and slain, and their forces were partly destroyed. Only by a supreme effort were the survivors able to hold the line of the Ebro and prevent the Carthaginians from conquering all of Spain.

It was, however, this disaster which ultimately cleared the way for the rise of the conqueror of Carthage. In 210, the young Publius Scipio, son of the slain proconsul of the same name, sought and obtained election to the Spanish command which his father had held. As he was only twenty-five years old, and had never held any office above the aedileship, it required a special law to legalize the choice. In him Rome at last found the military genius whom she needed to end the war with victory. He had an unusual gift for winning the affections of both the Romans and the Spaniards, and no sooner had he taken command than the Roman cause in Spain began to prosper again. Early in 209, he made a lightning dash to the southward and captured New Carthage, the capital of Carthaginian Spain. Immense spoil was taken, and in addition he got possession of the hostages whom the Carthaginians had taken from the Spanish chiefs to secure their obedience. By restoring these hostages to their relatives Scipio at once won many allies. He rearmed the legionaries, giving them swords of the type used by the Spaniards, and by extensive drill he introduced new tactics which rendered the Roman infantry a far more effective striking force than it had ever been before. In the next three years he defeated the Carthaginians in two pitched battles and drove them from Spain. One of the defeated generals, Hasdrubal the brother of Hannibal, slipped away northward with twenty thousand men and a large sum of money, and in 208 followed the route formerly taken by his brother toward Italy. The brilliant exploits of Scipio in Spain had heartened the Roman people and removed one source of Carthaginian reinforcements for the war in Italy, and it had brought Scipio himself into the public eye as a man fit to cope with the dreaded Hannibal. He had, it is true, been unable to prevent the escape of Hasdrubal from the peninsula, but long before he returned to Italy, Hasdrubal was dead and his army had ceased to exist.

*Hasdrubal's Italian Expedition: The Metaurus*

The prospect of a second Carthaginian army coming to reinforce the already invincible Hannibal caused great alarm in Rome, but alarm soon gave way to grim determination. Three armies were stationed in northern Italy at the beginning of the year 207, with the consul Marcus Livius Salinator in supreme command in that area. Meanwhile Hasdrubal had experienced a remarkably easy march through Gaul, and after wintering west of the Alps, had crossed into the Po Valley with little or no loss. This was largely due to the fact that the Gauls now knew that his expedition was not directed at them, and that lucrative mercenary service was to be had in his army. Having rested his men and raised their numbers to about thirty thousand by enlisting Gauls, he attempted to slip past the northern Roman armies to join his brother in Lucania. But the other consul Gaius Claudius Nero, who had been commanding the southern armies of Rome, learned through the capture of Hasdrubal's messengers what he was attempting to do. Detaching seven thousand men from his southern command, he hurried northward to join Livius. Their united forces brought Hasdrubal to bay at the River Metaurus, a small stream northeast of the Apennines, destroyed his army, and slew him. For the first time since the beginning of the war a Roman army had won a pitched battle in Italy. With Spain lost, the prospect of future reinforcements for Hannibal was now gone, and he had to retire to Bruttium, in the "toe" of the peninsula. The danger was past. Rome breathed more freely, but even then her generals did not dare face Hannibal in the open.

*The African Campaign: Peace*

In 206, Scipio returned to Rome to stand for the consulship, and easily secured it. His plan was to end the war by invading Africa and humbling

*Bettmann*

HANNIBAL

Carthage on her own soil. In instituting this policy he encountered difficulties. A strong party of senators favored the continuation of Fabian tactics, and only after much trouble did he gain permission to take charge of Sicily, with the option of invading Africa if he saw fit. As a preliminary precaution, the Macedonian War was closed by a treaty which left Philip V unpunished, and allowed each party to keep whatever territories it possessed at the time (205). During the remainder of 205, Scipio prepared an army of twenty-five thousand men and a suitable fleet, and the next year crossed to Africa.

During the first year of his African campaign Scipio did little but feel his way. To the west of Carthage lay the vassal state of Numidia, whence Hannibal had drawn his best cavalry. Two claimants disputed for its throne, Masinissa and Syphax. The latter had the upper hand, and although he had formerly given Carthage much trouble, he was, in 204, her staunch ally. Scipio took up the cause of Masinissa, whose partisans speedily furnished him with a force of the famous Numidian cavalry. In 203, Scipio used his own forces and those of his allies to win an astonishing series of victories. Syphax was taken prisoner, and Masinissa became king of Numidia. Utica, Tunis, and other cities fell into Scipio's hands, and the Carthaginians were beaten in two decisive battles. The supplies of Carthage were cut off, and famine threatened her. In desperation she sued for peace, and while the negotiations were in progress she summoned Hannibal home. At length Scipio concluded the treaty which, while severe, still left Carthage her independence and a few shreds of dignity. But she was not fated to get off so easily.

Early in 202, after the terms of peace had already been ratified at Rome, the starving Carthaginians plundered a fleet of transports which was on its way to provision Scipio's army, and encouraged by the presence of Hannibal, refused redress. War was renewed, and the following autumn the Romans under Scipio faced the army of Hannibal near the inland town of Zama. Each army had between thirty-five and forty thousand men, but Hannibal was now much the weaker in cavalry. To compensate for this he had eighty war elephants, with which he hoped to throw the Roman infantry into confusion. But now for the first time he faced a general who could cope with him. Scipio captured or routed the elephants with little difficulty and his cavalry drove that of Hannibal from the field. Then, leaving his front line to hold the enemy in check, he deployed the rear ranks, sending half to the right and half to the left, where they fell upon the uncovered ends of the enemy center. His cavalry then returned and attacked the enemy's rear. The Carthaginians suffered the same fate as the Romans at Cannae. Hannibal and seventy cavalrymen were all that survived of his once invincible army.

Peace was now made in earnest, and its terms spelled the doom of Carthaginian greatness. Carthage surrendered her elephants and all but ten of her warships, undertook to pay an indemnity of ten thousand talents in fifty annual installments, and renounced all claim to her former possessions in Spain. In Africa she acknowledged the independence of Numidia and of some other tribes in what is today Tripoli, and promised to restore to Masinissa all lands which he or his ancestors had ever held. She was never again to make war outside of Africa, and in Africa only with Rome's consent. Although still nominally independent, she was thenceforth to be, in fact, a vassal of Rome.

### *The Effects of the War upon Rome and Italy*

Rome had won the sternest duel which she was destined ever to fight. She was now without a rival in the region west of the Adriatic Sea and the

Sicilian Narrows. Her actual annexations at the close of the two Punic wars were small, including only Sicily, Sardinia, Corsica, and southeastern Spain, but no first-rate power now barred her from further annexations in the region west of Sicily. Indeed within fifteen years after the battle of Zama the two greatest of the Hellenistic monarchies, Macedonia and the Seleucid Kingdom, had shared the fate of Carthage. It is with justice that a contemporary Greek poet prophesied for her "A throne and scepter ruling both land and sea."

But the victory had not been won without heavy cost. Hundreds of thousands of men had fallen in battle. The whole southern third of the peninsula of Italy had been ravaged, year after year, for fourteen years. Villages had vanished, and their people were dead, in slavery, or had left the country. The Greek cities of the south were reduced to mere shadows of their former selves. Never again did this region regain the prosperity which it had before Hannibal came.

Among both Romans and Italians the war had produced psychological and moral effects similar to those which have grown out of the great struggles of the twentieth century A.D. Only the transcendent heroism of the Romans and of a majority of their allies could have made possible the final victory. This indomitable devotion to duty was apparent not only in the battles and sieges, but also in what contemporary slang terms "the home front." The civilian population submitted to enormous increases in taxation, to forced loans, and to strict government regulation of its activities. The state commandeered slaves to serve in the army, appropriated the trust funds of widows and orphans, and levied a special graduated property tax to support the fleet. Yet when all these exactions had been met, contractors could be found who volunteered to furnish the armies in Spain with provisions on a promise of payment after the war, and the Italian cities contributed large quantities of arms and equipment to supply Scipio's army for the invasion of Africa.

Nevertheless the strain of the conflict bore heavily upon the poise and self-possession of the people. There was a widespread feeling that the anger of the gods had produced the disaster which befell Italy in the early years of the war, and the idea gave rise to stories of portents and prodigies, which the Senate expiated by frequent sacrifices and other rites. The *Sibylline Books* were often consulted, and at their command sacred feasts and other acts of worship were performed in honor of various Greek gods. Finally, in 204, a still more drastic step was taken. The black meteoric stone which represented the Asiatic "Great Mother of the Gods" was brought to Rome and a group of eunuch priests came with her to care for her worship. The new cult was marked by such weird, colorful rites and orgiastic emotionalism that it was soon carried on only under severe legal restrictions. But about the same time, and without the permission of the government, the Greek cult of Dionysus was introduced into the capital from southern Italy. It also contained an orgiastic strain expressed in nocturnal ceremonies, noisy processions of drunken men and women, and, so its enemies said, immoral excesses. About fifteen years after the close of the war the government made it the object of a bloody persecution, and thereafter allowed it to continue only under strict regulations.

As might be expected, unprincipled rascals occasionally tried to take advantage of the public distress to enrich themselves at the expense of the state. Since the government insured the ships and cargoes which the contractors were sending to Spain to supply the armies, some of the shipowners used worthless vessels for the purpose, and then claimed damages when they sank. So great was the audacity of these rogues that they even used force in an effort to prevent their condemnation by the courts.

*Changes in Domestic Government and Federal Relations*

Rome's domestic government emerged from the ordeal unchanged in form but considerably altered in spirit. The Senate had by tacit consent assumed and exercised many powers to which it had no clear legal title, and had consecrated its usurpations by the successful outcome of its policies. Capable consuls and praetors, such as Marcellus, Fabius Maximus, or Scipio Africanus, had been kept in command of armies for years at a time by repeated re-elections or as proconsuls and propraetors, and Scipio's first command in Spain had been granted him, as we have seen, by a special law in defiance of all precedent. Therein lay the germs of future danger from autocratic war lords, but not until a century later did the peril become acute.

The Roman spirit became noticeably harsher and sterner under the strain of the conflict, and the change is to be seen in the treatment of both enemies and allies. Not since the capture of Veii had conquered towns been treated with the deliberate severity accorded to Capua, Tarentum, or Syracuse. When twelve Latin colonies, exhausted by the constant drains upon their man-power, professed their inability to supply their usual contingents for the army, they were punished by the curtailment of their treaty rights, and had thereafter to pay tribute to Rome. The rights of loyal allies were as a rule scrupulously respected, but they were treated with a brusque authoritarianism which showed all too clearly that they were the subjects of a mistress who demanded obedience as well as co-operation. When the war closed, many allied communities in southern Italy had been irretrievably ruined if not completely destroyed. Rome appropriated as her own over 4000 square miles of land which had been devastated during Hannibal's occupation of the region. The ancient custom of dividing the spoils with the remaining allies by founding Latin colonies was followed in only a few cases, involving only a fraction of the land. The Roman Federation still existed, but it was more like a collection of subjects, and less like a league of free allies than before. The scarred but triumphant Rome of 200 B.C. was well on her way to imperial domination of the Mediterranean World.

# 12

# *Rome Dominates the Eastern Mediterranean World (200-167 B.C.)*

## The Eastern Situation About 200 B.C.

### *Rome's Broadening Horizon*

With the defeat of Carthage, Rome suddenly became the strongest military and naval power in the civilized world. In this position she was forced to acquire a broader outlook than formerly, and to substitute definite foreign policies for the haphazard opportunism of the previous period. Preventive imperialism — the practice of attacking and defeating potential enemies before they became dangerous — became a recognized feature of her foreign relations, but she still clung to the view that wars were intended for defense and not for conquest. Up to about 200 B.C. Rome's relations with the Hellenistic states had been limited to a few transactions with the Ptolemies and to the circumstances growing out of the Illyrian and First Macedonian Wars, but she now came into direct relations, whether friendly or hostile, with all of them, and as a necessary consequence of these relations, became involved in their endless quarrels and wars. From these new series of wars she emerged, thirty-four years after the Battle of Zama, with an ascendancy in the eastern Mediterranean almost as complete as that which she already enjoyed in the West. To trace the growth of that ascendancy is the task of the present chapter.

### *The Hellenistic States*

In the eastern Mediterranean the dominant powers about 200 B.C. were, as we have seen,[1] the three great Hellenistic monarchies — Macedonia and

[1] Chapter 8.

the Seleucid and Ptolemaic Kingdoms. Of these Macedonia was the most stable because of its sturdy homogeneous people and able national dynasty, but its small population and area rendered it much weaker than Rome. In fact, in the First Macedonian War the Romans had been able, with some help from their allies, to fight Philip V to a standstill with only a fraction of their forces. The Seleucid state, under the aggressive Antiochus III, had just regained nominal possession of its eastern provinces, which had slipped out of its grasp many years earlier. This achievement had greatly increased the prestige of Antiochus in the Hellenistic world, but as his hold on these outlying provinces was not firm, his strength had not been proportionately increased thereby. The Ptolemaic state was nominally ruled by the infant Ptolemy V, but its actual government was in the hands of a corrupt and inefficient regency. Also a native Egyptian reaction against the Greeks was in progress, still further weakening the state. Both the Seleucid and Ptolemaic states were held together by mercenary armies of foreigners, and by Greek and Macedonian colonists. By 200 B.C. it had become difficult to secure an adequate supply of recruits for either the armed forces or the colonies. Hence it became necessary for their sovereigns to rely more and more heavily upon their non-Hellenic subjects, and upon persons of pure or mixed Greek descent long settled in the country. None of these people were as staunch or reliable fighters as the Greeks of the Aegean region.

There was also a number of small Hellenistic states which played important parts in the history of the region during the third and second centuries. In Greece proper there were the Achaean and Aetolian Leagues and Athens. In the Aegean region was the Republic of Rhodes, which had a strong navy and great wealth, and was highly respected for her honest and responsible dealings with her neighbors. In Asia were the small states of Pergamum, Bithynia, Cappadocia, Pontus, Galatia, and Armenia. All of these had been founded upon lands which either had once belonged to the Seleucids, or were coveted by them. On the coast the former possessions of the Ptolemies were now either wholly or largely free states. However these petty Asiatic states might differ from each other in other respects, they had one thing in common — fear of aggression and conquest by their larger neighbors.

This apprehension was heightened by the aggressive policies of Antiochus III. Plainly he intended to reconquer all of the lost territories of his house, and among them Asia Minor was likely to occupy a prominent place in his thinking. Then came a move which drove Pergamum, Rhodes, and the Aetolians to a new understanding. In 203 or 202, Antiochus and

Philip formed an alliance, the object of which was to seize and partition the extra-Egyptian possessions of Ptolemy V. Antiochus quickly invaded and conquered Syria and Palestine, while Philip fell upon the cities of the Aegean region which he coveted, regardless of whether they belonged to Ptolemy or not. His course was marked by a savage cruelty and a disregard for the rights of others rare even in Hellenistic annals. Rhodes and Pergamum united to stop his progress, but with little success. Philip then added to his list of Greek enemies by declaring war on Athens — an unpopular move — for because of her splendid cultural achievements, Athens enjoyed great prestige in the Greek world. In the meantime the Battle of Zama had made Rome supreme in the West, and to her, Attalus I of Pergamum, the Aetolians, Egyptians, and Rhodians turned for protection against their formidable neighbors. This was a fateful decision, for it was to bring the Romans into the Hellenistic state-system as arbiters of its destiny, and once there, they were unlikely to withdraw.

## The Second Macedonian War and Its Consequences (200–194 B.C.)

### *Rome Goes to War with Philip V*

At Rome neither Senate nor people were at first inclined to interfere in this far-off quarrel, which concerned them so little. But before long, under the expert manipulation of the Rhodian and Pergamene ambassadors, the Senate was won over to the view that Philip must be humbled. We can only guess at the motives which actuated its members. Some of them, including the Scipios, were enamored of Greek culture, and may have argued that they were defending the free Greeks against an aggressor. Others may have remembered vindictively that when Rome was struggling with Hannibal, Philip had tried to stab her in the back. Still others, knowing of the pact between Philip and the supposedly formidable Antiochus, would feel that it was better to strike down the nearer ally before the more distant one could come to his aid. At any rate, a Roman embassy was sent to stir up the continental Greeks against Philip (in which they had but little success), and a consul asked the Assembly of the Centuries to declare war upon him.

It required ingenious verbal juggling to make out a valid case for the proposal now before the assembly. It was a fixed Roman policy never to go to war unless attacked, either directly or through allies of the state. Philip had not attacked the Romans, and they had no allies in the area in which he was carrying on war. But the Greeks had a type of international relationship unknown to the old Roman custom, called "friendship."

Friends were merely bound not to attack one another, and to arbitrate their mutual disputes. Each party could, if it wished, maintain its neutrality in a dispute in which the other was engaged. Apparently Rome had some "friends" among the Greeks who had been attacked, and to the assembly these seem to have been represented as allies. At first the proposal, even in this form, was unsuccessful. The people, weary of wars and still suffering from the effects of the preceding one, unanimously voted it down. Then the senators returned to the attack, representing Philip as a real threat to Rome's safety. At length, quite reluctantly, the declaration of war was voted. To fulfill the formalities, an embassy was sent to present an ultimatum requiring Philip to promise never again to attack Egyptian dependencies or free Greek cities, and to make reparations to Rhodes and Pergamum for the damage he had done them. Philip indignantly refused, and the war began.

Of the two contestants, Rome was infinitely the stronger. Philip could scarcely hope to put into the field an army of over thirty thousand men at any time, and Rome could, when necessary, arm six times as many. Philip had very few allies, while Rome had many, and her fleet far surpassed his in size. But Philip had the advantage of an easily defensible position. Between Macedonia and the Adriatic shore was a range of high mountains, pierced by few passes, and the equally intraversable Cambaunian Mountains shut her off from Thessaly. Thus he could be attacked at only a few points, and if he could hold off the Romans for one or two years, avoiding disastrous defeats, they might become disgusted with the war and consent to a compromise peace. That was the best he could hope for.

### *The Conduct of the War*

At the beginning of the war, the Greeks were uncertain which side would win, and so remained neutral. In 200, a Roman army landed on the eastern coast of the Adriatic and made a successful raid into Macedonia, while a Roman fleet aided Athens against Philip, who was attacking her. In 199, the raid was repeated, Philip was beaten in a skirmish, and the Aetolians, presuming that they could now distinguish the coming victor, joined Rome. But no permanent gains were made, and late in 199, the invaders again retired to the Adriatic coast.

By the beginning of 198, the Romans had at last discovered a man fit to cope with the Macedonian situation, Titus Quintius Flamininus, whom they elected consul and assigned to the command of their eastern army. He was a genuine admirer of Greek culture, with a tact and persuasiveness which won the hearts of the sensitive Greeks. He made it plain to them that Rome was fighting only to free them from Macedonian rule, and when Philip tried to make peace, put forward terms laid down by the Senate which made the evacuation of the Greek peninsula a prerequisite to further negotiations. When Philip broke off negotiations, Flamininus followed up his advantage to the utmost. Before the year was out, Philip had nothing left in the Greek peninsula except the small western district of Acarnania and the three fortresses of Chalcis, Corinth, and Demetrias. Soon Flamininus defeated him in a skirmish and drove him back into Macedonia. The Romans retained their able consul in command the next year with the title of proconsul.

In the spring of 197, Philip, in desperation, sought a decisive battle. With twenty-five thousand men he marched southward into Thessaly, where Flamininus awaited him with twenty-six thousand men, of whom nearly eight thousand were Greek allies. After some marching and skirmishing, the two armies met accidentally on the slopes of a range of hills known as Cynocephalae. Philip's right wing routed the Roman left, while the Roman right wing drove back Philip's left. Then one of Flamininus' military tribunes acting without orders detached a body of men from the rear lines of the victorious Roman wing, led them to the other side of the field, and fell upon the rear of the victorious Macedonian wing. Of Philip's army eight thousand men were killed and five thousand were taken prisoners. The tactical revolution, which Scipio Africanus had effected in the closing years of the Second Punic War, had rendered the Roman legions immeasurably superior to the decadent phalanx formation used by the Hellenistic generals of the second century B.C. All that was left for Philip was to accept such terms as he could get.

### *Peace: The Settlement of Greece*

Flamininus found it hard to bring about a settlement. His Aetolian allies, who had been so slow to join the war, now wanted to continue it until the Macedonian kingdom was destroyed. To this policy Flamininus would not agree, for it would leave Greece open to invasion by northern barbarians or to conquest by Antiochus III. His aim was to humble Philip, but to leave him all of his Macedonian lands without diminution. Peace was finally made on the following terms. Philip was to surrender all of his holdings in Greece and his recent conquests, to be disposed of as Rome saw fit. He was to surrender all of his prisoners, deserters from the Roman army, and his navy. And he was to pay an indemnity of 1000 talents of silver, half in cash and half in annual installments. Under the circumstances he had gotten off easily. The way now seemed clear for the restoration of Greek freedom.

But the peacemakers had still to face baffling obstacles. The Aetolians, feeling that the victory over Philip was largely their work, claimed that they should recover possession of a long list of places which they had once held but had lost to Macedonia, and of others which they had captured during the war. This claim was not allowed. Again, if the Romans evacuated Greece, was there not danger that Antiochus would move in as soon as they had moved out? But if they remained in occupation of the country, the champions of Greek independence would be mortally offended. After considerable hesitation, the Senate left the question of holding or surrendering Greece to ten commissioners whom it appointed. They seem to have favored continued occupation of the fortresses of Chalcis, Corinth, and Demetrias (the "Fetters of Greece"), but Flamininus overruled them, and secured the support of the Senate for his views. To end the tension between Rome and her Greek protégés, he determined to stage a dramatic proof of his country's good intentions. At the Isthmian Games of 196, he caused a proclamation to be issued that Rome, acting through him, "freed, released from tribute, and allowed to live under their own laws," the peoples of continental Greece whom Philip had formerly ruled. To the Greeks this appeared to be complete independence, and, wild with enthusiasm, they showered Flamininus with honors. About the same time, in answer to an appeal of the Asiatic Greek cities of Smyrna and Lampsacus, the Senate also proclaimed that the Greeks of both Europe and Asia were to be free and autonomous. Rome had now become the champion of Hellenism everywhere. Graeco-Roman relations never again reached such a pitch of cordiality.

Unfortunately, matters could not rest there. Governments had to be provided for the liberated states of continental Greece, and whatever form Flamininus and the commissioners proposed for a given state was certain to offend either the aristocrats or the commons. They soon found that a Greek's most cherished right was that of settling his quarrels by war, and the Greeks were always quarreling. The Boeotians for a long time were obstinate in their attachment to Macedonia. A feud between the Achaean League and Nabis, Tyrant of Sparta, had to be settled by a military expedition, and when Nabis was defeated, the Achaeans were angry because Flamininus did not completely destroy their enemy. In general the Romans favored the aristocratic elements rather than the commons, and the latter accordingly became bitterly and violently anti-Roman in sentiment. It also began to dawn upon the Greeks that the proclamation of 196 had not restored complete independence to them, but only the liberty to conduct their own governments so long as the Romans saw fit. Bitter was the disillusionment of all classes when the discovery was made, and the good feeling which Flamininus had caused to spring up quickly vanished. After two more years of negotiating, arbitrating, threatening, and fighting, it seemed that a degree of order had been restored to this Hellenic pandemonium, and Flamininus gladly sailed for home. Already the Aetolians were weary of a regime which cut short their career of conquest and aggression, and were ready to welcome any outsider who would free them from the hated restraint.

## The War With Antiochus (192–189 B.C.)

### *Causes and Background*

All the while that the Romans had been fighting with Philip V and reorganizing Greece, their relations with Antiochus III had been growing steadily worse. It was not that Antiochus wanted war with Rome, for he had plenty of reason to realize the formidable character of her power. But he was bent upon restoring his ancestral dominions to their fullest extent, and to achieve this end he had to reconquer the western coast of Asia Minor and a few places on the Thracian side of the Hellespont. He was fully convinced that in doing so he was within his rights, and was unwilling to allow a foreign power to interfere with him. The Romans on their side looked with apprehension upon the expansion of the Seleucid Kingdom, and were not averse to applying to it their new policy of preventive imperialism. Furthermore, Antiochus was reconquering the Greek cities of Asia ("enslaving" was the Roman phrase), and it seemed inconsistent that they should allow Antiochus to rule over Greeks when they had just fought a war with Philip V to prevent him from doing so. At first they were also inclined to take the part of Ptolemy V, who had been despoiled of his Asiatic possessions, but Antiochus forestalled them by concluding a treaty of alliance with Ptolemy, and by giving him his daughter in marriage. The quarrel was further fomented by Eumenes II, the new king of Pergamum.

Eumenes, it will be observed, had a personal interest in the matter. His territories had once belonged to the Seleucids, and although Antiochus had promised not to molest the lands which properly belonged to Pergamum, the reconquest of the neighboring lands would shut Eumenes off from all further expansion, and place him at Antiochus' mercy for the

*Galloway*

RESTORATION OF THE ALTAR OF ZEUS

*Built by Eumenes II*

future. Furthermore, Eumenes had established a protectorate over some cities outside of his kingdom, and Antiochus had not promised to spare them. Hence it was to Eumenes' advantage to see Antiochus humbled, and Rome was the most likely agent for the purpose.

Beginning in 200 B.C., when a Roman embassy arrived at the Seleucid court, the relations of the two powers had become increasingly strained. Until the defeat of Philip V, the Romans had been careful not to provoke Antiochus' enmity, but in 196, when his envoys visited Flamininus at Corinth, they were bluntly informed that their master must not "enslave" any more Greek cities. The next year a new cause of strife developed when Hannibal sought refuge with Antiochus.

For several years after the Battle of Zama, the great Carthaginian had lived in retirement, but in 196 he was once more in public life, this time as a politician. Carthage was at that time governed by a corrupt and oppressive oligarchy, which not only levied heavy taxes, but spent money so dishonestly that the state was on the verge of bankruptcy. Hannibal was elected to the office of *suffete*, which corresponded loosely to the Roman consulate. From this point of vantage he led an attack on the oligarchs which resulted in their losing most of their power. He then reorganized the finances of the state so efficiently that without any new taxes he was able to discharge all of its obligations. But his enemies did not rest until they had ruined him. They sent reports to Rome, accusing him of plotting a new war, and in 195 a Roman embassy was sent to lay a formal complaint against him before the Carthaginian Senate. Hannibal, realizing that he could not resist the forces opposing him, secretly fled and sought refuge at the court of Antiochus. His presence there was certain to heighten the hard feelings that already existed between Antiochus and the Romans.

The continental Greeks were also interested in stirring up a new war. The settlement made by Flamininus and the Roman commissioners had aroused universal dissatisfaction, and among the malcontents the most prominent were the Aetolians. Soon their representatives approached Antiochus and besought him to aid them in freeing Greece — this time, from the Romans. In 192, they took the final step and tried to form a league with Philip V, Antiochus III whom they elected general of their league, and Nabis of Sparta against the Romans. Philip, remembering their many hostile acts against him, rudely rebuffed them, and Nabis, showing his hand too soon, was defeated by the Achaeans with Roman aid. But Antiochus, without waiting to survey the situation or to collect his forces, landed in northern Greece with only ten thousand men. Even then he probably intended no more than an armed demonstration, but the result was war.

### *The War in Greece*

In the beginning Antiochus seems to have had no coherent plan of action. Hannibal, with characteristic audacity, urged him to rouse Carthage to a new war and to attack Italy, offering to head the enterprise himself. Antiochus would not adopt this plan, and merely set about consolidating his position. North-central Greece quickly espoused his cause. But Philip V, who remembered how Antiochus had failed him a few years before, and who had no love for the Aetolians, heartily supported the Roman side. Early in 191, a Roman army of twenty-two thousand men commanded by the consul Manius Acilius Glabrio, landed in western Greece and marched across the mountains into Thessaly where it was joined by a contingent of Achaeans.

The war in Greece was soon finished. Glabrio forced Antiochus to evacuate Thessaly, and he fell back to the historic pass of Thermopylae, where he made a stand. The Romans, using the same strategy which Xerxes had employed in 480, crossed the mountains by the path which the Persians had traversed, and fell upon the enemy's rear. So decisive was their victory that the Seleucid monarch at once abandoned Greece and returned to Asia. The Romans spent the remainder of 191 in reorganizing the state system of continental Greece, and in collecting a fleet with which to aid them in the invasion of Asia.

### *The War in Asia*

As the struggle could not be ended with victory until Antiochus had been defeated in his own dominions, the Romans turned to their ablest general, Scipio Africanus, to take charge of the campaign against him. Since Scipio had been consul only three years before, and could not legally be re-elected so soon, they gave the consulship to his mediocre brother Lucius, and attached Africanus to his staff as an aide. The Aetolians obtained a truce which was equivalent to a surrender, and a Roman fleet, aided by Rhodian and Pergamene squadrons, cleared the Aegean of Antiochus' ships. Foreseeing defeat, the Seleucid king sued for peace, but Africanus offered such harsh terms that he broke off negotiations. Then the Roman army, with the support of Philip V, marched through Macedonia and Thrace, and entered Asia Minor by way of the Hellespont where it was joined by Eumenes II. In January 189, at Magnesia in Lydia, Antiochus gave battle.

In numbers the Seleucid king had a great advantage — seventy-five thousand men as against thirty thousand Romans and allies. His most effective troops were his armored cavalry, but he had also fifty-four elephants. The remainder of his force was not especially formidable, although it included a phalanx of the Macedonian type, and a number of scythed chariots. The Romans massing their cavalry on their right wing, defeated Antiochus' left, while his right wing defeated the Roman left. But whereas he pursued the enemy right up to their camp, the Roman right wing wheeled about and fell upon the unprotected flank of his phalanx, which was cut to pieces. In all he lost about fifty thousand men, while the Romans and their allies lost only about three hundred and fifty. He had now no army, and his subjects in Asia Minor began to surrender *en masse* to the victors. His only recourse was to seek peace on whatever terms the conquerors chose to grant him.

*Peace: the Reorganization of Asia Minor*

The Treaty of Apamea, by which Antiochus closed the war, humbled him once and for all. He had to renounce all of his lands north and west of the Taurus Mountains, to surrender his elephants and all but ten of his ships, and to pay an indemnity of fifteen thousand talents in annual installments. He was to surrender Hannibal and several Greek agitators who were with him, but the Carthaginian (no doubt by prearrangement) escaped and took refuge with King Prusias of Bithynia. Antiochus promised never to fight again in Asia Minor, Europe, or the Aegean Islands, except that he might defend himself against attack, if he did not annex lands conquered in the forbidden areas. In other respects he was still independent, and his lands southeast of the Taurus Mountains were not affected. In view of the alliance which he had made with Ptolemy V, the Romans did not even insist that he restore Syria or Palestine to the latter. The Seleucid state was, with many vicissitudes, to drag out its existence for yet another century, but it never recovered from the disaster at Magnesia. The later history, a sad record of discord and dissolution, will be traced in a subsequent chapter.[1]

Having rid themselves of their chief enemy, the Romans now proceeded to organize the lands which they had taken from him. For themselves they kept nothing but the movable spoils of war and the indemnity previously mentioned. Friends were rewarded, and enemies, whether open or secret, were punished. Philip V had aided the victors loyally and he was rewarded by the remission of the unpaid balance of the indemnity which he owed, and by permission to keep several places which he had taken from the enemy in Thessaly. The Aetolians, whose intrigues had brought Antiochus into Greece, escaped with less punishment than they might have expected. They lost some territory, paid an indemnity of 500 talents, and bound themselves to Rome by a close and burdensome alliance.

A similar reckoning was held in Asia. Eumenes was rewarded with so much land in Asia Minor that his dominions were nearly quadrupled in size, and he became one of the most important of the Hellenistic princes. To the Rhodians went an extensive tract in southwestern Asia Minor. Upon the intercession of Eumenes, the King of Cappadocia was absolved from blame for the aid given to Antiochus with only the moderate fine of 300 talents.

There remained one problem which the Hellenistic monarchs had never been able to solve decisively. The Galatians, after nearly a century of

[1] Chapter 13.

residence in Asia Minor, still plundered the lands of their neighbors whenever possible. In 188 the consul Manlius, aided by Pergamene troops, invaded their country and broke their power. Their lands were devastated, their strongholds were stormed, and many thousands of them were sold into slavery. Manlius and his army, by methods which were not always above reproach, acquired a stupendous amount of spoil. Thereafter, however, the Galatians ceased to be a menace to their neighbors, and soon acquired the arts and habits of civilized life. Late in 188 the Romans withdrew from Asia, and left the princes and peoples of the region to work out their own destinies.

The defeat of Antiochus had removed Rome's last important competitor in the Mediterranean region, and left her supreme. Of the great Hellenistic monarchies, only Egypt had not felt her heavy hand. But the Ptolemaic state was far gone in decline, and within a few years it drifted slowly and peacefully into the position of a Roman client-state. As far away as Asia Minor, where she had not a single soldier, Rome's word was law. Thus when Prusias of Bithynia attacked Eumenes of Pergamum, it needed only a word from Rome to make him desist, and as Hannibal was supposed to have instigated the strife, his surrender was demanded. The great Carthaginian, knowing that his last refuge was gone, committed suicide to avoid falling into the hands of his implacable enemies (183). Yet Rome did not intervene often, and never without being invoked. The greedy kings and quarrelsome city-states of the Hellenistic East might yet have worked out their salvation if they had chosen to do so. That they did not so elect, was their own fault.

## Greece and Macedonia Between Two Wars (188–171)

### *The Greeks Lose Rome's Friendship*

In the years that followed the defeat of Antiochus III, Roman friendship for the Greeks underwent a sharp decline. This revulsion of feeling was principally due to two factors. The first of these was the fall from power of the Hellenophile Scipio family, and the rise of the matter-of-fact and nationalistic Cato. The second was the constant quarrels and disorders in Greece, with consequent appeals to Rome, which alienated former friends of the Greeks.

The popularity of Scipio Africanus did not long survive the end of the war with Antiochus. With all of his personal magnetism and the prestige conferred by his brilliant military record, he had made many enemies. Chief among them was the dour, close-fisted, and conservative Marcus

*Brown Brothers*

SCIPIO AFRICANUS

Porcius Cato, a born fighter in both war and politics. Perhaps what offended him most about the Scipios was their love of the Greek ways and their disregard of national traditions. Cato himself, while by no means ignorant of Greek culture, had a very poor opinion of the Greek people and their national character. He felt that their influence was corrupting the morals of the Romans, and he believed that Rome should have as few dealings with them as possible. When such dealings could not be avoided, the Greeks should be treated frankly as inferiors, who were to receive the orders of their betters and obey them. By a series of well-planned attacks delivered through the courts and assemblies, Cato drove the Scipio family from public life, and in 184 he himself attained the censorship, the highest regular office which the Roman state could bestow. Under his influence the Romans began to give up their indulgent attitude toward the Greeks, and to adopt an imperious tone.

In Greece, the mortal ills from which the country had so long suffered gave rise to the usual aimless bickerings between states and parties. The Achaeans, whose league, it will be remembered, had always championed the cause of the propertied classes in the age-old struggle with the proletariat, periodically fought with Sparta, whose kings Cleomenes and later Nabis had championed social revolution. The latter, indeed, had gone so far as to seize Argos about the time of the Second Macedonian War, and had been forced to release it only by the intervention of Flamininus. Throughout southern Greece the suffering poor looked upon this royal demagogue as a champion who might deliver to them the property of their rich neighbors. Although Nabis was assassinated by the Aetolians during the war with Antiochus, his program lived after him. For a time Sparta had been forced into the Achaean League, but in 188 she was again at war with it. Atrocities of the most shocking kind were perpetrated by both sides. Philopoemen, the leading spirit of the Achaean League at the time, dismantled the Spartan fortifications, sold three thousand of Nabis' former partisans into slavery, and destroyed the traditional Spartan social system. When Rome intervened to mitigate these horrors, the Achaean aristocrats, who had formerly been her friends, began to hate her.

But the trouble did not stop with Sparta. In 183, the Messenians seceded from the League, and when Philopoemen tried to force them back into it, they captured and poisoned him. His successor Callicrates reversed the previous policy of the League completely. Having gone to Rome as an envoy, he showed the Senate how to make the Greeks docile. Rome was to state her wishes in strong terms, and to uphold the authority of those Greek politicians who were subservient to her. This advice was directly in line with the view of the dominant party in Rome, and it was followed without hesitation. The Achaeans, although they hated Callicrates as a traitor, submitted to his dictation, but the majority of them felt deeply the humiliation of being mere lackeys of the Roman Republic. Plainly the political life of continental Greece was becoming more envenomed than ever.

### *Macedonian Recovery: War Threatens*

Meanwhile, Macedonia was staging a splendid recovery from her defeat. Philip V spent the remainder of his reign in developing the resources of his kingdom. New settlers were invited into the country. Mines were worked, the royal estates were developed, and the army was enlarged and disciplined. All this did not escape the notice of the Romans, who suspected that Philip was plotting a new war. Relations were not always pleasant, and he often had to bear slights inflicted by Roman envoys, but he bided his time. When he died in 179, he had a large army and more money than any of his predecessors except Alexander the Great.

His successor Perseus (179–167) had some of his father's energy and ability, but with it a strain of headstrong folly which hastened if it did not cause his ruin. He began to meddle once more in Greek politics, posing as the champion of the lower classes, the anti-Roman faction. He contracted a marriage with the granddaughter of Antiochus III, and gave his sister in marriage to King Prusias of Bithynia. This activity, in view of the increased strength of Macedonia, was a source of uneasiness, not only among the Romans, but to their Pergamene client, Eumenes II. In 172, the latter came to Rome to stir up enmity against the Macedonian king. On his way home he was injured, and claimed that Perseus had tried to have him murdered. The Senate, always suspicious of Macedonia, sent envoys to Greece to form a coalition against her. A final embassy was sent to Perseus himself with demands for submission, but although he did not want to fight, he refused to make the desired concessions. In 171, Rome declared war.

## The Third Macedonian War (171–167)

### *A Three-Year Stalemate*

As in the Second Macedonian War, Rome had a large preponderance of strength, but for some time she did not use it effectively. In continental Greece the Aetolians, Achaeans, and most of the Boeotians took the Roman side, and of course Eumenes of Pergamum did the same. Except for a few semi-barbarian tribes on his northern and eastern frontier, Perseus was without allies. The Roman fleet controlled the sea. As against the huge reserve of man-power controlled by the Roman Republic, Perseus could put into the field a maximum of only about forty-three thousand men.

Nevertheless, during the first two years of the war the Roman offensive was so poorly conducted that it nearly ended in disaster. The first army to cross the Adriatic consisted of only about thirty-seven thousand men, under an indifferent commander. As a result, Perseus won a considerable success in a cavalry battle, and the Romans did nothing to restore their prestige. Perseus, knowing the risks that he ran, once more offered to treat, but was rebuffed. The next year, although Rome's fortune improved somewhat, she won no victories. A third year followed with only minor successes.

Such a stalemate was certain, under the circumstances, to have serious repercussions among the Roman allies. Signs of dissatisfaction began to appear. Eumenes himself seems to have had negotiations with Perseus, although he tried to conceal the fact and clung to the Roman side. Prusias of Bithynia, who was under no obligations to the Romans, openly suggested a negotiated peace. From later developments we may judge that there was evidence of disloyalty among the Aetolians, and perhaps among the Achaeans also. The Rhodians, who had preserved neutrality, decided to offer their mediation between the contestants. To maintain her credit and to end a costly struggle, Rome had to take the war seriously in hand.

### *The Fall of Macedonia and the Third Settlement of the Greek World*

The campaign of 168 showed that she was at last awake to the seriousness of her task. The consul Lucius Aemilius Paullus, who was put in command of the Macedonian theater of war, was an able leader, with a tolerance toward Greek ways reminiscent of the Scipios and Flamininus. At the same time the army was adequately reinforced. Immediately matters took a turn for the better. Operating from Thessaly, Paullus by a brilliant maneuver forced his way into Macedonia, and in June, 168, Perseus met him in battle near the coast town of Pydna. The result was a complete Roman victory, the entire Macedonian army being destroyed or scattered. Perseus fled, but was soon captured and in a few days all Macedonia was in the hands of Paullus.

It now remained for the Romans to make yet another attempt to settle the Graeco-Macedonian question. In Macedonia their decisions were radical, but not oppressive. Although Perseus and his family were dethroned, Macedonia was not made a province. Instead, it was divided into four republics, none of which were to allow rights of commerce or marriage to citizens of the others. The Macedonians were to pay to Rome, in lieu of a war indemnity, half the tribute which they had been accustomed to pay to their kings. For reasons not understood now, the royal gold and silver mines were temporarily closed, while the exportation of timber and the importation of salt was forbidden. As the Macedonians had never had a republican form of government, the arrangement may have been ill-suited to them, but it seems to have worked reasonably well.

In Greece, however, no such moderation was shown. The Romans were still unwilling to annex Greek territory, but they were thoroughly exasperated at what they felt was treachery and ingratitude on the part of many of the Greek people. Hence they determined to teach these turbulent protégés a lesson. A reign of terror ensued, the pro-Roman party everywhere perpetrating judicial massacres of Macedonian sympathizers among their fellow citizens. In Aetolia alone, five hundred were slaughtered. While the Achaean League had shown itself officially loyal, it seems, there had been individual exceptions. Acting on the advice of the unscrupulous Callicrates, the Romans deported to Italy one thousand of the most prominent men of the Achaean Confederacy, among whom was the historian Polybius, pretending that they were to be tried for treason to the Roman cause. Actually, no effort was made to try them, but they were interned in Italy for seventeen years.

Upon Epirus was inflicted the greatest punishment. The nature of the offense is not clear, but it was evidently considered far blacker than anything perpetrated by the other states. Acting on orders from the Senate, Paullus in a single day rounded up 150,000 captives — nearly the whole population of the country — and sold them as slaves.

Nor did Eumenes II and the Rhodians win complete immunity. The former had been the recipient of many favors from Rome, and in the hour of her need had attempted to play her false. Although he was still allowed to rule, he never regained favor. He was forbidden to come to Rome to plead his own cause, and when he sent his brother Attalus, the Senate tried to incite the latter to conspire against him. Attalus refused to take advantage of his brother's plight, but Prusias of Bithynia and other neighbors were not so considerate. As soon as they found that Eumenes was out of favor, they hastened to attack him, and the last years of his reign were stormy ones. Rhodes was ingeniously punished by the erection of a free port at near-by Delos, where the shipowners could land and transship cargoes without paying the customs duties and harbor dues which the Rhodians charged. In a short time the revenues of Rhodes from these sources had shrunk from 1,000,000 drachmas a year to 150,000. Henceforth the Greeks could no longer doubt who were their masters.

At the same time the Roman citizen body received a tangible reward for its sacrifices and exertions in recent wars. In 167, the income from indemnities, spoils, provincial tributes, and other sources had so filled the treasury that the *tributum*, or land-tax paid by Roman citizens, was abolished, not to be re-established until four and a half centuries later. It was for them a cogent proof that imperialism could be made to pay dividends.

## The Roman Provinces (200–167 B.C.)

While the Romans were establishing their hegemony in the East, they were not neglecting the task which they faced as lords of the western Mediterranean shores. There the first half of the second century B.C. found them engaged in setting up new provincial governments, and in reducing to order the peoples of the lands over which they had already asserted their authority. During the whole of the period, Sicily seems to have been quiet and prosperous under the system of government established for her in 227 and 210, but Cisalpine Gaul, Corsica, Sardinia, and Spain all had to feel the weight of the Roman arms, and to be introduced to Roman methods of administration.

### *The Reconquest and Romanization of Cisalpine Gaul*

When the Second Punic War closed, all that remained of Rome's previous conquests in the Po Valley were the colonies at Placentia and Cremona, and in 201, the former of these was wiped out by a native uprising. But as soon as possible after the close of the war, the Romans began the tedious and laborious task of reconquering the Po region. In a series of campaigns extending from 197 to 187, the power of the Gauls was broken. The Cenomani, whose lands lay north of the Po and just west of Venetia, returned to their former Roman allegiance. The Insubrians, whose capital was Mediolanum (Milan), submitted to a harsh treaty which forever excluded them from the hope of attaining Roman citizenship, while the Boii, who lived south of the Po, seem to have left the country and migrated into central Europe. Everywhere the Roman state acquired large tracts of land which could be used for the settlement of colonists.

On the south side of the Po were founded a series of Roman and Latin colonies among which were Bologna, Mutina (Modena), and Parma, while Cremona and Placentia each received large reinforcements. To connect these new settlements with Rome, the Aemilian Road was built northwestward from Ariminum (the terminus of the Flaminian Road) to Placentia. This road was so important a factor in the development of the region through which it passed that a portion of this district still bears the name of Aemilia. In time other roads pierced the lands beyond the Po. Ditches were dug to drain the swamps, and in general the reclamation works of the Etruscans were revived. Much of the Roman public land was not settled as formal colonies, but was granted in small tracts to individual Roman and Latin settlers. By degrees the remaining Gauls were

*Bettmann*

ROMAN SIEGE CATAPULT

either pushed out or absorbed, and the Latin language and culture completely dominated the province. Thus the Po Valley became a cultural annex of peninsular Italy, and it has remained so ever since. In later times it was to furnish Rome with tough, virile soldiers, and with several of her greatest writers, including the poets Catullus and Virgil and the historian Livy.

But the process of rounding out the frontier of Italy did not stop there. To the east were the Veneti, who had been Roman allies for more than a century. With them she had no trouble, for the alliance continued until, in the first century B.C., they became Roman citizens. But they needed her protection against their neighbors, the mountaineers of the Alps and the coastal tribes of the adjacent peninsula of Istria. To check these marauders, the Romans, in 181, founded the Latin colony of Aquileia, and waged a series of wars which ended with the conquest of Istria.

### *The Ligurians, Sardinians, and Corsicans*

Because of the mountainous nature of their country, the Ligurians were an even more persistent problem than the Gauls. Wars against them went on throughout the first quarter of the second century, and were marked by great cruelty and many alternations of success and failure on both sides.

Ambitious Roman generals attacked them merely for the purpose of gaining a military reputation, and made such ridiculous claims of victories that the phrase "a Ligurian triumph" came to be a synonym for empty pretense. After 180, when the consuls deported forty thousand Ligurians from their homes to a deserted tract in Samnium, they ceased to be a major problem.

Up to this time Sardinia and Corsica had never been thoroughly conquered by either the Carthaginians or Romans. Their pacification was a slow process, impeded by the stupidity, cruelty, and rapacity of some of the praetors whom the Romans sent out to the province. Beginning about 181 B.C., a series of native uprisings convulsed both islands for five years, and for a time required the presence of a consul with two legions of soldiers. At length the able Tiberius Sempronius Gracchus subdued Sardinia, whose inhabitants he punished by doubling their tribute. Corsica remained unsettled until 163 B.C.

### *The Spanish Wars and Provincial Government*

By far the most troublesome of the Roman provinces were those in Spain. There, as the result of the victories of Scipio Africanus, Rome fell heir to the possessions of Carthage, and she had either to retain them or see them reoccupied by Carthage. Her troubles in governing these arose equally from the nature of the country and that of the people. Except in the Ebro Valley of the northeast and in the area now called Andalusia, it was almost entirely a land of mountains and of high, desolate plateaus. Yet its mineral wealth was fabulous — gold, silver, copper, mercury, and iron — and in the southern river valleys was fertile soil capable, when cultivated, of producing large crops of grain, olives, and grapes. Except in the districts penetrated by the Carthaginians, the people were barbarians of various races and tongues, whose only effective units of political organization were the clan and the tribe. They did not always make a good record when fighting by ordinary methods, but they were tricky and dangerous guerrillas, who harassed their enemies with raids, skirmishes, and ambushes. The very instability of their institutions helped to bewilder their enemies, for when a tribe was beaten and had to make a treaty of submission, it would quickly dissolve. Then its component parts would reorganize into new and totally unrecognizable political units, which would renew the fight. Nowhere were the powers of Roman generalship so severely taxed, and nowhere else did Roman armies make so poor a showing.

In 201, Rome held only the eastern coast of Spain and the valley of the Guadalquivir River in the south, and she may have intended to go no farther with the conquest. But the free barbarians of the interior raided the provincial lands and stirred up rebellions among the inhabitants. Hence arose punitive expeditions, which could be effective only when they led to the extermination or conquest of the offenders. Here again was the traditional Roman dilemma of defense ending in conquest which in turn gave rise to new wars of defense on behalf of her new subjects, but in Spain it was far harder to deal with than elsewhere. In the end it had an unfortunate influence upon the character of the Roman officials involved. As they dealt with inveterate treaty-breakers, they too learned to break treaties when it suited their purposes. With the provincials, whom they no doubt felt to be secretly disloyal, they adopted methods of shocking brutality. Many a praetor saw, amid the riches of this far-off land, endless opportunities to enrich himself by trickery and spoliation, and no doubt acquired something of the attitude expressed by the modern proverb, "the ten commandments do not exist east of Suez." Harshness and injustice on their part bred new and bitter revolts. All combined to give Spain the poorest government of any of the Roman provinces.

Not until 197 did the Romans give to their Spanish possessions a regular provincial organization. Roman Spain was divided into two parts. Of these, Hither Spain comprised a strip of land along the eastern coast stretching from the Pyrenees Mountains to a point below New Carthage, while Farther Spain included roughly the same area as the modern region of Andalusia. Each province was governed by a praetor, who was kept in office for two years instead of the customary one year.

In the same year a general revolt broke out in the Spanish provinces. In 196 Hither Spain was allotted to the consul Marcus Porcius Cato, with two legions, but although he subdued his own province, Farther Spain continued to give trouble. Gradually, the Romans, working from the latter province, pushed northward into the central plateau, and before 190 they had occupied a strip of land along the south bank of the Tagus River which included Toledo. At the same time, but much more slowly, the boundaries of Hither Spain were moved westward to the headwaters of the Ebro River. In 180–179 Tiberius Sempronius Gracchus, later the conqueror of Sardinia, governed Hither Spain with such fairness and firmness that he secured peace all along the borders. For the next twenty-five years there were no more disturbances of note, but this was only a breathing space in a struggle which was to last, with interruptions, for nearly two centuries.

Meanwhile a few attempts had been made to Romanize these provinces by planting Roman and Latin colonies. Already in 206, Scipio Africanus had founded a citizen-colony at Italica, near the site on which Seville was later to stand. Gracchus himself founded another colony at Gracchuris on the river Ebro, and in 171 a Latin colony was planted at Carteia on the southern coast, for the children of Roman soldiers and Spanish women. Three years later Corduba (Cordova) was founded on the upper Guadalquivir River. Rome had taken the first steps — although only the first — toward the conquest and Romanization of Spain.

# 13

## *Conquest Replaces Domination: Roman Foreign Relations (167-133 B.C.)*

### THE HELLENISTIC EAST IN VASSALAGE AND DECLINE

#### *A New Roman Foreign Policy*

WITH THE OVERTHROW of the Macedonian monarchy and the ensuing punishment of its real or fancied Greek supporters, a new era opened in Roman foreign relations. For about seventeen years after these events, the peace was disturbed only by a few minor frontier wars. But about 150 B.C. there began a new series of wars and diplomatic crises involving Macedonia, Greece, and Carthage. In the settlements which grew out of these disturbances the Romans, while not everywhere abandoning their old policy of indirect control over their foreign satellites, came more and more to use strong, brutal methods and in several cases substituted their provincial system for the earlier protectorates. In the Hellenistic East, Roman interference, barbarian invasions, and native rebellions against the Greeks accelerated the decline of the Seleucid and Ptolemaic kingdoms, and helped to bring about a sharp decrease in the area dominated by the Hellenistic culture. These topics, together with the expansion of the Roman provincial system in Spain, form the subject matter of the present chapter. Because a knowledge of conditions in the Hellenistic world helps one to understand many of the events here narrated, we will give it full consideration.

#### *The Seleucid State under Seleucus IV and Antiochus IV*

The Treaty of Apamea struck a heavy blow at the Seleucid state, but did not by any means destroy its independence. As we have seen,[1] it definitely

[1] Chapter 12.

removed Asia Minor north of the Taurus Mountains from Seleucid control, and moreover, its repercussions were felt throughout the dominions of Antiochus III. The Greek and Iranian rulers upon whom Antiochus had imposed his suzerainty took advantage of his defeat to resume their independence, thus undoing most of the work which he had performed during his great eastern expedition of 212–204. However he still controlled Media and other provinces along the western edge of the Iranian plateau, and with them Babylonia, Mesopotamia, Syria, Palestine, and Cilicia. Under favorable circumstances he and his successors might hope to build up within these lands a strong and virile kingdom. But the fates and the Roman Senate had disposed otherwise, and within fifty years after the loss of Asia Minor the Seleucid power had shrunk to a mere shadow of its former greatness.

Antiochus III did not live long after his defeat at Magnesia. In 187, he was killed while attempting to seize a temple treasure in the Iranian province of Elymais. His son and successor Seleucus IV (187–175) undertook to restore the strength of the state by refraining from costly foreign ventures and by pursuing a program of peaceful internal development. He carefully avoided all disputes with the Romans, and with this end in view, refrained from participation in the troubled diplomacy of the Mediterranean world. This careful policy was beginning to bear fruits when, in 175, Seleucus was murdered and the kingdom threatened with a war of succession. He left two sons, of whom Demetrius, the elder, was at that moment a hostage at Rome, and the younger, Antiochus, was a mere baby. But Seleucus also left a brother, Antiochus, who had been for some years a hostage at Rome and was now at Athens. With the aid of Eumenes II of Pergamum the uncle seized the vacant throne which by right belonged to his nephews.

Antiochus IV (175–163) is known to many in the Christian world as a persecutor of the Jews; but this is merely magnifying one incident in his reign to the exclusion of other and more important ones. Personally he was a mixture of energy, ability, and spectacular personal eccentricities. He had a coherent policy for the strengthening of his kingdom, which, given an opportunity, might have done much for it. Realizing that a prime source of its weakness lay in the heterogeneous character of the population and their lack of any common rallying point for the building of patriotic sentiments, he attempted to find remedies for these deficiencies. To secure a more uniform culture among his subjects he pursued an aggressive program of Hellenization, refounding a number of decayed Hellenistic cities, and reorganizing on Greek lines Asiatic cities in which the natives had been deeply influenced by Greek culture. This policy brought him into a conflict with the Jews, of which more will be said presently. To promote a common patriotism he sponsored worship of himself as a god, assuming the title of *theos epiphanes*, or "God in Human Form."

### *Egyptian Wars: The Circle of Popilius*

During the reign of Antiochus IV the century-old rivalry of the Seleucids and the Ptolemies broke out again. The ministers of his nephew, the young Ptolemy VI, planned to attack Antiochus with a view to the recovery of Palestine and southern Syria, but he forestalled them and, in 169, invaded Egypt. Ordinarily he would have had to fear the interference of the Romans, who were determined that the Seleucid power would never again grow strong, but they were now busy with the Third Macedonian War and could do nothing. Breaking the frontier defenses of Egypt, Antiochus reached Memphis and captured his nephew. The Alexandrian mob, which often intervened in times of political crisis, then set up a younger brother of the captive as Ptolemy VII. Antiochus, thinking that he could promote a civil war between the brothers without further exertion, released his prisoner and withdrew, but they disappointed him by agreeing to rule jointly. The next year he returned and besieged Alex-

*Bettmann*

ROMAN SOLDIERS IN BATTLE

*Relief from the Great Ludovisic Sarcophagus*

andria. By now, however, his opportunity to conquer Egypt had gone, never to return. The Battle of Pydna had ended Rome's preoccupation with Macedonia, and she was now free to act. A senator named Popilius Laenas visited Antiochus, with an order that he immediately withdraw from the Nile Valley. When Antiochus asked for time to consider the matter, Popilius drew a circle around him in the sand with his staff, and bade him return an answer before he quitted the circle. Realizing that he could never stand against the might of Rome, Antiochus swallowed the insult and withdrew. It was plain that the Roman Republic was now the arbiter of the destinies of the remaining Hellenistic states, and that they were free only to the extent that she chose to let them be.

### *Antiochus IV and the Jews: the Maccabean Revolt*

The struggle with the Jews, which left so deep a mark upon their subsequent history, was an outgrowth of Antiochus' policy of Hellenization. They had been in close contact with Greek civilization since the days of Alexander the Great, and it had made a strong impression upon them. Even in Jerusalem and its neighborhood the Greek language was widely understood, and among the colonies of Jews who had settled in Alexandria and other Hellenistic cities outside of Palestine it had entirely displaced the Hebrew and Aramaic tongues used by their ancestors. Greek names were common, even among the priests of Yahweh at Jerusalem, and a rage for Greek fashions had grown up among the Jerusalem aristocracy.

It had always been a Seleucid policy to transform the temple-states into Hellenistic cities whenever possible, and there were strong reasons for doing so in this case. With a hostile Egypt as a permanent neighbor, the presence of an imperfectly controlled temple-state on this perilous border was not to be tolerated, and it seemed that no great difficulty would be encountered in transforming it into a Hellenized city-state. To accomplish this, it was necessary to uproot the narrow and exclusive Jewish religion, and this Antiochus determined to do. Yahweh's temple was to be turned over to the worship of the Olympian Zeus, and the Jewish law was to be cast aside. As evidence of the change, all Jews were ordered to eat pork whenever called upon to do so.

A large portion of the Palestinian Jews seemed ready to submit, among them some of the priests. But the more scrupulous ones, particularly a sect called the *Chasidim* ("Pure Ones"), stood firm. A priest named Mattathiah and his five sons began a rebellion against the king, massacring many apostate Jews, and collecting a band of outlaws to aid them. One of the sons, Judas Maccabaeus, assumed command of the movement, and defeated several detachments of the royal troops. Antiochus, who was now intent upon planning a campaign in the east, could not spare the time to suppress Judas and his bands. A compromise was proposed, by which the Hellenized Jews and their stricter brethren were to live peacefully together in the land, with the worship of Yahweh restored in the Temple. Judas and his followers accepted those terms of the agreement which favored them, but refused to abide by the others.

From that time on the Maccabean movement was never entirely rooted out. Its leaders stood ready to profit by every civil war or disputed succession which rent the Seleucid state, selling their support to the highest bidder and frequently changing sides. In 161, they made a treaty with Rome, by which they gained a degree of recognition as an independent political unit. The next year Judas was killed, but in 152 his brother Jonathan was made High Priest of Yahweh, a position which made him in effect the ruler of Jerusalem and Judea. Gradually the lands subject to him and his descendants grew larger as one successful seizure or usurpation followed another, until they came to include all of Palestine and even some lands outside. Jonathan and his descendants (who are known in history as Hasamoneans) ruled Palestine until late in the first century B.C. Judaism had survived a great peril. To contemporary observers the Maccabean wars probably seemed of minor importance compared with other events of the time, but their outcome assured the future of one of the world's most important religions, and through it, helped to make possible the growth of Christianity.

### *The Later History of the Seleucid State*

Meanwhile Antiochus departed for Babylonia, Media, and Armenia, where he attempted to duplicate the exploits of his father by recovering the lost dominions of his house. After some successes, he died before coming to grips with the Parthians, his chief enemies. Demetrius Soter (162–150), a son of Seleucus IV, now seized the throne, and for twelve years strove hard to uphold the failing fortunes of his family, but in vain. His energetic measures offended many of his subjects, and aroused the jealous suspicion of the Romans and the neighboring kings. Attalus II of Pergamum set up against him a pretender, Alexander Balas, who claimed to be the son of Antiochus IV. Demetrius fell in battle, and Balas became king. He was utterly worthless, however, and in a few years was overthrown in turn by a true Seleucid, Demetrius II. From that time on the decline of the

Seleucid Kingdom was steady and rapid. The Parthians conquered the last vestiges of its Iranian possessions, and in 129 entered Babylon. The Seleucids now controlled only Syria, with an uncertain suzerainty over the turbulent Jewish state, and soon even these remnants of their dominions began to slip away. By the beginning of the first century B.C. they were powerless, and Syria had lapsed into anarchy.

*The Ptolemaic State: Problems and Sources of Weakness*

In the Ptolemaic state a similar but less drastic decline occurred. After 200 B.C., it controlled only Egypt, Cyrene, and Cyprus. As a whole the kings who followed Ptolemy IV were inefficient, and frequently vicious. Although the Ptolemies had never suffered defeat by Rome, they fell more and more under her influence and every important issue was likely to be settled as she wished. Native unrest continued, and had an unfortunate effect upon the prosperity of the country. The area of land under cultivation continually shrank, as civil wars and the inefficiency of the government caused the irrigation system to decline. The government strove to meet the hostility of the native Egyptians with a mixture of firmness and conciliation, putting down revolts with a strong hand, and endeavoring to redress the grievances which provoked them. At best this policy was only partly successful. Although commerce with the East still flourished, the income of the government declined. The monetary situation of the country — a sure index to its prosperity — grew steadily worse. The coinage of silver for domestic circulation was discontinued, and the copper coinage was debased in weight.

Dissensions rent the royal house, and produced a lurid series of conspiracies, rebellions, and murders. Thus from 164 to 145 Ptolemy VI (*Philometor* or "Mother-lover") had to defend his throne against his brother Ptolemy VII (*Physcon* or "Big-belly"). On two occasions the Romans intervened to settle the dispute, and wound up by awarding Egypt to Philometor and Cyrene to Physcon. When Philometor died, leaving a widow Cleopatra (who was also his sister) and two children, Physcon promptly married the mother, murdered the son, and became king. He then discarded Cleopatra and married her daughter. Later the injured queen drove him from Alexandria, but he took revenge by murdering the son she had borne him, cutting the body in pieces, and sending it to her as a present. In the end he was restored, and died in peace. Although not all of his successors were as repulsive as he, their annals continued to be full of civil war, vice, and crime.

### *The Decline of Hellenism: Graeco-Oriental Cultures*

As Hellenistic political power declined in Asia and Egypt, the native states and cultures became ever more aggressive. The revival of Jewish nationalism and the growing unrest in Egypt have been noted, but they were far from being the only examples. About 130 B.C., the Sacae, a horde of nomads from the Steppes, overran the Greek Kingdom of Bactria, and obliterated all traces of Hellenism in eastern Iran. We have seen how the Parthians conquered the Seleucid possessions in western Iran and the Tigris-Euphrates Valley. They were not consciously hostile to Greek civilization, for Greek cities like Seleucia on the Tigris continued to exist in their dominions, and they even made official use of the Greek language. But they ceased to give to the Hellenistic element that active support without which it was sure to be submerged by the mass of the Medes, Persians, and the Semites among whom it was planted, and although Hellenism lingered a long time in favored spots, it ultimately succumbed. Only in the Indus Valley did a semi-Greek state manage to prolong its existence far down into the first century B.C. Armenia had never been colonized by Greeks to any appreciable extent. Between the Parthian frontier and the borders of Syria there grew up a series of small oriental kingdoms — Adiabene, Osrhoene, and Commagene. Thus, in southwestern Asia the area of strong Hellenistic influence was contracted until it included only Syria and the coast of Palestine.

In eastern and central Asia Minor there had grown up a curious Graeco-Oriental culture, represented by the states of Bithynia, Pontus, Cappadocia, and Armenia. The royal families of these states, while not of Greek descent, spoke the Greek language and tried to appear as Greeks to the outside world. They employed Greeks in their service, and founded Greek cities in their dominions. Bithynia, where the native culture resembled that of the Greeks, became thoroughly Hellenized, but in the other states, where kings and aristocracies were of Persian descent, Hellenism remained a veneer. Oriental methods of government, polygamy, emotional religions, and many other features all showed that they belonged to the East rather than to the West.

### *Pergamum*

The Kingdom of Pergamum, after the troubled years of the crafty Eumenes II, saw better days with the accession of his brother Attalus II in 159. The new king was ideally suited to his position as a Roman vassal.

While not offensively subservient like some of the other Hellenistic kings, he took good care never to offend the Senate, and always loyally performed his obligations. On matters in which the Romans had no interest, he pursued an independent policy. They supported him by diplomatic means in a war which he fought with Pontus and Bithynia, and he made a victorious peace. At home he developed the resources of his kingdom and increased its prosperity. When he died in 138, he was succeeded by Attalus III, an illegitimate son of his brother Eumenes and the last sovereign of the Pergamene house. The five years of his reign were enough to reveal him as a thrifty financier and progressive agriculturist, with a marked strain of personal eccentricity. At any rate he took a step hitherto unprecedented when he bequeathed his dominions to the Roman people. Of this famous will and its fateful consequences more will be said in another place.[1]

## The Final Subjection of Macedonia and Greece

### *Macedonia a Roman Province*

As a whole, the governments established in Macedonia in 167 were more successful than might have been expected. Although born of a great national calamity, and foisted by a foreign enemy upon a people unaccustomed to self-government, the four republics into which the country had been divided functioned reasonably well for fifteen years. During this time the Roman Senate seems to have treated them indulgently, for in 158 it granted them permission to reopen the gold mines, and later permitted them to coin their own money.

But many years of peace would have been required to give this system of government any real strength, and about 150, the peace was rudely broken by the appearance of a pretender to the vacant throne. A certain Andriscus, who claimed to be Philip, the son of Perseus, appeared and laid claim to the heritage of his alleged ancestors. For many years he had been engaged in unsuccessful agitation, and had on one occasion been captured and sent to Rome. He escaped, raised an army in Thrace, and invaded Macedonia. Either from real distaste for him or because they feared the Romans, the republics resisted, but he defeated two of them and secured the submission of the remainder. A small Roman force which tried to unseat him was defeated and its commander was killed.

The Romans now took the matter seriously in hand. In 148, they sent out an army of two legions under the command of the able Quintus

[1] Chapter 15.

Caecilius Metellus, who soon overthrew and captured the pretender. It now seemed unsafe to re-establish the previous form of government, and the Romans took the only other step possible when they declared Macedonia a province. It was to be administered by a governor of praetorian rank, who was also to have charge of their possessions in Illyricum and Epirus. The republics were of course not re-established, but the other arrangements made in 167 were left intact. A Roman army now protected the vulnerable northern frontier of Macedonia, and the Egnatian Road, the oldest Roman road east of the Adriatic, was built across the country from west to east. Macedonia was the first regularly organized Roman province in the Hellenistic world.

### *The Achaean Revolt: the Settlement of the Greek Question*

It was not long before the Greek question had to be dealt with in an equally decisive fashion. The removal of the Achaean political prisoners to Rome in 167, had temporarily cowed the faction opposed to Callicrates, and for some years he swayed the Achaean League unopposed. Relations with Rome were outwardly friendly, for every command of the Senate was punctually obeyed. But the calm was deceptive. As years passed and the prisoners were neither tried nor released, it became apparent that the Romans had no real charges to bring against them, and the injustice with which they were treated aroused the indignation of their fellow countrymen. The support given Callicrates by the Romans added fuel to the flames, for he was everywhere despised as a traitor. At last, in 151, the three hundred surviving Achaean political prisoners were released and allowed to return home. While they seem not to have taken any part in subsequent anti-Roman agitation, their presence served to remind their countrymen of the great wrong which had been done them, and so increased the tension. The next year Callicrates died, and the last bond which held the Achaeans in subjection seemed to have been snapped. The stage was now set for the final act of the Greek tragedy.

Throughout continental Greece the hatred of the lower classes against Rome had now risen to fever heat, and after the death of Callicrates they gained control of the Achaean League. For this the Romans themselves were largely to blame. The men whom they had so long imprisoned were the natural leaders of the upper class, whose absence, of course, favored the rise of the masses to power. This trend was further helped by Rome's connection with the despised Callicrates. Two demagogues, Diaeus and Critolaus, now forged to the front, and began a campaign of deliberate provocation against the Romans.

Sparta, too, was never a willing member of the League, and the Romans had always endeavored to mediate in her favor. In 150, the Spartan separatist movement flared up again, and in his efforts to repress it, Diaeus so alienated the Senate that it decided to teach him and his supporters a lesson. Because of involvements in Spain, Africa, and Macedonia, it allowed the matter to drag on for three years, and then sent an embassy to Greece to announce that not only Sparta, but Corinth, Argos, and two other cities were to be detached from the League. The Achaeans insulted the embassy, and refused redress for the outrage. Both sides prepared for war.

Such a contest could only end in an overwhelming Roman victory, but to the last minute the Romans strove to avoid it. Metellus, who was still in Macedonia, sent envoys to try to effect a settlement, but in vain. The Achaeans, made confident by the knowledge that they enjoyed the support of the Boeotians and Euboeans, collected an army and advanced north of the Isthmus. Metellus moved southward, while another Roman army under the consul Lucius Mummius crossed over from Italy. The war was quickly over. Metellus defeated and killed Critolaus, while Mummius administered a final and crushing blow to another Achaean force near Corinth. Corinth itself was taken in 146.

This time the Senate determined to settle the nagging Greek question permanently by a severe example. Corinth, the city in which the embassy had been insulted, was sacked, all of its inhabitants who had not fled were sold into slavery, and the city itself was destroyed. For another century the site of Corinth remained desolate. Its art treasures became the spoil of the victors. Polybius, who was present, told of seeing Roman soldiers using priceless paintings as dice-boards. Another story was that Mummius, who was entirely ignorant of artistic matters, contracted with certain shipmasters to transport the finest of the captured statues and paintings to Rome, and inserted into the contract a clause, "that if any of them were lost, destroyed, or damaged in transit, the carriers must replace them with others equally valuable."

Although continental Greece might now have been made a province, this step was not taken. The settlement of its affairs in 146, while more drastic than any preceding one, was like them, based upon a desire to leave the Greeks as much freedom as they seemed capable of putting to good use. Persons who had fought or plotted against Rome were executed and their goods confiscated. The Boeotian, Euboean, and Achaean leagues were dissolved, and their member-states contracted individual alliances with Rome. Greeks were not allowed to hold real estate or transact business in more than one city. Each state had to adopt an aristocratic constitution, and abolish its popular assembly. The propraetor of Macedonia was made responsible for the maintenance of order and the settlement of disputes. In a few cases tribute may have been levied in lieu of war-indemnities. While the settlement was in progress, the historian Polybius, who had great influence at Rome, acted as a disinterested mediator between the Greeks and their conquerors, and mitigated the hardships which his countrymen would otherwise have had to suffer.

Although the individual Greek cities retained the power of self-governing commonwealths, they had lost the last traces of real independence. Yet, sad as was their fate, it is hard to pity them. It was the natural culmination of several centuries of wars, revolutions, conspiracies, and betrayals of the national cause through the alliances of Greeks with foreign enemies. Even after the Romans began to interest themselves in their affairs, the Greeks might still have retained a large measure of self-government if they had used it well. But they had persisted to the last in a series of senseless disputes, in which one side or the other was constantly soliciting Roman intervention. It was this course which had gradually chilled the generous enthusiasm that men like Flamininus and the Scipios had felt for the cause of Greek independence. It was a Greek, Callicrates, who reduced his people to the position of vassals to the Romans. As the Romans were forced to use ever stronger and more brutal methods in their efforts to solve the Greek tangle, the Greeks only stiffened their necks and hardened their hearts. The last independent gesture of the Achaean League was to declare war upon the Greek cities of Sparta and Heraclea. Only when the foreigners had completely subjugated them did the Greeks unwillingly sink into a state of peace.

## The Third Punic War and the Fall of Carthage (149–146)

### *The Revival of an Old Feud*

The year which saw the destruction of Corinth also witnessed the end of Carthage and the organization of its territories as a Roman province. Fifty years elapsed between the end of the Second Punic War and the beginning of the Third, and during much of this time the old feud between Rome and Carthage had appeared to be dead. But in the minds of the Romans, at least, it had only been dormant, and when at length it broke out again, the result was a fight to the death.

In the generation which followed the flight of Hannibal, Carthage, although shorn of her foreign empire, was still prosperous. The Romans were so little interested in commerce and finance that they had offered no serious competition to her trade, and the failing Hellenistic world was in no position to do so. In addition to commerce, her agriculture still flourished as of old. Political power was in the hands of the oligarchic party, which was friendly to Rome, and it lost no opportunity to display its good will. In the wars against Macedonia and Antiochus III, Carthage had aided the Romans, and her conduct had on all occasions been scrupulously correct. On the Roman side the fear and hatred generated by the great peril of the Second Punic War still lingered, but in time this too might have been dispelled had it not been for the disturbing influence of Masinissa.

### *Carthaginian-Numidian Relations*

The fifty years which followed the Battle of Zama had witnessed a great transformation in the Numidian state. Masinissa's masterful and statesmanlike rule had resulted in its thorough unification and had promoted the cultural advancement of his people. Agriculture took the place of herding as a means of livelihood, and cities grew up. But above all he was ambitious to gain new lands, and in this enterprise the Carthaginians were the most likely victims. Hence the relations of Numidia and Carthage resolved themselves into a long series of aggressions on the one hand, and of unsuccessful appeals to Rome on the other.

This situation grew out of two clauses in the treaty which ended the Second Punic War. The first provided that Carthage should return to Masinissa all lands which either he or his ancestors had ever held, and the second forbade Carthage to wage war, even in Africa, without Rome's consent. Both provisions were made for Masinissa's advantage and he did not fail to use them. One by one he gathered in the isolated Carthaginian cities along the North African coast from Cyrenaica to the Atlantic Ocean, and then began to encroach upon the block of land immediately behind Carthage herself. The victim's repeated appeals to Rome brought senatorial commissions to arbitrate the disputes, but the decisions were uniformly in favor of Masinissa. By far the greater part of the territory left to Carthage in 201 was thus seized before the Carthaginians were finally driven to desperation. Some of them, seeing the hopelessness of the situation, began to favor coming to an understanding with their tormentor, but the popular party, regaining power, exiled the advocates of the pro-Numidian policy. The fugitives fled to Masinissa, who ordered them restored to Carthage. War ensued in 150, and Carthage suffered a crushing defeat. However, in appealing to arms without Roman authorization the Carthaginians had broken the treaty of 201 and were thus at Rome's mercy.

### *"Carthage Must be Destroyed"*

At Rome the feeling against Carthage had recently been growing stronger and its chief exponent was Marcus Porcius Cato. His motives, in spite of much speculation in both ancient and modern times, must remain a mystery, but there can be no doubt about his feelings. In 153, he had been sent to Carthage as an envoy, and while there had been greatly impressed by her wealth and the size of her population. On his return he reported to the Senate that Carthage was a potential danger to Rome and ought to be destroyed. Failing at first to gain his point, he is said to have closed every speech, whatever the subject, with the statement "and furthermore, Carthage should be destroyed." In spite of the influence of the Scipios, who urged a more generous policy toward a fallen rival, he finally convinced the Senate. Hence when Carthage, after her defeat by Masinissa, sought pardon for her breach of the existing treaty, she encountered a thoroughly hostile attitude.

### *Roman Deception: the Third Punic War (149–146)*

The Romans were determined to destroy the wealth and power of Carthage, but they wished to do so without the trouble of a war. Hence they adopted a policy which, while technically justifiable, made this one of the blackest chapters in their history. They mobilized an army and then sent envoys to Africa to demand redress for the offense which the Carthaginians had committed. The latter in terror asked how they could gain pardon and were told that it might be had by making proper amends. The Carthaginians gave three hundred hostages to the Romans and surrendered all their arms. When at last it seemed that they had deprived themselves of all power of resistance, the Senate delivered its decision. Carthage must be destroyed, but the inhabitants might rebuild their city wherever they wished so long as it was at least ten miles from the sea.

This dishonorable jockeying failed of its purpose. When the Carthaginians found that they had been tricked, they rose up with the blind fury of the Semite to defend their homes. Utica and other neighboring Phoenician cities at once deserted to the Romans, but this did not deter them. By working day and night they replaced the arms and armor which they had surrendered. Noble women willingly gave their hair to be made into strings for bows and catapults. When at last the consuls of 149, Censorinus and Manilius, were ready to attack the city, it was as strong as before and had a field army outside to send in provisions and worry the enemy.

The siege of Carthage lasted three years. Censorinus and Manilius were poor generals, and their attempts to storm the city or starve it into submission were repeatedly baffled. Masinissa, now ninety years old and near death, was apathetic and gave no aid to his Roman suzerains. Hasdrubal, the commander of the Carthaginian field army, inflicted several minor defeats upon the besiegers. Indeed matters might have been worse for the Romans, had they not at that moment received competent guidance from their countryman Scipio Aemilianus, the son of Aemilius Paullus and the adopted grandson of Scipio Africanus. Happening to be in Africa as the executor of the will of Masinissa, who had just died, he was able on two occasions to rescue the Roman army from imminent danger.

### *Scipio Aemilianus and the Fall of Carthage: Africa a Province*

When the consular elections for the year 147 were held, the Roman people determined to end this costly and unseemly struggle. Scipio Aemilianus was too young to be eligible for the consulship and was seeking election as an aedile. However, he was put forward for the consulship, a special law was passed to authorize his candidacy, and he was elected. Another special law assigned him to the command of the army in Africa.

At once the Roman prospects began to improve. Military discipline was restored and a close blockade was drawn about the doomed city. An improvised Carthaginian fleet was defeated and in the spring of 146 the besiegers breached the walls. A ferocious hand-to-hand fight raged through the streets, the Romans driving the desperate Carthaginians from street to street and from house to house toward the citadel. After six days and nights of uninterrupted slaughter, the fifty thousand survivors surrendered and were sold as slaves. Carthage was burned to the ground, the fires raging for seventeen days. Her site was plowed up and sown with salt and a solemn curse was pronounced against anyone who would try to rebuild the city. The aim of Cato had been realized, but Rome had little reason to glory in her deed.

The remaining Carthaginian lands, some five thousand square miles, were divided. The Romans gave large tracts to the cities which had deserted to them and made a temporary grant to the sons of Masinissa for some grudging aid which they had rendered. The few cities which had resisted to the end were destroyed and their dominions became Roman public land. For the whole area a new province was set up with the name of Africa.

## The Spanish Wars

Although the Spanish provinces of Rome were quiet from about 179 to 154 B.C., the conditions for a lasting peace were wanting on both sides. Among the Romans there were numerous crafty, unjust, and grasping praetors who aroused the hatred of the provincials and the free natives alike. The Spanish tribesmen, to whom the plundering of weaker neighbors was a common and honorable custom, raided the provinces whenever possible. Under such conditions the wonder is that the peace lasted as long as it did.

### *The Lusitanian and Celtiberian Wars*

Beginning in 154, the praetors of Farther Spain were occupied for fifteen years in a desperate struggle with the Lusitanians, who lived along the Atlantic coast north of the Tagus River. The war began with a Lusitanian raid into the province. Three years later the praetor Galba, unable to beat the marauders in fair fight, adopted a dishonorable scheme. Having made a treaty with the Lusitanians in which it was stipulated that they were to receive lands, he first disarmed and then treacherously massacred thousands of them. Among the few who escaped was Viriathus, who became the hero of his people during the remainder of the war. Galba was later tried for his crime at Rome, but was acquitted.

Viriathus, collecting the remnants of his people, became a guerrilla leader and defeated one Roman army after another. The Celtiberians, who lived on the upper Duero and Ebro rivers, joined him, and in the end nearly all the tribes of the central plateau placed themselves under his banner. In 141, Viriathus surrounded a consular army of two legions and allowed it to escape only after extorting a favorable treaty from its commander. The treaty was at once disavowed. Three years later the Romans bribed some of Viriathus' friends to assassinate him, and Lusitanian resistance collapsed.

The Celtiberian War lasted, with one long interruption, from 153 to 133, and the fighting centered around the native stronghold of Numantia.

The first period (153–151) was marked by indecisive results, due largely to the incompetence of the Roman commanders, and by shameful treachery on the part of the praetor Lucullus. After eight years of peace the Celtiberians were again in arms, this time as the allies of Viriathus. But even after the Lusitanians surrendered, their Celtiberian allies fought on. Metellus, the conqueror of Macedonia, won some successes at the outset, but after his recall there followed a long series of disgraceful Roman disasters. The Numantians, with a force which never exceeded eight thousand men, fought off one Roman army of thirty thousand and in 137 surrounded another of twenty thousand and forced its capitulation. Its commander, the praetor Mancinus, saved his army and himself by agreeing to a treaty favorable to his captors; the Senate, however, disavowed the treaty and satisfied its sense of honor by handing Mancinus (but not his army) over to the Numantians. The Spaniards refused to be satisfied with the arrangement and the war went on.

Again the Roman populace took matters into its own hands by choosing Scipio Aemilianus, this time to the difficult post of Hither Spain. His first task was to restore discipline to his demoralized troops, and when this was partly completed he besieged Numantia with an army of sixty thousand men (late 134). The blockade continued throughout the winter, and the besieged, having exhausted their supplies, were reduced to cannibalism. At last, after a desperate defense lasting eight months, most of the survivors committed suicide, and the remainder surrendered. Numantia was destroyed.

The last important center of native resistance to Roman rule in Spain had now been taken. Only the mountainous corner of the peninsula between the Duero River, the Atlantic, and the Bay of Biscay still resisted conquest, and the Romans did not penetrate that region until after another century had elapsed. The wars of conquest had been savage and Roman governors had appeared at their worst in Spain. Service in the Iberian peninsula had become so unpopular that prospective recruits used every device to keep from being sent there. Even so, we may wonder whether the blessings of peace, order, and superior civilization may not have recompensed the provincials for their sufferings.

# 14

# *Roman Civilization (265-133 B.C.)*

## An Era of Change and Readjustment

While the Romans were winning the lordship of the Mediterranean world, they were also making drastic readjustments in their institutions, intellectual attitudes, and ways of living. Wars and conquests raised new and perplexing political problems. Changed economic conditions bore heavily upon many of the population, but presented the fortunate few with undreamed-of wealth and opportunities for enjoyment. Contacts with the more mature Hellenistic civilization acquainted them with its art, literature, philosophy, luxury, and vice, and they were forced to undertake the task of accepting the good and rejecting the bad features of this strange new world. As in every age of rapid change, violent contrasts and frequent maladjustments were to be seen between conservatives and progressives, rich and poor, Roman and provincial, free and slave. In this age were generated some of the disputes which were later to overthrow the Republic, but in it Rome also began to broaden and enrich her native civilization so as to make it worthy of an imperial people. To all these developments the present chapter will be devoted.

## Domestic and Imperial Government

In so far as the framework of domestic government was concerned,[1] the period treated in the present discussion saw few changes, except for some minor adjustments to meet new conditions or to correct abuses. Although there was no diminution in the powers of the assemblies or the magistrates, the Senate nevertheless dominated the government and did

[1] Chapter 6.

everything possible to make its position permanent. In this it encountered more difficulties from the magistrates than from the assemblies. As long wars became common and difficult administrative tasks called for continuity of policy, the state made increasing use of proconsuls and propraetors, or even of private persons to whom *imperium* had been given by special laws when occasion demanded. These persons were often left at the same post for years at a time, as we have seen in the careers of Scipio Africanus, Aemilius Paullus, Scipio Aemilianus, and Flamininus. But the Senate was fully aware of the danger that some of its members should gain undue prominence through successful tenure of such posts, and took all possible precautions against it. With few exceptions it made good its right to assign magistrates and pro-magistrates to administrative posts. For the same reason the dictatorship, with its extensive and ill-defined powers, was not filled after 202, and stringent regulations were enacted regarding the higher offices. The *Lex Villia Annalis*, passed in 180, provided that they should be held in the following order: quaestorship, aedileship, praetorship, consulship, with a two-year interval between each. Re-election to the consulship was legal only ten years after the close of the first term, and no one was eligible to it until he had attained the age of forty-two. Finally, about 150, re-election was forbidden entirely.

In other respects the senatorial aristocracy became narrow and exclusive. The Claudian Law, passed in 218, forbade senators to own ships large enough for overseas trade, and custom prohibited their lending money at interest. The only legitimate form of investment for them was in land or in domestic business ventures operated through plebeian or freedmen agents. Progressively fewer "new men" forced their way into the charmed circle, for the expense of candidacy for a curule office was high and chances of reimbursement by honest means were few. Furthermore, the magistrates in charge of an election could disqualify any prospective candidate at will. The class of businessmen which had grown up during the Second Punic War, to whom the misleading name of *Equites* (literally "horsemen") was gradually coming to be applied, was naturally loath to undertake careers which necessitated the surrender of many lucrative business connections. Family influence also played a large part in determining the outcome of elections, hence the mixed patrician and plebeian aristocracy which furnished the official personnel of the state soon came to include a nearly fixed group of families who collectively guided the policy of the government.

*Finance and Law*

State finance underwent sweeping changes. The treasury was still operated by the quaestors, but the funds which passed through their hands had increased enormously and new methods of raising money had come into use. The voluntary conditional loan of 242–241 has been mentioned; [1] and during the Second Punic War the state resorted to even more drastic expedients. Compulsory loans were levied, the trust funds of widows and orphans were borrowed by the government, and supplies were bought on credit. But victory eased the strain, and by 187 all of the war debt had been paid. Thereafter, income rose with every new victory and every new province. A modern estimate places it for the year 187, at 610,600,000 denarii, of which only 20 per cent came from the citizen-tax and the rent of the Italian public lands. The remainder was derived from war indemnities, spoils taken in war, royalties from the Spanish mines, provincial tithes, and other sources which had grown out of conquest. The same estimate places the annual expenditure at 555,000,000 denarii, of which 85 per cent was for past and current wars. Even after 167, when the land tax in Italy was discontinued, the treasury still had a handsome surplus to spend on roads and public buildings.

Law kept pace with the needs of a changing society. A science of jurisprudence, which looked beyond specific situations to the general principles of human conduct, came into existence. One of the causes of this development was the necessity for removing or modifying the primitive and archaic features of the Laws of the Twelve Tables, which still formed the basis of the Roman legal structure. In a few cases these laws were changed or supplemented by legislative enactments, but more was accomplished by reinterpretation of those which already existed.

Originally, only the pontiffs had been the interpreters of the law and the arbiters of legal procedure. However, about 250, they began to hold classes in this subject, to which any person who wished instruction was admitted, and thus a number of trained lawyers grew up outside the priestly colleges. These men acquired great influence with the magistrates, many of whom were completely untrained in either law or court procedure, and in time their opinions came to be considered a part of the law itself. Apparently it was these lawyers who designed a method by which a son could gain freedom from *patria potestas* without being disinherited, and another by which a woman could secure freedom from the perpetual legal inferiority to which custom consigned her.

[1] Chapter 11.

A second means of imparting flexibility to the law developed from the *Praetorian Edict*. It was customary for each urban praetor, upon entering office, to publish an edict stating the laws which he intended to enforce and the principles which would guide his decisions. As a rule, each incoming praetor copied almost exactly the edict of his predecessor, and so in time the text of the edict became fixed, and acquired the force of law. The *praetor peregrinus*, who dealt with suits involving foreigners of various nationalities, made a third contribution to the science of law. Much of the Roman civil law did not apply to the dealings of these non-citizens with each other — and no other single body of law could be made to do so. Hence this official had to fall back upon those elemental rules of conduct which all civilized men recognized as binding, the "law of nations." Gradually its precepts also were intruded into the Roman law, where they exerted a humanizing and civilizing force of great importance. Thus the Roman legal system was expanded, humanized, divested of archaic and useless technicalities, and transformed into a set of principles fit to govern a great empire with justice.

It was only natural that in time outstanding lawyers would undertake to sum up in book form what they knew about their subject or those parts of it in which they were chiefly interested. In a previous chapter we have seen how Appius Claudius initiated this type of literature with his *Legal Procedure*. About 200 B.C. the brothers Publius and Sextus Aelius Paetus composed a systematic exposition of Roman law which passed under the title *Tripertita*. Marcus Cato also appears to have tried his hand at the same subject. Some years after 150 B.C. the task was taken up by Mucius Scaevola, probably the greatest lawyer of his day, and the first of three men of that name to write on jurisprudence. These were but a few of the many second-century Romans who wrote upon a subject which was of as great interest to their people as philosophy was to the Greeks.

### *Municipal Government in the City of Rome*

The city of Rome had grown enormously, but its government, which still remained simple, was by now inadequate. Except for the servants and attendants of the aediles, there was no police force, and in spite of its excellent and abundant water supply, it had no fire department. In public works, however, the city was less backward. In 144, a third aqueduct was built, and Marcus Porcius Cato, while censor, let contracts for a comprehensive system of drains and sewers. In 142, a stone bridge was built over the Tiber to supplement the prehistoric wooden *Pons*

*Sublicius*. Paved streets began to appear, along with stone temples, basilicas, and colonnaded walks. It now became the custom to adorn public buildings with paintings and statues brought home as plunder from eastern campaigns. Buildings and pavements alike were usually made of the unsightly volcanic rock now called tufa, and were plastered with stucco, but concrete or travertine limestone was used occasionally. For private dwelling-houses sun-dried brick was still the commonest material. Indeed, Rome, for all her wealth and power, had no building fit to rank with the best in Capua, Syracuse, or the Hellenistic East.

### *The Latins and Italians*

Throughout the period under discussion Rome continued to be the head of a federation of Latin and Italian allies, but her relations with them changed noticeably for the worse. During the Second Punic War many of the allies in southern Italy had revolted and been reconquered, while twelve of the Latin colonies had refused to furnish their quotas of troops and had suffered punishment for the offense. Thus by the end of the war a large portion of the allied population had forfeited the good will of their suzerain, and some had lost the rights secured to them by their original treaties. But this was not all. As province after province was organized overseas, the allies had to furnish their share of troops to defend these acquisitions, while the provinces and the emoluments arising from them belonged to Rome alone. So far from being better off for their exertions, the allies were now the victims of outright discrimination. Thus, a law passed in 177 provided that in distribution of bonuses from the sale of booty, allied soldiers were to receive only half as much as Roman citizens, and in the assignment of lands in Cisalpine Gaul, citizens received ten *jugera* each, but allies only three. Roman officials came increasingly to interfere in the internal affairs of the allied communities. In short, after 200 B.C., the Latins and Italians gradually sank from the position of allies to that of subjects.

But the fault did not all lie with Rome, nor did she entirely abandon her earlier efforts to act fairly toward her former allies. While some of them were still prosperous, others were declining in population and wealth. After the close of the Second Punic War there were for many years constant calls for colonists, and in many of the colonies large allotments of land were to be had for the asking. It is not surprising that thousands of Latins embraced these opportunities, and other thousands left their homes to settle in Rome. Shortly after 200, a number of Latin cities complained that so many of their citizens had emigrated without legal authorization that they could not meet their military quotas. To relieve this condition the censors expelled thousands of Latins from Rome and sent them back to their native communities. The military quotas were likewise revised on the basis of a census, so that their obligations could be made to conform to their man-power. These acts, it will be observed, were for the benefit of the Latin cities and to the detriment of Rome. They indicate a desire to be fair, at least with the Latins. Apparently the Italians were treated with somewhat less consideration, but even they must not have experienced any striking unfair treatment. In fact, until the beginning of the land reforms of Tiberius Gracchus in 133, there was little evidence of discontent in the Federation.

### *Provincial Government*

Provincial government, as established in the lands conquered after 264 B.C., was in a sense a makeshift, designed to meet a condition which had no parallel in the Roman past. After the end of the First Punic War, when governments had to be set up in the areas taken from Carthage, the Romans pondered the matter for more than a decade, and not until 227 did they take the first steps toward the solution of their problem. At that time they erected an administrative district in their Sicilian lands and made another of Sardinia and Corsica. Two additional praetors were elected each year, one to be assigned to each of the extra-Italian districts under Roman control. In 197, when Hither and Farther Spain were organized, the number of praetors was raised to six, and one was assigned to each of the Spanish provinces. When Macedonia and Africa were made provinces, another device was adopted to provide them with governors. The Senate assigned ex-consuls or ex-praetors to them with the rank of proconsul or propraetor, and this became the rule in all provinces subsequently formed under the Republic. It had long been customary, when an official was restricted to a specific sphere of duty, to refer to it as his *provincia*. Thus Italy was often the *provincia* of one or both of the consuls. Under this arrangement, one of the praetors had the administration of Sicily assigned to him for his *provincia*, while another took Sardinia and Corsica. In time the word became associated with the territory rather than the official, and nearly lost its former meaning.

The praetor, propraetor, or proconsul had to perform his task in accordance with a provincial charter, which was drawn up by a committee of ten senators appointed for the purpose, and was then passed by the

Senate. The basic principles of such a charter were: (1) the paramount authority of Rome, as represented by her officials; (2) the unequal distribution of burdens and privileges in accordance with merit; (3) local self-government in each provincial community; and (4) in most cases, tribute instead of military and naval service.

The provincial governor represented the Roman state. With him were one of the quaestors, who had charge of the financial side of the government, and from one to three deputies (*legati pro praetore*) to perform such tasks as he might delegate to them. The quaestor was of course elected by popular vote at Rome, but the deputies were appointed by the governor who was responsible for their acts. He also took with him a group of "companions" (*comites*) of his own choosing — young Roman aristocrats who wanted to gain experience in government, to see the world, or to pick up dishonest gains.

The population of the province was carefully graded with regard to both burdens and privileges. At the top were a few communities which deserved special consideration from the Romans, often by aiding them when they invaded the country. These were called "free and allied" (*liberae et foederatae*), and their status was almost exactly that of an Italian ally, with complete independence in every sphere except foreign relations, and fixed military and naval obligations. Over them the praetor had no direct control. In Sicily only three of the sixty-five communities were thus favored, and Sardinia contained no privileged communities of any kind. Next in order were the "free and immune" (*liberae et immunes*) class, which were exempt from tribute and enjoyed varying degrees of self-government, but only as long as the Roman state so desired. Sicily contained five communities of this class.

By far the most numerous class was the "tithe-paying" or "stipendiary" communities. In Sicily, Hiero II and the Carthaginians had worked out a system of taxation based upon Seleucid and Ptolemaic practices, by which the landowners paid the state one tenth of each crop in taxes, or a fixed sum per head for livestock on pasture. To aid in the collection of the tax, the officials of each community compiled a census, but the state, instead of making collections through its own officials, farmed the task out to contractors. In each district bids were received, the highest bidder undertaking to pay the government a certain sum, which was to constitute its whole income from the tax in that community. After having paid the state the amount of his bid, he collected the tax, keeping all that he received. Let us suppose, for example, that in a certain city-state the normal expectation of income from the tribute would be about 100,000 denarii, or its equivalent in grain. *A* bids 95,000, *B*, 95,500, and *C*, 95,650. *C* is the successful bidder, and he at once pays the state the amount of his bid. He then collects the tax, which in this particular year yields 98,500 denarii. He spends 2000 denarii in making collections, so his profit amounts to 850 denarii. Government officials were expected to protect the taxpayer against fraud and extortion, and to compel recalcitrant landowners to pay.

In the East this system was based upon the theory that the state was the owner of the land, and that it collected rent rather than taxes. The Romans adopted the system because it was convenient, and disregarded its implications. Not until long afterward did they come to regard the provincial landholders as tenants and the tax as rent. In Sicily the collection was in the hands of native collectors, and for nearly two centuries we hear nothing of dishonest practices in connection with it. Later, when it was applied to the province of Asia and the collectors came to be heartless and extortionate Roman *publicani*, it acquired and deserved a bad name. In Spain, Macedonia, and some of the other provinces, each community paid a fixed sum (*stipendium*), which could be collected by the quaestor without the intervention of contractors. Thus the entire province of Macedonia paid an annual *stipendium* of a hundred talents, which was raised by the local governments. In addition the governor was entitled to certain supplies for his support, and to maintenance from the communities through which he passed.

The last category of provincial land was *ager publicus*, owned by the state and rented by the censors like public land in Italy. The tenants were usually natives, and were often the former owners of the land or their descendants. Customs duties were also collected on both exports and imports at the provincial frontiers just as in Italy, and this work was likewise let by contract. The rates were low, ranging from 2½ to 5 per cent, and no effort was made to hamper the free movement of goods.

The character of provincial government varied with the time, the place, and the governor. His power during his term of office was little short of absolute, for even when he exceeded the authority granted him by the provincial charter, he could not be called to account until he was once more a private citizen. Even if this had not been so, he was usually too far away from the home government for it to have any accurate information about his doings. He was forbidden by law to condemn Roman citizens without a fair trial, and if both parties were citizens he was expected to submit the case to a citizen jury. In Sicily there was also a measure of protection for provincials, but in some of the other provinces the governor's power over non-citizens was absolute and there was no appeal from his decisions, however cruel and unjust they might be. His temptations were as great as his authority. His power of life and death over individual provincials enabled him to reap heavy gains from false accusations and the sale of pardons, or from goods confiscated and never reported. Provincial community governments were an equally easy prey. Even allied cities found it expedient to placate him and his staff with gifts. By threatening to quarter his soldiers upon a town, he could easily wring a gift of money from it. He had no regular salary, but he could pad his expense accounts to the detriment of the Roman state. Add to this the fact that a praetor had incurred heavy election expenses in Rome and expected to have others when he stood for the consulship, and we may see why so many cases of maladministration, extortion, and corruption existed. Indeed, the wonder is that they were not more numerous. Then, too, there were many mistakes due to ignorance. Except for a few years in the Spanish provinces, the term of office was only one year, from which must be deducted the time spent in traveling to and from the province. Before a governor could become moderately well acquainted with his task, he had to resign it to his successor.

It is only fair to say that the home government made constant attempts to improve the quality of the provincial governments. The Senate on several occasions righted wrongs done in Spain, where the worst mistakes and crimes were committed, and in 148, a permanent "court of recovery" was established to try governors accused of disobedience to orders, or mistreatment of provincials. It became customary for the people of a provincial community to choose a "patron" among the senatorial aristocracy to look after their interests, and it was his duty to prosecute the complaints brought by his clients. Moreover, the general character of Roman public men did not begin to deteriorate sharply until the latter part of the second century B.C., when political strife at home had weakened the state and brought to the front a class of politicians intent only on gaining advantages for themselves and their respective parties. Until then the interests of the provincials were usually protected by the governor's integrity and sense of duty.

## Social and Economic Development

### *Disparity of Wealth and Living Standards*

One of the most striking effects of the increased power and wealth of the Roman people was the unequal distribution of this new wealth between the rich and the poor. The senatorial aristocracy acquired wealth by more or less legitimate means, despite the fact that each adult male member had to give many years of his life to the state without pay as a soldier or official. The commons, on the other hand, lost rather than gained from the performance of their official duties.

Most of the outstanding political and military leaders acquired relatively large fortunes. Scipio Africanus at the time of his death had an estate of about 1,000,000 denarii, while Amelius Paullus was considered rather poor with only 370,000. Marcus Cato, although he had been poor in his youth and was notoriously honest, had extensive holdings in land and mortgages. The middle class also accumulated fortunes of varying sizes from government contracts, speculations in the sale of spoil, rents from urban properties, and income from agricultural lands. That this wealth was not more evenly distributed among the population of Italy was primarily due to the undeveloped state of commerce and manufacturing. The rising standard of living naturally increased the expenses of the wealthy, and had Italy produced the things which they desired, these articles would probably have been purchased there. Again, if the import trade had been in the hands of Romans and Italians, its profits would have remained in the country. In some few places, such as Pompeii or the Etruscan city of Arretium, manufactures and commerce did at least partly keep pace with increasing wealth, and the result was that such places enjoyed a great and rather evenly distributed prosperity. In Rome itself a certain amount of small-scale manufacture grew up, but this was the exception rather than the rule. Italy produced hardly enough food stuffs for her own use, and the bulk of her manufactured goods came from the Hellenistic East. Hence much of the wealth gained by successful imperialism was immediately drained off to foreign lands without reaching the masses of the people at all, and its temporary presence in the country only rendered their lot worse by raising prices of the articles which they had to buy.

This disparity of wealth was reflected in living standards. The poor were unable to live better than their ancestors and were fortunate if they did not sink to an even lower level. In the second century B.C., the small farmer, for causes which will be considered presently, frequently had fewer of the necessities of life than his ancestors had enjoyed a century earlier, and many of this class sold or abandoned their lands to migrate to the cities or the provinces. Those who moved to the cities could take up handicrafts, but they faced great handicaps. Slave labor, then as always, depressed wages and built up a prejudice against manual labor. In Rome the poor were housed in rickety tenements, so poorly constructed that there was always danger of their burning or even collapsing under their own weight. At best they had only an indifferent chance to earn an honest living. At this point many of them yielded to the temptation to exploit the advantage which their presence in the city gave them as voters. Candidates for office frequently gave them free food, baths, and amusements, and the government itself undertook to see that they had an adequate supply of grain at a rather low price. Despite their precarious means of livelihood, they seemed to have succumbed to the spell of city life, so that all efforts to attract them back to the farm with offers of free land usually failed. In addition to the native Italians, Rome also attracted a large group of free Greeks, Asiatics, and other foreigners, while thousands of slaves from all parts of the Mediterranean world gained their freedom and swelled the numbers of the new urban proletariat. But the economic demoralization of this group was not completed until later, when party strife led to competitive bidding for their support.

It was the people of large and moderate fortunes who profited by the improvement in living standards. Many of their houses were built on a larger and more commodious scale than ever before. A few of them had, behind the *atrium*, an open courtyard surrounded by a complex of rooms and a cloister, or *peristylium*, which ultimately gave its name to this whole section of the house. The courtyard might be planted with grass, flowers, and shrubbery, and sometimes had a fountain in the center. Here the family could enjoy the combination of open air and privacy dear to the Italian heart, then as now, and here all of the commoner activities of family life were carried on, leaving the *atrium* for formal occasions. As early as 184 B.C., some householders had water piped into their houses from the city aqueducts, and bathrooms of the Greek type were fitted out. Well-to-do men no longer performed manual labor, but the women of the household still kept up many of their traditional activities, such as spinning, weaving, and sewing. Food became more varied, and was prepared by professional cooks — slaves who brought high prices on the market. White bread took the place of the porridge of earlier times, and bakeshops made their appearance. Silver plate and other expensive tableware came into use.

For rich and poor alike, public festivals and amusements grew ever more numerous and varied. In addition to sacrifices and religious games, other events of a purely secular character were given. Triumphal processions of victorious generals assumed great significance, and sometimes lasted several days. From Etruria or Campania came the brutal custom of gladiatorial combats, first held in Rome in 264 B.C. So slowly did this practice take hold of the Roman fancy that we hear of only three exhibitions of this kind before 200 B.C., and they did not become common until the end of the period under discussion. The first *venatio*, in which men fought with wild animals, was held in 186. Horse races, acrobatics, and theatrical performances also had their part in amusing the populace.

### *Social Life: the Family and the New Slavery*

Social customs and family life reflected the changed conditions. Women by various legal fictions made good in law the freedom which they had long enjoyed in fact, and the forms of marriage in common use were usually those which did not confer upon the husband the absolute power over his wife's person and property which he had previously enjoyed. Especially in the group which took up Hellenistic fashions, were educated women to be found, such as Cornelia the daughter of Scipio Africanus. She was a woman of high character and broad culture, who entertained visiting Greek and Hellenistic celebrities, and who had the unique distinction of having rejected an offer of marriage from one of the Ptolemaic kings of Egypt. She gave personal attention to the education of her children, providing them with Greek as well as Roman instructors. Not all of the women of the upper classes, however, took their freedom as temperately as did Cornelia. Divorce, which was unheard of before 264, was on the increase in the second century, although still relatively rare. Celibacy, with the moral looseness that usually accompanied it in the ancient world, was on the increase among men of the senatorial and equestrian classes, and the voluntary limitation of families was beginning to cause concern among thoughtful persons.

Another sign of the times was the extension of slavery. In an earlier chapter [1] we have seen how slaves were treated in early Rome. But the Punic and other foreign wars changed all that. The First Punic War threw some seventy-five thousand foreign slaves on the market, and the Second Punic War, several times as many. In the early second century the sack of Epirus alone brought in a hundred and fifty thousand. The increased numbers and foreign origin of these slaves brought about a sharp change in the Roman attitude toward them. Gradually it became customary to look upon them not as dependents but as chattels, to be used, worn out, and discarded. Prices varied enormously, from five hundred denarii for an ordinary farm laborer to perhaps three thousand for a handsome

[1] Chapter 7.

and accomplished dancing-girl, and even more for a skilled cook. Larger and larger staffs of slaves with specialized functions came to be maintained in the households of the rich. Although some might suffer mistreatment, their life in general was an easy one, and the slave usually had a good opportunity to save money for the purchase of his freedom, or to win it as a reward for faithful service.

Such was not the case with field slaves on the capitalistic farms. There a slave was not, as a rule, in personal touch with his master, and was regarded as an investment which had to yield dividends. On this point our chief authority is Marcus Cato, whose book on agriculture is a description of plantation economy. His slaves were under the personal charge of a steward (*vilicus*) and his wife, who were slaves themselves. They were to be kept busy from dawn until dark, even on religious holidays. In food and clothing they were not stinted unduly. Their ration consisted of some two pounds of wheat a day (with slightly more in summer), windfall olives, fish-pickle, vinegar, a little olive oil, and a half pint of the cheapest wine. Probably they also raised some vegetables for their own use. Every second year each man received a tunic and a pair of wooden shoes. The steward was himself under the watchful eye of his master, who insisted that he treat the other slaves justly. But these drudges had little or no hope of gaining their freedom, and Cato advised that all who were old, worn out, or ill be sold for whatever they would bring. Refractory ones were worked in chains, and on at least some estates the slaves were lodged at night in noisome underground dungeons (*ergastula*). The harshness of the new system is measured by the frequent attempts at revolt in the second century. Half-savage slave herdsmen varied their labors by robbing and murdering travelers, or ran away and formed gangs of bandits. When captured they suffered the horrors of crucifixion. The presence of this mass of human misery bred fear and distrust in Italy up to the beginning of the Christian Era.

### *The Plantations (Latifundia)*

The plantation system, of which Cato's model farm was an example, was growing in importance all over Italy, but was especially prevalent in southern Italy and Etruria. It owed its origin to various causes. When the Second Punic War ended, Rome found herself in possession of thousands of square miles of land in southern Italy, from which almost the whole population had vanished. Everywhere the war had taken such a toll of lives that few *bona fide* colonists were available, and the south-

Italian lands were much less attractive than the rich loam of the Po Valley. Hence the censors were glad to rent it out in large tracts to wealthy Romans for use as pasture or farm land. There is reason to suppose that even at that time the law forbade any individual to rent more than one thousand *jugera*, but the limit was often exceeded, or even disregarded. As the tendency was for leases to be repeatedly renewed, such lease-holds came in time to be considered private property, and were sold, bequeathed, given as dowries, or mortgaged. In central Italy the demand for military service and the gradual exhaustion of the soil on the small independent farms caused many of the owners to sell out to persons with plenty of capital, who could thus amass holdings of several hundreds of *jugera* each. Such farms could be worked with profit because of the more abundant capital, constant supply of slave labor, and progressive agricultural methods at the disposal of the owners. In Etruria, large estates had apparently always been the rule, but the Etruscan landlords were now being replaced by Romans, and the former servile peasant class by slaves.

The new type of landed estate (*latifundia*) was operated on a frankly capitalistic basis. The purpose of their owners was not to produce food and other necessities of life for family use, but rather to secure as large a cash profit as possible. With this end in view, they concentrated on profitable crops such as wine, livestock, olives, garden vegetables, and poultry. Grain was usually produced only as a secondary crop, for the use of the master and his slaves. At times both grain and clothing for the slaves might be bought in the open market, but Cato cautioned his readers that a farmer must be more inclined to sell than to buy if he were to make a profit on his operations.

Two kinds of capitalistic farms, neither of which had been common in the third century, now became increasingly prominent: the plantation and the stock ranch. Cato wrote for proprietors of estates of from 100 to 240 *jugera*, engaged principally in the culture of grapes and olives, but with numerous side crops, such as willows for basket-making. Even on such farms as this, some livestock was kept for milk, meat, wool, and the manure which they would furnish. For their feed he advised the use of clover, vetch, and other legumes, which also served to restore the fertility of the land on which it grew. If these did not last the year out, leaves were picked from the trees and stored for fodder. Wine and olive oil might be pressed out on the estate, or the olives could be sold on the tree to contractors. Such a farm required a large staff of workmen. An olive grove of 240 *jugera*, on which six oxen, four asses, a herd of swine, and one hundred sheep were also kept, required the service of thirteen persons, while

100 *jugera* of vineyard (also with some livestock) was worked by sixteen. Obviously very little effort was made to raise the efficiency of the individual worker by the use of machinery. The hoe, mattock, spade, and a crude, ox-drawn plow were employed by Cato's slaves just as they were by the small-scale, independent farmers. The greatest efficiency of the new system must be sought in the more extensive knowledge of the owners and in the natural advantages of large-scale over small-scale operations.

On the poorer lands of southern Italy relatively large stock ranches grew up, often consisting of several thousand *jugera* each. In many cases the same man owned several of these tracts, and thus could follow the old Italian custom of driving his stock to the mountain pastures in the summer, and back to the lowlands in the autumn. The horses, cattle, sheep, goats, and swine reared in this manner found a ready market in Rome and other large Italian cities, while wool, cheese, and similar products were always in demand.

We must not, of course, assume that the small independent farmers disappeared from rural Italy. In large areas where local conditions were favorable, they continued to exist in numbers, and gradually adapted themselves to the new conditions. They even continued to raise grain with profit, for although the government imported considerable amounts from Sicily, Sardinia, and Africa, this was a small portion of the total requirement, and in places located a few miles inland the cost of transportation neutralized its advantage over local grain. In fact, throughout most of Italy the local product had the market entirely to itself. The presence of *latifundia* in a neighborhood might be a positive advantage to owners of small tracts near by, for in rush seasons the ordinary staff of laborers on such estates was not sufficient, and additional workers were hired.

But the changed conditions had introduced slaves in numbers sufficient to have a profound effect upon Italian life. They gradually modified the racial character of the rural population, and formed an even greater portion of the urban proletariat. Contact with them probably influenced the character and attitude of the old Roman and Italian stock. Slavery placed a stigma upon honest labor, and hindered the progress of mechanical inventions. The children of the upper classes grew up among slave nurses and servants who must obey their every whim, and as a result lacked the self-control which had played so great a part in the character of the old-time Roman. It is possible that we may see in this fact at least one of the causes of the growing harshness and arrogance of the Roman Senate in the first century B.C. Even at best, the slave could not know and appreciate the "customs of the ancestors" which had done so much to shape the old Roman character; but instead infected the rising generation with the habits and ideas of the Orient whence most of the house servants had come. At worst, a slave found it advantageous to ease his lot by teaching his masters those vices which tend to accumulate in the lower purlieus of every long-civilized society. These influences, of course, operated unevenly, for then, as now, there were aristocratic families in which the number and influence of the servants were small, and in which the parents preserved as much as possible of the traditional virtues.

## The Birth of a New Culture

Under the impact of these influences Rome began to evolve a new culture, broader and more sophisticated than the old. Throughout the last half of the third century the demands of military service had brought large numbers of Romans into contact with Sicilian and Italian Hellenism, and after 200 B.C. soldiers and ambassadors had visited Greece and Asia Minor in much the same way. Greek immigrants, both free and slave, came to Rome, and some of the slaves were men of considerable education. Even

*Metropolitan Museum*

CYBELE

*The Great Mother of the Gods*

in the third century there were senators who took pride in their knowledge of the Greek language and literature. Conquest brought in many masterpieces of both classical and Hellenistic Greek art as spoil, and many Romans either learned to appreciate such work or affected to do so. Greek artists began to work for the Roman state or for individual Romans. Members of the great Hellenistic philosophical schools came to Rome, often as ambassadors, and captivated the intellectual coteries of the capital by the fluency of their language or the profundity of their ideas. The New Comedy was translated or imitated and gained a mild popularity on the Roman stage. Greek gods and forms of worship made even greater inroads upon the traditional Roman religion. From the East came the colorful and wildly emotional cults of the Great Mother, Ma Bellona, Isis, and Serapis, to find worshipers among the humble slum-dwellers or middle-class persons of foreign extraction.

### *Foreign Religious Influences*

Religious changes were of two kinds, official and popular. In the crises of the Punic wars the Senate constantly attempted to find new means of averting divine displeasure, and these expedients frequently took the form of adopting Greek cults and ceremonies. The Sibylline Books were often consulted, and the measures which they prescribed usually called for sacrifices to Greek gods offered according to Greek customs. Several embassies were sent to consult the Delphic Oracle. But in 204, in response to a command in the Sibylline Books, envoys were sent to Asia Minor to bring to Rome the sacred black stone which represented the Great Mother of the Gods. She was an old Anatolian divinity, worshiped by eunuch priests with wildly emotional rites. When the Romans discovered the true nature of their divine guest, they restricted her worship to a single festival each year and forbade Romans to enter her priesthood on pain of death.

Other Greek and Asiatic cults came uninvited, brought by immigrants, slaves, or returning soldiers. The orgiastic worship of Bacchus was introduced during the Second Punic War. His rites were celebrated at night, with wild excitement and drunkenness. Although the association of his cult with hopes of a blessed hereafter gained it wide popularity, charges of immoral conduct were brought against his devotees. In 185, the Senate investigated the matter, caused the execution or suicide of several thousand allegedly guilty persons, and restricted the celebration of Bacchic rites for the future. Of the other emotional cults little was heard until after the end of our period. The fact was, however, that the cold, impersonal, Roman official cults were losing their popular appeal, at least in the cities, and colorful deities, who were thought to care for the welfare of their worshipers in this life and give them eternal happiness after death, were certain to grow in popularity. The upper classes continued to give lip-service to the official cults, but some of them lost all positive religious beliefs and turned to philosophy as a substitute.

### *The Origins of Roman Literature*

It is one of the ironies of history that the father of Roman literature was a Greek freedman. When Tarentum was taken at the end of the war with Pyrrhus, Marcus Livius Salinator acquired a Tarentine slave named Andronicus, who when freed took the name of Livius Andronicus. Either before or after his manumission he entered the teaching profession, but his work was hampered by the fact that there was no reader available in Latin comparable to the Homeric poems. To remedy this defect, he translated the *Odyssey* into Latin Saturnians, an old native verse form in which each foot consisted of alternating stressed and unstressed syllables. His translation seems to have been a spiritless literal rendering, but it served its purpose so well that it was still in use two centuries later. Subsequently its author took to translating Greek tragedies and comedies into Latin, with adaptations made necessary by Roman conditions. As late as 207 he was commissioned by the state to compose a hymn to be sung in a religious procession. His importance lies chiefly in the stimulus which he supplied to the native Italians and Romans who fell under his influence, and who in many cases had far greater talents than their teacher.

A somewhat younger contemporary of Livius Andronicus was the Campanian, Gnaeus Naevius (*ca.* 270–199 B.C.), who spent most of his adult life in Rome and wrote in Latin. Naevius not only made Latin adaptations of Greek tragedies, but originated the *fabula praetextata*, an historical drama with a Roman setting. Two of his works were the *Rearing of Romulus and Remus*, and the *Clastidium*. In his later years he employed the Saturnian meter in an epic poem which he wrote on the First Punic War, a mediocre performance, at best, if we are to judge it by the surviving fragments. Yet this epic has a certain importance for the student of Virgil, because the latter drew heavily upon it when composing his immortal *Aeneid*. In the later years of the Second Punic War, Naevius incurred the displeasure of the powerful family of the Metelli, who caused him to be imprisoned. Later, he was released, and died in exile. He was the last

Latin poet to use the Saturnian meter. Increasing Greek influence caused his successors to adopt the measures long in use east of the Adriatic.

A much greater poet, whose works displayed a mature blending of Greek and Roman elements, was Quintus Ennius (239–169). He was a native of Calabria, and had become acquainted with three languages, Oscan, Greek, and Latin. He fought in the Roman army during the Second Punic War, won the friendship of several important Romans, and became a Roman citizen. His knowledge of Greek literature and philosophy must have been considerable. Like his predecessors, Ennius translated Greek tragedies into Latin, but at least in some cases he adapted them so drastically that they might almost rank as original works. Like Naevius, he wrote Roman historical plays. From the Epicureans he had imbibed a philosophic atheism, which he expounded in his prose treatise *Euhemerus*. But it was his *Annales*, a history of Rome in hexameter verse, that made him beloved by succeeding generations of Romans. In eighteen books he carried the story from the landing of Aeneas down to within a few years of his own death. It was a stately pageant, the characters delineated in heroic proportions, and the lines so catchy that over six hundred of them have been preserved as quotations, although the poem, like almost all other Roman literature up to this time, has perished. Among the extant lines may be noted one on Fabius Maximus, "One man by de-

*Galloway*

ROMAN MASKS

*Tragic and Comic*

laying saved the state," another on Manius Curius Dentatus, "Whom none could vanquish by either steel or gold," and a third on the causes of Rome's successes, "Rome's fortunes are rooted in old customs and in her men." As a pioneer in the use of Greek meters, Ennius naturally produced some lines that grate on the sensitive ear, but his rugged strength, occasionally relieved by delicate satire and frank skepticism, endeared him to the Roman people as long as they could appreciate the heroic virtues of the men of old whose praises he sang. He was not the last of the Roman tragedians, but when he died it had been demonstrated that tragic drama would never find a congenial home in Rome. The future lay with comedy.

### *Roman Comedy: Plautus and Terence*

Roman comedy first attained the dignity of true literature in the hands of Titus Maccius Plautus (*ca.* 255–184), an Umbrian whose mature years were spent in the capital. In his earlier career he had seen the seamy side of life as a stage carpenter, merchant, and laborer in a flour mill. He knew human nature at first hand, and above all, he was conversant with the tastes of the Roman theater-going public. He was credited with the authorship of 130 plays, but Roman critics listed only about twenty of unquestioned authenticity.

At first glance one might easily conclude that Plautus was no more than a translator of plays from the Greek New Comedy, for that was what he claimed to be. "The Greek name of the play is *The Ass-Driver*; Demophilus wrote it; and Maccius translated it into a foreign tongue," he says in the prologue to his *Asinaria*. Characters and plots alike were Greek, and there is much that was not only foreign to the Roman scene, but shocking to Roman sentiments. Like his originals, he usually employs stereotyped incidents and stock characters. Old men, whose traits are drawn in terms of extremes of greed or indulgence, young men in love (as Greeks understood that term), slaves, who by sly rascality help their young masters out of scrapes or speed the course of romance, "parasites" who live by their wits, greedy and depraved dealers in female slaves, boastful but cowardly soldiers, courtesans, and shrewish married women — such are the *dramatis personae* of most of his works. Romantic love in the modern sense hardly existed. In fact, Plautus' love stories have a frankly sensual character which is not surprising in countries where marriages are contracted by parents of the participants, for reasons of pure convenience. Thus far he follows his models, and the society which he describes is, if it ever existed anywhere, third-century Greek.

Yet his originality was far greater than it seemed. He was one of the greatest verbal artists in all literature. His Latin vocabulary included words of people from all walks of life — slaves, courtesans, soldiers, priests, physicians. He coined words in a manner which reminds one of modern slang — such as "tooth-crackers" for fists, "nut-crackers" for teeth, and "rod-tickler" for a slave who is often beaten. His whole technique and dramatic outlook differed widely from those of Menander and the other writers of the New Comedy. Many of the rôles in his plays were sung, while the New Comedy was entirely recited. His Greek prototypes attempted psychological analysis and character study, and in them, the plots had a fair amount of importance. But for Plautus a plot was a mere peg on which to hang a series of humorous incidents, each of which was good for a laugh without reference to the final outcome of the play. Many of his scenes might, with no more than a change of names, be transferred from one play to another without loss of unity. His humor had more of the gargantuan robustness of Aristophanes than would have found favor in refined and decadent third-century Athens. Horseplay, puns, mistaken identity, sharp tricks, beating of slaves, and similar devices amused the Roman commons upon which Plautus depended for a living.

Yet he did occasionally deviate from his usual practice. In the *Captives* he tells the story of a man whose nature had been soured and hardened by the loss of his sons, and of the self-sacrificing devotion of a slave for his master. The *Amphitruo* tells the story of the birth of Hercules in broad and vulgar burlesque. It was not patterned after the New Comedy at all, but after a variety of tragicomedy popular at Tarentum. Modern readers of Plautus may be repelled by his vulgarity, and his love stories hardly ever rise above the level of the white-slave traffic. However, in spite of these and other faults, his work has enjoyed a certain popularity in every generation from his own time to the present.

Some years after the close of the Second Punic War a young Carthaginian slave was purchased by the senator Publius Terentius Lucanus. The boy showed talent, and his master first educated him and afterwards gave him his freedom. He then assumed the name Publius Terentius Afer. Terence, as he is known to the modern world, became a favorite of the literary coterie of which Scipio Aemilianus was a member, and they protected and encouraged him. In fact, there were ill-natured rumors abroad that what passed for his plays were partly or wholly their work. He died in 159, leaving six comedies, all of which have survived.

Terence was much more dependent upon the New Comedy than Plautus. Psychological analysis and character study form a large part of his comedies, and there is little or none of the boisterous good nature and uproarious fun which we find in Plautus. His vocabulary is also less rich than that of his predecessor, but it has a purity and exactness of expression that were later to make his works a mine of striking quotations. A favorite device with him was "contamination," the transposition of a scene from one play to another. For this his critics attacked him, and he found it necessary to defend himself in his prologues.

His themes vary considerably. In the *Phormio* we see a quick-witted and obliging rascal help his two young friends gain the objects of their affections. The *Mother-in-Law* describes the clearing-up of a serious misunderstanding between a young married couple. The *Self-Tormentor* and the *Brothers* both consider the age-old theme of whether a father should be severe or indulgent with his sons, while the *Eunuch* tells the story of a courtesan's loyalty and tender care toward her adopted sister.

As pure literature, Terence's plays have always enjoyed a high reputation, but they were not especially successful on the stage. Perhaps his intimacy with the Scipionic circle, and its strong philhellenic leanings, led him to neglect the expedients employed by Plautus to make his dramas

Bettmann

SCENE FROM A COMEDY OF TERENCE

*From the Codex Vaticanus*

popular. At any rate, when the *Mother-in-Law* was presented, the audience deserted it to attend an acrobatic performance. Yet his plays have always had admiring readers, and in the eyes of later Roman critics he ranked along with Plautus as one of Rome's two great dramatists. Several other comedians are known by name, but their works have not come down to us.

### *Satire and History*

Although drama was largely an imported and exotic creation, satire was essentially an original product of second-century Rome. It was a medley of prose and verse, in which the foibles and vices of the age were denounced or ridiculed and moral principles laid down. Some of its elements go back to classical Greek literature, but the Greeks never achieved the finished product. Ennius had tried his hand at it, but the first to follow it exclusively was probably Gaius Lucilius (*ca.* 180–102). His work was divided into thirty books, in which he not only treated moral and social questions, but expressed his political views and attacked individuals of whose conduct he disapproved. About 1300 scattered lines have survived in the form of quotations by other authors, and they prove that Lucilius, while a keen critic and clear thinker, was a very mediocre poet. Not until nearly a century later did satire come into its own in the hands of the great Horace.

By 200 B.C., educated Romans were conscious of the importance of their country's past, and during the next fifty years several attempts were made to record it in writing. In the beginning, either because they looked upon Latin as a barbaric tongue or because they wished to appeal to the reading public of the Hellenistic world, most historians wrote in Greek. The first of them, Fabius Pictor, began his work with the founding of Rome, and carried it down to a point somewhere in the Second Punic War. Polybius, who had occasion to use the history as a source, says that it was disfigured by national prejudice, but that Fabius wrote with an honest desire to tell the truth. His sources, which were pontifical records, treaties, laws, family records, and oral tradition, were naturally of unequal value, the documentary evidence being in general reliable, while family records in particular were full of inaccuracies and outright falsehoods. Three other histories of Rome, written like his, in Greek, appear prior to 150 B.C., but they were poor performances, and soon dropped out of use. Meanwhile, a school of Latin historians had developed, headed by the redoubtable Marcus Porcius Cato. His work was marked by a plain and rugged style, and as a reaction against the hero worship which had for so long surrounded Scipio Africanus, he made it a point never to mention the personal name of any army commander or other public figure, but only his official title, such as consul or praetor. It is said that the only individual mentioned by name in his work was an elephant of unusual bravery in the Carthaginian army. A documentary source of some importance for later historians was formed, when Cato collected and edited about 150 of his own speeches on public questions. None of the histories written at Rome during this period have survived, but they were used by later Roman historians whose works still exist. From such quotations and from the statements of essayists and literary critics, we derive all our knowledge of these early Roman efforts at historiography.

# 15

*****************************************************************************************************

# *The Decline of the Republic (133-79 B.C.): The Era of Party Strife*

## The Dawn of the Age of Revolution

In preceding chapters an effort has been made to portray the civilization of the Roman people in the second century B.C. The year 133 ushered in a new age in which the dominant notes were strife, disorder, and political change. This troubled period was to last for a century, to sink the Roman world deeply into civil war and bloodshed, and to end with the overthrow of the Republic. It may be divided logically into three parts, each of which marks a step in the destruction of republican government and the establishment of a monarchy. The first part was dominated by a political and social struggle in which the middle and lower classes attempted to overthrow the senatorial aristocracy and deprive it of its privileged position. It ended in 79 with the triumph of the Senate and the promulgation of the constitution of Sulla. The second (79–44) saw the gradual eclipse of the political parties by the great leaders who strove, individually or collectively, to dominate the state. Its culmination was reached when Julius Caesar eliminated his rivals and gained the headship of the Republic, and it ended with his death. The third (44–30) was marked by strife between leaders who sought to take over Caesar's power, and ended with the establishment of a new form of government by his grandnephew, later to be known as Augustus. Only the first step in this process will be treated in the present chapter.

The new age was marked by a sharp change in the Roman national character. Gradually the old sense of fairness, moderation, and respect for law vanished. Aristocrats and commons alike put forth extreme claims, disdained compromise, and resorted to trickery and violence as everyday political weapons. Corruption at home and shameless oppression in the provinces prevailed. Finally came a series of civil wars in which both Romans and provincials suffered. Individualism in many instances replaced the old reverence for the "customs of the ancestors," producing brilliant but selfish and ruthless leaders who used party names, did lip service to party ideals, and committed hideous crimes for their own private ends. The Roman people were still virile, enterprising, and creative, and in such fields as literature and the fine arts their great age was yet to come. But they were rapidly losing the traits of character which had made it possible for them to carry on a republican form of government.

## The Gracchi and the Era of Land Reforms (133–121 B.C.)

### *Tiberius Gracchus and the First Land Law*

For eighty years after the Battle of Cannae the Senate was, with few exceptions, in control of the Roman government and there was no organized opposition to it. Only when crises arose which required more competent leaders than those who could be provided through regular channels did the Assembly of the Tribes assert itself, and even then there is no evidence that it did so in outright opposition to the Senate. Under senatorial leadership wars were fought, treaties made, and provinces organized. Not until new issues arose to make the Roman commons class-conscious was senatorial control challenged.

The issue which brought this era of harmony to an end was the land question, and the leader who raised it was Tiberius Sempronius Gracchus. He was an aristocrat, descended on his father's side from a long line of able plebeian senators and soldiers, and on his mother's side from Scipio Africanus. He had enjoyed a broad education, not only in war, government, and law, as became a Roman, but also in Greek literature and philosophy. In temperament he was a mixture of the idealist and the practical man, with an honest desire to aid the downtrodden poor and a shrewd understanding of his country's need for more soldiers. However, Gracchus was never a deep or logical thinker, and circumstances sometimes pushed him into steps fraught with danger for the state.

The land problem was the result of prevailing economic trends, and of the public land policy of the government, both of which have been treated.[1] As small farms gave way to large ones and free landed proprietors to slave labor, Rome acquired a large class of wretched proletarians who, under existing laws, did not own enough property to render them

[1] Chapter 14.

liable to military service. It seemed to Tiberius Gracchus that the state ought to repossess the public lands held illegally by aristocratic Romans, and to distribute them in small tracts to poor citizens. This step would at the same time relieve distress and increase the number of potential recruits for the army. In 133, when he took office as plebeian tribune, he undertook to secure the passage of a land law embodying these points.

The land law sponsored by Gracchus was carefully framed to cover all contingencies and to meet all objections. Privately owned land was not affected by it. To the public lands, he wished to apply the provisions of the Sexto-Licinian Laws of 366 B.C., with additions to meet the conditions of his own time. Each leaseholder was to be allowed to retain five hundred *jugera* of public land (or one thousand if he had two sons) and was to receive a clear title to it. All land held in excess of the lawful amount was to be surrendered, the state reimbursing the holder for improvements which he had made upon it. The repossessed land was to be granted in tracts of thirty *jugera* each to actual occupants, as hereditary inalienable leaseholds for which they were to pay the state a small rent. The law was to be administered by a board of three members chosen by popular vote.

The bill was in no sense revolutionary, but its introduction at once provoked a very bitter struggle. As the senators held most of the land to be repossessed, there was no chance of their passing the measure. Gracchus, seeing this obstacle, took the bill straight to the Assembly of the Tribes. The Senate, offended anew by this tactless act, resorted to a device which in the past had usually blocked radical tribunician measures. A colleague of Gracchus, Marcus Octavius, was induced to veto the bill. But Gracchus was very much in earnest and refused to admit defeat. Having first tried indirect pressure upon the Senate without result, he proceeded to a truly revolutionary step. Stating that when two tribunes disagreed the Assembly might judge between them and depose the one of whose policies it disapproved, he invited it to act as arbiter. The Assembly deposed Octavius from office, and the bill was passed. The commissioners chosen were Tiberius, his brother Gaius, and his father-in-law Appius Claudius.

The deposition of Octavius was a declaration of war against the aristocracy, for with it Gracchus had destroyed the only effective check which the Senate had upon the Tribal Assembly. The unprecedented bitterness of the strife which followed is explained by the fact that both contestants were playing for tremendous stakes. Many of the aristocracy faced the possibility of heavy financial loss, in some cases involving land which had been in their families' possession for generations. The Senate as a body saw its prerogatives taken over by the Assembly, and the powers of the magistrates transferred to the most popular and aggressive of the board of tribunes. For Gracchus, failure meant not only the loss of his cherished land reform, but also merciless punishment at the hands of his exasperated opponents. Hence, he adopted increasingly demagogic and radical measures as the struggle proceeded, while the Senate retaliated by granting the land commission insufficient funds and circulating the rumor that Gracchus wished to become king.

While the struggle was at its height, King Attalus III of Pergamum died, bequeathing his kingdom and personal estate to the Roman people. Gracchus at once introduced a bill reserving the personal estate of the dead king to provide funds to equip the holders of land allotments, and asserting the Assembly's right to settle the affairs of the new province. Although this proposal was not contrary to law, it had long been customary to leave such matters under the control of the Senate. It was now no longer a question of the land law, but an all-out struggle for political supremacy.

For the senators only one hope remained: Tiberius would be in office for only one year, and it was generally felt that a tribune could not lawfully hold office for two successive terms. Once he went out of office, they could nullify his acts and attack him in the law courts which they controlled. Thus, to protect himself and perpetuate his policies, Tiberius was compelled to take a further step along the path of revolution by becoming a candidate for re-election.

To the more reactionary members of the senatorial group this was the last straw, and they lost their heads completely. Led on by one of the Scipios, they formed a mob, armed themselves with clubs and staves, and fell upon Gracchus and his followers. He and three hundred of his adherents were clubbed to death. The Senate then formed an extraordinary judicial commission, which condemned to death or banishment many more of Tiberius' supporters who had escaped the first massacre. But they could not stop the work of the land commission until at least four years after it was set up, and there is evidence that it repossessed and granted out much land. At length it was deprived of its right to seize land, and for the time the program stopped. Whatever the merits of some of the Gracchan proposals, the Senate had placed itself clearly in the wrong by its violent and illegal acts, and it was later to suffer for its fault.

Perhaps the most permanent result of the tragic career of this ill-fated reformer was the emergence of the two parties whose struggle for supremacy was to dominate the political life of Rome for the major part of the following century, the *Optimates* and the *Populares*. The former was composed of members and dependents of the senatorial aristocracy, whose political and economic interests it represented. The Populares included all the elements among the Roman citizen body who wished to overthrow senatorial supremacy and to improve the lot of the lower classes by government action. Their leaders were, as a rule, discontented men of senatorial rank. The membership of these groups often fluctuated, for class interests were never as all-absorbing in Rome as in Greece, and even the common people would at times support the Optimates if displeased with the policies of the Populares. Before the introduction of the land law of 133, the Populares can hardly be said to have existed, and the Optimates were so firmly intrenched that they scarcely needed a name or party organization. But after 133, both parties remained self-conscious and aggressive until they were submerged by the triumph of military autocracy.

For ten years no worthy successor of Tiberius Gracchus appeared, but these were not years of peace. Some Latins and Italians had been lessees of public land, and the danger of losing their holdings, added to their other ills, made them appeal to Rome for redress. Scipio Aemilianus took up their cause against the Populares. Shortly afterward he died mysteriously, and rumor had it that he had been murdered by his wife, the sister of Gracchus. Demands began to be heard that Roman citizenship be extended to the allies. Then in 125, the Latin colony of Fregellae revolted, and was destroyed. At some time during this period the re-election of the tribunes was legalized, but when or how is not known.

### *Gaius Gracchus (123–121 B.C.)*

In 124, Gaius Gracchus, the younger brother of Tiberius, was elected tribune, and the tempo of the quarrel between the Optimates and the Populares quickened. In character he differed greatly from Tiberius. He had the same lofty patriotism and sympathy for the unfortunate, but to these he added a fiery temper and a truly Italian thirst for vengeance. He entered office with a comprehensive plan, the principal purpose of which was to destroy the power of the senatorial oligarchy.

Gaius' first measure was designed to avenge his brother's blood, and to vindicate his memory. Although Scipio Nasica, the ringleader of the senatorial mob, was dead, Popilius Laenas, consul in 132 and a leading persecutor of the Gracchan faction, was forced into exile. Then a law was carried prohibiting the Senate from erecting extraordinary criminal courts to try political offenders. Furthermore, the land law of 133 was re-enacted and put into working order.

*Bettmann*

ROMAN GRAIN SHIP

With these measures went a comprehensive social program, patterned in many instances after Hellenistic models. To assure an adequate food supply for the common people of the capital, Gaius secured the passage of a law whereby the state undertook to furnish each citizen with a bushel of wheat a month at a low price, but one which was far from constituting a dole. As it stood, this step was probably intended to do no more than stabilize and control the cost of cereal foods. Later on, however, this practice became a means of buying votes, and the grain was given free. In addition, an extensive program of public works, including some of the most important Italian roads, was undertaken to relieve unemployment.

Administrative and judicial machinery also came in for a general overhauling. The senatorial juries in the "Recovery Court," before which provincial governors were tried for maladministration, had recently acquitted several persons commonly believed to be guilty. There were rumors that bribery had been used. After first trying to remedy matters by a strict law against such corruption, Gaius, through his friend the tribune Acilius, carried a bill which completely reorganized this important tribunal. The text of the law is mutilated and some of its important provisions have to be inferred. It is certain, however, that senators, members of their families, and magistrates were barred from the juries, which were probably to be made up of citizens with a minimum property qualification of four hundred thousand sesterces. Whatever the details of the plan, it granted a monopoly of the juries to the middle-class businessmen popularly known as equestrians.

His favors to the businessmen did not stop there. The newly organized province of Asia had for many years been disturbed by the appearance of a usurper named Aristonicus, who claimed to be an illegitimate member of the old Pergamene royal house. After this adventurer was overthrown, other troubles had delayed the establishment of a settled government for the province. Gaius Gracchus now carried a law which applied to Asia the tithing system used in Sicily with important variations. Instead of letting the contracts for the collection of the Asiatic tribute in small units and on the spot, so that natives of the province could bid them in, the government was to let them in a single unit and in Rome. This step threw them into the hands of the equestrians who formed large companies of *publicani* to carry on the business. With the juries and the taxes of Asia in their hands, the equestrians rapidly consolidated into a self-conscious social and political class, generally at odds with the Senate and formidable by reason of its wealth, intelligence, and wide contacts at Rome and in the provinces. Both this and the change in the jury system were injurious to the provincials. The new jurors were, if anything, more corrupt than the old had been, and the *publicani* were notoriously dishonest and oppressive. In a court composed of their fellow equestrians they ran little risk of conviction, while governors who opposed them were in constant danger of false charges prepared by them.

In all these measures Gracchus had not been guilty of any illegal act, since there was no hard-and-fast rule which delimited the respective spheres of government exercised by the Senate and the Assemblies. But the net result was none the less revolutionary in character, for by custom these matters had always been handled by the Senate. He followed up his advantage by habitual invasions of the senatorian sphere of government. Finance and the assignment of provinces were now almost entirely monopolized by the Assembly, encouraged by an all-powerful tribune whom none dared challenge and who could be re-elected for an indefinite number of years. If this state of affairs continued, Rome would soon have as a single chief executive the most popular member of the college of the tribunes.

Thus far Gracchus had antagonized only the Senate and could still count on the support of both equestrians and commons. He was triumphantly re-elected for the year 122. But his enemies were not ready to admit defeat. They cast about for a means of undermining and overthrowing him, and in 122 they had a plan ready. It was simple and devastatingly effective — to instigate another tribune to outbid him for the favor of the mob on whom he had to depend for votes. Among the tribunes elected for 122 was Marcus Livius Drusus, a partisan of the Senate and a shrewd, unscrupulous schemer. To him was committed the task of undermining Gracchus' position by proposing measures more to the popular taste than those already brought in, and by giving credit to the Senate in each case. Drusus advocated land allotments of such prodigal liberality as to surpass anything the Gracchi had sponsored. It may be noted that these allotments were merely proposed, and so far as can be judged, were never actually put into effect; however, they served the purpose of the Senate.

But the greatest opportunity for Drusus and the Senate came when Gracchus brought in a bill for the extension of Roman citizenship to the Latins, and of Latin rights to the Italians. The bill proved as offensive to the Roman commons as to the Senate, and Drusus seized upon it. He interposed a veto against it, and this time the veto was not overridden. In its place he proposed the elimination of a few minor grievances for the Latins. The popular conscience was satisfied, and the Gracchan measure was dropped. The unpopularity of Gracchus was increased a few months later when he attempted to found a colony (Junonia) on the site of Carthage. Subtle and mendacious propaganda was employed to turn the populace against the scheme, and when the elections for the year 121 were held, Gracchus was not re-elected.

The Senate could not stop there. The aristocracy felt that they would have no peace as long as the trouble-maker was alive. Early in 121 a carefully planned riot broke out, for which the blame was thrown upon Gracchus and his supporters. The consul Lucius Opimius received a command from the Senate to quell the disorder. The equestrians did nothing for their benefactor, and the populace gave him but little help. A pitched battle was fought in which Gracchus and many of his supporters were killed, and afterwards the surviving members of his party were massacred in cold blood.

Whether for good or ill, the work of Gaius Gracchus survived him. The equestrians, although they had deserted his cause, kept all that his laws had gained for them, and the populace still had its lands and its grain law. In 111, a third land law was passed giving all holders of public lands (outside of Campania) a clear title to their allotments, and granting to the beneficiaries of the Gracchan laws the right to sell their holdings. No doubt most of this land soon passed once more into the hands of the aristocracy by more or less honest purchase. To the Optimates had gone a partial victory in the first round of the battle, but they had not regained all of their lost powers. The equestrians retained control of the courts, the populace their grain law, and the African colonists their land. Little had been accomplished by the Senate except the destruction of the Gracchi and the temporary blocking of further reforms.

## THE JUGURTHINE WAR, MARIUS, AND THE NEW ARMY

### *The Senatorial Restoration: Transalpine Gaul*

For some years after the death of Gaius Gracchus the Senate again controlled the government with the tacit consent of the other classes, but the quality of its rule had not improved and no effort was made to solve the problems which beset the Republic. The same arrogance, selfishness, and dishonesty which had precipitated the Gracchan troubles and prevented their peaceable solution were still apparent. In foreign affairs, however, the period was marked by a striking series of military victories over the Gauls, and the formation of a new province on the Mediterranean coast of Gaul. As early as 125 an army had been sent to protect Massilia against her Ligurian neighbors, and the Celtic tribes farther north were soon drawn into the struggle. In this war prominent places were taken by the Celtic Allobrogians who lived southwest of Lake Geneva, and by the Arverni from north of the Cevennes Mountains. In 121, the proconsul Lucius Domitius Ahenobarbus inflicted a crushing defeat upon these two tribes and captured the Arvernian king Bituitus. All the tribes between the coast, the summit of the Cevennes, the upper Rhone, the Alps, and the Pyrenees submitted to the victors. Since Rome had long desired a land route between Italy and Spain, the conquered territory was organized into the province of Transalpine Gaul, and Massilia was richly rewarded for her past assistance with gifts of land. At Aquae Sextiae and Narbo, Roman colonies were founded, and a road, the *Via Domitia*, was built along the coast from the borders of Italy to the Spanish side of the Pyrenees.

### *The Jugurthine War*

When the Populares next attacked the established order, it was because of the senatorial blunders and misfortunes in handling the affairs of the client kingdom of Numidia. In 118, Micipsa the son of Masinissa died. By his will the kingdom was divided among his two sons Hiempsal and Adherbal, and his nephew Jugurtha. The sons were men of little ability, but Jugurtha had all the craft, ambition, unscrupulousness, and persuasiveness of his grandfather. He promptly slew one cousin and drove the other from the country. The fugitive appealed to the Roman Senate, which, however, showed suspicious favor toward Jugurtha. To him it awarded the more valuable western part of the kingdom, while Adherbal received the less productive eastern section with Cirta as its capital. A few years later Jugurtha besieged Adherbal in Cirta, put off two senatorial embassies with fair words, and finally took the city in 112, killing Adherbal and a number of Roman and Italian traders resident in it.

Although this was an unpardonable offense, again the Senate seemed ready to condone it. A storm broke out in Rome. The Populares, headed by the tribune Gaius Memmius, roundly accused the senators of bribe taking, and pushed the charge so vigorously that the Senate was forced to support a declaration of war against the Numidian king. But the war was only a pretense. In 111, the consul Calpurnius Bestia secured a sham submission from Jugurtha, and in return allowed him to keep his kingdom. Memmius asserted that Bestia had been bribed, and with more zeal than propriety summoned Jugurtha to Rome to tell what he knew about the alleged corruption. The Senate, however, secured the services of another tribune, who forbade the Numidian to testify. To climax the whole disgraceful affair, Jugurtha secured the assassination of a relative who was living in Rome. Even the Senate could not endure this outrage. The culprit was ordered to leave Italy at once, and war against him was resumed. In 109, Jugurtha defeated the consul Spurius Albinus and captured his army. Thereupon the Assembly, imitating the Senate's tactics, set up a special court of investigation which condemned Bestia and Albinus.

Here was an unparalleled and disgraceful record of senatorial bungling, with every indication that senatorial magistrates had sold their country's cause for gold. Goaded at last into serious action, the Senate sent Quintus Caecilius Metellus, an honest senator and fair general, to subdue Jugurtha. He was efficient but slow, since he lacked cavalry with which to conduct desert warfare. When nearly a year had passed without the capture of Jugurtha, the suspicious Populares again began to accuse the Senate and its general of dishonesty.

It was at this crucial moment that Gaius Marius came forward as a popular leader, and the feud of the Optimates and Populares entered a new stage. Marius was a "new man," the son of a day laborer. After winning distinction as a soldier, he had gained the offices of quaestor, tribune, and praetor, and had also been in business, thus forming connections with the equestrians. He owed many favors to the aristocratic clan of the Metelli, and in 108, was serving on the staff of Quintus Metellus in Numidia. Metellus had aroused the hatred of Marius by treating him as a lowly dependent, and thereafter the two were irreconcilable enemies. Returning to Rome, Marius became a candidate for the consulship. In his campaign speeches he bitterly criticized both the Senate and Metellus. The populace not only elected Marius, but in defiance of the Senate's wishes designated Numidia as his province.

*The New Army*

In recruiting additional forces for the campaign, Marius adopted a new and fateful policy. For many years it had been increasingly difficult to secure enough recruits from the diminishing class of small farmers on whom the principal burden of military service had hitherto fallen. In fact, the provincial wars required the presence of the same personnel for several successive years, and for such service these unwilling draftees were unsatisfactory. Marius abandoned the old plan and called for volunteers. To stimulate enlistments, he promised them bonuses in land and money besides their regular pay. Thousands of landless freemen answered the call. Later on Marius elaborated the system still farther, subjecting recruits to rigorous training.

Once the military effectiveness of the new system became apparent, it was generally adopted, and its consequences were epoch-making. A minor result was that the hard-pressed small Italian farmer was relieved of one of his greatest burdens, for the old system of conscription was seldom applied thereafter. The volunteer was usually a poor man who fought to gain the bonus which would render him financially independent. The commander who enlisted him was personally responsible for the fulfillment of the promises made when he entered the service, for neither then nor later did the Senate make any general provision for them. Thus a special law had to be passed to reward each army, and the commander was compelled to become a politician in order to secure its passage. This meant that the

*Metropolitan Museum*

BRONZE FIGURINES REPRESENTING FARM ANIMALS

loyalty of his men centered upon the commander rather than the state, even though it involved rioting or civil wars in his behalf. As we shall see presently, the system finally resulted in making every important military commander a veritable war lord who could ride roughshod over constitutional machinery.

Once in Africa, Marius pressed Jugurtha so hard that the latter took refuge with his ally, King Bocchus of Mauretania. Marius then sent his quaestor Lucius Cornelius Sulla to demand the surrender of Jugurtha. After some hesitation, Bocchus complied and, in 107, the war was at an end. Jugurtha perished in a Roman dungeon and his kingdom was divided. Bocchus received the extreme western portion, while the remainder was given to Gauda, a weak and unambitious relative of the dead king. Thus ended an incident which made the reputation of Marius, and mercilessly exposed the weakness and corruption of senatorial rule.

### *The Cimbrian War*

Hardly had the Numidian war ended when the Romans were called upon to meet a severe crisis along their northern frontier. In northern Germany near the base of the peninsula of Jutland, there lived, about 120 B.C., two Teutonic tribes, the Cimbri and the Teutons. For reasons not definitely known, they set out in search of more productive lands and wandered off to the southeast. About 113 they appeared on the northern bank of the Danube and attacked the Taurisci, a Celtic tribe allied with Rome. A Roman force sent to oppose them was badly defeated, but with typical inconsequence the Cimbri and Teutons did not follow up their victory. Instead they turned westward along the Danube Valley and soon afterward entered Gaul. In 109, they appeared on the frontier of the new Roman province of Transalpine Gaul. There they defeated one Roman army after another, topping their exploits with the Battle of Arausio (Orange), in 105, where sixty thousand Romans were killed. The way to Italy was now open, but the victors wandered off into independent Gaul which they pillaged from end to end.

Again the Roman aristocracy and the conscript armies of the Republic had been tried and found wanting, and as usual in such cases, the Assembly took matters into its own hands. Marius, although legally ineligible for re-election to the consulship, was re-elected for the year 104, and in 103, 102, and 101, held third, fourth, and fifth terms. Fortunately for the Romans, the enemy was for several years engaged in ravaging Gaul and in attempting to invade Spain.

Marius now had plenty of time to develop a new army on a volunteer basis. The legion was reorganized so that it consisted of six thousand men, divided into ten cohorts of six hundred men each, commanded by *legati*, and sixty centuries of a hundred men each, commanded by centurions. Experts from the gladiatorial schools taught the men swordsmanship, while hard drill, long marches, and manual labor toughened the soldier's muscles and enabled him to use his weapons with deadly effectiveness.

In 102, the respite granted to the Romans by the aimless wanderings of the enemy was at an end. The two tribes recrossed the Pyrenees and undertook a concerted attack upon Italy from different directions. The Teutons and some of the smaller groups crossing Transalpine Gaul, approached their objective from the west, while the Cimbri circled through central Gaul, followed the valleys of the Danube and the Inn, and entered the Po Valley by the Brenner Pass. Marius cautiously followed the Teutons and at Aquae Sextiae attacked and annihilated them. In the meantime, his aristocratic colleague Catulus had been defeated by the Cimbri, who then ravaged Cisalpine Gaul north of the Po. Being consul once more in 101, Marius joined Catulus, and at the Battle of the Raudine Plains destroyed the Cimbri. The civilized world was once more saved from the threat of a barbarian invasion, and the star of Marius reached its zenith.

While Rome was trembling before this threat of invasion, she also had to face a slave revolt in Sicily. In 104, under the leadership of Salvius and Athenion, two of their own number, the plantation slaves of the island rose against their masters, and for three years they kept the upper hand. Many of the proletariat of the Sicilian cities joined them. At its height the rebellion was supported by an army of twenty thousand infantry and two thousand cavalry. But the victory of Aquae Sextiae released part of Marius' professional army to be used against them, with competent commanders. In a short time the rebellion had been put down, and the surviving slaves restored to their masters.

### *The Marian Army in Politics: Saturninus and Glaucia*

The military efficiency of Marius' army was now generally admitted, but its political influence had yet to be demonstrated. Now that victory had been won, Marius was obligated to redeem his promises, and he could do so only by securing the passage of a law granting them the stipulated bonus. This necessitated another consulship for him, and the aristocracy was determined that he should not have it. Again he had recourse to the Populares whose leaders, in 102, had helped him to gain his fifth consulship, and had secured a grant of land in Africa for the veterans of the Jugurthine War. Hence, in 101, we find Marius in close alliance with Lucius Appuleius Saturninus and Gaius Servilius Glaucia, two questionable characters who at that time enjoyed the leadership of the city rabble. Marius was a candidate for the consulship, Saturninus for the tribunate, and Glaucia for the praetorship.

The election of 101 was stormy. Marius had the support of the equestrians, and his veterans were on hand to riot in his behalf. By these means and by bribery he and Glaucia were elected, and Saturninus achieved the same end by securing the murder of his most popular opponent. After taking office, the trio proceeded to introduce a legislative program which was a sadly vulgarized version of that of the Gracchi. To please the populace a provision was inserted reducing the price of grain to a purely nominal figure. Another clause granted to the volunteers of Marius the land devastated by the Cimbri in Cisalpine Gaul. Apparently Italians as well as Roman citizens were to be eligible for allotments, and Marius himself was designated to take charge of the distribution. A special proviso prescribed that every senator must, within five days after the passage of the law, take an oath to uphold it. The program was not enacted into law without violence. After trying legal obstructionist tactics, the Optimates began a riot, but in this they counted without the veterans of Marius, who speedily overcame all opposition and secured the passage of the law. Marius, who as consul had to administer the oath to the senators, took final revenge upon his former patron and friend Metellus by tricking him into refusing to swear, and then forcing him into exile.

But the coalition, although all-powerful for the moment, was soon to disintegrate. In spite of their demagogic practices, Saturninus and Glaucia were not popular with the Roman masses, and before the year was over they had alienated both the equestrians and Marius. When the elections of the year 100 were held, Marius was not a candidate, but Glaucia was standing for the consulship, and Saturninus for another tribuneship. As Glaucia's candidacy was strictly illegal, and his opponent Gaius Memmius was a popular politician, Glaucia had Memmius murdered on the day of the election. The equestrians, disgusted with such violence, joined the Senate in an attempt to restore order. Saturninus, Glaucia, and their partisans entrenched themselves on the Capitoline Hill, while the Senate instructed Marius to put down the revolt. Apparently he also felt that his former allies had gone too far, for he gathered a force, besieged them, and compelled them to surrender. He promised that the lives of the prisoners would be spared, but a crowd of young equestrians and senators surrounded the building in which they were imprisoned, tore off the roof, and stoned them to death. As their laws had been passed by illegal methods, they were declared void. Marius, who had offended all parties, was thoroughly discredited, and sank into obscurity. Two years later the triumphant aristocracy secured the passage of a law which provided that no bill could deal with more than one subject, and that an interval of at least seventeen days must elapse between the introduction of a bill and its final passage.

## Livius Drusus and the Revolt of the Allies

Although the peace was not again broken for nine years (100–91 B.C.), the issues which had so long agitated Roman public life had not been settled. The land question was, it is true, somewhat less prominent than formerly, but the equestrians still controlled the juries, and the agitation among the allies continued unabated. The corruption and venality of the equestrian juries was displayed in a glaring light by their treatment of Rutilius Rufus. In 98, this cultured and humane senator was for a time left in control of the province of Asia. There he repressed the exactions of the *publicani* with a strong hand, and treated the people with kindness and justice. Five years later he was accused of having practiced extortion in the province, convicted, and subjected to a ruinous fine. To show the falsity of the charge, he retired to the very province which he was accused of having oppressed, and lived in honor among the people. Both the jury question and that of citizenship for the allies came to a head in 91, the year of the tribunate of Livius Drusus.

### *The Program of Livius Drusus*

Drusus was the son of the tribune who had opposed Gaius Gracchus. He was a thinker and a theorist rather than a practical politician, but he understood the problems which beset the Roman state, and undertook to solve them by peaceful compromise. It was obvious that if the government were ever to become stabilized, it must have the united support of the senatorial and equestrian orders, which had for a generation been quarreling over the control of the law courts. To remove this bone of contention, Drusus proposed that the Senate be enlarged by the addition of three hundred equestrians to its ranks, and that the juries should thereafter be composed of equal numbers of the Senate and the remaining equestrians. New and stringent rules were to be made against bribery. Moreover the complaints of the allies were becoming so insistent that it was plain that Rome faced a crisis within her confederacy. For them Drusus proposed an immediate extension of Roman citizenship, which would include both Latins and Italians. However, this measure had to be voted by the Assembly of the Tribes, and the extension of citizenship was especially likely to prove offensive to the Roman commons. To bribe them into acquiescence, Drusus undertook to found new Roman colonies in both Italy and Sicily, and included in his program a proposal for cheaper grain.

This plan, which was intended to conciliate all factions of the citizen body, ended by offending all of them in varying degrees. The equestrians saw little gain for themselves in a measure which would confer a doubtful benefit upon three hundred of their number and lessen the influence of the whole remaining group. In the Senate it gained some support, but many senators feared that the new members would form a "bloc" which would dominate senatorial policies. All classes of citizens were hostile to the extension of the suffrage. Even among the Italians, who were otherwise his wholehearted partisans, fear that some public land would be repossessed for the planting of the proposed colonies caused alarm. Goaded to desperation, Drusus combined several of his measures in a single bill and succeeded by violence in forcing its passage. The Senate declared this "omnibus bill" invalid. Then, just as the dauntless tribune was preparing for a second attempt to push the proposals through one by one, he was mysteriously assassinated and no effort was made to discover the assassin. Livius Drusus was the last Roman civilian reformer. The blind selfishness and narrow prejudices of his contemporaries rendered his failure inevitable. Only by "blood and iron" could the tangle be resolved, and thenceforth the reformers were to be men of war, who often paid scant deference to constitutional forms.

### *The Revolt of the Allies, 90–88 B.C.*

The murder of Drusus and the failure of his plan for the extension of Roman citizenship made civil war in Italy almost inevitable, and the Senate made it doubly certain by creating an extraordinary commission to investigate the agitation among the allies. Goaded to desperation, the Italians formed a confederacy of their own, with its capital at the eastern Italian town of Corfinium, renamed Italia, and with a government modeled closely after that of Rome. The league included most of southern Italy, reaching to Campania on the west and the edge of the Sabine country on the north. The Latin colonies and Greek cities, however, did not join in the movement. In the north some of the Picenes rebelled, but the Etruscans and Umbrians, while dangerously discontented, did not immediately take up arms. The resulting struggle (known variously in history as the "Social War," "Italian War," or "Marsic War") produced the most dangerous crisis which the Romans had had to meet since the invasion of Hannibal. The rebels were men of military experience, thoroughly acquainted with Roman tactics and discipline, and their leaders were skillful generals. Against them Rome could lead armies about as large as their own, but she had the additional advantage of being able to draw upon the provinces for both money and auxiliaries. Everything depended upon the attitude of the Etruscans and Umbrians, for if they revolted, it seemed likely that the rebels would win.

With forces so evenly balanced, the first year of the war was a checkered series of victories and defeats for both sides. In the south the rebels occupied most of Campania, Apulia, and Lucania. In the north the Romans were more successful, but before the end of the year it became evident that Etruria and Umbria were ready to revolt. This was too much, and the following winter the consul Sextus Julius Caesar carried a law which granted the coveted citizenship to all allies who had not yet revolted, or who would immediately return to their allegiance. By this timely concession, the spread of the rebellion was checked.

The year 89 saw a decided turn in the tide. A second concession was made to the rebels in the *Lex Plautia-Papiria*, which granted citizenship to all Italians, whether rebels or not, who would claim it within sixty days. Thereafter desertions from the rebel forces must have been numerous, and this fact, together with the brilliant generalship of Lucius Cornelius Sulla, broke the back of the movement in the south. One by one, the districts occupied by the rebels were reconquered, until when the year closed only Samnium and the adjoining sections of Campania were still in arms. Sulla was rewarded with the consulship for the year 88. Due to their prolonged resistance, there were still some Italians outside the pale of Roman citizenship, but they, too, gained it within the next few years.

Yet in spite of its victorious close, the war had left a vexatious heritage of problems for Roman statesmen to wrestle with. At home, it intensified the strife between the Senate and the equestrians, who had by this time assumed the leadership of the Populares. So acute was the financial stringency in the year 88, that public land within the city of Rome had to be sold to raise funds for the treasury. Many senators, deprived by the war of the income from their estates, were in debt to equestrian money-lenders, and when the praetor Asellio tried to place legal obstructions in the way of the suits to collect debts, he was murdered in broad daylight by a mob headed by a tribune. The murderers were never brought to justice. Even more important was the question of voting arrangements for the Italians. Having granted them citizenship, the old citizens seemed determined to condemn the Italians to permanent inferiority by enrolling them in only eight tribes, a custom closely resembling that observed toward freedmen. Such treatment was keenly resented, and promised to bring on an early renewal of the war. But while the Romans were busy with disorder and sedition at home, a grave peril was threatening them in the East. In 88 Mithridates Eupator, the king of Pontus, invaded and conquered the province of Asia, and from thence passed on into Greece.

## The First Mithridatic War (88–84 B.C.)

Mithridates VI (121–63 B.C.) came of a family which had for several generations been Roman client kings. He was a man of great energy and some ability, and a typical product of the mixed Hellenistic and Oriental civilization of eastern Asia Minor. He spoke Greek, had Greek ministers and generals, and posed as the protector of Greek civilization; but his harem, his frequent fits of callous brutality and blood-lust, and his arbitrary methods of government all belonged to the Asiatic rather than to the Greek world. In the early years of his reign he had been an obedient Roman vassal and had done good service to the Greek cities on the northern shore of the Black Sea. When the Scythian and Sarmatian tribes of the Steppes had attacked these far-off outposts of Hellenism, he had sent an army to their aid which had defeated the barbarians and secured peace for their Greek neighbors. In return he had gained possession of the "Kingdom of the Cimmerian Bosporus" which included the region around what is today called the Straits of Kertch. Later on, his ambition led him to attack two of his fellow vassals, the kings of Cappadocia and Bithynia, but Sulla, then propraetor of the new Roman province of Cilicia, had forced him to withdraw. The Social War gave Mithridates his opportunity. In 88, the king of Bithynia, encouraged by the proconsul of Asia, made an unjustified attack upon the Pontic ruler, and in revenge the latter invaded the Roman provinces.

The invasion caught the Romans unprepared, and for a time it carried all before it. Only in Lycia did the invaders meet with successful opposition, although in a few weeks Mithridates had occupied the whole province of Asia, and the people, ground down by the exactions of the Roman *publicani* and proconsuls, received him as a deliverer. To play the part convincingly, he conferred various benefits upon them. Then not trusting their gratitude, he decided to bind them to him by implicating them in an unpardonable crime. By his orders, and on a set day, the people of Asia murdered in cold blood some eighty thousand Romans and Italians who were living in the province. After this hideous massacre, Mithridates swept on across the Aegean. Rhodes withstood him, but by way of compensation he gained a convenient base in Greece when Athens espoused his cause. Through her port he poured an army into Greece, and soon the southern and central parts of the peninsula were under his power. His fleet controlled the Aegean, and with its aid he conquered Euboea and attacked Thessaly. In this region a deputy of the governor of Macedonia temporarily checked his advance, but there was every reason for the Romans to think that if they did not act quickly, they would lose their land east of the Adriatic and that even Italy might not be safe.

### *Civil War in Rome*

The crisis, instead of producing unity in Rome, merely provided the occasion for further suicidal civil war. A commander had to be chosen for the army which was to be sent against Mithridates, and the matter became a political issue. The Senate chose Sulla, who was to set out as soon as his consulship had expired, but the Populares would have none of him. As the war seemed likely to be a fairly easy one with plenty of spoil, the aged Marius came forward to ask for the command. At this point a tribune, Sulpicius Rufus, advanced a legislative program designed, like that of his friend Livius Drusus a few years before, to settle all outstanding problems. Although not previously allied with the Populares, Rufus put forward a series of proposals which exactly embodied their views. The Italians were to be distributed through all of the tribes, and the command against Mithridates was to be given to Marius. The commons were to be conciliated with a land and grain bill and the equestrians by provisions which would compel delinquent senatorial debtors to meet their obligations. Mindful of the fate of Drusus, he surrounded himself with a guard of six hundred young equestrians whom he called his "anti-Senate." The Senate, determined to prevent the passage of such a program, summoned the consuls Sulla and Pompeius Rufus to Rome, where they proclaimed an indefinite suspension of public business. Had Sulpicius Rufus heeded their prohibition, the passage of his laws would have been impossible, but instead, he started a riot in which the son of Pompeius was killed and Sulla was saved only after he had taken refuge in the house of Marius. Then through violence the whole series of laws was enacted.

Up to this time Sulla had not been closely connected with either party, but he was a stubborn individualist, to whom the wealth and glory to be gained from the eastern command appealed irresistibly. He had no intention of being thus cavalierly thrust aside, and as the election of Marius had been the work of the Populares, he espoused the cause of the Optimates. Returning to his army at Nola, he laid the cause before his soldiers. Like all other armies of the day, they were volunteers, recruited on the plan worked out by Marius. They were Sulla's men, and if Marius were to take command against Mithridates, they would, of course, be left behind and a new army recruited. Like their commander, they anticipated an easy war and large rewards in spoil and pay. Hence they rose up as one man and demanded that their chief lead them to Rome to destroy their enemies and his. Sulla was easily persuaded. Entering the city, he overpowered all opposition, and completely undid the work of Sulpicius. The leaders of the Populares were outlawed, and rewards were offered for their destruction. Sulpicius himself was slain, but Marius, after a series of hairbreadth escapes, reached Africa in safety. Sulla and his partisans in their turn carried a series of laws intended to assure their position in the future. To Sulla himself went the eastern command. To prevent further demagogic tribunician legislation, it was decreed that in the future all bills presented to the Assembly of the Tribes must be authorized in advance by the Senate, and the rights of the tribunes were somewhat curtailed. The new citizens lost their right to be registered in all the tribes. Yet, when the consuls for 87 were elected, Lucius Cornelius Cinna, one of the opposition party, was chosen. Having done what he could to secure his position at home, near the end of the year 88, Sulla sailed for Greece.

### *The Marians Gain Control of Italy*

Hardly had Sulla left Italy when his enemies regained power. Cinna quarreled with his colleague, Gnaeus Octavius, who drove him from the city. But the fugitive gained the support of one of the armies in Campania, and by large promises he attracted thousands of Italians to his standard. Marius, after wandering for months in Africa, returned and levied an army in Etruria. In a short time he and Cinna entered Rome in triumph, and a reign of terror ensued. Marius, infuriated by the hardships which he had suffered, and perhaps no longer wholly sane, went about with a band of armed slaves butchering all of his real or fancied enemies in cold blood. At last, Cinna stopped the bloodshed by massacring the slaves. Amid these ghastly scenes, Cinna was re-elected to the consulship, with

Marius as his colleague. The old warrior had hardly entered his seventh consulship when he died, having tarnished his earlier fame with the crimes of his last days. For the next three years, Cinna and a small clique of his supporters governed Italy quietly enough, but corruptly, inefficiently, and in flat defiance of constitutional precedents. Their sole purpose during these years was to forestall the attack which they knew that Sulla would eventually launch against them, either by depriving him of his command or by gathering an army strong enough to overpower him.

*The War in Greece and Asia*

For Sulla, these years were full of difficulty, danger, and achievement. The triumph of the Marian faction in Rome had left him without hope of reinforcements or of financial support, while his enemies did everything possible to hamper him. He had no fleet, while Mithridates had a large one. Yet in the face of these handicaps he led his men from victory to victory. He supported his army by plundering the treasuries of the Greek temples, and by ruthless requisitions upon the people. Slashing across the peninsula, he made straight for the enemy base, and besieged both Athens and the Piraeus. After a long and hard-fought siege he captured Athens early in 86, massacred many of the inhabitants, and forced the Pontic general Archelaus to abandon the Piraeus. Whirling about to the northward, he annihilated two Pontic armies, the smaller of which was twice as large as his own. By midsummer of 85, Greece and Macedonia were cleared of the enemy, and the prestige of Mithridates had suffered a fatal setback.

While still engaged in the siege of Athens, Sulla had been compelled to face a threat of intervention by his enemies at home. Early in 86, Cinna sent to Greece Marcus Valerius Flaccus, the successor of Marius as consul, with an army and orders to supersede Sulla. But the soldiers of Flaccus were unwilling to attack their fellow countrymen, and whether from fear or patriotism, Flaccus marched eastward through Macedonia for an independent campaign against the enemy. At Byzantium he crossed into Asia, but his soldiers, angered at his efforts to restrain them from plundering, murdered him and chose in his place his deputy, Gaius Flavius Fimbria. This man, lawless and violent but a capable commander, reconquered the northwestern portion of Asia Minor, including Pergamum.

Having expelled Mithridates from Greece, Sulla had to wait until a fleet could be collected before invading Asia. In 86, he sent his deputy, Lucius Licinius Lucullus, to solicit ships and crews from Rome's clients in Egypt, Cyprus, and Phoenicia. After a year of disheartening rebuffs,

Lucullus finally succeeded in collecting a small fleet, with which, in 84, he gained control of the Aegean, the Hellespont, and the Bosporus. Sulla was now free to follow the forces of Flaccus and Fimbria into Asia.

To Mithridates it was plain that his cause was lost. The Asiatics, sadly disillusioned by his acts of cruelty and oppression, and fearing punishment from Sulla and Fimbria, were beginning to plot against him. Every day that Mithridates continued the war made his ultimate defeat all the more certain. Sulla, on his side, had no desire to proceed to extremities. Fimbria's army was more a hindrance than a help to him, and he wanted his hands free for the coming civil war with the Marian faction. By the Treaty of Dardanus, peace was made between the Romans and Mithridates, on very moderate terms. Mithridates was made to evacuate all of his conquests in Asia, to surrender prisoners, deserters, escaped slaves, and half of his fleet, and in addition to pay an indemnity of two thousand talents. In return for these promises, he was pardoned and admitted once more to the position of a Roman ally. For the Asiatics, Sulla had no mercy. They had slaughtered Roman citizens, and any fate short of outright massacre was good enough for them. The few communities which had resisted the invader and preserved their friendship for Rome were suitably rewarded. For the rest, a fiendishly ingenious punishment was devised. During the winter of 84–83, Sulla's army was quartered upon the province, the householders to furnish subsistence, clothing, and pay for the soldiers. In addition, the province had to pay the stupendous sum of 20,000 talents as an indemnity. To secure this sum, the provincials had to borrow from Roman moneylenders at rates of interest which left them in virtual slavery for years.

Fimbria and his outlaw army were quickly dealt with. Sulla demanded their unconditional surrender, and the men had no desire to fight. Fimbria committed suicide. A few of the soldiers were incorporated in Sulla's army, and others escaped to Mithridates. The remainder were condemned to remain in Asia for an indefinite term, to act as a garrison.

## Civil War, Proscription, and Dictatorship

### *Sulla Reconquers Italy*

Even before the end of the Mithridatic War, Sulla had begun to plan measures to get the better of his enemies in Italy. In a letter to the Senate, he rehearsed his services to the state and the wrongs which he and his friends had suffered, and announced that he was going to take vengeance upon his enemies. He added, however, that he would respect the concessions made to the new citizens by Cinna and his friends. The Senate, now under the control of the Populares, made half-hearted efforts to mediate, but achieved nothing, and both sides prepared for war. Cinna took Gnaeus Papirius Carbo as his colleague, and an army was gathered to uphold their cause. It was Cinna's purpose to forestall Sulla by crossing over to Greece and fighting out the quarrel there, but his troops mutinied and murdered him. Carbo decided to await Sulla in Italy.

The next year (83) Sulla landed at Brundisium with forty thousand men, all of whom had sworn an oath of personal loyalty to him. Immediately supporters began to flock to his standard. Gnaeus Pompeius, the son of Pompeius Strabo, one of the consuls of 89, raised three legions in Picenum, where his family had large estates, and made his way to Sulla's camp. Marcus Licinius Crassus, a young man who had fled to Africa to escape Marius and Cinna, brought in additional troops, and other members of the Optimate party did likewise. In the opposing camp all was confusion. Quintus Sertorius, the ablest of the Marian generals, was sent to Spain, and the leaders who remained to fight Sulla were decidedly second-rate men, if not worse.

Sulla's conduct of the civil war was marked by the same mixture of shrewdness, audacity, and ruthlessness that had characterized his campaigns against Mithridates. During the remainder of 83 he secured all of southern Italy except Samnium, while his lieutenants made headway against the enemy in Cisalpine Gaul, Umbria, and Picenum. For 82, the Populares chose as their leaders Carbo, and Gaius Marius, the son of the conqueror of Jugurtha and the Cimbri. While they were probably the best men available in the party, they could not turn the tide. Early in the year, Sulla marched into Rome, defeated Marius, and besieged him in Praeneste. Then leaving an army to carry on the siege, he seized Rome, and marched northward into Etruria. Everywhere the enemy was defeated, and soon the north was in his power. A Samnite army, marching to relieve Praeneste, was unable to break the siege, and its leaders in desperation resolved to make a dash on Rome. A last desperate battle was fought under the walls of the city (called the Battle of the Colline Gate), in which the Samnites almost defeated Sulla, but in the end he vanquished them, took eight thousand prisoners, and massacred them in cold blood. Praeneste fell, and Marius committed suicide. Except for local resistance, the war in Italy was over. Carbo fled to Africa, where he was captured and killed by the young Gnaeus Pompey, whom Sulla sent in pursuit of him. For this feat Pompey demanded and received the right to enter the city in triumph, and Sulla (perhaps in jest) gave him the surname of *Magnus* ("The

Great"). Only in Spain did a remnant of the beaten faction remain in arms under the formidable Quintus Sertorius.

*The Proscriptions: the Punishment of the Italians*

Having disposed of armed opposition, Sulla proceeded deliberately to exterminate both his actual and his potential enemies. As the Roman commons had always submitted to the leadership of senators and equestrians allied with the Populares, it was among these two classes that he sought and found most of his victims in Rome. Many Italian communities had opposed Sulla's progress, and had, according to his view, merited punishment. Vengeance and greed alike urged him to extreme severity. A wave of political assassinations followed his entry into Rome, and when his friends urged him to quiet the anxiety of those against whom he had no grudge, he adopted the infamous device of proscription. A regular list was drawn up and posted, of persons condemned to death and confiscation of property. Rewards were offered for their arrest or murder, and those who sheltered them were to be severely punished. Even the sons and grandsons of proscribed persons were deprived of the right to hold office or sit in the Senate. The horrors to which this practice gave rise defy description. New names were continually added to the list, some by Sulla himself, and others to please his friends. Men were proscribed because Sulla's adherents coveted their property, or because of private grudges. Criminals murdered men and then cleared themselves by having the names of the victims placed on the proscription list. Ninety senators and twenty-six hundred equestrians suffered death or banishment, along with some two thousand persons of other classes.

The Italians who had taken sides against Sulla fared no better. Samnium was almost depopulated, and Etruria suffered a wave of deaths and confiscations. On some communities ruinous fines were levied, while others had to surrender part or all of their lands, on which colonies of Sulla's veterans were then settled. The most obstinately rebellious towns were destroyed, and large numbers of the Italians were deprived of their newly won citizenship, receiving in its place a form of Latin rights which placed them at a very serious disadvantage. But the new citizens, as a whole, did not lose their rights to be registered in all the tribes and centuries. That question, at least, was settled.

For his friends, Sulla did well. Every soldier who had fought under his banner received a cash bonus, with a farm in addition if he desired it. All the leaders who had aided him in the civil war were rewarded with choice prizes from the confiscated estates. Although such property was nominally sold at auction, none dared bid against the friends of the new war lord. Crassus in particular laid the foundation of his enormous fortune by purchasing such estates at bargain prices. One of Sulla's freedmen bought in an estate worth 6,000,000 sesterces for 2000, and there were no doubt many other such cases. Ten thousand slaves of proscribed persons were freed, and all took the clan-name Cornelius, with Sulla as their patron.

### *The Sullan Constitution*

To Sulla, now that he was lord of the Roman world, there fell the task of restoring order to a government which had for fifty years been racked by party strife. Late in 82 he extorted from the Assembly a law legalizing all that he had done up to that time including the proscriptions. For the future a new office was created for him, that of "dictator to set the state in order." No term of office was specified; he was to be the supreme head of the state until his death or voluntary abdication. Armed with these unprecedented powers, Sulla undertook the reconstruction of the Roman constitution.

In the three years during which he held the dictatorship, Sulla gave to Rome the first logically integrated constitution she had ever had. In character it was strongly aristocratic, having as its basic principle the supremacy of the Senate. To undo the ravages made in its ranks by war and proscriptions, three hundred equestrians friendly to Sulla's cause were added to it, and provision was made for its maintenance at about six hundred members. The assemblies were retained, with the old forms of organization, but no bill could be introduced into either of them without the consent of the Senate. Likewise the power and dignity of the tribunate, which had in the past cost the Optimates so much trouble, were greatly decreased. Although tribunes still retained the right to release persons from arrest they could no longer dominate the legislative activities of the Assembly, and the tenure of this office made one permanently ineligible for any other. Thus men of ambition would naturally shun it. The juries in the Recovery Court, on which the equestrians had sat for forty years, were restored to the Senate. A series of new courts, also with senatorial juries, were set up to deal with various forms of crime, and rules were established for their procedure. This feature of Sulla's work outlasted practically all his other reforms.

Other magistrates had their independence severely curtailed. The laws regulating the tenure of the curule magistracies were re-enacted with more stringent provisions. The minimum age for quaestor was thirty; for praetor, forty; and for consul, forty-three. Twenty quaestors were chosen each year, and at the end of their terms of office they were admitted to the Senate for life. The number of praetorships was raised to eight. There had to be a lapse of two years between the tenure of a curule office and entry into the one above it, and ten years between a man's tenure of the consulship and re-election to it. The censorship was abolished.

Provincial government was likewise systematized. There were now ten provinces, although to complete the number Cisalpine Gaul had to be retained, in spite of the fact that all of its inhabitants were now either Roman citizens or Latins. Each year the Senate assigned to each of the ex-praetors and ex-consuls of the preceding year, one of the provinces which he would govern for a year. By this arrangement, the consuls and praetors lost control of the military forces, for they had to spend their time in Italy, where no forces were stationed. To the propraetors and proconsuls fell the control of all military activities. Thus the powers of the higher magistracies were greatly lessened, and because the civil and military powers were almost completely separated, the Senate was in a much better position than formerly to govern both. Little if any effort, however, was made to end the shocking abuses common in provincial government, and for the next fifty years they grew worse rather than better.

Having rewarded his friends, punished his enemies, and placed a friendly Senate in control of the government, Sulla, in 79, abdicated his dictatorship and retired to Campania, where he spent his last year of life in a combination of refined leisure and coarse debauchery. When he died in 78, he had, in spite of the blood and tears which he had caused to flow, accomplished little. He had defeated Mithridates, but the Pontic king was still dangerous. He had placed the Senate in control of the government, but it was to lose the place in less than a decade, just as it had lost it before he became dictator. With the two crying evils and deadly perils of the state, the professional armies and corruption in provincial government, he had not even tried to deal. Finally in achieving his ends, he had raised up a group of able, unscrupulous, ambitious officers, such as Pompey, Crassus, and Catiline, who a few years later were to take leading parts in undoing his work. After all, his motives seem to have been chiefly, if not exclusively, personal. Almost everything that he did can be accounted for by his desire for wealth and leisure, or by motives of gratitude and revenge. On the base of his statue in Rome was the inscription which he himself had written, to the effect that no friend had ever done him so great a favor, and no enemy so great a wrong, but that each had been fully repaid. With it we may well sum up his career.

# 16

# *The Decline of the Republic (79-49 B.C.): Personal Politics and Foreign Conquest*

## The Overthrow of Sulla's Constitution

In spite of the care with which Sulla had framed his constitution, it remained intact for less than a decade. The causes of its overthrow are not hard to find. The senatorial aristocracy, whose incompetence and corruption had reduced the state to chaos before his time, had learned nothing and forgotten nothing. As a group it originated hardly one worth-while measure in the generation that intervened between Sulla and Caesar. This failure was not due to lack of problems. Professional armies and politician-generals were as great an evil as ever, and the corruption of provincial government increased. Nor can it be said that there were no able individuals in its ranks, for all of the important leaders of the day except Cicero came of senatorial families. Caesar, Pompey, and Crassus were all men of as great ability as any of the statesmen of earlier centuries. But whereas such men had once shaped the destinies of the state through the instrumentality of the Senate, and had strengthened its position, they were now forced into the ranks of its opponents. This fact, in addition to the power which a strong leader could exercise through the possession of a personal army, made the period following Sulla's retirement one of political free-lances, who used and discarded the old party names at will, and cared chiefly for personal aggrandizement. For a generation such men dominated the government by increasingly violent and irregular methods, until Caesar eliminated or survived the others, and gave Rome a monarchy.

### *Lepidus and Sertorius*

Trouble began even before Sulla abdicated, when Marcus Aemilius Lepidus was elected one of the consuls for 78. He had served in Sulla's army, but was known to be opposed to the new constitution. Once in office, he found a pretext to raise an army in Etruria, and late in 78, marched on Rome. His program, which he forwarded to the Senate, included the return of confiscated lands to the Italians, the restoration of the tribunate, and a second consulship for himself. His colleague Catulus was helpless alone, but with the aid of the young Pompey he raised a force and defeated Lepidus, who fled to Sardinia with the remains of his army. There Lepidus died, and his followers, under his lieutenant Marcus Perperna, went on to Spain, where they joined the rebel Quintus Sertorius.

Affairs in Spain had long been going badly for the government. When, in 83, the Marians had sent their ablest general Sertorius there, they had sowed the seeds of future trouble for their aristocratic foes. Sertorius displayed remarkable skill in conciliating the natives and gaining their confidence. Although he had been driven out by Sulla's lieutenants, he soon returned, and led the Lusitanians (who lived in what is now Portugal) in a revolt against Rome. Using his Roman companions as drill masters, Sertorius built up a formidable army of Spanish natives who could use Roman or guerrilla tactics equally well. To impress his rude allies, he posed as an inspired prophet. Rigorous measures were adopted to prevent his Roman followers from oppressing the Spaniards, and a school was founded in which the children of native chiefs could learn both Latin and Greek. In short, Sertorius was founding a Hispano-Roman state, and the idolatrous affection which the Spaniards felt for him gave promise that within a few years it would be too solidly rooted to be easily overthrown. Sertorius won an astonishing series of victories over the Sullan governors of the Spanish provinces, and in 77 they had to appeal to Rome for help.

Such a crisis as this quickly exposed the weakness of the Senate's position. It had no standing army, and all that it could do was to appoint a commander who either had a personal army at his disposal or could easily raise one. At that moment, the only person qualified for the command against Sertorius was Pompey. He was, in 77, the real commander of the army which had defeated Lepidus, and although legally ineligible to hold a proconsulship because he had never been elected to any urban magistracy, he demanded the Spanish command. The Senate had no choice but to obey. Pompey was made governor of Hither Spain, with Metellus Pius as his colleague in Farther Spain.

We have already seen the beginning of Pompey's spectacular career. Although he had begun as a lieutenant of Sulla, he was temperamentally unfitted to play the part of a docile servant of the Senate. As a general he

*Bettmann*

POMPEY

was able but not brilliant, and although capable of occasional acts of perfidy and cruelty, he was normally both honest and humane. Yet in the tricky game of Roman politics he was, when acting alone, hopelessly inept. Perhaps the chief reason was that he seldom saw beyond his own personal career, and had little interest in either constitutional niceties or political issues. He had entered public life in an irregular manner, and never learned to fit himself completely into the structure of Roman government. He preferred to serve the Senate, but to be contented he had to be vested with extraordinary powers, or hold some office for which he was by law disqualified. Hence, it is not strange that he drifted from party to party, made and broke political alliances, suffered great humiliations, and never gained from the Senate the gratitude due the great services which he rendered to it.

Pompey arrived in Spain in 76, but for the next four years he did little to increase his reputation. Sertorius with brilliant generalship inflicted repeated defeats upon both Pompey and Metellus, but they were usually able to win victories over his subordinates whenever they could force them to fight pitched battles. In 74, Pompey, in despair, wrote to the Senate to beg for reinforcements, and predicted that if they were not sent, Sertorius might even invade Italy. At last, however, superior numbers and equipment turned the tide in favor of the government forces. Perperna, who had conducted the remains of the army of Lepidus to Spain, had the rebel hero assassinated. Thus ended the career of a man who, but for the accident of political strife, might have done much for his country. In 72, Perperna himself was captured and put to death by Pompey. The war in Spain was at an end, and Pompey was recalled to meet a pressing danger in Italy, of which more will be said presently.

### *Lucullus and the Third Mithridatic War*

In the East, the Mithridatic War had flared up again. With one slight exception, the peace established by Sulla lasted nine years. But in 75 Nicomedes III of Bithynia died, leaving his dominions by will to the Roman people, and Mithridates undertook to forestall the Romans by himself occupying Bithynia, and attacking both Asia and Cappadocia. The next year the Senate sent to the East the two consuls, Lucius Licinius Lucullus and Marcus Aurelius Cotta. The latter was a man of small ability, but Lucullus, a former lieutenant of Sulla and a staunch partisan of the Senate, won victory after victory. With a small army of mutinous and discontented soldiers he chased Mithridates from Bithynia, invaded and captured Pontus, and forced the Pontic king to take refuge with King Tigranes of Armenia. When the latter refused to surrender his guest, Lucullus invaded Armenia and inflicted a series of smashing defeats upon Tigranes. For six years he pursued his triumphant career, but at no time did he bring the end of the contest within sight. Every victory seemed to lead to a new advance into the enemy's country, and Lucullus, with a haughty disregard for the feelings of his men, would neither enrich them with the plunder of the occupied countries nor hold out to them the hope of an early discharge from service and the customary rewards accorded to discharged soldiers. Many of them were former soldiers of Flaccus and Fimbria, who had served in the East since 86, and they were weary of this enforced exile. In 68, a dangerous mutiny compelled Lucullus to abandon his Armenian campaign, and thereafter disasters multiplied. Mithridates returned to Pontus and ousted the Roman army of occupation, and Lucullus found himself helpless to turn the tide. During the next two years he fought a losing battle against hopeless odds, until it became necessary to replace him with a man in whom both the soldiers and the Roman public had more confidence. Yet his campaigns had not been fruitless. Both Mithridates and Tigranes had been so crippled by his blows that only a slight additional effort was necessary to break their power. This task was reserved for the more fortunate Pompey.

While Lucullus was in the East, he promulgated a measure for the relief of the people of Asia which won for him the undying hatred of the Roman equestrians, but which at the same time marked him as a shrewd and humane statesman. As we have seen, the hapless Asiatics had been compelled to borrow from Roman bankers the money needed to pay the staggering indemnity levied by Sulla. So harsh had been the terms of these loans that by 71, when Lucullus took the matter in hand, the debt had risen, in spite of continual payments, to the fantastic sum of a hundred and twenty thousand talents. So great was the distress of the people that they were even selling their children into slavery in order to raise money. Lucullus lowered the rate of interest to 12½ per cent a year, and struck off all interest which exceeded the amount of the principal. He then decreed that each debtor was to pay to his creditors one fourth of his income for four years, after which the debt was to be considered paid. The province was effectually relieved, but thereafter the equestrians lost no opportunity to circulate derogatory rumors about Lucullus, and aided greatly in undermining his reputation.

### *The Revolt of Spartacus*

While Pompey was in Spain and Lucullus in the East, a dangerous outbreak in Italy called attention to the weakness of senatorial rule, and to the seething mass of human misery which was the direct result of the Roman slave system. In 73, a band of gladiators, headed by a Thracian named Spartacus, broke out of a gladiatorial training school at Capua and took up their quarters on Mt. Vesuvius. Breaking open the slave prisons on the near-by estates, they freed and armed their occupants, and soon had an army which rumor magnified to a hundred and twenty thousand men. These desperate wretches, who knew that death by crucifixion awaited them if captured, defeated several improvised armies sent against them. Spartacus, who knew that he could not hold out indefinitely against the mighty Roman Republic, tried to influence his men to march northward to the Alps, whence they could travel in small bands to their old homes, but in vain. The prospect of easy plunder was too much for them, and they remained in Italy. Before long, they controlled the whole southern part of the peninsula except the coastal towns. The Senate in desperation turned to another ex-officer of Sulla, Marcus Licinius Crassus, to whom it entrusted the conduct of the war.

Crassus by severe measures restored discipline in his demoralized forces, and soon began to make headway against Spartacus, but in the meantime the Senate, which doubted his ability to master the situation, recalled Pompey from Spain to co-operate with him. Crassus, who had seen success just within reach, had no desire to be robbed of the resulting glory. After a series of successful skirmishes, he met the slaves in a pitched battle in Apulia. Spartacus and all but five thousand of his men were slain or captured. The survivors were met by Pompey, who annihilated them, and as a warning to others, six thousand prisoners were crucified along the Appian Road between Rome and Capua. The splendid but hopeless fight by Spartacus and his fellow slaves for freedom was ended. Its chief result was to give Crassus a military reputation which, when considered along with his great wealth, made him a worthy rival of the showy Pompey.

### *The Consulship of Pompey and Crassus*

When the consular election for the year 70 approached, the Senate was in an awkward position. Pompey and Crassus were bitter personal enemies, and each had an army under his command. Both were certain to be candidates for the consulship, and while Pompey was not legally eligible, the presence of his army made it necessary to legalize his candidacy. However, since there was bitter opposition to both, they found it necessary to ignore their differences and form an alliance. To secure their election they made liberal promises to the classes which had suffered most heavily from Sulla's policies — the equestrians and the commons. Both were chosen.

The consulship of Crassus and Pompey saw the destruction of the more significant features of Sulla's constitution. To the tribunes were restored all the powers of which he had deprived them, so that they became once more the effective leaders of the commons. The juries were reorganized, so that thenceforth they were to consist of one third senators, one third equestrians, and one third *tribuni aerarii* — a class which apparently ranked just below the equestrians in wealth and political power. A third measure of great importance was the restoration of the censorship, which Sulla had abolished probably because it would open a way for talented individuals to enter the Senate by irregular means. No effort was made to recall the exiled Marians or to restore confiscated property, but the Senate nevertheless lost, through fear of the swords of two war lords, what the sword of Sulla had gained for it. Whatever the nominal form of the government, it was plainly the sword which ruled the state.

### *Provincial Misgovernment: Verres*

The same year, 70 B.C., gave to the Romans striking proof — if indeed any were needed — of the corruption and oppression that prevailed in some of the provinces, for it witnessed the trial of Gaius Verres, the ex-propraetor of Sicily. He had been in office there from the beginning of 73 to the end of 71, and had made for himself an unusually bad name through his extortions, injustice, and dishonesty. Hardly had he returned from Sicily when the outraged provincials demanded his punishment. But he had influential friends at Rome who used every means in their power to protect him. The prosecution was conducted by Marcus Tullius Cicero, a rising young orator who had gained the good will of the Sicilians as provincial quaestor. By a mixture of shrewdness and energy he frustrated the efforts of the defense to delay the trial until the next year (when Hortensius, Verres' attorney, would be consul), and in August brought the case to trial. The culprit, not daring to face certain conviction, went into exile before it was completed.

The evidence showed that in the three years which he spent in Sicily, Verres had stolen or extorted forty million sesterces, and that he had committed numberless acts of cruelty and oppression. Acting in collusion with the *publicani*, he had ordered the provincials to pay whatever these harpies demanded from them, and then to seek redress in his courts if they were overcharged. As he shared in the gains of the tax-farmers, no redress was ever granted. When the government sent money to Sicily to purchase grain, he kept the money and extorted the grain from the provincials. Other enormous sums were extorted under cover of his right to levy provisions for the support of himself and his court. Justice was sold to the highest bidder, and false accusations were lodged against wealthy men. In such cases Verres either sold verdicts of acquittal, or confiscated their property and kept it for himself. Provincials and Roman citizens alike were imprisoned, tortured, or even crucified, in flat defiance of the law. Verres pretended to be a connoisseur of art, and either seized outright or bought at his own price numerous statues and paintings, sometimes even plundering temples. To these crimes he added outrages against the honor of families, and led a life of scandalous immorality. He boasted that of the three years of his stay in Sicily, he intended to keep only the takings of one year, reserving those of the second year for his subordinates, and the third year for his jurors. Of the two *Verrine Orations* composed by Cicero, only the first was actually delivered. The second, which contains the foregoing lurid summary of Verres' misdeeds, was circulated in pamphlet form after his flight from Rome.

It must not be thought that all provincial governors were as vicious as Verres. Instances to the contrary might be found, but there is evidence that provincial government in general was both oppressive and corrupt. There were excellent laws to protect the provincials, and courts to enforce them, but to no avail. The too-great powers of governors and *publicani*, the decline of Roman morality, and the weakness of the home government, all combined to render laws and courts alike useless. It is significant that at his trial Verres had the support of many of the leading men of Rome, who nearly secured his acquittal, and Cicero himself, on other occasions, seems to have defended men equally guilty. In short, the aristocracy was seldom shocked by the vices of its members. For it, only genius was an unpardonable sin. Not until Julius Caesar and (later) Augustus gained control of the government did the lot of the provincials undergo measurable improvement.

## The Ascendancy of Pompey (70-62 B.C.)

The quality of senatorial government, which as we have seen had been none too good under the constitution of Sulla, deteriorated steadily after the changes made by Crassus and Pompey had weakened its position. In fact, for some years after their joint consulship, both were allied with the *Populares* and used their influence accordingly. As before, when critical situations arose, they could only be met by entrusting extensive powers to military leaders, and the Senate was loath to take this step. The commons, on the other hand, demanded efficiency in military and civil affairs, and were willing to use the services of the war lords to achieve it. About this issue some of the most severe political struggles of the next decade were to be waged.

### *The Suppression of Piracy: the Gabinian Law*

Aside from the Mithridatic War, the most pressing problem of the day was the prevalence of piracy in the Mediterranean Sea. In earlier times the navies of Rhodes, Ptolemaic Egypt, and Carthage had kept down this ever-present menace. But the Romans had destroyed Carthage and weakened Rhodes, while the decadent Ptolemies had dismantled their fleet. At the same time, the Roman conquests had driven thousands of bold and desperate men from their homes, leaving them only piracy as a means of livelihood. From their bases in southern Asia Minor, Crete, and the Balearic Islands, they practically controlled the seas. Not content with capturing merchant ships, they also raided coast lands and carried off thousands of captives, whom they held for ransom or sold as slaves. For a long time little attention was paid them, for the Romans had few commercial interests, and the pirates were welcome purveyors of slaves.

There had been, it is true, occasional feeble efforts to deal with the scourge. In 102, after a pointed protest by King Nicomedes of Bithynia, the Roman government had sent a fleet and army into Cilicia and reduced part of the district to the form of a province. In 78, probably because of the services rendered by these marauders to Mithridates, another raid had been made on the Cilician coast, and two efforts (the first completely unsuccessful) were made to conquer Crete. But in spite of these timid gestures the evil grew steadily worse, and began to affect the interests of the Romans themselves. Grain ships from Africa and Sicily were captured in such numbers that famine threatened the capital. Coastal areas in Italy were raided, and rich Romans were either held for ransom or killed. The equestrians and commons alike demanded action. It was obvious that the time for half-measures had passed, and that nothing but a large-scale drive would make the seas safe.

To do this a unified command would have to be created under a leader with sweeping powers, and only the Assembly of the Tribes was willing to take such a step. In 67, the tribune Aulus Gabinius proposed that the war against the pirates be entrusted to a single commander to be chosen by the Senate from among the ex-consuls. He was to have entire control of the Mediterranean and Black Seas for three years, and all provincial governors whose provinces fronted upon these seas were to be subordinate to him. He was to have the right to name twenty-five lieutenants of senatorial rank, and to have twenty legions of soldiers, five hundred ships, and six thousand talents in money. Obviously the post was intended for Pompey, and the *Optimates*, who saw that the holder of such gigantic powers could easily become the master of the state, opposed the bill bitterly. But Gabinius was in earnest, and after overriding a tribunician veto by reverting to the tactics of Tiberius Gracchus, he secured its passage. Pompey received the appointment.

His success was rapid and spectacular. Having first made the grain supply of Rome safe, he divided the Mediterranean into districts, with a squadron to operate in each. All efforts were closely co-ordinated, and in forty days, the sea west of the Sicilian "Narrows" was free. Another fifty days sufficed to drive the pirates from the eastern Mediterranean and to storm their strongholds in Cilicia. Leniency toward captives sped the progress of the work. Those who surrendered voluntarily were neither killed nor enslaved, but were settled in colonies far enough from the sea to discourage a return to their old calling. In three months the pirate problem had been disposed of. Pompey was lauded to the skies, and the *Populares* were ready to raise him to still greater powers and honors.

### *Pompey and the Mithridatic War*

The next move was to give Pompey the task of settling the tedious Mithridatic War. Lucullus had failed, and the Roman public had lost confidence in him. Moreover, the equestrians mortally hated him, and were anxious to replace him. Hence, in the spring of 66, a tribune, Gaius Manilius, introduced a bill giving Pompey the command against Mithridates, with powers more sweeping than any he had yet held. He was to continue in possession of those powers previously held, and in addition was to receive the governorship of Bithynia and Cilicia, with a large increase in his forces and in the number of his lieutenants, all of whom he was to appoint. No Roman had ever held such tremendous authority before, and his position, if the bill were passed, would be dangerously near to that of despot. Scarcely any opposition was encountered, and the bill became a law.

In spite of his egregious vanity, Pompey was a conscientious public servant, and he spent the next five years in settling Rome's problems in the East. Having taken over the armies of Lucullus — with unnecessary tactlessness and impoliteness, it is true — he resumed the attack upon Mithridates. The power of the Pontic king had been all but broken by Lucullus, and his only hope lay in substantial aid from Tigranes. Pompey, by forming an alliance with the Parthians, succeeded in keeping the latter busy, and Mithridates was soon driven from his kingdom again. The fugitive took refuge in his possessions north of the Black Sea, to which he could not be readily followed. Pompey then turned against Tigranes, who immediately submitted, and thus saved his crown. By the end of 65, Pompey had broken the opposition in the north.

In 64, he turned his attention to Syria and Palestine. The Seleucid

State had sunk into complete impotence and although Tigranes had for a time ruled both Syria and Cilicia, Lucullus had compelled him to relinquish his hold upon them. Both districts were now prey to anarchy and disorder. Pompey destroyed the brigands who harassed the people, slew or deposed the tyrants who had seized their cities, and organized Syria and Phoenicia as a Roman province. He then passed on into Palestine, where two Jewish princes, Hyrcanus and Aristobulus, were contending for the high-priesthood of Yahweh and the kingship of their country. Pompey took the side of the weaker elder brother Hyrcanus against the ambitious Aristobulus, and captured Jerusalem after a short siege. Hyrcanus was installed in the coveted position, but he lost much territory and ruled the remainder in strict subjection to Rome.

While Pompey was in the south, the last act in the tragedy of Mithridates had been played. Misfortune had only accentuated the stubborn savagery of the Pontic king's nature, and he was now dangerous to all his associates. Like Hannibal, he was planning a desperate attempt to gather an army, and invade Italy by way of the Danube Valley and the Alps. But defeat had destroyed the confidence of his subjects. A favorite son, Pharnaces, revolted, and the Greeks of the Kingdom of the Cimmerian Bosporus — now Mithridates' only subjects — supported the rebel. True to his nature, the fallen king had all of his wives and children within reach murdered to prevent their capture, and then caused a Celtic mercenary to kill him. Pharnaces sent the corpse to Pompey, who had it buried with honor.

Asia Minor was now organized as thoroughly as Syria and Palestine had been. Bithynia and western Pontus were combined as a single province, and the province of Cilicia was greatly enlarged. In addition, Pompey founded, re-established, or changed the rulers of a host of client states stretching all the way along the eastern frontier, including Pontus, Galatia, Cappadocia, and many more. Temple-states, tribal domains, and free cities were all set in order. Not since the days of Alexander the Great had western Asia been so systematically pacified.

But Pompey's work did not stop there. In the lands he conquered he undertook methodically to revive and strengthen the Greek element, which had been declining for a century and a half. Old Hellenistic cities that had lost heavily in population were recolonized, given new names, and provided with new governments. New cities were founded, with nuclei of Greeks or Hellenized Orientals to rule them. A good example of this work is to be seen in Palestine, where the Greek cities both east of the Jordan and along the coast, which had been weakened or destroyed by the Maccabean princes, were rebuilt. Due to his efforts, Hellenistic influence in Asia was stronger and more vigorous for three centuries after his time. In all he claimed to have conquered twelve million people, to have taken spoil worth eight hundred million sesterces, and to have raised the total of provincial tribute from two hundred million sesterces to three hundred and forty million.

### *Roman Politics: Crassus, Cicero, and Catiline*

But the years that Pompey spent in the East were not peaceful ones in Rome. Politicians realized that he had strength enough to seize dictatorial powers whenever he chose, and it was feared that if he did so he would imitate Sulla by proscribing and murdering his personal enemies, of whom the most prominent was Crassus. There were, however, many others, and the apprehension which prevailed among them poisoned Roman political life for several years. To this fact we may attribute several of the most significant events of the times.

Crassus was not the man to await supinely the stroke of fate. Instead he bent his energies to secure for himself a military command and an army capable of resisting the Pompeian forces. Usually he worked through agents of various kinds, such as needy senators who owed him money, desperadoes bent upon revolution, and equestrian business associates. For this reason his moves cannot always be traced back to their author.

Chief among the coterie of Crassus was a man who was later to eclipse both himself and Pompey, Gaius Julius Caesar. He was born in 100 B.C., of one of Rome's most aristocratic families, but his leanings were all toward the *Populares*. His aunt had married Marius, and his own first wife was the daughter of Cinna. When Sulla had ordered him to divorce her, he had braved the anger of the Dictator by refusing to do so, and for this show of independence he narrowly escaped proscription. He spent his fortune recklessly in entertaining the commons, and soon found himself heavily in debt, but he also had more honorable ways of appealing to their hearts. When his wife and aunt died, he delivered funeral orations in which he praised both Cinna and Marius, and when elected aedile, he restored the monuments and trophies erected in honor of Marius and overthrown by Sulla. He prosecuted a few of the murderers employed in the Sullan proscription, and even proposed to restore political rights to the children of proscribed persons. Later he was to prove one of Rome's greatest generals and statesmen, but in the sixties he still followed the lead of Crassus, to whose schemes he was no doubt a party.

Crassus' first move was designed to secure a hold upon the Spanish provinces. In 66, three disappointed candidates for the consulship formed a plot to murder their successful competitors and install two of their number in office. The ringleader of the plot was Lucius Sergius Catilina, a reckless adventurer and débauché who had formerly served as one of Sulla's executioners. The plot failed, but it is significant of senatorial ineptitude that no action was taken against its backers. Indeed, one of them, Gnaeus Calpurnius Piso, soon gained the office of propraetor in Hither Spain. Crassus had had no part in the plot, but he apparently saved its authors from punishment, and Piso went to Spain as his henchman. Piso was soon killed, and this move came to naught.

In the same year Crassus tried again, this time in Egypt. It was alleged that Ptolemy X, who was murdered in 80, had left a will bequeathing Egypt to the Roman people. The Senate had not taken possession of the

*Galloway*

CICERO

bequest, and Egypt had fallen into the hands of a usurper, Ptolemy XI, a worthless and tyrannical ruler known by the nickname "The Piper." A tribune introduced a bill providing that Caesar should be sent to annex the Ptolemaic lands, and naturally enough, he would require an army to support him. But Cicero, the only member of the *Optimates* who at this time showed the slightest trace of statesmanship, was convinced that the interest of his party and all of the state lay in conciliating Pompey and attaching him once more to the senatorial cause. Largely through his efforts, the bill was defeated.

Undiscouraged by two failures, Crassus tried a third time. In 64, he supported for the consulship Catiline and a nonentity, Gaius Antonius. But Cicero, with the grudging, last-minute support of the aristocracy, won first place in the election, and Antonius was chosen as his colleague. Cicero next made a bargain with Antonius by which the latter practically surrendered his liberty of action and agreed to support all of Cicero's policies.

The year 63 witnessed the culmination of Crassus' efforts. A tribune named Rullus introduced a most extraordinary land-law, which was to devote practically the whole of the state's funds to finding farms for the urban poor. Even the income from Pompey's conquests was to be used, although Pompey's soldiers were to have no part in the allotment. The law was to be administered by a board of ten members with powers as sweeping as those of Pompey, and with an army to enforce its decisions. It required no great prophetic gifts to see that if the bill passed, Crassus and nine of his adherents would be members of the board. The commons were indifferent, and Cicero, by mobilizing the reluctant Senate, was able to defeat the proposal.

But the chief event of the year was the second conspiracy of Catiline. Again he was an unsuccessful candidate for the consulship. He had now broken with Crassus, and was on his own. Accordingly, he formed a new plot to murder Cicero, set fire to the city, and assume the consulship himself. A small army was recruited in Etruria by a lieutenant, Lucius Manlius. To attract followers, he promised a general abolition of debts, and several needy senators, along with a number of ruined men from various parts of Italy, were thereby drawn into the movement.

Cicero, in spite of the apathy of the Senate, foiled the conspirators at every point. He kept himself informed of their plans, and in an open meeting of the Senate, at which Catiline himself was present, exposed the plot in the blistering speech known as the *First Catilinarian Oration*. The arch-plotter left the city for the camp of Manlius, and the Senate declared him a public enemy. Early in December, Cicero made use of a Gallic embassy in the city to secure conclusive evidence against five of the conspirators (including Publius Cornelius Lentulus, a praetor), and arrested them. A month later Antonius attacked and annihilated Catiline's army in a ferocious battle near the Etruscan city of Pistoria. Catiline himself was among the slain.

Meanwhile the arrest of the conspirators had produced an awkward dilemma. Since they had not carried out their plot, there was little evidence to lay before an ordinary court. The Senate had no right to sentence them, but Cicero felt bound to refer the case to it. Opposing the death sentence were Crassus and Caesar who had had no part in the plot — Crassus had even furnished information to the government. Experience had shown that Crassus was an expert in the art of bribing juries, while Caesar (now praetor-elect) protested vigorously against a sentence of death for the plotters, threatening, on behalf of the *Populares*, a dire vengeance against any magistrate who would slay citizens without a trial. For a moment the Senate wavered, but Marcus Porcius Cato, the great-grandson of the Censor, soon recalled it to sterner measures. The death-sentence was voted, and Cicero immediately caused it to be carried out. He was greeted with well-deserved applause at the time, but a few years later his enemies were to exile him for this necessary but illegal act.

### *The "Harmony of the Orders"*

Cicero's services to the state did not stop there. He attempted to build up a triple alliance of senators, equestrians, and Pompey to support the existing government, and for several years worked assiduously (and in the main intelligently) to achieve this end. In the heat of the Catilinarian crisis, the first two elements of this alliance had reached an understanding which Cicero did his best to render permanent, and his efforts to prevent hostile measures against Pompey were directed toward the same goal. Such an alliance, if it could have been achieved, would have rendered the existing government impregnable. Its failure was ultimately due to the errors of others, rather than those of Cicero.

Late in 62, Pompey landed at Brundisium, and his return proved a rather ridiculous anticlimax. After having kept Roman political circles in suspense for five years, he quietly disbanded his army, and humbly petitioned the Senate to confirm his acts in the East and to reward his men. Here was the crowning good fortune of the "Harmony of the Orders," and had the Senate known how to consolidate its position, its troubles would have been over for a long time to come.

That nothing of the sort happened was due to perverse short-sightedness in senatorial circles. In the past Pompey had been guilty of a number of high-handed acts against other generals and provincial governors, among whom was Lucullus. The aristocracy in general resented his unconventional career, and saw only that here was an opportunity to put him in his place. Hence, it was decided to pass upon his settlement of the East item by item, and no move was made to reward his soldiers. For Pompey there was no retreat. His faith was pledged to the men who had fought for him, and his reputation was staked upon his acts in the East. He was thus driven once more into the ranks of the *Populares*, and the coalition lost its military support.

Soon afterward the equestrians also deserted the alliance. In 61, a company of *publicani* who had bought the right to collect the taxes of Asia complained that they had bid too high, and asked for a remission of a third of their obligation. Cicero, although privately convinced that the demand was unjust, supported it, but the uncompromising Cato secured its rejection. By this and similar measures the equestrians were alienated. In short, every point in Cicero's program was sabotaged by aristocratic politicians who would have benefited most by its success.

The failure of Cicero's plan cleared the way for the rise of Caesar who, in 63, was elected praetor and also *pontifex maximus*. At the end of his praetorship he was so deeply in debt that Crassus had to underwrite his obligations before his creditors would allow him to leave the city for his province of Farther Spain. Once in the province, however, Caesar gained a good reputation both in war and civil government, and, more important, he secured money enough to pay his most pressing debts. When he returned to Rome, just before the consular elections for the year 59, he found Pompey still vainly striving to save his reputation and fulfill his obligations, just as he had been two years before, and Crassus agitating the claims of the equestrians regarding the taxes of Asia. Here was political capital of which Caesar could make good use.

## The First Triumvirate and Its Consequences (60–49 B.C.)

It was now obvious that the Senate was committed to the policy of repressing every political leader who rose above mediocrity, and that no man of first-rate ability could either serve it or live on peaceable terms with it. Caesar himself had two immediate objectives, for both of which he would have to secure senatorial consent. His military exploits in Spain entitled him to a triumphal entry into the city, and he wished to be a candidate for the consulship. But to gain the first he had to remain outside the city until authorized by the Senate to enter, and as declarations of candidacy had to be made in the city and in person, the two objectives were incompatible unless a special dispensation was accorded absolving him from his personal declaration of candidacy. The Senate would not make this harmless concession, and Caesar, who saw clearly which of his aims was the more important, waived the triumph and became a candidate.

*The Formation of the Triumvirate: Caesar as Consul*

He then went to work to build up an invincible anti-senatorial coalition. He reconciled Pompey and Crassus, and allied both with himself. Each had certain elements of strength to contribute to the alliance. Crassus had wealth, and also the support of the equestrian order; Pompey had a military reputation and the support of his veteran soldiers; while Caesar

*Galloway*

JULIUS CAESAR

had the audacity, the organizing ability, and the knack of swaying the Roman commons which both the others lacked. The objectives of Crassus and Pompey have been mentioned, but it must be added that Caesar, in addition to the consulship, wished to secure the proconsulship of one or more provinces for a number of years, with the command of an army. Thus, and only thus, he might win the military reputation indispensable to a successful Roman public career, with wealth and the personal devotion of soldiers. Cicero was invited to join the coalition, but refused. Although the resulting "ring" had no legal standing, it came to be called the First Triumvirate, or "Committee of Three."

From the first, Caesar's election was assured, but the aristocracy was determined to render him harmless in advance. By wholesale bribery they secured the election of Marcus Calpurnius Bibulus, a narrow-minded and stupid aristocrat, as his colleague. With such a colleague in the consulship it was hoped that he could do little. But worse was to come. The Senate was compelled by law to assign provinces each year to the incoming consuls before the elections, to be governed in the year following their consulship. Its members, foreseeing the election of Caesar, relegated the consuls of 59 to the inglorious supervision of state forests and cattle-paths in Italy. It was a foolish move, for Caesar was not a man to yield tamely to such unfair discrimination, and his only means of reversing its decision was to break its power through a resort to the Assembly and Pompey's veterans. Whether Caesar wished it or not, he was compelled to enter his consulship as an enemy of the aristocracy, and of all that it stood for.

Accordingly, he spent the year of his consulship in paying his political debts and assuring his own future. After a vain attempt to win the support of his enemies, he openly defied both Bibulus and the Senate and resorted to the Assembly. When Bibulus attempted to veto his colleague's acts, he was driven from the forum by a mob of commoners and Pompey's veterans. He then retired to his house and announced before each meeting of the Assembly "that he was taking the auspices," an act which, until completed with favorable results, precluded the transaction of public business. But such tactics had no influence upon Caesar, and orators who opposed him fared no better. Thus, when Cato attempted to denounce his measures, Caesar had him arrested and imprisoned, and tribunician opposition was disregarded. In quick succession he carried bills embodying the wishes of his colleagues in the Triumvirate. The public lands in Campania were assigned to Pompey's veterans and to needy commoners, while Pompey's organization of the eastern provinces and client-states was confirmed. Crassus secured the remission of the portion of the Asiatic tribute which he demanded. Lastly, a tribune named Vatinius carried a measure assigning to Caesar the provinces of Cisalpine Gaul and Illyricum for five years, together with three legions of soldiers; while shortly afterward the Senate, acting under pressure from Crassus and Pompey, added the province of Transalpine Gaul with an additional legion. A special clause in each of these acts gave him the right to take possession of his province while still consul. At the end of the consulship he had shown himself both clever and unscrupulous, but none of his measures displayed far-sighted statesmanship. Yet from that time on his future career was, in a sense, determined. He had his opportunity to win military fame, and he had committed so many flagrantly lawless acts that he could never again retire with safety into private life. His only security from prosecution and ruin lay in the continuous tenure of some official post, for Roman law forbade the arraignment of any magistrate while in office. It was this stern necessity which later drove him to fight a civil war and to become the uncrowned king of Rome.

Before setting out for his provinces, early in 58, Caesar took pains to protect himself from attacks at home. To Pompey he gave his only daughter Julia in marriage. The consuls of 58 were tools of the Triumvirate, and Caesar took Calpurnia, the daughter of one of them, as his third wife. But one more measure was necessary. So long as Cicero and Cato were in Rome, and Caesar was absent, there was danger that they would rally the *Optimates* and oust the Triumvirs from power. Accordingly, it was decided that both must be removed from the scene. Cato was sent as a lone ambassador to superintend the annexation of Cyprus to the province of Cilicia, and prudence or a sense of duty made him accept. Cicero, for whom Caesar felt great respect, and to whom the latter was under strong obligations, was courted assiduously by the Triumvirs, but he refused to succumb to their blandishments. To silence him Caesar at last turned to Cicero's bitter personal enemy, the violent and unscrupulous Publius Clodius, who wished to be tribune, but whose patrician birth disqualified him for the office. However, Caesar arranged a fraudulent adoption into a plebeian family for him, and he was elected tribune. He at once carried a law to distribute grain free to the Roman proletariat, and thus became a popular idol. He then introduced another bill sentencing to banishment all persons who as magistrates had put Roman citizens to death without trial. The measure was patently aimed at Cicero, who, after vainly seeking aid from Pompey, retired into exile. Clodius, who by this time had gathered a gang of hoodlums with which he could set the laws at defiance, secured a supplementary decree banishing Cicero at least five hundred miles from Rome, and burned his house. Cicero retired to Greece, a martyr to the cause of an aristocracy which could neither save itself nor rally around capable leaders when they tried to save it. In April, 58, Caesar having disposed of all possible sources of opposition, set out for Transalpine Gaul.

### *The Conquest of Gaul: Country and People*

So important a part did Gaul play in Caesar's subsequent career and in the later history of Rome, that we may well pause to consider the land and its people. Independent Gaul was bounded on the south by the Roman province and the Pyrenees, on the west by the Atlantic Ocean and the English Channel, and on the east by the Rhine River. The main body of the people were Celtic in speech and culture, but there were two large exceptions. On the north the Belgae, a group of tribes living north of the Seine and Marne rivers, included some Germanic elements; and in the southwest the Aquitani spoke a non-Indo-European tongue akin to modern Basque. In their material and intellectual culture the people were just emerging from barbarism. They practiced both agriculture and stock raising, and they were skilled in metal working. Towns were numerous, and commerce was carried on by the natives and the Roman provincials settled in the country. Society was profoundly aristocratic, with striking resemblances to that of later France. There were three classes — nobles, priests, and commons. The nobles were great landlords, who held the commons in a state little better than slavery. The priests were the famous *Druids*, who had a close organization, an elaborate educational system, and great power. In some of their rites they performed human sacrifices, to the great disgust of the Romans. The art of writing had been learned from the Greeks of Massilia, and the Druids, at least, used the Greek alphabet. Some of the tribes coined money, but they usually did no more than imitate Greek and Roman coin types.

But in government the Gauls were hopelessly weak. Political organization was based upon blood-kinship, the smallest unit being the clan. Except in Aquitania, the clans were united in large tribal groups, which must have numbered nearly a hundred in all. In Central Gaul the most important tribes were the Aedui, Arverni, Sequani, Helvetii, and (in modern Brittany) the Veneti, while in Belgic Gaul, the Bellovaci, Nervii, Treveri, and Eburones were outstanding. Inter-tribal wars occurred frequently, and to wage them, loose alliances were formed, often including

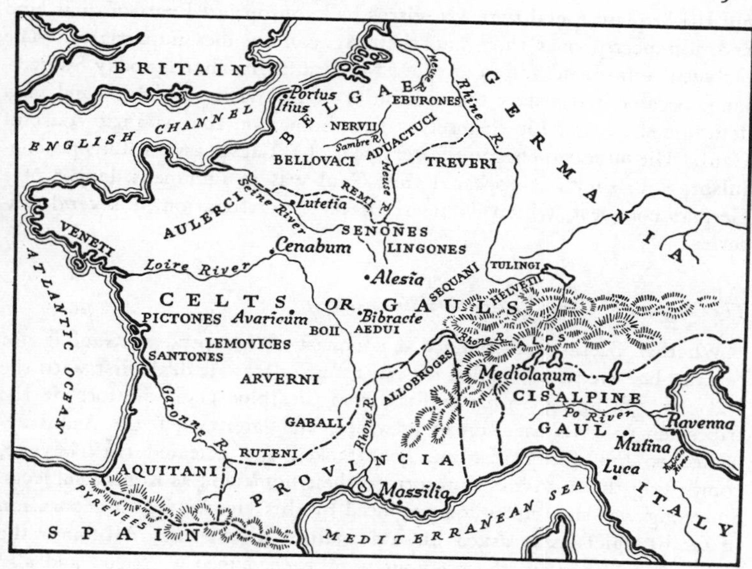


GAUL AT THE TIME OF THE ROMAN CONQUEST
*About 50 B.C.*

many tribes. But such groups usually were temporary arrangements, because of internal dissensions. Until a few years before Caesar's time the average Gallic tribe had been governed by a king, but except in a few distant corners of the land, the monarchies had everywhere given way to turbulent aristocracies, whose members either waged private wars or schemed to get personal control of their respective states. Of national patriotism there were few traces, and even tribal loyalty was so weak that an invader could usually count upon the support of some of the malcontents from almost every tribe.

To add to the prevailing disorder, Gaul was undergoing a series of invasions by the Germans from across the Rhine. We have seen how the Cimbri and the Teutones had ravaged the land. About 70 B.C. another and formidable inroad began. The Aedui, who had long been allies of Rome, were at war with the Sequani, and the latter had called to their aid a band of German warriors from the tribe of the Suevi, under the leadership of a chief named Ariovistus. The coalition decisively defeated the Aedui, but the Sequani found that Ariovistus had appropriated part of their land and domineered over them and their Aeduan enemies impartially. The Helvetii, who lived across the Jura Mountains in what is today Switzerland, became alarmed at the proximity of Ariovistus and his band, and determined to find for themselves new homes on the Atlantic coast of Gaul. The migration began the very year that Caesar assumed his proconsulship. In short, it appeared that Gaul was in imminent danger of a German conquest, which would set back her civilization by several centuries.

### *The Conquest of Gaul: Preliminary Encirclement*

Whether Caesar had planned a conquest of independent Gaul is not certain, but events compelled him to act at once. He dealt first with the Helvetii. Bringing up his legions from Cisalpine Gaul, he forbade the tribesmen to cross the Roman province, and later, when the Aedui appealed to him for protection, he attacked and defeated the Helvetii, compelling the survivors to return to their homeland as Roman subjects. So strong was the impression produced by this victory that a deputation of Gallic chiefs next asked his aid against Ariovistus. Although the German chief had, in the previous year, been named a "friend and ally of the Roman people," when Ariovistus refused to abandon his rule in Gaul, Caesar took the matter in hand and attacked and defeated him, driving the survivors of his army across the Rhine. In both these cases he could have claimed to have acted with perfect propriety, having waged war to protect Rome's Aeduan allies. Thus, in one campaign, he had freed Gaul from the German peril, but when winter came, he placed his legions in quarters among the Sequani. It was a manifesto to the Gauls: Rome intended to keep what she had won, and for the Helvetii and Sequani the days of chaotic independence were over.

The advance of the Roman frontier to the Rhine was viewed with alarm by many Gallic chiefs, and particularly by the Belgae, whose lands adjoined those of the Sequani on the north. In the winter of 58–57, they formed a confederacy which included all of this division of the Gallic people except the tribe called Remi, whose territory lay about the modern town of Rheims. Rumor placed the strength of the Belgic army at nearly three hundred thousand men. As in the previous year, Caesar carefully observed the proprieties. Waiting until the Remi had placed themselves under his protection, and the confederates had in turn attacked them, he led his army into the Belgic territory.

For all of its great size, the army of the Belgic confederacy soon broke up. After watching and skirmishing with Caesar's men for some time, they found that their provisions were running low, and that Caesar's Aeduan allies were about to raid the territories of the Bellovaci. Thereupon they decided to separate and return to their homes, with the promise that all would gather to defend any tribe which Caesar would attack. But by rapid raids into their territories, Caesar was able to reduce most of them piecemeal, without hindrance from the other allies. Only twice did he encounter serious opposition. The Nervii, the most prominent of the Belgic tribes, delivered a surprise attack against him at the Sambre River, but after a murderous battle were almost annihilated, and submitted. The Aduatuci, a German tribe living in Gaul, pretended to surrender and then made a night attack upon his army. They were sold into slavery. Finally a legion sent into the districts later known as Normandy and Brittany brought the tribes of these two districts into submission.

If we plot the campaigns of Caesar's first two years in Gaul on a map, we will discover that he had laid a solid foundation for the conquest of the land, and had laid it with consummate skill. A great circle of conquered land bordered the Rhine and the English Channel and marked out the new frontier, but the tribes of central Gaul had not fought at all. In fact both then and later Caesar fought against Germans more often than Gauls and when, for reasons of policy, he found it necessary to display cruelty, this treatment was regularly reserved for German invaders of Gaul. Being surrounded on all sides by Roman territory, the tribes between the Roman province and the Seine made their initial submission without a struggle. When at last they discovered the significance of his strategy, they rose in revolt, but by this time Caesar had the tremendous moral advantage of dealing with rebels rather than with men fighting to retain their independence. To overcome such rebellions was to require six more years of fighting, negotiating, and organizing.

Aware of the difficulties that still awaited him, Caesar, in 56, secured an extension of his proconsulship for five more years, and then returned to his task. The third campaign was devoted to the repression of a formidable rebellion among the Veneti on the coast of what is now Brittany, but Crassus' son, one of Caesar's lieutenants, also conquered Aquitania for him. Great efforts were made to teach the neighbors of the Gauls that Gaul was now Roman property. In 55, when two wandering German tribes crossed the Rhine and demanded lands in the new province, Caesar refused, and then, on a flimsy pretext and by very dishonorable methods, attacked and annihilated them. The same year, and again in 53, he led his army into Germany by bridges which he built over the Rhine, but the Germans did not oppose him, and he soon retired. In 55 and 54, he undertook to overawe the Celtic Britons by invading their country, but no permanent conquests were made. Yet in spite of his repeated victories, Caesar's hold upon Gaul was insecure, and a final war for Celtic independence was certain to occur sooner or later.

### *The Conquest of Gaul: The Final Struggle and Its Results*

It was fortunate for him that when the Gauls made their final struggle to overthrow Roman supremacy, it came in two parts and in two different years. The first broke out in the winter of 54–53 among the Belgae, where the Eburones under their chief Ambiorix besieged a Roman detachment in its camp, and then, luring it out by treacherous negotiations, attacked and annihilated it. A similar attack was made upon another detachment, commanded by Quintus Cicero, the brother of the well-known orator. But Cicero beat them off, and the next summer Caesar took a terrible revenge upon the Eburones and their allies. Their lands were mercilessly ravaged and a large part of the tribe destroyed, although Ambiorix himself escaped. This severe lesson so cowed the Belgae that the next winter, when the tribes of central Gaul revolted, they had to do without much aid from the region north of the Seine.

The revolt in central Gaul was supported chiefly by tribes which had not yet been in arms against the Romans. Vercingetorix, a young chief of the Arverni, formed an extensive conspiracy, which came to include practically all of the tribes between the Seine and the Garonne rivers and southeastward to the boundaries of the original Roman province. The rebellion broke out while Caesar was in Cisalpine Gaul and his troops were in winter quarters, and every effort was made to keep him from rejoining his army. As tribe after tribe joined the movement, and preparations were made to invade Rome's province on the southern coast, it seemed as if her supremacy beyond the Alps was tottering to a fall. But Caesar once more showed himself equal to the emergency. Before the winter had ended, he had foiled the attempts to invade the province, and had forced his way through to his army. In quick succession he took town after town, culminating in the capture and destruction of Genabum (Orleans) and Avaricum (Bourges). Titus Labienus, the ablest of his lieutenants, meanwhile defeated the tribes along the Seine. Vercingetorix then attempted to resort to guerrilla tactics, for which his preponderance in cavalry especially fitted him, and the Romans suffered severely from want of provisions. At last even the Aedui joined the movement. But in the end Caesar's superb military genius turned the tide. Forcing Vercingetorix into the town of Alesia, he besieged him there, and when a large force of Gauls gathered to relieve the town, Caesar beat them off and starved the rebels into surrender. The rebel chief was taken to Rome, where six years later he was put to death; otherwise Caesar displayed great clemency toward the defeated.

The fall of Alesia broke the back of the rebellion, but it required yet another year of fighting to stamp out the embers of the conflagration. In this work Caesar displayed such tact and humanity that the conquered people were thoroughly conciliated, and did not revolt again until many years afterward. In conquering them Caesar had killed or enslaved nearly a million persons, but many of these were Germans from beyond the Rhine. In the end the Gauls were really the gainers, for the cessation of German raids and inter-tribal wars soon allowed them to repair the damage caused by the conquest, and both wealth and population continued to increase for centuries thereafter. The Roman yoke was a very light one. Caesar imposed only a small tribute, forty million sesterces a year, which was collected by native magistrates and not by *publicani*. No land was confiscated for Roman colonies, and aside from the tribute and some general police powers, local self-government went on as before. No effort was made to Romanize Gaul, but Roman civilization spread gradually as the Gauls adopted it.

For the Romans the conquest was of major importance. It gave them in the northeast a "scientific frontier" which they urgently needed. The Gauls were a virile and intelligent people, who could easily be assimilated into the Roman body-politic, and Rome had use for such material. The conquests of Pompey had so greatly increased the number of Orientals under her sway that she was becoming top-heavy in that direction. Caesar's conquests restored the balance by bringing into her possession millions of Europeans capable of furnishing excellent fighting men for her future armies. In a wider historic sense, the conquest decided for all time to come that the region between the Rhine, the Alps, and the Pyrenees was to be Latin rather than German in culture. Because of this, we may say that Caesar was one of the most influential shapers of the course of medieval and modern European history.

For Caesar himself, the conquest marked a turning point in his career. It gave him wealth, military reputation, and the devotion of an army, which lifted him to a plane of equality with Pompey. No Roman before him had ever won such an ascendancy over a body of soldiers, inspired them with such unconquerable morale, or drilled them to such a pitch of efficiency. In Gaul he forged the weapon with which he was to beat down all opposition and make himself lord of the Roman world. Indeed, it was in Gaul that Caesar ceased to be a mere politician and became a general and statesman.

### *Roman Politics, 58–53 B.C.*

Meanwhile, political conditions in Rome had seen their full measure of confusion. No sooner had Caesar left the city in 58 than Crassus and Pompey resumed their quarrels. Clodius, probably incited by Crassus, assumed a hostile attitude toward Pompey, and although the latter was anxious to secure the recall of Cicero, Clodius and his outlaws succeeded in preventing action on the measure until September of 57. As a countermeasure, Pompey backed a rival tribune, Titus Annius Milo, who took the only possible means of opposing Clodius by gathering a gang of gladiators who would meet violence with violence. Through the joint efforts of Pompey and Milo, Cicero was recalled, but his power was broken, and for some years he was a dependent of the Triumvirs. Yet the Triumvirate itself had become dangerously weakened, and Pompey was veering about once more toward an alliance with the Senate. Such an alliance would have been dangerous to Caesar in particular, for it would no doubt have cost him his Gallic command. In reality, however, none of the Triumvirs could afford to let their understanding lapse.

Again Caesar took the matter in hand. After spending the winter of 57–56 in Cisalpine Gaul, he arranged, before beginning the campaign of 56, to have both of his allies meet him at the town of Luca, in the extreme southern end of the province. Other politicians attended the conference in large numbers. Again Caesar reconciled Crassus and Pompey, and worked out a new plan to govern their mutual relations and to preserve peace. For himself he asked a second five-year term in his provinces. Crassus and Pompey were to be consuls again in 55. At the close of their consulship, each was to have a proconsulship comparable in duration and opportunities to that of Caesar. Crassus was to have Syria, and Pompey, the Spanish provinces and Africa, and each was to have an army of his own.

The conference at Luca patched up the rifts in the coalition, and left the Senate once more helpless. Pompey and Crassus secured the consulship of 55 by preventing an election until after the year had begun, and then had themselves elected by the aid of the officers in charge of the voting.

All of the decisions of the conference at Luca were carried out. Before the year had closed, Crassus was on his way to Syria, where he hoped to pick a quarrel with the Parthians, and to win victories as showy as those of Caesar.

But fate had ordained otherwise. Ill-luck dogged Crassus from the start. He knew nothing of desert fighting, and was poorly supplied with cavalry. Pushing straight across the Syrian Desert, he was assailed near the city of Carrhae by swarms of light cavalry, who picked off his infantry with their arrows and refused to come within range of the Roman javelins. His own cavalry, commanded by his son, was surrounded and annihilated. In 53, Crassus himself, although fully aware of the fate that lay in store for him, was compelled by his men to hold a conference with the Parthian leaders, at which he was treacherously murdered. Hardly a fourth of his men reached Syria, although many more were spared and taken as captives to Parthia. The victors failed to follow up their success, and when later they invaded Syria, they were easily beaten off. Disastrous as the Battle of Carrhae was to the Romans, it did not cost them a single city. The significance lay in the effect upon the Roman political situation.

The death of Crassus broke up the Triumvirate, and paved the way for a new civil war. Three ambitious war lords might preserve a mutual equilibrium, but two such as Caesar and Pompey never could. The break was hastened in 54 by the death of Caesar's daughter Julia, who had acted as a peacemaker between her father and husband. Neither desired a break, but each had grown so powerful that the Roman world could not hold them both. The wonder is that the war was delayed as long as four years after the Battle of Carrhae.

### *The Rivalry of Pompey and Caesar*

Meanwhile, Pompey was gaining powers more sweeping than any held by a Roman since Sulla's time. As early as 57, he had been appointed "Curator of the Grain Supply" to deal with a local famine, and with this office had gone a large appropriation, the right to name fifteen lieutenants, and a commission to interfere in any province for the purpose of securing grain. His proconsulship in Spain and Africa has been mentioned, but we must further note that Pompey instituted a new practice by remaining in Rome himself, while governing the province through his lieutenants. Still more was to come. The gangs of Clodius and Milo were still engaged in intermittent hostilities, and in January, 52, a brawl occurred between them on the Appian Way near Rome, in which Clodius was killed. So great was the disorder that no magistrates had been elected, and the gangs of Clodius, backed by the Roman proletariat, indulged in an orgy of murder, plunder, and arson. In despair the Senate turned to Pompey, to whom it granted a dictatorship under the thinly veiled name of "consul without a colleague," with the right to name a colleague when and if he chose. Armed with these powers, Pompey quickly brought soldiers into the city and restored order. Milo was brought to trial, and in spite of Cicero's efforts in his behalf, was exiled. The henchmen of Clodius fared no better. Although Rome had order once more, Pompey was now so powerful that only Caesar stood between him and complete control of the state. Even after his consulship ended, his powers were not visibly diminished. In effect he was the chief executive of the Roman state, and his method of obtaining supreme power by holding a number of offices at one time furnished many a precedent for the later principate of Augustus. Further, Pompey was now reconciled with the Senate, and as its agent he exercised his prerogatives. Little by little he was led to see that only by eliminating Caesar could his power be consolidated and rendered secure. Hence, while for a long time he took no active steps against his former friend, he was either a benevolent neutral or a tacit supporter of the anti-Caesarian moves made by others.

The attack upon Caesar began with a series of laws apparently designed to reform the government. A measure against bribery, but retroactive to 70 B.C., was so framed that the legality of Caesar's election to the consulship could be questioned. Another law made it necessary for a praetor or consul to wait five years after quitting his office before becoming a proconsul or propraetor. While this second law was ostensibly intended to discourage bribery at elections, it meant that Caesar would ultimately find himself out of office, and therefore open to legal attack for the lawless acts committed during his consulship. This was a direct personal attack. He would be eligible for a second consulship in 49, and he intended to hold his Gallic command until he could secure election to the consulship. To do this, he would have to become a candidate *in absentia*, and his enemies, intent upon forcing him into private life so that they could ruin him, determined to prevent his doing so. In 52, a law had been passed legalizing his candidacy on these terms; however, soon afterward another was enacted requiring a personal appearance of all candidates. His enemies claimed that the second law abrogated the first, but this Caesar would not admit.

In both 51 and 50 B.C., one of the consuls was hostile to Caesar, and although he had the support of the tribunes against his enemies, attacks upon him multiplied. It now became the object of the senatorial faction to deprive him of his Gallic command before he became eligible for his second consulship. Several proposals to this effect were brought up, but in each case tribunician vetoes prevented action. In 50, his chief agent in Rome was the tribune Gaius Scribonius Curio, who had been elected because he was Caesar's violent enemy, but whom Caesar bribed by paying his many debts. Curio, posing as a disinterested patriot, pointed out continually that to deprive either Caesar or Pompey of his army would mean that the other would become the master of the government, and demanded that both lay down their powers at once. At the same time he vetoed all measures aimed against Caesar alone. Late in the year, he actually succeeded in having his proposal enacted into a law by the Senate, but it proved impossible to put it into effect. The next day Pompey was chosen commander in chief of all Roman soldiers in Italy and was commanded to defend Italy against invasion, by one of the consuls, who acted without authority. Events were now moving rapidly toward an irreparable break.

Yet neither Pompey, Caesar, nor the Roman people wanted war. The memory of the horrors perpetrated by Marius and Sulla was in every mind, and everywhere men feared that they would be repeated. Nor were the chiefs themselves bent upon destroying each other. Pompey wanted no more than to force Caesar into a subordinate position which would complete his own control of the state, while Caesar did not dare to accept such a position. Once he had given up his army, he would be helpless, and he could not trust Pompey to protect him against his enemies. Given a continual round of urban offices and provincial governorships, he would, no doubt, have been content. Hence the month of December, 50, was spent in fruitless negotiations. Caesar, who saw more clearly than his opponents that war was inevitable and wished to put them in the wrong, offered the fairest possible terms, which were promptly rejected.

The coming of the year 49 brought the quarrel to a head. As usual, Caesar had among the tribunes two staunch partisans, and when, on January 1, the Senate met to consider the Caesarian question, a letter from Caesar himself was read. Although calm and moderate in tone, it was an ultimatum. Caesar would disband his forces and retire to private life if Pompey would do the same. If, however, his terms were rejected, he would yield no farther, but would fight. For a moment the Senate wavered, but Pompey himself rallied it. Declaring that if it retreated from its position he would no longer defend it, he secured a decree ordering Caesar to hand over his army and his provinces to successors by a certain day, with outlawry as the alternative. When Caesar's friends among the tribunes attempted to veto the motion, they were ejected from the senate house, and succeeded in escaping only by assuming the disguise of slaves. Caesar could now claim to act as the savior of the constitution and the protector of the rights of the tribunes.

When the fugitive tribunes reached Caesar, he was at Ravenna, on the Adriatic coast in the extreme southern part of the province. He had with him only one legion, but with characteristic audacity, he determined to act at once. Setting forth to his soldiers the violent and illegal conduct of the aristocracy, he ordered them to cross the Rubicon River, which separated his provinces from Italy. This act was in itself a declaration of war. Between the two remaining Roman war lords, the sword was to decide which would be the sovereign of the state.

# 17

# *The Decline of the Republic (49-30 B.C.): Civil War, Dictatorship, and Wars of Succession*

## The Civil War of Caesar and Pompey (49–45)

When Caesar led his troops across the Rubicon River, he is said to have exclaimed: "The die is cast." The saying, whether authentic or not, is a true evaluation of the situation. The time for intrigue, negotiation, and compromise had passed, and only the sword could now decide the quarrel. But although most of the senators seem to have thought that the issue was between the republic and a monarchy, the real question was whether Caesar or Pompey should found the monarchy which had now become inevitable, and which of them should determine its character.

### *The Resources of the Contestants*

Neither contestant was prepared to wage aggressive war. Pompey had hoped to the last to frighten Caesar into submission, and Caesar, although expecting war, had delayed preparation so as not to seem the aggressor. Pompey had, it is true, armies in Spain and Africa, and the decree of the Senate gave him command over the two legions stationed in Italy, with authority to draft recruits. His fleet controlled the Mediterranean, but the fact that he was in theory a senatorial agent was a mixed blessing. It gave him the support of the *Optimates*, but it also compelled him to govern his moves by the advice of the council of senators in his camp, and the advice which they gave was uniformly bad.

Moreover, they were animated by a fierce partisan hatred, and talked constantly of proscription and confiscation, to the great disgust of moderates like Cicero.

On Caesar's side was the most effective fighting machine of the age, hardened by years of warfare and animated by a blind devotion to its commander. No man knew as well as he how to inspire soldiers and officers to the endurance of hardship or to heroism on the battlefield, and their idolatrous affection for him and his cause played an important part in Roman politics long after his death. He was very popular, especially in Cisalpine Gaul, but his authority did not extend beyond the Gallic provinces and Illyricum, and he had practically no fleet. In the beginning, the Italians saw in him only an outlawed general, supported by questionable characters who might secure the confiscation of property and the abolition of debts. He had hardly a general of respectable ability in his camp, for Titus Labienus, his most efficient lieutenant in the Gallic wars, had deserted to the Pompeians. His political henchmen, likewise, were usually men of no reputation. But this fact ultimately worked to his advantage, for it freed him from the necessity of taking unwelcome advice, and gave him an iron control over the members of his party. Lastly, Pompey was a hopelessly vacillating and inept politician and only a moderately able commander, while Caesar was a genius in both politics and war. This difference in the personal characters of the leaders was a decisive factor in shaping the outcome of the struggle.

### *Caesar's Conquest of Italy and the West*

Having begun by taking the offensive, Caesar conducted the war with his usual dash and brilliance. Hastily summoning two additional legions from Transalpine Gaul, he pushed forward into Picenum, Umbria, and Etruria. Here so many untrained recruits, raised by the Pompeians, fell into his hands that he was soon able to form them into three new legions for his own service. When the troops from Transalpine Gaul arrived, he had an army of forty thousand men. At Corfinium, the former capital of the Italic Confederation, he besieged and captured a Pompeian force of fifteen thousand men. Pompey with his two legions could do little or nothing to check him, and winter weather prevented him from securing reinforcements from his provinces. He quickly evacuated Rome, and the Senate decreed outlawry against any of its members who refused to follow him in his retreat. By the middle of March he had sailed for Greece, and all Italy was in Caesar's hands.

No less astonishing than the swiftness of the conquest was the moderation of the victor. Pompeian officers who surrendered were set free without conditions, and no confiscation of property took place. Neither pillaging nor the mistreatment of civilians was tolerated. This incredible gentleness proved, in the long run, to be a wise policy. Men compared it with the stark ferocity of Caesar's opponents, and soon the law-abiding people of Italy were won over to his cause. But many of the captured Pompeian officers abused his good nature, and were afterward found fighting in the ranks of his enemies.

The conquest of Italy was only a beginning. Before he could come to decisive grips with Pompey, Caesar would have to organize a government in Italy, consolidate his position in the West, and find ships to carry his army across the Adriatic Sea. As matters stood, the Pompeian army in Spain could easily attack him in the rear by invading Gaul and Italy while he was in the East fighting Pompey; also the provinces of Sardinia, Corsica, Sicily, and Africa which had come under Pompey's control as curator of the grain supply, controlled the flow of food-stuffs to the capital. Hence, he must begin by mastering these if he were to rule Italy securely.

The improvisation of a makeshift government for Italy was quickly carried out. Although the senators who remained in Rome were either hostile or apathetic, he put the city in charge of a praetor, and appointed a commander for his army of occupation. To raise money, he commandeered the treasure stored in the *Aerartium Saturni*, the only act of forthright illegality in this part of his career. Having thus made Italy reasonably safe from both invasion and anarchy, he set out for Spain.

Caesar's Spanish campaign of 49 was a severe test of his military genius. He planned to use nine legions and six thousand cavalry against the seven legions and forty-five thousand Spanish auxiliaries of his opponents. But when Massilia espoused the Pompeian cause, he had to leave three legions to besiege it. However, his advance guard quickly seized the passes of the Pyrenees, and the remainder of the campaign was fought out along the Ebro. For a while flood waters cut Caesar off from his provisions and nearly brought him to disaster, but he soon extricated himself. Then, by a series of masterly movements he brought his enemies to bay and, without a single pitched battle, forced them to capitulate. Officers and men were allowed to go to their homes unmolested. The surrender of Farther Spain, where Caesar had many friends, followed as a matter of course. On his return he found that Massilia was ready to capitulate. The old Greek city was punished with the loss of some of its territory and privileges, and had to pay an indemnity, but otherwise it was not molested, and remained a free Roman ally. In the autumn of 49, Caesar was back in Rome.

His lieutenants, who had attempted to drive the Pompeians from the grain-producing provinces, had had varying fortunes. Although Sardinia and Sicily surrendered without trouble, it was otherwise in Africa. There the Pompeians not only had a well-organized army, but were strengthened by the forces of the Numidian king Juba. The invasion was intrusted to Caesar's friend, the former tribune Curio. Rashly undertaking to fight when only half of his force had arrived, Curio was defeated and killed, and his army exterminated. Thus, Africa remained in Pompeian possession for a long while, until Caesar in person could take the matter in hand.

While still in Spain, Caesar had, at his own request, been named dictator. He held the office only long enough to have himself elected consul for the year 48, and to secure the passage of a few needed laws. Among them was one restoring political rights to the descendants of persons proscribed by Sulla, another recalling those exiled by Pompey, and a bankruptcy law so equitable that it was retained permanently. Having entered upon his consulate, he set out in pursuit of Pompey.

### *The Campaign in Epirus and Greece*

The task before him was not easy. Pompey had an army of some forty-seven thousand men in Epirus, of whom thirty-six thousand were legionaries and seven thousand were cavalry. His fleet kept him well supplied with provisions, and he had the support of the wealthy eastern provinces and vassal kingdoms. Only half of Caesar's army — about twenty thousand men — had crossed the Adriatic when bad weather and the Pompeian fleet prevented the remainder from crossing. Later, Marcus Antonius (who later became the lover of Cleopatra) succeeded in joining him with reinforcements, but his army was still inferior in size to that of Pompey. Throughout the campaign, Caesar's men lived on short rations, while their lack of cavalry (of which they had only one thousand) repeatedly threatened to bring them to disaster.

The first phase of the campaign ended in Pompey's favor. Caesar found him entrenched on the Adriatic coast near Dyrrachium (modern Durazzo), and failing to bring him to a pitched battle, attempted to besiege him in his camp. For some time this move seemed to promise success, although Caesar's men were so short of provisions that they had to make bread from roots gathered in the fields. But the line of the besiegers was too thinly held, and Pompey broke through it. Caesar suffered heavy losses, and his forces might have been annihilated if Pompey had pursued his success energetically. Caesar retreated eastward into Thessaly, followed by his rival.

Near the city of Pharsalus the two armies again came into contact, and Pompey, flushed with his previous success and urged on by his senatorial advisers, determined to give battle. The Battle of Pharsalus is perhaps the finest example of Caesar's skill as a tactician. Pompey's forty-seven thousand men were drawn up so that their right flank was protected by a ravine and their left by their seven thousand cavalry. It was his plan that his infantry should merely hold the line against the attack of Caesar's twenty-one thousand infantry, while his cavalry should drive Caesar's one thousand cavalry from the field and attack the Caesarians in the rear. But Caesar, having foreseen this move, was prepared for it. Behind his threatened right flank he posted a reserve of two thousand chosen legionaries, with orders to attack the Pompeian horsemen when they came within reach. The plan worked perfectly. As Caesar's cavalry retreated, the Pompeian cavalry were caught between them and the infantry reserve and defeated so badly that it fled from the field. The Caesarian reserve then turned Pompey's left flank, and his whole army fled to its camp. Caesar, who was always quick to follow up a success, stormed the camp. Pompey hastily fled eastward, and his leaderless soldiers soon surrendered. Some of the Pompeian senators escaped and others were put to death. The lower officers and soldiers were pardoned, and either sent home or incorporated into Caesar's army. The victors lost only two hundred men killed; the vanquished lost fifteen thousand.

While the Battle of Pharsalus dealt the Pompeians a staggering blow, it left them far from conquered. Many of the chiefs escaped to Africa, among them Pompey's eldest son Gnaeus, Marcus Cato, and Titus Labienus. Pompey himself made his way to the Aegean coast of Thessaly, where he crossed to Mytilene. With his wife and younger son Sextus, he then sailed southward to Rhodes and Cyprus, trying to collect men and money as he went. But the news of his misfortune had preceded him, and when he reached Syria he found that it had declared for Caesar. In an evil hour, the fugitive decided to seek refuge in Egypt.

### *Caesar in Egypt and Asia*

The Ptolemaic kingdom happened at that moment to be engaged in one

BATTLE OF PHARSALUS

of its many civil wars. The contemptible and oft-exiled Ptolemy "the Piper" had died, leaving his crown to his daughter Cleopatra and his son Ptolemy XII in joint tenure. Ptolemy had just driven his sister-wife from the kingdom, and it was to him that Pompey appealed for permission to land. The young king's family were under deep obligation to the suppliant, but his ministers saw only that to receive him might embroil them with Caesar, while to rebuff him might be dangerous if his fortunes ever rose again. They compromised by luring him ashore and murdering him. When Caesar, in hot pursuit, arrived in Alexandria, the head of his former friend was brought to him. Although Pompey's death was a stroke of good fortune for Caesar, he buried the head and punished the murderers.

But Caesar was far from being done with Egyptian affairs. Intervening in the dynastic quarrels of the royal house, he undertook to bring about a settlement between Ptolemy and his sister. He soon ceased to be an impartial judge. Cleopatra, who was twenty-two years old, so charmed the fifty-two-year-old and thrice-married Caesar that he became her lover, and tarried at Alexandria to assure her of the crown. It was a dangerous move, for he had only a small force, and the Alexandrian mob, aided by the royal troops, launched a furious attack upon the foreign intruder. During the latter part of 48 and the first part of 47, Caesar and Cleopatra were besieged in the "Royal Quarter" of the city, and came within a hair's breadth of disaster. From this perilous situation he was rescued by Mithridates of Pergamum, a free-lance soldier and son of Mithridates of Pontus. Raising a motley force of Syrians, Arabs, and Jews, this adventurer invaded Egypt from the east. Pelusium and Memphis fell into his hands, and he effected a junction with Caesar. The forces of Ptolemy XII were defeated, and he himself perished in flight. The crown went to Cleopatra and another brother, Ptolemy XIII, a mere child of ten or eleven years.

From Egypt Caesar went to Asia Minor, where Pharnaces, the son and successor of Mithridates, had tried to take advantage of the Roman civil war to recover his paternal kingdom, and to commit various hostile acts toward his neighbors. In a five-day campaign ending with the Battle of Zela, Caesar annihilated his opponent's army. Pharnaces' lands were given to Mithridates of Pergamum as a reward for his services. So rapid had been Caesar's settlement of the Pontic question that he summarized it in his famous dispatch: "I came, I saw, I conquered." In July of 47 he was back in Rome, where he had to solve the accumulated problems of his eighteen months' absence.

While in the East he had again been named dictator, and the powers attached to the office were no greater than the situation demanded. Some of his supporters still agitated for the abolition of debts. He quickly put these radicals in their places, but to soothe their feelings he carried a law remitting a year's rent on certain properties in Rome and Italy. The troops left in Italy during the eastern campaign had mutinied, demanding their bonus and immediate discharge. Caesar appeared before them, told them that their demands were granted, and announced that they were discharged. When he ended by addressing them as "Citizens" — a term which showed that they were no longer in his service — they broke down and begged to be taken back. The ringleaders were punished, and the rest were returned to duty. A few other measures looking toward permanent changes in the government were taken at this time, but they must be described elsewhere. At length, in the spring of 46, Caesar set out to destroy the Pompeian forces in Africa.

### *The African and Second Spanish Campaigns*

Since the defeat of Curio in 49, Africa had become a Pompeian stronghold. The nominal commander was Metellus Scipio, the father of Pompey's fifth and last wife, but with him were Cato, Labienus, and other prominent leaders. Their army numbered fifty thousand men, while that of Juba, their Numidian ally, was thirty thousand strong. Caesar as usual operated with much smaller forces. He had as allies Bogud and Bocchus, two Moorish chiefs on Numidia's western frontier, and Publius Sittius, a former Catilinarian who for years had operated in North Africa with a fleet and army of his own. In general the odds were heavily against Caesar, and only his genius and the high quality of his soldiers restored the balance. Bad weather and the small size of his fleet caused his army to arrive in detachments, and for some time he was in grave peril. But Caesar's allies distracted Juba's attention, and as soon as possible the Caesarians took the offensive. The Pompeians were lured into a pitched battle at Thapsus, where Caesar won an easy and overwhelming victory. Only fifty of his men fell, but fifty thousand of his enemies were slain in battle or massacred by his infuriated soldiers. Juba, Cato, Metellus Scipio, and others killed themselves to escape capture, while Labienus and the sons of Pompey escaped to Spain. Numidia was divided, the greater part being organized as a Roman province, while Bogud, Bocchus, and Sittius shared the remainder.

On his return to Rome, Caesar celebrated a triumph of four days' dura-

*Brown Brothers*

THE GREAT WALL AT THAPSUS

*Cross-Section Showing Roman Fortifications*

tion and unprecedented magnificence, over the Gauls, Egyptians, Pharnaces, and the Numidians. In keeping with custom, no mention was made of the Roman armies which he had beaten in the civil war. The populace was amused with feasts, gladiatorial combats, wild beast hunts, and a naval battle on an artificial lake in the Campus Martius. Both soldiers and civilians received large presents in cash. The fête was probably intended to signify the return of peace after foreign and civil wars; peace, however, had not yet come.

The Pompeians who escaped from the field of Thapsus had made their way to Spain, where people were weary of the misgovernment of Caesar's lieutenants. There they won over part of the army, and called up for service the former soldiers of Pompey who had settled in the province. The Caesarians lost ground at every point, and it soon became plain that only Caesar himself could recover what his subordinates had lost. In November, 46, he set out for the province, and in March, 45, brought his enemies to bay at Munda, on the southern coast. A murderous battle ensued, in which the last Pompeian army was defeated and destroyed. Labienus died fighting, and Gnaeus Pompeius was soon hunted down and slain. His brother Sextus escaped, but for a long time was powerless.

There was no longer a Pompeian party, and Caesar's supremacy was thenceforth unchallenged.

## The Dictatorship and the Death of Caesar

### *Caesar's Offices and Titles*

Having traced Caesar's rise to supreme power, we must now survey his career as an autocrat and a statesman. Since he was the sole survivor of the group of soldier-politicians who had so long dominated the state, he was now in effect a monarch, and to him fell the task of reorganizing the government. As his career of victory had rolled on, the Senate and people had heaped upon him office after office, and honor after honor. In 48, he had only held the consulship, but soon afterward he was again made dictator, and held the office by various grants for the remainder of his life. During most of this time he also held the consulship, but the office had necessarily shrunk to a mere name. In fact, Caesar twice resigned from consulships to appoint his friends to the place, so that as many of them as possible would have consular rank; and even when a consul died at noon on the last day of the year, he appointed a man to fill out the unexpired term. In 46, he was given the powers of a censor with the title of "prefect of morals." To cope with opposition from the tribunes, he acquired the powers pertaining to their office for life and also their personal inviolability. He had been *pontifex maximus* since 63 B.C., and through this office could control the state religious cults. In the Senate his vote was taken first, a practice which led timid and self-seeking men to vote as he did. By special laws, he could make war and peace on his own initiative, appoint provincial governors and some of the city magistrates, collect taxes and spend state funds at will, conduct elections (thus controlling them), and raise individuals from plebeian to patrician rank. Together these powers and offices gave him a status equivalent to that of an absolute monarch, and with them he had a series of honorary titles such as "Father of his Country" and *Imperator*, which denoted the supreme power and worth of their holder. But he did not stop there. Our Greek and Roman authorities assure us that he allowed himself to be worshiped as a god, and that a priest was appointed to conduct the cult. The seventh month of the year, previously called Quintilis, was renamed Julius, a name which it still bears throughout western Europe. By these grants, the Senate and the people legalized the powers which Caesar had won by the sword. Most of the grants were for life, and there was no prospect that he would surrender them. All that he now lacked was the title of "king," and there was serious agitation for him to assume this also.

### *The Caesarian Program of Government*

Armed with autocratic powers, Caesar could now undertake to treat the ills which had so long affected the Roman people and their subjects. In the short interval between campaigns, and in the few months between his return from Munda and his death, he promulgated or sponsored an amazing volume of legislation. Unlike the laws passed during his first consulship, these were no mere partisan measures, but the framework for a new and grander Rome, a true world state, which was to be formed under his benign and absolute power.

At home the chief problem to be solved was a social one. In the capital 320,000 persons received a monthly dole of free grain, while both in Rome and the rest of Italy, slave labor had for a long time been restricting more and more the opportunities for free labor to find employment. Caesar began by inducing 80,000 of the poorer citizens to accept places in the colonies which he was founding in Italy and the provinces. By this means, and by depriving undeserving persons of their grain allotments, the total number of recipients was reduced to 150,000. Employment was given to many on public works, and a law was enacted requiring the owners of stock ranches to employ, for at least one third of their herdsmen, free men. But he made no other attack upon the institution of slavery, which was one of the cornerstones of ancient society.

Although Caesar did not attack the social privileges of the senatorial aristocracy, he viewed its political position with disfavor. In an autocracy such as he was founding there was no place for a powerful Senate, and its functions were gradually taken over by him. Provincial government, finance, control of foreign relations, and others of its time-honored prerogatives, passed into the hands of the Dictator, and seemed likely to remain there. Yet such was the strength of the tradition of the Senate's greatness that it could neither be abolished nor too openly humbled. It was, therefore, essential that he secure its acquiescence in his program, and to achieve this end various expedients were adopted. Pompeians who seemed likely to live quietly under his government were invited to return to their seats. There were many gaps in its ranks, and Caesar, by virtue of his office of *praefectus morum*, proceeded to fill these with his personal adherents. In doing so he sometimes conferred senatorial rank upon centurions from his army, and upon other persons of low birth. His enemies even accused him of promoting Gauls to this coveted position. A slower but more effective method was his increasing the number of magistrates. The praetors were increased to sixteen and the quaestors to forty. Some of these Caesar appointed outright, and all of them owed their places to him. But his general policy was to bring the Senate and the magistrates whom it had formerly controlled into public contempt, and to absorb their functions himself.

The equestrian order did not fare essentially better than the Senate. As their wealth and power had, in large part, been won at the expense of the provincials, any step toward better conditions in the provinces was certain to injure their position. He planned (and in Asia carried out) a reorganization of the system of tax collection whereby all the provinces would be put under the system that already prevailed in Spain and Macedonia — one of fixed contributions collected by magistrates, and paid to the provincial quaestors directly. Whether the equestrians were to receive compensation in some way is not clear.

Before his death, Caesar had conceived a gigantic plan for the ordering of every phase of Roman life, but had barely begun to realize it. To make Rome a fitting capital for a world empire, he began to adorn her with splendid buildings, and laid out the new Julian Forum, which was far more magnificent than the old forum. Roman law was to be codified with sharply increasing penalties for the more common crimes, and rigid provisions against luxurious living. This task was not completed until nearly four centuries later. But certain phases of this program, which were actually realized, demand special consideration, and will be mentioned separately.

The calendar in use at Rome had hitherto been a lunar one, with a year of 355 days, which was kept in approximate agreement with the solar year by annexing an additional intercalary month every third year. Because of the confusion which preceded Caesar's rise to power, the intercalations had not been made regularly, so that in 46 the official year was ninety days ahead of the solar year. With the aid of the Alexandrian astronomer Sosigenes, Caesar remedied the defect by adding three months to the year of 46, and, beginning with January 1, 45, he instituted the Julian calendar. It was worked out on a solar basis, with a year of 365¼ days, the fraction of a day being added to the month of February as an extra day every fourth year. In Greek Orthodox countries the Julian calendar is still used in its original form, and in western Europe and America it survives with a slight modification.

In Italy, the grant of Roman citizenship to the allies had not been accompanied by any systematization of local government, and Italian interests had generally been neglected by the central power. Municipal and tribal institutions of various kinds flourished side by side, and the relations of local authorities to the Roman state were ill-defined. By the Julian Municipal Law (*Lex Julia Municipalis*), Caesar created a uniform pattern for local government, although it did not have to be followed slavishly. Grandiose public works and reclamation projects were planned, including the drainage of the pestilential Pontine Marshes, and large additions were to be made to the system of roads. A number of new agricultural colonies were established, but without any such spoliation as had marked Sulla's work in the same field. Lands used for the purpose were either parts of the state domain, or were purchased from their owners. This was the first real effort made since the extension of the rights of citizenship to integrate the Italians fully into the Roman body politic.

The same care was shown for the interests of the provincials. Caesar

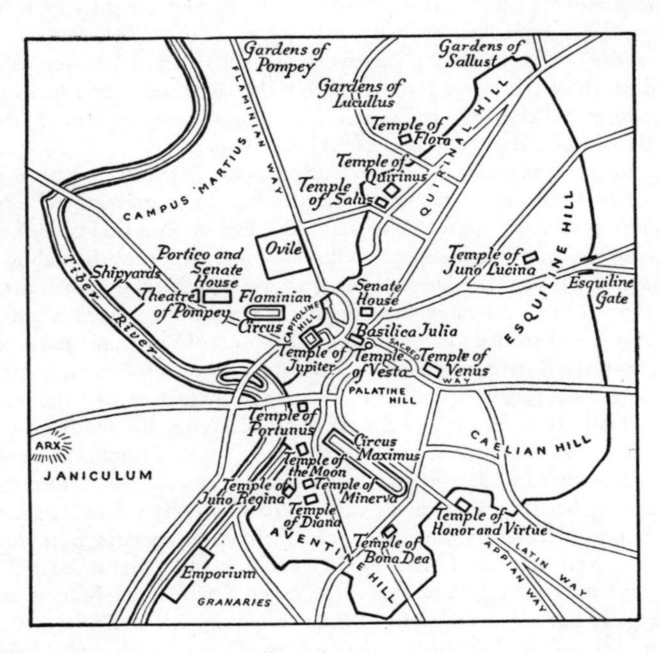


REPUBLICAN ROME

carried a new and severe law against extortion by Roman governors, and as has been indicated, began to reform the system of tax-collection. He was always lavish with grants of Roman citizenship, and where this was not practicable, of Latin rights. Especially, Sicily and Narbonese Gaul profited by his liberality. He also founded many citizen-colonies in the provinces. In 46, exactly a century after their destruction, he refounded both Carthage and Corinth, populating them with veteran soldiers, freedmen, and needy proletarians. Other colonies were settled at Heraclea and Sinope on the Black Sea, and at various points in Africa, Spain, and Narbonese Gaul. All this foretold the day when the line of demarcation between citizen and provincial would be obliterated, and all inhabitants of the Roman world (except slaves) would be equal under a common master. But to complete this process would have required many years, and Caesar lived only a few years after his defeat of Pompey. After his death, as we shall see, a reaction took place, and three centuries were to elapse before his apparent policy was carried out.

Meanwhile, Caesar was meditating still grander schemes of war and conquest. A gigantic expedition, led by himself in person, was to avenge the defeat of Crassus by the Parthians, and thereafter the barbarians who lived north of the lower Danube were to be chastised. Enormous forces were to be collected for the purpose, and Caesar was to leave Rome for the East in 44. But fate had decreed otherwise.

As time passed and it became evident that the Republic was undergoing drastic and permanent changes, the number and bitterness of Caesar's enemies constantly grew. Not only the former Pompeians, but many who had until this time supported him, began to feel that the public good demanded his death. There was, of course, no open opposition to his policies. More and more extravagant honors were heaped upon him. His statue was erected among those of the kings of Rome; he had a golden throne in the Senate house; and other evidences of subserviency were not wanting. His person was declared sacred and inviolable, and the senators individually took an oath to defend him and avenge his death if he were murdered. All the while, in the winter of 45–44, rumors were afloat that he intended to assume the title of king. His real intentions cannot be known, but for the moment, at least, he resolutely refused the dangerous honor. However, the suspicions of his secret enemies were not disarmed. Sixty senators formed a plot against his life, and it is significant that not only former Pompeians like Gaius Cassius and Marcus Brutus took part, but also Caesarians of long standing such as Decimus Brutus. Their task was made easier by the fact that Caesar, with a fine disregard of personal danger, kept no guards about him, and refused to listen to warnings. On the Ides of March (March 15) of 44, he was inveigled into attending a meeting of the Senate. As he was on his way, two warnings were given him, but he paid no heed to them. At a preconcerted signal the conspirators attacked him with their daggers, and after a brief struggle he fell dead at the foot of Pompey's statue, pierced with twenty-three wounds.

It is usual to look upon Caesar as the destroyer of the Republic and the founder of the Empire, but this view is not entirely valid. The fall of the Republic was a gradual process, in which not only Caesar, but also the Gracchi, Marius, Sulla, Pompey, and Crassus all played parts. Some form of monarchy had probably been inevitable ever since the failure of Cicero's "Harmony of the Orders." Pompey himself had, as we have seen, been something very like a monarch in the years before the Civil War, and Cicero had predicted when the war began that a Pompeian victory would lead to the establishment of an autocracy. But while we cannot hold Caesar entirely responsible for the triumph of one-man power in Rome, he was the first Roman politician to found an outright autocracy with the apparent intention of making it permanent. Certainly he formulated one of the two concepts of monarchy which, when he was killed, were all that the Roman people had to choose from. Pompey had envisioned a government in which the Senate, the people, and the magistrates would still remain important parts, with himself as "first citizen," caring for tasks which were too great for the regular machinery of the state. In his system the privileged position of the Roman citizen-body would have been carefully preserved. Far different from this was the Caesarian autocracy, in which one will dominated all, and citizens and provincials were in process of being reduced to a common level beneath the sway of an autocrat. The terrible years that followed Caesar's death were to decide who would be his successor, and which of the two systems would be adopted.

### The Last Struggle of the Republic (44–43 B.C.)

The conspirators who had slain Caesar had personified in him all the forces making toward monarchy, and imagined that his death would automatically restore the Republic. They were soon bitterly undeceived. The other senators fled in terror from the scene, and the Roman mob shrank from the assassins. When Mark Antony, Caesar's colleague in the consulship, called a meeting of the Senate a few days later, the conspirators dared not attend. No doubt the majority of those senators who were present would have liked to declare Caesar a tyrant and his acts void, but they had not the courage to do so. Upon the validity of his work depended the land-grants of the veterans, and to question these would rouse them to rebellion. Every official held his place, directly or indirectly, through the will of the dead dictator, and if their tenure of office were questioned, the whole state would be reduced to anarchy. At length the Senate compromised lamely by confirming his acts and granting an amnesty to his murderers. At the funeral further proofs of Caesar's posthumous power were seen. When his will was read it was found that several of his assassins were among his heirs, while his private gardens were given to the public for a park, and each citizen was to receive a substantial sum in cash. Antony artfully worked upon the public sympathy by having read the decrees of the Senate in Caesar's honor, and the vows taken by the senators to protect and avenge him. Step by step, he roused the feelings of the mob to fury, and at the opportune moment, the dead man's gashed and bloody toga were shown to them. Seizing the corpse, they conducted the funeral themselves, burning in addition the Senate house where the murder had occurred and the houses of the conspirators. The dead Caesar had proved as powerful as the living one had been.

### *The Senate and the Caesarians*

From this point, there can be no doubt that if the Caesarians had been able to agree among themselves, they would have been masters of the situation; this they could not do. In his will Caesar had bequeathed the bulk of his estate to his grand-nephew, the eighteen-year-old Gaius Octavius, whom he also adopted as his son. Octavius was the natural leader of the party, but his youth was against him, and he was absent with Caesar's army in Epirus. The only other person with any claim to influence in the party was Antony, the surviving consul. As the Senate in its fright had given validity not only to the acts that Caesar had performed, but to his plans for the future, Antony felt that his course was an easy one. Seizing his dead master's papers and money, and raising a guard, he pretended to carry out Caesar's plans, and in general acted as if he had inherited the dictatorship. But in this he reckoned without Octavius, now Gaius Julius Caesar Octavianus, who took his position as Caesar's heir very seriously. Coming to Rome, the young man demanded possession of his adoptive father's estate, which Antony refused to give up. By selling his own personal estate, Octavian was able to pay

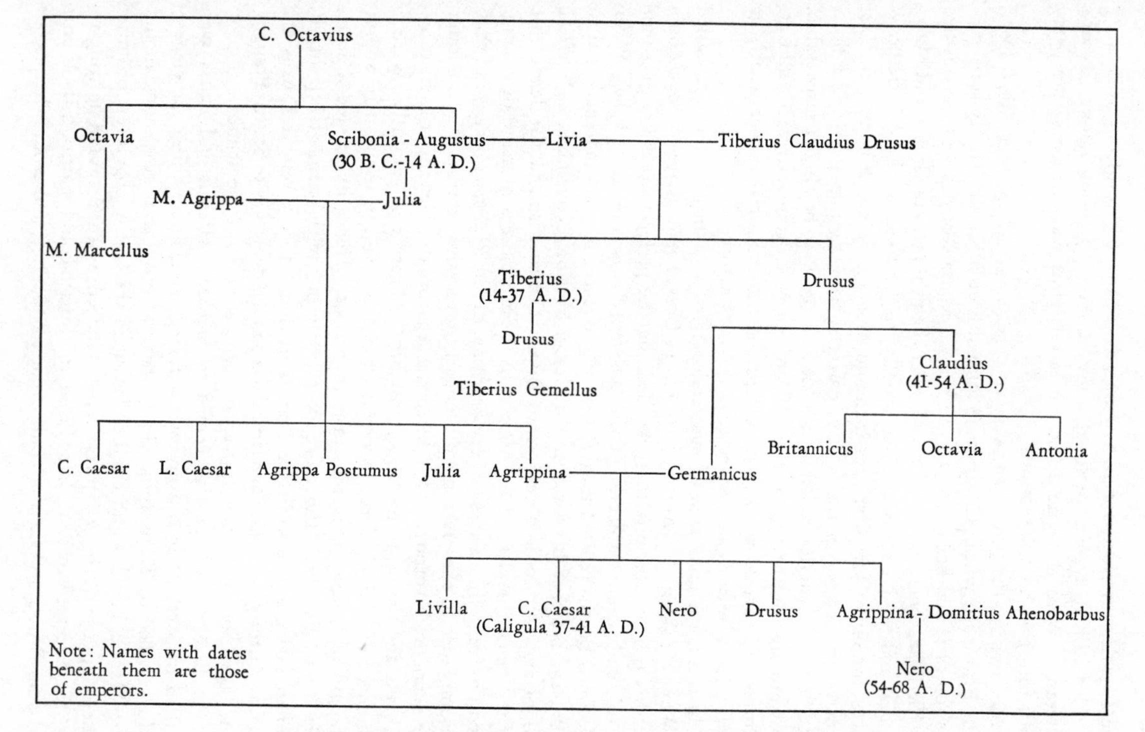


GENEALOGICAL CHART OF THE JULIO-CLAUDIAN FAMILY

the legacies provided for in Caesar's will, and his resulting popularity enabled him to raise a personal army of several legions among Caesar's veterans. With these he defied Antony. Thus was the Caesarian party split into two hostile sections.

Meanwhile, the Senate and Caesar's assassins had not been idle. Decimus Brutus, to whom Cisalpine Gaul had been allotted, hastily took possession of it and began to raise an army. Marcus Brutus and Cassius fled to the East, where the former took over the provinces of Greece and Macedonia, and the latter, with great cruelty, began to scour the Asiatic provinces and client kingdoms for men and money. Sextus Pompey, the last remaining member of his family, emerged from hiding, gathered a fleet, and began to practice piracy on a scale so large as to be almost respectable. Toward the end of the year 44, Cicero emerged from retirement and attempted to rebuild the shattered structure of senatorial power which he had tried vainly to save some twenty years before.

In Italy, the confusion of men and parties was shown by the so-called "War of Mutina." Antony, to whom Caesar had assigned Macedonia for his proconsular province, decided that he preferred to have Cisalpine Gaul, and secured a decree of the Assembly awarding it to him. When Decimus Brutus refused to give up the province, Antony marched against him, and besieged his forces in the city of Mutina (November, 44). With all of the war lords absent from Rome, Cicero assumed the leadership of the Senate, and tried to infuse into it once more a measure of courage and wisdom. In a series of fiery orations, called *Philippics* because of their resemblance to the orations of Demosthenes against Philip of Macedonia, he denounced Antony, and induced the senators to order the consuls of 43, Hirtius and Pansa, to march against him. Cicero was painfully aware of the need of military force to support his cause, and to secure it he sought the aid of Antony's enemies in both parties. Hence he secured a decree giving to Octavian the office of propraetor, with membership in the Senate and orders to join the consuls in their effort to relieve Brutus and defeat Antony. At the same time Cicero made overtures to Sextus Pompey, and to various provincial governors who controlled the armies.

For a while this policy seemed to succeed. Hirtius and Pansa were killed in battle, but Antony was defeated, and, abandoning the siege of Mutina, fled to Transalpine Gaul. Several provincial governors, including Marcus Lepidus and Lucius Plancus in the Gallic provinces, promised their support to the senatorial cause. Indeed, with Octavian fighting for it, there seemed to be a chance that the Senate could maintain itself until Marcus Brutus and Cassius could come to its relief, and would then regain control of the government. But in reality, however, no such chance existed. The Optimates, then as always, were their own worst enemies. After the victory at Mutina they grew over-confident and committed every imaginable blunder. They slighted Octavian, whom they hated for his Caesarian connections and despised because of his youth. Marcus Brutus, as much a stickler for political proprieties as his father-in-law Cato, railed at Cicero for accepting aid from Caesar's adopted son. Cicero himself who, although guilty of several blunders, was the most realistic member of the party, tried in vain to stem the tide. When the Senate refused to waive the minimum age limit for the consulship so that Octavian could be elected to it, his army marched on Rome and compelled it to yield. He and his cousin Quintus Pedius were elected in place of Hirtius and Pansa, and immediately secured the condemnation of Caesar's murderers to banishment and confiscation of goods (43).

### *The Second Triumvirate and the Proscription*

Worse was to come. The armies of Lepidus, Plancus, Antony, and Octavian were made up almost entirely of Caesar's veterans, and they had a better sense of party solidarity than their self-seeking leaders. When Antony came to Transalpine Gaul, his soldiers and those of Lepidus quickly reached an understanding. The leaders were compelled to make common cause, and Plancus could only join them. Decimus Brutus, now heavily outnumbered, tried to flee to Macedonia, but was captured and killed. It was now only necessary for the Caesarians to secure the support of Octavian, and this was easily done. In November, 43, he met the others near Bologna where plans were made for the future. Antony, Octavian, and Lepidus were to assume joint control of the state for five years, with the title of *Triumviri rei publicae constituendae*, or "The Board of Three to Set the State in Order." Octavian was to resign his consulship. All leaders of the opposition, and all personal enemies of the triumvirs were to be put to death in a general proscription, and their property confiscated. Antony and Octavian were then to lead armies against Marcus Brutus and Cassius.

There followed scenes of horror recalling the worst deeds of Sulla. Octavian surrendered Cicero to Antony's wrath, Antony gave up his uncle, and Lepidus and Plancus each gave up a brother. As usual when danger exposes naked human nature to view, the extremes of heroism and baseness were seen. There were wives who betrayed their husbands, and those who risked their lives helping their husbands escape. A father appealed to Antony on the ground that his son was Antony's friend, only to be told that the son had suggested his name for proscription. Debtors murdered or betrayed creditors, and rich men were killed for their property. Cicero and his male relatives were sought with peculiar malignity. He first decided to flee, but later came back and calmly awaited his fate. His head and hands were cut off and nailed to the speaker's stand from which he had so often addressed the people, and Fulvia, Antony's virago wife, thrust a pin through the tongue. In all, three hundred senators and two thousand equestrians were proscribed, but a large number of them escaped, either to Brutus and Cassius, or to Sextus Pompey, while others remained hidden until the danger was past. Some of them later achieved high offices and honors.

Putting aside our disgust at its horrors, we must scan the proscription for its political effects. It broke the Optimate party once and for all; the survivors either accepted the rule of the triumvirs loyally, or were broken men from whom little active opposition was to be expected. It likewise ended the career of the Senate as an effective instrument of government, for thereafter it was chiefly a puppet, which did and said what the masters of the state ordered. Octavian himself in his later years tried vainly to make it assume a part in the government, but in spite of strenuous efforts largely failed to do so. Yet the triumvirs were not wholly without justification for this terrible massacre. As they themselves cynically put it, Caesar had shown mercy to his enemies, and they had slain him. Sulla before him, and (we may add) Octavian after him, used terror to cow their foes, and both died in their beds.

Having sated their blood-lust and raised what money they could from confiscated estates, the triumvirs next undertook to deal with those who still resisted their power. Supplementing their funds by levying taxes and forced loans, Antony and Octavian gathered two armies, and leaving Lepidus in control of Italy, they set out against Marcus Brutus and Cassius. The latter had meanwhile shamelessly despoiled the Asiatic provinces, and had gathered an army of one hundred and twenty thousand men. The triumvirs, with a nearly equal number, met them near Philippi on the coast of Macedonia. There, in the autumn of 42, two battles were fought. In the first, Brutus defeated Octavian, while Antony captured the camp of Cassius. The latter, thinking that his cause was lost, committed suicide. It would thereafter have been to Brutus' advantage to have delayed fighting, for the winter was approaching, and the triumvirs were short of provisions. But desertions from his army alarmed him, and in despair he again gave battle. His forces were cut to pieces, and he committed suicide. The common soldiers of the defeated army were usually spared, but most of their leaders were mercilessly slain, and their corpses were denied burial.

## From Triumvirate to Monarchy (42–30 B.C.)

After the battles of Philippi, only the sea-power of Sextus Pompey stood between the triumvirs and complete control of the Roman world. From that moment, the real question was which of the three would succeed in surviving, ousting, or killing the others, and thus gaining the undivided inheritance of Caesar. Immediately after the battles, Antony and Octavian divided the Roman dominions. Antony took the eastern provinces and Transalpine Gaul. Octavian received Spain, Numidia, Illyricum, the immediate government of Italy (which however remained a joint possession of the three), with Sardinia and Sicily when and if he could take them from Sextus Pompey. Lepidus at first got nothing, but later the province of Africa fell to him.

The division was a fateful one, for since Lepidus had never had much strength, it was obvious that the real contest would be between Octavian and Antony. By taking the East, Antony put himself out of touch with Rome and Italy, and condemned himself to rely more heavily upon the support of the Hellenistic and Oriental peoples. Thus, whatever his original sentiments, he had to follow the cosmopolitan policy of Caesar, and his association with Oriental kings strengthened his natural leanings toward autocracy in government. Octavian, on the other hand, was able to maintain close contact with the Roman citizen-body, and to become its leader; but to do this he had to make himself the champion of its privileged position, and to renounce the autocratic tendencies of his adoptive father. Hence, in time, Antony became the proponent of the type of monarchy for which Caesar had stood, while Octavian came to represent a form of government very much like the disguised monarchy of Pompey. It was as a champion of the Roman citizen-body that Octavian was later to win the struggle, but in 42 it appeared that he had much the worse part of the bargain. His hold upon Italy was slender, and it appeared that Antony's only purpose in conceding it to him was to make him assume the hateful and dangerous task of finding land in the peninsula for a hundred and seventy thousand discharged soldiers.

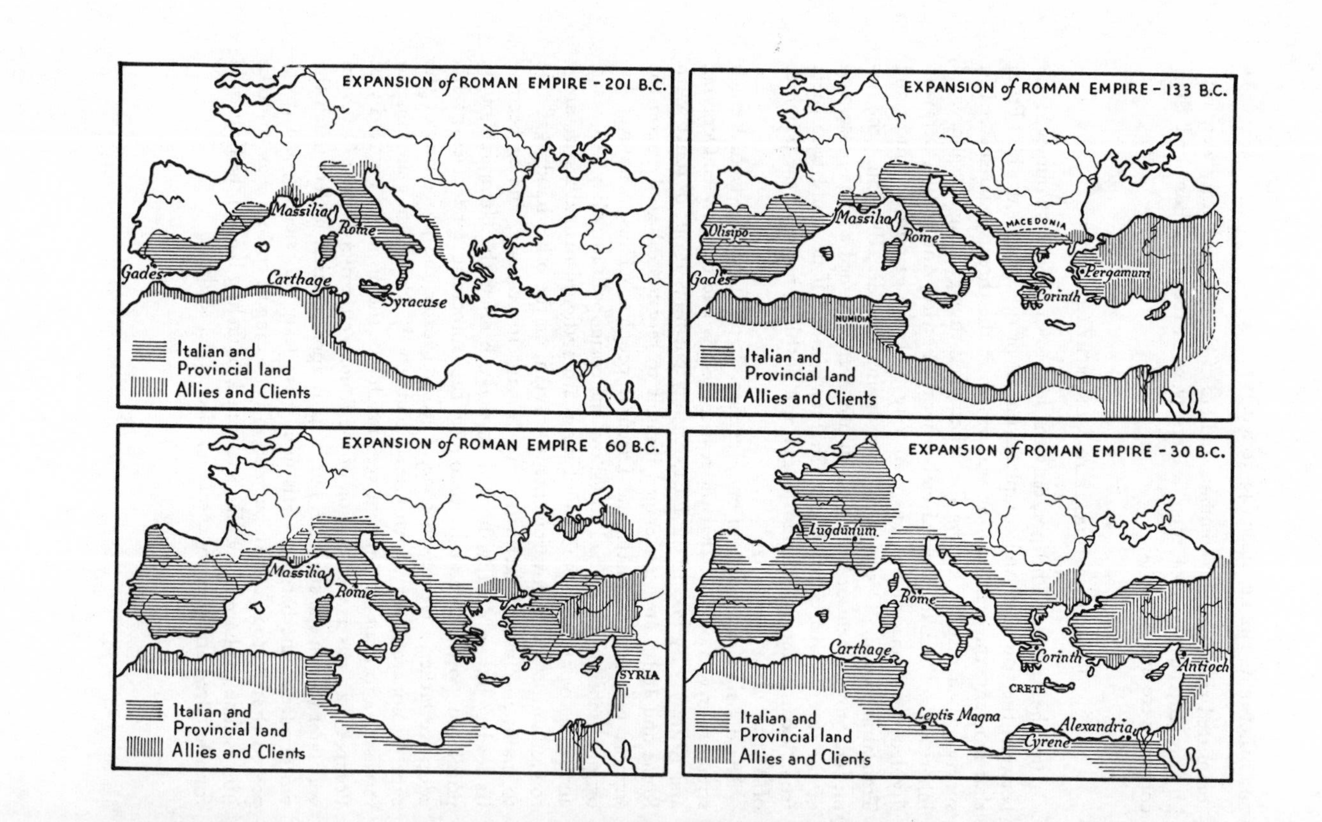
EXPANSION of ROMAN EMPIRE - 201 B.C.
Massilia
Rome
Gades
Carthage
Syracuse
Italian and
Provincial land
Allies and Clients
EXPANSION of ROMAN EMPIRE - 133 B.C.
Olisipo
Massilia
Rome
MACEDONIA
Pergamum
Gades
Corinth
NUMIDIA
Italian and
Provincial land
Allies and Clients
EXPANSION of ROMAN EMPIRE 60 B.C.
Massilia
Rome
SYRIA
Italian and
Provincial land
Allies and Clients
EXPANSION of ROMAN EMPIRE - 30 B.C.
Lugdunum
Rome
Carthage
Corinth
Antioch
CRETE
Leptis Magna
Alexandria
Cyrene
Italian and
Provincial land
Allies and Clients

### *Joint Rule of Antony, Octavian, Lepidus, and Sextus Pompey*

Meanwhile, from Philippi Antony went to Asia. Cassius had just wrung ten years' tribute from its luckless inhabitants in one year, and Antony completed their ruin by taking an additional nine years' tribute in two years. All the Oriental kings and free cities also paid dearly for their support of Caesar's murderers.

Among the culprits was Cleopatra of Egypt, who was to prove a very important factor in bringing on Antony's destruction. When the murder of Caesar occurred, she was living in Rome as his mistress, but she had immediately returned home. In the recent war she had given aid to Cassius. When called upon to explain her conduct, she met Antony at Tarsus and immediately gained the upper hand. Whether at this time her charms or her treasures captivated him the more is not known, but he followed her to Egypt, where he spent the winter of 41–40. This was the beginning of his decline, for while he was there Octavian in the West and the Parthians in the East began to undermine his power.

Octavian returned to an Italy which was steeped in misery and seething with rebellion. To satisfy the troops he seized the lands of eighteen cities, founding military colonies upon them and turning their former owners out penniless. He did not thereby satisfy the soldiers, and nearly ruined himself. Fulvia, the wife of Mark Antony, and Lucius his brother, undertook to stir up against him the veterans on the one hand, and the dispossessed landholders on the other. The result was the savage "Perusine War," so called because it ended with Octavian's driving his enemies into the Etruscan city of Perusia, which he besieged and took in 41. Lucius and Fulvia were released, but many of the other malcontents were killed, and Perusia was burned. The net result was to strengthen Octavian's hold upon Italy. Soon afterward, when Antony's governor of Transalpine Gaul died, he acquired that province also. Octavian now controlled a solid block of land covering all of southwestern Europe.

These gains had really been made at Antony's expense, and there was danger that he would break with his ambitious colleague. In 40, it seemed that this might soon happen, for Antony, forming an alliance with Sextus Pompey, came to Italy and besieged the port of Brundisium. Again, however, the soldiers and officers of the two armies intervened to make peace, and Antony, who wished to devote his energies to a war with the Parthians, consented to a compromise. A line was drawn from north to south through the Illyrian city of Scodra, the lands east of it going to Antony, and those west of it to Octavian. Both were to recruit soldiers in Italy. To seal the treaty, Octavian's widowed sister married Antony, who was now a widower. A few months later, at the promontory of Misenum, the two came to an agreement with Sextus Pompey, whereby he promised to cease his blockade of Italy, to keep the seas clear of pirates, and to expedite the shipment of grain to Rome. In return, he was to be compensated for his father's property, permitted to stand for the consulship, and allowed to keep Sicily, Sardinia, and Corsica. Thus Octavian emerged from the affair the equal of Antony; Sextus had gained a legitimate position of considerable importance; and Lepidus had not even been consulted.

The treaty of Misenum was soon broken, and for four years Octavian fought out his quarrel with Sextus Pompey. In the course of this war he suffered many reverses at sea, both from the enemy and from storms, but his indomitable courage and persistence at last brought him victory. Realizing his own deficiencies as a commander, he came to rely heavily upon his friend Marcus Agrippa, one of the most talented generals of the time. In 37, he held another meeting with Antony at Tarentum, at which the Triumvirate was renewed for five more years, and Antony in return for twenty thousand soldiers to be furnished by Octavian, lent him a fleet of one hundred and twenty ships. The next year Octavian concerted measures with Lepidus for a decisive attack upon Sicily. In a naval battle fought near Naulochus, Agrippa sank or captured all but seventeen of the Pompeian ships. Lepidus landed in western Sicily, while Octavian invaded it from the east. Sextus Pompey in desperation fled to Antony, who received him kindly, until shortly afterward he detected him in hostile acts and had him put to death. Thus died a leader who had at times played an important part in the Roman civil wars, and in whom one must feel a sympathetic interest because of his misfortunes, although at best he was never able to rise above the rôle of a pirate chief.

At the same time Lepidus fell from power. After the conquest of Sicily he attempted to keep the prize for himself, but his soldiers deserted him, and he had to throw himself upon Octavian's mercy. His life was spared, and he was allowed to keep the title of *pontifex maximus*, which he had usurped after Caesar's death. However, his armies and provinces were taken from him, and he lived for twenty-three years as a state prisoner. Octavian now controlled the whole western basin of the Mediterranean.

### *The Rivalry of Antony and Octavian*

With this victory, a sharp change took place in Octavian's methods and policies. He restored to the magistrates many of the powers of which they had been deprived under the Triumvirate, excused himself for his part in the proscriptions, and promised to lay down his powers in the near future. By strenuous efforts, he put down the lawlessness which had afflicted Rome and Italy since the beginning of the civil wars, and brought back security of life and property. He ceased to display the jealous cruelty which had disgraced his early years, and became kindly and benevolent. Thus, Octavian began to assume the position of a Roman national leader, at the very time when Antony, now his only competitor, was becoming more and more a stranger to the Romans, and was aggravating the situation by assuming Oriental manners and promoting foreign interests.

For Antony, the four years following the treaty of Brundisium were relatively uneventful. He seems not to have paid any attention to Cleopatra, and lived principally in Greece. During this time his lieutenants repulsed several Parthian attacks upon the province of Syria, but after the treaty of Tarentum had secured Antony's interests in the West, he undertook to deal with the Parthian problem in person. Octavia returned to Italy, and in 36, her husband, with eighteen legions of infantry and seventeen thousand cavalry, began his campaign. Unlike Crassus, Antony took the northern route through the mountains of Armenia, whose king was his ally. But bad fortune pursued him. His Armenian ally proved treacherous, and the enemy captured his baggage train and exterminated two of his legions. When he at last made good his retreat to Syria, he had lost thirty-two thousand men, and his prestige was severely shaken. It helped him but little when, two years later, he invaded Armenia, captured its king by treachery, and occupied the country.

The Armenian disaster threw Antony completely into the hands of Cleopatra. Even before he embarked upon his first campaign, he had summoned her to Antioch, married her (without divorcing Octavia) and acknowledged the children whom she had borne him during their first *liaison*. Ancient writers unanimously attributed his acts to love, while some skeptical moderns insist that he needed the treasures of Egypt for his wars and found this an easy way to secure them. Between these two opinions each reader may make his own choice. At any rate, Antony fell more and more deeply under Cleopatra's influence. As the help which Octavian had promised him at Tarentum never came, he became estranged from Octavia, and, in 35, divorced her. Thereafter, Alexandria was his real capital.

In the winter of 34–33, the world received concrete proof of Cleopatra's influence upon Antony. A great gathering was held in the Egyptian metropolis, at which he announced a new order of things in the East. Caesarion, Cleopatra's son by Caesar, was acknowledged as her consort on the throne of Egypt, to which were added Cyprus and southern Syria. To one of his own children by her he gave Cyrene; to another, northern Syria and Cilicia; and to the third, Armenia. All but the last of these were Roman provinces. Octavian carefully circulated the report of these scandalous doings in Rome, and gradually convinced the Roman public that Antony was no longer one of them, but an Oriental king. A wave of outraged Roman nationalism arose, and grew in volume as reports came that Antony had abandoned the Roman costume for Oriental robes, allowed himself to be addressed as the Greek god Dionysus or the Egyptian Osiris, and spent his time in debauchery. He still had friends among the Roman upper class, to whom he occasionally held out hopes of the restoration of the Republic, but the masses of the people began to rally around the solid, common-sense Octavian. Even among the Romans stationed with Antony at Alexandria discontent was rife, and grew gradually greater. Cleopatra unwittingly furthered this feeling by assuming haughty airs with her husband's Roman friends.

### *The Overthrow of Antony and Cleopatra*

In 32, the growing estrangement of the two war lords came to a head. The second term of the Triumvirate had expired, and this time it was not renewed. Octavian, finding that Antony had made his will and deposited it in Rome, had it seized and read in the Senate. It confirmed the stories afloat about Antony's subservience to Cleopatra. The consuls and part of the Senate favored Antony, but they fled from Rome, leaving Octavian the master of the situation. Without difficulty he then secured a declaration of war against Cleopatra (which tacitly included Antony, as well) and caused the inhabitants of the lands under his rule to take an oath of personal allegiance to him. The final struggle for the mastery of the Roman world was on. It was a clash of ideals as well as of men — the Caesarian cosmopolitan autocracy against a limited (or disguised) monarchy, in which the Senate and Roman citizen body would hold privileged positions.

On the decisive campaign of 31, this clash of ideals exercised a profound influence. Antony, with an army and fleet gathered from all parts of the eastern lands, advanced to the western coast of Greece. Cleopatra was with him, directing his actions. There is some evidence that she did not want her husband to overthrow his antagonist, but rather wished him to retire to the East and build up a purely Oriental state which she would share with him. On the other hand, his Roman officers and soldiers wished him to win a decisive victory, which would enable them to return to Italy. At any rate, she constantly clashed with them, and Antony's plans were effectively sabotaged by the resulting factional strife. Desertions from his ranks became increasingly numerous. Late in August, Octavian and Antony encamped on opposite sides of the Bay of Actium, and on September 2, both prepared for battle.

The stories told of the Battle of Actium vary so widely that we cannot be sure exactly what happened. It was entirely a naval action, the armies being mere spectators. The victors afterward asserted that Cleopatra caused the Egyptian fleet to desert at the beginning of the action, and that Antony in mad infatuation followed her. This statement is questionable, but it seems beyond doubt that Antony and Cleopatra both fled, and their leaderless fleet and army soon surrendered.

After this victory, all that remained for Octavian was to gather in its fruits, and he did so with relentless thoroughness. In 30, he took the road through Asia Minor and Syria toward Egypt, while another force invaded Egypt from the west. Antony and Cleopatra first tried to negotiate, and then to fight; but Octavian was inexorable, and their troops were thoroughly demoralized. Alexandria was taken after only a trifling skirmish, and the cause of Antony was lost. Cleopatra, ready to try one last desperate expedient, attempted to abandon Antony and to charm Octavian as she had his two Roman predecessors in Egypt. On receipt of a false message that she had killed herself, Antony fell upon his sword, but Octavian refused to be moved by her wiles. Learning that he intended to take her to Rome to adorn his triumph, she ended her life — rumor said by the bite of a snake which was brought to her in a basket of fruit. Octavian took possession of her kingdom by right of conquest.

At last Rome had a master. The long agony of the Roman civil war was over, and a new age had begun.

# 18

# *Roman Culture in the Late Republic*

## Prevailing Tendencies of the Age

In the midst of the disorder, uncertainty, and misery which marked the last century of the Roman Republic, a new civilization was growing to maturity in Italy. It was a hybrid product, composed of an Italic base, upon which had been grafted elements borrowed from Hellenistic Greece and the Orient. We have already seen some of these foreign influences at work among the Roman intelligentsia in the previous period, and they continued to operate throughout the later days of the Republic. As the process neared completion, it became evident that the new culture, despite its mixed origin, retained its essential Italic character, although greatly enriched and much changed in appearance. Rome began to produce some of her greatest literary masterpieces, and evolved art forms which combined grandeur with beauty.

Yet these developments were not all good. The unsettling of traditional beliefs and moral standards by contact with those of foreigners, the natural temptations which go with newly won wealth and power, and the cruel trials of the proscriptions and civil wars, all combined to reduce a large portion of the citizen body to depths of self-indulgence and moral depravity never reached before. Religion decayed dangerously, and among the proletariat of the capital poverty, idleness, and dependence upon charity wrought terrible havoc. In short, in this period of political crisis the Roman people were also passing through a moral and intellectual crisis closely connected with it and no less severe.

### *The Roman Attitude Toward Greeks and Greek Culture*

A peculiar feature of the Roman viewpoint in the first century B.C. was the combination of a brutal contempt for the Greek people with an unbounded admiration for both Classical and Hellenistic Greek civilization. On the one hand, the Greeks were subjected to the most shocking oppression, and cultivated Romans like Sulla and Cicero spoke and thought of them as an inferior people. But at the same time Greek philosophy, literature, science, art, and luxury were all the rage. Young Romans went in great numbers to complete their education at Athens, Rhodes, or the Asiatic cities, and those who could not do so often took lessons from Greek teachers in Rome. Many a Roman of means supported in his house a Greek scholar, who taught his host oratory or philosophy, celebrated his deeds in histories or laudatory verses, acted as his adviser in buying or stealing works of art, or introduced him to the polished luxuries and vices of the East, as their mutual tastes dictated. Greek art was popular in many forms: originals, acquired by various means; commercial copies, made either in Greece or Rome, but in any case by Greeks; and adaptations which employed Greek technical processes but were dominated by the taste of an Italian public. Greek and Oriental slaves, of whom every aristocratic family had a number, cared for the children, shaped the character of the housekeeping, and often cared for the business affairs of their masters. In all, it is not surprising that the Roman aristocracy became deeply tinged with Hellenism.

In the realm of pure intellect the Greeks seemed to dominate everything. Many of the better Romans were interested in philosophy, but they did nothing original, and were content to take instructions from Greek teachers. In literature, it was Greek verse forms, mythology, drama, history, and sentiments to which men turned for inspiration, and which they imitated. From Greek sources they acquired new ideas, which their own matter-of-fact Latin tongue could not express, and for which they took over Greek loan-words or translated others literally into Latin.

In everyday life a similar influence was felt. Housekeeping, manufacturing, commerce, amusements, and vices required new words of Greek origin to express new ideas and to name new objects unknown to former generations. Wealthy men, and the bankrupt spendthrifts who aped them, began to use, in coarse forms, luxuries invented for Hellenistic kings and nobles, and all who could afford to do so adopted those household comforts and decencies which had long been known in the Greek world, but of which most Romans were ignorant.

Even political life felt the all-pervading Hellenizing influence. Greek political thought helped to shape the characters and determine the policies of leaders as different from one another as the Gracchi, Sulla, Caesar, Cato, and Brutus. Greek ideas of social reform probably helped to shape the policies of the Populares in the early stages of the struggle, and one cannot read the awful story of the proscriptions without feeling that such acts were far more at home in a Greek city than in Rome. Captive Greece was avenging her sufferings upon her rude conqueror by infecting him with the political ills which had brought on her own downfall; with them went a knowledge of the remedies which her own philosophers had proposed for them.

## Society, Morals, and Religion

By 50 B.C. all free Italians had gained Roman citizenship, and Rome was the social and cultural as well as the political center of the Italian peninsula. Political needs and the colonizing activities of the state had spread the use of Latin throughout the peninsula, and the other Italic dialects, while still used in backward communities, were gradually dying out. The upper classes in the Italian communities were acquiring senatorial or equestrian rank as Romans, and everywhere Roman patriotism had taken the place of the earlier local loyalties. The growth of this Roman-Italian nation vastly increased the importance of the city of Rome, both in population and influence.

### *The City of Rome*

In the middle of the first century B.C., Rome was a large, sprawling, polyglot metropolis, with a population numbering somewhere between half a million and a million persons. It had outgrown its earlier walls, and was reaching out into the country on every side. But its growth had been without plan, and it had, as a consequence, little of the grandeur proper to so important a place. Private houses and business blocks were still built largely of sundried brick, and the streets were narrow and crooked. On the Palatine Hill, and in a few other sections of the city, were the showy palaces of the rich, but most of the dwellings were of the class called *insulae* ("islands") — apartment buildings or tenement houses several stories high, in which one might rent anything from a luxurious apartment at ten thousand sesterces a year down to a single room on the top floor of a rickety human rookery for about two hundred. Some even had water piped into them from the city system, although the poor had to depend upon neighborhood fountains, from which they carried water in jars. There was a fair system of sewers, and some effort was made to keep the streets clean, but neither fire nor police protection

*University Prints*

ROMAN WALLS
*Showing Methods of Facing Concrete with Stone or Brick*

existed. Crime was rampant, and until Pompey put it down with military force, there was little protection for individuals other than what they could furnish for themselves with armed slaves or clients. Evidence of the general lack of supervision, and of the extreme poverty of many of the people, was the fact that near the Esquiline Gate was a combination "city-dump" and "potter's field," where the corpses of the friendless poor were buried in shallow pits along with the carcasses of horses and donkeys. But the government undertook to see that the capital was supplied with at least the most indispensable foods, selling grain to those who could pay for it, and giving a monthly ration to those who could not.

*Aristocratic Society in Rome*

The senatorial and equestrian orders formed collectively what might be termed the "good society" of the capital — an aristocracy to which either birth, wealth, or literary ability gave admission. They lived on a scale of comfort unknown to their ancestors. Indeed, many of the richer members and the spendthrifts who strove to imitate them at times adopted gaudy splendor and coarse luxury which was the scandal of their own and later times. Eating, drinking, flashy clothes, expensive furniture, handsome slaves, and gambling cost these worthies enormous sums, and they went to the most absurd and revolting lengths to procure the objects of their desire. Thus, Lucullus, who returned from Asia a very rich man, had tunnels run through a mountain to let the sea into the ponds where the fish for his table were reared, and we hear of others who threw disobedient slaves into their ponds to be eaten alive by the lampreys which the masters later consumed. A single dinner cost Lucullus 50,000 denarii. Young dandies wore togas so elaborate that Cicero compared them to sails; they perfumed themselves and practiced a whole series of other ridiculous measures in order to make themselves attractive. Dining tables cost as much as 1,000,000 sesterces each, and worse pleasures cost still larger sums.

As many undertook to live in luxury who had not the money to do so, debts grew to astronomical proportions. Cicero, although never immoral or luxurious according to Roman ideas, was constantly borrowing money. Caesar at one time owed 25,000,000 sesterces (principally spent on his political career), while Antony owed 40,000,000, and Curio 60,000,000. This accumulation of debts was a fact of political importance. Crassus gained great influence by financing embarrassed politicians, and Catiline's conspiracy won many adherents among debt-ridden men of fashion. In fact, economic bankruptcy was almost as prominent a symptom of the decline of the Roman aristocracy as was political bankruptcy, and the two were closely connected.

Morals in general were at a very low ebb. In spite of a superficial air of refinement, aristocratic society had shockingly coarse manners. Even in the Senate, politicians hurled charges of the foulest crimes at each other, and these do not seem to have been greatly resented by the accused. Malicious gossip spared the reputations of neither men nor women. Divorce was so common as to cause no comment, and misconduct on the part of the wife was frequently the pretext. When the husband was at fault, it was not considered sufficient ground for a divorce. Many senators and equestrians did not marry at all, but kept slave mistresses. The civil wars naturally aggravated the disorder. During the proscriptions many men were murdered because favorites of the party in power desired their property, or at the behest of relatives who wished to be rid of them. Sons even disposed of inconvenient fathers in this manner. Cruelty, especially toward slaves and provincials, had become an ingrained trait of the Roman character. No description can do justice to the horrors visited upon the hapless Italians by Sulla and the Second Triumvirate, or upon the followers of Spartacus by Crassus. Since 105, gladiatorial shows had ceased to be confined to funerals, and were given for amusement on all important public occasions. Not only were combatants often killed in the actual fighting, but it had become customary for the audience to vote upon the fate of a beaten contestant, with the result that he was in many cases slaughtered by his victorious opponent. Bribery of voters and juries had likewise become a commonplace.

But we must not suppose that such manners were universal. We catch glimpses of a class of honest and respectable men and women, who, as always, gained less attention than their vicious contemporaries, but were probably more numerous. Cicero, Marcus Terentius Varro, the scholarly lieutenant of Pompey, and Cicero's friend Titus Pomponius Atticus were men of unspotted records for honesty and decency. Nor can we forget those who practiced the precepts of Stoicism. In the late second century Panaetius of Rhodes had reinterpreted the teachings of Zeno, omitting most of his nebulous speculations upon the nature of the universe, and inculcating a homely and practical type of virtue. In this form Stoicism gained many adherents among the Roman equestrian and senatorial classes, and their moral tone was greatly improved by it. Marcus Cato and his son-in-law Marcus Brutus were both Stoics, and although woefully lacking in common sense, they were models of pure and honorable conduct. In its original form, Epicureanism was also capable of exerting a moral influence, and Lucretius (96–54), whose poem we shall later discuss, felt that it could regenerate Roman society. But it was easy to pervert the quest for happiness into a mere pursuit of bodily pleasures, and Cicero assures us that in at least one case its emphasis upon pleasure was made to sanction a life of vice.

The emancipation of women was now an accomplished fact. By various legal fictions most married women had been freed from the power of their husbands, and were free to manage their affairs as they pleased. Many of them became socially prominent, and a few even attained political influence. Then, as in other ages and countries, the majority of women probably used this freedom wisely, but there were glaring and notorious examples to the contrary. In passing judgment upon these emancipated women we must remember that Roman gossip seems to have been virulently poisonous, and that much that we hear about them is at best wildly improbable. When all of these precautions have been taken, there is still evidence enough to paint some shocking pictures. Clodia, the sister of the notorious Publius Clodius, was a woman of learning, wit, and charm, but she was an unfaithful wife, and was accused of several serious crimes. Praecia, the mistress of Cethegus, was, to quote Plutarch, "a famous wit and beauty, but otherwise little better than a prostitute." [1] Servilia, the mother of Marcus Brutus, was at least the target of much ill-natured talk. Against these and similar cases, we must place the excellent Aurelia (the mother of Julius Caesar), Porcia the wife of Marcus Brutus, and other women of high character, great intelligence, and gracious manners who were a credit to the strictest Roman traditions.

### *The Common People and the Slaves*

But what of the shopkeepers, artisans, laborers, and paupers, who made up the vast majority of the population? Our evidence as to their condition is scanty, for Roman writers paid them little attention. One fact is true of them all: among them there was a very large proportion of foreign blood, principally Greek or Oriental. Some of these had come as free immigrants drawn by the lure of large profits or wages, but the majority seem to have come as slaves, and to have remained as freedmen. Except for a few articles of luxury, Rome produced nothing for export. Her commerce consisted of the importation of necessities and luxuries from abroad, to be paid for with cash gained from Italian agriculture or with the spoils of empire. Hence, there was little or none of that large-scale production which in the modern world employs so many millions and helps to distribute wealth throughout the social structure. Slave competition also narrowed the opportunities of the poor freeman, and kept wages low. A room in a tenement, a diet of wheat porridge with a few vegetables, scanty and threadbare clothing — such was the living standard of the Roman workman; but his life had its compensations. Amusement was provided free by the government or by ambitious politicians in the form of chariot races, gladiatorial shows, wild-beast hunts, feasts, and religious pageants. At election time, the candidates outdid each other in courting the mob upon whose votes they depended. The mild Italian climate enabled the poor to spend much of their time in loafing at the baths or on street corners, so that their mean living quarters were used only as places for sleeping or eating. At worst, there was always free grain furnished to those who could not afford to buy it, and one could get the other necessities in some way or other. But there were many who neither worked nor wished to work. Rome had an enormous pauper population, whose numbers may be judged from the fact that after

[1] *Lucullus*, c. 9.

Caesar had eliminated all possible names from the relief rolls, and had sent eighty thousand persons to his colonies abroad, one hundred and fifty thousand were still receiving free food from the government.

Although strikes and collective bargaining were out of the question in a society in which the price of slave labor set wages, one means of self-help was left to the working man. By organizing and pooling their slender resources, they could render each other great services. Such an organization was called a *collegium*. Some of these were trade associations, such as fullers or bronze-workers, while others appear to have been called into existence by common needs. Their purposes were social, religious, and benevolent, one of the most important being that of procuring decent burial for poor and otherwise friendless persons. But since they could also be manipulated by unscrupulous politicians, the state was always jealous of them. In 63, following the conspiracy of Catiline, they were suppressed. Publius Clodius later carried a law legalizing the *collegia*, but Caesar abolished all except a few of the oldest and most respectable.

Slaves continued to lead a precarious existence, but if attached to an urban household their lot was neither hopeless nor very uncomfortable. They no doubt lived better than did the poor freemen, for it was to their masters' interest to keep them in good condition. They were sometimes shockingly mistreated, but most of them were Greeks or Orientals, who were long inured to oppression and not resentful. By way of compensation, Roman custom made it easy for them to gain their freedom, and many thousands of them did so. As freedmen they might enter industry or commerce, and the more capable ones often became wealthy. Their children ranked as high as other free-born Roman citizens. Country slaves usually led as hard a life as ever, although some signs of alleviation appeared. In some localities they were being displaced by tenants, who were often freedmen. Varro, the standard authority for agriculture in this period, advises that slaves be allowed to contract regular marriages, and that each well-behaved slave be given the opportunity to own cattle or cultivate a tract for his own use. This advice marks the first step in the transformation of slaves into serf-tenants with privileges and property of their own.

### *Industry and Agriculture*

In the Italian towns, industry was on a much sounder basis than at Rome. Pottery was produced on a large scale, but unlike Greek ceramic wares, it was made in molds, each of which could produce hundreds of

*Bettmann*

ARRETINE CRATER

*From Capua*

pieces of identical appearance before being discarded. The best-known pottery of this type is the so-called Arretine ware, a red-glazed product made principally at Arretium in Etruria. Tanners, bakers, fullers, cabinet-makers, gold- and silver-smiths, and many other tradesmen were to be found in these places, where they often gained comfortable fortunes. Apparently they did not suffer from the stigma which was attached to businessmen and workers by the Roman aristocracy, for they often rose to the highest municipal magistracies. Most of the workmen seem to have been slaves, but the proportion was not as high as in Rome.

Agriculture suffered less than one might suppose from the confiscations and re-allotments of land which accompanied the civil wars. The military settlers sent out by Sulla, and probably also those of Pompey, Caesar, and the Second Triumvirate, seem not, as a rule, to have been successful farmers. Many of them must have sold or mortgaged their land at the earliest opportunity, and less than twenty years after the Sullan settlements were made, some of his colonists were so embarrassed financially that they were ready to take part in the schemes of Catiline. However, small farms continued to exist in many places, and some of the large estates were broken up into tenant farms. Grapes, olives, and livestock continued to be the most popular products, but grain culture was not entirely discontinued, and was even revived during the years when Sextus Pompey cut off the supplies from Sicily and Africa. Varro, writing about 40 B.C., speaks with enthusiasm of the high state of cultivation throughout the peninsula.

*Religion*

Religion underwent both change and decay. The upper classes had long since lost interest in the state cults except as part of the routine of government, and the common people found in them neither present consolation nor hope for the future. Temples fell into ruins, and priesthoods were left vacant for years at a time. Atheism, which to all intents was a part of the Epicurean philosophy, seems to have gained many adherents among the reading public, and skepticism was practically universal.

The spiritual needs of the educated Roman were, of course, met either by Greek philosophy or not at all. But for the common man, philosophy had no charms, and the Greeks who taught it in Rome made little effort to reach him. For him, especially if he were of Oriental descent or living in contact with Orientals, religions imported from the eastern Mediterranean served the same purpose as did Stoicism and Epicureanism among his richer neighbors. There were already Jews in Rome before the death of Caesar, and although they made few full converts, many Gentiles attended their synagogues and accepted their doctrines concerning God, morality, and the future life. But the most popular Oriental religions at this time were the vegetation cults, which deserve special treatment.

The vegetation cults had originated in Asia Minor, Syria, Egypt, and Babylonia, and represented, in a personalized form, the story of the annual death and resurrection of plant life. The myths connected with them bore a strong resemblance to one another. In each there was an immortal, omnipotent goddess, with whom was associated, either as lover or husband, a god of a peculiar character. The god had once met a violent death, but his divine consort had raised him from the dead and made him immortal like herself. In Asia Minor, men worshiped the Great Mother of the Gods, with whom they associated the divine youth Attis. The story was that he had once scorned her proffered love, and in revenge she had driven him mad, so that he emasculated himself and died of his hurt. But the Great Mother had restored him to life, and to commemorate the event her eunuch-priests (*Galli*) each year celebrated a wild festival. Clad in gaudy robes they went through the streets, shrieking, clashing tambourines, whipping themselves until the blood ran, and begging money. This cult, as we have seen,[1] had been brought to Rome by a decree of the Senate during the Second Punic War, but when its true nature became known, it was discouraged by severe restrictions.

The Isis cult had originated in Egypt. Osiris had once been the divine king of the country, with Isis as his wife. His evil brother Set had murdered him, but Isis had restored him to life, and he had become the ruler and judge of the world to come. There he judged the souls of the departed according to the deeds done in life, and gave them fitting rewards or punishments. Again we find the annual festival of death and resurrection, the wild emotionalism, and the powerful priesthood. Ptolemy I had partially Hellenized the cult, changing Osiris' name to Serapis, and suppressing many features offensive to the Greek taste. As these two cults were the most important of their kind, and were typical of the rest, it is needless to treat the others individually.

Except for the Great Mother cult, none of these Oriental religions received much encouragement from the government, and most of them were mildly discouraged. Although they could not be carried on publicly inside the city, no attempt was made to suppress them. Isis had a temple on the Campus Martius as early as 80 B.C., but when her worshipers built one on the Capitoline Hill, in 58, it was destroyed. Subsequent destructions in 53, 50, and 48 show the persistence of her votaries in rebuilding their shrines, and the continued hostility of the Senate. In 43, the Triumvirs compromised by building her a temple with public funds, but outside the *pomoerium*.

The influence of these religions was a mixture of good and evil. Their emotionalism no doubt served as an outlet for the pent-up discontent of the poor and downtrodden. They assured men of divine interest in their personal affairs in this world, and promised happiness in the life to come. Judaism, at least, improved the morals of its followers. But the vegetation cults had less pleasing aspects which in part justified the attitude of the Senate. A suspiciously large number of loose characters were found among their votaries, and apparently nothing was done by the priests to reform them. The latter were themselves grasping and dishonest, if nothing worse. Gross and obscene symbols played a large part in the rites. Certainly they turned the attention of their followers away from the useful career of a citizen and a soldier, and hence aggravated the ills

[1] Chapter 14.

which afflicted the state. But these religions had come to stay, and under the Empire their influence was constantly on the increase.

## Art

It is an evidence of the growing sophistication and national self-consciousness of the Romans in the last century of the Republic, that they found original means of self-expression in both the fine arts and literature. In Rome and in the Italian towns alike, architecture, sculpture, and painting flourished, being supported by both public and private patronage. History, poetry, oratory, and the didactic essay lent luster to Roman literature, and many great masterpieces were produced in these fields.

Roman art was the product of many influences, Etruscan, Hellenistic Greek, Italic, and Asiatic; but in this period it had already begun to assimilate these, and was placing upon the resulting products the stamp of the Roman character and taste. As always, its greatest works were in the field of architecture. Efforts to adorn the capital with worthy public buildings had begun under the kings and had continued at intervals throughout the Republic, but it was only in the age following the Gracchi that they began to transform its general appearance.

### *Roman Architecture*

As we have seen, the Romans had already begun to evolve an architectural style of their own for such practical purposes as bridge and aqueduct building, and they had borrowed from the Greeks the plan of the basilica. But for temples and other pretentious public buildings they were still dependent, principally, upon Etruscan and Greek models until the late second century B.C. Indeed, the temple of Jupiter on the Capitoline Hill, and many imitations of it which were erected in Roman citizen colonies, always preserved its Etruscan plan, even though Sulla, when he rebuilt it after its destruction during the civil wars, provided it with lofty Corinthian columns in the Greek style. The new temples, however, of which great numbers were begun throughout Italy in his time, represented a new style. The deep portico characteristic of Etruscan temples was preserved, but whereas the Etruscans had extended their colonnades along the sides of the building, the first-century Roman architect often reduced these to mere vestigial remnants — ribs set in the side walls and carved like half-columns. These "engaged" columns became a recognized feature of the Roman architecture of the Empire period.

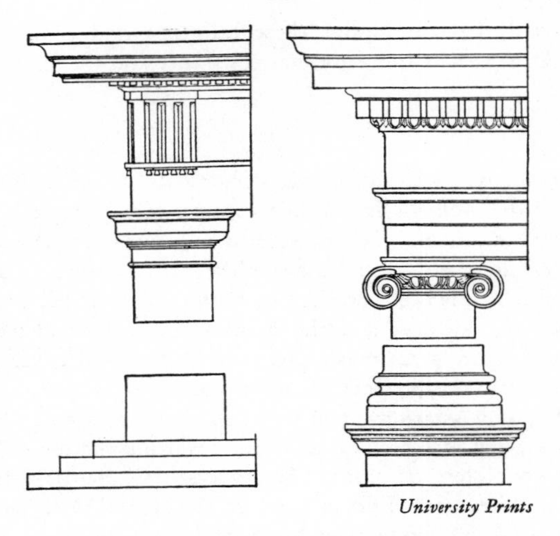

*University Prints*

ROMAN ARCHITECTURAL STYLES
*Doric* *Ionic*

The floor plan was also altered. In Etruscan temples the ratio of length to width was 6 to 5; the new style called for a ratio of 2 to 1, making a much longer and narrower structure. The Etruscan custom of placing a temple on a high platform (*podium*), with steps only at the front, was continued in preference to the low Greek *stylobate*, which had steps on all sides. Builders began to use concrete for the cores of the foundation walls, which were, however, usually faced with stone. Later on this practice was extended to the superstructure, and made possible the gigantic vaulted creations of the first three centuries of the Christian era.

Basilica architecture also began to assume a specifically Roman character. The Basilica Julia, built by Julius Caesar, was one of the most pretentious of his public works, being some 326 feet in length and 117 feet in width. It stood on a raised platform, and was approached by a flight of steps. It was entered at the side which faced the Forum, through a portico which consisted of a two-story arcade in place of the traditional colonnade. The building itself was made up of a nave, above which was a clerestory, and two side aisles, each of which, like the portico, contained a two-story arcade. The clerestory walls were supported by massive piers. Other basilicas differed somewhat from this

*University Prints*

ROMAN ARCHITECTURAL STYLES

*Corinthian* *Composite*

plan, but the combination of nave, clerestory, and side aisles was so useful that it came to be widely employed, and was later included in the construction of Christian churches.

To Pompey the Romans owed their first permanent stone theater, which was built outside the city on the Campus Martius. In reality the theater was only a part of a rather complex structure, which included a temple of Venus, a covered promenade, and several rooms, one of which was large enough to serve as a meeting place for the Senate. The theater proper was built upon Greek models, but these were not followed slavishly. Thus instead of making the stage and the auditorium separate structures, as a Greek would have done, Pompey's architect planned them as a unified whole. The stage was roofed, but the auditorium was open to the sky. Taking into account the negligible part played by the chorus in contemporary drama, he also decreased the size of the orchestra.

To Caesar the Romans also owed the beginning of the system of *fora*, or public squares, which were later to be one of the most striking features of the city. Somewhat to the north and west of the old Roman Forum was laid out the Forum Julii, with a splendid temple of "Ancestral" Venus (from whom the Julian clan traced its lineage) in the center.

*University Prints*

RESTORATION OF THE BASILICA JULIA

The old Forum was also remodeled, and was surrounded by a series of public buildings, of which the Basilica Julia was one. Both public and private business was thenceforth transacted elsewhere; and the *fora* became mere show places.

*Sculpture*

Sculpture flourished during the last century of the Republic and assumed a number of widely different forms. Second-rate Greek artists made numberless copies of Classical and Hellenistic masterpieces, which found ready sale among wealthy Romans. Those who could afford to do so bought originals from financially embarrassed Greek cities, and the less scrupulous art fanciers sometimes stole them outright. But great as was the admiration of the Romans for Greek art, they had ideas of their own which they insisted upon carrying out in work done under their supervision or patronage. Portrait sculpture had long flourished in Italy, and although Greek technical processes were used, the work done had a strongly original character. In contrast to the Greek tendency to idealize the subject, the Roman artist practiced a merciless realism. In some cases he even copied the wax death masks preserved by aristocratic families, reproducing the evidences of illness or senility which they displayed without any attempt at evasion. Work modeled from the living subject was no less frank. A bust of Pompey shows us a plain face, with snub nose, small eyes, and broad head; while on the other hand the statues of Caesar, of which several are extant, have caught for us the striking features and commanding presence which literary sources assure us that he possessed. Even the lowly tombstone cutters partook of the realistic tendency. A baker, Vergilius Eurysaces, caused his tomb outside the city to be adorned with a frieze showing the operation of his plant, from the cleaning of the wheat to the sale of the bread, while similar scenes are to be found carved on the tombs of others, both in Rome and in the Italian towns.

*Painting and the Lesser Arts*

Painting, like sculpture, was a composite of Greek and Italic elements. While easel pictures done in encaustic were no doubt common, we have

*University Prints*

WALL DECORATION

*From the House of Silenus. Pompeii*

*Bettmann*

ROMAN TABLE ON MOSAIC FLOOR
*Pompeii*

to draw our knowledge of the art from frescoes used as wall decorations in dwelling houses, of which specimens have been recovered in both Pompeii and Rome. In some of these (the so-called "Architectural Style") a flat wall is treated with a view to creating the illusion that the spectator sees a wall broken by columns or pilasters, and pierced with windows through which he sees rural landscapes or urban street scenes. In the best of them, the effort is very successful. Again, the central scene is taken from Greek mythology or legend, and may be a reproduction of some great Hellenistic masterpiece. Successful generals had elaborate battle scenes painted to be carried in their triumphs, but of these none have survived.

Subsidiary arts flourished. The tables of the wealthy were lavishly adorned with gold and silver plate, elegantly decorated with naturalistic engravings. Gems and cameos were likewise plentiful, and the workmanship of surviving specimens is of a very high order. Mosaic working had been introduced from the Hellenistic world, and even in a small town like Pompeii a wealthy citizen could have his dining room floor adorned with a mosaic reproduction of the great Hellenistic battle-piece "Alexander at the Battle of Issus." For people of small or moderate means there was artistically decorated glassware, or pottery molded with raised figures and finished with red glaze.

## Literature

Both in prose and poetry the Romans began to produce work which subsequent ages have enthroned among the world's great masterpieces. Again it was Greek examples which gave the stimulus and provided models for imitation, but in this, as in other things, what the Romans borrowed they stamped with their own character and gave it to the world as a new creation. Drama languished, producing little except mimes which displayed first-rate ability, but oratory flourished amid the turmoil of political strife, and historiography throve in an age which was making history with unparalleled rapidity. In philosophy, the Romans produced nothing which can be called original, but Cicero explained Greek thought to his countrymen in charming prose essays, while Lucretius made it the subject of an immortal poem. Satire became, in the hands of Marcus Terentius Varro, a work of art and a means of moral improvement. Catullus and several others whose works have been lost sang of love and wine, as well as of more serious subjects. Taken as a whole, the Roman literature of this period far surpassed anything that the Greek world had to offer, and is a worthy monument to the genius which produced it.

### *Oratory*

Roman oratory was a native Italian product, remodeled under Greek influence. The assemblies, the Senate, and the law courts had trained men to be vigorous and convincing speakers, but not until the second century B.C. had Greek rhetorical skill been brought into play to improve either style or delivery. In the days of Cicero, Pompey, and Caesar every aspirant to honors as an orator took extensive training from Greek rhetoricians, from whom he attempted to learn the niceties of form and delivery long taught and practiced at Athens, Pergamum, and Rhodes.

Three schools of oratory had developed in the Greek world, and all had their representatives at Rome. The Attic school took as its model the sober, restrained, and plain style of the Athenian orator Lysias, and advocated a quiet, dispassionate delivery. Its Greek exponents encouraged the use of the Attic dialect of about 400 B.C., but their Roman pupils merely insisted upon conservative Latin vocabulary unmarred by slang. The Asiatic school practiced an ornate style, with metaphors, similes, antitheses, striking phrases, and an impassioned, sing-song delivery. At Rhodes a middle course was advocated, with some of the features of each of the other schools, but without their more extreme tendencies. The Romans at first favored the Asiatic school, of which the great Optimate politician Quintus Hortensius (114–50) was the chief exponent. But the prosecution of Verres gave the first place to Cicero, who favored the "Middle" school, and he in turn was succeeded in favor by representatives of the Attic style. With the fall of the Republic, oratory ceased to hold an important place in Roman life.

*Galloway*

HOUSE IN POMPEII (RESTORED)

*Peristyle of the House of the Golden Cupids*

As Cicero was pre-eminent in several fields of literature, we may well survey his literary career as a unity. The modern world knows him best as an orator. His speeches, of which fifty-six survive, generally follow (although not rigidly) the traditional four-fold division into introduction, narration, argument, and conclusion. The language has an inimitable quality which is hard to describe and almost impossible to counterfeit. Without assuming the form of verse, it is highly rhythmical, and each sentence ends with a definite cadence. Grammar and vocabulary are marked by an easy correctness. Characteristic is his use of the "period" — a complex and closely knit sentence, the sense of which is not complete until the last word has been uttered. On ordinary occasions he was inclined to use the plain, straightforward style of the Attic school, but when he wished to be impressive he adopted the elaborate and ornate manner of the Asiatic school, although seldom going to extremes in either direction. Illustrations, jests, pathos, and scathing denunciations — such are a few of the characteristics of the most brilliant oratorical style ever attained by any Roman. The faults of this style were its virtues overdone. Verbosity, and occasional over-ornamentation were the most obvious of them to a modern reader, although they probably annoyed the Romans less than they would a present-day audience. Perhaps the greatest tribute to his skill and power as a speaker is the fact that in an age of force and violence they enabled him to become for a time the leading figure in Roman politics. A list of his chief political and judicial speeches is in itself a running commentary upon twenty-five years of Roman history — the *Verrine Orations* (*In C. Verrem*), the *Oration for the Manilian Law* (*Pro Lege Manilia*), the *Orations on the Land Law of Rullus* (*De Lege Agraria*), the *Catilinarian Orations* (*In Catilinam*), the *Defense of Milo* (*Pro Milone*), and the *Philippics*.

### *Cicero: Essayist and Letter-Writer*

At intervals in his busy public career Cicero wrote a series of essays which, if he had written nothing else, would have entitled him to a high place in Roman literature. First, in point of originality, must be placed the seven which deal with the theory and practice of public speaking, of which the *Orator* (*De Oratore*) and the *Brutus* are the most important. During the enforced leisure brought about by the First Triumvirate and the dictatorship of Caesar, he composed two treatises on political theory — the *Republic* (*De Re Publica*) and the *Laws* (*De Legibus*). The first defends the Roman constitution, but suggests the addition of a single chief magistrate (*moderator rei publicae*) who would guide the destinies of the state by wise counsel rather than by power. Whether this last feature was intended to refer to either himself or Pompey, or whether it was purely theoretical, is not known. The *Laws* is a reasoned discussion of Roman government and jurisprudence. Both have come down to us in fragments. In 45, after the death of his beloved daughter Tullia, he sought consolation in the study of Greek philosophy and in the next year he produced an astonishing series of philosophical essays, which popularized for Roman readers the teachings of Greek thinkers. In doing so he laid no claim to originality. "They are only copies," he wrote to his friend Atticus, "and quite easy to write. I just supply the words; and I have plenty of them." [1] These are popularizations in the best sense of the word, and they are written with an inimitable Ciceronian charm which many of the Greek prototypes (notably Aristotle) lack. On pure philosophy we have the *Academics* (*Academica*), an exposition of Platonism; the *Definitions of Good and Evil* (*De Finibus*), which discusses the nature of the chief good; and the *Tusculan Disputations* (*Tusculanae Disputationes*) on miscellaneous subjects. In practical philosophy he produced the work usually called *Offices* (*De Officiis*), but more properly *Duties*, a handbook of ethics for the use of his son; *Old Age* (*De Senectute*); and *Friendship* (*De Amicitia*). Religion also claimed his attention in the *Nature of the Gods* (*De Natura Deorum*) and *Divination* (*De Divinatione*). Most of them are cast in the form of dialogues — a form which enables Cicero to do an occasional fine character sketch. From these essays subsequent generations of Romans, and later scholars of medieval Europe, were to gain almost all their knowledge of Greek philosophy. He found the Latin language woefully deficient in abstract terms suitable to the discussion of philosophy, but by coining new words or giving new meanings to old ones he largely remedied the defect. Many of the words which he thus added to the Latin vocabulary have passed into the tongues of modern Europe and America.

Lastly, over eight hundred of his letters, together with many written to him by others, were published after his death. Here we have Cicero's mind in its everyday dress, without any formality, for when they were written he had not expected to have them published. Particularly frank and unreserved were those which he wrote to his banker friend, Titus Pomponius Atticus, to whom he confided his most private business as well as his judgment on men and affairs, for over twenty years. Not only do we learn about the events of the time from these letters, but they are marked by an easy geniality and an unparalleled richness of humor. Yet

[1] *Ad Atticum XII*, 52, 2.

because they display the writer's vanity, weakness, and uncertainty at certain stages of his career, they account for much of the modern criticism of his character and policies. Rome was to produce several other great masters of prose, but none of them ever quite equaled Cicero.

### *Varro: Scholar and Satirist*

One of the most prolific and versatile writers of the ancient world was Marcus Terentius Varro (116–27). Although for many years he commanded armies and governed provinces, this senator from the Sabine Hills managed to write nearly fifty works, both long and short, on such diverse subjects as history, grammar, law, agriculture, philosophy, religion, and literary criticism. So all-inclusive was his learning, that Caesar seems to have appointed him to head the great library which he intended to build in Rome, but the daggers of Brutus and Cassius prevented the realization of the project. Of Varro's many works, all that survive are a portion of his treatise *The Latin Language* (*De Sermone Latina*), and his short work on *Agriculture* (*De Re Rustica*). The former is a ponderously learned discussion, treating the subject in what a modern philologist would call an unscientific manner, but crammed with information which even his critics find useful. His *Agriculture*, written when he was eighty years old, is a delightful little book. The style is plain and familiar, and the contents are a rare combination of theoretical and practical knowledge. In his own day Varro was better known for his *Antiquities*, an encyclopedic hodgepodge of history, anthropology, and religious ritual in forty-five books; and his *Portraits* (*Imagines*), a set of illustrated biographies of famous Greeks and Romans. But it is nothing less than astonishing that this research scholar should have produced the *Menippean Satires*, a series of humorous discussions of ethics and of life in general, which he modeled after the works of the Cynic philosopher Menippus of Gadara. The fragments of these lost works which have come down to us make us regret the more that they have not been preserved entire.

### *Memoirs and History: Caesar and Sallust*

From the last years of the Republic date the oldest Roman historical works now extant. In these we must not expect to find the disinterested objectivity which characterized Thucydides and Polybius. True to their utilitarian bent, the Romans did not seek truth for its own sake, but rather as a means of forming character, or glorifying their country or political party. Hence, Roman historians never attained the scientific accuracy of the best Greek work, and in their worst moments they produced what may more fittingly be called propaganda than history.

Then, as always, political strife and civil wars produced a tendency to memoir writing, for both generals and politicians found it desirable to explain and justify their acts to the world. Rutilius Rufus, Sulla, and other public men wrote autobiographies, but these have not been preserved. In fact, the only surviving work of this class is that high-school acquaintance of so many modern youth, Caesar's *Commentaries on the Gallic War* and *Civil War*. The author protested that these were not histories, but only notes for the use of later historians. This claim is far too modest, for Caesar was a master of prose style, and a competent historian. His real aim was to justify his highly controversial career to the educated public of his own day, and he set about the task with consummate skill. His *Gallic War* tells the story of the conquest of Gaul down to the fall of Alesia with such lucidity and seeming artlessness, never arguing or pleading, but letting the facts which he presents speak for themselves, that the reader is irresistibly borne to the conclusion which Caesar meant he must reach. The same course is followed in the *Civil War*. Yet this is not to cast doubt upon the essential truth of his narratives. He may have suppressed or colored an occasional unpleasant fact, but his enemies, some of whom had served under him in Gaul and had every opportunity to detect falsehoods in that part of his work, never attempted to discredit it. Both works are incomplete. Aulus Hirtius, a friend of Caesar and one of the consuls of 43, wrote a continuation of the *Gallic War* in which he told the final incidents of the conquest, while unknown authors did the same for the Egyptian, African, and Spanish campaigns. All of the sequels are readable and fairly reliable, but they lack the magic of Caesar's touch.

Among the members of the Caesarian party was Gaius Sallustius Crispus (86–34). He had a stormy public career, being expelled from the Senate in 50 on a charge of moral turpitude, but Caesar restored him to his seat, and later made him governor of Numidia. There he made a large fortune, which enabled him to spend the last years of his life in luxurious retirement. The only works of Sallust to survive entire are two monographs, the *Jugurthine War* and the *Conspiracy of Catiline*. In style he imitated Thucydides, but there the resemblance ended. Both were partisan documents, written in the interest of the Populares in general and of Caesar in particular. In the former he skillfully brings out the corruption and inefficiency of the Senate, as a foil for the great deeds of Marius, while the latter work, without justifying Catiline or condemning Cicero, omits all mention of Caesar's supposed complicity in the plot. This amounts to an indirect denial of the story afloat among the Optimates that both Caesar and Crassus were implicated in the affair. He specializes in character sketches and moral observations, and occasionally, as in his battle scenes or in his account of the debate over the fate of Catiline's accomplices, he produces masterly descriptions. His history of Rome from 78 to 67 B.C., which was apparently written for the same purpose as the others, has come down to us in fragments. Two letters and a speech also attributed to him are of doubtful authenticity.

### *Poetry: Catullus and Lucretius*

The last century of the Republic produced several poets who were well known and admired in their time, but of these only two have left works which are now extant. Catullus and Lucretius both rank very high on the list of the world's poets, and although entirely different in temperament and outlook, each presents to us interesting phases of the life of this troubled age.

Gaius Valerius Catullus (87–*ca.* 47) was a native of Verona, a town in Cisalpine Gaul, where his father had both wealth and social position. As a young man he came to Rome, where his ready wit and literary genius at once made him a social favorite. He soon fell madly in love with Clodia, the beautiful, charming, and immoral sister of the gangster-tribune. Although she was married, for several years Catullus was her favored lover. To her (under the pseudonym of Lesbia) he addresses a wonderful series of love lyrics — *Kisses*, *Lesbia's Sparrow*, and the one which begins "Let us live and love, my Lesbia," being among the best known. In spite of the guilty nature of the affair, Catullus seems to have felt for her a pure and unalloyed affection not at all in keeping with the circumstances, but his happiness came to a sudden end. Another lover, Cicero's friend Caelius, supplanted him. Naïvely astonished that a woman who had been untrue to her husband would also be faithless to her lover, Catullus voiced his agony and cursed the deceiver with a truly Italian fluency. "I hate and love," he complains, "How can that be? I do not know, but I feel it and am tortured." [1] And again, "I loved you then, not as a man loves his mistress, but as a father loves his children. Now I know you, and although my love burns more fiercely, you mean far less to me than before." [2] Finally his love turned to hate, and he called Clodia the vilest names that can be applied to a woman.

[1] *Elegies*, LXXXV. [2] *Ibid.* LXXII.

*Keystone*

THE PORTLAND VASE
*The Marriage of Peleus and Thetis*

But Catullus did not confine himself to poems of love and hate. After his break with Clodia he went to Bithynia on the staff of a Roman propraetor. While there he wrote the *Attis*, a highly colored and graphic picture of the orgiastic rites of the Great Mother, ending with the hopeless lament of one of her eunuch-priests over his separation from home and friends. A visit to the tomb of his brother who had died in Asia inspired another splendid elegy. His marriage songs are full of stately beauty and noble thoughts, and his *Address to Sirmio*, which celebrates his return to Cisalpine Gaul after the journey to Bithynia, will stir the heart of anyone who has ever thrilled at the sight of home after wandering in a foreign land. Catullus owed much to Classical and Hellenistic Greek models, but his depth and range of feeling, and the beauty of diction, were seldom if ever surpassed in the ancient world.

Very different was Titus Lucretius Carus (*ca.* 95–52). Like Catullus, he was a man of good family and abundant means, who remained entirely aloof from politics. But whereas Catullus moved in the capital's fast and giddy society, Lucretius seems to have lived in retirement. The multiplied ills of his country moved him deeply, and like a good Roman he sought a remedy. He thought that he had found it in Epicurean philosophy, and to expound it to the public he wrote *The Nature of Things* (*De Rerum Natura*), one of the greatest didactic poems in the world.

*The Nature of Things* consists of six books, written in dactylic hexameter. Parts of it were never finished. The author's purpose was to rid men of two unfortunate habits of thought to which he attributed the disorders of the time: greed of wealth, power, and pleasure in this world, and fear of the world to come. He pictures religion as a monster before which men cowered in abject terror, not daring to look it in the face. It incited them to crimes and immoral acts such as human sacrifices, and made their lives miserable. He closes his scathing indictment with the memorable line, "Such are the crimes to which religion incites men." But the Greek philosophers dared to examine the monster, and found that its terrors were all imaginary. To understand the true nature of the universe and of man is to banish fear and to gain inner peace. Our poet then expounds the atomic theory, which Epicurus had made the central point in his explanation of the universe. All matter, including man himself, is composed of atoms, which combine, disintegrate, and recombine in a series of ever-changing forms. The soul, like the body, is a collection of atoms which at death separate, destroying man's personality so completely that it can never live again. Hence, after death there is no future world to fear. There are gods, but they dwell apart from the world which they created, and never interfere with its operation. Thus, within limits, each man is the maker of his own happiness or woe. He has his period of life, from which he should gain the greatest possible amount of happiness, and when the time comes to depart, he should go without repining. Happiness is not gained by idle pleasure hunting. In terms almost applicable to the twentieth century A.D., he pictures the man who restlessly seeks new sensations, and is bored with each in turn because he has nothing worth while within himself. Greed, ambition, sensuality, and romantic love alike fail to give one the key to the good life, which can be gained only by following the precepts of Epicurus. In the fifth book Lucretius, with a brilliant flash of intuition, describes the life of primitive man, picturing his savage condition and upward climb toward civilization in terms almost identical with those used by modern anthropologists. Here the poem really ends, for the sixth book was never completed. Legend says that the poet, driven insane by a love-potion, wrote it in the intervals of his madness, and committed suicide before it was done.

It is a powerful poem, but one lays it down with a feeling that here was no remedy for the desperate plight of the Roman world. Not by passive renunciation, but by active reform, were the problems of the day to be met, and Augustus, rather than Epicurus, was to be its savior.

# 19

## *The Augustan Principate (30 B.C.-14 A.D.)*

### Augustus: The Man and His Problems

After a century of turmoil the Roman state had, in 30 B.C., at last fallen into the hands of a constructive statesman. Octavian — or Augustus, as we shall soon have occasion to call him — was thirty-three years old when he won his final victory over Antony. There was in him little of the superficial brilliance of Julius Caesar, but in quite another way he was one of the world's great personalities. Physically, he was small and delicate, with fine features and piercing eyes. His health was always poor, but by careful living he managed to attain the age of seventy-seven. Probably there was not in all Italy a better example of the middle-class Italian character, nor one who understood that character more fully. He had all of its conservative devotion to the "customs of the ancestors" in religion, politics, and social outlook. He ruled his oddly assorted family with the benign despotism of an old-time Roman, while at the same time he often proved himself a charming companion, even engaging in a little genteel gambling. He would tolerate the plainest speech from those about him, but behind his unassuming exterior was a quiet force which made him master of any situation.

Although brave when the occasion demanded, Augustus was a planner and a manager rather than a soldier. He had the clarity of vision to see both the needs of the Roman state, and the most feasible means of satisfying those needs. His judgment of the abilities of subordinates was seldom mistaken, and he could bind the ablest men to him by bonds of friendship which insured their loyalty. Indeed, much of his success in war and provincial administration was due to the able and unselfish service of his boyhood friend Marcus Agrippa and his two stepsons Tiberius and Drusus Claudius Nero. At the same time he had for an adviser on civil affairs a wealthy but unassuming Etruscan of equestrian rank, Gaius Cilnius

Maecenas. No doctrinaire prejudices clouded his judgment, and his measures were never hasty or ill-considered. At last, Rome had found in him a physician fit to cope with her ills.

The defeat of Antony had entailed upon Augustus the task of providing the Roman world with a stable, efficient government. In undertaking this work, however, he was not entirely a free agent, for the Roman people had certain principles and prejudices which he could not safely disregard. The events of the preceding twenty years had proved that the Republic was dead and could not be restored. On the other hand, the fate of Caesar and the fall of Antony had demonstrated that the Roman citizen body would not tolerate any world-embracing despotism which would reduce them to a common servitude with provincials. Some form of one-man power was inevitable, but it must be cloaked in republican forms and guarantee to the Romans that privileged position which the blood of their ancestors had won for them.

## The Office of the Princeps

Whether or not Augustus ever wished to retire to private life, he could not have done so without reducing the state to anarchy. To found a government which would serve the needs of all classes and stand the test of actual use, was a work requiring careful planning. In keeping with his character, Augustus waited nearly three years before undertaking to make permanent arrangements. In the meantime he governed the state by means of the war powers assumed for the struggle with Antony, and strengthened by annual tenure of the consulship. At the beginning of the year 27 B.C., he was ready to proceed toward a permanent organization. The office of *princeps* (meaning "chief," the title by which the new head of the state came to be known) took shape gradually, as circumstances produced new needs, or as experience pointed out new lessons. At first, it was only a varying collection of republican magistracies, powers belonging to other magistracies, and honorary titles, all gathered into the hands of one man. Not for a considerable time did the list become stereotyped. Only by analyzing them and then considering the material and moral resources at the command of their holder can we understand the nature of the office.

### *The Proconsular Power*

The conclusion of the civil wars had left Augustus the military autocrat of the Roman world, with about five hundred thousand professional soldiers under his command. The principle of professional military service was too thoroughly established to be abolished, and at least half of this force was needed permanently for police service and frontier defense. Since this was Augustus' personal army, it was necessary to continue his control of it on a legalized basis. On January 13, 27 B.C., Augustus resigned his virtual dictatorship and restored the command of the armies to the Senate. Recognizing its incompetence to control this force and to administer the government through the ordinary magistracies, the Senate then invested him with the powers of proconsul over Syria, Hither Spain, and Transalpine Gaul for a period of ten years. He already held Egypt by right of conquest, and he probably continued to do so without a senatorial grant. With the exception of one legion in Macedonia and another in Africa, the Roman armies were now completely under his control. At the end of the ten-year term this power was renewed, and thereafter he held it for terms of five or ten years for the remainder of his life. As new provinces were formed or old ones required the presence of armies, they were put into the possession of the *Princeps*. In a few cases, peaceful provinces were restored to the Senate, but as a rule the number of imperial provinces steadily increased, while that of the senatorial provinces remained stationary or decreased. Hence his control of the bulk of the military forces and of the most troublesome provinces was now firmly established by constitutional means.

This grant of proconsular power was not in itself a radical departure from tradition, for Lucullus, Crassus, Pompey, and Caesar had held similar grants during the late Republic. But none of them had come so near to commanding all of the armed forces of the state except Caesar in the last days of his life, and his grant had been, really, the result of conquest. Up to 23 B.C., Augustus was able, by virtue of his consulship, to exercise paramount authority over the senatorial provinces as well as direct authority in his own, and after that date he achieved the same end by other means. Consequently, through this and allied powers he had effected control or rights of supervision over the whole Roman world outside of Italy. It was only a logical outgrowth of this state of affairs that, in 22 B.C., the Senate granted to him the right to declare war and make binding treaties without asking its consent.

### *The Government of Rome and Italy*

Experience had demonstrated the need of a strong executive in domestic as well as in foreign affairs, but the Roman people were sensitive and suspicious toward any institution that smacked of monarchy. Accordingly, Augustus experimented for several years before devising a satisfactory system for the control of this field of government. In 28 B.C., he revised the senate-roll (in his capacity of consul), placing his own name at the head of the list. The holder of this distinction was called *princeps senatus*, a title which corresponds to some extent to that of *dean* in a modern legislative body, in the sense of "ranking member." The only privilege which it conferred was that of speaking first on any question before the house. Yet so tremendous was the personal prestige of Augustus that, although he never discouraged reasonable opposition to his expressed opinions, very little was ever offered. Up to 23 B.C. his tenure of the consulship enabled him to introduce business at its meetings, and when he resigned this office, the same right was conferred upon him by special enactment. His motions took precedence over all others. As we shall see presently, none but those acceptable to him were likely to become senators. Hence, his control of senatorial legislation was, in effect, complete whenever he chose to exercise it.

As a more positive means of controlling the government of Rome and Italy, Augustus, as we have seen, held the consulship continually from 31 to 23 B.C. This practice, however, was open to grave objections. As a consul he had a colleague of equal powers, who might at times resort to obstructionist tactics. It also necessitated annual re-elections, and continual tenure of a curule office was contrary to tradition. Moreover, it did not give him control over the Assembly of the Tribes. Hence, in 23, this plan was given up. He resigned the consulship, and in return received the tribunician power for life. This was not the office of tribune, but only the powers and privileges belonging to the office. His person was legally guaranteed against injury and indignity. He could convene the Senate or the Assembly of the Tribes, put motions to them, veto their acts or those of the magistrates, and release prisoners from arrest. In short, this power enabled him to control the whole machinery of the state without having to stand for re-election or attend to small administrative details. Although he and his successors held the tribunician power for life, they numbered their years of tenure as if they had been annually re-elected. The other state magistracies, completely overshadowed by powers so sweeping, soon sank into insignificance, and became mere honorary distinctions or municipal offices of the city of Rome.

We have seen that in Rome the worship of the state gods was an important function of the government, and that the *pontifex maximus* was the head of all the state priesthoods. Until 12 B.C. this office was held by the

*Bettmann*

PRIMA PORTA AUGUSTUS
*30 B.C.–14 A.D.*

former triumvir Lepidus, who had seized it shortly after the death of Caesar, but after his death Augustus secured his own election to it. He likewise held several less important priesthoods. Indeed, his hold upon the state religion was of the greatest service to him in his campaign for social and religious reform, of which we shall hear more.

### *Honorary Titles and Extra-Legal Powers*

In addition to an enumeration of his powers and offices, the list of titles of a Roman emperor contained several elements which did not confer any specific prerogatives upon him, but gave the general impression that he was a person of superhuman greatness or goodness. The first of these was *imperator*, used instead of a given name. As a title following the name it had been conferred upon victorious generals by their soldiers, and when thus granted it entitled the holder, with the consent of the Senate, to celebrate a triumph in Rome. In the beginning Augustus used this title in the ordinary way, with a numeral indicating the number of triumphs which he had celebrated or to which he was entitled. In 38 B.C., however, he dropped his given name and replaced it with *imperator*, although he still continued to use it in its original sense as well. Thus he became *Imperator Caesar*, *divi filius*. On January 16, 27 B.C., the Senate gave him the additional title *Augustus*, by which he was always afterward known. Its meaning was rich with implications, but indefinite enough to escape being offensive to republican sentiment. Apparently derived from *augere* (to cause to increase), it had hitherto been reserved as an epithet of certain gods in their capacity of givers of prosperity. Great men had in the past been honored by the Senate with surnames (e.g. *Felix*, "the Lucky," to Sulla, or *Magnus*, "the Great," to Pompey), but in no previous case had it been implied that the person honored was the equal of the gods. Finally, in 2 B.C., he was proclaimed *pater patriae*, Father of his Country. Thus, a titulary of Augustus as of 14 A.D. reads: "*imperator Caesar*, *divi filius Augustus*, *pontifex maximus*, *consul* XIII, *imperator* XX, *tribunicia potestate* XXXVII, *pater patriae*." This may be loosely translated: "The Triumphant Caesar Augustus, son of the divine Julius, Chief Pontiff, thirteen times consul, winner of twenty triumphs, holder of the tribunician power for thirty-seven years, Father of his Country." Much as this may sound like vain boasting, it was not so. Those titles which do not confer concrete powers hint at another phase of the imperial power which demands attention.

Broad as were the enumerated powers of a Roman *Princeps*, they did not, by any means, indicate the full extent of his real power. He was the wealthiest man in the Roman world many times over, the heir of Caesar, and the conqueror of all rivals before he received from the Senate the grants which are commonly treated as constituting his title to rule. The provincials, ten times more numerous than the Roman citizens, did not understand the legal theory of the Principate at all, and simply regarded Augustus as a king. Many, indeed, went further, and worshiped him as a god. In short, the *Princeps* had behind him an overwhelming preponderance of material resources and moral support which would have enabled him to play the absolute monarch if he had been so minded. His adherence to constitutional forms was, therefore, in large measure, voluntary, for there was no power strong enough to compel him to observe them. Therein lay the strength and the weakness of the Principate. It enabled a man like Augustus to display a benevolence, a moderation, and a respect for the rights of others which he would have found it hard to show if he had been struggling with a powerful opposition, but in the hands of weak and unprincipled successors, such power became an instrument of tyranny.

## Domestic Government

### *The New Class System*

The government of the Roman Republic had always been organized on a class basis, and that of the *Principate* continued to be so. Augustus, however, with that fine creative genius which marked his every public act, set about to revamp the system so that the causes of class war would be eliminated. Each class was to have a political career marked out for it, peculiar to it and adequate for its abilities and ambitions. These classes were not to be closed castes, for men of ability might, by acquiring wealth and holding offices, rise from one rank to another. Especially was this possible through the favor of the *Princeps*.

In spite of its past incompetence and the losses in wealth and personnel which it had suffered during the civil wars, the Senate still represented the best character and political talent to be found among the Roman people. Accordingly, it retained much of the importance which it had had under the Republic. It was from the Senate that the *Princeps* drew the legal authorization to hold most of his powers, and in addition it enjoyed a large share of nominally independent authority. To fill this position with credit, it needed to be purged of the less desirable characters added to its ranks by Caesar and Antony. Hence in 28 B.C., 18 B.C., and 4 A.D., Augustus, acting by virtue of various offices which he held, revised the Senate roll. The qualifications for membership were stiffened, and its number reduced to six hundred. Henceforth, to be a senator one had to be a Roman citizen by birth and a resident of Italy, to have an estate valued at 1,000,000 sesterces ($90,000), to have held certain minor city offices, to have served as a legionary tribune in the army, and to have been chosen to the quaestorship. Flagrant immorality or dishonorable conduct theoretically barred men from membership. Since many otherwise suitable men were too poor to meet the property qualifications, Augustus made up the sums which they lacked out of his own pocket. This, together with his revision of the Senate roll and his practice of recommending certain candidates to the voters, enabled him, in point of fact, to appoint all members of the Senate. Men of senatorial families were given preference for curule offices, and they enjoyed numerous social privileges, including the right to wear togas bordered with broad purple stripes. With few exceptions the highest offices in the imperial service were filled with men of senatorial rank. After holding one of the quaestorships a senator became eligible for election to the aedileship or the tribunate, the praetorship, and the consulship. As propraetor or proconsul he might govern a senatorial province.

Nominally the sphere of activity reserved to the Senate was very extensive, and it might have been much more so in fact than it was if the Conscript Fathers had proved equal to their opportunities. Actually, there were elements of weakness in the senatorial position which made this impossible. The Senate represented an ideal of government which was understood only by the Roman people, and even among them it had been weakened by a century of class strife. The provincials did not understand this ideal at all, but tendered whatever loyalty they felt for the Roman state to the *Princeps*. Thus the legal theory of the Principate, with its division of powers, was not understood by the great body of the people who lived under it. Consequently, the Senate lacked the backing of a strong public opinion, which alone would have enabled it to hold its own against the tremendous resources of its partner in the government. In addition, many of the senatorial aristocracy refused to do their share of the necessary work. Too often they begged for financial support from Augustus, or devoted themselves to pleasure or vice. In its ranks there still lurked a doctrinaire hostility to the new government, which, although largely disarmed by the tact and personal charm of the *Princeps*, probably tended to paralyze its energies, or to direct its stronger spirits into conspiracies against him. Many of the functions assumed by Augustus would never have been taken over if the Senate had not failed to perform them. On the other hand, many of the aristocracy seem to have accepted the new regime wholeheartedly, and among them Augustus found able provincial governors and military commanders.

Under the Republic the equestrian order as a class had never achieved an assured political position comparable to that of the Senate. Hence its members seem to have accepted the Principate loyally. In the Augustan system an equestrian had to be a free-born Roman of good character, eighteen years of age, to have an estate valued at not less than 400,000 sesterces ($36,000). To each man who possessed these qualifications the state entrusted a horse. His insignia consisted of a toga with a narrow purple border. Equestrians were subject to an annual inspection, at which unworthy members were reproved or dropped from the rolls.

The political career of an equestrian began with military service as commander of an auxiliary corps, and as tribune of a legionary cohort. Having satisfied this requirement, he could then aspire to a series of offices known by the general name of procuratorships, connected with the financial administration of the *Princeps*. In a few of the less important provinces the procurators had complete charge of the government. The prizes of the equestrian career were the prefectures of the grain supply, of the police, of Egypt, and of the praetorian guard. These offices equaled any of those open to senators in importance and remuneration, and their holders were frequently promoted into the Senate. Indeed, so attractive did the equestrian career become that Augustus found it hard to secure enough candidates for the quaestorship among those to whom both careers were open.

The popular assemblies, recruited from the proletariat of the city of Rome, were the weakest element in the new government. Accustomed to bribery and intimidation, and lacking both character and education, their members did little more than endorse the decisions of the *Princeps* and his advisers. The lack of a representative system made it impossible for the Roman citizens of Italy and the provinces to participate in legislation. This was an unfortunate fact, for the quality of these men was, as a rule, much higher than that of the residents of the capital.

### *The City of Rome*

Preoccupation with political strife and the affairs of the Empire had prevented the Romans from working out a suitable government for the city of Rome. Toward the end of the first century B.C., although it was the largest city in the Mediterranean world, it still lacked police and fire protection, and had few worthy public buildings. The provision of a food supply was a function of government, but it was often neglected, with famines as a result.

When Augustus resigned the consulship in 23 B.C., he seems to have intended to leave the administration of the city in the hands of the Senate and the magistrates. If such was his plan, he was soon compelled to abandon it by repeated and disastrous breakdowns of municipal services. The most critical of these were police, fire, and the grain supply. In the first four years of senatorial rule three serious riots forced Augustus to give up his *laissez-faire* policy, and to intervene to restore order. His first step was to place three cohorts of his praetorian guard in Rome. Later, three *urban cohorts* were organized to act as supplementary police. Their number

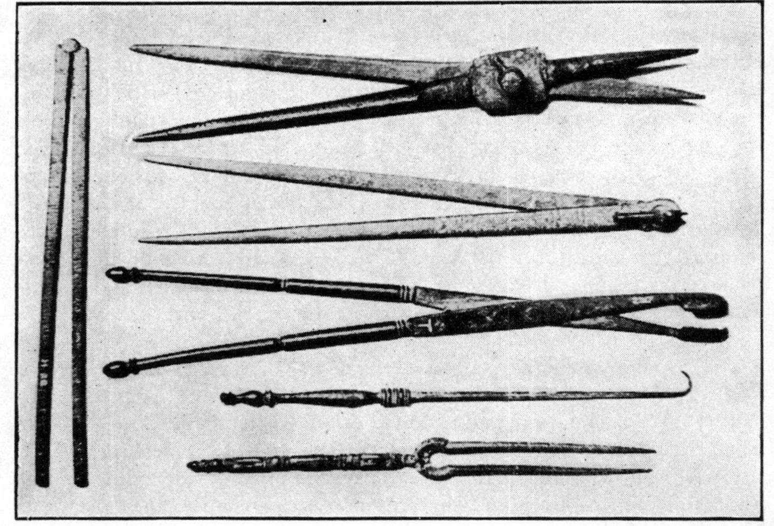

*Bettmann*

ROMAN SURVEYOR'S INSTRUMENTS

was forty-five hundred, and they were commanded by a senatorial official, the prefect of the city. Disastrous fires in 14 and 7 B.C. produced similar results in that area of administration. After an unsuccessful attempt to form a fire department manned by public slaves, he organized seven cohorts of *vigiles*, whose duties combined fire fighting and night patroling, under an equestrian prefect. The management of the grain supply broke down in senatorial hands as early and as disastrously as did the other branches of municipal government. Within a year of his retirement from the consulship, Augustus was forced by a famine to resume control of this important function, and in 6 A.D. another famine caused him to appoint a permanent equestrian official to control it (*praefectus annonae*). For purposes of local administration Augustus divided the city into fourteen sections (*regiones*), each of which was subdivided into wards. Over each ward was a *master*, elected by the people. The Emperor's activities as a city-planner and builder in the capital will be considered elsewhere. All in all, there is no better example of senatorial decadence and imperial efficiency than this.

## The Financial System of the Principate

*Senatorial and Imperial Spheres of Action*

The financial administration of the Roman state under the Principate, like other phases of government, was divided into two parts. The Senate still controlled the revenues from its provinces and from Italy, and stored the proceeds in the *aerarium Saturni*, as before. Augustus, on the other hand, did not as yet have a centralized treasury department to handle his financial affairs. Each of his provinces had its own fiscal organization, and in addition there was a central office to handle his private property. These provincial treasuries very early acquired the name of *fisci* (purses or baskets), but not until later was a central fiscus established at Rome. From the revenues at his disposal the Emperor met the expenses of provincial government, but the drain was a heavy one, and necessitated frequent drafts upon his private fortune.

By 6 A.D. the cost of the military establishment had produced a crisis. New sources of revenue had to be found, for the existing tax rates could not be safely increased; but Italy, the wealthiest part of the Empire, would not submit to direct taxation. A new treasury, the *aerarium militare*, was established, and Augustus inaugurated it with a large gift from his private funds. After much haggling, the Senate consented to approve a tax of 5 per cent on inheritances left to Roman citizens, with exemption for small estates and bequests to near relatives. Another tax of 5 per cent was levied upon the price of manumitted slaves, and a sales tax of 1 per cent upon the proceeds of auction sales. These two affected Roman citizens and provincials alike. The income from these taxes was paid into the new treasury, and for a long time proved adequate to meet the expenses of the army and navy.

*Numismatic Society*

SPANISH DENARIUS

*Obverse: Head of Augustus. Reverse: Civic Wreath*

The right of coinage was divided between Augustus and the Senate, but it is significant that after 15 B.C. he had a monopoly upon the issue of gold and silver, while the Senate issued only bronze. Numerous city mints survived, especially in the East, and these were only gradually abolished. The coinage of Augustus was honest and dependable. The standard [1] was as follows:

| | | | |
|---|---|---|---|
| 2½ asses | 1 sestertius | silver | .09 |
| 10 asses | 1 denarius | silver | .36 |
| 25 denarii | 1 aureus | gold | $9.00 |

## Social and Religious Reforms

### *A Regenerated Citizenry*

In the eyes of Augustus, the keystone of the imperial structure which he was rearing was to be the Roman citizen body, which was to rule, through him, over the provincials. To fill their exalted place with credit, they would have to recover those virtues which had made Rome great in previous ages. His first step was to stop the contamination of the blood of the conquerors through mixture with their subjects. Hence he reversed the policy of Julius Caesar, and restricted, as far as possible, the granting of citizen rights to provincials. Whereas between 70 and 28 B.C., the number of citizens increased from 450,000 to 4,063,000 (over 900 per cent, largely due to grants of citizenship to Gauls, Spaniards, and other provincials, by Julius Caesar), from 28 B.C., to 14 A.D., a period of exactly equal length, the figure rose only from the last figure to 4,937,000 or about 21 per cent. Senators were forbidden to marry freedwomen, although it was found impossible to enforce this restriction upon the other classes. The right of owners to free their slaves was severely restricted, and freedmen were barred from political activities. On the other hand, every possible inducement was offered to citizens to marry and rear families. By the Julian Law of Marriage of 18 B.C., marriage was made a duty of every Roman and those who shirked it suffered various disabilities, such as ineligibility to receive legacies. Fathers and mothers of families were favored in various ways. Other laws were enacted against luxury and immorality, with drastic penalties attached. Above all, Augustus strove by precept and (to some extent) example to make the family virtues stylish and popular. In

[1] The values of Augustan silver coins in American money have been computed in terms of their ratio to gold, and the worth of the *aureus* on the basis of the present price of gold — $35.00 an ounce.

some cases he furnished impecunious young aristocrats with money wherewith to set up housekeeping. His daughter, stepsons, nieces, and nephews all married young, and most of them reared large families. But the times were against him. His own daughter and granddaughter were banished for rank immorality. Twenty-seven years after his first marriage-law he sponsored a second, the Pappian-Poppaean Law (*Lex Pappia Poppaea*), but the consuls who secured its passage were both bachelors. Not until fifty years after his death, when Italians and provincials began to fill the ranks of the aristocracy, did the moral tone improve noticeably.

Probably the worst economic and social evil at Rome was the presence of a beggarly proletariat over two hundred thousand strong, whom the government had to feed, clothe, and amuse. Although he recognized the seriousness of the evil, Augustus did nothing to remove it, and actually aggravated the situation by doles of money and lavish shows in the amphitheaters. Yet every effort was made to revive agriculture, and to check the flow of population from the country to the cities. A campaign of literary propaganda, of which Virgil's *Georgics* are the classic example, was initiated to make country life popular. More effective was the system whereby discharged soldiers were given allotments of land and money with which to begin farming. Here again Augustus was working against the dominant tendency of the age, and in Italy the effort failed. In the provinces as a whole the settlement of discharged soldiers in colonies was a marked success.

### *The Revival and New Growth of Religion*

A revival of religion was part of the plan for social reform. The times were more favorable to this, for the nationalistic revival upon which Augustus had ridden into power was hostile to those foreign cultural elements which had been influential in undermining the Roman national religion. The restoration of order in Italy was likewise conducive to the revival of religious rites, and the genius of Virgil soon gave to the ancestral worship what it had always lacked, an immortal poem which would popularize it wherever read.

The "drive" to restore the popularity of the old gods had begun even before the Battle of Actium, with an onslaught upon the Egyptian cults that had become popular in the cities of Italy. While the war spirit was at its height the worship of Isis and Serapis was forbidden inside the *pomoerium*. The repair of temples and the reorganization of decadent priesthoods followed. In 28 B.C. alone Augustus restored eighty-two shrines, and this was but the beginning. Soon there rose on the Capitoline Hill the splendid sanctuary of Jupiter Optimus Maximus, the chief of the state gods, and on the Palatine another dedicated to Apollo. In the Forum of Julius Caesar stood a temple of Venus, the reputed ancestress of the Julian clan, while in the Forum of Augustus the temple of Mars the Avenger commemorated the return of the Roman standards and prisoners lost by Crassus and Antony. The Pantheon of Agrippa will be treated separately. Each of the two hundred and fifty-six wards of the city had its own shrine dedicated to the Lares and the Genius of Augustus. The facility with which the Romans deified abstractions provided other gods whose worship would shed glory upon the Princeps, such as the Augustan Peace or Mercury Augustus.

The priestly colleges, many of which had ceased to function for a generation or more, were reorganized, and every effort was made to attach social prestige to membership in them. Augustus himself, in addition to being chief pontiff, was a member of the Board of Fifteen on Sacred Rites, the Board of Seven on Feasts, an Arval Brother, a Titian Brother, and a member of the College of Heralds. As these ancient organizations were reconstituted, all the resources of antiquarian research were taxed to revive their rituals and functions as of old. A drastic purification of the Sibylline Books took place, and two thousand volumes of unauthorized prophecies were burned.

The Augustan literary revival will receive detailed treatment elsewhere, but it may here be remarked that Virgil, Horace, and even the cynical Ovid contributed by their works to popularize the movement. The deep hostility with which the Christian clergy later viewed the *Aeneid* is itself enough to show how potent an influence this masterpiece was to be in awakening the religious fervor of its readers.

Religion was to be made the handmaid of social reform. The Etruscans had taught the Romans to believe that the gods divided human history into distinct epochs, at the beginning of each of which the human race enjoyed a fresh start, free from the accumulated evils of the preceding era. Therefore, to signify that the age of disorder, irreligion, and immorality had closed and that a new and better age was at hand, Augustus in 17 B.C. caused the Secular Games to be celebrated. In a splendid festival lasting three days and three nights the opening of the new age of peace and virtue was signalized, and for it Horace wrote the *Secular Hymn*.

But a new religion was making itself felt in the Roman world, which demanded careful and tactful handling. The worship of living kings had become a common practice in the Hellenistic East, and early in 29 B.C., the cities of Asia Minor requested permission to pay divine honors to Augustus. If properly controlled, this practice could well be used to build up an imperial patriotism among the provincials, but since it savored of absolute monarchy, the upper classes at Rome were certain to oppose its introduction into Italy. By an ingenious compromise Augustus both accepted and rejected the proffered worship. In the East he allowed and encouraged the cult of himself and the goddess Roma (the personification of the Roman state, long worshiped by the Greeks), and later he sponsored the same cult in the Gallic provinces. A great altar was built at Lugdunum, where deputies from the local governments of Gaul gathered annually to worship the deities which personified the state and its visible head. Subsequently the same cult was established in the other provinces, and after the rise of Christianity officials used it as a test to discover the guilt of persons suspected of belonging to the forbidden sect, since no Christian would participate in it. In Rome and Italy the worship of Augustus was not permitted; but after 12 B.C., the cult of the *genius* of Augustus — his divine double and guardian spirit — was instituted in conjunction with that of the Lares. In the Italian municipalities this phase of Augustus-worship was in charge of boards of six men (the *seviri Augustales*) to which freedmen, although barred from all other offices were eligible. Thus even the freedmen were not entirely deprived of opportunities for distinction in the Augustan system.

In the lifetime of Augustus his efforts probably elicited nothing better than lip service from the cynical and sophisticated Roman aristocracy, but that is not to say that they were entirely fruitless. His influence can be traced with certainty in the revival of religious fervor which became apparent in the late first century A.D., and he no doubt helped to prolong the life of the ancestral paganism for many generations.

## The Military and Naval Services

When the Principate was founded, professional armies were an accomplished fact against which it was useless to struggle. The state needed a large army to defend its far-flung frontiers, but at the same time the avenues must be closed through which popular commanders had been able to attack the government whose servants they professed to be. In short, the army must be "removed from politics." Augustus began, immediately after the fall of Antony, by demobilizing half of the five hundred thousand men under his command, giving them land or money from his private funds. The remainder he distributed through the provinces under his jurisdiction. It required about thirty years for him to work out a permanent military system, which may be summarized as follows.

### *The Field Army*

The army was to consist of three classes of troops — legionaries, auxiliaries, and praetorians. The first two were to constitute the field army, while the third was to be the bodyguard of the *Princeps* and the garrison of Italy. Legionaries had to be Roman citizens at the time of enlistment, and when, in times of stress, a few provincials were enlisted in this branch of the service, they received citizenship at once. They were enlisted for a term of twenty years. Ultimately Augustus had in service twenty-five legions, each having a paper strength of 120 cavalry and 5880 infantry. When discharged from service a legionary received a bonus in land or money. This, with the donatives distributed to him by the government, booty taken on campaigns, and savings from his regular pay, rendered him financially independent. The auxiliaries were recruited from among the more belligerent provincials, and their total strength was about equal to that of the legionaries. Their period of service was twenty-five years, and when discharged they received Roman citizenship. They were organized into corps called *cohortes* and *alae*, consisting respectively of 480 infantry or 960 cavalry. In arms and discipline they resembled the legionaries, with whom they were constantly associated in the camps and on campaigns.

In times of peace, the field army was usually garrisoned upon the frontiers. There it formed a bulwark against invasions of the uncivilized peoples outside, which would otherwise have reduced the Empire to chaos and rendered its civilizing work impossible. But the army had other functions as a promoter of culture which it would be hard to overestimate. Gauls, Pannonians, Moors, Spaniards, and others were kept for a quarter of a century under Roman discipline, commanded by Roman officers, and associated constantly with Latin-speaking legionaries. They not only became citizens when discharged, but had also learned Latin of a sort and developed an imperial patriotism. This was the principal avenue through which Augustus allowed the entry of provincials into the citizen body. It assured the gradual increase of the number of citizens, and trained the newly enfranchised ones in Roman ways. The army not only fought battles, but built roads and public buildings. Around its frontier camps, important cities gradually arose whence Roman civilization was to radiate to surrounding regions, and some of these former legionary camps are still among the most important cities of Europe.

### *The Praetorian Guard and the Fleet*

The praetorian guard, although not without parallels in the time of the Republic, was really an innovation pointing toward monarchy. It consisted of nine cohorts of one thousand men each, commanded by two equestrian prefects. Praetorians had to be of Italian birth. They served for sixteen years, received double pay and had easy conditions of service. Under Augustus, six of these cohorts were stationed in Italian municipalities, and the remainder, as we have seen, in Rome. The three urban cohorts were strictly a police force, and need not be treated further.

The destruction of rival sea powers had freed the Romans from the need of a large navy, but the piracy of the later Republican period had proved the necessity of an adequate marine police force. The fleet organized by Augustus was designed for this purpose, and was therefore of small importance in comparison with the army. It was manned almost entirely by freedmen and slaves, and its commanders were equestrians. Naval bases were maintained at Misenum and Ravenna in Italy, and at Forum Julii (Frejus) in Gaul. Flotillas on the Rhine and Danube were a part of the system of frontier defense.

Augustus did not flatter the soldiers, and was a strict disciplinarian. He sternly repressed outrages upon civilians, and made the warriors who fought for him earn their pay and allowances. He did not entirely remove the danger of military domination of the government; indeed, in organizing the praetorian guard he contributed directly to aggravate this peril. For at least a century society had an opportunity to live in peace and safety, and when, in 68–69 A.D., a military revolt came, the tradition of order was too strongly established to permit such a movement to last long.

## The Provinces and the Frontier Problem

In the provinces the task of Augustus was not merely to end the disorder caused by the civil wars. He had to provide what Rome had never had — an orderly and practicable system of government for her dependencies. Under the Republic, the government of the provinces had remained a series of makeshifts, too clearly apparent in its straggling boundaries, clashing authorities, and wretchedly inefficient administration. Under the new order, control of the provinces was, as we have seen, divided between the *Princeps* and the Senate, but in point of fact, Augustus was able to give the senatorial provinces a much more efficient supervision than they had previously enjoyed. The character of provincial government everywhere underwent an immediate change for the better, and the far-sighted frontier policy took the place of the haphazard measures to which the Senate had been accustomed to resort.

*Government in the Imperial Provinces*

In the "imperial" provinces (at first Syria, Transalpine Gaul, Hither Spain, and Egypt), Augustus himself was the proconsul, and the actual governors were his deputies. In the first three, they bore the title of *legatus Augusti pro praetore* and were of senatorial rank. They were appointed and dismissed by him and received regular salaries. An able and trusty man might be kept in one province for a long time. Under each of these imperial governors were a varying number of legionary commanders, who acted as his subordinates. All of these officials were kept under close control, and they were liable to summary trial and punishment for any kind of misconduct. Opportunities to make independent military reputations did not exist, for any victories which they won were credited to Augustus, under whose auspices they served. One branch of provincial administration was entirely outside their hands. In each province was an imperial *procurator*, who collected taxes, took charge of the money, and was not under the control of the governor. As these procurators were of equestrian rank, they had no class sympathy for the governors, and they thus formed independent sources from which the *Princeps* could get information about local conditions. As other provinces were annexed, all of them fell to the lot of Augustus and his successors to administer, and the same system was usually applied to them. In a few cases, however, where only auxiliary troops were stationed in a province, the procurator (sometimes called prefect) had the whole task of government to himself.

Egypt was in a class by itself. Its defensibility, its importance as a producer of revenue and foodstuffs, and the peculiar character of its people, made it a crucial point. No senator could enter this province without a special permit, and its equestrian prefect, unlike others of his class, had legionary soldiers under his command. The highly organized Egyptian bureaucracy, taken over from the Ptolemaic kings, supervised the economic life of the country in such a way as to wring from the people an enormous revenue, exceeding that of any other province. Its grain alone fed the Roman people for four months out of the year. Augustus governed it in general more as a private estate than as a public trust.

### *The Senatorial Provinces*

In the senatorial provinces, while the old system of government, discussed in our treatment of the Republic, continued, its spirit soon changed for the better. Probably the old system of tax-farming continued for a time, but the proconsuls now received large fixed salaries, and both they and the *publicani* were under close supervision. Infractions of the law were more often reported to the Senate and their perpetrators punished. A comprehensive census of the whole Empire was taken, with periodic revisions. This rendered arbitrary taxation difficult. After 6 A.D., the presence of imperial procurators in the senatorial provinces to collect the taxes reserved for the military treasury rendered the supervision over their governments even closer than before.

### *Provinces and Frontiers — Spain and Gaul*

When Augustus assumed control of Hither Spain the struggle of the natives against Rome had been in progress for nearly two centuries, but in the mountainous northwestern part of the peninsula the Cantabrians, Asturians, and Gallaecians still retained their independence and plundered the settled areas of the province. In a series of campaigns lasting intermittently from 27 to 19 B.C., Augustus and his lieutenants crushed the rebels, transplanted the more refractory ones to the plains or sold them into slavery, and planted colonies and garrisons to secure the work of pacification. Thereafter Spain was at peace, but a force of several legions was permanently stationed in the north to prevent further trouble. The present city of Leon takes its name from the fact that a legion once had its camp on the site.

The organization of the Gallic provinces, which had never been put into good order by Julius Caesar, occupied Augustus at intervals from 27 to 13 B.C. Since Narbonese Gaul was peaceful and largely Romanized, it was soon handed back to the Senate. However, the recently conquered area (known as "Long-haired Gaul" in contrast to the old province, where men wore their hair short in the Roman fashion) required special attention. There Augustus established the three provinces of Aquitania, Lugdunensis, and Belgica, which included respectively the southwest, the center, and the north of the country. Apparently these provinces continued under a single governor throughout his life, although with separate administrations. Little change was made in the existing local governments. The sixty-four principal tribal units (known to the Romans as

ROMAN EMPIRE ABOUT 14 A.D.

*civitates*) continued to enjoy local self-government, and the native nobility held much the same privileged position as in the days of independence. Only one Roman colony was founded, that of Lugdunum (Lyons). However, the cessation of German raids and civil wars made Gaul so prosperous that many of the native towns grew to large proportions and later attained the rank of cities.

*The Alpine and Danubian Lands*

Above all things, the security of Rome's Gallic and Balkan provinces depended upon her attainment and maintenance of a defensible northern frontier. It is proof of the haphazard imperialism of the Republic that in spite of its far-flung conquests in Asia, Africa, and Europe, the Alpine regions at the very door of Italy were still in the hands of barbarians who murdered and plundered in the Po Valley and interrupted communication by land between Rome and Gaul. A similar situation existed along the borders of Macedonia, where the Illyrians and Celts taxed the skill and courage of every Roman proconsul. To govern these areas with a minimum of expenditure, the Romans needed a short, strong line of defense on their northern frontier. When Augustus came into power such a frontier had been attained only along the Rhine. He spent a large part of his active career attempting to complete the solution of the problem.

In 25 B.C., the Salassi, a robber tribe living southeast of Lake Geneva on the Italian side of the Alps, were annihilated, and their territory occupied by a colony of discharged praetorians. Farther south a trustworthy native chief, Cottius, founded a kingdom for which he became a vassal of Rome. These two strokes freed the road between Italy and Gaul from molestation. Ten years later the Rhaetians and Vindelici, who occupied the Alps north and northeast of Italy, were attacked and conquered by Tiberius and Drusus, Augustus' two stepsons. Their lands became the imperial provinces of Rhaetia and Noricum, which extended to the upper Danube.

The situation on the middle and lower Danube had been taken in hand somewhat earlier. In 29 B.C., Marcus Crassus, proconsul of Macedonia, had conquered the Moesians, who lived along the lower Danube, and turned their land over to a vassal Thracian prince. Later in the Principate of Augustus it was made a province under the name of Moesia. But between Noricum and Moesia lived the Pannonians, who had been at war with Augustus shortly before the outbreak of the final struggle with Antony. In 12 B.C., his elder stepson Tiberius led an army against them, and in two years of hard fighting subdued them. Although their lands were not organized as a province for some years thereafter, they were subjects of Rome from that time on. Rome now had, for the first time in her history, a defensible northern frontier, which followed throughout its length the courses of two navigable rivers.

### *The Conquest and Loss of Germany*

Here the progress of Roman conquest in Europe might well have stopped, but the northern frontier was not yet wholly satisfactory. The Germans across the Rhine occasionally raided the borders of Gaul. The Rhine-Danube frontier was long and awkward, containing, as a glance at the map will show, a re-entrant angle near the upper courses of the two rivers. A better solution seemed to be that of making the Elbe rather than the Rhine the northeastern frontier of the Empire. The Elbe-Danube line was about three hundred miles shorter than the Rhine-Danube line (2150 miles as compared with 2450), and it was more nearly straight. For over twenty years Augustus strove to attain it. After six years of campaigning (12–6 B.C.), first by Drusus and after his death in 9 B.C., by Tiberius, the land between the two rivers was organized into the province of Germany, with the exception of the mountainous region known in modern times as Bohemia. There the matter rested for more than a decade (6 B.C.–6 A.D.), during which time an able chief of the Marconanni, Maroboduus by name, founded a strong and progressive kingdom in the unoccupied area. When in 6 A.D., Tiberius undertook to round out the new line by conquering the kingdom of Maroboduus, he was interrupted by a savage revolt of the Pannonians and Dalmatians in his rear. Three years were spent in subduing this outbreak, but before Tiberius could resume his German enterprise a disaster occurred which put an end to any thought of further conquest in that direction.

In 9 A.D., Publius Quintilius Varus, the governor of Germany, was entrapped by rebels in the marshy Teutoberg forest with three legions and an equal force of auxiliaries, and the whole force was annihilated. The rebellion which led to this disaster was the work of a young German chief known to the Romans as Arminius, who, after fighting in the Roman army for some years and gaining the rights of a citizen, formed a secret coalition of malcontents and struck for his country's independence. The disgrace to the Romans was great, but there was little real danger, either to Italy or Gaul. The coalition which had destroyed the army of Varus soon broke up, and between 11 and 17 A.D., first Tiberius, and later his nephew Germanicus, won a series of brilliant successes against the enemy. But the strain upon the man-power of the Empire was too great. Augustus, realizing this, laid down the maxim that the Empire should not be extended farther, and on this frontier the advice was put into effect. In general, the Rhine remained the boundary between Roman and German.

### *The Eastern Frontier, and the Parthian Question*

In the East the crucial problem was the Parthian state, and anything like a "scientific" frontier was impossible. At the beginning of the Principate of Augustus, Rome possessed in this region the provinces of Bithynia-Pontus, Asia, Cilicia, and Syria. Central Asia Minor was in the hands of the vassal kings of Galatia (Amyntas) and Cappadocia (Archelaus), while eastern Asia Minor contained the vassal states of Pontus, Armenia, and several smaller units. In 25 B.C., however, after the death of its king, Galatia was made a province. South of the Taurus Mountains were other vassal kings, whose relations with Rome were carried on through the governors of Syria. Among these were Commagene, Damascus, Judea, and the Nabatean Arabs. The advantage of a frontier covered by these vassal states was so great that Augustus continued and strengthened it. The characters of the rulers of these states varied considerably: there were enlightened rulers like Polemon of Pontus, and spendthrifts like the Cappadocian monarchs. Josephus has left us a full-length literary portrait of one of Rome's vassals, Herod of Judea. He was a colorful villain, the murderer of his wife and sons, and hated by his subjects, yet so astute was he that after espousing the losing causes of Cassius and Antony he was each time able to make peace with the victor and emerge from a dangerous crisis with improved fortunes. After Herod's death in 4 B.C., ten years of misgovernment under his son ended with the annexation of most of his kingdom as a province under a procurator. It was in the last days of Herod's reign that Jesus of Nazareth was born at Bethlehem of Judea, and he grew to manhood in the petty principality of Galilee, under the rule of Herod Antipas, a son of Herod the Great.

The Parthian problem could never be permanently solved. When Augustus came into power the Roman people were still smarting from the defeats of Crassus and Antony, and public opinion demanded revenge. Augustus, more anxious for solid results than for spectacular strokes, took a more profitable but less glorious course. The Parthian royal family was rent with dissensions, and their king, Phraates IV, was too weak a ruler to play a strong part. Augustus shrewdly worked upon this situation. In

20 B.C., Phraates allowed Tiberius to establish a Roman candidate upon the throne of Armenia without opposition, and surrendered to him the captured Roman standards and prisoners. This well-advertised diplomatic victory marked the beginning of an era of uneasy peace between the two powers, during which there was usually a son of Phraates at Rome as a hostage. The Armenian question, however, could not be settled to the satisfaction of all. Roman candidates were repeatedly made kings of the country, only to be driven out soon after by native rebellions with popular or Parthian aid. In 4 A.D., Gaius Caesar, grandson of Augustus, was mortally wounded while on such a mission.

### *Egypt and Africa*

Egypt, with her irrigation canals repaired by Augustus and her government once more in efficient hands, throve and prospered under his rule. The predatory Ethiopians on the south were reduced to vassalage, and an unsuccessful attempt was made to conquer the spice country of Arabia. Commerce with India served to enrich the merchants of Alexandria.

In the old province of Africa, wars with the Moors along the borders harassed the country throughout the reign of Augustus, and for a long time afterwards. He completed the recolonization of Carthage, which had been decreed by Julius Caesar. In 25 B.C., the province was greatly enlarged by the annexation of the Numidian kingdom, whose sovereign, the learned Juba II, was transferred to Mauretania (modern Algiers and Morocco). There his court became a center of culture, and Juba himself wrote many books. His wife was Cleopatra Selene, the daughter of Antony and Cleopatra.

Augustus gave to the Empire an intelligible plan of imperial government, but he virtually ended the age of conquest. Henceforth the energies of the state were to be expended upon defense and consolidation.

## The Succession

Although each of the powers and offices which formed part of the Principate was the gift of the Senate and the people, Augustus realized that unless the state was to relapse into anarchy, provision would have to be made for the succession during his lifetime. Family pride prompted him to seek his successor among his own kindred, and the nominally elective character of the Principate made it necessary that his successor, to receive immediate and peaceful possession, should already be the holder of its powers before he was called upon to exercise them.

*The Husbands and Sons of Julia*

A daughter, Julia, was Augustus' only child. Livia, whom he married after divorcing Julia's mother, had two sons, Tiberius and Drusus, by her former husband. His sister Octavia had a son, Marcus Marcellus. As long as possible Augustus based his succession arrangements upon the husbands and children of Julia. Her first husband was Marcellus, who soon died. Shortly afterward his sixteen-year-old widow was married to her father's trusted friend, Marcus Agrippa, who was compelled to divorce Julia's cousin before becoming her husband. She bore Agrippa three sons, Gaius Caesar, Lucius Caesar, and Agrippa Postumus, and two daughters,

*University Prints*

AGRIPPA

Julia and Agrippina.[1] Augustus adopted the two older sons, but until they would be old enough to govern the state a regent would be necessary, and Augustus' poor health made him constantly apprehensive of an early death. For this purpose he secured the tribunician and proconsular powers for Marcus Agrippa in 18 B.C., but Agrippa after receiving them continued to act in the same subordinate capacity as before. In spite of his poor health Augustus outlived both Agrippa and his two elder sons. After Agrippa's death in 12 B.C. the unwelcome post of imperial son-in-law was forced upon Augustus' elder stepson, Tiberius. He was compelled to divorce a wife whom he loved and marry a woman whose immoral life he detested, to act as guardian for stepsons who would sooner or later push him aside. From 11 to 6 B.C., he stuck to his odious task, but at length he found Julia's vices intolerable and fled to Rhodes, where he remained for seven years.

Augustus now began to push the fortunes of his grandsons, and started them upon a political career, culminating with a grant of proconsular power to Gaius in 1 A.D. The young man was sent to the East to settle the Armenian question once more, but died soon afterward of a wound received in battle. Lucius Caesar had previously died while on a mission to Spain. In 2 B.C., Augustus had at last discovered what all the world except himself knew — the shameless conduct of his daughter. With a ferocity equal to his former affection for her, he banished her to an island, and sentenced her to live there under severe hardships. Some of her accomplices suffered death. As Agrippa Postumus grew up he proved to be of subnormal mentality. Later the younger Julia was convicted of conduct like that of her mother, and shared a similar fate. Agrippina, the younger daughter, was virtuous and respected, and her husband Germanicus, a nephew of Tiberius, was a talented young man, but he was too young to assume the duties which the advancing age and poor health of Augustus compelled him more and more to delegate to others. Tiberius had returned to Rome, and although Augustus had apparently never cared much for him, he was compelled to push him forward. In 4 A.D., Tiberius received the tribunician and proconsular powers and was adopted by Augustus. Even then the dynastic ambitions of the old Princeps were strong enough to make him arrange that the succession should, after the death of Tiberius, go to Germanicus and Agrippina. But throughout the remainder of Augustus' life the fortunes of Tiberius rose, and when, on August 19, 14 A.D., the old man breathed his last, Tiberius was ready to assume the vacant place.

[1] See genealogical table, p. 327.

## The Significance of Augustus' Career

All sorts of judgments have been passed, both in ancient and modern times, upon the character and policies of Augustus. Was he a hypocrite, or was he sincere in his professions? In his political testament (the *Res Gestae divi Augusti*, written shortly before his death, and surviving as an inscription at Angora, Turkey) he states that he restored the Republic, and that he excelled others only in prestige. On the other hand Tacitus, writing about 110 A.D., treats him as one who by cunning founded a monarchy.

It is idle to weigh these terms too closely. He was a practical statesman, who evolved a workable system of government embodying some of the features of both a republic and a monarchy. If we view the overwhelming physical force at his disposal, his absolute power in the provinces, his wealth, and his influence at Rome, we may choose to call him a monarch. If we remember that his powers were granted by the Senate and people, and that he scrupulously respected the rights of these law-making agencies, we may think of him as a republican magistrate. But any attempt to solve this problem involves quibbling which serves no useful purpose. More important is the fact that he took hold of a chaotic and miserable world, and left it orderly and prosperous. His was a creative mind which brought order into every phase of human life that it touched, and for two centuries after his death the Roman Empire was substantially what he made it. The question of his sincerity is, naturally, one which we can never answer with finality. But one may well wonder if anyone could have preserved the appearance of sincerity and consistency through a long life if he were himself conscious that he was acting a part other than what he professed.

There were indeed flaws in his plan. Undoubtedly the partnership between *Princeps* and Senate rested on a weak foundation when the one was so much stronger than the other, for his successors were free to play the tyrant whenever they chose. The army had not been eliminated from politics, as later events were to show all too clearly. Society did not take kindly to reform by legislative fiat. Some of these faults were due to errors of judgment on his part, but many others were the outcome of conditions which he was powerless to alter. The Republic was dead before he came upon the scene, and the Senate had lost its hold upon the respect and affections of the masses. Probably no one else could have done as well as Augustus, and when a grateful people enrolled him among the gods, we may say that he deserved the honor as much as any man that ever governed the state.

# 20

# *The Augustan Age in Society, Art, and Literature*

## Social and Intellectual Outlook

When, after a century of strife and disorder, the Roman world again found peace and good government under the rule of Augustus, it quickly began to erase the scars of the struggle, and to build for itself a new and greater prosperity. With astonishing rapidity Italy and the eastern provinces regained the wealth which had been lost or destroyed, while Spain, Africa, Gaul, and the lands newly conquered by Augustus redoubled the exploitation of their soil and other natural resources. In the West and along the Danube new cities were being founded and old native towns were everywhere growing in population and wealth. Commerce on the Mediterranean Sea revived, and the expanding system of Roman roads opened up new areas to the activities of the trader.

### *Prevailing Attitudes: (I) Optimism*

Amid these scenes of reviving and expanding prosperity two opposing mental attitudes were to be found among the people of the Empire. The middle and lower classes, both Roman and provincial, were inclined to be optimistic, and outside of areas where the process of conquest was very recent, enthusiastically loyal to the new government. There was a feeling that the fabled "Golden Age" had returned, and that for this Augustus was to be thanked. An incident related by his biographer Suetonius illustrates the strength and spontaneity of this sentiment. Shortly before his death, while Augustus was staying at Puteoli, an Alexandrian merchantship arrived. "The passengers and crew," says Suetonius, "clad in white, crowned with garlands, and burning incense, lavished upon him good wishes and highest praise, saying that through him they lived, sailed the seas, and enjoyed their liberty and fortunes." [1]

Augustus and his aides did everything possible to heighten this "era of good feeling." Those who still cherished the lost cause of the Republic were not molested, but the task of healing their wounded feelings was left to time and a sense of benefits received. So long as free speech did not actively promote sedition, it was not curbed. On the other hand both poets and prose writers of ability were given liberal patronage without having to surrender too much of their independence. Special consideration was given to those who wrote on patriotic themes or moral improvement, but these were subjects as welcome to sentimental republicans as to the government. Neither Augustus nor his friend Maecenas (who usually handled literary matters for him) tried to pose as literary critics, but both with rare good sense confined themselves to occasional suggestions as to subjects on which they would welcome new work, and left the development of these themes to the initiative of their protégés themselves. Hence there is little wonder that some of the men who had fought under Brutus at Philippi, or who had lost relatives in the proscriptions, forgot and forgave the past.

### (II) *Pessimism*

But neither optimism nor loyalty was quite universal. In Greece peace could do little to revive the exhausted country, and even among the Roman citizen body there were many whose feelings had been too deeply lacerated to recover readily. Impoverished senatorial and equestrian families who had lost their property by confiscation and their relatives by legalized murder harbored many a bitter memory, and saw in the very strength of the Principate proof that they would never recover the property and influence they had lost. A few hatched conspiracies, but the remainder either lived in philosophical retirement, plunged into excitement and sensual enjoyment, or fawned hypocritically and begged favors from Augustus. The loss of freedom, although every effort was made to conceal it, heightened the feeling of discouragement, and although some of the former ruling classes found adequate opportunities for employment and advancement under the new regime, there were others who refused to take part at all in public affairs. Never had moral corruption among the aristocracy been so widespread, so shameless, or so little censured. Many a young man who

[1] *Divus Augustus*, c. 98.

in a former generation would have been too busy in war or politics to have done more than indulge in an occasional debauch, now found himself without serious employment, a prey to the feeling that life held nothing for him but the pleasure of the moment. Among the lovers of Julia, the daughter of Augustus, were a Claudius, a Gracchus, a Lepidus, and a Scipio, as well as other bearers of old and glorious names, who were themselves but worthless libertines. The old Roman ambition to marry and rear a family meant nothing to men who had ceased to believe in the worship of the deified ancestors, and who saw no chance that their descendants would be anything more than the idlers that they themselves were. Hence celibacy grew even more common, and the marriage laws of Augustus did not check it. Light women — many of them as high-born as Julia herself — shared the revels of the men. To such an effete and overripe aristocracy, romantic pessimism came as natural as it was later to do among the upper classes of France in the nineteenth century.

Moreover, the feeling of world weariness penetrated even the attitudes of the active middle class of the Italian towns. A hint of their outlook may be gained from a Greek motto engraved on a silver cup found near Pompeii, belonging, apparently, to the country estate of one of its citizens: "While you live, enjoy life, for the future is uncertain." The epitaphs of this class also bear testimony to the prevalence of the same viewpoint. A sign of the times was the increased number of suicides, often caused by no misfortunes greater than age and ill-health, or mere disgust with life. Prosperity could not hide from men the fact that no great improvement in the general conditions of life was to be hoped for; that generation after generation would tread the same weary round of life, ending with the world no different from and no better than it had been when they came into it. Hence the mild and shallow epicureanism of their outlook. Each of these viewpoints produced its school of literature in this period. To the buoyant optimism of the new age we owe the immortal *Georgics* and *Aeneid* of Virgil, and some of the more stirring odes of Horace, while to the languid pessimism and lascivious romanticism of a portion of the upper and middle classes we must attribute the elegies of Tibullus, Propertius, and Ovid. Pessimism, too, underlies much of Livy's matchless *History*.

### *Romanization of the Provinces*

In the western provinces the process of Romanization progressed rather rapidly during this time. Southern Spain and Narbonese Gaul were almost entirely Latin in speech, dress, and customs. In "Long-Haired" Gaul it would seem that only the aristocracy had been deeply touched by Roman influence, but many if not all of the Gallic nobles were already Roman citizens. Roman education had begun to spread among them. Shortly after Augustus' death we hear of a school called the *Maeniana* ("Galleries") at Augustodunum, the capital of the *Aedui*, to which came the sons of the Gallic chiefs. It was to have a long and distinguished career, and it was probably only one of several such "colleges" in Gaul. Among the Gallic commons, as we have seen,[1] contact with the auxiliary corps of the army and with traders was beginning to introduce the Latin language, although the progress of Roman culture was much slower than among the upper classes. In the Danubian lands, and in the newly conquered province of Numidia, Romanization had as yet made little progress, and in some areas it was destined never to proceed far. One thing was still lacking to make the western provincials loyal subjects of Rome. She might give them peace and prosperity, but her dominion still lacked a moral basis, and so long as it did so, it was after all nothing but the rule of superior force. It was to supply this lack that Augustus seems to have encouraged the worship of himself and the goddess Roma by the provincials, but more was needed. Unconsciously but none the less surely the great writers of the Augustan Age, especially Virgil and Livy, supplied educated provincials with a rationalization of Roman rule which enabled them to support it loyally and still retain their self-respect. In the eastern provinces, where king-worship was a well-established institution, the need was not so obvious; and although Latin literature was never read by Greeks or Orientals to any great extent, philosophy was later to perform the same function that poetry and history did in the West.

## Augustan Art

In the fine arts, the establishment of the Principate produced no strikingly new styles, but rather a development of existing ones. There was, however, an unexampled outburst of activity, either sponsored or stimulated by the government, and a large amount of work done either for local governments in Italy and the provinces or for private persons. Just before his death Augustus boasted, "I found Rome a city of sun-dried brick. I leave it a city of marble."[2] As regards private buildings this was certainly not true, but enough was done in replanning and rebuilding the capital's public structures to warrant the boast. Of these grandiose works

[1] Chapter 19. [2] Suetonius, *Divus Augustus*, C. 28.

so many were subsequently either destroyed or rebuilt that we have relatively few remains by which to judge his accomplishment.

*City Planning in Rome and the Provinces*

For the first time in its history the city of Rome was subjected to a program of comprehensive planning designed to produce a striking effect when viewed as a unity. The boundaries of the *pomoerium* were extended to include the Campus Martius, upon which a series of beautiful public buildings was erected. Toward the northern end was the mausoleum of the imperial family, a round structure covered with a mound of earth, like an Etruscan tomb. Farther south Agrippa erected the Pantheon, but although it still exists, drastic reconstruction in the second century A.D., has made it impossible for us to determine its original shape and appearance. South of the Pantheon were the splendid "Baths of Agrippa." Midway between the Pantheon and the Mausoleum was the Altar of Peace, whose

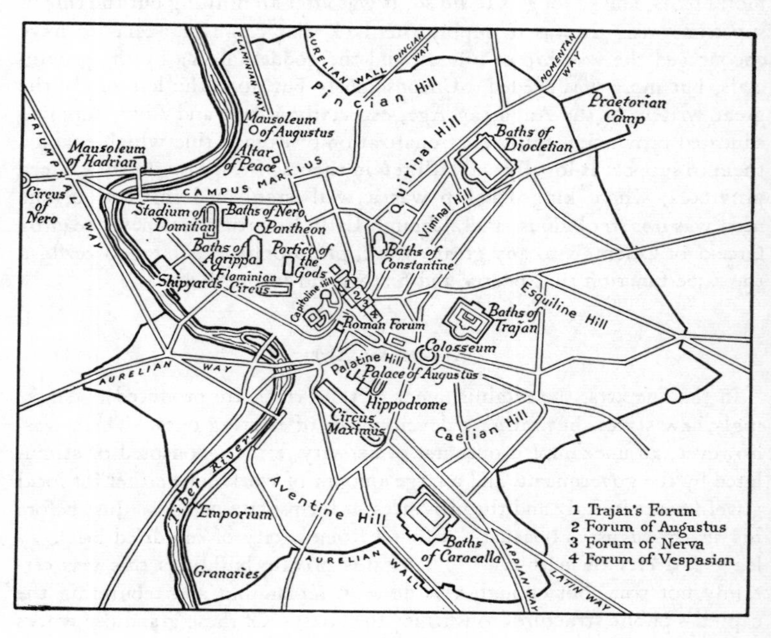


IMPERIAL ROME

sculptures will be considered separately, and at the extreme southern end, near the old city wall, was the magnificent Theater of Marcellus, erected in honor of Augustus' nephew and son-in-law. Within the older portion of the city, between the Capitoline and Esquiline hills, the Forum of Augustus was laid out, with the Temple of Mars the Avenger as its central feature. Many of the buildings planned but not completed by Julius Caesar were taken in hand, and on the old Roman Forum a temple was built in his honor. On the Palatine Hill a new temple was built in honor of Apollo, near which Augustus had his own rather modest residence. In all, eighty-two temples were repaired in the year 28 B.C. alone. On the Esquiline Hill Maecenas covered the old "city dump" and pauper burying ground with a thick coat of earth, on which he laid out a splendid park, the "Gardens of Maecenas." The city water system was improved by the

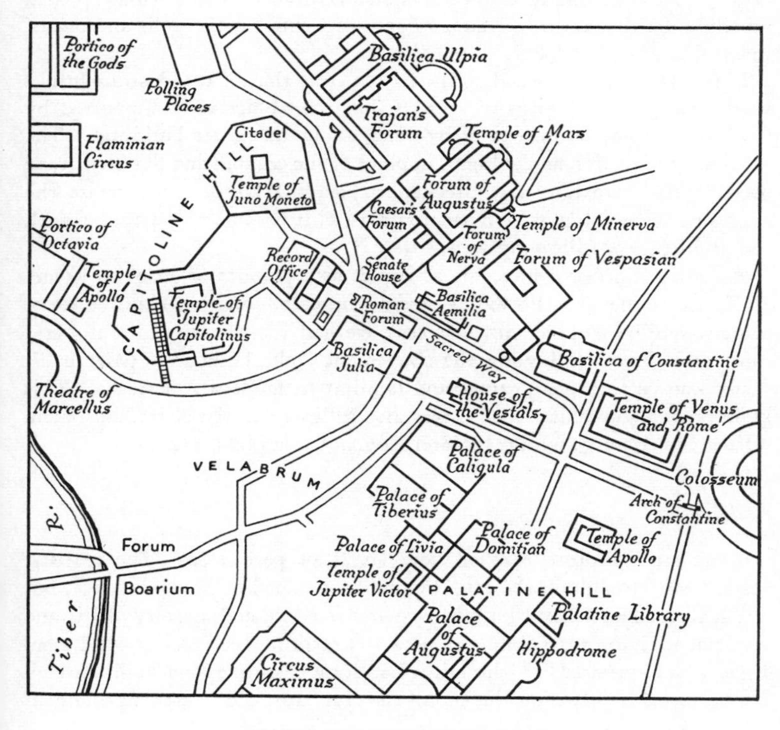


DETAIL MAP OF IMPERIAL ROME

repair of the old aqueducts and by the construction of three new ones. By these and many other less important steps, the capital of the Empire was made worthy of her great position. The beauty of the new buildings was, in many cases, enhanced by the addition of facings of white marble from the quarries of Carrara, then being extensively worked for the first time, and in a few instances, imported marble of various colors was used for decoration.

Only a few significant examples of Augustan architecture can be described here. The Temple of Mars the Avenger, in the Forum of Augustus, was laid out on a modified Italic plan. It stood upon a high platform, with steps only at the front, and the proportion of length to width was 25 to 18. It had a deep portico, and a colonnade around three sides, each side consisting of eight Corinthian columns (the corners being counted twice). At the back, instead of a blank wall, was a semicircular apse, in which stood the statue of Mars, a figure of Venus on his right and one of Julius Caesar on his left.

In the Theater of Marcellus, the façade, like that of the Basilica Julia,[1] was composed of a series of arcades, but the arches were supported by Corinthian columns instead of by piers, as in the earlier building. The combination of arch and column, in place of the column and flat architrave used by the Etruscans and Greeks, enabled the builder to increase the spaces between columns, and for that reason, it became very popular with the architects of following ages.

Augustus did not confine his activities as a planner of cities to Rome. At Turin, in the upper Po Valley, and at Augustodunum, in Gaul (both of which were built under his auspices), we find whole cities carefully laid out, with streets following the convenient "checkerboard" pattern already known in Roman camps and familiar to modern Americans. This style proved so popular that it was also followed in the cities laid out in Africa and other provinces by later Roman town planners.

### *Sculpture*

Augustan sculpture reached new levels of perfection. The realistic tendency noticeable in the late Republic continued to be in evidence, but the sculptor had achieved a much greater freedom and mastery of life and movement than ever before. A new and striking tendency toward symbolism had appeared. Although it had long been in evidence in the Hellenistic world, only after the end of the civil wars did it gain a prominent

[1] See Chapter 18.

*Galloway*

BREASTPLATE

*From Prima Porta Statue of Augustus*

place in Rome and the West. In part, this was a spontaneous expression of the feelings of the people, but there can be no doubt that it was also used by Augustus and his friends as a subtle form of propaganda, to mold public opinion on many questions. It was at all times employed with moderation and good sense, and for that reason was probably all the more effective.

An excellent illustration of the dominant trends in this field is the famous Prima Porta statue of Augustus, which dates from the decade between 20 and 10 B.C. Here the *Princeps* is represented as a man of between forty and fifty years of age, bareheaded and barefooted, clad in armor, from beneath which protrudes his military cloak. His right arm is raised, while his left (a modern restoration) clasps a spear or scepter. His face is strikingly individual, with finely modeled features, firm chin, and deep-set eyes. The air and facial expression are those of a ruler of men, and the pose is that of a victorious general addressing his soldiers. Only the bare head and feet, which are out of place under the circumstances, are conventions borrowed from Hellenistic art; the rest is a masterpiece of Roman realism. But there is also a strain of allegory, aptly placed among the embossings of the armor. At the top is the Sky, represented as a bearded man with widespread cloak. Beneath the Sky, the Sun in his chariot pursues the Moon and the Goddess of Dawn, a symbol of the coming new day. In the third register we see the symbols of the military achievements of the Principate. In the center a bearded Parthian wearing a royal diadem presents a Roman eagle-standard to an armed and helmeted Roman, a reminder of the surrender of the captured Roman standards to Tiberius.[1] At each side sits a dejected figure, the one on the left holding out an empty sheath, while that on the right has a Gallic trumpet and a standard shaped like a wild boar. These are symbols respectively of the final conquest and disarming of Spain and the suppression of a revolt in Gaul. In the fourth register appear Apollo and Diana (guardian spirits of Augustus and the Empire), while at the bottom is Earth, a reclining goddess holding a horn of plenty. It is hardly possible to conceive of a more effective portrayal of the achievements of Augustus and his government.

Relief work can best be studied in connection with the Altar of Peace (*Ara Pacis*), erected between 13 and 9 B.C. The altar proper was surrounded by a wall some ten feet high, enclosing a square 88 feet 8 inches on a side, with entrances at the east and west sides. The inside of this wall was decorated with a series of heavy garlands of foliage, hanging from ox-skulls, while the outside carried an Ionic frieze representing the festivities attending the return of Augustus from Gaul in 13 B.C. At the right of the western entrance was a group portraying the sacrifice of the famous white sow by Aeneas.[2] To the left was another of the she-wolf suckling Romulus and Remus. Similarly, the eastern entrance was flanked on the right by a figure symbolic of Rome, and on the left by another which probably represented Italy, and shows traces of having been inspired by the famous eulogy in Book II of Virgil's *Georgics*. A beautiful woman is shown sitting on a rock, holding in her ample lap two infants between whom is a heap of fruit and grapes. To the left and right of her are two small female figures, whose robes stand out as if blown by strong winds. Below and to the left, water flows from an overturned jar forming a stream from which a swan rises, while an ox lies chewing its cud and a sheep grazes beside it. A dolphin beside the right-hand female figure suggests the sea.

But the center of interest is the sacrificial procession depicted in the

[1] Chapter 19. [2] *Aeneid*, Book VIII.

*Bettmann*

ITALY, THE FOSTER MOTHER
*Relief from the Ara Pacis*

frieze on the northern and southern sides. The artist was probably inspired by the Panathenaic procession on the walls of the Athenian Parthenon, but his treatment of it was entirely Roman and original. Instead of idealizing his subjects, he depicted them as they were, first Augustus himself with his lictors and attendant priests, then the imperial family, followed by the Senate, with a crowd of citizens bringing up the rear. The imperial family and the other notables are drawn with such striking individuality that we must conclude that here are actual portraits. Not a detail has been slighted. Even the children appear with such close attention to juvenile psychology that we almost seem to see before us a motion picture reel of the procession frozen into eternal stone. Such work, while deeply indebted to the Greeks in more ways than one, could not have been done by a Greek. Only Rome — the Rome of Augustus — could be its home.

Many other specimens of Augustan sculpture have been found in Rome, Italy, and the provinces. True to the tendency to follow the lead of the capital in everything, the Italian and provincial artists usually did no more than copy or adapt the masterpieces which adorned Rome, but such

*Metropolitan Museum*

PROCESSIONAL

*Relief from the Ara Pacis*

copies served a double purpose, spreading both the knowledge of advanced artistic technique and the imperial gospel which the artists, like the poets and historians, were helping to shape.

### *Painting and Jewelry*

Painting showed no marked advance over that of the preceding period, but in metal-working and cameo-cutting striking triumphs were achieved. The contrasting ideals of the age are nowhere better shown than in the series of cups found at Boscoreale, near Pompeii, and dating from about the time of Augustus. The "imperial gospel" is taught in the engravings of a silver cup, on which Augustus is pictured as receiving gifts from the gods and the homage of conquered German tribes. But from the same collection comes another, adorned with skeletons, a ham, a wine bottle, and musical instruments, bearing the cynical motto, "Get and use." Two splendid cameos, known from the places where they are now preserved as the Vienna Cameo and the Cameo of France, represent respectively the triumph of Augustus and his reception into Heaven while Tiberius and his mother Livia rule the earth. The workmanship and form of expression is Hellenistic rather than Roman, but the ideas are purely Roman and Augustan in character.

## Latin Literature

From the last days of the Republic the Romans inherited, as we have seen, two types of poetic composition: didactic poetry, exemplified by the work of Lucretius, and the elegy, already made popular by Catullus. Didactic poetry, aside from Virgil's *Georgics*, never gained popular favor during the Augustan Age, but a whole school of elegists arose, including three of its great poets — Tibullus, Propertius, and Ovid. All of them gave their attention chiefly to amorous themes, although on a distinctly lower plane than their great model. Virgil, the greatest poet of the age, did his first important work in the Hellenistic medium of the idyll, but passed from that to didactic poetry, and ended by producing a great national epic, while Horace found his inspiration in the lyrics of sixth-century Greece. In prose we see oratory declining as political autocracy closed one of its chief fields of endeavor, and the philosophic essay ceased for a time with the death of Cicero. However, in history, Livy was to produce one of the world's greatest prose masterpieces.

### *Poetry: The Elegists*

Albius Tibullus (54–18 B.C.) deserves but brief mention. He was a man of gentle but melancholy disposition, with sufficient means and no political ambition. His two books of elegies are divided among his love affairs with a series of wayward beauties (chiefly one whom he called Delia), descriptions of country life, eulogies of his friends, and one patriotic poem. Although his style is smooth and pleasing, he produced nothing of first-rate worth.

His fellow elegist, Sextus Propertius (born about 51) displayed the same melancholy and amorousness, but he was a stronger and more vehement character. Having in childhood lost his father and having had his family estate confiscated by the orders of Octavian, he went to Rome to study law, but soon gave it up to write poetry. He fell in love with a professional courtesan whom he called Cynthia, quarreled with her many times, and

CUP FROM BOSCOREALE

made up the quarrels almost as often. Neither was faithful to the other. It was all sordid enough, and Propertius confesses that he frittered away his life. He quotes an alleged prophecy on his career:

> Write elegies, a deceitful task. There lies your warfare. You shall bear the seductive arms of Venus, and be an easy foe for Venus' sons. Whatever successes you win by your toils, one girl will elude your grasp; and although you may shake the hook from your mouth, the rod shall still hold you fast with its barb.[1]

But at last he became disgusted with Cynthia, and left her with a parting curse:

> I shall weep as I go; but my wrongs outweigh my grief . . . May weary age make you stoop with the years you have concealed! May ugly wrinkles mar your beauty! May the mirror mock your furrowed visage until you wish to tear your white hairs out by the roots! And when you have become a hag, may you lament your misdeeds! [2]

In later life, Propertius wrote elegies on more serious topics. Book IV (the last of his collection) contains much patriotic poetry, including

[1] *Elegies, II*, 34 ff. [2] *Ibid. III*, 25, ll. 7–16 (condensed).

praises of Augustus. Like Tibullus, he had always been haunted by thoughts of death and decay. In fact, one of his finest poems is a consolation addressed to the senator Aemilius Paullus, whose wife had recently died. With restrained but masterly pathos he represents the departed as addressing her bereaved husband and children. Step by step she recounts the vainness of grief which cannot recall the dead to life, her proud pedigree, virtuous life, and love for her family. Finally come her injunctions for the future:

> Now I commend to you our children, the tokens of our love. This care lies yet unburned in my ashes. Father, be to them also a mother. When you kiss away their tears, add other kisses for me. The whole household is now your burden. If you must grieve, do so in secret; and when they come, receive their kisses with dry cheeks. . . . Rise, witnesses who weep my loss while beneficent Earth tenders me the reward of my life. Heaven itself is opened to the virtuous.[1]

Such words belong to no single age, but will retain their power as long as men grieve for their dead. In spite of his unbalanced character and occasional bad taste (he once described a friend drowned at sea as "strange food swimming among the distant fishes") he attained the first place among the Augustan elegists.

Publius Ovidius Naso (43 B.C.–17 A.D.), the last of the elegiac school, was a poet of more pleasing personality but of less real talent than Propertius. Comfortably well-to-do, with a good education and no great ambition except in literature, Ovid was, for many years, the poet of fashionable society, and in this his success was phenomenal. Without being especially immoral himself, he catered to the immoral tastes of a circle whose lives were loose even when judged by the easy standards of the age.

Ovid began, like his predecessors, with a series of love elegies addressed to a certain Corinna. He later collected and published these poems as the *Loves*. There is so little real feeling in them that we may well doubt Corinna's existence, but the versification is easy and almost flawless. In fact, Ovid brought elegiac verse to such formal perfection that it is customary to speak of him as the founder of a new school of poetry. Catering to the prurient tastes of his circle, he next wrote the *Art of Love*, a pseudo-didactic poem instructing his readers on means of winning the affections of the opposite sex, not even neglecting professional etiquette for courtesans. With the skill of a French novelist, he produced a thoroughly pernicious book, whose influence was certain to be bad, without at any point descending to gross or vulgar language which would shock people of

[1] *Ibid. IV*, 11 ff.

good taste, and attempted to disarm critics by prefixing to the book a warning to good women not to read it. Following this came the *Remedies of Love*, which taught the art of extricating one's self from disreputable affairs of the heart. In the midst of this amatory literature he penned the *Letters of Heroines*, a series of epistles purporting to have been written by the heroines of mythology and legend to their husbands or lovers. It is a clever trifle, amusing if read in small sections.

His *Metamorphoses* go still farther into the realm of mythology. Heeding the advice of the Alexandrian Callimachus against long poems, he collected some two hundred and fifty stories of miraculous transformations of persons or things into other forms, and published them in fifteen books. Each story is complete within itself, and the whole is really not one poem, but a series. The material, all drawn from Greek sources, had already been treated so often as to be hackneyed, yet Ovid with his fresh and sparkling style gave it a new interest. Probably as a concession to Augustus' interest in the restoration of religion, he also began the *Fasti*, a Roman religious calendar in verse.

But in 8 A.D., a sudden and irreparable misfortune struck down this fashionable poet. Possibly because of his *Art of Love*, but more probably on account of some indiscreet act which neither he nor Augustus cared to make public, he was exiled to Tomi, a semibarbarous town on the coast of the Black Sea. All appeals for permission to return proved vain, and Ovid died in exile. In these last years he wrote the *Letters from the Pontus* and the *Poems of Sadness*, in which he begged for mercy, bewailed his fate, and described his new home. While not lacking in interest, they have not the sparkle and zest of his earlier works.

Ovid was neither a great poet nor a great man, but his influence upon subsequent times was enormous. His erotic poetry has served, for better or worse, as an example for others from his time to the present. He did for Greek mythology what Cicero had done for Greek philosophy, making it accessible in a popular form to Roman readers. In the long medieval centuries, when few scholars in western Europe knew the Greek language, his poems were the medium through which they could most easily learn the myths which he had culled from it, and modern students of Roman religion find his *Fasti* all but indispensable.

### *The Circle of Maecenas: Virgil*

Meanwhile a more serious school of poetry had arisen and flourished under the patronage of Augustus and Maecenas. As previously indicated,

*Bettmann*

VIRGIL

*Mosaic found near Tunis*

this government patronage was liberal and by no means oppressive, and it did not attempt to degrade poetry to the mere level of propaganda. The chief figures of the circle of Maecenas were Virgil and Horace, although Propertius seems to have belonged to it for a time.

Publius Vergilius Maro (70–19 B.C.) was a native of Cisalpine Gaul, born and reared on a farm near Mantua. His family were of the middle class, and gave him an excellent education in the schools of Cremona, Milan, and Rome. His first ambition was to practice law; but he soon abandoned this interest for Epicurean philosophy, and later for poetry. Some of his earlier poems have survived; but they are not his greatest work, and may be disregarded here. Then, in 41, came a great calamity. In the confiscations instituted after the Battle of Philippi to find land for the soldiers of the Triumvirs, his paternal estate, although not marked for confiscation, was seized, and in spite of the efforts of several influential friends, was never recovered. But his *Eclogues* were already making him famous, and he was soon taken under the protection of Maecenas. His losses were made good by the gift of an estate on the Bay of Naples and a house in Rome. During the last twenty years of his life he was the favorite poet of Augustus. In 19 B.C. he was taken ill while on a journey to Greece, and died at Brundisium. He was a man of shy and retiring disposition, pure morals, and great kindliness. His fame rests chiefly upon three works: the *Eclogues*, the *Georgics*, and the *Aeneid*.

The *Eclogues*, published in 38, were a series of ten poems modeled upon the *Idylls* of Theocritus. In them we meet the too-familiar singing and sentimental shepherds, who usually bewail unhappy loves. Virgil's originality, however, was greater than such a description would suggest. He imitated the pastoral settings of Theocritus, but his own knowledge of south Italian scenery was so extensive that he depicted it with a sure personal touch. Nor was Virgil blind to the world of his own day in other respects. In the *First* and *Ninth Eclogues* he describes the woes of the luckless Italians who were being driven from their homes to make way for discharged soldiers. In the *Fourth*, written between 40 and 38, he foretells the birth of a prince who will restore the Golden Age. Its real significance is unknown, but in the Middle Ages, when Virgil had come to be considered a prophet and magician (the spelling of his name was changed from *Vergil* to *Virgil* so that it would appear to be derived from *virga*, a magician's wand), it was looked upon as a prophecy of the approaching birth of Christ. The *Tenth* is a consolation addressed to his friend Cornelius Gallus, whose mistress had deserted him. Although they were not Virgil's greatest poems, they alone would entitle him to a high place among Roman poets.

Virgil never lost his love of the simple country life of his boyhood, and when his friends and patrons attempted to rehabilitate Italian agriculture, it needed only a hint from them to induce him to sing the praises of a calling which interested him so deeply. The *Georgics*, or "Farmer's Guide," which he completed about 30, was a labor of love. Into its four books of hexameters he wove his own experiences, directions culled from textbooks, and allusions to myth and legend. The resulting picture was neither idyllic nor unreal. It was a survey of Italian conditions as he knew them, bad as well as good. Plowing, sowing, reaping, stock-raising, beekeeping, and other activities of the farmer were described at once with realism and with a delicate, poetic insight. Rural religion drew a large share of his attention, and we find that, however blasé and skeptical the urban aristocracy might be, the small farmer (for whom Virgil wrote) still retained a living faith in the gods and spirits who ruled over their calling. Centuries later it was to be this rural religion, not the cults of the Roman state, which offered the toughest and most persistent opposition to Christianity. The author's enthusiasm for his beloved Italian countryside breaks forth in a famous eulogy:

> She is full of rich harvests and of Massic wine dear to Bacchus, of olive-trees and of thriving herds . . . Here spring is broken only by summer. Twice a year the flocks bear young, and fruit trees yield two crops. No tigers or fierce lions are found; and no aconite deceives its unhappy gatherers. No scaled serpent trails upon the ground his endless coils, or twists his body into spirals.[1]

Not only the land, but the people, merit his praise:

> She has borne this virile breed of men — Marsians, Sabellians, Ligurians inured to poverty, and javelin-bearing Volscians. Decii, Marii, great Camilli, hard-fighting Scipios, and you, Greatest Caesar, who now hurl back the unwarlike Indian from Rome's frontiers in the uttermost parts of Asia.[2]

When he uses Greek mythology, it is as a background — often a contrast — to his Italian picture.

### *The Aeneid: A Roman Epic*

But Virgil's greatest work, the *Aeneid*, was yet to come. Although the primitive Romans knew nothing of any Trojan ancestry, the story that Aeneas had been the ancestor of the Roman people had now been current for several centuries, and was generally believed. Hardly had Virgil finished the *Georgics* when he undertook to write an epic upon the wanderings and wars of Aeneas, and he was still at work on it when stricken with his last illness. In his will he directed that the unfinished manuscript be destroyed, but Augustus overrode his wishes, and by so doing preserved the poem for the world.

The *Aeneid* is an epic poem in twelve books, written in dactyllic hexameter. It tells the story of the fall of Troy, the roundabout journey of the survivors from Asia to Latium, and the wars by which Aeneas established himself and his companions as lords of the country. In both form and subject matter the author borrowed liberally from Homer and many other poets. The general plan resembles that of the *Odyssey;* but the romance of Aeneas and Dido in the fourth book was suggested by an incident in the *Argonautica* of Apollonius of Rhodes, while Ennius, Naevius, and other Roman writers are laid under contribution. The *Aeneid* is no naïve story

[1] Book II, ll. 143–153 (condensed). [2] *Ibid.* ll. 167–172.

of an old-time hero, told for the entertainment of a half-barbarous audience. Instead, it was the product of a civilized and sophisticated society, and had to be planned for reading as well as recitation. Hence it demanded a perfection of plot, a depth of thought, and a nobility of ideals which Homer's audience would neither have understood nor appreciated. Both the Homeric and other elements which Virgil borrowed and incorporated into the poem are so thoroughly welded together by the fires of his genius that the completed work is a truly original product, and its superficial resemblance to the Homeric poems is less important than the fundamental differences.

Aeneas is depicted by Virgil as a man entirely dominated by the quality which the Romans called *pietas* — a sense of duty to the gods, the state, and his family. All of his other qualities are subordinated to this one. He fights bravely, but only when he is sure that he is obeying the divine will in doing so. He is naturally kindly and merciful, but when the gods so order, he can also be cruel. He loves Dido, but does not hesitate to desert her when his love for her interferes with the mission which the gods have committed to him. Fate, working through the gods, had chosen Aeneas to perform a great and glorious task — to found in Italy a kingdom from which Rome was one day to arise a Rome predestined to rule the world. Hence, every act of Aeneas must be directed toward this goal, and the gods would never allow their servant to rest until it had been attained. They snatched him from the flaming ruins of Troy when in despair he would have fought to the death, drove him from Troy to Thrace, from Thrace to Crete, from Crete to the unknown West. When he tarried at Carthage, they compelled him to abandon the woman whom he loved and resume his wanderings, with a brusqueness which amounted to brutality. In the murderous war which he had to fight with the Latins and Rutulians, the gods decided his every move. Juno, who hated Trojans, was determined to balk the plans of her fellow deities, and fought bitterly against Aeneas. But in the end even she had to surrender, and the decree of Fate was executed. Thus, Aeneas had little in common with the predatory, brawling, deceitful, and thoroughly individualistic heroes of Homer's poems, and as a man he was less interesting because of this fact. But the true meaning of the *Aeneid* lay deeper than the story of Aeneas: it was Rome and Rome's predestined rule over the world of which Virgil sang.

A splendid example of the predestinarian tone which pervades the *Aeneid* occurs in the sixth book, where Aeneas, like Odysseus, visits Hades. There the ghost of his father Anchises points out to him the souls of the unborn heroes of later Rome — Romulus and Remus, Brutus, the founder of the Republic, the warriors and statesmen who were to make her the mistress of the Mediterranean world, Caesar, Pompey, Augustus ("Who shall restore the Golden Age in Latium"), and finally, in a passage of deep and powerful pathos, Augustus' nephew Marcellus, who at the time it was written had recently died. Succinctly, Anchises states Rome's mission in the world:

> Let others mould more gracefully the breathing bronze, or fashion faces from marble, plead law cases more cunningly, measure the motions of the skies, and describe the rising of the stars. Your task, Roman, is to rule the world with power, and to establish peace. Your victories shall be to spare the submissive and beat down the proud.[1]

Yet the grandeur of the theme must not blind us to the literary beauty of the treatment. No Roman before Virgil, and certainly none after him, ever gave to the hexameter such majestic dignity and stately splendor. His descriptions are not always good, but at his best, as in his story of the sack of Troy, he is unsurpassed. In telling the story of Dido's love for Aeneas he uses divine intervention to account for the outcome, but he traces the growth of her passion with such acuteness of psychological analysis as to render the divine agency unnecessary. A master of restrained pathos, his sympathy reaches out to the unfortunate ones of all lands — Greek, Trojan, Carthaginian, or Latin. Often a line or two carry within them the suggestion of a whole tragedy, such as Priam's nameless and headless corpse lying unburied, Andromache's shameful servitude, or the restless ghost of the drowned Palinurus. We are told that when Virgil read Book VI to the family of Augustus, and came to his eulogy of the dead Marcellus, Octavia the mother of the dead youth fainted, overcome by the poignancy of the funeral scene which he described. Such are a few of the gems which stud the poem from beginning to end.

The success of the *Aeneid* was immediate, great, and lasting. For the Romans of the Empire it made Virgil what Homer had long been to the Greeks — the poet of poets. It was eagerly read by all who could read, both in Italy and the provinces. It helped to reconcile thinking provincials to Roman rule, for what shame was there in yielding, not to a foreign conqueror, but to the decrees of Fate? In the later Empire its author had become a semidivine figure, and superstitious persons told fortunes by opening a roll at random and reading the first line which they happened to see. Christians naturally hated the poem, for not only was it packed with pagan lore from beginning to end, but Virgil, unlike Homer, had made the

[1] *Aeneid, VI*, ll. 847–853.

*Galloway*

THE CAMEO OF FRANCE

gods quite respectable. Yet even Christians fell under its spell. Saint Augustine and many another devout churchman read it, trembled for the safety of their souls, and returned to read again. Fantastic legends sprang up, making Virgil a sort of pre-Christian Christian, a prophet who had foretold the birth of Christ. To Dante he was the embodiment of all which was best in human nature, and from him the Florentine poet took the inspiration, not only for his *Divine Comedy*, but for the political theory of his *De Monarchia*. In modern times Virgil has had critics as well as admirers, but the consensus of opinion places him in that select company of the world's greatest poets with Homer, Dante, Shakespeare, and Milton.

*Horace*

But the circle of Maecenas also included a poet of a very different character. Quintus Horatius Flaccus (65–8 B.C.), known to modern readers as

Horace, was a native of the Apulian town of Venusia, where his father, a freedman, was a petty official. The family had a modest estate, and Horace's father, a man of high principles and great ambition for his son's future, sent him to school at Venusia, Rome, and Athens. Horace was studying philosophy at Athens when Marcus Brutus gave him a commission as legionary tribune in the army which he was gathering to fight the Triumvirs. He ran away from the battlefield of Philippi, and returned to Italy to find his parents dead and his property confiscated. For a time Horace had to support himself by acting as a scribe in a quaestor's office, but he had already begun to write poetry, and his genius in this line soon changed his fortune. Virgil and other friends succeeded in interesting Maecenas in the young poet, and a few years later he was presented with a small but sufficient estate in the Sabine country. He continued to write poetry until his death, and enjoyed the favor of both Augustus and Maecenas throughout his life.

Horace began his career by writing *epodes*, a form of verse imitating the works of the sixth-century Greek lyricists Archilochus and Alcaeus. His themes, in keeping with his fortune, were not always pleasant ones, including some bitter personal denunciation, and a lament for Rome's strife-torn condition in which he advises the Roman people to desert their homes and seek new ones far away. But as his position improved, so did his outlook on life. The later *Epodes*, while by no means his best work, display the mixture of genial wit, patriotism, and sincere but not servile gratitude to his benefactors which were to characterize his prime.

His next published works took the form of the *satire*, already rendered illustrious by Ennius, Lucilius, and Varro. In the *Satires* we see an Epicurean Horace, by no means puritanical in his tastes, who views human faults and foibles with amusement unalloyed by any trace of indignation. Misers who are never satisfied with their share of this world's goods, rakes who get themselves into trouble by amorous escapades, gourmets who live only to eat, talkative bores, fortune-tellers — such are a few of the persons who come in for a share of his kindly ridicule. He does not even spare himself, but repeats an imaginary conversation in which one of his slaves, using the freedom accorded to his kind at the *Saturnalia*, mercilessly exposes the difference between the poet's high sentiments and his lazy, luxurious, and loose way of life. Again he praises the quiet life of the country and contrasts it with the unseemly noise and hurry of Rome. Such themes have been popular with satirists in all ages, but seldom have they been treated with so deft a touch, or with such keen observation.

The masterpieces of Horace's career, however, were four books of *Odes*

*Keystone*

THE ROUND TEMPLE OF MATER MATUTA
*Rome*

(*Carmina*). Both form and subject matter vary widely, the form generally imitating once more the verse-forms used by the early Greeks, while the subjects range over the whole of the contemporary scene, and also include some fine hymns to the gods. He celebrates the fall of Antony and Cleopatra with a song of joy:

> Now let us drink, and with light feet beat the earth. Now, my friends, let us adorn the tables of the gods with feasts of the Salian Priests.[1]

When he heard that some of the captives taken at the time of Crassus' defeat had married Parthian wives and become subjects of an Oriental king, he gave vent to his indignation in the noble ode beginning, "We believed Jupiter to be a god when he thundered in Heaven," [2] in which he compares these spiritless traitors to the patriotic martyr, Regulus. Several of the odes are eulogies to Augustus. The elegies of Tibullus, Proper-

[1] *Odes*, *I*, ll. 1–4. [2] *Odes*, *III*, 5, l. 1.

tius, and their school also find an echo in the Odes. Under a variety of pseudonyms, several women, the objects of his not-too-delicate affections, are praised, blamed for inconstancy, or warned to love before old age spoils their beauty.

The *Odes* marked the high point in Horace's career, and after the death of Virgil he held a place similar to that of an English poet laureate. Hence, in 17, when Augustus caused the Secular Games to be celebrated, he induced Horace to compose for the occasion the *Secular Hymn*, a florid and showy poem which does not rank among the author's best work. Lastly, Horace has left us a series of *Epistles*, written to friends (among them Maecenas, Augustus, and Tiberius), including a whimsical *Address to his Own Book*, and the famous *Art of Poetry*. In these later years he achieved a mellow maturity of thought, mingled with a lurking melancholy, which led him (perhaps independently) into the same train of thought as Lucretius. Addressing himself in one of his latest works, he says: "You have played enough, and have eaten and drunk your fill. It is time to depart." [1] The Romans produced no worthy successor to him in the field of lyric poetry. It was not an exaggeration when he said, "I have built me a monument more lasting than bronze." [2]

### *Augustan Prose*

While the Augustan Age produced much prose literature, very little of it has survived the ravages of time. Augustus, Agrippa, and other prominent persons of the day composed memoirs, but of these the only survivor is a brief epitome of those of Augustus known as the *Res Gestae divi Augusti*, or *Monumentum Ancyranum*, preserved in the form of inscriptions at Angora, Turkey, and elsewhere. But in Titus Livius ("Livy," 59 B.C.–17 A.D.) the age produced a historian who for literary artistry ranks with the greatest masters of his craft in the world.

Livy, like the other stars in the Augustan firmament, was an Italian but not a Roman. He was born at Patavium (Padua) in Cisalpine Gaul, and lived there most of his life. Little is known about his career, although it is certain that he was acquainted with Augustus, who took a personal interest in his work. He was trained in rhetoric and oratory, but whether he taught these subjects is not known. Like many of his contemporaries, he had a profound respect for the Rome of the Republic, and felt that his own age was a degenerate one. However, he accepted the Principate loyally. To embalm the memory of the past, and to provide moral instruc-

[1] *Epistles, II*, 2, ll. 214–215. [2] *Odes, III*, l. 1.

tion for the present and future, Livy wrote a history of Rome from its foundation to the death of Drusus, the stepson of Augustus (9 B.C.). It reached the unbelievable length of a hundred and forty-two books, of which thirty-five are extant, while the others are known through brief epitomes.

Livy did not approach his task in the spirit of the modern scientific historian. His use of documents was scanty, and of the many inscriptions then extant he seems to have consulted only one, to which Augustus drew his attention. For the earlier portion of his work he relied entirely upon tradition, as recorded by previous writers. He frankly warns his readers that he takes little stock in the stories of the founders.

> The events which occurred before the city was founded or thought of have been handed down in a haze of poetic fable rather than as reliable history; and I do not propose to confirm or deny them.[1]

But he tells them just the same, not without poking a little sly fun at them. After the Gallic invasion of 390, his literary sources become a little fuller and more reliable. Livy never questioned the reliability of any source if he could find a satisfactory and rational account of events in it. He even uses Valerius Antias, an author whom he frequently stigmatizes as untruthful and unreliable. When his authorities disagree, Livy does not always decide between the conflicting statements. "In such remote events," he says on one occasion, "let them be accepted as true if they appear true." Like both Greek and Roman historians before him, he composes speeches for his characters to deliver on all sorts of occasions. This practice was not intended to deceive his readers, who understood its true nature. No one supposed that the speeches were genuine; they served to describe a situation, to bring out the character of the speaker, or to sum up the reasons for and against a proposed course of action.

Whatever his failings as a historian, Livy as a master of prose is as unapproachable as Virgil in poetry. The proof of his mastery is the number of stories of early Rome which are today household possessions among educated men and women, and which are taken exclusively from his pages. Romulus and Remus, Brutus the founder of the Republic, Lucretia, Virginia, Scipio Africanus, and a host of other characters are unforgettable acquaintances to anyone who has read his work. His story of the Second Punic War has the majestic sweep of an epic, as he shows us the towering Roman heroes — Fabius Maximus, Marcellus, and the Scipios — in the act of turning disaster into victory by their patriotism, valor, and per-

[1] *Preface*, ll. 25–29.

sistence. In unspoken contrast to the supine and spiritless Senate of his own time he pictures for us the strong and purposeful Senate of the early Republic — the "assembly of kings" of which Pyrrhus' ambassador spoke. Hence, whatever failings he may have had as a recorder of facts, his artistic genius is transcendent. Nor must we suppose that Livy at any point knowingly falsified his statements. The evidence shows that he told the truth when his sources furnished him with it, and when he failed to do so, it was their fault and not his.

The influence of Livy's work would be hard to overestimate. Originally the Romans had had a number of traditions about their early history which were flatly at variance with his, but Livy effectually drove them out of current circulation. His work ranked along with that of Virgil as a shaper of the ideals of the millions of new citizens arising in the provinces, and thus, he did something to realize the picture of old-time Roman morality and patriotism which he had painted. So great was his fame in his own lifetime that we are told of a Spaniard who made the journey to Italy merely to see him, and who after seeing him returned immediately to Spain without paying any attention to the other sights of the capital. We can now no longer agree with Dante's statement "Livy who errs not," but he still ranks reasonably high as a historian, and as a story-teller he is as inimitable as ever.

## Greek Literature

While this brilliant culture was flowering in the Latin portion of the Roman Empire, Hellenistic civilization was at a low ebb. Continental Greece had been exhausted by wars and oppression, and bled white by emigration, while Asiatic Greece had just begun to recover from similar ills. The Hellenistic kings who had formerly patronized artists and literary men were no more, and the Roman government paid little or no attention to Greek literature. Thus the cultural sterility of these lands is not surprising; yet even in this age it was not complete. If no authors of the first rank appeared, literature of a sort continued to be produced.

Dionysius of Halicarnassus (died 7 B.C.) was a rhetorician who had taught for many years at Rome, and who, like Polybius before him, felt that his countrymen should know more about her political institutions and historic past. As Polybius had already described her rise to empire after 264 B.C., Dionysius in his *Roman Antiquities* undertook to fill in the gap before that date. His history contained twenty-two books, of which eleven are extant. His sources were much the same as those of Livy, and his statements are about as reliable as Livy's. But his style is not without charm, and the surviving portions of the work contain much curious and interesting lore. In addition he wrote some essays on literary criticism which for breadth of understanding and lucid good sense were hardly equaled in the ancient world.

Strabo (64 B.C.–*ca.* 24 A.D.) was a Hellenized Asiatic from Pontus. He traveled widely, including in his journeys Asia, Egypt, Greece, and Italy, and he used the knowledge thus gained, together with all that could be collected from works previously written, to compose the oldest geography now extant. It covers the whole world known to him, and of its seventeen books, sixteen are entire, completely preserved, while the remaining one is known from an epitome. It is of very unequal value. Strabo could and did give interesting and instructive descriptions of what he had seen, but for what he had not seen he used any source that came to hand, in some cases books centuries old. He sketches in the historical backgrounds of the countries which he treats, and in doing so preserves data from Greek historical works now lost.

Syria produced a Greek historian in the person of Nicolaus of Damascus, who enjoyed the acquaintance of Augustus and the patronage of King Herod of Judea. He seems to have turned his attention from subject to subject as Herod's whims varied, and only a portion of his *Life of Augustus* has survived. As may be suspected from his position, his standards were not high, and his work has little worth.

In Sicily, in the days of Julius Caesar and Augustus, lived Diodorus of Agyrium, better known as Diodorus of Sicily. Of original research he did little, but he rendered a great service to subsequent historians by compiling a *Historical Library* of excerpts from the works of other writers, covering everything from mythical beginnings down to Caesar's conquest of Gaul. Fifteen of his forty books are still extant.

## An Evaluation

In the Augustan Age the bilingual civilization of the Roman Empire reached maturity. The Latin and Greek languages each had a cultural domain which they were to retain with little or no change until the end of the ancient world. As we have seen, the Principate of Augustus found the Greek world in a temporary decline, while the Romans were winning their greatest triumphs in both art and literature. But in some respects the Augustan Age, for all its showy achievements, failed to keep pace with previous generations of Greeks and Romans. In philosophy, the Greeks had exhausted their originality, and were content to repeat and interpret the sayings of the creative thinkers of an earlier day, while the Romans had never risen above the level of students and imitators. The interest of the Greeks in the natural sciences had fallen to a much lower level than in the third and second centuries B.C.; the Romans had never wished to do more than to appropriate for practical purposes the individual discoveries of Hellenistic investigators. Oratory could not flourish in a world from which all real freedom had vanished. In its place came empty displays of rhetorical skill by lecturers who had little to say and took infinite pains to disguise the fact with showy delivery.

Yet an age which produced Virgil, Horace, Livy, the Prima Porta statue of Augustus, and the reliefs of the Altar of Peace cannot be denied the praise due to great achievements. Despite their lack of interest in science and philosophy, the Romans of the Augustan Age had a rare combination of aesthetic sense and realism. A few of its finer spirits added to these a tremendous moral earnestness which grew stronger as a reaction against the prevailing self-indulgence and vice. To varying combinations of these qualities the cultural triumphs of this period may be traced.

# 21

# *The Principate Under the Julio-Claudian and Flavian Emperors (14–96 A.D.)*

## General View

When Augustus died the Principate was an established fact, with forty years of successful government to lend it prestige. Its character was fairly well defined, and it had developed a system of military and civil administration. But it had also certain weaknesses, which must be understood before one can appreciate the difficulties encountered by Augustus' successors and the strife which so often, during the first century A.D., stained their hands with the blood of their fellow citizens.

The first of these was the lack of a workable political theory which would rationalize the existence of the Principate and define its place in the state. Augustus himself had been a successful opportunist, who had, as occasion demanded, played the part of a republican magistrate to the citizens, a successful war lord to the army, and a god-king to the provincials. But his success had been due to circumstances — among them, his unexampled personal magnetism and tact — which not all of his successors could bring to their aid. The first century A.D. accordingly found them involved in strife with a large section of the aristocracy, which had no positive program of its own, but refused to lend its support to the emperors personally. This opposition at times took the form of plots against their lives, at others fomented dissensions in their families, and again invented and circulated slanders against their personal characters. Usually such opposition provoked reprisals in the form of prosecutions for treason, which produced a recurring reign of terror that ended with the practical extermination of the old senatorial families. On the other hand, the position of the Senate under the Principate was, as we have seen,[1] so weak and that of the Emperor so strong, that it had no means of asserting itself if he undertook to play the tyrant.

Again, the army remained a potential danger to both Emperor and people, but only once during the first century A.D., did it attempt to upset the established order. When this happened (in the civil war of 68–69), the inability of the various armies to work together led to a destructive struggle, but the victory of Vespasian quickly brought them under control.

A third weakness, also mentioned before, was the narrow base upon which Roman government rested. Not more than one tenth of the population of the Empire were Roman citizens, and the members of the Senate were almost all from Rome or its immediate neighborhood. Not until near the middle of the first century was any large increase made in the citizen body by the enfranchisement of provincials, and not until after 70 A.D. were many citizens of Italian or provincial origin admitted to the Senate. In the meantime, both the legions and the civil administration had to be recruited entirely from a small section of the population. The influence of these weaknesses upon Roman government, efforts to correct them, and the usual wars along frontiers or rebellions within the provinces, make up the bulk of the history of the Roman Empire in the period under discussion.

## The Julio-Claudian Emperors (14–68 A.D.)

### *Tiberius (14–37 A.D.): Accession and Character*

Augustus had provided for the succession so well that when he died, Tiberius had no difficulty in securing the vacant Principate. Julia and Agrippa Postumus, either of whom might have been the rallying-point for malcontents, were quietly put out of the way. The Senate, with bad grace but great alacrity, granted Tiberius the legal powers which he still lacked. Thus, within less than a month after the death of Augustus his successor was in secure possession of the post.

At first it seemed as if the armies might not accept Tiberius quietly. The legions on the lower Rhine and those on the middle Danube mutinied, demanding a shorter term of service, higher pay, and other concessions. The Rhine mutineers even invited their commander, Tiberius' adopted son Germanicus, to lead them in a march on Rome. But the government, while conciliatory, was firm. Germanicus soon recalled his men to their

[1] Chapter 19.

duty, and Tiberius' son Drusus quelled the outbreak on the Danube. The other armies made no trouble.

The new Emperor was fifty-five years old, and had been in public life for nearly forty years. He was proud, reserved, and inclined to be puritanical. Although a very capable subordinate, he was hesitant and timid when acting on his own initiative. His previous career had tended to instill into him a sad skepticism and a poor opinion of human nature. During the lifetime of Augustus he had been alternately courted and flattered, or snubbed and despised, by the crowd of self-seekers who surrounded the Emperor, as his fortunes rose, fell, and rose again. None but an incurable optimist can survive such an experience without becoming cynical, and Tiberius was no fool. For most of his fellowmen he had only contempt, and he did not always conceal the fact. He was tight-fisted in ordinary dealings, although generous to the needy and deserving. Thus he was very unpopular with all classes in Rome where Augustus had spent money lavishly. Taxes, however, were collected justly, government debts were promptly paid, and a fire in Rome or an earthquake in Asia would move him to send huge sums to the sufferers.

### *Provincial Government*

Provincial government, which to the great majority of his contemporaries was the most important aspect of his reign, need not detain us long. It was honest, efficient, and conservative. The frontiers were made safe, but no conquests were attempted. In Africa a dangerous rebellion under the native chief Tacfarinas was put down, after three years of fierce guerrilla warfare, and the rebel leader was slain. The Asiatic client-kingdoms of Cappadocia and Commagene were made provinces, and the Roman hold upon the untrustworthy vassal state of Armenia was strengthened. With one slight exception, the peace with Parthia continued unbroken. Corrupt and oppressive governors or procurators were mercilessly punished. Indeed, Tiberius himself is said to have laid down for their guidance the rule, "A good shepherd shears his flock, but does not skin them." The road system was extended energetically, soldier labor being used wherever possible. In short, the provinces enjoyed at least as good government as in the days of Augustus, and were duly grateful for it.

### *The Imperial Family and Domestic Politics*

It was in his family affairs and his dealings with the Roman aristocracy that Tiberius was uniformly unfortunate, and this fact cast an air of tragedy and horror over much of his reign. The roots of the trouble were twofold. The lack of a fixed rule of succession and the dynastic policy of Augustus had thrown upon his hands an unfortunate situation, and he lacked the tact and personal magnetism to deal adequately with it. Although Augustus had been forced to accept Tiberius as his immediate successor, he intended that the Principate should eventually return to his own descendants, and of these the only one of sound mind and good character was Agrippina, the wife of Tiberius' nephew Germanicus. She was a woman of great ambition, violent temper, and a moody obstinacy which in later years may have degenerated into madness. Her husband was a superficially brilliant man, universally popular, good-natured, a fairly good general, and a poet of sorts. It will be remembered that when Tiberius was adopted by Augustus he was compelled to adopt Germanicus. As Tiberius already had a son Drusus, the arrangement naturally did violence to his feelings, and his enemies at once assumed that he would discriminate against Germanicus and in favor of Drusus. Prominent among his critics was Agrippina.[1]

Yet so long as Germanicus lived, Tiberius with dour fidelity stuck to his unwelcome bargain. When Augustus died Germanicus, as commander of the Rhine armies, already held the proconsular imperium, the first step toward the succession. For more than two years Tiberius allowed him to push the invasion of Germany, but although he won some successes, he made little progress toward the reconquest of the lost province. In 17 Tiberius decided that it was time to stop the expenditure of men and money, and recalled his nephew to Rome. The friends of Germanicus insisted that this step was the result of jealousy, but events proved that this was not so. He celebrated a magnificent triumph, was chosen consul, and received an even more important position than the former one. Affairs in Asia demanded the presence of a commander with sweeping powers, and Germanicus was sent thither with a proconsular imperium valid over the whole eastern part of the Empire. With him went Agrippina and their children. His routine tasks were successfully performed: a new king was installed in Armenia, a treaty was made with the Parthians, and the recently acquired provinces of Cappadocia and Commagene were duly organized. Otherwise, however, his conduct was marked by tactless blunders. He visited Egypt without permission, and assumed powers there which probably did not belong to him. Added to this, he quarreled with Gnaeus Piso, the governor of Syria. Then he suddenly fell sick and died at Antioch in 19 A.D.

[1] See genealogical table, p. 327.

*University Prints*

AGRIPPINA THE ELDER

His death precipitated a crisis. Agrippina and her friends affected to believe that he had been poisoned, and accused Tiberius of having used Piso as an agent to commit the crime. When the Emperor failed to be sufficiently demonstrative in his grief for his nephew, it was accepted as proof of his guilt. Piso was put on trial, charged with poisoning and with official misconduct. The poisoning charge broke down, but since he was obviously guilty on the second count, he committed suicide to escape condemnation. Agrippina was thenceforth openly hostile to Tiberius.

Tiberius was now free to promote the fortunes of his son Drusus, and he proceeded to do so. But once more Fate dealt unkindly with him. Drusus died in 23, leaving only an infant son as his heir. Tiberius now fell back upon the sons of Germanicus, whom he brought forward for the succession. But this step did not disarm the hostility of Agrippina.

The death of Drusus left the way clear for the rise of Lucius Aelius Sejanus, an equestrian of Etruscan ancestry who had commanded the Praetorian Guard since the death of Augustus, and who had distinguished himself by his unscrupulous readiness to serve his master. For some years he held an office very much like that of prime minister in a modern state. Acting on his advice, Tiberius concentrated the Praetorians in Rome, where a special camp was built to house them. Sejanus displayed great zeal in ferreting out conspiracies, and as Agrippina became more and more disagreeable, Tiberius seems to have relied upon him to neutralize her efforts against the government. Finally, in 26, the old Emperor became so disgusted with Rome that he withdrew to the island of Capri, off the coast of Campania. Sejanus was left to administer the government, subject to his master's orders, and for the next five years he was all-powerful.

Meanwhile, trials for treason had become unpleasantly frequent. The "Law of Majesty," which defined the offense, was vague and sweeping, making no distinction between actions directed against the welfare of the state and those injurious to the Emperor, who was at its head. It also took cognizance of acts or words disrespectful to him, the so-called "constructive treason." This was bad enough; the means of enforcement were worse. The Romans had no public prosecutor, but depended upon private informers to prosecute offenders, and rewarded them for securing convictions with a portion of the fines collected. In treason cases this amounted to a fourth of the estates of the culprits. A few of these informers may have been public-spirited citizens, but the majority were unscrupulous and bloodthirsty scoundrels. Such cases, when they involved senators, were tried before the Senate, and, whether from fear or from a desire to render Tiberius unpopular, it rarely acquitted anyone without his special personal recommendation. In his early years he often intervened in behalf of accused persons, but when he was absent from Rome many glaring injustices were perpetrated. If an accused person committed suicide before conviction, his estate was saved for his heirs, and as death and confiscation were the usual punishments, such suicides became very common. The evil grew much worse after Tiberius retired to Capri.

Apparently Sejanus harbored designs upon the Principate himself, for he set to work methodically to remove all other possible claimants. Agrippina and her sons were banished or imprisoned, with the exception of the youngest, the future Emperor Gaius, who managed to retain his liberty. Except for Tiberius, there seemed to be no real obstacle between the ambitious minister and the goal of his desires. By 30 A.D. he had begun to intrigue for the tribunician and proconsular powers, and was asking permission to marry the widow of Drusus. Once these were granted he would need only to remove Tiberius in order to gain his object.

The Emperor's suspicions at last became aroused, but so great was Sejanus' power that he did not dare attack him openly, and resorted to craft. Without stirring from Capri he succeeded in removing Sejanus from the command of the Praetorians, and ordered his arrest. That was enough. The servile Senate condemned the fallen minister and his children to death. His divorced wife, maddened by the destruction of her family, committed suicide, but before doing so wrote a note to Tiberius saying that Drusus had been poisoned as the result of a plot between his wife and Sejanus. Whether or not the accusation was true, Tiberius believed it.

For Tiberius the shock was so great that he never recovered from it. From that time forward he devoted himself more and more to vengeance upon his enemies. Drusus' widow was handed over to her mother, who starved her to death. An orgy of executions and suicides swept away the adherents of Sejanus. Agrippina and her oldest son died in exile, and her second son was starved to death in the palace. Finally only two candidates for the succession remained — Tiberius Gemellus the son of the dead Drusus, and Gaius the son of Germanicus and Agrippina. Tiberius, after making them his joint heirs, died on March 16, 37.

Later Roman historians dealt harshly with his memory. Neglecting the good government which Tiberius had given the provinces, they dwelt upon the executions and suicides which disfigured his reign, pictured him as a crafty and cruel tyrant, and accused him of the foulest and most unnatural vices. Of his cruelty, when aroused, there can be no doubt, but few if any men have had so much provocation as he. That he was personally immoral seems impossible for many reasons.

### *The Birth of Christianity*

It was during the latter years of Tiberius that the Christian religion was born. In the far-off province of Judea a young Jewish carpenter named Jesus began to preach to his countrymen a new concept of God and of righteous living. His was a doctrine which substituted love, brotherhood, and right thinking for the narrow legalism of the Jewish hierarchy, and he taught that God is a merciful father to men rather than an exacting and inexorable judge. When the priests, scribes, and Pharisees, the religious leaders of the Jewish people and the beneficiaries of the existing order of things, opposed him, he denounced them bitterly. For a time the common people, entranced by his winning personality and reputation as a miracle-worker, thought that he was the hero-king or Messiah, who, they hoped, would free them from Roman rule and make the Jews the masters of the world. When Jesus had preached for three years, matters came to a head. He was arrested by the municipal authorities of Jerusalem and brought before the Roman procurator, Pontius Pilatus. Although he had not violated any Roman law, he had referred to himself as a king, and his accusers hinted that if he were acquitted they would accuse Pilate of condoning treason. Since Pilate was no doubt a henchman of Sejanus, who had just fallen, to play safe, he had Jesus crucified. It is doubtful if news of so obscure a happening reached Rome at the time. But the matter did not end there. The inner circle of Jesus' followers declared that he had risen from the dead, and that he would soon return to earth to establish his kingdom. For some years they were merely another sect of Jews, but later they made their faith in Jesus the basis of a new and powerful religion.

### *Gaius Caesar (Caligula, 37–41 A.D.)*

The news of Tiberius' death made the Senate and people mad with joy. His grandson was thrust aside, and the imperial office was given to Gaius Caesar, better known to later ages as Caligula ("Little Boots," a nickname given him by the soldiers along the Rhine when as a child he had visited them with his father Germanicus). The new Emperor was twenty-five years old, but as yet had had no experience in government. His political philosophy, which had been formed by Oriental princes like the Jewish Herod Agrippa, with whom he had associated in his adolescent years, was one of absolute monarchy. With the amiability of his father he combined much of the mad ambition and pride of his mother. His prodigal generosity was for a time a welcome contrast to the tight-fisted economy of Tiberius. He began his reign by recalling exiles, remitting taxes, and displaying great respect for the Senate. The bones of his mother and brothers were buried with befitting pomp, while his sisters and his uncle Claudius were loaded with distinctions. It was felt that the golden days of Augustus had returned.

Then suddenly everything changed for the worse. Before the end of his first year Gaius fell ill, and when he recovered it was obvious that his mind was deranged. He began to play the part of an Oriental despot, and to indulge in acts of vainglory, cruelty, lust, and arrogance on an unheard-of scale. All persons who seemed likely to endanger his position were murdered, often with tortures. Tiberius had left a huge cash surplus in the treasury, but in a year it was squandered. Then came accusations for treason against senators and equestrians, increased taxes, confiscations of property, with the extortion of money by every kind of dishonorable expedient. Caligula assumed the airs and titles of a god, and compelled the

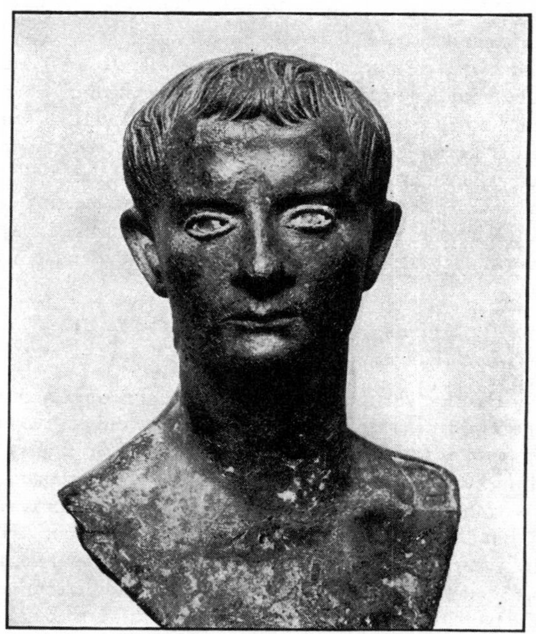

*Metropolitan Museum*

CALIGULA

*37–41 A.D.*

Roman citizen body to worship him. Aside from an abortive expedition against Britain, and a short stay on the Rhine, he paid no attention to the provincial armies. For nearly four years this mad tyranny continued, and the civilian population was powerless to resist it, until a tribune of the Praetorians whom he had insulted proved less docile. In January, 41, he was cut down, along with his wife and daughter.

### *Claudius (41–54 A.D.): Accession, Character, and Policies*

As the conspirators had not agreed upon a successor to their victim, the death of Caligula was followed by chaos. The Senate wanted to abolish the Principate and restore the Republic, but wasted its time in idle discussion. This delay ruined the project. As the masterless Praetorians were looting the palace, one of them found Tiberius Claudius Germanicus, the uncle of the dead Caligula, hiding in a closet. Recognizing him as the only surviving male of the imperial family, the soldiers saluted him as Emperor. The Senate had no choice but to submit as gracefully as possible, and Claudius began a reign which was to last more than thirteen years (41–54).

Prior to his accession, Claudius had been despised by his family as a man of uncouth appearance, physically weak and probably mentally deficient. For this reason he had before the accession of Caligula been kept in obscurity, but even so he had developed considerable talent as a historian, and had delivered some very creditable orations. Under his unprepossessing exterior, there lurked much common sense and breadth of mind, which combined to make him one of Rome's great emperors. His worst faults were superstition, credulity, and physical cowardice, by means of which he became an easy dupe for his wives and freedmen. To them was due a long series of disgraceful acts which besmirched an otherwise able and efficient government.

With his accession, and probably because of his personal convictions, there began a new and broader policy toward the provinces in general and the western provinces in particular, the aim of which was to assimilate into the citizen body at least the most enlightened of the provincials. Like Augustus and Tiberius, Claudius had great respect for the Senate, but he did not intend that it should remain exclusively Roman, or even Italian. In 47, he assumed the censorship, and in making up the Senate roll did not hesitate to add the names of distinguished Gallic nobles. In fact his liberality in granting citizenship to the provincials was notorious. He defended this policy in an oration delivered in the Senate which, if not a model of eloquence, displayed a deep understanding of the sources of Rome's greatness. Other great empires, he said, had fallen because the ruling people refused to assimilate their subjects. Rome had from the beginning freely admitted foreigners to her citizenship, and owed much of her greatness to the fact. In this respect Claudius reversed the narrow policy of Augustus and reverted to the broader one of Julius Caesar, and from that day forward the movement which he had begun never stopped until the whole Empire had become politically Roman.

Wherever the Senate was willing to perform duties he allowed it to do so, but he insisted that the work be done efficiently and justly. If it failed to perform its work well, he assumed the functions himself. In legislation the Senate was very active, passing decrees upon legal questions of many kinds. But at the same time imperial officials assumed charge of many public works in and about Rome, and Claudius conferred large powers upon his procurators in the senatorial provinces. Roads were built, swamps and lakes were drained, and harbors were constructed. Judicial business was attended to promptly, with Claudius himself sitting as judge for hours at a time. Although his detractors told many humorous stories about his absurd decisions, the truth seems to be that he interpreted the law with essential fairness, equity, and liberality.

Under him was formed a cabinet of freedmen ministers, something that none of his predecessors had had. The ministry of finance (*a rationibus*) was held by Pallas, a strong and unscrupulous character, who first gave the *fiscus* a central office in Rome. He used his place to amass enormous wealth, and his brother Felix, while procurator of Judea, even dared to take the wife of a client-king and marry her himself. Next came the ministry of correspondence (*ab epistulis*), held by Narcissus. There was also a ministry of petitions (*a libellis*), a ministry of judicial affairs (*a cognitionibus*), and another (*a studiis*) whose functions are not so well known. With these, and with a greatly increased staff of procurators (also freedmen in many cases), Claudius could exert more power than any of his predecessors had done.

*Provincial Government and Conquests*

In the provinces Claudius ruled ably and humanely wherever his freedmen did not sabotage his efforts. Taxation was equalized, while abuses were removed or mitigated. Conquests were made on a scale unknown since the days of Augustus. When in 46 the client-kingdom of Thrace fell into disorder, it was organized as a province. Britain was still divided into warring tribal states, as in the days of Julius Caesar. Every Roman statesman for a century past had felt that its conquest was necessary to the peace of Gaul; and in 43 the time seemed ripe. A powerful army under an able commander, Aulus Plautius, was detailed to the task, and in a short time had subdued the region south of the Thames. Claudius himself made the journey to Britain, where he received the submission of many of the native chiefs. The conquered area, which was steadily expanding throughout his reign, was organized as the province of Britain, and colonies of Roman citizens were planted at several points, including London. The frontiers were secured by a ring of vassal states, and in 51 Caractacus, the leader of the native resistance, was captured. It was in memory of this conquest that Claudius took the name *Britannicus*.

*Bettmann*

CLAUDIUS

*41–54 A.D.*

In North Africa he had to settle another frontier problem, which he had inherited from his predecessor. Caligula had put to death his cousin, King Ptolemy of Mauretania, and had declared his kingdom a province. But Aedemon, a freedman of the murdered Ptolemy, led a formidable revolt, which was not put down until 42. Mauretania was organized as two provinces, Caesariensis in the east and Tingitana in the west.

A Jewish problem of dangerous proportions was another inheritance of Claudius from the regime of Caligula. In Palestine, Syria, Egypt, and Cyrene alike, the Jews were at odds with their Hellenistic and Oriental neighbors, and the Imperial Government was constantly compelled to act as arbiter. The usual result was that the peacemaker gained the ill will of both parties. The administration of the province of Judea was also a cause of ill feeling on the part of the Jews, for unlike most provincial governors, these procurators were usually corrupt and oppressive, with no regard for the religious sensibilities of the people. Ever since the death of Tiberius, the leader of the Jews had been the wily Herod Agrippa, the grandson of King Herod the Great. From Caligula he had acquired Galilee and other Palestinian territories, to which Claudius added Judea. When he died, in 44, Judea was again made a province. As the quality of Roman government did not improve, the Jews became more and more stubborn and fanatical. The stage was being set for the great rebellion of 66 A.D. Such cases, however, were exceptional, and among the provincials generally Claudius was popular.

*Domestic Problems*

In Roman eyes his successes as a statesman and administrator were partly nullified by his inability to rule his own household. His freedmen abused his confidence by selling judicial decisions, appointments, and any other favors which they could induce him to grant, and as we have seen, stole shamelessly from his treasury. His wife, Valeria Messalina, led a life of unblushing immorality. Both empress and freedmen secured the condemnation and execution of senators and equestrians who stood in their way, or whose property they coveted. However, in 49, Messalina overreached herself. She became infatuated with Gaius Silius, a handsome and ambitious senator, and together they plotted to dethrone Claudius. Narcissus, the least objectionable of the freedmen, nipped the plot in the bud by securing from Claudius a death-warrant for both of them and then personally carrying it out. But the various freedmen now began to intrigue for the upper hand, each pushing his own candidate for the vacant position of empress, and Pallas won by inducing Claudius to marry his own niece, Agrippina the younger. She was more astute than Messalina, and fully as dangerous. By previous marriages Claudius had two daughters, Antonia and Octavia, and a son, Britannicus. Agrippina had a son, Lucius Domitius Ahenobarbus, who was through her a great-great-grandson of Augustus. She determined to push Britannicus aside and secure the succession for Domitius. Backed by Pallas, she induced Claudius to adopt Domitius, and to marry him to Octavia. All important offices were filled with her partisans, and her son was rapidly pushed forward in his political career. In 54, when her son (now called Nero) was seventeen years old, she was ready to act. Claudius died suddenly, and no one doubted that

Agrippina had poisoned him. A stranger mixture of strength and weakness, of wise statesmanship and imbecility, than Claudius, never wore the imperial purple.

### *Nero (54–68 A.D.): The First Five Years*

Under his mother's expert guidance Nero had no trouble in seizing the vacant Principate. The real government of the state was of course in the hands of others: Agrippina, his tutor the philosopher Seneca, and the praetorian prefect Sextus Afranius Burrus. Again the aristocracy entertained wild hopes that it would be freed from the terrors of false accusations and from the humiliation of having to pay court to freedmen, and again, as at the accession of Caligula, it prophesied the dawn of the Golden Age.

For five years (54–59), it seemed that these hopes had been realized. Nero himself, coached by his regents, was the soul of modesty and clemency. Abuses were righted, oppressive customs were abolished, and senators were employed in some of the posts which Claudius had filled with freedmen. But although the Senate was flattered, it really gained little power from the change of emperors. In fact Seneca and Burrus brought the imperial office nearer to absolute monarchy than ever before. Nero, for all his charming manners, began to show erratic and bloodthirsty tendencies, which were the preludes to his later crimes. In 55, he poisoned Britannicus. Agrippina was soon pushed aside, and while Seneca and Burrus carried on the work of government, Nero divided his time between a series of mistresses and the fine arts. He wrote poetry, played musical instruments, and sang operatic parts. Flatterers whetted his zeal to the point of inducing him to give public recitals — from the Roman point of view an inexpiable disgrace. In 59, a new mistress, Sabina Poppaea, so roused his indignation against his mother that he had her murdered, and his regents, to maintain their influence, publicly excused the crime. Three years later Burrus died, and Seneca, loaded with wealth, retired from power. Octavia was divorced, and Nero married Sabina. He was now his own master, and he signalized the fact by appointing as Burrus' successor a Sicilian named Tigellinus — a villain of the deepest dye.

### *An Imperial Tyrant and Artist*

For the remainder of his reign the Empire was subjected to a capricious tyranny, which did not by any means affect all its parts alike. In some of

*Bettmann*

NERO
*54–68 A.D.*

the provinces capable and conscientious civil servants seem to have carried on the government with efficiency and justice. But at home it almost seemed as if the evil days of Caligula had returned. Extravagance drained the treasury and to refill it Nero resorted to the usual judicial murders and confiscations. His divorced wife Octavia was put to death on a false charge, and several descendants of preceding emperors shared her fate. Meanwhile Nero was striving to make an immortal reputation as poet and musician, and was organizing contests in his chosen fields like those popular in the Hellenistic world.

In 64, Rome was visited with a calamity for which Nero was popularly (and no doubt wrongfully) blamed. A fire broke out in the city, and raged unchecked for nine days among the flimsy tenements and apartment buildings which housed so much of the population. When it was finally stopped, over half of the city was in ruins. Nero, roused for a moment from his mad career, did his best to relieve the homeless sufferers, but in the public mind his efforts did little good. A story was circulated and believed, to the effect that he had had the fire started so that the burning city would serve as an artistic setting in which he might recite his poem on the sack of Troy. Terrible as it was, the fire was a blessing in disguise. When the devastated districts were rebuilt, it was with broader, straighter streets and more substantial buildings. Nero, however, nullified some of these benefits by seizing a large tract of land in the heart of the city and constructing on it a grandiose palace, the "Golden House," and a splendid park. His expenditures on these projects disorganized his finances still further.

It was in an attempt to clear himself of the charge of having burned Rome, that Nero instituted the first government-sponsored persecution of the Christians. By this time Rome had a small Christian congregation, whose secretive ways and novel religious practices had aroused popular hatred. Relying upon their unpopularity, he caused a number of them to be arrested on the charge of having started the fire, and put them to death with revolting tortures. Later legend said that the apostles Peter and Paul perished in this persecution. It failed to convince the Roman populace, who instead began to sympathize with the victims; but it seems to have had one important result. It was probably at this time that a law was enacted making it a capital offense to be a Christian, for such a law was in existence a few years later, and was not repealed for two and a half centuries. Upon it later measures of persecution were based.

### *Provincial Government: Rebellions and Wars*

In provincial administration and foreign relations Nero's government was one of mixed tendencies. As previously indicated, many provinces continued to be well governed, but there were signs that all was not well. The frontier along the Rhine and the Danube continued to be quiet, but in Britain the oppression of the natives by money-lenders, tax-collectors, and soldiers produced a murderous outbreak. Led by Boudicca, the widowed queen of the Iceni, the rebels stormed three Roman colonies and massacred 70,000 Roman citizens. Suetonius Paulinus, the governor of the province, was absent on a campaign in the west when the rebellion broke out, but he soon returned and put it down. Boudicca, defeated in battle, took poison, and we hear of no more revolts in Britain for many years.

Toward the Greeks Nero was extremely indulgent, restoring nominal independence to the Greek peninsula and the Aegean islands. For this and other reasons he enjoyed an almost idolatrous popularity in the eastern provinces, so that long after his death men entertained wild hopes that he would some day return. War with Parthia broke out again during the last year of Claudius' reign — as usual, over the Armenian question. Vologeses, the Parthian king, taking advantage of the venality and incompetence of the Roman governors in the neighboring provinces, invaded Armenia and placed his brother Tiridates on its throne. Seneca and Burrus sent thither Gnaeus Domitius Corbulo, an efficient soldier and an honorable man, to restore Roman influence. Corbulo won a series of victories, but was later compelled by the irresolute attitude of the home government to make a compromise. In 63, it was agreed that Tiridates was to be king of Armenia, but he was to receive his crown from Nero, and to rule as a Roman vassal. This settlement was by no means a Roman triumph, yet it was not too damaging to Roman prestige, and solved the Parthian problem for a long time.

In 66, the Jews, irritated by years of misgovernment, economic depression, and bickerings with their neighbors, had reached the limit of endurance. The fanatical Pharisees got the upper hand of the pro-Roman Sadducees; and bands of outlaws, who united religious zeal with blood-lust, infested the country. When the procurator, Gessius Florus, seized part of the temple treasure, a revolt broke out. The Palestinian Gentiles took the side of the Romans, and massacred the Jews who fell into their hands. A Roman force which was sent to restore order was routed by the Jews, and the movement spread like wildfire. The extreme Pharisees (known as "Zealots") got control of the rebel forces, and prepared for war to the death. Nero in desperation sent Titus Flavius Vespasianus, a veteran commander schooled in the British wars, with a large army to suppress the rebels; but four years were to elapse and a revolution to occur before the task was accomplished.

### *The Last Years*

Meanwhile Nero was rushing headlong to his ruin. In 65, a formidable conspiracy was formed against him by the senator Gaius Calpurnius Piso, who drew in many senators and equestrians. However, the plot was betrayed, and an orgy of executions and suicides followed. Chief among the victims were the aged Seneca and his fellow Stoic, Paetus Thrasea, although it is almost certain that neither had any part in the conspiracy.

Anyone who had aroused Nero's hatred or jealousy by reason of literary rivalry with him, descent from Augustus, or even pre-eminent virtue in the midst of a corrupt society, was certain to be killed or exiled. Nero was now definitely the enemy of the senatorial aristocracy, and seemed bent upon exterminating it.

His thirst for fame as a poet, singer, and athlete had become a mania. In 66, he set out for a tour of Greece, where he hoped that his talents would be better appreciated than in Rome. The tour lasted about fifteen months, and was a light farce in the midst of tragedies. The facile Greeks arranged to hold all of their national games in the year 67 so that he might compete in them, and he won every contest. His superiority was proclaimed in chariot-racing, poetry, and singing. However, in the midst of this holiday he found time to summon Corbulo and several other able generals to Greece, and to murder them as soon as they arrived.

The Empire had now had its fill of Nero. In the spring of 68, the governor of Gallia Lugdunensis, the Romanized Gaul, Gaius Julius Vindex, rebelled — not against Rome but against an emperor who disgraced the Roman name. Sulpicius Galba, governor of Hither Spain, supported the rebel. The Rhine legions easily suppressed the movement, and immediately thereafter saluted as emperor their commander, Verginius Rufus. He declined the dangerous honor, but revolt was in the air. After the fall of Vindex, Galba had himself proclaimed emperor, and Marcus Salvius Otho, the governor of Lusitania, gave him help. Meanwhile Galba's agents were busy in Rome, where they persuaded the Senate and the Praetorians to recognize their master and repudiate Nero. The Imperial Tragedian, faced at last with real tragedy, fled to the villa of one of his freedmen, and there, on June 9, 68, committed suicide, exclaiming in his last moments, "What an artist the world is losing!"

Thus perished the last of the Julio-Claudian emperors. Although the magic of Augustus' name had lent luster to the line, the crimes of Caligula and Nero had at last broken the spell which he had thrown about the Roman people. As a whole, in spite of all their shortcomings, they had given the Empire a century of peace and at least tolerable government, but the same cannot be said for their influence upon the Roman aristocracy. Many of the older families had been exterminated by executions and forced suicides, while others undoubtedly allowed their race to die out rather than rear children amid such terror and uncertainty. Their vacant places were being taken by a group of new families, from whom were to spring the emperors and senators of the following century. The Principate had been too firmly established to be overthrown, but there still remained the task of making it a responsible and beneficent office of state instead of an instrument of tyranny.

## The "Year of the Three Emperors" and the First Civil War (68–69 A.D.)

With the death of Nero, opposition to Galba collapsed, and for a moment it seemed that he might be permitted to rule the Empire in peace. But such was not to be the case. The revolution which overthrew Nero had let loose forces which had not yet spent themselves, and which would not permit the immediate establishment of a stable government. As the Roman historian Tacitus was to write a generation later, "A new political secret was then discovered for the first time. It was perceived that emperors could be invested with sovereign power elsewhere than in Rome." [1] What the Spanish legions had done could be imitated by the armies on the Rhine, the Danube, or the eastern frontier. Until the pretenders put forward by these groups had fought out their respective claims to the Principate, there could be no peace, and this process was to require more than a year of disorder and suffering.

Galba himself was a disappointment to his supporters. He was more than seventy years old, and a man of hard and inflexible disposition. His ideas of right and wrong were purely theoretical, and he made no attempt to accommodate them to actual conditions. Although he posed as a champion of the Senate, he offended many of its members. All who opposed him were punished with callous brutality. He refused to give the soldiers the bonus customarily distributed by a new emperor, and he snubbed the Rhine legions by removing their beloved commander Verginius Rufus from office. Otho had expected to be named his successor, but he passed him over and chose instead a young aristocrat without political experience. These mistakes sealed Galba's doom. In January, 69, a revolt broke out on the Rhine, where Aulus Vitellius, the governor of Lower Germany, was hailed as Emperor. Before Galba could march against the rebels, Otho had him murdered by the Praetorians in Rome on January 15, 69.

Otho, an old comrade of Nero and a former husband of Sabina Poppaea, was a man of engaging manners and kindly disposition. He won the idolatrous affection of the Praetorians, and was speedily recognized by all the armies except those stationed on the Rhine. But although he was no general, he was compelled to take up the war against Vitellius, whose partisans were advancing through Gaul toward Italy. As soon as spring

[1] *History*, I, 4.

had opened the Alpine passes, the Vitellians under Valens and Caecina crossed into the Po Valley, and Otho, without waiting for the reinforcements which were on their way from the Danube, engaged them in two pitched battles. Both were fought near the village of Bedriacum, not far from Cremona. In the first Otho was victorious, and in the second he was defeated. But while the issue was still undecided and the detachments from the Danubian garrisons were not far away, Otho's nerve failed him, and he committed suicide. While not a vicious man when judged by Roman standards, Otho was too weak for the place which he had won.

However, Italy had not yet drunk her fill of misery and disorder. The victorious Vitellians treated her as a conquered country, and committed shocking outrages. Vitellius himself, another former intimate of Nero, was a weakling whose chief pleasure in life was eating. Between April and December of 69, he spent nine hundred million sesterces on food alone. Over his officers and soldiers he had no control at all, and their fighting strength melted away as they lived at free quarters in the Italian towns.

### *The Triumph of Vespasian*

Yet another storm was gathering. The Danubian and Asiatic armies had not yet had their turn at emperor-making, and they were determined not to forfeit it. The only person of high standing and strong character among their commanders was Vespasian, whom Nero had put in charge of the army in Judea. On July 1, 69, he was proclaimed Emperor by the prefect of Egypt, and the other governors and armies east of the Adriatic soon followed suit. A large force, gathered from the camps on the Danube and led by Antonius Primus, invaded Italy on his behalf. On the Vitellian side all was confusion. The soldiers fought bravely, but the generals were either fainthearted or treacherous, and Vitellius himself did nothing. By a series of savage blows the Danubian army pushed them back upon Rome, until early in December, Primus was close to the city.

The last of the war was at hand. Vitellius attempted to save his life by abdication, but his soldiers would not permit it. In a ferocious riot they burned the Capitoline Temple, murdered Vespasian's brother, and defied the invaders. Antonius Primus then stormed the city, massacred the Vitellian troops, and allowed Vitellius himself to be tortured to death. Vespasian's title was confirmed by the Senate, and the Empire once more had a strong master.

## The Flavian Emperors (69–96 A.D.)

With the accession of Vespasian a new era began in the history of the Roman Empire. As we have seen, the Julio-Claudian emperors had given it a century of internal peace and order. Vespasian ushered in a second century of stability, characterized by even better government than the first, and by foreign conquests that gave to the Roman state the widest boundaries which it was destined ever to reach. Although inferior to the Augustan Age in cultural achievements, it produced some very creditable work in both art and literature, and witnessed the spread of Roman civilization over much of the barbarian West.

### *Vespasian (69–79 A.D.): Character, Policies, and Problems*

Vespasian had little in common with his predecessors in character or social background. He was not a Roman by birth, but came from a middle-class family in the Sabine town of Reate. At the time of his accession he was sixty years old. His adult years had been spent in war and government, with occasional ventures into private business to relieve financial embarrassment. He was plain, unpretentious, and matter-of-fact, with strong common sense, and a quick but coarse sense of humor. His parsimony was so well known that it became the subject of many a funny story, but he could and did spend liberally on worthy causes. No grandiose schemes, doctrinaire notions, or wild ambitions ever lured him away from his task of making the Empire safe and prosperous. His sense of duty was so strong that even in his last moments he declared, "an emperor should die on his feet," and died while struggling to rise from his bed. If not a brilliant ruler, he was certainly a capable and conscientious one.

The outlook, at his accession, was not rosy. The Jewish revolt was by no means crushed, and at the other end of the Empire the civil wars had given rise to a formidable rebellion among the Gallic and German tribes along the Rhine. Everywhere the armies would have to be reduced once more to obedience. Internal problems were no less pressing. The extravagance of the emperors who followed Tiberius had so depleted the finances that Vespasian estimated that forty billion sesterces were needed to balance the treasury accounts. The Senate was depleted in numbers, and demoralized by the disorders of the preceding generation, so that it stood in need of a thorough reorganization, and of the introduction of much new blood.

Political unrest had also begun to agitate the senatorial order. A new

*Bettmann*

VESPASIAN

*69–79 A.D.*

philosophy of government had appeared, which was destined to cause Vespasian and his sons great trouble, and to dominate the state throughout most of the second century A.D. It was probably of Stoic origin, and hereafter will be referred to as the "Stoic Theory." It taught that there were only two kinds of rulers — kings and tyrants. The king, according to this theory, is the best man in the state, to whom the government has been committed, and he rules entirely for the welfare of the people. A tyrant is a lawless individualist, who exploits his subjects in order to serve his own vicious pleasures. Drawing upon the unfortunate experience of the Roman people with the Julio-Claudian emperors, the Stoic group asserted that hereditary succession can only produce tyrants, since an heir-apparent is certain to be spoiled by flattery and luxury, and because the hereditary principle treats the state as a piece of property. Instead, each emperor must adopt as his son the person best fitted to succeed him, so that the succession of the "best man" will be assured. But how can such a person be discovered? To these Roman aristocrats the answer was easy: let him be chosen by the Senate. It will be observed that this school of thought did not seek to limit the imperial power, but only to see that it was used in the public interest. Its chief advocate in Vespasian's day was Helvidius Priscus, a senator of uncompromising virtue but of little tact or common sense. Joined with him were many senators, and a number of Greek and Roman publicists who preached the doctrine in Rome and the provinces. With most of their conclusions Vespasian would probably have had no quarrel, but he was determined that his sons should succeed him, and on this point would not yield.

### *Wars and the Provincial Government*

Vespasian attacked his problem with energy and wisdom. The armies were speedily brought to order. The Gallo-German revolt was likewise taken in hand. The Batavians, a client tribe of Germans who furnished auxiliaries to the Roman army, had rebelled under the leadership of Julius Civilis, a Batavian who had gained Roman citizenship and the command of a cohort of his countrymen. A confederacy was formed of tribes from both sides of the Rhine, and the Roman garrison on this frontier, weakened by Vitellius' withdrawal of men from them for his invasion of Italy, were quickly overwhelmed. For a time it seemed as if a new Gallo-German state might be formed, which would embrace all the land between the ocean, the Rhine, the Alps, and the Pyrenees. However, a Roman expeditionary force was sent against the rebels early in 70, and before the end of the year, the rebellion had been crushed. The Batavians were not punished, but to check similar outbreaks in the future, auxiliary troops were usually stationed far from their homes and were commanded by Roman equestrians rather than by tribal chiefs.

The Jewish war lasted until near the end of 70. When Vespasian left Judea he put his older son Titus in command of the army and the latter pressed the siege of Jerusalem with great energy. The rebels, encouraged by wild hopes of divine intervention in their behalf, fought savagely, but wherever the opportunity offered they did not hesitate to fight among themselves as well. After a siege of five months (described in horrible detail by the Jewish historian Josephus, an eye-witness), the Romans forced their way into the doomed city, burned the temple, and leveled the other buildings to the ground. Over a million Jews perished in the struggle, and many others were made slaves. However, the survivors of the Jewish nation were everywhere allowed to retain their freedom of worship. Titus celebrated a splendid triumph in Rome, in which the "Seven-branched Candlestick" and other sacred objects were exposed to view. The Jewish question was settled for the moment, but the stubborn spirit of the race was not crushed. Fifty years later it was to flare up again in another ferocious rebellion.

Elsewhere, the eastern provinces were less troublesome, but they were flaming with discontent. Vespasian was insulted when he visited Alexandria. Disorders broke out in continental Greece and in many of the other "free" districts bordering the Aegean, giving Vespasian a plausible pretext to reduce them to the status of provinces again. Several pretenders who claimed to be Nero appeared and gained large followings. In the West, Vespasian had better success. There he initiated what amounted to a peaceful revolution in the make-up of the Roman state. Wherever possible he bestowed either Latin rights or Roman citizenship upon the provincials, and from them and their descendants drew more and more recruits for the legions. From that time forward Italy contributed few if any of the common soldiers, but most of the officers. Thus the Principate could claim the active support of a large body of new citizens in most of the western provinces, where their presence would serve as a natural deterrent to revolt.

### *Domestic Government*

At home, as a counterpart to his provincial policy, Vespasian began to fill the Senate with men drawn like himself from Italy, or even from the provincial aristocracies. As the old aristocracy was extinct, and even the families ennobled by Caesar and Augustus were rapidly dying out, this policy greatly changed the tone of Roman aristocratic society. The new senators had been reared far from the luxury and vice of the capital, and their coming greatly improved the prevailing standard of morals. Unlike their predecessors, they were willing to co-operate actively in the government of the Empire, and instead of regarding the provinces as domains to be exploited for their benefit, they tended to look upon them as parts of the Roman body-politic, to which just and equitable treatment was due. In time this policy was to result in making the whole Empire Roman both in citizenship and allegiance.

Toward the Senate as a body Vespasian's attitude was friendly, but perfectly realistic. He dated his accession from the day when he had been proclaimed by the army in Egypt rather than from his recognition in Rome. He doggedly refused to recognize the Stoic theory of succession, and when Helvidius Priscus made himself offensive in his advocacy of it, he was banished and executed. The Stoic and Cynic agitators who had preached the theory in the city were also banished. To make his intentions perfectly plain, Vespasian caused Titus to be invested during his lifetime with both tribunician and proconsular powers. He tolerated great freedom of speech from senators, and did not revive the treason trials which had disgraced the reigns of his Julio-Claudian predecessors.

In financial matters, he showed both efficiency and good sense. Realizing that high taxes were better for everyone than bankruptcy, he greatly increased and in some cases doubled existing rates, at the same time watching expenditures with an eagle eye. Yet he spent liberally for roads and public buildings, including the great "Flavian Amphitheater" (now known as the Colosseum), and he even endowed professorships in Greek and Latin oratory. When he died, on June 23, 79, he left a financially solvent state, and one greatly strengthened by his ten years of patient effort.

### *Titus (79–81 A.D.)*

The reigns of Vespasian's two sons were mere pendants of his own, dominated for the most part by the same problems. Of these Titus the older son survived his father by only a little over two years. Before his accession he had acted, while co-regent with his father, in an efficient but high-handed manner which led men to expect the worst from him, but as Emperor he completely reversed his conduct. Scrupulous care for the rights of others, together with liberality and beneficence, made him, as his Roman biographer puts it, "the delight and darling of the human race." [1] Whether he could have maintained this phenomenal popularity if he had lived longer is doubtful, but he had the supreme good fortune to die before his personal glamour had worn thin, and was, like his father, promptly deified by a grateful people.

Yet his reign was marked by two shocking calamities — the destruction of Pompeii and Herculaneum by the eruption of Mt. Vesuvius, and a disastrous fire at Rome. Vesuvius had been quiescent for many centuries, but in 63 it gave warning of reviving life in an earthquake which shook much of

[1] Suetonius, *Divus Titus*, c. 1.

*University Prints*

TRIUMPHAL PROCESSION

*Relief from the Arch of Titus*

the surrounding country. On August 23, 79, it burst forth into an eruption which buried the land along its seaward side for some eight or ten miles under a shower of pumice stone and volcanic mud. Herculaneum, Pompeii, and Stabiae, the three towns nearest to the crater — were all buried to a depth of twenty or more feet. Although most of the inhabitants seem to have escaped, none of these places were ever completely excavated or rebuilt in ancient times. Hence, the mementoes of their daily life were sealed up intact for the modern archeologist — amphitheaters, shops, temples, private houses — each exactly as it was when the eruption began, except for the inevitable destruction of roofs and the decay of perishable materials. Nowhere else can the life of ancient Italy be seen in such startling vividness. The fire at Rome destroyed much of the northern part of the city, including the often-burned Capitoline Temple. In both cases Titus made heroic efforts to relieve the sufferers, and spent liberally to repair the damage.

*Galloway*

RUINS OF POMPEII

*Showing Vesuvius in Background*

*Domitian (81–96 A.D.)*

Domitian has left a tarnished name upon the pages of history, but in spite of being neither a brilliant statesman nor a paragon of the virtues, he was neither worthless nor fundamentally vicious. It was his fate to have to face several unhappy situations from which death had rescued his more fortunate brother. Chief among these were a series of frontier wars, and an irrepressible conflict with the senatorial opposition.

*Provincial Government and Wars*

In his provincial administration, Domitian made a good but not brilliant record. His officials were closely supervised, and misconduct among them was rare. In Britain, his able lieutenant, Julius Agricola, completed the conquest of the island up to the Firth of Forth, but when he asked permission to conquer Ireland, was recalled. On the Rhine frontier, the inconvenient salient between the Upper Rhine and the Danube was annexed, and a frontier wall built to protect it. This district — the *Agri Decumates* or "tithe-lands" — was colonized with settlers from Gaul, and remained in Roman hands for nearly two centuries. In 88, when Antonius Saturninus, the governor of Upper Germany, revolted, the movement was easily put down. To prevent such uprisings in the future, Domitian made it a rule that no more than one legion could be stationed in any camp at one time. Other minor wars along the Rhine resulted in Roman victories.

Along the Danube, the danger was greater, and the successes won were fewer and less decisive. A movement of tribes far back in the barbarian North pushed the Marcomanni, the Quadi, and other Germanic tribes on the Bohemian plateau against the Danubian frontier. Farther down the Danube, the Dacians, a Thracian tribe living in the Transylvanian highland, had formed a strong state under a king named Decebalus. In 85, Decebalus invaded Moesia and killed its governor. When the praetorian prefect was sent to the Moesian front with an army, he too was slain. Three years later, a new Roman army invaded Dacia, while Domitian in person turned against the Marcomanni and the Quadi. The Dacian expedition was a success, but Domitian was defeated and had to compromise. Decebalus gave up his booty and prisoners, and was enrolled as a Roman ally; in return he received an annual subsidy and Roman military engineers to supervise the equipment of his army. It was an easy settlement for Rome, but not an honorable or decisive one, and a few years later it had to be revised with the sword.

### *Domestic Government: Domitian's Quarrel with the Senate*

At the beginning of his reign, Domitian displayed the same engaging qualities which had made his brother popular. He reformed private morals and administrative methods, built extensive public works, and spent lavishly to amuse the people. Feasts, gladiatorial shows, public games and distributions of cash to the soldiers and people were greater than at any time since Nero's death. The libraries destroyed in the fire of Titus' reign were rebuilt and restocked.

But in one thing Domitian blundered disastrously. The senatorial opposition still confronted him as it had his father, and with the same platform. Because he had inherited his place they were certain to feel ill will toward him, but Domitian made no effort to conciliate them. Instead he flouted their dearest principles, insisted on being addressed as "Lord and God," founded a priestly college (*Flaviales*) to worship his divine father and brother, and himself affected the airs of an autocrat. The result was open opposition from the Stoic leaders, and conspiracies by their sympathizers. He struck back by encouraging informers, and the all-too-familiar round of treason trials, executions, and suicides began again. The chiefs of the Stoic group were executed or banished, and the surviving philosophers were again driven from Rome. When treason charges failed, his victims were accused of religious offenses, and it is possible that the practice of Jewish or Christian rites were among the charges. When the Senate seemed hesitant to convict the accused, he surrounded it with soldiers.

The end of such a career was almost foreordained. Repeated conspiracies made Domitian suspicious of all about him, including his relatives, friends, and officials, and they in turn became afraid of him. Fear for their own lives at last nerved his wife, his Praetorian prefect, and other close associates to form a new and well-laid plot to kill him. On September 18, 96, he was lured away from his attendants and murdered. His death was not the work of the Stoic opposition, but to them was to go the profit of the deed.

### *The Flavian Period: a General View*

In general, the period of the Flavian emperors was, as we have seen, one of good government and prosperity. Except along the lower Danube, no crucial frontier problems arose, and the revolts in Judea and the Rhenish provinces, both of which had been in progress at Vespasian's accession, were successfully suppressed. In most of the provinces, the age was one of prosperity. From the viewpoint of government, it was an age of transition. The accession of an Italian family to the Principate, the entry of large numbers of Italian and provincial aristocrats into the Senate, and liberal grants of Roman citizenship to provincials marked the passing of the narrow Augustan concept of a privileged citizenry ruling over subject provincials, and the approach of an era when all inhabitants of the Empire except slaves would be members of the Roman body-politic. The base of the imperial structure had been greatly broadened by the enlistment of Roman citizens from provincial communities in the legions, and by the admission of men from the same group into responsible positions in the civil administration. A natural result of these measures was the growth of imperial patriotism among the landed aristocracies and urbanized classes of provincials. In these respects the age was one of constructive statesmanship.

One pressing problem remained unsolved. The mutual relations between the Emperors and the Senate were still undefined, and until this tangle had been resolved, the two chief agencies of government could never be at peace with each other. The uneasy reign of Domitian and his tragic end demonstrated all too clearly how this situation could hamper the activities and nullify the efforts of an otherwise able ruler. The solution of this problem was to be one of the crowning glories of the succeeding age.

# 22

# "The Five Good Emperors" (96–180 A.D.)

## Introduction

WITH THE ASSASSINATION of Domitian, the struggle between Emperor and Senate came to an abrupt end. The next five emperors all subscribed more or less fully to the theory of government advocated by the aristocracy, and governed their conduct accordingly. An understanding based upon the Stoic theory was arrived at, by which the Principate was recognized as a necessary magistracy of state, the holder of which was not above the laws, but rather subject to them. Hereditary succession was replaced — at least temporarily — by adoptive succession with senatorial approval. Each emperor was expected to take an oath at his accession that he would not put a senator to death, but would leave the trial of senatorial offenders entirely to the Senate itself. Vainglorious titles, such as Domitian's "Lord and God," were dropped by the ruler, and with them the stiff and formal court etiquette which he had established, and the emperors mingled with the senatorial aristocracy as equals. Freedom of speech prevailed, so that a man might speak or write as he pleased. Under these conditions, with few and short exceptions, internal harmony reigned, and the provinces were governed with efficiency, equity, and mercy.

This reconciliation of the emperors with the Senate did not diminish the imperial power, for (as indicated in the preceding chapter) such had never been a part of the Stoic program. Instead, it actually grew stronger by the elimination of opposition. Without antagonizing the Senate the emperors of this period assumed new functions or broadened old ones, built up an elaborate and efficient bureaucracy, and narrowed the sphere of senatorial activities in Rome, Italy, and the senatorial provinces.

The rise of the provincial aristocrats to influence and power in the government, which had begun under Claudius and continued under the Flavian emperors, progressed without a break. Of the five emperors who reigned during this period, four were of provincial birth or ancestry. All four were men of strong character, marked ability, and conscientious devotion to duty. The Senate, too, continued to receive provincial members, not only from the Latinized western provinces, but also from the Hellenistic East; and provincials came more and more often to hold important military commands and provincial governorships. Thus the supremacy of the Roman-Italian stock was progressively undermined, and the position of the other peoples of the Empire correspondingly improved. The armies were kept under strict control, and until near the end of the period the provinces were relatively safe from foreign invaders. Under such conditions wealth could accumulate, and the creative energies of the people could find expression in new and splendid cities, active commerce, and improved standards of living. Yet the calamities with which this brilliant age closed were to show conclusively that there was a darker side to the picture. Culturally, the peoples of the Empire produced very little that was worthy of comparison with the achievements of the Greeks and Romans of the preceding ages. In fact, it was during this age of splendor and material well-being that the decadence of ancient civilization first became sharply apparent.

## NERVA AND TRAJAN (96–117 A.D.)

### *Nerva (96–98)*

The murderers of Domitian had attempted to secure their own safety by choosing, in advance, a successor to their victim from whom they might hope for protection. Their choice fell upon Marcus Cocceius Nerva (96–98), a senator over sixty years of age, of mild disposition and blameless character, who was a strong believer in the Stoic theory of government. The dead tyrant was officially condemned, his acts annulled, and his statues destroyed. Exiles were recalled, and the more prominent informers were punished. The Praetorians and the populace were probably mollified by a donative, and acquiesced in the new regime, as did the provincial armies.

But Nerva, although amiable, was too irresolute to overcome the initial weakness of his government and to grasp firmly the power that had been thrust upon him. A number of administrative reforms were successfully undertaken, including the reorganization of the grain and water supply of

*Sawders–Combine*

NERVA

*96–98 A.D.*

the capital, the foundation of agricultural colonies for the Roman proletariat, and a plan for the relief of the poor in Italy, of which more will be said presently. In these matters the Senate was consulted, and Nerva enjoyed its support. But there were dangerous forces at work, which he had not the strength to control. The senatorial proconsuls, freed from Domitian's eagle-eyed scrutiny, began to rule corruptly and oppressively. The Praetorians, who regretted his death, mutinied, and slew his assassins in spite of Nerva's efforts to protect them. If civil war and chaos were to be avoided, a stronger hand was needed to guide the destinies of the state.

To supply this need Nerva adopted as his son Marcus Ulpius Traianus, the governor of Upper Germany, and induced the Senate to grant him the title of Caesar (a recognition of his membership in the imperial family), together with the tribunician and proconsular powers. The Emperor-elect was a Spaniard, from the Roman-citizen colony of Italica. He was over forty years old, and had already held the consulship, as well as a number of appointments in the provinces. His military talent was of the highest order, and he was a man of firm but kindly character. In all, it would probably have been impossible to have found a person better fitted to command the friendship of the Senate on the one hand, and the support of the armies on the other.

### *Trajan (98–117 A.D.)*

Three months after the adoption, Nerva died, and Trajan succeeded to the vacant office without trouble. The task which confronted him was twofold: he must reduce the internal government of the state to order, and settle a series of vexing frontier problems inherited from his last two predecessors. These problems included bickerings with the German tribes east of the Rhine, the menace of the Dacian Kingdom along the lower Danube, and unrest among the Parthians and their satellite states in the East.

### *Domestic and Provincial Government*

The more pressing internal problems were quickly disposed of. Summoning the leaders of the recent Praetorian mutiny to his camp on the Rhine, Trajan had them summarily executed. For the next ninety years the Guard gave no more trouble. Not until more than a year after his accession did he visit Rome, but when he did, his frank and unassuming character made him immediately popular. Carefully humoring the senators, he secured from them a mandate to right the worst abuses in the senatorial provinces — a task at which he worked during the remainder of his reign in the intervals of freedom from military duties.

We are fortunate in being able to secure an intimate view of this process in the case of one of the most corruptly governed provinces of Nerva's reign — Bithynia. To it he sent Gaius Plinius Secundus, known to modern scholars as Pliny the Younger. From the official correspondence of Trajan and Pliny one can see the problems that beset both Emperor and governor. Cities spent enormous sums on public works so poorly constructed as to be useless. Municipal funds were lent to individuals who "forgot" to repay them. Lawsuits for interpretations of the provincial charter and a host of details were reported at once to Trajan with requests for his advice or decision. In many cases the Emperor immediately authorized Pliny to act as he saw fit. In every instance, we find the governor

*Bettmann*

RELIEFS ON THE ARCH OF TRAJAN

meticulously careful of the welfare of his charges, and inordinately timid about acting on his own initiative. As a whole, the picture of Roman provincial government is a favorable one indeed.

From this correspondence comes one of our earliest accounts of the persecution of the Christians. When Pliny arrived in Bithynia, there were already so many Christians in the province that temples were neglected and sacrifices were not regularly performed. He issued an edict reminding the people that the new religion was illegal, and at once accusations (many of them anonymous) began to pour in. Suspects were arrested, and to discover the nature of Christian beliefs he examined them, sometimes under torture. He found no evidence of actual wrongdoing, but only what he describes as "an absurd and excessive superstition," which included the worship of Christ as a god, and pledges to refrain from evil conduct. Persons arrested were asked to sacrifice to the state gods, to curse Christ, and to sacrifice before a statue of Trajan. If they did this, they were released, for it was well known that no Christian would perform these acts. Those who refused were warned of the consequences, and if they persisted, were executed, "because, I was persuaded, whatever the nature of their opinions, a rebellious and inflexible obstinacy deserved correction." [1] Trajan in answer laid down a rule that was to govern the relations of the Roman government to the Christians for nearly a hundred and forty years. No effort was to be made to seek out Christians, he said, and no attention was to be paid to anonymous accusations. If a person were accused in due form, he was to be given an opportunity to clear himself by the procedure which Pliny had used, and if he did so, he was to be freed, regardless of his past conduct. If he refused, he was to be punished. While this rule made persecution of the Christians possible at any time, it also made certain that there would rarely if ever be a general persecution so long as it was in force.

Economic conditions in Italy had become alarming, and as a result, population was on the decline. A permanent measure of relief (apparently begun under Nerva) was put into effect under Trajan. A large sum was drawn from the treasury and lent in small amounts to poor landowners, who were to pay interest at 5 per cent. (The usual rate was 12 per cent.) This interest was to be paid to the debtor's native municipality, which was to use it to subsidize poor parents with large families to support. The plan was later extended by private bequests to the municipalities as well as by further imperial grants. Trajan also repaired the Italian roads, and extended the Appian Way southward from Capua to Brundisium. A new harbor was constructed at the mouth of the Tiber to supplement that already built by Claudius, and several other coast towns were similarly favored. In Rome itself a lavish building program was carried out, including the great Forum of Trajan, and better provision was made for the food supply. Magnificent shows and gifts of cash delighted the populace.

### *Trajan's Wars*

But Trajan was above all a warrior, and the times afforded him ample scope for his talents. The German tribes along the Rhine had already felt the weight of his hand at the beginning of his reign, and thereafter they gave no more trouble. But Decebalus of Dacia was becoming increasingly aggressive, and was even attempting to form an alliance with the Parthi-

[1] *Letters*, X, 97.

ans. Furthermore, he had inflicted upon the Romans defeats which were still unavenged. Hence, in 101, Trajan set out to deal with him decisively. In two campaigns he invaded Dacia, defeated its king in battle, and penetrated to his capital. Decebalus sued for peace, and Trajan, willing to make a last effort to conciliate him, granted it upon hard conditions. Decebalus became a Roman client, surrendered his implements of war and Roman deserters, destroyed his fortifications, and received a garrison of legionaries in his capital. Yet even then he would not remain quiet, and by 105 he had provoked another war. This time Trajan saw that only the conquest of Dacia would settle the dispute. Building a stone bridge across the Danube (of which the ruins still exist), he once more invaded the enemy's country. By the autumn of 106, he had beaten down opposition, driven Decebalus and his principal nobles to suicide, and thoroughly occupied the Dacian plateau. In the conquered land he organized a province which was to remain in Roman possession until about 270. As the land had been almost depopulated by the wars, thousands of colonists from the Danubian provinces and Asia Minor crowded in to acquire lands, and Latin soon became the spoken language. So thoroughly was the work of Romanization done that to this day the inhabitants of the region — the modern Rumanians — speak a language of Latin origin. The rich gold and silver mines of Dacia became imperial property, and these, together with the captured treasure of Decebalus, furnished Trajan with the funds needed for other enterprises. In Rome a huge memorial column was erected in the Forum of Trajan to signalize the conquest, and on its surface was carved a spiral band of relief running from bottom to top, telling the story of the Dacian wars in pictorial form.

It was on the eastern frontier that Trajan was destined to have his last war, in which he had only partial success. During the early years of his reign the East had remained quiet, the only event of note being his annexation of the Kingdom of the Nabatean Arabs, a small state south of the Dead Sea. But, in 113, the Parthian question flared up again, when these eastern neighbors tried to depose the King of Armenia and set up their own nominee in his place. For Trajan this was enough. He set out for the East, intending to settle this dispute as decisively as he had that in Dacia.

At first he carried all before him. By the end of 114, he had occupied Armenia, which he made a province, and the region immediately southwest of it, which became the province of Mesopotamia. The next year he descended the Tigris-Euphrates Valley, took the Parthian capitals of Seleucia and Ctesiphon, and followed the rivers to their mouths. East of

*Bettmann*

TRAJAN
*98–117 A.D.*

the Tigris he organized the province of Assyria. Thus far he had experienced little opposition, although he had made greater conquests than any previous Roman general in this area. However, at this point his good fortune deserted him. Even while he was in Babylonia, the Parthians had invaded Mesopotamia, where they stirred up a dangerous revolt and annihilated a Roman detachment. Trajan's lieutenants put down this movement, but other troubles came thick and fast. From Britain and other parts of the West came news of invasion and unrest. The Jews chose this moment to rise in revolt in Cyrene, Egypt, Palestine, and other provinces in which they were found in large numbers, and massacred many thousands of their Gentile neighbors. To crown the other misfortunes, Trajan was stricken with paralysis. Beaten at last by this concourse of mishaps, he started to return to Italy, but he never arrived. On August 9, 117, he breathed his last at Selinus, a city in Cilicia.

Trajan's last campaign had come very near to failure, and had put the resources of the Empire under a severe strain. Even so, he had been one of Rome's greatest emperors. His conquest of Dacia was a real service to the Empire, and its effects were to be felt for a long time. At home he had founded and strengthened a regime of peace and order which was to outlast his death by many years. Centuries later, when the senators wished to pray for all possible blessings for a new emperor, they would ask that he be "More fortunate than Augustus, and better than Trajan."

## HADRIAN (117–138 A.D.)

The Emperor's death revealed once more a glaring weakness in the Roman Principate. Trajan was childless, and up to the very end had made no provision for the succession. Only quick thinking and resolute action saved the Empire from a repetition of the civil wars of 68–69. He had a cousin, Publius Aelius Hadrianus, to whom he had entrusted several important posts in the civil and military services, and who at the time of Trajan's death was governor of Syria. Immediately it was given out that Trajan had on his deathbed adopted Hadrian. Later gossip had it that Trajan's wife Plotina had fabricated the story of the adoption, and assigned her the most dishonorable motives. But Plotina was a woman of too high a character to be guilty of base acts, and even if the adoption was fraudulent, it certainly saved countless lives and prevented untold suffering and destruction. Whether genuine or not, the adoption served its purpose. Hadrian's troops at once saluted him as Emperor, and by a little tactful manipulation he secured recognition from the Senate. The crisis passed, and the new reign began peacefully.

### *Character, Problems, and Policies*

In many respects, Hadrian was the opposite of his predecessor. At the time of his accession he was forty-one years old. While well versed in military science and a brave soldier, he loved peace, and fought only when compelled to do so. His chief interest was statesmanship — the organization of government and the development of law. Yet this was only one aspect of a many-sided character. He had been thoroughly educated in both Greek and Latin letters, and had an insatiable curiosity about the lands and peoples over which he ruled. Never before or after him did Rome have an emperor who visited so many parts of the Empire. His physical strength and energy were tireless, leading him to travel bareheaded and in all kinds of weather over thousands of miles of land and sea.

Beneath a tactful and pleasing exterior lay an imperious and masterful will, which insisted upon having its own way in everything. In his old age sickness and suffering were said to have made him cruel and bloodthirsty, but of this there is no decisive proof.

The Empire was, at his accession, in a critical condition. Trajan's Parthian War had drained its available man-power, and had imposed heavy burdens upon the people. It was time to abandon the policy of conquest, and to allow both land and people an opportunity to recuperate. Hence, Hadrian fearlessly surrendered the new provinces won by Trajan in his Parthian War, gave the Armenians another vassal-king, and made peace with Parthia. Once more, the Roman boundary stood at the Euphrates River and the Syrian Desert. But Trajan's work was not wholly undone. The Parthians had had a lesson which kept them quiet for nearly forty years. Dacia was not abandoned, for it already contained thousands of Roman settlers, was strategically an asset to the Empire, and economically profitable.

At home the abandonment of Trajan's policy of conquest produced a serious conspiracy, headed by Lusius Quietus, an old friend and former officer of the dead Emperor. He, with three other men of consular rank and a number of lesser figures, planned to assassinate Hadrian, but the plot was exposed before it had gone far, and its four chiefs were condemned to death in Hadrian's absence by a decree of the Senate (118).

### *Travels, Provincial Government, and War*

The world knows Hadrian chiefly for his travels about the Empire, and certainly no other emperor ever traveled so much on other than military business. In two tours (121–126 and 128–133), he visited practically every province, inspected army camps and frontier defenses, and personally investigated the workings of provincial government, with tireless energy. His style of travel was simple and unaffected, for he did not want to be a burden to the provincials. In fact, now that military expenses were reduced to a minimum, he had money to spend upon provincial public works, and did so without stint. Large numbers of provincial cities received from him temples, public baths, aqueducts, amphitheaters, or other testimonials of his regard. Along with government business, he had time to indulge his interest in countries and peoples. Twice he essayed mountain climbing, ascending Mt. Casius in Syria, and Mt. Etna in Sicily, in both cases to enjoy the view from their summits. In his love of the grand and sublime aspects of nature, he stood almost alone in the ancient world. At Athens, he was initiated into the Eleusinian Mysteries, held the archonship, added a whole new quarter to the city, and adorned the older sections of Athens with public buildings.

Above all, Hadrian's policy was one of peace, and with few exceptions he was able to maintain it throughout his reign. After a few minor barbarian raids had disturbed Britain, he reorganized the defense of the northern frontier of the province, fortifying it with a stone wall running from sea to sea. In Mauretania, he personally led a punitive expedition against the free natives because of their raids into the province. The Jewish revolt at the beginning of his reign was quickly put down, although the Jewish problem remained to plague his later years, and to end in a frightful catastrophe.

In 130, while passing through Judea, he noticed that Jerusalem had not been rebuilt after its destruction by Titus.[1] He decided to found on its site a Roman colony, for which he designated the name *Aelia Capitolina*, and to place a temple of Jupiter on the site of the Temple of Yahweh. Led by a professed Messiah (*Bar Cochiba* or "The Son of the Star"), the Jews began a savage rebellion, which ended with the slaughter of five hundred and eighty thousand rebels, the utter depopulation of the country, and a law forbidding Jews to enter the new colony of *Aelia Capitolina* except on a single day each year. But in spite of their rebellion, the surviving Jews still enjoyed freedom of worship.

The army was not neglected, in spite of the prevailing peace. Discipline and equipment were carefully maintained. A new system of recruiting for the legions seems to date from Hadrian's reign, whereby the Empire was divided into enlistment districts, each of which had to supply recruits for the legions stationed within it. The step ultimately had important political consequences, but these did not become apparent until much later. To the existing legions and auxiliary formations he added bands of irregular soldiers of provincial or barbarian origin, who were commanded by their own chiefs and armed with the weapons of their native districts. Such bodies were called *numeri*, and were to grow in importance in the following reigns.

Provincial government continued to be honest, efficient, and liberal in character. Grants of Latin rights to provincial municipalities were frequent, and they were likewise allowed to receive bequests from private persons. From this source many of them were later to build up substantial endowments for the performance of various services to their citizens free of charge. Members of municipal councils were exempted from capital

[1] Chapter 21.

*Bettmann*

HADRIAN
*117–138 A.D.*

punishment in all but the most extreme cases. With the cessation of Trajan's wars and the removal of the burdens caused by them, prosperity blossomed in most of the Empire, particularly in North Africa where the reclamation and settlement of lands formerly barren received a strong impetus.

*Domestic Government, Administration, and Law*

In Italy the system of aid to dependent children (*alimenta*) was extended. The administration of justice was likewise improved by the appointment of four circuit judges (*consulares juridici*) of senatorial rank, each of whom was to hear and decide cases in one of the four districts into which Italy was divided. As a supplement to the reform of the judiciary went a reform of the law. Up to this time it had been customary for each praetor when entering office to issue an edict stating the laws which he meant to enforce and the procedure which he would follow. In practice, however, each praetor had tended to copy the edicts of his predecessors, and Hadrian, with the consent of the Senate, appointed the jurist Salvius Julianus to draw up a permanent edict, binding upon all future praetors. Thereafter legal reforms would have to be made by the Emperor, the Senate, or by new interpretations given to existing laws by the jurists, and the legislative power was confined either to the Emperor or to agencies which he could control. As a legislator Hadrian was very active, covering a large number of subjects. His work is marked by lenience and common sense, and it was not without reason that when Roman law was finally codified, his laws were the oldest to be included in the codes.

An even more revolutionary step was taken in the organization of the administrative bureaucracy. We have seen how this corps of officials originated under Augustus and Claudius. But the latter had left the "cabinet" offices in the hands of freedmen; and they continued, with occasional exceptions, to be held by this class until Hadrian's accession. There were grave objections to this condition; for slavery was hardly a state calculated to train a man in honesty or self-respect, and the Roman aristocracy felt humiliated in having to show deference to these powerful but socially inferior officials. Hadrian revolutionized his administrative staff completely. All important non-senatorial offices were thereafter to go to equestrians, and the imperial service was so organized as to offer this class an attractive and lucrative career. Before that time no equestrian could hold one of the higher posts without performing military service — a fact which rendered a government career unpopular with many persons. As a substitute for military service, Hadrian instituted the office of *advocatus fisci* (prosecutor in suits brought by the treasury). After holding it a young equestrian was eligible to procuratorships of various grades, and in the end might aspire to one of the three great prefectures — of the Praetorian Guard, of the Watch, or of Egypt. These were equal in importance to any office within the reach of a senator. Salaries were of four classes — 60,000, 100,000, 200,000, or 300,000 sesterces a year. To add dignity to the equestrian career, a series of new titles were devised. Just as a senator was addressed as *vir clarissimus* ("Most Famous Man") so an equestrian was *vir egregius* ("Excellent Man"), and when he held an office he was addressed as *vir prefectissimus* or *vir eminentissimus*. With such a staff of well-educated, loyal, and self-respecting civil servants, the Emperor was in a position to supervise all phases of government much more closely than any of his predecessors. Yet the reform contained the germs of evil as well as good. Eventually (in the third and fourth centuries) this bureaucratic staff was to become so powerful as to get out of hand, oppressing the people and flouting the commands of the emperors.

With the Senate collectively and the aristocracy as individuals Hadrian tried to preserve good relations. Its prerogatives (which were scanty enough after two centuries of encroachment by emperors) were carefully respected, and he left to it exclusive jurisdiction over its own members. When in Rome he attended its meetings, consulted it on all important matters, and had legislation promulgated by senatorial decrees rather than by his own. Few if any offices formerly held by its members were taken from them by his equestrian staff; and they were treated as social equals, without offensive formalities. But somehow Hadrian never fully conciliated the aristocracy, and after his death it required strong efforts by his successor to prevent a senatorial decree of condemnation against him and to secure his official deification.

### *The Last Years*

Not until 134 did advancing age compel Hadrian to desist from the more strenuous activities which had occupied him since his accession. Then he built a magnificent villa at the picturesque suburban town of Tibur, equipped it elegantly, and adorned it with art treasures. However, his old age was not destined to be happy. His last two years were tormented by an illness so painful that he sought in vain for a means of suicide to end his sufferings. By 137, he was barely able to attend to routine business, and death was obviously not far off.

In these last days, it was imperative that he provide for the succession. From the first, he seems to have intended to have as his ultimate successor a young man of senatorial family and Spanish descent, Marcus Annius Verus. But in 136, when the first steps were taken to deal with the problem, Verus was only fifteen years old, and therefore a conscientious guardian would be needed to hold the place for him until he was grown up. Hadrian's first choice for the position was a peculiar one. For unknown reasons he selected Lucius Ceionius Commodus, a man of poor health and light character, whom he adopted, and for whom he secured the tribunician power and proconsular imperium. After his adoption Commodus

*Brown Brothers*

HADRIAN'S TOMB

*(Now known as the Castel' Sant' Angelo)*

bore the name Lucius Aelius Caesar, and *Caesar* from that time forward was the title regularly given to the heir-apparent to the Principate. To protect the interests of Verus Hadrian caused him to be betrothed to the daughter of Aelius Caesar. But the arrangement was not destined to stand unchanged for long. On January 1, 138, the Caesar died, leaving a young son, Lucius Verus. This time Hadrian acted with vigor and good sense. He now adopted as his son Titus Fulvius Boionius Aurelius Antoninus, an uncle by marriage of Marcus Verus, and a man without sons of his own. To Antoninus now went the title of Caesar and the powers which had belonged to the dead Aelius Caesar. Turning the administration of the government over to Antoninus, Hadrian retired to the Campanian coast, where he died on July 10, 138. Rome was to have other emperors of outstanding merit, but few of them were to display the wisdom, energy, and creative ability which had been his.

## The Antonines (138–180 A.D.)

### *Antoninus Pius (138–161)*

After so colorful a reign as that of Hadrian, the twenty-three years in which Antoninus Pius (138–161) held the Principate seems almost a blank. He was fifty-two years old at his accession, and had held a number of important offices under preceding emperors, both at Rome, in Italy, and in the provinces. He was a quiet, good-natured person, solid rather than brilliant, with the best of intentions and common sense enough to translate them into measures for the welfare of the state. During his entire reign he seems not to have stirred out of Italy, and usually lived in or near Rome. He had no military ambitions, and was content to leave the framework of government much as he had taken it over from Hadrian.

His whole reign was one of peace, disturbed only by a small border war in northern Britain and a few unimportant provincial rebellions. None of these called for much exertion, and all were handled by provincial gov-

*Bettmann*

ANTONINUS PIUS

*138–161 A.D.*

ernors. His relations with the Senate were uniformly friendly. Everywhere prosperity seemed to smile, and no great misfortunes befell either him or the state. Thus matters continued to the end of his life.

A constant factor in this reign from beginning to end was the steady rise of Marcus Annius Verus — now Marcus Aurelius Antoninus Caesar. Before Hadrian's death Antoninus had adopted him, and soon after he was betrothed to Antoninus' daughter Faustina. In 145 they were married, and the next year Marcus Aurelius received the tribunician and proconsular powers. Thereafter until the death of his adopted father he participated in the government of the Empire, serving a sort of apprenticeship in the place which he was to fill. During Pius' lifetime he held two consulships, and had entered upon a third one. At the same time Lucius Verus was adopted and given two consulships, but otherwise he remained undistinguished. When the old Emperor died, on March 7, 161, Marcus Aurelius already held the most important imperial prerogatives, and easily acquired the rest.

### *Marcus Aurelius: Accession and Coregency with Lucius Verus*

Marcus Aurelius Antoninus (161–180) is one of history's finest characters. Mentally he was not brilliant, and his health was poor. But he was a man of lofty ideals, utter unselfishness, and steadfast purpose, who with the aid of his own very modest talents carried the Empire safely through nearly twenty years of frightful disaster and tremendous stress. From his early youth he had studied philosophy, and a philosopher he remained to the end of his days. But although he preferred a life of quiet study and ascetic self-denial, he was ready at the call of duty to plan campaigns, to lead armies to victory, to spend weary hours hearing lawsuits, and to attend meetings of the Senate or of his private council. He was very careful to avoid laying unnecessary burdens upon the people, and was constantly solicitous for their welfare. Even the gladiators were protected during his reign by a law compelling them to fight with blunted weapons. At intervals in his busy career, he jotted down in Greek a book of meditations, which in ancient times went under the name *To Himself*, and which is still extant. In it we see this pagan Emperor searching his innermost soul, pondering the nature of good and evil, studying the riddle of the universe, recording the virtues of his relatives and associates, and acknowledging his debt of gratitude to them. It is with a start that we realize that such thoughts were recorded at spare moments in a hard-fought campaign against the barbarians north of the Danube.

The new reign opened with an unexpected act on the part of Marcus Aurelius. On his own motion, and contrary to the arrangements made by Antoninus Pius, he secured for his adopted brother Lucius Verus the same titles and powers which he enjoyed except that of *pontifex maximus*. The act had unfortunate consequences, for Verus was a happy-go-lucky person of light morals and no great ability. But for the eight years that their joint rule lasted (161–169), Marcus Aurelius shielded his brother's reputation, promoted his interests, and tolerated his shortcomings. In spite of their dissimilar characters, they lived in complete harmony, and in 163 Verus married Marcus' daughter Lucilla.

### *Wars and Pestilence*

Hardly had the new Emperors taken over their powers, when the long era of prosperity was broken by a series of dreadful calamities, of which the first was a new Parthian war. In 162, Vologeses III of Parthia invaded Armenia, defeated a Roman relieving force, and slew its commander. Marcus Aurelius sent the incapable Verus to act as titular commander-in-chief in the East, but he himself worked out a plan of campaign and sent along a group of the best generals in the Empire. Although the armies seem to have fallen into such disorder during the reign of Antoninus, that the Parthians at one time invaded Syria, the enemy was now forced back, and in 164, their capitals of Seleucia and Ctesiphon were taken and destroyed. Two years later a Roman invasion of Media forced the Parthians to sue for peace, which was granted on terms that gave the Romans some territory in the upper Tigris-Euphrates Valley. The eastern frontier was safe, and Verus returned to celebrate with his adopted brother and colleague a magnificent triumph.

The victory brought little joy. In the East the Roman army had become infected with a frightful epidemic disease, which soon spread through the Empire. It raged intermittently until 180, its last known victim being Marcus Aurelius himself. At least one fourth of the population of the Empire, both soldier and civilian, died, and in many localities its ravages were never repaired. In fact, it is practically certain that it dealt the Empire a blow from which as a whole it never recovered. At the same time, crop failures for several successive years brought famine to parts of Italy.

Plague and famine were not the only misfortunes. A formidable war broke out on the Danube, which was to last until after the end of the reign. Under the leadership of the Marcomanni and Quadi, two German tribes along the northern bank, a coalition was formed which included peoples all the way from the source of the Danube to the Black Sea. In 167, the forces of the coalition crossed the river, overran Rhaetia, Noricum, and Pannonia, and before the end of the year were besieging the city of Aquilea in northeastern Italy. Another wave swept into Dacia, where it did terrible damage.

Marcus Aurelius met the crisis with unflinching courage and tireless energy. In true Roman fashion he began by conciliating the gods, but this was only a preliminary. To spare his suffering people further financial burdens, he raised money for the war by auctioning off palace furniture, art treasures, and even part of the imperial wardrobe. New legions were organized by enrolling volunteers, slaves, gladiators, and criminals. In 168, both Emperors were at the front, and before the end of the year, the enemy had been driven from northern Italy and Pannonia. In January, 169, as Marcus Aurelius and his brother were returning to Rome, Lucius Verus died suddenly, but the circumstance was rather an advantage than otherwise. As soon as the funeral was over, Marcus Aurelius was back at the front, and step by step, with indomitable persistence and in the face of several serious setbacks, he pushed the enemy back across the Danube. By 172, this part of his task was completed, but he did not stop there. If the provinces were to be safe in the future, punishment must be meted out to these disturbers of the peace. So the Roman armies crossed the Danube and attacked the Germans and Sarmatians in their own country. With grim determination, the Philosopher-Emperor ravaged their lands, defeated them in pitched battles, and broke their power. The Marcomanni submitted first, followed by the Quadi and the Sarmatians. One hundred and sixty thousand captives taken in the Roman provinces were released (although this was not nearly all that had been taken), and the barbarians were compelled to give up all of their livestock to take the place of what they had stolen. By 175, Marcus Aurelius had paved the way for the organization of a new province between the Danube, the Carpathians, and the Bohemian Forest.

### *Later Years: Rebellion, Wars, and the Coregency*

But Fortune had not yet dealt her last blow. One of his ablest officers was the Syrian, Avidius Cassius, who had distinguished himself in the Parthian War, and who for eight years had governed his native province, to which had been added Cilicia and Palestine. In 175, for unknown reasons, he revolted and had himself proclaimed Emperor. Egypt at once joined him, thus threatening the food supply of the capital. Hurriedly,

Bettmann

MARCUS AURELIUS
*161–180. A.D.*

Marcus Aurelius made peace with the Germans and Sarmatians, and set out to meet the new danger. Luckily it proved to be short-lived. After a few months' reign, Cassius was assassinated by a soldier, and the movement collapsed. The rebels were treated leniently, and after spending a year in the East, Marcus Aurelius returned to Rome. While engaged in restoring order he had lost his wife Faustina, who died while accompanying him through Asia Minor.

It was now time to secure the succession, and Marcus Aurelius, unlike any emperor since Vespasian, had a son to succeed him. The young man, Lucius Aurelius Commodus, became consul in 176, and the next year received the titles and powers which made him the full coregent of his father. He was then seventeen years of age, and Marcus Aurelius determined to give him a training for the task of government similar to that which he had himself enjoyed. For the next two years he generally accompanied Marcus Aurelius in his campaigns, and shared the credit of the victories won.

Meanwhile, the war on the Danube had broken out again in 177, and once more Marcus Aurelius took the field in person. This time he intended to carry his work to completion by erecting the province which he had planned to organize several years before. His success was as great as ever, and at the beginning of 180, it was said that another year would suffice to complete the work. But the year was not to be his. On March 17, 180, he died (probably of the plague) in his camp near the site of the present city of Vienna. With his death ended the prospect of further annexations in the Danubian area, but the power of the German tribes had been broken for many years to come. Spain had also suffered grievously from the invasion of the Moorish tribes of North Africa, but these had been repulsed by his lieutenants.

Thus, the period of the "Five Good Emperors" ended in calamity, and the Empire, about 180, presented a far from prosperous appearance. Whole provinces had been devastated, and the population had been reduced by war and pestilence. In fact, its decline had already set in, and it was not entirely due to the disasters of Marcus Aurelius' reign. In many regions its prosperity had always been more apparent than real. Italy, Egypt, and the Greek peninsula had been, for very different reasons in each case, the victims of hard times through the best days of Hadrian and Antoninus Pius. The physical vitality of several of the culture groups had been sapped, so that their numbers were declining even before the plague. The finances of the imperial government had also been in an unhealthy condition throughout this period, if we are to judge by the steady decline in the value of the coinage. Thus, at Trajan's accession the silver *denarius* contained 10 per cent of copper alloy; he raised the proportion to 15 per cent and under Marcus Aurelius it stood at 25 per cent. Gold coins held up better, but did not entirely escape debasement. Arrears of taxation accumulated to a dangerous extent under Trajan, and again under Marcus Aurelius. Even in Hadrian's reign depopulation had become so apparent that he began the practice of inviting barbarian tribes to settle on deserted lands, and Marcus Aurelius settled large numbers of his prisoners of war on tracts devastated by the plague and the invasions. Rome at the end of the period, had nearly three centuries of empire left to her, but her greatest age was over, and her decadence had begun.

# 23

****************************************************************************************************

# *The Military Monarchy and the Military Anarchy (180–285 A.D.)*

## An Age of Military Government

When Marcus Aurelius died, the Roman Empire had enjoyed two centuries of almost unbroken internal peace and order, and of real or apparent prosperity. Thereafter, it entered upon a century of steadily mounting violence and calamity, which was to culminate in the ravaging of its fields, in the depopulation of vast areas, and finally, when the storm had passed, in permanent weakness, despotism, and decadence. This century of disorder falls into two well-defined divisions, each about fifty years in length, conventionally termed the Military Monarchy (180–235) and the Military Anarchy (235–285). In the former period, the Emperors repudiated the senatorial theory of government and based their right to rule upon the consent of the army. The results were imperial assassinations, the constant spoliation of the civilian population for the benefit of the soldiers, and increased hardship and uncertainty for all except the military caste. About 235, even this system began to collapse. Civil wars increased in number and intensity, and a series of invasions from the north and east devastated the Roman world. These calamities, together with pestilence and economic bankruptcy, resulted in the almost complete prostration of the imperial government, the separation of the Western and Oriental provinces from the Empire, and the temporary occupation of wide areas by foreign enemies. At last, in the 270's and 280's, a series of able generals and administrators from the Illyrian provinces seized the imperial office, drove out the invaders, restored imperial unity, and brought back a semblance of order. Such, in brief, is the story of the calamitous era which we shall now consider in detail.

## COMMODUS (180–193)

### *Character and Problems*

Lucius Aurelius Commodus, the son and successor of Marcus Aurelius, was the first emperor since Domitian to owe his position to hereditary succession. This fact was in itself enough to offend the champions of adoptive succession, who were therefore inclined to scrutinize his acts with hostile eyes. If he had possessed tact and good sense, this enmity might perhaps have been overcome, but in these qualities Commodus was conspicuously lacking. By nature he seems to have been both amiable and easily influenced, and he had gathered about him more than the usual crowd of worthless and self-seeking courtiers and parasites. Into their hands he surrendered the conduct of government business, and from them he took advice. His own interests lay mainly in training for the profession of a gladiator (in which he engaged personally), and in a series of mistresses, some of whom acquired great influence. He was greedy of spectacular and vainglorious titles, but instead of the conventional ones he preferred such as "The Roman Hercules," or "The Victor Over a Thousand Gladiators." Like Nero (whom he greatly resembled in character), he was capable of fiendish cruelty toward real or fancied enemies. He hated the hardships of military life, and after the first few months never showed himself to the armies. Thus instead of disarming his opponents, he furnished them with ample material for criticism.

Marcus Aurelius had beaten the tribes beyond the Danube so thoroughly that a little more campaigning would have made possible the organization of their territories into a province. Commodus abandoned the attempt, and left Rome's late enemies their independence. So good an opportunity to end their depredations never came again. In October, 180, he was back in Rome, and thereafter he never traveled far from it.

### *His Quarrel with the Senate*

Before long he was at odds with the Senate. In 182, his sister laid plans for her stepson to murder him, but the plot miscarried after the young man had rushed up to him, brandishing a dagger and crying, "The Senate sends you this." From that time on, the long-disused machinery of informers, treason trials, forced suicides, executions, and confiscations was in constant use against any members of the aristocracy whom he suspected of hostile designs. Favors were showered upon his worthless satellites, and upon the Praetorians, who in return gave their support to all that Commodus and his coterie did.

For nearly thirteen years (180–193) the Roman Senate and people cowered under the terror, and endured the wild freaks or repulsive vices of their ruler. Then, like Domitian before him, he began to entertain suspicions of his immediate associates, and suspicion bred reality. One day Marcia, his favorite mistress, found that she was among a group that he intended to put to death. On the last night of the year 192, she, with the Praetorian Prefect Laetus and the Chamberlain Eclectus, assassinated him.

## THE SECOND CIVIL WAR (193–197)

### *Pertinax, Julianus, and the "Sale of the Empire"*

The slayers of Commodus hastened to provide for their own safety by choosing a successor to their victim. Their choice fell upon Publius Helvius Pertinax, an elderly senator of low birth but good character and distinguished standing. But their hopes were doomed to disappointment. Although Pertinax had many of the qualities of a good ruler, the times were against him, and he had neither the tact nor the patience to master the adverse forces. His efforts to reform the discipline of the Praetorians failed, and on March 26, 193, they mutinied, and murdered him.

Then ensued what was perhaps the most disgraceful scene in Rome's long history. The Praetorians, acting collectively, put the imperial office up for auction, and finally knocked it down to Didius Julianus, a senator of doubtful reputation. The price charged was 25,000 sesterces per man of the Guard. Julianus was accordingly hailed as Emperor. This scandal, however, was so great that he was hardly recognized outside of Italy.

### *The Contest of Severus, Albinus, and Niger*

As the news of Julianus' accession got abroad, a wave of indignation swept the frontier armies, and those of Britain, the Danubian provinces, and Syria each undertook on its own responsibility to take vengeance upon the effeminate soldiers of the Roman parade grounds. The British legions put forward their commander, Decimus Clodius Albinus, a senator of African descent but a man of old and distinguished family. The Danubian armies saluted as Emperor the governor of Upper Pannonia, Lucius Septimius Severus. Like Albinus, he was a native of Africa, but his family was of equestrian rank, and so little Romanized that some of them could hardly speak Latin. The Syrian legions conferred the same honor upon their general, Gaius Pescennius Niger, an Italian of middle-class ancestry. Once more, after a lapse of a century and a quarter, the provincial armies had undertaken to fill the imperial office; and then as earlier, the fact made civil war inevitable.

In this contest all the advantages lay with Severus, and he used them to the utmost. He had both the largest army of the three, and the one nearest to Rome. By adroit diplomacy he secured the adherence of the Rhine legions, and made an agreement with Albinus by which the latter was adopted as Severus' son and given the title of Caesar. With his rear secure, Severus then set out for Italy, which he entered in May, 193. Julianus was quickly disposed of. With no force at his disposal except the wretched Praetorians, he made no defense worthy of the name, and was slain by the men who had raised him to power. Early in June Severus entered Rome.

Posing as the avenger of Pertinax and the protector of the Senate, he easily secured senatorial confirmation of his title, and took the traditional oath not to put a senator to death by summary process. He next dealt with the Praetorians. Surrounding them with an overwhelming force of his legionaries, he roundly denounced their recent conduct, confiscated their horses and arms, and disbanded them. Their place was taken by men drawn from his own army. Pertinax was deified and honored with a public funeral.

With Italy secure and his title legitimized, Severus could now fight out his quarrel with Niger. His generals won a series of smashing victories over the Syrian legions, and by the middle of 194 Niger himself had been captured and killed. Byzantium, which had espoused the losing cause, did not surrender until 196. The eastern adherents of Niger were punished with fines, confiscations, loss of civil rights, exile, and in some cases with death.

Having secured the eastern provinces, Severus found it necessary to chastise the Parthians, who had aided Niger, incited disloyalty among the client-kings, and encroached upon Roman territory. In 194 and 195 he punished the vassal-kings by annexing enough of their lands to form the new province of Mesopotamia, and extorted a favorable treaty from the Parthians themselves. The settlement proved to be a mere truce, but at the time Severus had to abandon his eastern campaign to take in hand the case of Clodius Albinus.

The bargain struck by Severus with Albinus must, in the nature of the case, have been a mere makeshift. The former had two sons, and it must have required a certain naïveté on Albinus' part to suppose that they would be set aside for his benefit. Yet he kept his side of the bargain until late in 195, when suspicious senators seem to have brought him to a realization that Severus' next step would be to eliminate him. He then assumed the title of Augustus and crossed over into Gaul. Severus, who was still in the East, served notice of his real intentions by causing the army rather than the Senate to declare Albinus a rebel. A little later the soldiers proclaimed their Emperor's adoption as the son of Marcus Aurelius, and gave to his elder son Bassianus the name of Marcus Aurelius Antoninus, with the title of Caesar. Severus then marched westward through the Danubian provinces against Albinus. In February, 197, the two joined battle near the Gallic city of Lugdunum, with armies numbering about a hundred and fifty thousand men each. Albinus suffered a crushing defeat, and committed suicide to avoid capture. Lugdunum was sacked and destroyed.

### *The Destruction of Severus' Opponents*

Severus was now master of the whole Empire, and he proceeded with cool calculation and callous cruelty to annihilate his opponents. Contrary to his oath of 193, he executed twenty-nine senators who had taken the losing side. In Gaul, Britain, Spain, and Italy a "reign of terror" took place, the former friends of Albinus being killed or exiled and their property confiscated. As this persecution struck with particular savagery at the landed aristocrats and the urban middle class, who in previous ages had been the mainstays of Roman civilization and the chief supports of imperial patriotism in the western provinces, its effect was therefore profound and far-reaching. Nearly a decade elapsed after the battle of Lugdunum before this man-hunt was ended. The wealth acquired from confiscated property did not pass into the ordinary imperial treasury, but into the personal possession of Severus, and to care for it a new treasury — the *res privata* — was set up.

## The Dynasty of the Severi (193–235 A.D.)

### *A New Order of the Empire: Military Monarchy*

The fall of Albinus ended the opposition to Severus. He now made it plain that he intended to base his power upon the army rather than upon the Senate and the civilian population. As a final repudiation of the Stoic theory of government, in 198, he caused his elder son Marcus Aurelius Antoninus to be proclaimed co-emperor by the army, and gave to the younger, Publius Septimius Geta, the title of Caesar. As a reward for its support, the army was showered with gifts and privileges. The soldiers' pay was raised, and they were allowed to contract legal marriages while in service. In all of the great frontier camps married quarters were established, in which the men could live while not on duty. Centurions, when honorably discharged from service, automatically acquired some of the privileges of equestrians, along with the ability to transmit these privileges to their heirs. Senatorial influence in the army was sharply curtailed by the placing of equestrian prefects over some of the legions in place of senatorial *legati*, and in provincial government by the extensive use of equestrian procurators in the place of senatorial governors. Thus the army became indirectly a recruiting ground for the most influential branch of the imperial military and civil services.

The privileged position of Italy was also attacked. In addition to the new Praetorian Guard, she received a legionary garrison, which was stationed on Mt. Alba, not far from Rome. The jury-courts for the trial of civil and criminal cases were abolished, their places being taken by a Praetorian prefect acting as a judge. To this office, Severus and his successors appointed a series of Rome's greatest jurists, and as the power of legislation was now concentrated entirely in the hands of the emperors, they had a unique opportunity to reshape the whole Roman legal structure. It is to the credit of both emperors and prefects that in their hands it became better organized, more flexible, and more humane than ever before. Indeed, it was largely because of their labors that Roman law acquired its lasting value as a fountain of wisdom and justice, and that it later became so influential in the states that succeeded the Roman Empire in Western Europe.

Harsh as his treatment of certain provinces and of certain classes of provincials had been, Severus did a great deal to raise the position of the non-citizen class in general. Grants of citizenship to provincial communities were frequent, and sometimes carried with them the *Ius Italicum*, which exempted them from provincial tributes. In Egypt, the capital of each nome was made a regular municipality with a council and magistrates of its own, and jurisdiction over the lands of the nome. Africa (his native province), Syria (the home of his Empress Julia Domna), and the Danubian provinces were all highly favored and enjoyed marked prosperity. His legislation was consistently favorable to the lower classes of the provincials, whose rights were now better protected than ever before. Only in regard to taxation, forced levies, and the abuses which arose from them, was the whole Empire decidedly worse off.

In finance, the system established by Severus was marked by huge increases in both receipts and expenditures. His income had been swollen by the proceeds of his confiscations and by much higher taxes, but his military expenses were far larger than those of his predecessors, and he spent enormous sums for buildings. In the end, he was unable to meet his obligations, and further devalued the coinage, bringing the proportion of alloy in the denarius up to 50 per cent. His successors were to find still further debasements necessary, for the military monarchy was by its very nature bound to lead to ever higher and higher pay and emoluments for the soldiers, who were the real sovereigns of the state.

### *Severus' Wars: His Place in History*

Having ended the civil wars, Severus again set out (late in 197) against the Parthians. In a war lasting two years he repeated the exploits of Trajan and Lucius Verus by taking Seleucia and Ctesiphon, the latter of which he destroyed. The Roman province of Mesopotamia was now definitely organized, and the eastern boundary was everywhere settled in Rome's favor. This and subsequent defeats so damaged the prestige of the Parthian kings that the way was clearly paved for their overthrow by the Persian natives nearly thirty years later. On his way back to Rome he spent some time in Egypt, which he reorganized as we have seen. In 208 (largely to get his sons away from the temptations of life in the capital) he took his whole family and went to Britain to campaign against the natives of what is today Scotland. As a whole his success was indifferent, but he remained in Britain until his death in February, 211.

Although Severus proved himself an astute, ruthless, and successful politician, as a statesman he does not rank very high. It would seem that his chief aim in refounding the Principate upon a military basis was to make it hereditary. In so doing he brought many ills upon the Empire, and did but little good. Under his successors the quality of the army deteriorated, and the cost of maintaining it rose steadily until it became an insupportable burden. His humiliation of the Senate, which had seldom if ever checked his predecessors, did little or nothing to increase his actual power. Furthermore, dependence upon the army subjected both Emperor and people to a galling and capricious tyranny, and ultimately made it impossible either to maintain peace within or provide protection against enemies from outside the frontiers. His political creed may well be stated in his dying words to his sons, "Be harmonious, enrich the soldiers, and pay no attention to anyone else." [1]

[1] Dio Cassius, LXXVII, 15, 2.

*Caracalla (211–217)*

It had been Severus' intent to leave his power to his sons jointly, but this plan was sabotaged by their deadly hatred of each other. Marcus Aurelius Antoninus (generally known as *Caracalla*, from a Gallic garment which he liked to wear) ruled in conjunction with his brother Geta for a year, during which each sought an opportunity to remove the other. In February, 212, Caracalla inveigled Geta into a conference and murdered him. Geta's name was erased from inscriptions and state documents, and his friends were mercilessly hunted down. The great jurist Papinian, who had been Praetorian prefect in the last years of Severus, was murdered because he refused to compose a defense of the crime.

For the next five years Caracalla ruled alone, devoting himself entirely to pleasing the army. "No one should have any money but myself," he is reported to have said, "and I only want it to give to the soldiers." [1] Increased pay and privileges, together with relaxation of discipline, were their rewards for supporting his regime. He met the increased expenditures made necessary by this policy by large increases in taxation, and by reckless spoliation of the civilian population. A continuous round of prosecutions, confiscations, and executions removed all known relatives of preceding emperors and many of the senators. Those who escaped were compelled to furnish large sums for entertainments, public works, and military pay. Existing taxes were greatly increased, and in some cases (for example, the inheritance tax) they were doubled. To make all provincials liable to it, he issued a famous edict bestowing Roman citizenship upon all but a few of the free inhabitants of the Empire. This measure has been hailed as a great advance in the status of the provincials; in reality, such was not the case. The theoretical improvement of their lot was more than offset by the growth of a system of spoliation and oppression designed to satisfy the ever-growing demands of the military caste.

Practically all of Caracalla's reign was spent in warfare. In 213, he chastised the German tribes along the eastern edge of the *Agri Decumates*. From there he went to the East, where the internal dissensions of the Parthians promised to make them an easy conquest. Before attacking them, however, he went to Egypt where, for unknown reasons, he perpetrated a frightful massacre of the people of Alexandria. His Parthian campaign, while not a total failure, was but an indifferent success.

The usual fate of his kind awaited him. His Praetorian prefect, Marcus Opellius Macrinus, found that his own life was in danger, and undertook

[1] *Ibid.* LXXVIII, 10, 4.

*Bettmann*

CARACALLA
*211–217 A.D.*

to forestall the blow. On April 8, 217, Caracalla was struck down by officers whom Macrinus had incited to the deed. He was the first of a series of seventeen successive emperors to die violent deaths. Macrinus won the support of the army and succeeded his victim.

*Macrinus and Elagabalus (217–222)*

For a year the usurper was able to hold his position, and in that time he reformed some of the worst abuses of Caracalla's reign. Peace was made with the Parthians, taxes were reduced, and the Senate was once more treated with respect. But the work of the Severi had been so thoroughly done that it could not be abolished. Dynastic loyalty was strong in the army, and an opportunity to display it was not wanting. The family of the Dowager-Empress Julia Domna had been sent back to their native city of Emesa in Syria. There Julia Domna died, but she was survived by her sister Julia Maesa, who had two daughters, Julia Soemias and Julia Mammea. Soemias and Mammea were widows and each had a son. Varius Avitus, the son of Soemias, was, in 218, acting as priest of the sun-god, Elagabal, of Emesa. He was only fourteen years of age. Julia Maesa, aware of the affection of the soldiers for the house of Severus, gave out to the Syrian legions that the boy was really the illegitimate son of Caracalla. The response was immediate. Avitus was proclaimed Emperor. The soldiers deserted Macrinus, and he was soon captured and killed in June, 218, together with his son Diadumenianus, whom he had proclaimed co-emperor.

The new Emperor took the name of his alleged father, Marcus Aurelius Antoninus, adding to it the name of his god *Elagabalus*, by which he is commonly known. Since Elagabalus (218–222) was too young to rule alone, the government was in the hands of his mother and grandmother, aided by a clique of Syrian ministers. In 219, the family returned to Rome, where they were to spend the next sixteen years. Elagabalus proved to be one of the most abysmal failures in Roman history. He shocked soldiers and civilians alike by his devotion to his Syrian god, who replaced Jupiter as the head of the Roman pantheon. Weird and horrible vices were attributed to him, and he displayed a flightiness which nullified all attempts to render him popular. Low-born and corrupt companions of his debaucheries were promoted to the highest posts, and the administrative services fell into chaos. The Praetorians, who could tolerate a bloodthirsty emperor but not a psychopathic pervert, became restive. The crafty Maesa saw that the days of Elagabalus were numbered, and prepared to sacrifice him in order to save the family. Alexianus, the son of Mammea, was her next choice. In 221, when Alexianus was thirteen years old, Maesa compelled Elagabalus to adopt him, and to confer upon him the title of Caesar, with the name Marcus Aurelius Severus Alexander. To make matters certain, she gave out that Alexander also was the illegitimate son of Caracalla. Elagabalus, seeing what his relatives were planning, tried to kill his cousin, but the step only precipitated his own ruin. On March 11, 222, the Praetorians mutinied, slew Elagabalus and his mother, and proclaimed Severus Alexander Emperor.

### *Severus Alexander and the Senatorial Restoration (222–235)*

The situation which confronted Maesa and Mammea in 222, was anything but reassuring. The military monarchy had now been an established fact for twenty-five years, and its character and consequences were fully apparent. Military discipline had deteriorated to the point where the soldiers murdered any officer who tried to enforce obedience, while Caracalla alone had had to add the staggering sum of 280,000,000 sesterces a year to the military budget for increases in pay. All over the Empire the population from senators to peasants was groaning under the insolence of the soldiers, high taxes, compulsory levies of supplies, and forced services. Even the Emperor's person was not safe, for to offend these arrogant warriors meant certain assassination. It is to the credit of these Syrian women and their advisers that they saw the problem in something like its true light, and attempted to grapple with it.

Severus Alexander (222–235) is generally represented as a good-natured and conscientious ruler, but the fact is of little importance, for he was never his own master. His mother was a woman of strong and imperious will, who dominated his every move. In spite of the story told about her son's parentage, she seems to have been a woman of good morals, and her intellectual attainments were high. She was assisted by wise counsellors, of whom the Praetorian prefect Domitius Ulpianus, one of the greatest of the Roman jurists, was the chief.

The policy of Mammea and her advisers was to remove the cause of the trouble by deposing the armed forces from their position as the grantors of the imperial power, and raising the Senate once more to its former place of influence and privilege. If this could be done, then there was some reason to hope that the army might again be the servant rather than the master of the state, and that civil government might get the upper hand of military tyranny. Such a change would, as we have seen, involve no loss of power on the part of the Emperor, but would actually increase his freedom of action. However, it was a difficult and dangerous step to attempt. The army had become thoroughly class-conscious, and resented keenly the slightest diminution of its privileges, while the middle and upper classes, much as they might welcome such a restoration of civilian government, were discouraged and unwarlike. Above all, it could be carried out only by a strong and clever Emperor, and Severus Alexander never possessed the necessary qualities. Nevertheless, his regents made the attempt, and in spite of their handicaps, they probably came surprisingly near to success.

Their first step was to purge the Senate of unworthy members, and to replace them with worthy and substantial men. As the praetorian prefects were now primarily judicial officers, it was enacted that they might be senators, and a number of Roman municipal offices were thrown open to men of senatorial rank. The imperial cabinet ministers were now senators instead of equestrians, and imperial decrees were submitted before publication to a council composed of twenty jurists and fifty senators. But although the senatorial aristocracy hailed these steps with delight, the new policy did not increase their power. Indeed, it was about this time that Ulpian claimed absolute power for his master in the famous sentence, "Whatever pleases the Prince has the force of law." [1]

It was one thing to revive an old political theory, and quite another to secure its acceptance by the headstrong and mutinous military arm. The soldiers grew more and more obstreperous under the weak rule of a boy and two women. The government found it necessary to extort supplies for army use from civilians as mercilessly as ever. Septimius Severus had, as we have seen, allowed soldiers to marry and set up households while in the service. Alexander completed the immobilization of the frontier armies by granting to each man a plot of ground near the post in which he was stationed, on the condition that he defend it from invaders. They were now little better than hereditary frontier militia. Military discipline reached something like an irreducible minimum. The army in Mesopotamia murdered its commander Flavius Heracleo, who tried to discipline it, and when the historian Dio Cassius tightened the discipline of the Pannonian armies, the Praetorians demanded his dismissal from office. Later on, when Dio was consul for the second time, Alexander warned him that it would be dangerous for him to remain in Rome during his term of office because of their dislike of him. Ulpian himself was murdered during a mutiny of the Praetorians, and his slayers could not be punished openly. It was under these conditions that Alexander found it necessary to repel a series of invasions from the north and east.

One of the vassal-states in the loosely knit Parthian Kingdom was the Kingdom of Persia, where lived the national group whose ancestors had once ruled western Asia. Its royal family bore the name of Sassanids, and after 208, their head was Ardashir, who later changed his name to Artaxerxes. In 227, he took advantage of the weakness of his Parthian suzerains to overthrow them and to found the Neo-Persian Kingdom. This was more than a political revolution, for with it went the revival of the Zoroastrian faith. As usual in the Orient, the new ruler at once set out upon a career of conquest, which aimed at nothing less than the repossession of all lands once ruled by the Persian Empire. In 230, he invaded the Roman province of Mesopotamia and threatened Syria. Two years later Alexander made a strenuous effort to deal with the upstart, but succeeded only in checking him for the moment. Thus opened the duel between Rome and the Sassanid Kingdom which was to last four centuries.

[1] *Digest*, I, 4, 1.

From the East, Alexander and Mammea were called away to meet other perils in the West. The German tribes along the Rhine had taken advantage of Rome's Persian war to invade Gaul and the *Agri Decumates*. In 234, Alexander and Mammea arrived on the scene, and made the mistake of attempting to buy off the invaders. For the Rhenish legions this was an unpardonable offense. Early in 235, under the leadership of a Thracian officer named Gaius Julius Verus Maximinus, they mutinied and killed the Emperor and his mother. Both the real and pretended members of the House of Severus were now extinct, and the attempt of its last member to effect a senatorial restoration seemed to have failed.

## The Military Anarchy (235–285 A.D.)

### *Maximinus and the Revolution of 238 A.D.*

With the revolution of 235, there began a half-century of disorder and calamity worse than any that the Roman world had yet seen. Its characteristics have been outlined, but we must now follow the dismal story on a more extensive scale. It is to this period that the name "Military Anarchy" is applied, because one of its most prominent features was the disorderly condition of the army.

At the outset, it appeared that the death of Severus Alexander had done no more than insure the continuation of the Military Monarchy and the supremacy of the army. Maximinus, the leader of the rebellion, became Emperor, and soon gained recognition everywhere. His elevation was itself a revolutionary step, for he was not a senator, and probably never applied to the Senate for recognition. He was a true product of the Severan army — brave, capable, and energetic, but also ignorant, brutal, and thoroughly disdainful of unwarlike civilians. Over the army his influence was boundless, and he led it to a series of brilliant victories against the Germans along the Rhine and the Danube. Road-building and repair were pushed resolutely, but in his civil government Maximinus was little better than a barbarian. Senators were removed from most of the high administrative posts. His agents, in their efforts to raise funds for his campaigns, spared neither rich nor poor. "Every day," says a contemporary historian, "one might see persons, who had the day before been among the richest, begging for alms." [1] Not merely the property of individuals, but the corporate funds of the municipalities, were confiscated without pity. Executions, often with a fiendish refinement of cruelty, were becoming

[1] Herodian, VII, 3.

*Bettmann*

MAXIMINUS
*235–238 A.D.*

horribly common, the victims being in some cases guilty of nothing worse than friendship with the preceding emperor.

Three years of such tyranny brought the sufferings of the civilian population to the saturation point and produced a violent reaction. In Africa a group of young aristocrats, threatened with the loss of their estates by a zealous imperial procurator, gathered their supporters and slew their tormentor. They next hailed as Emperor their aged proconsul, Marcus Antonius Gordianus. Gordian at once took his son of the same name for co-emperor, and applied to the Senate for confirmation of his title. It responded with approval of the two new Emperors, and appointed a committee of twenty of its members to supervise the defense of Italy against Maximinus. In a few weeks, however, the Gordians were attacked by the governor of Numidia, who totally defeated their untrained followers and killed Gordian II. Gordian I took his own life.

There now began a short but brilliant resurrection of senatorial power which was a striking tribute to the completeness of its renovation by Alexander and his advisers. On hearing of the fall of the Gordians, the Senate promptly nominated two members of the Committee of Twenty — Marcus Pupienus Maximus and Decimus Calvinus Balbinus — Emperors in their places, with a grandson of Gordian I as Caesar. Letters were sent to all the provincial governors, ordering them to renounce their allegiance to the Tyrant. Maximinus was in Pannonia, and he hastened to invade northern Italy, but the Committee of Twenty did its work brilliantly. Ravaging the countryside in the path of the invader and fortifying the towns, it reduced Maximinus and his army to starvation. Brought to bay under the walls of Aquilea, he attempted to storm the town; but the attack was a failure. Then his own soldiers mutinied and slew him. Pupienus and Balbinus were everywhere recognized, and for the moment the Senate enjoyed far more prestige than it had had at any time in the three preceding centuries.

This civilian reaction against military rule was short-lived. The real difficulty, which was the class-consciousness of the soldiery, had not been removed, and could not be. On July 9, 238, the Praetorians murdered Pupienus and Balbinus, and hailed Gordian III as sole Emperor. The slain men had reigned less than a hundred days in all, and their death showed that the soldiers were again the arbiters of the Empire. Yet the revolution had not been entirely fruitless. For over twenty years thereafter, no emperor dared to flout the Senate as the earlier Severi and Maximinus had done. A tacit division of power was in effect, by which the army nominated emperors and the Senate confirmed them. In fact, the compromise had the worst features of both systems, for it irritated the army but did not protect the civilian population from outrage and spoliation. Thus the overthrow of Maximinus merely added to the confusion that was engulfing the Empire.

### *Calamity, Invasion, and Disunion*

Calamities now fell thick and fast. Along the northern frontier the "sea" of barbarian peoples which had always threatened to engulf the civilized world now began to pound ceaselessly at the weakened defenses of the Empire. A tremendous unrest agitated the population of northern Europe and Asia from the Rhine eastward to the border of China, and nearly all the civilized peoples felt the strain. No longer did the Germans assail the Roman provinces in small bands. Huge confederacies came into existence, each one composed of many tribes — the Franks and the Alemanni on the Rhine and upper Danube, together with the Goths, Burgundians, and other groups in the regions farther east. It was said that one of these confederacies alone could put into the field 40,000 cavalry and 80,000 infantry, while the mixed host that assailed the Balkan provinces in 268 was believed to number 320,000 men. These figures, it is true, represent mere guesswork on the part of contemporary Greek and Roman writers, but the actual strength of the attackers must have been very great indeed. One invasion followed another in quick succession for a generation or more, and each wrought frightful destruction. Cities were sacked and destroyed, fields were swept clean of crops and livestock; and enormous numbers of provincials were massacred, carried off into slavery, or died of famine and disease. Gaul, Spain, northern Italy, the Balkan provinces, and Asia Minor all felt the scourge. In the East the Persians also devastated Syria and part of Asia Minor. As if Rome's sufferings from the invasions were not enough, a pestilence raged unchecked through the Empire for fifteen years, so that at one time 5000 persons were dying every day in the capital alone. Economic prostration followed such paralyzing blows as a matter of course, and long before the end of the period the coinage had become practically worthless pewter washed with silver.

Under the stress of these crushing disasters the unity of the Empire at length gave way. In each region civilians and soldiers alike demanded protection from the spoilers, and when they found that the emperors could not be everywhere at once, they revolted and set up emperors of their own. Each revolt only aggravated the evil, for it meant that the pretender whom it had established would have to collect money to pay a donative to his soldiers, and then to fight a civil war with the legitimate emperor. If the pretender won, he would then have to assume the protection of the whole frontier as his predecessor had done, with revolts in other regions as an inevitable consequence. If he lost, his supporters would suffer punishment. In any case, he was almost certain to be murdered by discontented soldiers before he had reigned long, and the forces which should have repelled the invaders were frittered away in fruitless and fratricidal strife.

### *Ten Emperors in Fifteen Years*

Thus Gordian III (238–244) was succeeded by Philip the Arab (244–249), Philip by Decius (249–251), Decius by Trebonian Gallus (251–253),

Gallus by Aemilianus (253), and Aemilianus by Valerian (253–260). If one adds the four emperors who rose and fell in the disastrous year 238, ten men held the Purple between the outbreak of the Gordian Revolt and the accession of Valerian, a period of only fifteen years. This represents only those who gained general recognition, and does not include either unsuccessful pretenders or sons of emperors invested with nominal powers.

*Germanic and Persian Invasions*

Of these evils, foreign invasion was the most pressing and immediate. The northern frontier was unsettled all through the 240's, but not until 251 was it disastrously broken. A Gothic chief named Kniva ravaged Dacia, crossed the Danube, and laid waste both Moesia and Thrace. Marcianopolis, the metropolis of Moesia, was sacked and destroyed and Philippopolis, the capital of Thrace, shared its fate after being betrayed by a treacherous provincial governor. When the Emperor Decius attempted to repel the invaders, treacherous subordinates lured him to his death in a battle near the Danube Delta. His successor, who was accused of having been a party to his destruction, bribed the barbarians to withdraw, and allowed them to take with them both plunder and captives. Two years later they suffered a slight setback when they again invaded Lower Moesia, and thereafter shifted their operations to Asia Minor. Seizing a fleet from the Greek cities of the northern coast of the Black Sea, they carried their ravages as far as the Aegean coast of the peninsula. These inroads were several times repeated during the next fifteen years.

Along the Rhine and upper Danube also the invaders were steadily at work. In 254, the Marcomanni broke into Upper Pannonia and penetrated as far as Ravenna in Italy. A few years later a horde of Alemanni crossed the Alps and ravaged northern Italy as far as Milan. Until 257, the Emperor Gallienus held the Rhine frontier intact, but in that year a horde of Franks and other Germans swept across Gaul and Spain, where they destroyed Tarragona, and reached distant Mauretania before they were destroyed. Thereafter, the Gallic provinces suffered from repeated and destructive inroads for about thirty years.

On the eastern frontier, Persian depredations were equally disastrous. In 253, and again in 258, Sapor I ravaged Syria and destroyed Antioch. Armenia was lost to the Romans, while the southeastern provinces of Asia Minor suffered as severely from Persian inroads as the northern districts did from the Goths.

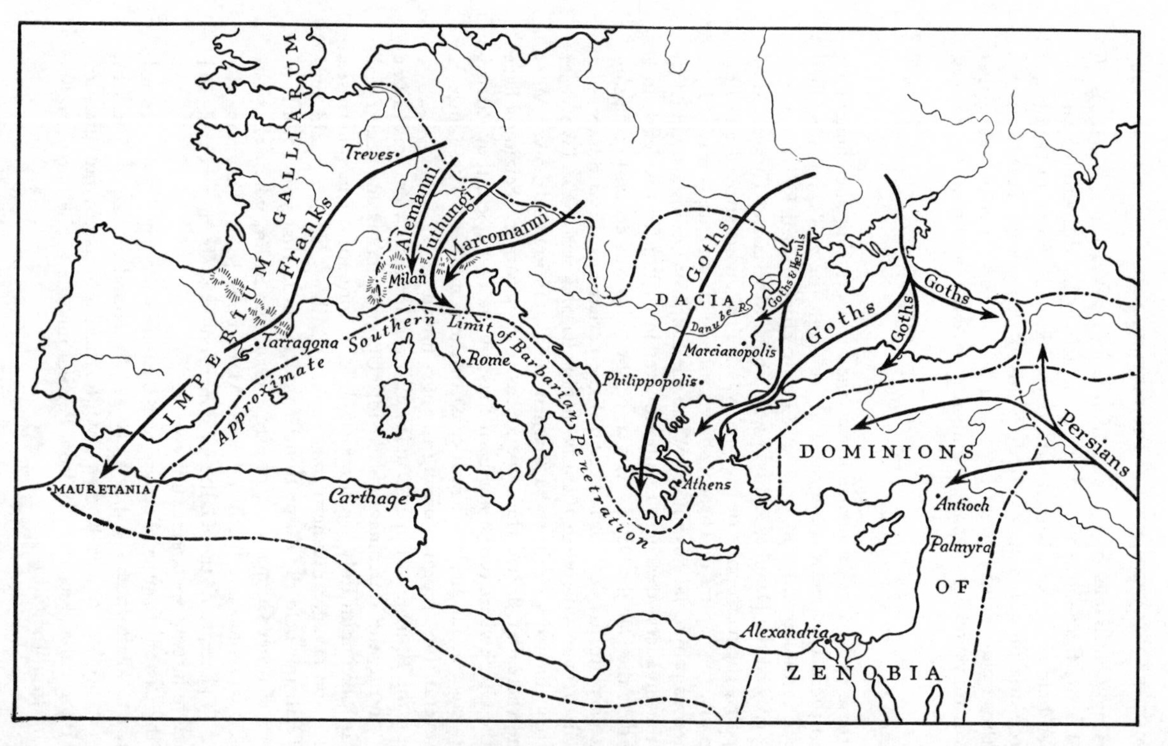


THE ROMAN EMPIRE DURING THE MILITARY ANARCHY

### *Valerian and Gallienus (253–268)*

It was under these discouraging conditions that Publius Licinius Valerianus (253–260) and his son Publius Licinius Egnatius Gallienus (253–268) became joint emperors. They belonged to an old and cultured senatorial family. Both were men of refined and civilized tastes, but while Valerian was weak and incapable, Gallienus was a hard-fighting and able ruler, to whom the Empire owed its ultimate salvation. During the early part of their joint reigns they were on good terms with the Senate. Valerian, like Decius before him, carried on a severe and methodical persecution of the Christians. While they reigned together Gallienus had charge of the northern frontier, where he repulsed a number of barbarian raids and began the fortification of the cities of the Rhine region. The great invasion of 257 occurred while he was absent in Italy. It shook his prestige severely in this region, but worse was to come. In 256, Valerian had gone to the East to organize a defense against Sapor and the Goths. There, in 260, he found himself facing the Persian host with an army ravaged by the plague. In an attempt to negotiate with Sapor, he was treacherously seized by the Persian king and led away to die in captivity. Christian legend has much to say about the humiliations which he suffered as a captive, but of his subsequent fate nothing is actually known. It was a staggering blow to Roman prestige in the East, and for the moment Sapor seemed irresistible. Gallienus was now left to face the storm alone.

The capture of Valerian seemed to assure the triumph of the forces of destruction. The people of Asia, the Danubian provinces and Gaul, maddened by their sufferings, began to set up usurpers in the hope of having emperors who would look after the interests of their respective districts. Along the Rhine, where Gallienus had left his son Saloninus in charge of the defense, a professional soldier named Postumus headed a rebellion in which the young prince was murdered. Postumus then assumed the government of Britain, Gaul, and Spain, which he ruled as a separate state, called by historians the *Imperium Galliarum*. So far as can be determined, he made no effort to conquer the remainder of the Empire. For eight years he reigned at Treves, repelling invasions, putting down piracy along the coast, and restoring a semblance of prosperity to his dominions.

In the East, the capture of Valerian was followed by two distinct separatist movements. Macrianus, a Roman army officer, set up his two sons Macrianus and Quietus as joint emperors. Asia Minor, Syria, and Egypt acknowledged their rule, and they invaded the Balkan peninsula. But their cause was in part ruined by the second movement, that of Odenathus of Palmyra. This city, located in the Syrian Desert east of Antioch, had been a semi-independent ally of the Roman Empire, and was a rich center of the caravan trade. Odenathus, like his ancestors, was its hereditary chief, and the family had long been Roman citizens. At first he attempted to save his city's commercial interests by negotiating with Sapor, but when the Persian rudely repulsed his advances, he gathered a force of Arab cavalry and attacked the Persians from the rear, driving them back to the Euphrates. Odenathus now assumed the title of King of Palmyra.

That the process of dissolution did not reach its logical conclusion was due to the ability and persistence of Gallienus. Even before his father's capture he had begun to reorganize the army and the civil administration. Since military officers of senatorial rank had proved themselves both incompetent and untrustworthy, Gallienus forbade senators to hold commissions in the army, and threw promotion open to men from the ranks. From his reign dated the rise of the school of brilliant generals, chiefly from the Danubian provinces, several of whom were to wear the imperial purple themselves. Both then and later, senators continued to find places in the civil service. To meet the need for a mobile army, the cavalry was greatly increased in numbers and was put under an independent command. At the same time a mercenary infantry force was created to supplement the immobile frontier armies. Towns in threatened areas were fortified, and the imperial fleet was repaired and put into action. By a mixture of kindness and firmness, discipline was re-established. In civil government, Gallienus at once put a stop to the senseless persecution of the Christians, and gave them freedom of worship.

Thanks to these astute measures, the movement toward dissolution was checked. Igenuus and Regalianus, both of whom had been proclaimed emperors successively in the Danubian area, were defeated and killed. When Macrian, after helping to defeat Sapor, invaded Moesia, he was met by Aureolus, one of Gallienus' commanders, who defeated and killed him. Meanwhile, Gallienus had reached an understanding with Odenathus. The Palmyrene chief was appointed "General of the East," with vague but sweeping powers over Syria, Cilicia, Palestine, and Mesopotamia. He also retained the title of "King of Kings" in Palmyra. Satisfied with the splendid position which Gallienus had given him, he remained faithful to Rome, stamped out the remains of Macrian's rebellion in Syria, and inflicted several stinging defeats upon the Persians. Up to his death, in 267, he continued to render excellent service to the cause of imperial defense. Toward Postumus, the murderer of his son, Gallienus made no overtures of any kind. He several times invaded the *Imperium Galliarum*, but here he enjoyed no success and finally contented himself with defending the Alpine passes. Thus he succeeded in holding the core of the Empire together, in preparing forces adequate to defend it, and in developing a staff of brilliant and energetic generals. If the general misery obscured these achievements at the time, we at least must do him justice by dating the beginning of Rome's recovery from his reign.

The end of Gallienus' career was in keeping with his own character and that of the age. In 268, a mixed horde of Goths and Heruli descended upon Moesia, Thrace, Macedonia, and Greece. With customary promptness the Emperor attacked them and won a promising victory. But treachery among his own followers was destined to cheat him of a complete success. First came news that Aureolus, whom he had left to defend the Alpine passes against Postumus, had gone over to the enemy. Whirling about, Gallienus defeated the rebel and drove him into Milan. While he was besieging the city his own staff turned against him. Since all of them were Illyrians, they were in all probability angered by his temporary withdrawal from the Gothic war and felt that an emperor of their own choosing would give their native provinces better protection than he had done. By this group, Gallienus was lured from his tent at night without his armor and stabbed to death. Thus perished the man whose personal culture, courage, energy, and wisdom rendered him worthy of a better fate. He was the last Emperor of refined aristocratic Roman stock. The future lay with the rude men of the sword whom he had trained and promoted, and who had stained their hands with his blood.

The murderers of Gallienus had already designated one of their number, Marcus Aurelius Claudius, as his successor, and in spite of the mutinous temper of the army when the crime was discovered, they had their way. The Senate, angered by Gallienus' unfriendly attitude toward it, murdered his surviving relatives and friends, but at length Claudius managed to put a stop to the massacre. By clever diplomacy, the new Emperor made the Senate his staunch supporter without restoring a single prerogative of which Gallienus had deprived it. At this time, Spain and part of southern Gaul voluntarily submitted to Claudius.

Leaving the Gallic and Palmyrene states to go their respective ways for the time, Claudius undertook to consolidate and defend the realm which he had taken over from Gallienus. Aureolus was quickly captured and put to death, and an invasion of the Alemanni, who had penetrated northern Italy, was hurled back. Claudius then undertook to destroy the Gothic host whose defeat Gallienus had been about to achieve the year before. By a series of masterly maneuvers he drove the surviving Goths back into the Balkan Mountains, killed a large part of them, and compelled most of the remainder to surrender. Many of the prisoners were enlisted in the Roman army, a dangerous practice which was to become more and more frequent from that time forth. News of another invasion of Italy, this time by Juthingi, called him back to the West before the Goths were quite "mopped up," but he was never to reach his destination. In January, 270, he died of the plague at Sirmium — the first emperor since Septimius Severus to die at liberty and in his bed.

### *Aurelian (270–275)*

On hearing of the death of Claudius the army in Italy and the Senate proclaimed his brother, Marcus Aurelius Quintillus, his successor, but the Balkan army offered the purple to Lucius Domitius Aurelianus, its commander and the ablest of Claudius' aides. Quintillus was quickly deserted by his men, and committed suicide. Thus to Aurelian (270–275) fell the task of completing the reintegration of the Empire. Like Claudius, he was an Illyrian of peasant stock, a stern disciplinarian and a military genius. Under his strong and able leadership the Roman world was to regain unity and a degree of order.

The situation which faced him was at first a perilous one. The Juthungi were pouring over the Brenner Pass into Italy. The Senate was bitterly hostile to the supplanter of Quintillus, and the civil administration was so disorganized that Aurelian even lost control of the workers in the Roman mint. Claudius had regained the voluntary allegiance of Spain and southern Gaul, but the core of the Gallic Empire was still independent. In the East, where Odenathus had been assassinated in 267, his place had been taken by his ambitious and energetic wife Zenobia, who ruled as regent for her son Vaballathus. During Claudius' reign she had occupied Egypt, and soon after, her forces invaded and conquered a large part of Asia Minor. At first Aurelian seems to have had an understanding with her, but she soon repudiated it and declared the complete independence of her state.

Aurelian of necessity began by consolidating his position in Italy. The Juthungi were driven out, but returned and administered a disastrous defeat to his army. Finally, after desperate fighting, they were again defeated and driven back across the Danube. A senatorial plot against him was brought to light and its participants punished. To overcome the mint workers and their supporters a regular civil war was necessary, and seven thousand men were killed before the rebels were crushed. Recognizing that future barbarian invasions of Italy were to be expected, he undertook to rebuild the walls of the cities, including those of Rome. The Roman wall was twelve miles long, and enclosed the whole of the ancient city. It was constructed entirely by the civilian stone- and brick-workers of the capital, and while only twelve feet thick and twenty feet high, it required a number of years for its completion. Its presence was a tacit admission that the whole system of frontier defenses was no longer adequate. Probably about the same time Aurelian withdrew the Roman armies and colonists from the exposed province of Dacia, beyond the Danube, and assigned them land on the southern bank of the river, which he organized into two new provinces, each of which likewise bore the name of Dacia.

With Italy and the Danubian frontier once more safe, Aurelian undertook to deal with Zenobia and Vaballathus. In 271 his general Probus (the future Emperor) recovered Egypt. The same year Aurelian himself crossed into Asia Minor, which he quickly reoccupied. Penetrating Syria, he defeated the Palmyrene army (composed largely of archers and armored cavalry) near Antioch, and pushed across the Syrian Desert to besiege Palmyra itself. After a bitter struggle, in which the Persians failed to send Zenobia the aid which they had promised, the city surrendered, and Zenobia with her son was captured. Her ministers, on whom she threw the blame for her rebellion, were executed, but she and Vaballathus were spared to adorn their captor's triumph, and were then given homes in Italy. Later, as Aurelian was returning to the West, a new rebellion broke out in Palmyra, in which the Roman garrison was massacred. When Aurelian crushed this movement he showed no mercy. Palmyra was destroyed, and never recovered its former importance.

Aurelian now turned to the Gallic Empire, which had been declining since the assassination of Postumus in 268. As we have seen, a large part of it had already been reoccupied by the legitimate line of emperors. The remainder was suffering from internal disorder and from invasion by the German tribes. In 273, Aurelian, acting on a secret invitation from the weak Gallic Emperor Tetricus, invaded independent Gaul, and the rebel state fell like a house of cards. Tetricus was spared, and later received a governorship in Italy. The Empire was now entirely reunited, and Aurelian with justice assumed the proud title, "Restorer of the World." A magnificent triumph celebrated his achievements.

In his civil government, Aurelian made valiant efforts to undo the harm wrought by the calamities of the preceding generation. To establish a moral basis for his own authority, he gave imperial patronage to the cult of the Oriental sun-god for whom he established a new college of pontiffs and built a magnificent temple, at the same time claiming to hold his power as the god's deputy on earth. No doubt he hoped in this way to free himself from the capricious demands of the soldiers. To improve the provisioning of Rome, he substituted distributions of pork, oil, and bread for the old-time grain ration of the poor. He endeavored to improve the coinage, but because of the disordered condition of the treasury, he accomplished little. Drastic steps were taken to protect the civil population from mistreatment by the soldiers.

But after the fall of Tetricus, Aurelian had only a short time to live. In 275, he set out on another campaign, this time against the Persians. While traveling the road on the north shore of the Sea of Marmora, he was assassinated by some of his officers, whom his private secretary had tricked into thinking that their lives were in danger. Rome had produced few men who were the equals of Aurelian in war and government, and none who were his superiors.

### *Tacitus and Florianus (275–276)*

Aurelian's death produced a curious situation. The army officers and soldiers, dreading another civil war if the widely scattered military forces attempted to choose a new emperor, referred the whole matter to the Senate. The latter, after some hesitation, chose Marcus Claudius Tacitus, a senator over seventy-five years of age. A poorer choice would be hard to imagine, but Tacitus did his best. In the six months of his rule he valiantly repelled a Gothic invasion of Asia Minor, and drove the barbarians out of the Empire. However, he had a bad habit of appointing his own relatives to high offices, and most of them made him enemies. In the spring of 276 he was assassinated by men who had previously killed his relative, the governor of Syria. His brother Marcus Annius Florianus attempted to succeed him, but the soldiers had had enough of the family. They chose Marcus Aurelius Probus to the vacant post, and killed Florianus.

### *Probus (276–282)*

The reign of Probus was devoted to preserving and strengthening the work of Aurelian. With the Senate he maintained good relations. Beginning in Gaul, which since the death of Aurelian had been invaded and largely occupied by the Franks and other Germans, he first restored and strongly fortified the Rhine frontier. He then followed the course of the

Danube, ejected the Vandals from Pannonia, settling a hundred thousand fugitive Bastarnae on devastated lands in Thrace, and reorganizing the governments of the border provinces. The robber tribes of Asia Minor were put down, and invaders from the desert were driven out of Egypt. Several pretenders in various parts of the Empire were suppressed firmly but without undue cruelty. The recovery of the Roman world from the calamities of the Military Anarchy had now progressed far enough so that Probus was able to take economic problems in hand. In an effort to restore prosperity he encouraged the planting of vineyards and the reclamation of swamplands, especially in Gaul and the Danubian provinces. Toward these enterprises he contributed a great deal of soldier-labor, but this proved his ruin. The army in Rhaetia mutinied and proclaimed the Praetorian prefect, Marcus Aurelius Carus, Emperor in his place. When Probus' soldiers at Sirmium heard of the revolt, they also mutinied and slew him. Our sources for this period are particularly bad, but in their turgid and tiresome way they picture Probus as a brilliant, masterful, and conscientious ruler.

### *Carus, Carinus, and Numerian (282–284)*

Carus was, like his three great predecessors, an Illyrian and a professional soldier. Although he reigned only eleven months, his military feats were by no means contemptible. He began by appointing his two sons, Carinus and Numerianus, Caesars. Leaving Carinus to govern the West, he set out with Numerian at the head of an army to punish the ever-restless Persians. On his way through the Danubian provinces, he defeated yet another inroad of the barbarians from beyond the frontier. Then falling upon the Persians, he beat them, took Seleucia and Ctesiphon, and prepared to invade the Iranian Plateau. Before he could do so, however, death overtook him, whether by a stroke of lightning or a conspiracy among his officers is not known. His son Numerian, now raised to the rank of Augustus, abandoned the campaign and led the army back toward the West. But he was a man of neither energy nor ability, and late in August, 284, he was secretly murdered by his Praetorian prefect, Arrius Aper. However, Aper stood alone in his crime, and when it was discovered, steps were taken to punish him. Disdaining Carinus, the army of the East chose as the successor of Numerian one of its own officers, Gaius Aurelius Valerius Diocletianus, who promptly slew Aper with his own hand. Carinus, who had meanwhile been discharging his duties in the West, refused to receive Diocletian as a colleague, and marched against him. Early in the spring of 285 the two armies met at Margus in Moesia and joined battle. In the midst of the struggle one of Carinus' officers avenged a private wrong by stabbing his master. Both armies now recognized Diocletian, and the Empire, scarred and battered by a half century of unparalleled calamity, entered upon its last revival of strength and prosperity. This period will be treated in subsequent chapters.

The Military Anarchy inflicted upon the Roman world wounds which were never healed. Population had shrunk appallingly. All over the West and much of the East ruined cities and deserted fields bore evidence to the severity of the recent catastrophe. With a worthless currency and no large-scale commerce, economic life had for the most part reverted to primitive levels. Worst of all, society seemed to have lost the power of recovery, and had instead sunk into resignation and apathy. Only two institutions displayed a capacity for further growth — the governmental bureaucracy, and the Christian Church, and these were to dominate the succeeding age.

# 24

# *The Civilization of the Early Roman Empire: (I) Government, Society, and Economics*

## Introduction

In the two hundred and seventy years between the death of Augustus and the accession of Diocletian, the Graeco-Roman civilization underwent a checkered course of growth, diffusion, and decay. Some aspects of this evolution have been touched upon in previous chapters, but we must now attempt to secure a unified picture of the whole process. Because of the infinite complexity of the scene, such a picture will have to be very generalized, touching only the outstanding lines of development. Furthermore, we must remember that it covers a period as long as that which separates Charles II of England and Louis XIV of France from the present day, and that in so long a time profound changes were certain to occur. With these reservations in mind we may proceed with the survey.

## Imperial and Local Government

### *Absolutism and Legal Reform: the Jurists*

Our previous study of the political history of the Principate has shown us that the main lines of development in imperial government were toward centralization, bureaucracy, and autocracy. These trends were, as we have seen, only slightly influenced by the periodically recurring struggle between the Emperors and the Senate. Trajan, Hadrian, and Marcus Aurelius, with the free consent of the Senate, extended their functions and encroached upon its prerogatives less obviously, but no less surely, than Septimius Severus or Caracalla. In senatorial eyes, the difference between good and bad emperors lay in their purposes and methods rather than in the preservation or diminution of senatorial prerogative.

Law-making had, from the beginning of the Principate, been entirely under imperial control, but as time passed the methods of the emperors became more and more direct. At some time during the first century A.D. the Assemblies lost their legislative functions to the Senate. The latter normally acted only upon proposals made by the Emperor himself or by other officials at his request, and always in accordance with his wishes. Septimius Severus abandoned this pretense of senatorial participation in law-making by giving to his own decrees the force of law.

No less important than the making of new laws, was the process of defining and explaining old ones. For many centuries Rome had been producing able jurists, who had written on both law and judicial procedure. Their influence had before the end of the Republic become so great that they had begun to reshape Roman law in the process of explaining it. To bring them under his own control, Augustus had granted to a few of the most eminent of these legal authorities the right to issue rulings which were binding upon the courts. Subsequent emperors continued the custom, so that there grew up a class of government-sponsored jurists whose writings were, in effect, authoritative rulings. These men were, of course, friends of the emperors and advocates of the imperial prerogative, and their interpretations of the law served constantly to increase the latter. Particularly during and after the reign of Septimius Severus, when the office of Praetorian prefect had become predominantly judicial rather than military in character, a succession of brilliant jurists held the post, and used it to create a science of law which was one of Rome's most significant contributions to the civilization of the world. Of these the chief were Aemilius Papinianus, Domitius Ulpianus, Julius Paulus, and Herennius Modestinus, all of whom lived during the period of the Severi. It is not surprising that they taught the world to see in a Roman emperor an absolute monarch. Under the new system jury trials were abolished and the entire conduct of the courts of justice was concentrated in the hands of the Emperor or his agents. It was a heavy price to pay for legal improvements, but the work which the jurists accomplished was of lasting benefit to mankind.

The science of jurisprudence, as embodied in the works of the jurists and in the codified *Praetor's Edict* and *Provincial Edicts*, undertook to lay down a broad and elastic set of principles for the government of human relations. While the use of precedents was admitted, it was assumed that all decisions must be reasonable, equitable, and just, and if the precedents to a given case did not point the way to such a decision, they could be set aside. Women, children, slaves, and the poor fared better under this system than ever before. Appeals might be taken from the lower courts to the Emperor himself, or the judge might refer a case to him before it had been tried at all for a statement of the principles that ought to govern a decision. The answer to such an appeal was a "reply" (*rescriptum*), which naturally had the force of law until set aside by a subsequent emperor or by the Senate after the death of the author. Augustus had begun the custom of issuing such documents, but it was not until the reign of Hadrian that arrangements were made to preserve them. After the death of Alexander Severus the growing despotism of the emperors and the barbarism of the age led to a practical cessation of works on jurisprudence, but a constant flow of rescripts continued to mold the law to meet new conditions.

### *Imperial Finance and Taxation*

In finance as in legislation the emperors soon came to overshadow their nominal partner, the Senate. Not only were the imperial provinces more numerous than the senatorial ones, but their population and resources were also greater. Moreover even in the senatorial provinces the emperors could collect the three taxes which supported the Military Treasury. The proceeds of confiscations went to swell the imperial funds, while the emperors were also the recipients of countless legacies and the heirs of childless persons who died intestate. From all these sources of income the Senate was excluded, and its income was never more than a fraction of that which flowed into the various imperial chests.

In theory, senatorial and imperial finance remained separate, but such was not the fact. From the days of Augustus onward, the emperors exercised almost as close control over the *Aerarium Saturni* as over their own treasuries. Thus Augustus, Claudius, Nero, and Vespasian each reorganized its administration — due in the main to the inefficiency of the senatorial management. It would seem that no emperor had any difficulty in diverting senatorial funds to his own use whenever he chose. Little by little the importance of this republican institution shrank until in the third century A.D. it had become merely the municipal chest of the city of Rome — a sure index to the decline of the body which was supposed to control it.

Meanwhile the imperial treasuries had been growing steadily in complexity of organization and volume of business. Augustus, as we have seen [1] had only provincial *fisci* and the Military Treasury. Claudius had

[1] Chapter 19.

set up a central *fiscus* in Rome. With the extinction of the Julio-Claudian family there arose the problem of dealing with its private estate, which had been swollen to huge proportions by confiscations and more or less voluntary legacies. Vespasian hit upon the idea of considering it a permanent state fund, to be used for the support of the Emperor and his family. As such it became the *patrimonium principis*, but an emperor might keep his private property separate from this fund. Septimius Severus, whose private fortune had grown to vast magnitude through the spoliation of his opponents, elaborated the system still further. He made the *patrimonium* a mere department of the *fiscus*, and for the care of his personal property organized the *res privata*. In this state the imperial financial administration remained until Diocletian reorganized the whole system.

Probably by far the greatest part of the property in the *patrimonium* and the *res privata* was in the form of land. The emperors, with estates totaling many millions of acres, were incomparably the greatest landlords in the Empire, and their holdings were to be found in practically all the provinces. To care for them, Vespasian, and later Hadrian, organized a "Land Bureau" under equestrian procurators. Its administrative methods did much, centuries later, to shape the practices of the medieval manorial landlords, and for that reason are worth a brief description. Individual estates were leased to contractors for fixed terms of years. Each estate was divided into two parts, of which the contractor farmed one and kept the entire proceeds, sub-leasing the other in small lots to free tenants. Leases usually ran for five years, and were renewable. In addition to a rent consisting of one third of his crop, each tenant had to do six days' work a year on the land held by the contractor. The procurators looked after the interests of the emperors, and, in theory, those of the tenants as well. In practice, the contractor could often bribe the procurator, and would then exact several times as much work and rent as the law permitted. This system, with its mixed obligation of rent and labor, was taken up by private landholders everywhere. Later, when high taxes and low returns made farming unprofitable, the tenants began to desert their lands and run away. It was then that the imperial government stepped in and bound them to the soil, although leaving them nominal freedom. With this step the essential characteristics of medieval manorialism were complete.

As with other states, ancient and modern, the financial history of the Roman Empire is one of a gradual but inevitable approach to bankruptcy. Thrifty emperors like Vespasian might check the process or even turn it back somewhat, but spendthrifts like Nero or Commodus more than nullified their efforts. In times of crisis, even competent rulers like Trajan or

*Bettmann*

ROMAN FARM IN NORTH AFRICA
*Mosaic. Early Second Century A.D.*

Marcus Aurelius found themselves compelled to spend far beyond their incomes. Yet, in general, the imperial financial system, despite its chronic weakness and the occasional acts of tyranny to which it gave rise, held up surprisingly well until the calamities of the reign of Marcus Aurelius, and did not place an intolerable burden on the people. It was only when pestilence and barbarian invaders decreased the taxable income on the one hand, and the Military Monarchy greatly increased expenditure on the other, that financial crisis became the normal condition of both government and people. A modern state in similar circumstances staves off the evil day by contracting bonded indebtedness, but the imperfect credit system of the ancient world left a Roman emperor no such resource. His only expedients were increased taxes, spoliation of his people in one form or another, and debasement of the currency. The first of these expedients was given a full trial by the Severi, but failed to yield sufficient returns. The second, in the form of confiscations of property in punishment for real or fictitious crimes, had been tried by occasional emperors ever since Caligula; and in the days of the Military Monarchy it too failed to meet the needs for funds. Imperial debasement of the currency had begun with Nero, and had proceeded slowly and irregularly up to the days of Septimius Severus, under whom, as we have seen, the denarius contained only 50 per cent silver. Under Caracalla its silver content sank to 40 per cent, and in the reign of Gallienus it was merely a silver-washed imitation, the core being made of an alloy of copper and other cheap metals. When at length Diocletian undertook seriously to stabilize the coinage, he reckoned 50,000 denarii as equal in value to a pound of pure gold, as compared with 1050 under Augustus. This represented a devaluation of 97.8 per cent.

There was another and more oppressive form of government financing which had long been used in certain places and for certain purposes, which came into continual and universal use under the Severi. That was the commandeering of goods and services from the civilian population for the use of officials and soldiers. It was an old custom in the Asiatic provinces and Egypt to compel those who lived near the great imperial roads to furnish animals and drivers without compensation for the transportation of state-owned goods or persons on public business. The oppressiveness of such a practice may be easily imagined, but although successive emperors strove to mitigate its evils, it was never abolished, and gradually spread to the West. The Romans had always levied provisions for the army from communities near the scene of military operations. This custom also spread under the Severi to all parts of the Empire. Unlike the regular taxes, these exactions could not be foreseen or allowed for in advance, and there was theoretically no limit to the amount except the absolute exhaustion of the population. Since it was the duty of the local officials to see that the prescribed payments were made, they fell with crushing weight upon the urban middle class and upon the peasants by whom, in the last analysis, the commodities had to be supplied. We shall have occasion to revert to this subject presently in connection with local government.

Another irregular levy, which had long been customary but which became much worse in the third century, was the so-called "crown gold"— a gift of money due from senators and municipal governments to each emperor at his accession and at times when he claimed to have won victories over foreign enemies. Naturally in an age of almost constant warfare, when no one cared to question imperial claims, this exaction almost attained the dignity of a regular tax, and its weight did much to ruin the classes upon whom it fell.

### *The Bureaucracy*

Aside from military needs, the chief item of imperial expenditure was the support of the civil bureaucracy. After the reform of Hadrian, its upper ranks were filled with equestrians, and the lower ranks usually with imperial freedmen. This establishment acquired much more extensive functions in the second and third centuries than in the first. In addition to the original provincial procurators, there were procurators who managed imperial estates and mines, others who collected imperial taxes in the senatorial provinces, still others who acted as provincial governors, and many who performed miscellaneous functions too numerous for special mention. As indicated previously,[1] the salaries of these officials varied from 60,000 to 300,000 sesterces, and there can be no doubt that they rose during the third century in something like an inverse ratio to the value of the coin in which they were paid. After the reign of Septimius Severus, more and more of these equestrian officials came from the ranks of discharged centurions, who were usually untutored residents of backward provinces, thoroughly imbued with the feelings of the military class. To such semibarbarians we must attribute much of the lawless violence of the government's methods during the Military Anarchy. The more cunning and fortunate members of this class became rich through imperial favor and corruption, acquired senatorial rank, and formed a new aristocracy — the senatorial class of the fourth and fifth centuries.

### *The Senate and the Senatorial Class*

Under the Principate, the Senate's lack of control over the military forces and over taxation condemned it to permanent weakness. After the death of Augustus, it pursued a checkered career, with its power and importance generally on the wane. Except in 238 A.D., it never took the initiative in resisting even the most tyrannical of emperors, and it repeatedly suffered terrible humiliations at their hands. Its government of the senatorial provinces was partly taken over by so good an emperor as Trajan; its share in the government of the capital did not at any time include control of the all-important police and grain supply; and under Septimius Severus, its mouthpieces the praetors and consuls lost control of the jury courts. Severus, as we have seen, even deprived it of its share in legislation. Under Gallienus, its members were excluded from official posts in the army. After the reign of Septimius Severus, few emperors bothered to

[1] Chapter 22.

take the oath not to put a senator to death by summary judgment. Diocletian merely put the seal upon an accomplished fact when he deprived it of all part in imperial affairs and left it only a small share in the administration of the city of Rome.

Yet the foregoing picture would hardly do justice to the influence of the senatorial aristocracy upon the history of imperial Rome. The Senate represented the point of view of the upper and middle classes of the civilian population, and it maintained this viewpoint for centuries, in spite of constantly changing personnel and the recurring persecutions to which it was subjected. Old senatorial families were always dying out or being exterminated, and the new members who replaced them were invariably chosen by the emperors. At first, the recruits came from Roman equestrian families, later, from the Italian municipal aristocracy, and still later, from the Romanized aristocracy of the western provinces or the Hellenized aristocracy of the East. In the third century A.D., the point was reached at which the sons or grandsons of semibarbarous professional soldiers could gain membership. But each new accession of personnel soon attained the stubborn intransigeance traditional to the group, and cherished the ideals of senatorial privilege, adoptive succession, and civilian supremacy over the army long after these causes had been irrevocably lost. Its members wrote or inspired the histories, picturing emperors as either good or bad according to their attitudes on these questions, and any emperor who could read these works, or who was anxious to stand well with posterity, was certain to be influenced by these ideals. Above all, there was a widespread feeling that only the Senate could legitimize an emperor's authority, and unless the emperor was willing to become a mere puppet of the soldiery, he was likely to render at least lip-service to this view. Thus, as a moral force, the Senate accomplished far more than as a factor in practical politics.

### *The Provinces*

The workings of the imperial government cannot be understood without reference to the provincial administration. In this field the most significant developments — aside from finance — were the growth of the equestrian bureaucracy and the separation of the civil and military functions of the provincial governors. Up to the accession of Septimius Severus, in spite of Hadrian's organization of a bureaucratic corps of equestrian civil servants, the system of provincial administration set up by Augustus had not been seriously interfered with. The provincial governors still combined civil and military functions, and were, in all but a few cases, senators. Severus placed the province of Mesopotamia under an equestrian prefect, and, in a number of instances, replaced senatorial governors with equestrian procurators who bore the additional title of "acting governor." Where a senatorial governor had had more than one legion under his command (as in Syria and Britain), Severus separated the province into two or more parts, giving each of the new governors one legion. Likewise, the procurators who served in provinces governed by senators began to take over more and more of the functions formerly performed by the governor. These trends — particularly the further subdivision of provinces — were developed by succeeding emperors during the next half-century.

Gallienus, as we have seen, instituted another revolutionary change in provincial administration. His exclusion of senators from military commands, to which allusion has already been made,[1] did not deprive them of the governorships which they had previously held, but merely withdrew from them all control of the armies. The civil and military powers were now completely separated, the latter being committed to professional soldiers with equestrian rank and bearing new titles.

### *The Army*

The army itself underwent equally sweeping changes. In previous chapters [2] we have seen how some of these took place, but for the sake of perspective these will be briefly recapitulated here. The first change was one of personnel. Under the Julio-Claudian emperors, recruits for the legions were secured almost entirely from Italy, while the auxiliaries were furnished by the provinces. Vespasian began to draw his legionaries from the Roman-citizen communities in the provinces, leaving the Praetorian Guard open to Italians, and continuing the old practice of recruiting auxiliaries from non-citizens. Hadrian made two innovations in the military system. He divided the Empire into enlistment districts, each composed of one or more imperial provinces, and each district had to furnish the soldiers who served in it. Under this system, fewer townsmen were drawn into the ranks, while their proximity to their old homes made it less urgent for recruits to learn or speak Latin. Furthermore, it became the rule that each legion had a fixed location, from which it could be withdrawn to meet an emergency, but to which it had to be returned when the emergency was over. This was the first step toward the immobilization of the legion — one of the outstanding developments of the Military Monarchy.

[1] Chapter 23. [2] Chapters 21, 22, and 23.

His second innovation was the use of bands of irregular soldiers called *numeri*, drawn from the more backward provinces or allied communities, armed with the weapons to which they had been accustomed and not subjected to Roman discipline. Examples of this class were the archers, slingers, and irregular cavalry found in the armies of the second century A.D.

With the coming of the Military Monarchy, the character of the army began to change rapidly. Septimius Severus, by allowing the legionaries and auxiliaries to marry and live outside the barracks, established bonds between his soldiers and the places in which they were regularly quartered, which made any permanent transfer of quarters entirely impracticable. It remained for Severus Alexander to complete the immobilization of the military forces by giving each soldier a small farm to cultivate during his spare time. Thereafter, the legionaries and auxiliaries were merely a border militia (*limitanei*), drawn from the least civilized part of the population, with interests hardly extending beyond that sector of the frontier on which the soldier happened to be stationed. This development, together with the systematic pampering to which the Severi had subjected the army, reduced its discipline and efficiency to a very low ebb, and goes far to explain the disasters which the Empire suffered under the emperors between Maximinus and Gallienus.

Such a condition was intolerable, and steps were soon taken to correct it. To Gallienus in particular should go the credit for the creation of a mobile army to supplement these turbulent border forces. In the Persian and German wars, *numeri* armed with specialized weapons — such as mounted archers or armored cavalry — became much more common. As they were composed of mercenaries, they were not, like the *limitanei*, tied to any one locality. In time of need, detachments (*vexillationes*) were

*Numismatic Society*

ANTONINIANUS

*Obverse: Head of Gallienus. Reverse: Trophy and Captives*

drafted from the legions and auxiliary regiments, and through continuous service such units became permanent organizations. As the original personnel was gradually eliminated, these companies, like the *numeri*, were filled with mercenaries, drawn from the more backward communities or from German or Moorish tribes along the frontier. Gallienus also organized a powerful cavalry force under a separate command. Collectively these forces formed a mobile army, ready to be used wherever necessary, and the *limitanei* merely supplemented it, or met the first shock of an invasion. The troops of the new army were well paid and privileged, loyal to the emperors, and divorced from local interests, but the expense of maintaining them was very high, and the burden of supporting the increased military establishment added greatly to the misery of the provincials. To supplement these measures, Gallienus and his successors caused the walls of the towns in threatened areas to be rebuilt. Thus a new system of "defense-in-depth" was substituted for the old, rigid, and inflexible one of frontier garrisons. The result was to be seem in the astonishing series of victories won over the invaders during the 260's and 270's.

Lastly, we must note the existence of a military police force (*Frumentarii*, *Speculatores*, and *Stationarii*), whose function it was to suppress civilian opposition to the government. Under the third-century emperors, its activities must have been a source of terror and oppression comparable to those of the secret police in modern collectivist states. For a civilian, the only means of self-protection against it was bribery, to which its members were notoriously open.

Such were the main outlines of the progress of the Roman government toward autocracy. While a few emperors, such as Septimius Severus and Maximinus, consciously fostered the harsh brutality and merciless greed of the government, the bad points of the system were mainly due to an inexorable necessity which drove good and bad rulers alike to use the same methods — often in spite of personal antipathy to them. The monotonous series of imperial assassinations which blots the annals of third-century Rome is in itself enough to show that the emperors were no more free agents than were their subjects. All had to bow before the tendencies of the age.

### *Municipal Government: the Curiales*

Thus far, we have been surveying imperial government, in which the population at large had no voice. Local self-government also continued to exist, both in Italy and the provinces, and to exert a strong influence upon community life. Under the Republic, as we have seen, it had in the provinces assumed a wide variety of forms, both municipal and tribal. This diversity continued to exist under the Principate. But everywhere the trend was toward urbanization, and this tendency had the full blessing of the imperial government. The reason is easy to discern. Municipal magistrates could usually be depended upon to maintain better order than tribal chiefs, and for such purposes as tax collection they could be used as instruments of the central power, performing their functions the more surely because of their intimate local knowledge, and saving the expense of salaries to additional imperial officials. Because of this encouragement, and also because of the initiative of the people, municipal government spread over provinces where, before the Roman conquest, it had been either weak or non-existent. Along the frontier, in particular, the army furnished a strong impetus to the movement. At every large garrison post there would spring up a settlement composed of persons who catered to the wants of the soldiers. To them would be added the families of soldiers,[1] and time-expired veterans who desired to be near their old comrades. Soon such a town would be large enough to receive municipal rights. Many of the cities of the Rhine-Danube area, in particular, owe their existence to this process.

It is well to remember that a Roman municipality was something more than a mere city in the modern sense. Each of them, like a Greek city-state, included a thickly settled area (a city in our meaning of the word), together with a more or less extensive tract of country in its neighborhood. This was called "attributed territory," and might be very large. Thus, Transalpine Gaul, with an area of about 240,000 square miles, was divided into 64 of these units, making an average of nearly 4000 square miles each — about the combined area of Delaware and Rhode Island. The smallest, however, had only a few square miles. The free inhabitants of these attributed areas might be citizens of the municipality, or they might be mere subjects. Often a Roman or Latin colony would have charge of several troublesome native tribes near-by, for whose tribute and good behavior it was responsible. Under favorable circumstances, such dependents would, in time, become fully merged into the citizen body.

In the West, and in Roman and Latin colonies everywhere, municipal institutions tended to follow closely those of Rome. At the head of each unit, corresponding to the consuls at Rome, was a board of either two or four men (*duumviri* or *quattorviri*), elected annually. With them served

[1] Although soldiers were not allowed to marry while in service, they frequently contracted irregular unions which were legalized when they were discharged.

several priests, and a number of subordinate officials. Every fifth year, these magistrates took the census, and to hold the office in a census year was an especial honor. At first, the choice of the magistrates rested with the municipal assembly, but in the second century most municipalities transferred it to the local senate.

Each municipality had its own senate (*ordo* or *curia*) which usually consisted of 100 *decurions*, chosen by the magistrates in census years, and holding office for life. This body advised the magistrates, shaped the policies which they had to follow, supervised finance, and acted as a court of appeal from judicial sentences which they had passed. To be eligible for membership one had to be a free-born citizen of the municipality, of good character, twenty-five years old (exceptions being permitted), and pay the usual entrance fee. He had also to own a small estate, and dared not engage in certain prohibited callings. Thus the decurions and their families formed a local aristocracy (*curiales*). The imperial government exempted them from certain cruel and disgraceful punishments, and gave them a few other privileges, but both local and imperial governments charged them with heavy responsibilities. In them we may see the sturdy, moral, and efficient middle class of the western provinces.

Of the municipal assemblies, little need be said, for they were of small importance. At first they had the right to make by-laws and to elect officials; however, in the second century most of them lost these powers to their senates, and gradually ceased to exist. But our whole picture is a general one, to which exceptions were both numerous and pronounced.

In the East, Greek influence was as strong as was Latin influence in the West. Here the old Hellenic cities preserved their earlier constitutions with great tenacity, and the Hellenistic cities of Asia usually copied one or another of the constitutions of the homeland rather closely. Thus, we hear of Asiatic cities with archons, generals, council, and assembly as at Athens, and of others whose constitutions had a Dorian character. Hellenistic accretions to these institutions were to be found in such offices as that of *agoranomus*, which corresponded to the Roman aedileship. In general, it may be said that the average Greek city had a council much larger than a Latin *curia* (often as many as five hundred members, or even more), and that the assemblies were more influential than in the West.

The powers of each municipality were determined by its charter. All had extensive jurisdiction over local affairs, but it is hard to find two in which their extent was identical. This tendency to discriminatory treatment, as we have seen in our study of provincial government under the Republic, had always been a feature of Roman policy, and it was compli-

*Metropolitan Museum*

MODEL OF A LUXURIOUS ROMAN HOUSE

*First Century A. D.*

cated by the frequent changes made in the status of individual cities, especially in the East. Some had the right "to live under their own laws," a phrase which apparently gave them control over all cases not involving imperial questions. Others could only legislate on less important matters, and were subject to the provincial governors in the more serious ones. All, except Roman colonies having the *ius Italicum*, had to pay tribute, and when a city's finances fell into disorder the governor stepped in to regulate them as a matter of course.

The pattern of municipal finance was, however, remarkably uniform. In very few cases were there any direct local taxes. Income was derived from indirect taxes such as tolls upon produce entering the city, rents from municipal lands and buildings, fines, forfeitures, gifts from rich citizens, fees paid by magistrates and decurions upon entering office, and income from endowments. The endowments were usually provided by gifts, and the income from each was earmarked for a particular purpose, such as providing feasts, baths, or shows for the citizens, or for the upkeep of public buildings. The generosity of the richer citizens toward their fellow townsmen was little less than miraculous, and was a factor of first importance in the financing and beautification of the cities.

In considering expenditures, we must begin by disposing of an item which bulks large in American municipal government — official salaries. Neither magistrates, decurions, nor priests received any remuneration for their services. On the contrary, all were expected to pay heavily for the right to hold their respective offices. These payments, which went under the name of *summa honoraria*, were set, in each case, by the charter. Thus, a seat in the curia of an Umbrian town cost 6000 sesterces, and the chief magistracy of a Sardinian town cost 3500. But a priesthood at Massilia cost 100,000 sesterces, and in an obscure African town, 600,000. Furthermore, if a candidate promised more than the minimum sum as an incentive to the voters to choose him, the additional amount was collectible at law.

Municipal services were numerous and expensive. Paved streets, a public water-supply through one or more aqueducts, disposal of sewage and garbage, public libraries, schools, and police protection all roughly parallel modern conditions. In addition, the city undertook to insure a supply of food at moderate prices, to keep up temples and provide for sacrifices, and to furnish entertainment in the form of theatrical performances, gladiatorial shows, wild-beast hunts, and feasts. Public buildings such as temples and baths were erected at lavish cost, and usually with an eye to making the city appear as much as possible like a small-scale repro-

*Metropolitan Museum*

MODEL OF GROUND FLOOR OF ROMAN HOUSE

duction of Rome. All in all, city life was rendered both comfortable and attractive for rich and poor alike.

But the imperial government also made considerable demands upon the municipal governments. To care for their interests, a succession of embassies had to be sent to the provincial governors or to the Emperor. These were costly and unpleasant, the envoys often had to travel long distances at their own expense, and to endure contemptuous treatment from imperial officials or from the Emperor himself. Each municipality was responsible for the maintenance of the roads in its territory, and for the provision of oxen, horses, vehicles, and drivers for the imperial postal service or for traveling government officials. This burden grew heavier, and became especially ruinous in the third century. Lastly, under the Military Monarchy and throughout the subsequent history of the Empire, the responsibility of the local officials for the collection of imperial taxes and forced levies of provisions became a veritable scourge. It was this straw which, in the end, broke the curial camel's back.

Some of these services, both local and imperial, were paid for out of city funds, but many if not most were performed *gratis* by the citizens. This brings us to the liturgical system, one of the most characteristic features of Roman government under the Empire. It was recognized in Roman political theory that every man owed to both the local and imperial governments certain services involving either the expenditure of money (*munera patrimonii*), personal labor (*munera sordida*), or both. These fell upon all classes. A poor man might be called upon to give five full days' work a year upon public projects without compensation, or to lend animals for the public postal service or transportation. A rich man was much harder hit. To him fell the thankless task of embassies abroad at his own expense, or of taking charge of some branch of local administration, either entirely at his own cost or with insufficient funds which he had to supplement. Even the holding of local offices was a duty which an unwilling candidate could be forced to accept. Worst of all, was the task of collecting taxes or provisions for the imperial government, with the prospect of having to make good any deficiency from one's own estate.

For the first two centuries of the Principate, the municipal system seemed to function very well. Even then, a few cases occurred in which no candidates for office came forward, and unwilling ones had to be drafted, but the reverse was usually the case. Due principally to the prodigal generosity of wealthy citizens, money seemed to be plentiful for all public purposes. Cities vied with each other in the splendor of their public buildings, and the lavishness of their entertainments. Beauty, culture, and comfort seemed to be ends in themselves, and to be easily attainable. It is true that in many places (as we have seen in the case of the Bithynian cities under Trajan), excessive and unwise expenditure early brought the cities into financial difficulties. In such cases, the Emperor would appoint a senator or equestrian in whom he had confidence to act as an adviser to the embarrassed community. This official bore the title of *curator rei publicae* ("guardian of the corporation"). Before the end of the second century A.D. almost every provincial and Italian municipality had thus fallen under guardianship. Then came the crash when, under the hard conditions of the Military Monarchy, it was found that the pattern of municipal services could not be easily maintained along with the increased imperial exactions. Compulsion was applied to stimulate the curials to shoulder their burdens. When they tried to escape by deserting their cities, the imperial government applied the doctrine that each man had a legitimate place of residence, to which he owed service and to which he could be forcibly returned to perform his lawful duties. This rule was mercilessly applied to all men of property. With the reign of Maximinus began the confiscations of the municipal endowments by the emperors, at the same time that imperial taxes and levies were becoming much heavier.

Heavy as were these blows, they were as nothing to the calamities of the Military Anarchy. All along the northern and eastern frontiers, and for hundreds of miles into the interior, cities were plundered and destroyed and their people were massacred, carried off as slaves, or died of the plague. When the storm began to abate, the cities in these regions had suffered a mortal blow. As they were rebuilt in the 270's and 280's, they were small and poor. The lands upon which the citizens had depended for their incomes were often barren wastes, or else were settled by barbarian serfs. The wealth which had made possible their earlier brilliant careers was gone, and the imperial government had become a devouring monster, which held the remaining curials at their posts to serve as the instruments for the satisfaction of its insatiable demands.

## Society and Economic Organization

### *Social Classes*

Our previous discussion has made it evident that the people of the early Roman Empire were, like those of other ancient states, divided into well-defined social classes. In Roman law, each class had a recognized set of rights, privileges, and duties. The gradations were many, and in their totality were so complex that only the main outlines can be described here.

Although Roman citizenship conferred some real and valuable privileges, the similarities of status between the citizen and the non-citizen members of the same class were much more apparent than the differences, and after 212, there was only a negligible number of non-citizens left. Hence, for the sake of simplification, the distinction between these two groups may be largely ignored in the present discussion.

*The Aristocracy*

At the top of the social structure stood the aristocracy which, among Roman citizens, was represented by the senatorial and equestrian orders, and among the provincials, by various types of rich landlords who in time gained citizenship and merged with their Roman counterparts. Whatever the differences of origin and tenure among the members of this class, they were all the possessors of estates which were cultivated by tenants or slaves. With abundant leisure and opportunities for education, this group everywhere tended to conform to one of two cultures — Hellenistic in the

*Bettmann*

ROMAN YOUTH HOLDING STYLUS AND BOOK

*Mural about 70 A.D. Pompeii*

East, or Latin in the West. Its members were well informed about public affairs, and, up to the end of the second century, exercised a strong influence upon the government of the Empire. Many of them drifted to Rome, and from their number came the emperors and most of the high-ranking officials of the government in the peaceful and prosperous period between Nerva and Marcus Aurelius.

However stable the condition of this class might appear to be, its personnel was constantly changing. The concentration of wealth in the hands of these aristocrats made them an easy prey for emperors such as Caligula or Nero, who supplemented their regular income by extortion and spoliation. The former is said to have confiscated the property of two wealthy equestrians in order to make good his losses in a game of dice, while Nero, hearing that six men owned half of the province of Africa, immediately caused them to be executed for treason and their holdings to be seized. Many other families became extinct through lack of descendants, or were impoverished by prodigal expenditure. At the same time, men of wealth had no difficulty in gaining equestrian rank, and equestrians were constantly rising to senatorial status. By such steps, the grandsons of slaves sometimes found it possible to become great aristocrats.

*The Curials*

However, the chief source of recruits for the aristocracy was the urbanized middle class of Italy and the provinces, the curials. In the Greek world and in Italy, this class might be either the owners of small estates or successful tradesmen, but in the western provinces they were more likely to belong to the former than to the latter group. While many of the curials belonged to old and well-to-do families, this class was even more accessible to recruits from below than was the aristocracy. Self-made businessmen, time-expired centurions to whom land had been granted and who had saved large sums of money, or prosperous peasants, all found their way into its ranks. Freedmen were barred unless their disabilities were removed by a special imperial grant, but there was nothing to keep their sons from attaining curial status. Like their aristocratic neighbors (although to a lesser extent), these people enjoyed excellent educational opportunities, and to them went the greatest advantages of city life. Their sense of civic duty was, until the end of the second century, unbelievably strong. To attain membership in the local senate, to be elected to a magistracy, to receive a complimentary decree from their fellow townsmen, or to enjoy the honor of a statue voted by the decurions, were aims for the realization of which they were willing to pave streets, erect buildings, or provide endowments for their cities out of their modest estates. Inscriptions tell us of many cases of magistrates who voluntarily paid far more than the legal *summa honoraria*. Their imperial patriotism was apparently equally strong. From their ranks, the emperors from Vespasian to Hadrian recruited the bulk of their legionary soldiers, and up to the accession of Septimius Severus, they furnished most of the lower army officers. Having absorbed one of the two great cultures of the Mediterranean world, they served as unconscious missionaries for its dissemination. Furthermore, their sense of the unity and grandeur of the Empire made them, like the aristocrats, effective agents for the prevention of rebellions and separatist movements.

Yet throughout the late second and third centuries, this class was on the decline, and the reasons are of great interest to any one who would seek the cause for the ultimate overthrow of the Empire. The immediate cause must be sought in the policies of the imperial government, which, as we have seen, loaded them beyond bearing with the task of carrying out its commands. But this was a symptom of still deeper social ills rather than a cause in itself. If the prosperity of the whole population had not been on the decline, they might even have survived the increased demands of the Military Monarchy. If one examines their economic relationships closely, it becomes apparent that they were, like the aristocracy, to some extent parasites whose support cost more than they gave in return. This is particularly true of the landed proprietors, who collected rents from their tenants without any appreciable improvement of agricultural methods or other measures to maintain and increase the fertility of the soil. In industry, no noticeable improvements were made throughout the entire period of the Roman Empire. Thus, in a society whose productive capacity was always low, the very steps taken to adorn the cities and to render city life attractive inevitably resulted in the diversion of labor from necessary channels to those which were desirable but not indispensable. Indeed, it is even arguable that the imperial government itself was, in spite of all the benefits which it rendered, a luxury too expensive for the existing social and economic conditions. At any rate, when the cost of imperial government rose and the taxable income of the people failed to rise proportionately, its only recourse was to absorb the personal fortunes of the class which acted as its local agents. This fact, added to the calamities which the cities suffered in the third century A.D., completed the financial ruin of the once-prosperous middle class. In the fourth and fifth centuries, its surviving members were no more than slaves to the state, chained to the unwelcome task of performing forced services, and wringing taxes from a proletariat who hated them for their efforts.

### *The Urban Proletariat*

Beneath the curials in the social structure was a much larger class of common freemen, some of whom were urbanized, while many others lived in the country. In Rome, the emperors had to take over the task of feeding and amusing the urban proletariat, for Imperial Rome had as little productive economic life as Republican Rome had had. But that was not the case in the Italian cities, much less in those of the provinces. The great metropolitan centers of the Hellenistic East — Alexandria, Antioch, Tarsus, Corinth, Miletus, and Smyrna — were thriving hives of commerce and industry, in which slaves and freemen alike toiled for a livelihood, and this activity was reproduced on a smaller scale in the urban centers of Africa, Spain, Gaul, Britain, and the Danubian lands. From an economic viewpoint, the lot of the free urban worker had both advantages and disadvantages. Industry was organized on a small-scale basis, the average unit consisting of a shop in which the master was assisted by members of his family, free laborers, or a few slaves. Machinery was scarce and simple, and hence did not require much capital. A man who displayed industry and thrift could easily obtain sufficient funds to set himself up, either from a wealthy neighbor or from one of the numerous banks connected with municipal treasuries. Bakers, carpenters, tanners, weavers, fullers, potters, and metal workers could find a ready market for their products in the immediate vicinity of their shops. But there was also a fairly large class who were unable to take advantage of these opportunities, and who thus remained hired laborers. Their lot was a hard one, except as they shared in the general blessings of city life. Their wages were irrevocably set at a very low level by the existence of slave competition. Indeed, a large proportion of them, especially in the West, were freedmen. A bare sufficiency of simple food, coarse and threadbare clothing, and crowded living quarters were for them, as for the workmen of Republican Rome, the ordinary lot in life. But in many places they too shared in the free entertainment, public baths, distribution of food, and other largesse provided by the local governing classes.

### *Trade and Benefit Societies: The Collegia*

A remarkable feature of the life of the early Roman Empire was the extension of the voluntary associations of tradesmen and of benefit societies (*collegia*). The principles upon which they were founded have been discussed.[1] Although the ban against secret societies still existed, it did little or nothing to hamper non-political organizations. In the second century A.D., every town worthy of the name was likely to have an organization of workmen for each of the principal trades flourishing openly with a recognized place in municipal life. Each was organized on a city-wide basis, and so far as can be determined, there was no connection between those of the same trade in different places. Their purpose was primarily social, and there was little resemblance between them and either a medieval guild or a modern labor union. On festival days the members of each organization marched in a body, and they held feasts at stated intervals. Provision was made for funeral services of members, and for the care of the sick or the poor. Some of them served as volunteer fire companies. Each group had its patron deity, for whose worship it made provision. Some of them, like the shipowners of Rome and Alexandria, were favored by the government because they performed functions necessary to the provisioning of the capital; but in the end its favor proved more deadly than its opposition. During the third century, when industry and commerce alike proved unprofitable, merchants and craftsmen were on the verge of being forced out of business. At that point the government stepped in, converted the *collegia* into organs of control, and forbade men to leave their callings. Thenceforth, both production and distribution were in effect conducted by slaves of the state.

There were also organizations which were not connected with any trade, and served merely to satisfy the wants of the poor. As a rule, each served the double purpose of a social club and burial society. A good example would be the second-century *Collegium salutare Dianae et Antinoi* at Lanuvium, not far from Rome. Its members were slaves and very poor freemen. An initiation fee of one hundred sesterces and a jar of wine secured admission, while monthly dues were three asses. A slave member who secured his freedom had to treat his fellows to a jar of wine. Each officer of the organization had, upon induction into office, to provide a dinner consisting of a piece of bread, four sardines, and wine for each member of the society. Disorder at meetings and breaches of etiquette at dinners were punished with heavy fines. Each member at death was provided with a funeral costing three hundred sesterces, unless he were in arrears with his dues or had committed suicide, in which cases nothing was done for him. Many of these societies maintained special *ustrinae* for the cremation of corpses, and *columbaria* in which the ashes of members

[1] Chapter 18.

were deposited, with provision for rites to insure the peace of their souls.

### *The Peasantry*

Much more numerous than the city proletarians were the peasants who cultivated the soil. It would be a mistake to project the conditions existing on Italian estates of the first century B.C. into succeeding centuries, and suppose that agriculture in the Roman Empire was carried on chiefly by slaves. Such conditions were no longer dominant even in Italy, and in most of the provinces never existed. Instead we find the agricultural work of the Empire principally in the hands of free tenants, who farmed on a share-crop basis which varied widely with the locality. The system in vogue on the African imperial estates, in which the peasant held his land on a five-year lease, paying a third of his crop and six days' labor a year to the landlord, would probably not be far different from the one in use on private estates in the same province, and the combination of rent and labor for which it called was no doubt employed in most places. On the landlord's *demesne* (to use a medieval term), some slaves were no doubt employed in addition to the peasants. With a primitive plow and few other labor-saving devices, the peasant must have had to work hard for a very modest return. Apparently in many places it was the custom to restore the fertility of the soil by allowing it to lie fallow at intervals and by using it for pasture, a practice that was to be characteristic of the medieval manors in later centuries. Necessary as this method was in areas where clover and alfalfa were not sown, it greatly decreased the yield of a given piece of ground over a term of years. As a rule, the peasant did not live on his farm, as an American farmer does, but in a village from which he could go out each day to his land.

In general, the lot of the peasant was a hard one, for he had not only to pay his rent, but also to meet heavy imperial taxes and such irregular exactions as working on the public roads and furnishing of draft animals for the imperial post. In fact, as long as possible, the curials managed to pass all imperial levies on to the peasant without suffering from them themselves. He had little or no part in the brilliant city life which gave the Empire the appearance of such great prosperity in the second century A.D., and his educational advantages were nil. Culturally, he was much more conservative than the urban commoner. Long after the city dweller had learned to speak broken Greek or Latin, the peasant continued to use the tongue of his ancestors. Like the Italian farmers of whom Virgil wrote, he worshiped his rustic gods with a stubborn persistence which long withstood the advances of Christianity, and of which our present word "pagan" (from *paganus* — "villager" or "rustic") is a survival. While not disloyal to the Emperor, the peasant had no intelligent comprehension of the Empire, and in the troubles of the third century, his short-sighted insistence upon the protection of the segment of the frontier nearest to him lent strong support to such rebellions as that of Postumus in Gaul. But even a peasant could, if he possessed the requisite qualities, rise in the world. By serving twenty-five years in the auxiliary corps, or twenty in the legions, he could gain Roman citizenship and a sum sufficient to set him up in life. Occasionally a peasant with good business ability would gain sufficient wealth to warrant his admission to the curia. However, only a few could take advantage of these opportunities. In the main, this class tended to sink rather than rise. Hundreds of thousands of country people must have been killed or enslaved, and probably as many more died of the plague, during the calamities of the Military Anarchy. The survivors were regularly stripped of their produce to feed the armies and pay taxes. Agriculture ceased to be profitable, and the farmers attempted to escape by flight. It was then that the government undertook to revive agricultural production by crude and violent means. Captive barbarians were settled upon desolated lands as serfs, and early in the fourth century the survivors of the native peasant population were probably bound to the soil. At the end of the third century, the peasant might still be, in the eyes of the law, a freeman, but his freedom was only a mockery.

### *The Decline of Slavery*

While all classes of freemen, except the very rich, were sinking into social and economic dependence, the lot of the slave was improving. The diminished supply and consequent high price of slaves were primarily responsible for this, but humanitarian ideas propagated by the philosophers also worked toward the same end. Only when the slave was cheap and easily replaced was his sullen, inefficient labor profitable. When his price rose, his owner had to find means to give him an incentive to labor willingly. It was no doubt this fact which led to the decline of agricultural slavery in Italy. Roman custom had always made it easy for a slave to gain his liberty, and under the Empire it became still easier. Shrewd slaves were often freed and set up in business, with their former masters as silent partners. The emperors also intervened to protect those who were still in slavery. Beginning in the reign of Hadrian, a series of laws took away the master's right to kill his slave, forbade inhuman punishments, and protected female slaves from dishonor. At the accession of Diocletian, household servants and many industrial workers were still slaves, but slavery as an institution had entered upon a decline which was, centuries later, to lead to its complete disappearance from western Europe.

*Manufacturing and Commerce*

In manufacturing and commerce, the Romans of the Empire generally followed closely the methods of the Hellenistic Greeks. Technical processes remained as primitive as ever, although in restricted fields, such as the manufacture of Arretine pottery, the mechanics of large-scale production were in existence. We have seen how small the shops were from which issued the manufactured goods of the time. This was not entirely due to the lack of capital, for when they saw fit, the Romans could undertake tasks calling for huge expenditures and elaborate organization of effort. Labor-saving machinery was practically non-existent, and if it

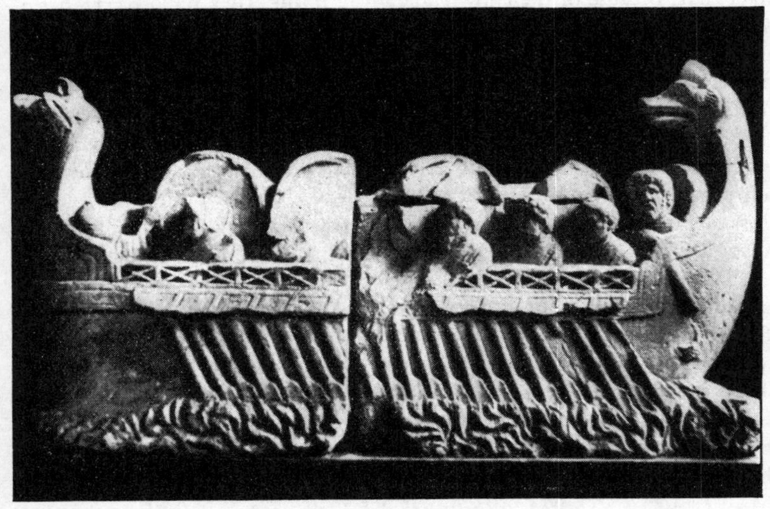

*Bettmann*

TRANSPORTING WINE CASKS ON THE RHINE

*Relief about 200 A.D. Neumagen, Germany*

had been available, there were no potential markets capable of absorbing the products. Indeed, as always in the ancient world, the great households attempted to be self-sufficient in both food and clothing, and on a smaller scale the middle class did much the same. With the rural population, poverty compelled men to produce as many as possible of their common necessities, and to buy very little. Only such articles as pottery, metal-work, leather, and luxury goods, which could not be economically produced at home, were likely to be bought at all in the open market, and of these, the last was out of the reach of the commoner. But transportation costs made it imperative that even these be produced as near as possible to their ultimate destination. Hence, manufactures spread from Italy to the western provinces, and by the end of the first century A.D., the Italians had lost control of the provincial markets for cheap merchandise.

Of luxury goods (such as "purple" dye or fine linen), Syria, Asia Minor, and Egypt produced a large share, but there were some which could be found only outside the Empire. Silk, spices, incense, and many other costly articles came from Arabia, India, and China. The chief drawback to all European commerce with these eastern lands has always been the fact that, because of their low standard of living, they import very little except the precious metals in payment for their exports. In the first century A.D., the Empire had, in its dealings with them, an average annual adverse trade-balance of about one hundred million sesterces. At the other extremity of the Empire, the German, Moorish, and other barbarian tribes outside the frontier were willing enough to buy Roman goods, but they had very little money or goods with which to pay, and could buy only in accordance with their means. Hence, the net result was a large loss of precious metals each year. During the Military Anarchy, currency disorders brought commerce with the East practically to a standstill.

If we attempt to sum up the data on the state of the Roman Empire about 285, gleaned from the foregoing pages, the picture is a dismal one. Society was coming more and more to be composed of only the very rich and the very poor, with the producing class chained to their occupations. To this fact must be added a bankrupt treasury, a worthless currency, ravaged lands, and depleted population, all under an autocratic emperor, backed by a mercenary army and a bureaucratic civil service. Nearly two hundred years were still to elapse before Rome's strength in the western Mediterranean area was broken, but her great days were over.

# 25

# *The Civilization of the Early Roman Empire: Art, Intellect, and Religion*

## Introduction

### *The Decay of Classical Culture*

For two centuries and a half after the death of Augustus, the Graeco-Latin culture of the Roman Empire continued to cherish the intellectual and artistic traditions of its great past, but the stream was running low, and its current was becoming progressively more feeble. During the first century of this period it produced much that was worthy to rank with the lesser triumphs of earlier ages. Then came a century of stagnation, and following it, a sharp and rapid decline. Literature succumbed to a taste for showy rhetoric and to blind worship of the past, and of the arts only architecture was producing anything which was destined to win the approval of later ages. Science and philosophy lingered a little longer, but before the accession of Diocletian they, too, had succumbed to the forces which were bringing the classical world to an end. The decline of economic prosperity, the breakdown of political order, the weakening of urban life, the growth of political absolutism, and a caste-ridden social order — all contributed to create an environment in which none of the distinctive products of earlier ages could flourish. Hence, they withered away, and men began to follow lines of thought more appropriate to the times.

### *New Tendencies: The Diffusion of Civilization*

The decline of classical culture did not bring about complete intellectual stagnation. We have seen that the third century A.D. produced many of

Rome's greatest thinkers in the field of law, and mystical religions had never before commanded so much attention. This was the age in which Christianity was weaving the great principles of its founder into a philosophy fit to captivate the intellects and win the allegiance of the educated classes throughout the Roman world. Ethics ceased to be a branch of philosophy and became associated with religion, thus placing moral guidance within easier reach of the masses than before.

Furthermore, this period witnessed the spread of Graeco-Roman culture over practically the whole of the Empire. West of the Sicilian Narrows, and in the Danube Valley, the Latin language and Roman civilization penetrated the more progressive communities, transforming the cities into slightly vulgarized replicas of Rome. In Asia and Egypt, Greek culture made a lasting impression upon the Oriental civilizations which were later to engulf it. In short, the cosmopolitan culture of the Roman Empire was becoming the common property of the whole known world.

## Art

### *Architecture: Temples, Amphitheaters, Triumphal Arches, Baths, and Fora*

It was in architecture that the artistic genius of the Roman people found the best opportunity for self-expression, and retained its creative power longest. The two hundred and fifty years following the death of Augustus witnessed the creation of the most impressive architectural monuments in Rome, and the spread of Roman styles of building over enormous areas in the provinces. Perhaps the most significant features of Roman architecture are a penchant for utilitarianism and a tendency toward massive grandeur of construction. In structural methods, the increased use of concrete made it feasible to produce those enormous masses of building which have withstood the strains of nearly two thousand years without collapse. But the Romans never allowed the ugly surface of the concrete to be seen in their more pretentious edifices. Instead, they faced it with sawed or hammer-dressed stone of the best quality and appearance that their means afforded. The use of the arch, vault, and dome grew more and more daring as the possibilities of the material came to be realized, until it produced such gigantic piles as the Pantheon, the Baths of Caracalla, the Tomb of Hadrian, or the Colosseum. Yet the foregoing are only a few of the most outstanding creations.

Although the original Pantheon (a temple built to honor the deities connected with the Julian clan) was the work of Marcus Agrippa, the building in its present form was constructed by Hadrian. It consists of a

*Metropolitan Museum*

MODEL OF THE PANTHEON
(*Hypothetical Restoration*)

tremendous round dome, which is entered through a portico. The dome itself is one of the boldest ventures ever undertaken by an ancient architect. Its inside diameter and height each measures 144 feet, while the walls are brick-faced concrete over 20 feet in thickness. A round opening nearly 30 feet in diameter, located in the top of the dome, admits light. The inside wall is relieved from monotony by the fact that it is divided by ring-cornices into three stories. The first two are cut by niches let into the thickness of the wall, while the uppermost is coffered to within a short distance of the opening at the top. The portico measures 111 feet by 44 feet on the floor, and its roof is held up by 16 Corinthian columns of granite, arranged in three rows. This imposing structure has suffered little damage in the eighteen centuries since its completion, and is today used as a Christian church.

Throughout the Romanized West, the craving for gladiatorial combats and wild-beast hunts produced amphitheaters of various sizes and degrees of artistic beauty, but of these, easily the first in size and magnificence, was the celebrated Flavian Amphitheater (commonly called the Colosseum) at Rome. It was begun by Vespasian shortly after the suppression of the Jewish Rebellion, and was finished by Domitian. It stands on the ground

*University Prints*

COLOSSEUM AT ROME

between the Palatine and Esquiline hills, and is elliptical in shape, with a long axis of 614 feet and a short axis of 512 feet, outside measurements. When intact, its outer wall had a height of 169 feet. The cores of the walls were made of concrete, and were originally faced on the outside with travertine stone and on the inner surfaces with various kinds of stone and brick. The exterior rose in a series of four stories, the three lower consisting of open arcades alternating with half columns. Those of the first story were Doric, of the second, Ionic, and of the third, Corinthian. The fourth story was a solid wall, ornamented with Corinthian pilasters. The arena, an elliptical space in the center of the structure, had axes measuring 271 feet by 176 feet. Beneath the floor of the arena were dens for beasts, cells for condemned criminals, and an elaborate drainage system. It was surrounded by a strong fence to protect the spectators. Between it and the outer wall were three tiers of seats, running completely around the structure, and accommodating some 45,000 persons. Above the uppermost story was a "grandstand" roof, on which about 5000 persons could find standing room. An elaborate series of entrances and exits permitted the crowds to leave it in only a few minutes. These are merely the more obvious points in the construction of the most massive and impressive monument bequeathed by the Romans to later times. Today, stripped and ruined though it is, the Colosseum moves the admiration of the spectator, an enduring reminder of "the grandeur that was Rome."

Another type of structure common in Imperial Rome was the triumphal arch. As early as the second century B.C., massive single arches had been erected to commemorate notable victories and the generals who won them. So far as the city of Rome is concerned, the earliest surviving arch of this kind is the one erected in honor of the Emperor Titus to commemorate his capture of Jerusalem. It is a single arch of Pentelic marble, which measures on the outside, 50 feet in height, 44 feet in width, 15 feet, 5 inches in depth. The opening is about 27 feet high, and 17½ feet wide. On the inner jambs are fine, spirited reliefs, one of which represents the spoils of the Temple of Yahweh borne in Titus' triumph, while the other portrays the Conqueror himself riding in his chariot and crowned by Victory. Later triumphal arches were usually built with triple openings, and a great many examples survive both in Rome and the provinces. Noteworthy are the Arch of Trajan at Beneventum, and the Arch of Septimius Severus at Rome, while the fourth century produced in Rome the Arch of Constantine. All of them are decorated with reliefs on a much more lavish scale than the one just described.

The building of temples continued, and when destroyed, they were rebuilt at government expense. The famous Capitoline Temple was several times burned and rebuilt. But perhaps the most remarkable architectural creation of the period in this field was the second-century Temple of Venus and Roma, designed by no less a person than the Emperor Hadrian. It stood on the "Sacred Way," just north of the Colosseum, on a raised concrete platform about 475 feet long and 325 feet wide. Its longer sides supported elaborate colonnades. The temple proper was placed on a low platform in the middle of the larger one. Its walls were built of concrete covered with marble, and it was surrounded by a Corinthian colonnade of Pentelic marble. It consisted of two cells, placed back to back, each ending in a semicircular apse. These rooms were entered at the ends, through *prostyles* of four columns each, flanked by elongations of the walls which the Greeks called *antae*. The roof was a barrel vault of concrete, covered with a temporary roof of tiles.

Experiments with various kinds of vaulting also produced interesting and important effects in Rome's most popular type of building, public baths. Smaller bathing establishments had long been known, but only in the post-Augustan period did the builders undertake the stupendous piles of concrete and stone which, even when in ruins, are awe-inspiring. Titus, Trajan, and Caracalla each attempted to erect a larger or more imposing bath than his predecessors. The celebrated Baths of Caracalla measured 704 feet by 691 feet, and could accommodate 1600 bathers at a time. The principal hall, which was 163 feet long and 79 feet wide, was covered with a barrel vault intersected by three cross vaults. At the ends of the cross vaults and the main vault, windows were placed. It contained a swimming pool, a warm bath, and a hot bath, with dressing rooms and drying rooms; but bathing was only one of the many forms of amusement carried on here. In the wings were open courts for athletic exercises, with complexes of rooms surrounding them. At one time this huge structure even housed a temple of the Oriental Sun-god Mithra. The enclosure in which the baths stood measured about 1150 feet by 1100 feet, and was surrounded by a wall, to the inside of which were attached porticoes, alternating with rooms used for restaurants and various other purposes. In the early fourth century, the Baths of Diocletian even surpassed the earlier baths in size.

Basilicas also played an important part in the communal life of Imperial Rome. Their general plan and purpose has been described earlier,[1] and no important changes were made in their construction until the fourth century. Among the largest erected during this period was the Basilica Ulpia built by Trajan on one side of his new forum.

Under the early Empire, Rome continued to be adorned with additional *fora*, all located in close proximity to those of the Republic and the Augustan Age. Somewhat to the southeast of the Forum of Augustus, Domitian began the construction of a long, narrow forum which, being unfinished at the time of his death, was completed by Nerva and bears his name. It was surrounded by a high wall, to the inside of which was attached a colonnade surmounted by sculptured panels. Even in its present ruined condition, it is a work of remarkable beauty. Northeast from the Forum of Augustus, Trajan laid out the one which bears his name, the largest and most ornate of all. It was in part excavated from solid rock, and consisted of a square court, surrounded on three sides by a colonnade, with the Basilica Ulpia on the fourth. In a small court beyond the Basilica stood the celebrated Column of Trajan, flanked by two libraries, one for Latin books and the other for Greek. Still farther to the north Hadrian built the Temple of the Divine Trajan.

The Column of Trajan is itself one of the wonders of the city. It is a hollow shaft of Parian marble, which, with its pedestal, reaches a height

[1] Chapter 18.

*Brown Brothers*

COLUMN OF TRAJAN

of 124 feet. The interior is lighted by slits cut into the wall, and it contains a spiral staircase of 185 steps. The outside of the shaft is decorated with a band of relief sculpture, which winds around it from the base to the summit, and which tells the story of Trajan's Dacian wars. To give it the appearance of uniform height throughout its length, the width of this band gradually increases from less than three feet to more than four feet. Originally a statue of Trajan crowned the monument, and the ashes of the Emperor and his wife rested in a chamber in the base. An obvious imitation of it is the Column of Marcus Aurelius, built on the same plan with the same dimensions, and relating in sculptures the history of the German wars of the Philosopher-Emperor.

### *Architectural Remains in the Provinces*

Provincial urban centers, while never able to vie with the capital in magnificence of their architecture, had many fine public buildings, aqueducts, bridges, baths, and amphitheaters. Except in Africa, few of the buildings have escaped the ravages of time, but surviving examples like the Capitoline Temple of Thugga or the *Maison Carrée* of the Gallic city of Nîmes, show that they sometimes attained both grace and beauty. Bridges, amphitheaters, and aqueducts have left more numerous and impressive traces. The bridge of Alcantara in Spain is still in use, and towers 197 feet above the surface of the Tagus River. The ruins of the aqueduct

*Keystone*

MAISON CARRÉE
*Nîmes, France*

of Nîmes (known to modern times as the *Pont du Gard*) rises on three tiers of arches 160 feet above the Gard River. The city aqueduct of Lugdunum was 52 miles long, receiving its water from the slopes of Mt. Pilat. The amphitheater of Pola in Dalmatia (one of many such provincial structures) accommodated 23,000 persons. These are only a few examples from the hundreds of similar structures which once adorned the cities of Rome's western provinces. Greek and Oriental centers were adorned with colonnaded temples, baths, libraries, and other public works.

### *Sculpture: Reliefs and Portrait Statues*

In the first and early second centuries, Roman sculpture continued to flourish, but soon after experienced a sharp decline. No doubt as a result of accident, we have no striking post-Augustan work earlier than the reign of Domitian, when the reliefs of the Arch of Titus were carved. In these we are introduced to a new style, which differs sharply from that prevalent under Augustus. They display the same technical mastery as the earlier works, but instead of the quiet dignity of the reliefs which decorate the Altar of Peace, they are full of life, movement, and emotion. On the south wall we see the laurel-crowned Roman soldiers bearing the Seven-Branched Candlesticks and the Table of Shewbread (familiar to readers of the Old Testament), behind trumpeters and standard-bearers, and amid a motley throng of spectators. On the north wall, we see Titus himself approaching in a six-horse chariot, accompanied by the symbolic figures of Honor and Worth. The faults of this work are easy to see. An attempt is made to attain depth by a use of perspective legitimate only in painting, and the effect is not entirely pleasing. But so magnificent is the sweep of the scenes that one can almost hear the stamp of the marching men and the roar of thousands of excited voices. If the artist's aim was to secure an illusion of reality, he has succeeded.

The reliefs of Trajan's Column were probably not more than twenty-five years later in time than those of the Arch of Titus. In general, they display the same mastery of technical detail, combined with a prosaic realism and power of composition which makes the whole spiral read like a written history of the Dacian Wars. Scenery is treated with what we may suppose is photographic exactness, the Danubian towns, the mountains and forests of Dacia, and the Danube with the imperial fleet afloat upon it. The artist portrays for us the various barbarian neighbors of the Empire with a realism which makes the column a mine of information for the historian and anthropologist. However, there is little or none of the dignity

*Galloway*

ARCH OF TITUS
*Showing the Spoils of Jerusalem*

of the Augustan sculptures, or of the excited animation of the Arch of Titus.

The Antonine Column marks a further decline in art. Perhaps because of the nature of the subject, no connected narrative is attempted, but the whole is organized into a series of scenes from the wars of Marcus Aurelius — the miraculous rain which saved the Roman army, the beheading of the German chiefs, and similar themes. The workmanship is often faulty, even descending to crudity, and there is an almost complete lack of creative power throughout the composition.

Portrait sculpture had meanwhile continued to develop throughout the first two centuries of the Empire, and it retained its power of characterization much longer than relief sculpture. There is an excellent series of imperial busts running far down into the third century, including those of

Vespasian, Trajan, Hadrian, Caracalla, and Gallienus. Among them is the excellent equestrian statue of Marcus Aurelius which is infused with the dignity and strength of the subject. Indeed, it is possible to see in these portraits the changing types of individuals who wore the imperial purple, from the erudite and masterful Hadrian to the brutal Caracalla and the barbarian Maximinus. But, by the end of the third century, even this field had fallen into the same decadence as the rest.

Sculpture of various kinds also flourished in Italy and the provinces. There we find little that can be called refined art, but when the provincial stone-cutters attempted to record the life which they saw about them, their matter-of-fact reproductions of familiar scenes acquired both a historical value and a beauty of their own. Whether in Italy or in the provinces, the common man was proud of his trade, and liked nothing better than to have himself portrayed on his tombstone as doing his daily task. Teamsters, smiths, small shopkeepers, potters, and other craftsmen, as well as soldiers, followed this practice, and it has left us a wealth of data on their everyday life. Bankers sit at desks counting their day's receipts; tradesmen haggle with customers; fullers stand in tubs tramping the dirt from clothing; or a cavalryman rides down a foe. Such reliefs are often crudely executed, but they represent the everyday life of the common people, and as such have a freshness and spontaneity which the more formal work often lacks.

### *Painting and Mosaic*

Of painting we naturally have few remains, and these few are principally from the buried cities of Pompeii and Herculaneum, and from the Catacombs where the early Christians buried their dead. The former group belonged to the so-called "fourth style," which is similar in spirit and execution to the reliefs of the Arch of Titus. There is the same tendency to restlessness, motion, and gay coloring. Many of these paintings are copies of Greek originals, but even in such cases the artist usually chose those which would represent struggles or incidents full of emotion. To vary these he would at times paint scenes of trivial prettiness, depicting cupids, satyrs, nymphs, and other cheerful figures from the world of gods.

Very different are the early Christian paintings from the walls of the Roman Catacombs. There the painter used the technique learned from his pagan teachers, but he was inspired by a new idea, and his works reflect this new attitude. In actual skill he did not equal his pagan contemporaries, but, like his fellow Christians, he was attempting to convey a message to those who saw his work. His themes were often symbolic: Christ as the Good Shepherd, a fish (the mystic symbol of Christ), or doves. Occasionally he painted the portrait of a dignitary of the church, and in a few cases these are masterful productions. When Diocletian became emperor, painting had sunk as low as sculpture, but in Christian painting there was hope for the future.

Mosaic work flourished long after good workmanship and creativity in the other fine arts had ceased. Especially in Africa, we find men of means decorating their homes with elaborate compositions showing them engaged in the daily business of life, or enjoying sports. For this reason, some of the mosaic floors from North African villas are exceedingly valuable documents in the study of social and economic history.

## Post-Augustan Literature

When Augustus died, the literary genius of the Roman people, which had blossomed so luxuriantly in the early part of his reign, was temporarily spent, and for a generation thereafter it produced little of merit. From the reign of Tiberius we have only the second-rate *History* of Marcus Velleius Paterculus, and the *Memorable Deeds and Sayings* of Valerius Maximus. The *Philippic History* of Trogus Pompeius, which seems to have been far superior to either of the foregoing, is only preserved in the form of a later epitome. The short reign of Caligula was utterly barren.

### *The Silver Age: Seneca, Lucan, and Petronius*

With the accession of Claudius, however, there began a revival of literary activity which was to last for nearly a century, and to which the appropriate name "Silver Age" is commonly applied. While it did not produce much that can be compared to the work of the great Augustan poets, or to the immortal prose of Livy, it has bequeathed to modern times numerous products of creditable worth, and several works of undoubted genius. Before 150 A.D., the great age of Roman literature was definitely past.

The earliest of the Silver Age writers was the Spaniard Lucius Annaeus Seneca (3 B.C.–65 A.D.), previously mentioned as one of the ministers of Nero. His private career was a queer mixture of good and evil, including a very questionable part in Nero's murder of his mother as well as other public acts of similar character. But in his later days, Seneca retired to a life of Stoic asceticism, and it was apparently in this last period of his life that he wrote the philosophic treatises and letters of advice which have been preserved. In this field, three long essays (*Benefits*, *Anger*, and *Questions about Nature*), together with some shorter tracts, and a hundred and twenty-four *Moral Letters* are known to have come from his pen. His style is labored and often artificial, while the thought is by no means always original. But when all this has been said, there remains a nobility of sentiment and a searching analysis of the vices and discontents of the jaded Roman aristocracy of his time which cannot fail to impress the reader. So close did he come at times to Christian ideas that later Church fathers felt as if he had almost belonged to them, and there grew up a legend that he had been in touch with the Apostle Paul. Many a reader, both ancient and modern, has found him a source of strength and comfort.

But Seneca was also a poet, dramatist, and satirist. Nine extant tragedies are attributed to him with certainty. They follow well-worn themes previously treated (and much better handled) by the Greek tragedians. As literature they rank very low, and it is well for Seneca's reputation that we do not have to judge him entirely by them. His one surviving satire is a spiteful burlesque on the Emperor Claudius, recounting the adventures of the absent-minded Emperor in the world to come.

A much better poet than Seneca was his nephew Marcus Annaeus Lucanus (39–65), who like him was a member of the court circle of Nero. For a time Lucan enjoyed Nero's favor, but literary jealousy soon produced a quarrel which caused the poet to join in the conspiracy of Piso. He was arrested, tried to make peace by betraying his accomplices, and then, finding this of no avail, died bravely. His only surviving work is the *Pharsalia*, an epic on the civil war of Caesar and Pompey. It is written in dactylic hexameter, and is divided into ten books. Lucan's public demanded a bombastic rhetorical style, sensational and shocking incidents, neat sayings, and high-flown sentiments. Although he satisfied this decadent taste to the full, a judgment based upon these faults alone would be unfair. He shows some originality in discarding the machinery of divine intervention employed by Homer and Virgil, and occasionally his rhetoric rises to the level of true eloquence or stirring pathos.

Nero's court also produced a great realist, who could record the low life of his day with convincing fidelity and without a touch of bombast. His name was Gaius Petronius, and although a friend of the Emperor, he was later forced to commit suicide. His only extant work is a portion of a burlesque novel, the *Satyricon*. The chief characters bear Greek names, and they are, whether men or women, both depraved and dishonest.

*Bettmann*

ARCH OF TITUS

Their speech is the Latin of the streets, which the author handles with easy mastery. But the book is not entirely given over to filth. Gems of literary criticism occasionally fall from the mouths of abandoned wretches, and it would be hard to find a more merciless exposé of professional legacy-hunters or of the vulgarity of rich upstarts anywhere in the literature of the world. *Trimalchio's Dinner*, the portion most often read by modern students, presents the picture of a multi-millionaire freedman, his ridiculous attempts at refined luxury and culture, and his crass and tiresome freedman friends.

### *Satire: Persius, Martial, and Juvenal*

Not all of the literature of Nero's reign was produced by the court circle. Aulus Persius Flaccus (34–62), a wealthy young equestrian from Volaterra in Etruria, undertook to satirize, from the Stoic point of view, the faults and failings of his fellowmen as he saw them. His model in this enterprise was Lucilius.[1] Persius lived a retired life, which precluded any intimate knowledge of the immorality and crime which Petronius portrayed in such glaring colors. His style is obscure, but the nobility of his thought, and the fervor with which he preaches it, command both sympathy and respect.

In addition to these wealthy men who employed their leisure in writing, there was, in Rome, a class of poor men of letters who knew the seamy side of life from personal experience. The smallness of the reading public and the absence of newspapers and periodicals prevented their earning a living by their pens, and they were forced to depend upon the bounty of wealthy men with literary tastes. If the writer had any pride, such a life was all but unbearable, for he was exposed to the insolence of the patron and his servants, and to the competition of lowbred freedmen or Greek adventurers who tried to monopolize the patron's scanty favors. To realize the degradation of such a life is to understand the bitterness with which it tipped the pens of Martial and Juvenal.

Marcus Valerius Martialis (40–105) was a Spaniard of poor family, who came to Rome about 64 and remained there for thirty-six years, supplementing the slender returns from his writings by the type of genteel beggary mentioned above. For this purpose he flattered all who would help him (including Domitian), and stabbed with barbed epigrams those who refused his pleas or gave too little. To cater to the tastes of a depraved society he wrote at times with shocking coarseness, and he never hesitated to ask for gifts. He won fame and eked out a living, but gained neither wealth nor social position. Finally, a wealthy Spanish lady gave him a small estate in his native country, and thither he returned to spend his last years.

Martial's favorite verse form was the epigram, which had long been popular among the Greeks, but up to that time not much used by Roman poets. In its Greek form it had been merely a short, expressive, occasional poem, which generally conveyed a serious sentiment. In a few cases, Martial followed the Greek custom, as in his noble description of the suicide of Paetus Thrasea and his heroic wife:

> When the pure Arria gave to Paetus the sword which she had drawn from her body she said: "If you will believe me, my wound does not hurt; but what you are about to do, Paetus, will hurt me."[2]

[1] Chapter 14. [2] *Epigrams*, I, 13.

However, most of Martial's epigrams have a witty, satirical point, meant to raise a laugh at the expense of the victim; some of them carry poisoned stings. Thus,

> You serve the best wines, Paulus; but gossip says they poisoned four wives for you. It isn't true of course; and I don't believe it. All the same, I don't want any of your wine.[1]

Ranting lawyers, ill-mannered patrons who neglect their poor clients, social climbers, old women who try to appear young, poor men who try to act the part of millionaires, and a great many other ludicrous figures are the butts of his raillery. He wastes no moral indignation upon his victims, but leaves that to his readers. He is often very brutal, but he must have been a popular figure in his own day. It is to him that we owe our present concept of the epigram as a vehicle for the expression of pointed satire.

Decimus Junius Juvenalis, a contemporary and friend of Martial, was a satirist of a different kind. Of his personal career we have few authentic particulars. It would seem that he was the son or adopted son of a rich freedman from the Italian city of Aquinum, and that he spent his adult years in Rome. Whatever his financial status, he seems to have been, like Martial, a hanger-on of wealthy patrons, and he can describe in strong colors the miseries of such a life.

From Juvenal's pen we have sixteen satires, written in hexameter verse. Each of them is a rhetorical essay upon some phase of Roman life, except the fifteenth, which relates an incident that had recently occurred in Egypt. In them we must not seek the gay spitefulness of Martial. Juvenal was a moralist who either hated, or affected to hate, the vices of Roman society, and he found it full of vice. Hence, he puts before us Rome at her worst — the home of luxury, immorality, flattery, faithlessness, and murder. We can see his anger rise to white heat as he describes the shameful deeds of her aristocrats, both men and women, but a further reading discloses that Juvenal has three pet dislikes: Greeks, women, and stingy patrons. He considers the first of these as hungry, oily-tongued, brassy hypocrites, who elbow poor but honest Romans out of the good graces of generous patrons. His famous *Sixth Satire* is a confused indictment of the whole female sex, in which he adopts the thesis that there are few good women, and that they are unendurable by reason of their pride. Murder and adultery are ranged side by side in his thinking with nagging, the affectation of learning, addiction to Oriental cults, and pride of ances-

[1] *Ibid.* IV, 69.

*University Prints*

THE MIRACULOUS RAIN

*Relief from the Column of Marcus Aurelius*

try. Of the patrons he says, in blunter fashion, about the same as Martial.

Occasionally Juvenal's grumbling rises to the level of genius. His *Third Satire*, which describes the ills of city life and lauds the country, is so eternally true to life that with a few minor changes it is as valid today as when it was written. In the eighteenth century of our era, Dr. Samuel Johnson used it, with only a little retouching, as the basis of his *London*. In the same way, *Satire X*, *On the Vanity of Human Wishes*, carries a message to every generation. We need not accept Juvenal's picture of Roman society as universally true, but no doubt he dragged into the light some of its most glaring and repulsive evils, and in so doing created some of the finest word-pictures in Roman literature.

### *The Pervigilium Veneris*

After Juvenal, the Roman world produced but one poetic genius — the unknown author of the second century *Pervigilium Veneris*, or *Venus's Eve*.

In both meter and vocabulary it shows a break with the classical tradition. The former is trochaic septenarian, once commonly used by Roman writers, but later crowded out by Greek meters, while the latter differs widely from that of the first century. It is the night before the spring festival of Venus, and the author is thinking of the brilliant pageant of the morrow:

> Tomorrow let him love who never loved; and who has loved, tomorrow let him love. Spring has come; tuneful spring; spring is the world reborn. Spring is the season of love and of mating birds, when the grove lets down its tresses, bathed by fertilizing showers.[1]

Tomorrow Venus, the mother of all nature, will hold sway upon her lofty throne, and all nature will break forth into beauty at her command. Roses, bathed in dew, will burst into bloom, and flowers will spring up spontaneously in the fields. Diana will cease her hunting and come to the festival, and nymphs will roam about, accompanied by Cupid who, for the day, will be deprived of his arms. At intervals, the florid beauty of the description is broken by the refrain, "Tomorrow let him love who never loved, and who has loved, tomorrow let him love." But there is no joy in the heart of the poet. "She sings, but we are silent. When will my spring come? When shall I, like the swallow, break my silence?"[2] Simple as is its structure, no translation can do it justice. It was the swan-song of Latin poetry. Thereafter Rome produced some creditable versifiers, but no great poets.

### *Latin Prose: Science, Oratory, and Letter-Writing*

Meanwhile, the use of prose as a medium of expression had not ended with Seneca. Scientific and near-scientific manuals became fashionable, and a number of them were written during the latter half of the first century. Thus Lucius Junius Columella, a contemporary of Seneca, composed an extensive treatise on agriculture, which combined practical knowledge with literary charm to a degree hitherto unknown in agricultural textbooks. More extensive and ambitious was the *Natural History* of Gaius Plinius Secundus (23–79), a native of the Po Valley, commonly known as the elder Pliny. While leading the life of a busy official, Pliny managed to compile this extensive encyclopedia, which contains twenty thousand separate articles, and for which material was drawn from two thousand volumes of reference. The style, as befits the subject, is bald and

[1] Lines 1–4. [2] Lines 89–90.

matter-of-fact, relieved at times by rather commonplace moralizing. Its distinguishing feature is the author's omnivorous credulity. He finds it possible to believe that there are men with only one eye located in the center of the forehead, men with dog's heads, and others who have only one foot. In recording these absurdities he was no worse and no better than his time. It was from him, directly or indirectly, that medieval writers drew wonder-tales with which to embellish their works, and some of his stories were believed until the days of the Renaissance. A few years after Pliny's death, Sextus Julius Frontinus wrote a booklet on the subject *Aqueducts*, based upon his own experience as superintendent of the Roman water-supply, and another on *Stratagems*. Neither one has great literary worth, but they are full of valuable technical knowledge.

A much higher place must be assigned to the *Orator* of Marcus Fabius Quintilianus (40–118). The author was a Spaniard who spent his adult years in Rome, where his teaching gained him an imperial pension and senatorial rank. His *Orator* is, in fact, a broad and comprehensive statement of his theory of education, as well as a discussion of training in his particular field. Not only does he adopt Cato's theory that an orator is "a good man skilled in speaking," but he also insists that the high character necessary to the ideal orator must be formed by a combination of pure home environment, careful teaching, and broad background. Such an education does not end when maturity has been reached, but continues throughout life. In the technical portion of his book, Quintilian tends to go back to Cicero as a model, and to discard the rhetorical ornaments with which speakers had overloaded their works since the days of Augustus. Thus, he was one of the earliest advocates of an archaistic trend which was to become dominant in Roman literature in the second century. But however much we may disagree with some of his views, those which deal with general education are with few exceptions as valid today as they were in the first century A.D.

Among Quintilian's students was Gaius Plinius Caecilius Secundus, the nephew and adopted son of the author of the *Natural History*. With ample means and assured social standing, the younger Pliny led a busy life as an official and devoted his leisure to literature. In 100, he was consul, and later, as we have seen, he was sent to govern Bithynia. Of all his voluminous works, only one oration (the *Panegyric*) and ten books of his collected letters have survived. Both show an effort to imitate Cicero in an age which had completely lost Cicero's spirit. The *Panegyric* is an elaborate, highly ornamented, and thoroughly tiresome address to the Emperor Trajan, which is interesting only because it is a statement of the Stoic theory of government. The *Letters* are far less affected, and are therefore of more interest to a modern reader as revelations of the author's personal character and of the society of which he was a part. Like Cicero (but with much less cause) he was inordinately vain, a fact which led him to collect his own letters for publication. Hence they lack the spontaneity and naturalness of Cicero's correspondence; nevertheless they portray their author as an honorable, industrious, and kindly gentleman. His letters to Tacitus on the eruption of Mt. Vesuvius (in which his uncle had perished) are graphic eye-witness accounts of the great catastrophe, while his correspondence with Trajan is among our most valuable evidence on the character of Roman provincial government under the Empire. His stories of private life among his friends and acquaintances are no less illuminating, and serve as a corrective to the denunciations of Juvenal. They show us Roman aristocrats who were moral, serious-minded, and benevolent people, with standards of conduct not very different from our own. Pliny himself was an affectionate husband, a kindly master to his slaves, and a lavish giver to public purposes of all kinds. Yet even he could callously torture Christian deaconesses to wring from them confessions regarding the character of their religious rites, and could order other Christians to death "because I had no doubt that, whatever the nature of their opinions, their obduracy and unbending stubbornness deserved chastisement." [1] Future ages may find equally serious and unsuspected faults in the good men of our own times.

### *History: Tacitus and Suetonius*

Among Pliny's many correspondents was Gaius Cornelius Tacitus (54–120), the last great Roman historian. Tacitus was probably a native of northern Italy who, like Pliny, held the consulship and a series of other important posts. His literary career began in his youth with a *Dialogue on the Orators*, and was continued in two monographs — a biography of his father-in-law Agricola and a treatise entitled *The People and Customs of Germany*. But he is chiefly known for his *Annals* and *Histories*. The first is a year-by-year account of Roman history from the death of Augustus to the overthrow of Nero, in sixteen books; the second continued the story down to the assassination of Domitian. Of the *Annals*, four books and parts of three others are lost, while only the first four books of the *Histories* and part of the fifth have been preserved.

As a recorder of facts Tacitus was no doubt conscientious and careful to

[1] *Letters*, X, 97.

*University Prints*

RESTORATION: INTERIOR OF THE BATHS OF CARACALLA

tell what he believed to be the truth. But he was dealing with untrustworthy sources, and his whole outlook had been poisoned by his own unhappy experiences in the last years of Domitian. To him the Principate seemed nothing but an instrument of crime and oppression, which corrupted the nature of every man who held it. Thus he painted his imperial characters in colors of almost unrelieved darkness, seeing bad motives behind even their best acts. His sketch of Tiberius is not accepted by the most careful modern historical scholars, but from the viewpoint of literature it is a masterpiece. He set out to portray for us a past-master of deception, cruelty, and vice, and such is his power of innuendo that he can in numerous cases lead the unwary reader to his desired conclusion without once giving a tangible bit of evidence to support it. His descriptions of the tragedies of Nero's reign are treated with less rhetoric and more factual data, and in them he rises to heights of lurid splendor seldom surpassed. But he has no more mercy on the corrupt and despicable Roman aristocracy than upon the emperors. Thus, in his story of the Conspiracy of Piso he uses the heroism of the lowly freedwoman Epicharis as a foil to set off the contemptible conduct of equestrians and senators who betrayed their accomplices to gain pardon for themselves.

His style is without a parallel. His phrases are so highly wrought that every word tells in determining their meaning. Prose epigrams are thickly scattered through his pages, such as his judgment upon Galba, "While a private citizen, he seemed to be too great for private station, and in the opinion of everyone he would have seemed fit to rule, if he had not ruled." [1] Read aloud in the original, his narratives have a rolling organ-tone of pathos inherent as much in his choice and combination of words as in the subject matter. Modern criticism has drastically revised many of his judgments, but his reputation as a literary artist is secure. Yet, great as was his genius, he did not influence his immediate successors. Not until the fourth century, in the work of Ammianus Marcellinus, do we find any effort to continue his narrative or imitate his style.

Far more influential was his younger contemporary Gaius Suetonius Tranquillus. Of him we only know that he was a friend of the younger Pliny, and that he later served as a private secretary to Hadrian. In this position he had access to the imperial archives, which he used freely in his *Lives of the Twelve Caesars*, a series of biographies of the emperors from Julius Caesar to Domitian. His style is poor, and he utterly lacked political insight. Each biography is arranged topically: birth, early life, public career, personal character, and death. His interest was entirely in personalities, and he collected everything which lent life and color to them, from autograph letters to trivial and scandalous gossip. In a similar manner he composed biographies of famous Roman literary men, but of these only fragments have survived. Poor as his biographies are, they suited exactly the decadent taste of the three succeeding centuries, and he had many imitators, including the so-called "Writers of the Augustan History" and Aurelius Victor.

Even in Suetonius' day Latin prose had already begun to suffer from tendencies which were to blight its subsequent development. Throughout the first century it had displayed a penchant for artificial rhetorical ornament which grew stronger as time passed. In the second century this bombastic turn was joined with a taste for archaic words and expressions, producing an intolerable mixture which all but ruined prose style. One of the best-known exponents of this style was Marcus Cornelius Fronto,

[1] *Histories*, I, 49.

an African who acted as tutor to Marcus Aurelius. His letters, part of which have been preserved, are written in this unpleasant literary jargon.

### *Apuleius*

The later second century produced a first-rate Latin novelist in the person of Lucius Apuleius, also a native of Africa. His *Metamorphoses*, or *Golden Ass*, is a series of weird stories of witchcraft and magic, interspersed with picaresque adventures and risqué stories in much the same manner as Boccaccio. The hero, having attempted to use a magic formula, makes a mistake in it, and as a result is transformed into an ass. After an astonishing career of misadventures, he regains his human shape with the help of the goddess Isis, and thereafter becomes her priest. Apuleius' vocabulary is very extensive and varied, and his style is marked by a sort of barbaric exuberance found in no other Latin work. The finest portion of the *Metamorphoses* is the immortal story of Cupid and Psyche.

### *The Revival of Greek Literature: Plutarch and Dio Chrysostom*

Meanwhile, the Greek world had been reviving from its exhaustion, and was once more assuming its rightful place in the culture of the Empire. In the late first century, it was again producing philosophers, scientists, historians, rhetoricians, essayists, and thinkers in other fields. While not as great as those of pre-Roman days, these writers were by no means to be despised. In fact, the Greek mind seems to have retained its classical heritage and creative ability longer than did the Roman mind.

About 100 A.D., Plutarch of Chaeronea held the first place in general literature among the Greeks. In his native Boeotian town his family was prominent and apparently wealthy. After studying at Athens and lecturing for a time in Rome, he returned to his ancestral home, where he spent the remainder of his life. He is best known for his *Parallel Lives of Illustrious Greeks and Romans*. As a patriotic Greek, Plutarch wished to prove that his people's heroes were not inferior to those of the Romans. To do so he arranged most of his lives in pairs — a Greek, a Roman whose career resembled that of the Greek, and then a comparison of the two. Such a purpose and method made it impossible for Plutarch to write objectively. His true aim was to produce moral biography. This objective, added to his habit of "pairing" the lives, results in a certain amount of distortion of both facts and perspective. Moreover, Plutarch had never lived under any government but that of the world-embracing Roman Empire, and was therefore unable to understand the turbulent political life of free Greece and Rome. But he used all the available sources, whether Greek or Roman, and for this reason has preserved much knowledge from works now lost. In addition he composed a long series of *Moral Essays* on miscellaneous topics, from which we may get a convincing picture of the shabby, decadent Greece of his time. His style is discursive if not garrulous, but he is usually interesting, and his works are marked by broad-mindedness and good sense.

In the same period, Asiatic Greece produced a notable orator and moralist in Dio of Prusa (commonly called *Chrysostom* or "Golden-mouth"). He traveled much, was exiled, and later became a friend of the Emperor Trajan. Eighty of his orations are extant. His style is often rhetorical and high-flown, but at his best he has a gift of graphic narrative and a moral earnestness which challenge respect. Many of his speeches are addressed to the people of particular towns, and in these he analyzes their failings as well as their virtues with a keenness which makes his picture of Asiatic Greek social and political life a valuable supplement to Pliny's *Letters*.

Syrian Hellenism in the reign of Marcus Aurelius brought forth a satirist of considerable power in Lucian of Samosata. Of all the later Greek writers, he came the nearest to writing pure Attic Greek, while his comic prose dialogues display both a wealth of imagination and a biting wit. Yet Lucian could be serious beneath his mockery. He exposes religious and philosophical cheats mercilessly.

### *Greek Historians*

The Greek world of the second and third centuries was the home of several very creditable historians, without whom our knowledge of the Roman Empire and other phases of ancient history would be much poorer than it is. Flavius Arrianus, a native of Bithynia and a provincial governor under Hadrian, wrote an excellent life of Alexander the Great. In it he made extensive use of the memoirs of Ptolemy and Aristobolus, together with Alexander's court diary and other source documents of first-rate authority. His *Indica* tells the story of the voyage of Alexander's admiral Nearchus from India through the Indian Ocean to Babylon. But Arrian was interested in the present as well as the past. He wrote an excellent account of the border defenses of the province of Cappadocia, and a *Tour Around the Black Sea*, based in part on personal observations.

One of Arrian's contemporaries was Appian of Alexandria (95–165), who, if not a great historian, was at least a very diligent compiler of historical facts. His *Roman History* (in twenty-four books) is a mediocre work, which originally began with the coming of Aeneas to Italy, and ended with the defeat of Sextus Pompey. Considerable sections are known only through epitomes. The plan is a peculiar one. Instead of a connected chronological account of the Roman past, he recounts the various wars which the Romans had waged abroad or among themselves, so that the events of a single year are often treated in two or more separate books, and as parts of different stories. His accuracy in details is not above reproach, but he usually follows the principal thread of each story correctly. For some parts of his narrative he is our only extensive source.

An even more ambitious work was the third-century *Roman History* of the Bithynian Greek, Cassius Dio Cocceianus. He was a Roman citizen and a senator, who had held two consulships and several provincial posts. His work was divided into eighty books, and covered the period from the landing of Aeneas to 229 A.D., the last forty-seven years being covered largely by his own personal experiences. Books XXXVI–LX and parts of the last three are extant in the original form, while the others are known in various Byzantine epitomes. Dio's style is very poor, and he used his sources uncritically; but he consulted good sources, and has thus, for example, preserved in indirect form much of the lost portion of Livy. A few years after Dio, a Syrian Greek named Herodian compiled a similar work covering the period from 180 to 238. Stylistically it is no better than Dio, but with care a historian can gain much useful information from both.

So universal was the use of Greek, that our only extant Jewish historian, Flavius Josephus (37–100), used it to relate the story of his people. His *Antiquities of the Jews* (in 20 books) carries his narrative from the creation to 66 A.D., while his *Wars of the Jews* (in seven books) describes the Jewish revolt of 66–70, in which he participated. His style is usually dry, but in his description of the siege of Jerusalem by Titus he attains a photographic realism. It is only fair to say that modern Jewish scholars question his honesty and accuracy.

## Science and Philosophy

Whereas the Latin writers who dealt with science seem to have been interested only in collecting curious and useful facts, the Greeks continued, until far into the third century, to make original investigations in medicine, astronomy, and mathematics. Although the works of the Hellenistic scientists have been almost completely lost, a number of treatises from the second and third centuries survived and were used by medieval and early modern scholars.

*Medicine, Geography, and Mathematics*

Chief among the physicians of the early Empire was Galen, an Asiatic Greek who was a friend and official of Marcus Aurelius. He was interested in philosophy as well as medicine, and his works contain a great deal of both. On the medical side he continued the work of Hippocrates, although on a lower level. From the latter he learned the theory that the

*Bettmann*

SURGEON TREATING A WARRIOR. SCENE FROM VIRGIL

*Mural Painting. Pompeii*

body is composed of four "Humors" (blood, phlegm, yellow bile, and black bile), and that for good health it must preserve a balance among them. These imaginary substances have given rise to the terminology by which we distinguish various kinds of temperament in mankind.[1] He also propounded the theory of "natural spirits," "vital spirits," and "animal spirits," which bears a shadowy resemblance to our ideas of digestion and the circulation of the blood. But there were many other prominent physicians, and the profession was divided into various schools, some of which practiced special types of treatment like our chiropractors or osteopaths. As a whole, the level of attainment in medicine was not rising, and in some localities it must actually have fallen.

Mathematics and astronomy continued to receive attention at Alexandria. In the reign of Antoninus Pius, one of the leading Alexandrian mathematicians was Claudius Ptolemaeus, one of the most influential figures in the history of science. Adopting the idea current among the Greeks generally, that the earth is the center of the universe, he proceeded to plot the courses of the heavenly bodies then known. His observations were few, and he made mistakes in some of them, but the completed system (which he embodied in a book known by its Arabic name of *Almagest*) was accepted by both the medieval Mohammedans and Christians. Only in the sixteenth century did Copernicus discredit it. Ptolemy's *Geography* was a compendium of existing knowledge about the earth, including instructions by which every reader could be his own map-maker. For each place named he gave the latitude and longitude as established by astronomical observations — a theoretically valid method, but in practice good only if the observations upon which it is based are accurate. As many of Ptolemy's calculations were quite inaccurate, his geography suffered accordingly.

In the field of pure mathematics, Menelaus (about 100 A.D.) wrote an excellent text on spherical trigonometry. A century and a half later, Diophantus made great progress in algebra, for which he worked out a fairly efficient system of algebraic notation.

### *Philosophy: Eclecticism and Neoplatonism*

Throughout the early centuries of the Christian era, men were far less interested in discovering new facts about nature than in solving the riddle of their own lives and destinies. Philosophy became more and more de-

[1] An example of these survivals is our word *melancholy*, which originally meant "having too much black bile."

voted to ethics and religion. These common interests tended to obliterate the differences between the traditional philosophic schools. Seneca, Epictetus, and Marcus Aurelius were Stoics; Plutarch was a follower of Plato; and Dio Chrysostom did not belong to any school. Yet all of them were chiefly interested in ethics, and all believed that man's greatest good is gained by avoiding vice and luxury and by serving one's fellowmen. It is probable that all recognized, behind the many gods of the popular religion, a single supreme deity. Among the educated classes of the Empire there must have been many whose views were similarly eclectic in character, and whose interest in a better life was equally strong.

In the mid-third century, the closer relations between mystical religion and philosophy were exemplified by the development of Neoplatonism. Its founder, Plotinus (203–262), was a Hellenized Egyptian, who after much study in the East settled in Rome and taught there until his death. His ideas are embodied in his *Enneads*, a work which he wrote, but which owes its present form to his disciple Porphyry. To Plotinus, the Platonic doctrines almost ceased to constitute a philosophy, and became a religion. Enlarging on Plato's concept of a single supreme god, Plotinus made him the author and embodiment of all that is good, wise, and perfect. But as such, he is so infinitely far from the world of men and nature that to us he is incomprehensible. Fortunately, there are between God and the world two intermediate entities, "the Divine Mind" and "the Universal Soul." From the latter, the souls of men are derived, and through it man can first regain touch with the Divine Mind, and then, by abstract contemplation, with God himself. Thus, the true philosopher can catch occasional glimpses of the perfect happiness which awaits him when, after death, he is reunited with God.

Neoplatonism had a peculiar destiny. Porphyry continued his teacher's work, but was gradually drawn into a struggle with the Christians. When the official headship of the school passed to the Syrian Iamblichus, it suffered a sharp decline. Forgetting the noble vision of Plotinus, he degraded Neoplatonism by using it to rationalize the pagan cults, and to render the fall complete, he himself assumed the rôle of a miracle-worker. In this debased form Neoplatonism became the rallying-point of the intellectual pagans in the fourth and fifth centuries. But the purer philosophy of Plotinus did not perish. Strangely enough, it was the Christians themselves who seem to have been most deeply influenced by it, and more than one of them found in it a stimulus to closer union with God. Its absorption by both of the warring religious systems is in itself highly significant. The world was entering upon an age in which all thought would tend to take on a religious form.

## Religion

### *An Age of Reviving Faith*

The same restless thirst for knowledge of man's place in the Universe and his eternal destiny, which drove so many disciples to the feet of Stoic or Neoplatonist teachers, sent far more to seek the same kind of knowledge from the priests and worshipers of the gods. The country folk, we must remember, had never lost their faith in religion, and the same may probably be said of many of the urban common people. The upper classes gradually returned to religion although not always to the old state cults which their forefathers had in so many cases abandoned. In all, the period between Augustus and Diocletian witnessed a phenomenal growth in religious fervor, which was to dominate Europe for many centuries to come.

In supplying this thirst for religious comfort and consolation, the official cults on the whole played only a minor part; nevertheless, it was not a negligible one. The old gods received sincere and even enthusiastic homage from worshipers all over the Empire. The Imperial Cult, which by its very nature could not be much more than a formality, was conscientiously carried on by local governments everywhere. Perhaps the secret of the vitality of these official cults is to be found in the fact that such worship could be readily supplemented by a resort to deities which came nearer to meeting the needs of the time.

All circumstances point to the fact that a new state of mind had taken possession of the Graeco-Roman world. Men were no longer content merely to purchase the neutrality or material favor of the divine powers, and then to rely principally upon their own efforts to solve their problems. The feeling of helplessness and resignation, which had for ages oppressed the Orientals, now asserted itself among the Hellenized and Romanized populations of the Empire. It had been the motivating force behind Stoicism and Epicureanism, but now these philosophies of resignation were themselves becoming inadequate. It was not enough for a man to fall back within the limits of his own personality. Even there he needed divine guidance and care in meeting the trials of this life, and the decreasing attractiveness of the present existence led him to long for the assurance of a blessed and eternal life after death. Superstition (particularly, astrology) flourished, and there was a widespread feeling that human nature was corrupt and unclean, so that it could never be rendered pleasing to the divine powers without an internal cleansing, symbolized by some outward rite of purification. Beyond a doubt, the Oriental cults were better fitted to meet this need than were the Graeco-Roman pagan cults, but to do so, even they had to acquire new characteristics and to assume a new significance.

*The Oriental Cults: Vegetation Deities, Mithra, and Yahweh*

Hence, the vegetation deities — Serapis and Isis, the Great Mother and Attis, and the Syrian Goddess — constantly grew in popularity, and to them were added a number of Oriental gods of another kind, such as Mithra and the Hebrew Yahweh. The vegetation cults have been discussed in earlier chapters,[1] but under the Empire they assumed an ethical character which they had never possessed in the days when the mistresses of the Augustan poets were among their participants. Mithra, a Persian sun-god, was the personification of the forces of light, righteousness, and order as opposed to darkness, evil, and chaos. All of them required of their regular worshipers an initiation preceded by rites of purification, and such rites were highly significant. Baths, fastings, abstinence from sensuality — all played a part. Even more impressive was the *taurobolium*. The candidate for purification was placed under a platform on which a bull was slaughtered so that the blood could run down over him. This bath of blood was supposed to free him from spiritual uncleanness, and after receiving it he was said to be "reborn to eternity." In this process of internal regeneration moral conduct came to play an increasingly important part. Jewish synagogues were very common in the cities, and while the severity of the Hebrew ceremonial law kept most gentiles from a full profession of Judaism, thousands of them attended its services, where they learned to believe in the Jewish God and in an eternity of happiness for the righteous. It was into this world of men longing for religious guidance, consolation, and hope, that Christianity came.

*Early Christian Missions and Institutions*

Christian missionary work among the gentiles began very early, and after the middle of the first century, was pushed energetically. Except for the data which we possess on the life of Paul of Tarsus, we know very little about this early missionary activity, but its results were apparent in the establishment of churches in Syria, Asia Minor, Greece, Macedonia, Egypt, and even Italy. They were entirely urban, for the country people were too conservative to be easily moved. In the cities, Christianity usually touched only the lower classes, or well-to-do persons who had risen

[1] Chapters 14 and 18.

*University Prints*

MURAL FROM THE CATACOMBS

*Christ as the Good Shepherd*

from them. Even in Rome, Greek was the language of their services, and it was the uncouth "common" Greek of the Hellenistic East. But the new religion had a driving force which the other religions lacked. It demanded of its adherents an undivided allegiance — unlike the pagan cults, which permitted their followers to participate in as many forms of worship as they chose, with no strong enthusiasm for any of them. It gave them a clear-cut promise of present help and future happiness which no other religion could give, and by its charitable activities the Church gave very material aid to the needy and afflicted. Every Christian was, to some extent, a missionary, and in the prevailing mental state of the age, their efforts were certain to bear fruit.

Before long, these Christian congregations began to develop institutions and forms of worship. By 150, these were fairly well crystallized and uniform. In each city there was a popularly elected bishop (*episkopos* — literally, "overseer"), assisted by a board of elders who, as the number of Christians grew, were delegated to take charge of separate congregations and so became priests. Financial matters were handled by a board of deacons. Traveling evangelists were common, and at first there were also *prophets*, who fell into trances and delivered what were supposed to be inspired sayings. But this office attracted so many fanatics and charlatans that it was soon abolished. The most prominent rites were baptism and the Lord's Supper, to which were added group singing, sermons, and Scripture reading.

Christian literature came into existence in the latter half of the first century. First came the pastoral letters of Paul and other great teachers of the faith. Then, between 70 and 100, the *Gospels*, *Acts*, *Revelation*, and other *New Testament* books were composed. At first such books were more numerous than at present, but utility and popular choice gradually narrowed the list to those now included in the collection. Later there arose a number of writers whose aim was to instruct their brethren in the Church, to combat the variant forms of belief (*heresies*) which arose, or to defend their views before the pagan public. The earliest Christian literature was written in Greek or Aramaic, but in the second century, Latin also came into use. Prominent among these "Church Fathers" were Irenaeus of Lugdunum, Tertullian and Cyprian of Carthage, and Clement and Origen of Alexandria.

### *Persecutions of the Christians*

The Christians were not long in attracting the attention of the Roman government. Quarrels with the Jews or with pagan neighbors frequently ended in the secular courts, and the authorities soon learned that the new sect was not identical with Judaism. Furthermore, the Christians were zealous in making converts, refused to take part in the Imperial Cult, and held secret meetings. They were accused of cannibalism and of shocking immorality. For a long time they refused to serve in the army, or to hold political offices. Tactless and unbalanced Christians made matters worse by smashing statues or profaning pagan rites. Hence it is not surprising that the whole sect was accused of shirking its duties and of "hatred of the human race." The first outbreaks against it were mere mob violence, but Nero's persecution of the Church in Rome probably had the effect of placing on the statute books a law making the profession of Christianity a capital crime, with pardon for all who would curse Christ or worship the Emperor. Trajan's edict,[1] while it reaffirmed the principle of persecution, greatly mitigated its severity by directing that Christians should be dealt with only when a regular accusation was lodged against them, and

[1] Chapter 22.

that the authorities were not to initiate such action. Thereafter, for a century and a quarter, they occupied an equivocal position, with few if any general persecutions launched against them, but with local persecutions constantly going on in certain provinces whose governors lent encouragement to informers. Not enough was done to impede the spread of the faith seriously, but the lives of its followers were in constant danger. It was a situation certain to keep out lukewarm or self-seeking persons, but calculated to attract those of tougher fiber.

In spite of some outbursts of severity in the reigns of Septimius Severus and Maximinus, it was not until the accession of Decius that a consistent, Empire-wide effort was made to stamp out this outlaw religion. By this time, however, it had begun to gain converts in high places, and its followers, while still a small minority, were powerful by reason of their zeal and close organization. Decius began by arresting and executing many of the clergy, and then set up officials in each community to compel all of his subjects to sacrifice to the state gods. Each person was thereupon given a certificate stating that he had obeyed the law. What would have happened if he had lived longer, we cannot tell, but his death in 251 put a stop to further efforts for a time. Valerian resumed the work in 257, and continued it until his capture in 260. Gallienus then reversed his father's policy, granted the Christians toleration and liberty to worship, and even restored some of their confiscated property. Thereafter, the Church was at peace with the government almost without a break until 302.

The Christians had suffered heavily in these catastrophes, both from executions and desertions. But the constancy of the martyrs attracted many new converts, and the clergy, by a mixture of tact and firmness, had managed to bring most of the delinquent brethren back to their duty. The very calamities of the time, which had stimulated the demand for persecution of the Christians to appease the angry gods, had brought home to millions the necessity of both spiritual comfort and material help. In both respects the Church was equipped to meet their needs. Even the intelligentsia no longer looked upon it with the same hostility as of old. Compared with the wild vagaries of some of the cults then popular, its sane and simple ritual seemed to be the embodiment of the old Hellenic moderation and common sense. It was now the only institution that had successfully defied the all-dominating hand of the imperial government, and instinctively, all who chafed under the bureaucratic tyranny must have been drawn to it. It still had a severe ordeal ahead, but its future position was assured.

# 26

# *Bureaucratic Despotism: First Period*

# *(285-395 A.D.)*

## DIOCLETIAN: THE MAN AND HIS TASK

### *The Task of the New Regime*

WHEN A FREAK OF FORTUNE gave to Diocletian the undisputed imperial title, he inherited the task of patching up the rickety structure of Roman government, so that it would afford to a distracted people a maximum of protection, order, and prosperity. In this enterprise, the possibilities of success were strictly limited, and the form which his regime must take was in many respects clearly indicated by the experience of his predecessors. Above all, the population of the Empire needed protection from external enemies and freedom from civil wars, and to gain these advantages it must be prepared to pay a heavy price in taxation and in despotic control of its activities. All that a statesman could do was to make the price as low as possible. The imperial office had already ceased to be a principate, and had become a military autocracy. But no way had been found to exert the imperial power efficiently at points where it was most needed, or to stabilize it by eliminating assassinations and civil wars. The imperial civil service had been developed along bureaucratic lines ever since Hadrian's reign, and a mercenary army, divided into two groups of frontier guards and mobile units, had been an accomplished fact since the days of Gallienus. Neither the bureaucracy nor the army had been fully developed, but the lines of their future evolution were clearly laid down. Both called for heavy expenditure. Hence, it was impossible to restore the relatively low and stable rates of taxation of the first and second centuries. Economic life had been so thoroughly demoralized by fifty years of disorder and calamity that the temptation to attempt its restoration by government fiat and by drastic regulation was well-nigh irresistible. In these respects, Diocletian had little choice, and his success or failure would be measured by his ability to build a lasting structure on these unpromising foundations. His achievement should be judged by the fact that the Empire, as he reorganized it, lasted for nearly two centuries in its entirety, and that the eastern portion endured for nearly a thousand years more.

### *The Man Diocletian*

The Emperor to whom this reorganization was due was one of Rome's greatest men. He was by birth a Dalmatian, the son of a freedman. He had enlisted in the army, and had risen by his own efforts to be the commander of Numerian's bodyguard. Yet his talents were not primarily military. He could command armies with fair success, but preferred to leave this task to others. He was above all an administrator and a manager of men. His judgment of subordinates was seldom mistaken. His aides were often headstrong and violent in their relations with each other, but they were putty in his hands. On occasion he could be callously cruel, but as a rule he inclined toward mercy. He had the ability to organize and systematize which the times so sadly needed. Most important of all, he was no selfish adventurer, but a statesman who worked for the best interests of everyone.

## The Tetrarchy (285–305)

### *Imperial Divinity and Coregency*

The first step of the new Emperor was a reassuring one. As soon as opposition to his rule ceased, he spared the vanquished adherents of Carinus, and even confirmed his appointees in their offices. In a short time, he had been recognized everywhere except in northern Gaul, where a group of homeless vagrants and discontented peasants — the *Bagaudae* — were in revolt. In less than a year, this rising was also crushed.

Like Augustus, Diocletian did not attempt to establish a new constitution by a single act, but introduced new measures as the need arose. He immediately put forth a new interpretation of his office, and carried it out consistently. According to this theory, the Emperor was a god — he himself being the earthly counterpart of Jupiter (*Jovius*), established by the King of the Gods to reduce the earth to order and to rule it. Drawing the logical consequences from this claim, he denied that either the Senate or the army had any part in the making of emperors or in ruling the state. The Senate thereafter, with a few brief exceptions, acted only as the city council of the capital. With this theory as a foundation, he proceeded to provide for the adequate government of the state and for the imperial succession. Very soon he selected as his colleague Marcus Aurelius Maximianus, an Illyrian officer considerably younger than himself. Maximian was a man of great military ability, but coarse, crude, stubborn, and cruel. To him was given the name *Herculius*, to signify that he also was a god, but subordinate in power and functions to his colleague *Jovius*. Diocletian adopted him as his son, and granted him powers in theory equal to his own; in fact, however, Maximian was thoroughly subordinated to his benefactor, and never questioned his authority. Each assumed the full list of imperial titles, and although Maximian had a definite set of provinces to rule, laws were issued in the names of both. In practice, Diocletian was the sole legislator.

In 293, a further change was made. The experience of the preceding eight years had proved that even two emperors were not enough to meet the needs of the time. Every important theater of military operations demanded the presence of an emperor, for otherwise a successful general was likely to be set up by his soldiers as a pretender to the purple, with a civil war as the result. If he already held a share in the imperial power, then the danger was removed. Furthermore, if there were to be at least two emperors in office at once, the successors of the reigning pair would have to be designated in advance and receive training in their tasks. For these purposes, Diocletian chose two *Caesars*, Gaius Galerius Maximianus and Flavius Valerius Constantius. Both were Illyrians, men of mature age and military experience. Diocletian adopted Galerius, who married his daughter, while Constantius married the stepdaughter of Maximian and was adopted by him.

The mutual relations of these four rulers formed an intricate pattern. Laws were issued in the names of all four, and each was authorized to strike coins bearing his own portrait and titulary. Each of them had his own guards and court. For the purposes of routine administration, the provinces were divided among them. Diocletian himself took charge of the Asiatic provinces and Egypt, with his capital at Nicomedia near the Bosporus. Galerius ruled the Balkan lands as far west as the border of Italy, with his capital at Sirmium. Maximian, whose capital was at Milan, governed Italy, Rhaetia, Spain, and Africa; while Constantius, from his seat at Treves, ruled Gaul and (later) Britain. Thus, to the younger and more active Caesars went the perilous Rhine and Danube frontiers, while the Augusti took charge of the less-turbulent interior lands. In practice, however, each of the four went where he was needed, without any hard-and-fast rule.

### *Court Etiquette: Imperial Ministers*

To carry out the illusion of divinity, Diocletian introduced the elaborate court etiquette of the Orient at all four imperial courts. Instead of the democratic simplicity of the early emperors, they practiced an ostentatious pageantry, with troops of guards, marshals, ushers, and chamberlains. Visitors had difficulty in gaining an audience, and when they did, had to kneel and kiss the hem of the imperial robe. Augusti and Caesars alike wore splendid costumes of silk and cloth of gold, and sparkled with precious stones. The Augusti were addressed as "Most Holy Emperors," and everything connected with the government was adorned with the adjective "holy." It must not be supposed that this practice was the result of a mere vainglory on the part of the rulers. Diocletian himself later showed how lightly he regarded it by retiring voluntarily to private life and raising cabbages with his own hands. It was in reality no more than an attempt to end the disgraceful series of imperial assassinations which had deprived the Empire of the services of so many of its most gifted rulers. In this aim it succeeded, and from that time forward assassinations became rare.

In addition to mere courtiers, each Augustus and Caesar had about him a body of high-ranking state officials who performed the same functions as the earlier cabinet ministers, but with more grandiose titles. Thus, the treasurers became "Counts of the Holy Largesses," while other titles such as "Master of the Holy Memory," and "Vicar of the Holy Council," appeared. These court officials, together with a body of lawyers, made up the *Consistorium* of each court, a combination of high court of justice and council of state. All of its members bore the title of *comites* (companions), from which the medieval and modern title of *count* is derived.

### *The Bureaucracy and the Army*

Diocletian completely reorganized provincial government. Throughout the Military Anarchy, the division of the provinces into smaller units had been going on. He now increased the total number to 101. Northern Italy lost the last remnants of her privileged position, while even central and southern Italy were subjected to certain financial obligations for the benefit of the city of Rome. The whole peninsula was organized into eight provinces. The city, while no longer an imperial capital, kept her grain doles and free shows, to which wealthy officials added much in the form of gifts and entertainments. At the other extreme, Egypt was divided into three provinces and apparently was relieved of some of her worst burdens. Over each province was placed a governor of senatorial or equestrian rank with the title of *praeses*, *corrector*, *consularis*, or (in two cases) *proconsul*. But the large number of the provinces prevented the Emperor from supervising each provincial government directly. To remedy this defect, they were grouped into twelve *dioceses*, each with a *vicar* at its head. Over the vicars were the four Praetorian prefects, who were directly responsible to their respective imperial masters. Of these officials, only the Praetorian prefects had any military functions. The others dealt exclusively with civil administration.

The separation of the civil and military powers, begun by Gallienus, was continued and made more distinct. Equestrian *duces*, some of whom ranked as equals of the imperial counselors, were placed in control of all but a few of the armed forces. The subordinate officers appear to have remained about the same as before.

In general, the army was developed along the lines laid down by Gallienus, with the two chief divisions of *limitanei* or border militia and *comitatenses* or mobile fighters. But the development of armament and discipline went on apace. Both classes were heavily increased in numbers, principally through the use of barbarian recruits, either mercenaries from outside the frontiers or colonists (*laeti*) settled in communities on desolate lands in the provinces. Two of the older branches of the service were in disfavor. The Praetorians sank to the position of municipal police in Rome, while the dreaded *frumentarii*, or secret military police, were abolished outright. Discipline was strict, and efforts were made to protect civilians from military oppression.

### *Finance and Taxation: The Munera*

Four imperial courts, an enlarged army, and an elaborate civil bureaucracy all called for increased expenditures, and to produce the necessary funds the revenue-collecting agencies and the system of taxation were reorganized. The new system was based upon the compulsory levies in kind which had been used to supply the armies, and not upon the regular taxes of the previous age. A comprehensive survey of all real estate was made, with provision for its correction every five years, and its complete revision every fifteen years. It was then divided into tax units, which might consist either of the land itself, of the people who worked it, or of livestock. The land unit was called a *jugum*, and varied in size from province to province, or according to its fertility and use. Thus, in Syria, five *jugera* of vineyard, twenty of first-class plow land, forty of second-class plow land, or sixty of third-class plow land, each equaled a *jugum*. A *caput* was equal in tax value to a *jugum*, and consisted of one man, two women, or a fixed number of animals of a given kind. Payment was made in produce, for the disordered state of the currency made payment in cash impracticable. Each year the government decided what funds were needed, and apportioned it *pro rata* among the *juga* and *capita* of the Empire. It was then the business of the governor of each province to see that the curials collected the required amount, and if, in a given municipality, this was not done, they had to make up the deficiency out of their own pockets. If the first estimate proved inadequate, other levies could be made in the course of the year. Customs duties, crown gold, and other special taxes were continued. Harsh as some of its features were, it bears witness to an honest effort to distribute the burden fairly, and a fourth-century writer tells us that under Diocletian it worked reasonably well.

As before, the taxes were supplemented heavily by *munera*, paid either in labor or in money. For the municipal proletariat, which paid no other direct taxes, the labor which was demanded was not excessive, but the curials did not escape so easily. The municipalities were forced by the imperial government to maintain all of their local functions, to which were now added the cost of building city walls, while the endowments which had formerly borne the cost of so many of these activities had long since been seized by the emperors or rendered valueless by currency inflation. Hence, the middle class, with much less wealth than before, found itself beneath a crushing weight of exactions designed to benefit both the local and imperial governments. From that time forward the lot of the people of the middle class became steadily worse, and as the government carefully closed all possible means of escape, they became little better than slaves of the state.

### *Currency Reform*

An earnest effort was made to reform the currency. The old silver-coated copper denarius was continued by Diocletian as a fractional coin, with a nominal value of 1/50,000 of a pound of pure gold — about one fourth of the figure set by Aurelian. Various multiples of the denarius were minted, including the *argenteus*, a pure silver coin worth forty denarii. Gold coins were struck at the rate of sixty to a pound. In the main, this system was honest, but the value assigned to the copper denarius was far too high, and prices quoted in it rose rapidly. To stop this trend, Diocletian issued his famous Edict of Prices (301), in which maximum prices were set upon all kinds of goods and services. Any person offering or asking more than the set price in any case was to be put to death. Large portions of this edict have been preserved, and are now used to determine the relative levels of wages and prices at the time of its issue. We must here confine ourselves to the immediate consequences of the measure. Merchants and workmen refused to abide by it, and blood was shed. At last, Diocletian recognized the futility of the edict and withdrew it. Years later, Constantine revalued the denarius at a little over one fifth of the figure adopted by Diocletian, and this time it was set at very nearly its true value.

Realizing the evils that naturally spring from autocracy and bureaucracy, Diocletian made strenuous efforts to protect his subjects from them. Officials were expected to conform strictly to the law, and appeal might be taken from their decisions to the emperors themselves. In order to seize private property, an official had to have a warrant under an imperial seal, and if he failed to produce it, the intended victim was privileged to beat him. But all such safeguards soon proved ineffective.

### *The Northern Frontier*

While Diocletian was reorganizing the Roman state, he and his colleagues were also busy resisting invasions, putting down rebellions, and restoring order. Gaul was one of the first regions to receive attention. The suppression of the Bagaudic Revolt has been mentioned, and in the next few years after its suppression, Maximian drove the Germans back across the Rhine, rebuilt the fortifications along the river, and restored peace to the country. The *Agri Decumates*, however, were not recovered.[1]

While the pacification of Gaul was in progress, misfortune befell the Roman cause in the North. The Channel fleet was under the command of a Gaul named Carausius, who, in 287, learned that Maximian intended to put him to death. He revolted, got possession of Britain, and, with a fleet at his disposal, bade defiance to the government. A fleet built by Maximian to fight Carausius was defeated, and in 290, the emperors had to make a truce by which the rebel's position in Britain was temporarily

[1] Chapter 21.

recognized. But when Constantius Caesar assumed command in Gaul, the fortunes of war improved. The strongholds which Carausius held on the coast of the continent were recaptured, and before long he was assassinated by Allectus, one of his officers, who took his place. In 296, Constantius invaded Britain, defeated and slew Allectus, and reunited the island to the Empire.

### *Wars in the East and South*

In the East and South, similar crises were successfully met. Until 293, peace prevailed between Rome and Persia, but in that year the warlike Narses I came to the Persian throne, and the irrepressible conflict between the two states broke out anew. The Roman army was commanded by the hot-headed Galerius, who, through carelessness, suffered a disastrous defeat. Diocletian, after publicly humiliating the culprit, sent him back with a fresh army to redeem his reputation. This time, Narses was completely defeated, and his wives and children fell into the hands of the Romans. Diocletian then arranged a favorable peace, by which Rome annexed a large strip of land on both sides of the Tigris. In Egypt, two revolts were put down, and along the Danube, invading German and Sarmatian tribes were repeatedly thrown back. Africa was, for a time, disturbed by a confederacy of Moorish tribes, but Maximian soon crushed this group and restored order. The last years of the Tetrarchy were, in general, years of peace.

### *The Persecution of the Christians*

One problem defied all of Diocletian's efforts. His later years saw the beginning of a struggle between the imperial government and the Christian Church, which he was destined to pass on unsolved to his successors. The reason for this resumption of persecution, after forty-two years of toleration, is not known. The Christians blamed Galerius, who was an intolerant pagan, but it is possible that they were not themselves entirely blameless. There were many of them at Diocletian's court, some of whom held high offices, and even his wife and daughter were alleged to be among their number. It may be that this group was involved in some intrigue against Galerius, but whatever the cause the truth is not known. At any rate, in 303, was issued the first of the series of edicts — each more severe than its predecessor — by which they were outlawed and subjected to dire penalties. Senators and curials had their privileges revoked; imperial councilors were reduced to slavery; churches and sacred books were destroyed; and meetings of Christians were forbidden. Supplementary edicts directed that the clergy were to be arrested and compelled to offer sacrifice to the state gods. Although some who refused were tortured or slain, in general the edicts were not zealously executed. Constantius, in his territories, destroyed only a few church buildings, while pagan officials elsewhere frequently did as little as they could. In all, the persecution remained in force for about eight years, and occasioned much suffering; however, it failed of its purpose. We shall later see how it finally collapsed.

### *The Abdication of Diocletian and Maximian*

Meanwhile, Diocletian prepared to put his system of government to the supreme test. It had probably been his intention from the beginning that he and Maximian should eventually abdicate, and, in 304, a severe illness left him too weak to carry on the government longer. The next year he and his colleague both laid down their powers on the same day, Diocletian

*University Prints*

RESTORATION OF THE PALACE OF DIOCLETIAN

*Spalatro, Yugoslavia*

at Nicomedia and Maximian at Milan. Galerius and Constantius became Augusti, and Diocletian before his abdication selected two new Caesars — Maximinus Daia in the East, and Flavius Valerius Severus in the West. Both were creatures of Galerius, who now assumed the dominant place in the Tetrarchy. Constantine, the son of Constantius by a concubine, and Maxentius, the son of Maximian, were both passed over — a fact which was to prove fatal to the arrangement. Diocletian retired to a magnificent palace which he had built on the Adriatic shore near his native Salona, where he lived quite simply until about 316. Maximian, with very bad grace, took up his residence in southern Italy.

Considering the unfavorable conditions under which he worked, and making a fair allowance for human fallibility, one may say that Diocletian's accomplishment entitles him to high praise. He had to deal with a society, a government, and a culture which were far gone in decline, and he inherited from the Military Anarchy institutions which were at once pernicious and indispensable. From these unpromising materials, he built a political structure which staved off the fall of the Western Empire for two centuries, and gave it an opportunity to produce some worthy fruits to compensate for its evils. It is doubtful if anyone could have done more.

## The Rise of Constantine (305–324)

### *The Breakdown of the Tetrarchy*

The Tetrarchy did not long survive the retirement of its creator. As absolutism and bureaucracy were suited to the conditions of the time, they remained permanent features of the Roman polity, but Diocletian's system of coregency and succession was too intricate ever to function when his commanding personality had ceased to co-ordinate its parts. After 305, it quickly broke down, although twenty years of disorder were necessary to demonstrate its entire impracticability. The history of this confused period is largely that of a return from tetrarchy to monarchy and hereditary succession.

Hardly a year elapsed after the succession of Constantius and Galerius before the first break in the system appeared. Galerius was the leading spirit in the new imperial group, but his harsh and arbitrary manners soon caused friction. At his court was Constantine, the son of Constantius, a young man of unusual courage and ability. While there he served as an informal hostage for his father's subordination to the eastern Augustus, but Constantius demanded his return, and early in 306 he arrived in Gaul.

The following summer, while on an expedition to Britain, Constantius died, and his army immediately proclaimed Constantine Emperor in his place. To keep the peace, he sought confirmation from Galerius, who reluctantly conceded to him the title of Caesar, at the same time raising Severus to the rank of Augustus.

One break invited others. As Severus had his capital at Milan, Rome was left with her Praetorian Guard but without an emperor. Galerius had recently proclaimed the extension of the capitation tax to the capital, and the people were discontented. Learning of Constantine's successful *coup d'état*, the people and Praetorians promptly saluted as Emperor Maxentius, the son of Maximian. When Severus marched on Rome, his army deserted him, and he was taken prisoner. Later Maxentius put him to death. Maximian, who had retired unwillingly, now reassumed his imperial title. When, in 307, Galerius invaded central Italy, he was deserted by part of his army, and narrowly escaped the fate of Severus. His supremacy was at an end. Constantine profited by the quarrel to marry Maximian's daughter and to receive from him the title of Augustus.

In this dilemma, Galerius sought the aid of Diocletian. A meeting was held at Carnuntum in Pannonia, at which Galerius, Diocletian, and Maximian were present. Diocletian, although urged to resume his former position, refused to do so, and compelled Maximian to retire once more. Maxentius was outlawed, and Constantine was once more reduced to Caesarship. As neither would submit, matters were as bad as ever. To take the place of Severus, Galerius named as Augustus Licinius, an Illyrian officer and an old friend of his (308).

### *The Rise of Constantine*

These disorders worked steadily toward the advancement of Constantine. In statesmanship, he almost equaled Diocletian, while as a general he was without a peer in the late Empire. He had inherited the attractive personality of his father, but had an iron will which Constantius had lacked. He was far-sighted, shrewd, able to organize and direct the efforts of others, and patient enough to await opportunities. He had a strain of religious mysticism which made him see visions and dream dreams, although under the spur of excitement or policy he could commit the blackest crimes. By reason of these varied vices and virtues he successfully rode out the storms which engulfed all his rivals.

At first Constantine possessed only Gaul and Britain, yet none of his five colleagues was much better off. Alone among them, he cultivated the

*University Prints*

COLOSSAL HEAD OF CONSTANTINE

*306–337 A.D.*

friendship of the Christians, although he had not yet embraced their faith. After the conference at Carnuntum, he received Maximian at his court, but the old man was like an unquiet ghost of the past, fit only to plague the living. After trying unsuccessfully to unseat Maxentius, he returned to Gaul and attempted the same thing with Constantine. The attempt miscarried, and in 310 Maximian committed suicide. Maxentius, who had for years been on bad terms with his father, nevertheless broke with Constantine after this affair, and the latter countered by seizing Spain.

Meanwhile, Galerius passed from the scene. In 311, worn out with work, disappointment, and disease, he died at Nicomedia. His last act was a confession of failure. Until then he had kept up the persecution of the Christians in his own territories and those of his satellites. Just before his death he issued an edict granting them the right to believe and worship as they chose on condition that they pray to their God for his welfare, their own, and that of the state. The persecution had cost many lives and much suffering, but it had failed in its purpose. The Church was still intact, and the government had had to yield.

The stage was set for a drastic reshuffling of territories. Constantine wished to eliminate Maxentius, whose territories lay in the path of his further expansion, while Licinius and Maximinus were at odds over the provinces vacated by the death of Galerius. When Maximinus promptly seized the coveted prize, Constantine had no difficulty in securing the alliance of the disappointed Licinius. This move isolated Maxentius, and Constantine could now attack him without fear of intervention from the other Augusti.

Fortune favored the allies. Constantine's Italian campaign was a whirlwind success. His army was much smaller than that of his enemy, but discipline, loyalty, and generalship were on his side. In the summer of 312, he quickly occupied the Po Valley, and by autumn, was pushing down the Flaminian Road toward Rome. Encouraged by a vision of the Christian God, he had his men inscribe the mystic monogram of Christ on their shields. On October 28, he met Maxentius at the Milvian Bridge, a few miles outside the city. A skillful flanking movement threw the enemy into disorder, and Maxentius, together with thousands of his men, perished in the swollen Tiber. The next day Constantine entered Rome as a deliverer: the West, as far as the Adriatic Sea and the Sicilian Narrows, was in his hands. The next year, Licinius defeated Maximinus, who died soon afterward. All of his lands fell to the victor. Of the six emperors, only two were left, and as both were grasping and unscrupulous, they were not likely to remain long at peace.

Immediately after his victory, Constantine began to court the favor of all who could aid him. The Roman Senate was treated with distinguished honor, and in return it conferred upon him the title of "Senior Augustus," with the sole right to legislate for the Empire. He immediately used this prerogative to stop the religious persecution which still raged in the provinces of Maximinus. The Edict of Galerius was extended to Italy and Africa, while everywhere confiscated church property was restored, and the imperial treasurers in the provinces were ordered to furnish the Church liberal sums of money. That winter at Milan he met Licinius, who married his sister Constantia and agreed to publish the pro-Christian edicts in his own provinces. Such was the famous "Edict of Milan" — technically not an edict at all, but a mere agreement between the two emperors. Thus, Constantine became the official protector of the Christians everywhere, and in return enjoyed their favor.

The peace between these two self-seeking men was of short duration.

Because the Roman world was not big enough to hold them both, a break was inevitable. In 314, when Constantine discovered that his ally had encouraged an attempt against his life, war was declared. It was short, but bitterly contested, and although not decisive, it gave Constantine a great advantage. Licinius ceded to him all of the European provinces except Thrace, and put to death a colleague whom he himself had appointed. For nine years an uneasy peace reigned; but it was in reality only a preparation for war. Constantine, on his side, appointed his sons consuls without consulting Licinius; the latter, realizing that the Christians everywhere were the partisans of his rival, began to persecute them. In 323, while repelling a Gothic raid, Constantine crossed over into Thrace, and Licinius took this as an act of war. The next year the crucial struggle began. Licinius was defeated in a savage battle at Adrianople, losing thirty-four thousand men. He fled to Byzantium. His navy was defeated by a fleet under Constantine's son Crispus, and he was compelled to cross over into Bithynia. There he was again defeated, and had to surrender. At the prayer of the prisoner's wife, Constantine promised to spare his life, but soon after found a pretext for putting him out of the way. The Roman world was once more in the hands of a single ruler.

## Constantine the Statesman

### *The Completed Autocracy*

After the final defeat of Licinius, Constantine was the autocrat of the Roman world until his death in 337. In his hands the "constitution" of Diocletian assumed its final form, which it was not to lose until the overthrow of the Byzantine Empire in the fifteenth century A.D. Some of the changes which he made were good, and many more were bad, but upon them Constantine must rest his claim to the title of statesman.

In his hands, the bureaucracy, as organized by Diocletian, became still more elaborate. He completed the separation of the military and civil powers by depriving the Praetorian prefects of their military functions, which he vested in specialized officers. The prefects now became the heads of the civil bureaucracy, responsible to the Emperor for the conduct of their subordinates, the vicars and provincial governors. At his death, the standard number of prefects was three, stationed respectively in Gaul, Italy, and the East; in times of stress a fourth might be appointed for Illyricum or some other district which needed special attention. The last channel of communication between the subject and his imperial master was broken by a law making the prefects the final judges of law cases arising within their respective jurisdictions. Whatever the advantages of this system, it greatly increased the corruption and oppression from which the people suffered, and made it harder for emperors to secure obedience from their officials.

Military reforms emphasized still more the separation of the *limitanei* from the mobile army. The frontier garrisons were denuded of their best personnel for service in the *comitatenses*, to whom were added new formations called *palatini*, with substantially the same sphere of service. To replace the Praetorians, he organized a new class of *scholae palatini*, consisting of barbarian cavalry. In fact, the barbarians now began to assume a dominant place in the army generally. Many tribes were settled inside the frontiers on waste lands, where they lived under their own governments and laws on condition that they furnish fixed numbers of recruits. As such undisciplined material made better cavalry than infantry, the relative importance of the cavalry grew constantly greater. Soldiers' sons had before them the option of entering either the army or a municipal senate, and the hard lot of the curials made the choice an easy one. Theoretically all free inhabitants of the Empire were liable for service in the army, but in practice this theory was only used as an excuse to collect a tax — "recruit money" — which was used to pay the mercenaries. The *limitanei* on each sector of the frontier were commanded by a *dux*, while the mobile forces were headed by a varying number of "masters of the soldiers." Barbarians living outside the frontiers were frequently subsidized to refrain from depredations themselves, and to fight Rome's enemies. In short, the command of the armies was so thoroughly subdivided that it was much more difficult for an ambitious general to rebel than it had been in the third century, while the army personnel (including high officers) were more and more drawn from barbarian sources. In both facts we may see symptoms of the increasing decadence of the Empire.

A new and elaborate hierarchy of court officials was created. At its head were two dignitaries, the *quaestor* and the *magister officiorum*. The former was the chief secretary of the Emperor. He combined the functions of the various imperial secretaries as established by Hadrian and his successors, except the portfolio of finance, which was under separate control. The latter corresponded roughly to the Praetorian prefect under the Principate, with command of the Guard, control of foreign affairs, and the position of master of ceremonies. Under his control were the new secret police (*agentes in rebus*), who took the place of the *frumentarii* and soon imitated their worst vices. Finance was controlled by a "count of the holy largesses," who handled state funds, and a "count of the private estate," for the Emperor's personal funds. Under these officials, corresponding to the procurators of the Principate, were provincial treasurers called *rationales*. The "Council of the Empire" (*Consistorium*) was continued. Court officials were minutely graded in rank, with titles such as "count of the first rank," "count of the second rank," and "count of the third rank," to indicate their order of precedence. As under Diocletian, chamberlains, ushers, and other palace servants were present in great numbers, and were carefully organized.

Constantine's financial policy included heavy increases in taxation, broadening of its base, and a greater dependence upon coined money than Diocletian had shown. The land tax was collected as before, but, in addition, senators had to pay a special impost called *follis senatoria* or *collatio glebalis*. Every five years senators, tradesmen, and curials had to pay in coin an assessment commonly called *chrysargyrum* or *collatio lustralis*; and "crown gold" was collected whenever a new emperor came into power. If the position of the taxpayer had been difficult under Diocletian, it now became all but unendurable for the middle and lower classes; and burdensome even for the aristocracy.

In one respect, Constantine wrought an improvement in conditions: he established a coinage which remained unaltered in the surviving portion of the Roman Empire for over eight centuries. In this system, the standard gold coin was the *solidus* which contained 1/72 of a pound of gold and was worth, in present American terms, about $5.25. Silver and silver-bronze coins, each with a nominal value very near its intrinsic worth, were also minted.

Chronic distress led men to make desperate attempts to escape from their obligations. Tradesmen, unable to meet expenses, closed their shops, while peasants and curials deserted their lands and fled. In accordance with long-standing custom, the curials were caught and forced to resume their duties, and when the Christian clergy were freed from some of the *munera*, curials were forbidden to take holy orders. The same restriction was now extended to the other classes except senators. By a law of 332, the peasants of many of the provinces were bound to the soil, retaining the other rights of freemen, but unable to leave their farms. Thus they became, in effect, serfs. For coercing the tradesmen, the state had recourse to their occupational *collegia*. Each man was bound to his trade and to its organization, which was collectively liable not only for taxes but also for furnishing the state with goods at a price which it fixed at a very low figure. It is possible that some of these measures had been adopted temporarily by Diocletian, or even by his predecessors, but now, for the first time, they were enacted into permanent legal form. In short, the financial need of the state reduced almost the whole population to hopeless slavery, in which it lived for the purpose of filling the treasury.

*Constantine and the Christian Church*

Constantine also took a long step toward the solution of the religious problem which had so long plagued the Empire. Diocletian's religious policy had had two chief objectives — the deification of the living emperors, and the crushing of the Christian Church. In the former, he had not won unqualified success, while in the latter, he and Galerius had failed completely. Yet in a society which, like that of the early fourth century, tended to think in religious terms, it was important to gain for the imperial power a divine sanction, and since the Church could not be destroyed, a way must be found to get along with it. Sentiment as well as expediency probably influenced Constantine's religious viewpoint. Because his mother was a Christian and his father had always been friendly to the new religion, Constantine had had an unusual opportunity to develop a sympathetic understanding of it; however, his innate caution prevented him from extreme measures in either direction. At any rate, he soon gained the support of the Christians, and never afterward lost it. When he defeated Maxentius, it was under a banner marked with the symbol of the Christian faith, and Christian support must have helped him greatly in his struggle with Licinius. Constantine, on his part, favored the Church as much as he dared in her warfare against paganism, and openly took her side against the heretics who were trying to destroy her unity. Under his government, complete freedom of religion prevailed, but the Church received large gifts from his treasury, and in addition enjoyed the right to acquire property by inheritance or gift. The wealth gained from these sources enabled it to engage in extensive charities, which in return won new converts. The clergy were freed from some of the most onerous *munera*, while bishops received the power to try certain law cases. The Church showed its gratitude not only in active support of its imperial friend, but by making obedience to his rule a religious duty. Although deification of a human being was contrary to Christian principles, there were in the Bible unmistakable injunctions to obey governments whose acts were in harmony with the divine will. The Christians recognized Constantine as "The Lord's Anointed" — a man chosen by God to rule the Roman Empire as King David had been chosen to rule Israel. Rebellion against such a ruler was sacrilege as well as treason. Constantine crowned his services to the Church by having his sons reared in the faith, and by receiving baptism himself when on his deathbed. Divine right monarchy in the Roman Empire was now an accomplished fact.

Constantine soon began to assume a tone of authority in his dealings with the Church, and circumstances encouraged him in this course. The orthodox clergy were engaged in a struggle with two groups of heretics, the Donatists and the Arians. In Africa, the hostility of the peasants toward the landlords had taken a religious form when the Donatists, a group drawn principally from the lower classes, propounded the view that the sacraments were not valid if administered by an immoral clergyman. To accept this view was to subject the clergy, who were drawn principally from the upper classes, to the moral censorship of the common people. But in the fourth century, when priests were coming to be looked upon as agents of God possessing a mystical sanctity, this view was unacceptable to the majority of the Christians. The Church, although no friend of clerical immorality, insisted that accused priests be subject only to the jurisdiction of their brother-clergymen. In 313, the Donatists appealed to Constantine, who referred the case to the clergy of Gaul and Italy. In 316, and in accordance with their decision, he condemned Donatism and began

*University Prints*

ARCH OF CONSTANTINE

to persecute its adherents, although five years later he admitted defeat and granted them toleration. This controversy, embittered by many lawless acts on the part of the heretics, lasted until Africa was lost to the Vandals, over a century later.

The Arian controversy began in Alexandria. Arius, a priest, disagreed with Alexander, his bishop, over the nature of Christ and his relation to God the Father. He maintained that the Son was created by the Father, is not co-eternal with Him, and therefore possesses divinity of a subordinate character. His bishop held that both are in every way equal. Constantine, still unbaptized, had little interest in the theological aspects of the question, but since it disturbed the peace of the Church he at last called a council of the clergy to meet at the Bithynian city of Nicea, under his personal presidency (325). There the churchmen drew up a creed which condemned Arianism, and Arius himself was banished. But the tables were soon turned. Constantine fell under the influence of Arian clergymen, and as Alexander was now dead, the leadership of the anti-Arian party had fallen to his successor Athanasius. The latter was banished by Constantine, and several times suffered a similar fate at the hands of Constantine's sons, but in the end he won his point, and Arianism was outlawed. Plainly the Church, which in the days of the persecutions had been independent, was slowly but surely becoming a mere department of state for the Empire. It was a high price to pay for victory.

*Constantinople*

The question of an imperial capital again became acute. Rome was poorly located to meet the needs of the day, when the Emperor found it necessary to be near to as many dangerous frontiers as possible. At that time, the points most in need of attention were the lower Danube and the Persian border, and Constantine undertook to find a suitable site, fairly near both of them, for his residence. After some consideration, he selected Byzantium, and, in 330, began to rebuild it on a lavish scale. Its name was changed to Constantinople, and everything possible was done to attract people to it. Beautiful buildings were erected, including an imperial palace, a senate house, and many churches.

The foundation of Constantinople was perhaps the most important act of Constantine's reign. It was what Rome had never been — a natural center of trade, and prosperous in its own right. But its foundation had unexpected consequences. As we have seen, the Empire was divided into a Greek East and a Latin West. Hitherto, except under Diocletian, the

West had been the seat of government, and Nicomedia was not well located for the purpose of an imperial capital. Now the East had a capital of its own, where Greek influence soon became dominant. It was so far from the center of the Empire that the West would necessarily have a capital and a government of its own. The way was paved for the permanent division of the Empire into a western and an eastern section, and thereafter, for the fall of the Western Empire.

### *Family Life and the Succession*

In his family life, Constantine was unhappy. He had by a concubine an elder son named Crispus, while his wife Fausta bore him three sons — Constantine, Constantius, and Constans. Crispus was a young man of great ability, who, in 317, was made Caesar along with Fausta's eldest son Constantine. But, in 326, a palace tragedy occurred. Acting on charges brought by Fausta, Constantine put Crispus to death. Vengeance, however, soon overtook Fausta. Not long afterward, apparently because of accusations made by his mother Helena, Constantine had his wife scalded to death in a hot bath. Legend has made much of this double tragedy, but many of its details are obscure.

As his younger sons grew up, Constantine conferred the title of Caesar upon each of them, while two years before his death he gave the same title to Dalmatius his nephew, and made Hannibalianus, another nephew, king of Pontus and Cappadocia. Each Caesar had a portion of the Empire assigned to him to govern under the Emperor's supervision.

In 337, while preparing for a war with Persia, Constantine fell sick and died at Nicomedia, receiving baptism on his deathbed. He had completed the task begun by Diocletian. The Empire was now a theocratic despotism, from which every trace of freedom had vanished, and under which every man was in some way chained to a task conducted for the benefit of the state. The succession had been temporarily restored to an hereditary basis, although this was to prove the most fleeting of his achievements. He left a thoroughly stagnant and decadent state, in which only the Christian Church was able to make further growth.

## The Dynasty of Constantine (337–363)

### *The Reigns of the Brothers: Constantine II, Constantius, and Constans*

For twenty-six years after the death of Constantine, his kinsmen wore the imperial purple. It was a period of disorder at home and invasion from without. Immediately, the garrison of Constantinople massacred the half-brothers and nephews of their dead master, including the Caesar Dalmatius. Only two of the nephews escaped, Gallus and Julian, both of whom were to rise to prominence in the years that followed. Constantine's sons then took possession of their respective inheritances. Constantine II received Gaul, Britain, and Spain; Constans secured Italy, Africa, and the lands along the Danube; while Constantius retained the Asiatic provinces and Egypt.

Strife and misfortune dogged their steps from the first. All of them were treacherous and grasping, making much of Christian theology, but with few traces of Christian ethics in their conduct. Constantine II and Constans, being in the West where Athanasian doctrines were strong, embraced them, while Constantius, whose subjects were principally Arians, was a bigoted follower of Arius. They did not long remain at peace among themselves. In 340, Constantine II attacked the Italian lands of his brother Constans, but was slain and his own provinces annexed by the victor. For the next ten years, Constans and Constantius were on terms of armed truce, and a final break was averted only by the calamities which both suffered in their other relationships. Constantius was at war with Persia, and suffered a series of defeats, while Constans was so hated for his vices that, in 350, he fell victim to a military conspiracy headed by Magnus Magnentius, an officer of barbarian origin. The murderer assumed the imperial title and took possession of the lands of his victim. He would probably have pushed eastward against Constantius if Vetranio, the elderly commander of the Danubian frontier, had not prevented such a move by assuming the purple himself.

Constantius met the threat with more energy than he had shown in his foreign wars. As he was childless, he provided for the succession and for administrative aid by elevating to the Caesarship his elder cousin, Gallus, whom he sent to the East. This done, he advanced against the enemy. Vetranio voluntarily surrendered his position to Constantius, who spared his life. In September, 351, Magnentius was defeated in a battle at Mursa, in Pannonia. Constantius pursued the usurper into Gaul, where, in 353, he committed suicide. The tattered fabric of the Empire was at last reunited under a son of Constantine as sole Emperor, but even then his troubles were not over. The next year, a mercenary captain named Claudius Silvanus (like Magnentius, a Frank by descent) rebelled in Gaul, but was immediately put down.

*The Caesarship of Julian*

Meanwhile, Constantius had killed one Caesar and appointed another. Gallus, who seems to have been mentally unbalanced, committed so many mad acts that, in 354, Constantius invited him to Italy and put him to death. Yet a Caesar was badly needed, for not only was the Persian menace still present, but the northern barbarians, who, for a generation, had been relatively quiet, were again pounding at the Rhine and Danube frontiers. On the Rhine the Franks captured Cologne, while farther south the Alamanni took Augustodunum. With these crises facing him, and with the Arian controversy engrossing his attention, Constantius tried once more to secure a helper. This time, his choice fell upon his cousin Julian, the brother of Gallus. The background of the new Caesar had been peculiar. Forced to remain out of politics because of the jealousy of his cousins, he had studied Greek literature and philosophy assiduously. He hated Christianity as the religion of his despised relatives, and as an enemy of the classical culture which he loved. Yet Julian, for all his zeal, was no true Hellenist. Through Neoplatonism he had imbibed a love of ascetic practices which a Greek would have scorned. He was honest and fearless, and he had no small share of military genius.

Being sent to Gaul, in 356, with a body of advisers who were likewise spies, Julian fell to work with tireless energy. In the next five years, he cleared the left bank of the Rhine of Germans, won a smashing victory over the Alamanni at Strassburg, restored the fortifications along the border, and invaded Germany itself. His achievements as an administrator equaled those in war. A glaring light is thrown upon the corruption of Roman government when we learn that he was able, merely by restoring honesty to the conduct of public business, to lower the capitation tax from twenty-four *solidi* to seven *solidi* per head. But he was not permitted to pursue his work unhampered. In 360, Constantius, who had met with more defeats in his Persian wars, ordered Julian to send the best of the Gallic troops to him. The soldiers took matters in their own hands and proclaimed Julian Augustus. For a year, neither he nor Constantius could spare the time and energy to fight out their quarrel. Then, in 361, Julian marched eastward, at the same time trying to negotiate with his cousin for the recognition of his new position. But before blood could be shed, Constantius died, leaving Julian in undisputed possession of the Empire.

### *Julian and the Pagan Revival*

The chief interest of Julian's brief reign (Nov. 361–June, 363) lies in his fruitless effort to restore paganism to the position of which Constantine and his sons had deprived it. His religious views have been mentioned. He now attempted to put them into effect by constructing a pagan church, incorporating into it those features which made the Christian Church strong, and throwing the weight of imperial favor into the scale on its behalf. True to his noble and humane — if somewhat impractical — character, he refrained from outright coercion of the Christians, although every indirect method was employed to weaken them. In preceding reigns, adherence to the Church had been the passport to imperial favor, but, under Julian, this was reversed. Christians were deprived of their control of education by a law which forbade them to teach the Greek or Latin classics. In this step, he had the thoroughly logical justification that they could not conscientiously explain the allusions to the pagan gods, of which the classics were full, without in some degree prejudicing their pupils against the state religion. The remaining pagan temples were protected from spoliation, and the Emperor personally conducted a campaign of propaganda in favor of his views. To fan the discord which raged in the Church, he recalled exiled clergymen of both Arian and Athanasian views, and allowed them to indulge their unseemly quarrels as long as they did not violate public order. But all his religious plans were doomed to failure. Corrupt as the Christian Church of his time was in certain respects, it met needs both spiritual and practical which paganism could not supply. It seems probable that if Julian had reigned longer, he might in desperation have resorted to a persecution as bloody and cruel as those of Valerian and Diocletian.

As it was, the unfinished Persian War left him little time to promote this quixotic scheme. In the spring of 363, he led his fleet and army down the Euphrates, and then crossed over to the Tigris. By-passing Seleucia and Ctesiphon, he attempted to strike at the heart of the Persian dominions. Another army, operating from a base in Armenia, was to meet him, but it failed to arrive on time. In spite of this disappointment, he was winning striking successes, when a chance wound, incurred as he was fighting like a common soldier, caused his death (June 26, 363). The army at once elected as his successor an officer named Jovian, who made peace with the enemy by ceding to them all the Roman possessions east of the Tigris, together with some districts between the Tigris and Euphrates. He also rescinded Julian's enactments against the Christians.

## The Dynasty of Valentinian and Theodosius (364–395)

### *Valentinian I and Valens*

When Jovian died, after a reign of only eight months, the army again took matters into its own hands. Resuming the powers of which Diocletian and Constantine had vainly attempted to deprive it, it chose as Emperor Valentinian, a Pannonian officer, with the recommendation that he select a colleague and divide the Empire with him. The new Emperor responded by elevating to the rank of Augustus his brother Valens, to whom he committed the government of the provinces east of the Adriatic Sea. Valentinian I (364–375) was a peculiar mixture of attractive virtues and revolting vices. He was an able general and a conscientious administrator, with a breadth of view which made him keep entirely aloof from the quarrels that rent the Church, and with a genuine sympathy for his suffering subjects. But he was easily angered, and when enraged, displayed demoniac ferocity. Indeed, he was said to have kept in his palace two savage bears, to tear in pieces anyone who offended him, and he put many persons to death for little or no reason. Valens (364–378) was a person of little intelligence or character, and a bigoted Arian who spent valuable time and energy persecuting the Athanasians when the Persians and Germans needed his undivided attention. Nominally both emperors were equal rulers of an undivided state, but actually the will of Valentinian was dominant.

The brothers faced a crisis of stupendous proportions. Taxation and official oppression had driven thousands of unfortunates to banditry, and had reduced the remainder to the utmost misery. From northern Britain all the way around to Africa, invaders were pounding the frontiers or devastating the border provinces. Pirates swarmed the seas. Nor was the imperial title which they enjoyed uncontested. In the East, Valens had, for a time, to struggle with doubtful success against Procopius, a collateral representative of the family of Constantine.

Valentinian and Valens made what headway they could against these evils. The invaders of Britain were expelled from the province, and the Germans were driven from Gaul. It is significant that when this had been done, Valentinian found it necessary to settle more German colonists on deserted lands inside the frontier, and to enlist still more Germans in the army, where they already outnumbered all other elements. In 367, to provide a permanent watch against further invaders, he elevated his young son Gratian to imperial status and stationed him at Treves. On the lower Danube the West Goths (*Visigothi*) were compelled to make peace. Again some of the defeated army were settled as dependent allies, this time in Dacia and Thrace. On the middle Danube, the Quadi were likewise brought to terms, while in Africa a Spanish general named Theodosius (whose son was later to become Emperor) put down a formidable uprising caused by imperial misgovernment. At home, in spite of his fiendish cruelty, Valentinian made some very useful reforms. By revoking the privileges granted to favored curials, he lightened somewhat the burdens of the whole class. To prevent the oppression of the municipalities by the bureaucracy, he established for each one an official representative called a "protector of the municipality" (*defensor civitatis*) who had extensive powers, including that of direct appeal from provincial functionaries to the Praetorian prefect on behalf of his charges. His tolerant religious policy did much to bring back to orthodox Christianity many lukewarm Arians, and permitted him to employ the services of able pagan soldiers and governors. In 375, a ruptured blood-vessel, caused by a fit of rage, ended his life.

Again confusion reigned. Gratian (367–383) was only sixteen years old when his father died, while Valens was by nature incapable of giving unity to the administration of the government. To add to the troubles of the disrupted Empire, the army in Illyricum saluted as Emperor Valentinian's eight-year-old son by his second wife, as Valentinian II (375–392). The boy's mother, Justina, was a fanatical Arian, and to her naturally fell the office of guardianship for him. But Gratian for a long time refused to grant him any independent authority.

*The Hunnish and Gothic Invasions*

It was while the Empire was thus deprived of competent leadership that an irreparable calamity befell it. Another wave of migration from the steppes of eastern Europe and Asia (of which the premonitory signs may perhaps be seen in the troubles of the preceding reign) was setting the northern peoples in motion. This time, the newcomers were a tribe of Mongoloid nomads, called Huns by their neighbors, who were conquering all that lay in their path. They were small in stature, with swarthy complexions, slanted eyes, and little or no beard. Their habits were filthy, and they spent almost their whole time on horseback. Moving with uncanny speed, they could outflank the defenders of a threatened district and devastate it before being caught. Their ferocity toward conquered peoples was such as to reduce their prospective victims to helpless panic. The Alans, a mixed tribe of German and Iranian descent who lived in the

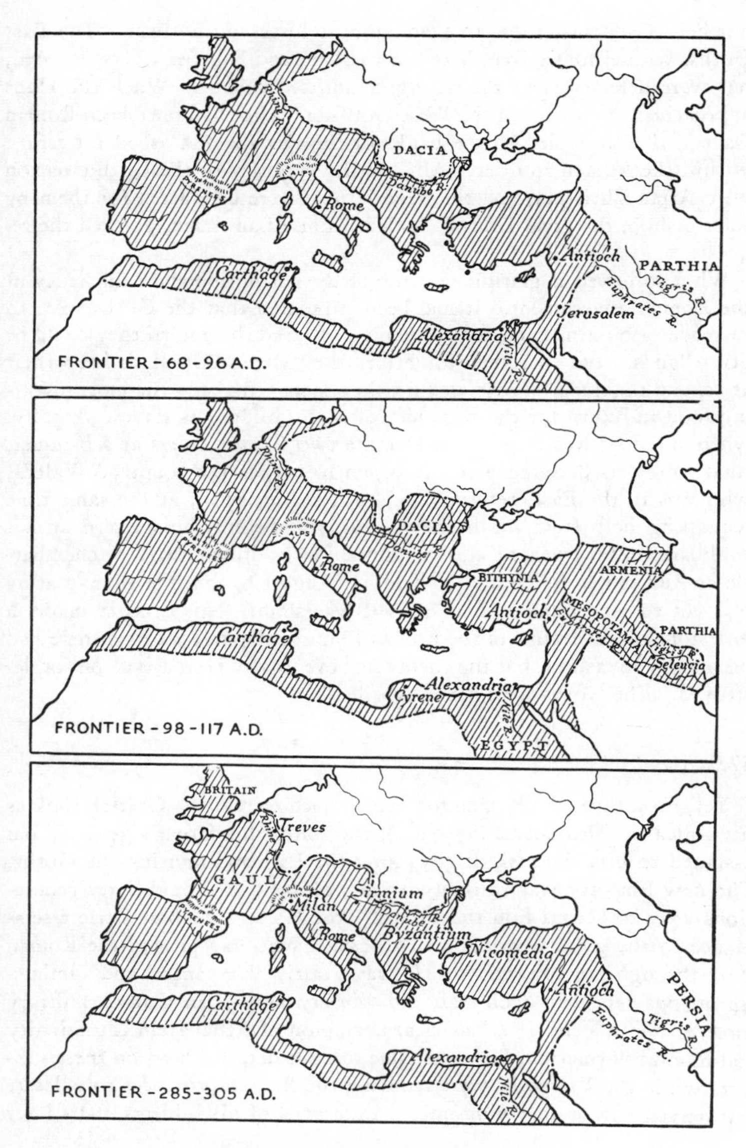


FLUCTUATION OF THE ROMAN FRONTIER

northern Caucasus, submitted and joined forces with them. The East Goths, whose homes were between the Don and Dnieper rivers, resisted, but were defeated, and their king committed suicide. When the Huns approached the homes of the West Goths (in what had once been Roman Dacia), the latter fled to the banks of the Danube and asked for refuge within the Roman frontier. Already the majority of the Gothic nation were Arian Christian, and the negotiations were conducted for them by their bishop, the great Ulfilas. Valens, himself an Arian, granted the request.

What followed is glaring evidence of the corruption and inefficiency of the Roman government. It had been stipulated that the Goths were to surrender their arms, and that Valens was to feed them until they could be given lands. But in return for bribes they were allowed to keep their arms, and the imperial officials furnished them with only the most revolting food in return for the surrender of their children as slaves. Finally, when an effort was made to assassinate two Gothic chiefs at a banquet, their followers declared war and began to ravage the country. Valens, who was in the East, returned and gathered an army, at the same time requesting help from his nephew Gratian. Before the western armies could arrive, however, he allowed himself to be drawn into a pitched battle at Adrianople in Thrace. There, on August 9, 378, the Roman army was cut to pieces and Valens himself was slain. This disaster marks a milestone in the decline of the Roman Empire. Up to that time there had been many invasions, but the enemy had eventually been driven out or destroyed. The Goths were never expelled.

### *Theodosius I*

Yet, for a time, the Roman fortunes seemed to revive. Gratian took as his colleague Theodosius (379–395), the son of his father's general, and assigned to him the task of governing the East and fighting the Goths. The new Emperor was thirty-two years of age. Although later generations were to accord him the title of "the Great," he bore little resemblance to the great warriors and statesmen who had piloted the Roman state through previous crises. He was a fairly able general and administrator, but depended upon craft and subtlety more often than on military force to win his ends. A fanatical champion of Athanasian Christianity and moral reformation, he found time to issue detailed laws on these subjects while the Visigoths were reducing the Balkan provinces to a desert and massacring or enslaving untold thousands of his subjects. His laws against immoral conduct were replete with punishments of frightful severity such as mutilation and burning alive. He was meticulously careful in his regulation of court etiquette and of official rank and precedence. In his dealings with his ministers and officials, he was, by turns, both suspicious and credulous, giving great power to advisers and following their counsel blindly, and later disgracing or abandoning them with no apparent reason.

For three years, Theodosius temporized with the Visigoths, occasionally fighting, but for the most part allowing them to roam at will over the lands between the Danube and the Aegean Sea. At last, in 382, he concluded a treaty with them by which he gave them land on the south bank of the Danube on condition that they become free allies of the Empire. The Romans paid the Visigoths tribute, in return for which the latter were to furnish recruits for the imperial army. They remained staunchly loyal to Theodosius as long as he lived, and affectionately termed him "the Friend of the Goths."

As Theodosius' fortunes rose, those of his colleagues fell. In 383, a usurper, Magnus Maximus, defeated and slew Gratian, and took possession of Britain, Gaul, and Spain, leaving the central provinces to Valentinian II. Theodosius, who could not afford civil war while the Goths were still in a position to make trouble, recognized Maximus as his colleague. But four years later, the usurper invaded Italy, driving Valentinian II and his mother to seek refuge at Constantinople. In 388, Theodosius defeated Maximus and put him to death, after which he sent his Frankish general Arbogast to recover the West for Valentinian. The Frank proved treacherous, and, in 392, the last representative of the family of the great Valentinian I was murdered.

As Roman public opinion would not tolerate an outright barbarian as Emperor, Arbogast conferred the title upon his secretary, the rhetorician Eugenius. The movement assumed the appearance of a pagan reaction, in which many of the aristocracy were implicated. In Rome, the statue and altar of Victory, which Gratian had removed from the Senate house, were replaced, and pagan rites were publicly resumed. But the triumph of the old religion was short-lived. In 394, Theodosius marched westward, and at the Battle of the Frigidus (in modern Carniola) Eugenius was defeated, captured, and executed. Arbogast took his own life. But the victor did not live to enjoy his success. Four months later, in the palace at Milan, Theodosius the Great breathed his last.

His death ended an era. Paganism was far from extinct, but the fall of Eugenius blasted its last hope of political supremacy. Henceforth, it could only decline, until, centuries later, its remnants were stamped out or absorbed into medieval Catholicism. Theodosius himself had sealed the victory of Athanasian Christianity, and thereafter Arianism was the creed of only barbarian Germans. The clergy were assuming some of their medieval rôle. In 390, the populace of Thessalonica murdered the Gothic commander of the local garrison, and Theodosius in revenge caused seven thousand of them to be massacred. Saint Ambrose, Bishop of Milan, assumed the position of censor of his master's conduct, and for eight months refused to admit him to the cathedral. Theodosius gave way and did public penance for his crime. Politically, also, the Empire was assuming a medieval appearance. Since the days of Valentinian I and Valens it had been divided, the line following in general the division between the Greek East and the Latin West, and Theodosius on his deathbed made the division permanent. Internal decay everywhere presented a sorry picture. A corrupt and unmanageable bureaucracy, an army composed principally of Germans, depopulated lands, and poverty-stricken provincials — all foretold its early fall, while the first contingent of free barbarian conquerors was already within its gates. The old order was nearly dead, and the next century was to see its obliteration.

# 27

# *Bureaucratic Despotism: Second Period*

# *(395-476 A.D.)*

## Dominant Trends

In the Roman Empire, the death of Theodosius I marked the transition from an era of decline and decadence to one of destruction and dissolution. The eighty-one years which followed this event witnessed its permanent division into two independent states, and the overwhelming of the Western Empire by the Germanic barbarians who had so long hurled themselves against its frontiers. In place of the Western Empire, the invaders set up loosely organized tribal states. The Eastern Empire, meanwhile, not only survived the calamities which destroyed her western sister, but achieved renewed strength and stability.

## The Theodosian Dynasty in the East and the West (395–457)

### *The Division of the Empire*

The reunion of the Roman Empire effected under Theodosius I, in 394, lasted but a few months. Before his death, which occurred in January, 395, he once more divided it between his two sons, Arcadius and Honorius. The line of demarcation was approximately that followed by Gratian, in 379. The East went to Arcadius, and the West to Honorius. Nominally, the division was only one of administration, for the laws were issued in the names of both emperors, and each year each of them chose one of the consuls. From a political viewpoint, therefore, it followed well-established precedents, and was in no sense a revolutionary step.

Yet, in fact, the partition of 395 had far-reaching consequences in both government and culture. Each section contained a capital city, which

*Numismatic Society*

ROMAN SOLIDUS

*Obverse: Head of Honorius. Reverse: Emperor Trampling an Enemy*

served as a natural center for its dominant culture. Although Rome had long ago ceased to be an imperial residence city, she remained the seat of the Senate and the magistracies which tradition had consecrated as emblems of the Roman state, while culturally she was the unquestioned center of the Latin West. Constantinople was, in quite another way, becoming equally prominent in the Graeco-Oriental East. Although Constantine had founded it as a "New Rome" with institutions copied from those of the city on the Tiber, its geographical situation soon attracted so many inhabitants from near-by areas that the Greek language and culture became dominant. Whereas Rome remained for a long time a center of paganism, Constantinople was, from the beginning, a Christian city. Hence, it was excellently adapted to the cultural leadership of an area in which a Christianized Greek civilization was rapidly taking shape. Since the subjects of Honorius were entirely Latin in culture, and those of Arcadius were almost all Greeks and Orientals, the presence of a capital city and a line of emperors in each section was enough to crystallize the existing cultural differences, and to make any lasting reunion of the two areas impossible. Therefore it is not surprising that, in spite of nominal unity, the two empires were in fact separate entities, always at peace and usually in alliance with each other, but pursuing independent policies and incapable of close co-operation.

In wealth and population, the Eastern Empire was by far the stronger of the two. Except for the provinces along the Danube, its territories had not been ravaged by an enemy for more than a century. Antioch, Alexandria, and a host of less important cities were busy centers of commerce and manufacturing. Through it, too, ran the trade routes to India, China, and central Africa, and to its people and government went the lion's share of the profits from foreign commerce. The Western Empire was, except for Rome and Carthage, devoid of first-rate cities, and in its European provinces, the urban centers were declining in both wealth and population. The periodic ravages of the barbarians had destroyed vast amounts of working capital and had depopulated whole districts. A manorialized rural economy was making the maintenance of government services in the West more and more difficult, and weakening its defensive strength.

### *The Dynasty of Theodosius: General Character*

In both East and West, the descendants of Theodosius I continued to wear the purple for over half a century. The Eastern Empire was ruled by Arcadius (395–408), by his son Theodosius II (408–450), and finally by Marcian (450–457), the brother-in-law of Theodosius II. In the West, Honorius (395–423) was followed by his nephew Valentinian III (423–455). With the exception of Marcian (who was not an actual descendant of Theodosius I), the same verdict may be passed upon them all. They were weak in both character and intelligence, and were utterly unfit to give the Empire the strong leadership it so badly needed. The actual government of the state was in the hands of their ministers and favorites, most of whom were unprincipled adventurers and intriguers. A leader of the caliber of Aurelian or Diocletian might have saved the state, but none appeared.

### *Alaric, Stilicho, and the First Sack of Rome*

At the beginning of the period, the chief danger seemed to threaten the dominions of Arcadius. His ministers were corrupt and incompetent court favorites, and the commanders of the army were barbarian mercenary captains of doubtful loyalty, of whom the most important were two Goths, Alaric and Gainas. Many, if not most, of the soldiers were Visigothic *foederati*, whose families were settled in colonies in the Balkan provinces. Before Arcadius had reigned a year, Alaric had gathered the Visigoths together and begun a revolt, the purpose of which was to wring better conditions of service from the imbecile government. For two years he ravaged Macedonia and Greece without mercy, until Arcadius consented to make him the commander of all imperial forces in the Prefecture of Illyricum. Then for several years he remained quiet.

In the West, the real ruler was Stilicho, a Vandal mercenary of considerable ability and unquestioned loyalty to his master, but incapable of cooperating with the government at Constantinople. It was because of quarrels between him and the ministers of Arcadius that Alaric had won his initial successes, and these same quarrels were to produce grave misfortunes in both East and West as long as he lived. Yet he put down a revolt in Africa, and until 406 defended the Rhine frontier successfully. With all his faults, he was the ablest leader of this sorry period.

In 401, Alaric again led the Visigoths in a revolt, and this time he turned his attention to the West. The next year he invaded Italy, where Stilicho defeated him but allowed him to return unmolested across the Julian Alps. A similar invasion, in 403, ended once more in defeat and a safe retreat. There is reason to suspect that Stilicho hoped to use Alaric to conquer for his master some of the lands of Arcadius, but whatever the reason, his failure to press his victories was the cause of irreparable misfortunes a few years later. Honorius, for greater safety, moved his capital from Milan to the swamp-girt city of Ravenna, which was to be the political center of Italy for over three centuries.

Stilicho remained at the head of the government of the Western Empire until 408. During that time, Alaric and his Visigoths lived quietly in Epirus and Dalmatia, although, in general, the period was one of disorder and calamity. Pannonia and Noricum were harassed by the Vandals and Ostrogoths. A mixed horde of barbarians under a pagan chief named Radagaisus hovered about the upper Danubian frontier, and, in 406, invaded Italy. In a fierce battle near Florence, Stilicho annihilated the invaders, but in doing so, he had denuded the Rhine frontier of troops, and this was the cause of the second irreparable break in the Roman line of defense. A swarm of Franks, Suevi, Vandals, and Alans crossed the river and fell upon defenseless Gaul, where they wrought frightful destruction. As a result of these misfortunes, in 407, Constantine, an imperial officer in Britain, assumed the purple and crossed over to take up the defense of the Gallic provinces. When, in 408, Alaric again approached Italy, all that Stilicho could do was to pay him the enormous ransom of four thousand pounds of gold [1] and to take him into the service of Honorius with all his followers. This was the last straw for the clique which surrounded the Emperor. They secured a warrant for the execution of the regent, and he was put to death.

Had the enemies of Stilicho been men of ability, they might still have retrieved the situation, but such was not the case. Alaric, who had now no strong opposition to fear, promptly led his tribesmen southward to the neighborhood of Rome, but withdrew upon receipt of another heavy ran-

[1] In intrinsic value, $1,512,000, but with at least ten times its modern purchasing power.

*Bettmann*

BARBARIAN HORSEMAN
*Hornhausen*

som — this time, five thousand pounds of gold, thirty thousand pounds of silver, and much costly merchandise. Each successful operation of this kind merely whetted the Gothic appetite for more. In 409, Alaric was back in the peninsula, this time to demand the cession of land upon which the Goths might settle, and food for their support. When Honorius, safe behind the walls of Ravenna, refused the demand, Alaric set up a Roman senator named Attalus as a puppet emperor. Since Attalus also proved obstreperous, the Visigoths at last moved upon Rome, and on August 24, 410, forced their way into the city. For three days they sacked and plundered, setting fires in certain quarters, but sparing the Christian churches. The extent of the damage is hard to estimate, but it cannot have been very great. Then the motley horde marched southward, their wagons loaded with spoil and captives, among whom was Honorius' half-sister, Galla Placidia.

Small as was the military significance of this disgraceful episode, its moral effect was tremendous. For eight centuries no foreign foe had set foot within the sacred *pomoerium*, and in that time the Roman arms had conquered the world. Many a patriotic Roman must have felt as St. Jerome did when the news reached his monastic cell at Bethlehem: "My voice is choked with sobs as I utter the words, 'Captive is the city which took captive the whole world.' " The pagans at once pointed out that this humiliation had come to Rome only after she had abandoned the worship of her old gods, and that the Christian God had not protected her. So damaging did this criticism appear that St. Augustine of Hippo spent thirteen years composing a reply, the famous *City of God*.

*The Visigoths in Gaul*

After leaving Rome, Alaric led his tribe to southern Italy, where he died. His successor Ataulf led the Gothic host back through the peninsula, and, in 412, the wanderers crossed the Alps into Gaul. There they fought for or against the Romans as circumstances dictated. Ataulf, who was anxious to remain at peace with the Emperor, married Galla Placidia, but, in 415, he was murdered. By that time Honorius was in competent hands. Constantius, an Illyrian general, had taken charge of his affairs, and was trying to retrieve the tottering fortunes of the Western Empire. The usurper Constantine had been defeated and killed in Gaul, and the Visigoths had been compelled to leave and cross over into Spain. There the Vandals, Suevi, Franks, and Alans, who had preceded them in 409, were already fast turning the peninsula into a desert, and, in 416, the Visigoths returned to Gaul. There they made peace with the Emperor, and enrolled as his soldiers. Galla Placidia returned to Italy, married Constantius, and became the mother of the Emperor Valentinian III.

The imperial government assigned the Visigoths a residence in southwestern Gaul, including the cities of Bordeaux and Toulouse, and a strip of land extending from the Garonne to the Loire. As this area was already occupied by Roman provincials, the government put into effect between the two peoples a system of relationships devised long before for use in similar cases. The provincials remained under the authority of Roman officials, and the Goths under that of their own kings. It had previously been the rule that a landowner in whose house a soldier was quartered had to surrender to the latter a third of his income. In this case, each proprietor gave up to the Visigoths the *ownership* of two thirds of his land. Hence, the territory occupied by the Visigoths was under a dual system of both land-ownership and government. It did not prevent further friction between Goths and Romans, who fought each other intermittently throughout the 420's and 430's, but it provided a precedent for the settlement of other Germanic tribes in Roman territory a little later. Not until 466 did the Visigothic king Euric finally repudiate Roman authority and undertake to build an independent Gothic state in Gaul and Spain.

### *Franks and Burgundians*

If much space has been devoted to the fortunes of this one tribe, it is because their conduct was largely typical of that of other barbarian groups. Thus, the Burgundians, who crossed the Rhine shortly after 406, began by founding a kingdom with its capital at Worms. But, in 436, an army of Huns in the Roman service defeated them so severely that they were glad to accept settlement as *foederati* to the south and west of Lake Geneva where one third of the land was allotted to them. Although they gradually extended their territories, it seems to have been by the consent of the government. In fact, they remained obedient to the Empire as long as it retained any authority in Gaul. In the north, the Salian Franks had been given lands by Julian, and they remained on them with little change in their condition until the Western Empire ceased to exist. Their kinsmen, the Ripuarian Franks, on the other hand, at an early date assumed an independent position, and took possession of much of the west bank of the Rhine. It was because the men of these tribes were soldiers in the Roman army that the Emperors were able to retain a dominant position in Gaul until about 460, when the *foederati* began to assert their independence.

### *The Germans in Spain and Africa*

A similar picture is to be seen in Spain. From 409 to 416, large parts of the peninsula were in the possession of the Vandals, Suevi, and Alans, but in 416, the Visigoths, fighting in the Roman service, attacked the other invaders. Before long they had driven the Suevi into the mountains of the northwest, exterminated the Silingian Vandals and most of the Alans, and compelled the Asdingian Vandals to acknowledge Roman suzerainty. This last group remained in the country until 429, when they departed for Africa. Thereafter, the Roman government controlled most of Spain until the Visigoth king Euric conquered it in 475.

The period of power and glory for the Vandals almost coincides with the reign of Gaiseric (429–472). Unlike the other German kings, he was not physically strong, but relied upon his powers as a schemer and a statesman. His diplomacy, cunning, and ruthlessness made him both feared and respected, and he ruled his people as an autocrat. In 429, Count Boniface the military commander in Roman Africa, was temporarily at enmity with the regent Galla Placidia, and to prevent her displacing him, he offered to share the African provinces with the Vandals in return for their aid. Gaiseric made the most of the situation. Taking possession of Mauretania, he swept eastward into Numidia. Boniface, once more on good terms with the Empress-Mother, resisted the invaders as best he could, and, in 431, he compelled them to raise the siege of Hippo. Four years later, Gaiseric secured a treaty giving him all of Mauretania on condition that he pay the Emperor tribute; for him such an agreement was, however, only a prelude to further advances. In 439, he seized Carthage, and in a few more years had occupied all of Roman Africa that was worth taking. He then built a fleet of small war-galleys, with which he ravaged the whole coast of the Mediterranean Sea. In 455, he sacked Rome. By 460, he had conquered Sicily, Sardinia, and the Balearic Islands, and from these bases he controlled the sea.

### *Huns and Germans in the Danubian Lands*

The provinces on the upper Danube were in chaos. After their first appearance, in the 370's, the Huns had settled down on the plain watered by the Tisza and the Danube, from which they exercised a loose suzerainty over German tribes around them. For a long time they were generally friendly to the Romans (to whom they furnished excellent mercenary cavalry), and they occupied little Roman land except the border province of Valeria. But their Germanic subjects — Ostrogoths, Gepids, and Heruls — ravaged the Danubian provinces repeatedly. Not long after 420, King Rugila united all the Huns under his rule, and in 424, the Eastern Emperor, Theodosius II, consented to pay him tribute. When Rugila died, he was succeeded by his nephews Attila and Bleda, but Attila murdered Bleda and reigned alone over an empire extending from the Rhine to the Volga or beyond. For some years, he pitilessly ravaged the provinces of the Eastern Empire, but, in 449, Theodosius II made peace with him on most humiliating terms. The Romans were to pay a tribute of twenty-one hundred pounds of gold a year, to surrender all fugitives from Attila's kingdom, and to leave a broad strip of land on the southern bank of the Danube completely uninhabited. The Western Empire, likewise, paid him tribute, but in return it was allowed to levy mercenaries among his subjects.

*Eastern and Western Empires 425–450*

A comprehensive view of the Western Empire in the second quarter of the fifth century would have revealed a sorry picture. With few or no exceptions, its provinces had all been invaded by the barbarians. Large tracts of land, especially in the strip which paralleled the northern frontier, had been swept almost bare of inhabitants. More than half of Gaul was occupied by barbarian *foederati*, who, at best, paid only a shadowy allegiance to the Empire, and who at times rebelled, killing or enslaving many of the provincials among whom they were settled. Similar enclaves of barbarians were to be found in northwestern Spain and the Danubian provinces, while Vandal Africa was an independent and hostile state. Over the shreds and patches of the provincial domain which were still in Roman hands, the Praetorian prefects, vicars, and governors maintained their authority irregularly and spasmodically. Under the system established by Constantine, these officials, who were drawn from the ranks of the senatorial aristocracy, had always been hard to control, and under the chaotic conditions which prevailed their demoralization was complete. Corruption, spoliation, and oppression of the middle and lower classes went on almost unchecked. Wealthy landlords assumed jurisdiction over their dependents, and set tax collectors and police officials at defiance. The income of the government shrank appallingly. A modern estimate places the return from the land tax at about $110,000,000 in 400, and at only $41,000,000 in 450. Military commanders had to depend upon turbulent and undisciplined barbarian mercenaries who supplemented their irregular pay by spoliation of the townspeople and peasantry. Driven to desperation, the victims formed bands of outlaws who lived by robbing their more fortunate neighbors. The Western Empire was rapidly becoming a mere federation of barbarian vassals and turbulent native aristocrats who paid only nominal homage to the weakling who wore the purple in Ravenna.

Valentinian III, the nominal ruler in the West from 423 to 455, was as weak as the other male descendants of Theodosius I. The real ruler was the Empress-Mother (until her death in 450), and the power behind the throne was the Patrician Aetius. Aetius was a remarkable military adventurer, the son of an Illyrian father and an Italian mother, who had spent some time as a hostage among the Huns. There he struck up a friendship with the barbarians which, in later years, enabled him to secure mercenary soldiers from them practically at will. He began his career in the service of John, a usurper, who had seized power in the West after the death of

*Galloway*

MAUSOLEUM OF GALLA PLACIDIA
*Fifth Century. Ravenna*

Honorius, but he later forced Galla Placidia to pardon him and give him the office of Master of the Soldiers. His chief rival was Boniface, previously mentioned as Count of Africa. Although the latter was the faithful friend of Galla Placidia, Aetius forced him into a civil war in the course of which Boniface died. Thereafter, Aetius was too powerful to be set aside. Hard and unscrupulous as he was, he upheld the tottering Roman cause in the West, and as long as he lived, he stayed the forces of dissolution.

Conditions in the Eastern Empire, while less critical than those in the West, were far from ideal. The land between the Danube River and the Balkan Mountains had been so thoroughly devastated that, by 450, it was a desolate and empty waste, while Greece, Dalmatia, Macedonia, and Thrace had suffered severely. The army, like that of the Western Empire, was made up principally of barbarian mercenaries, whose Gothic and Alanic commanders exercised a dangerous influence over the weak emperors. But the Eastern Emperors also had decisive advantages which their Western colleagues lacked. Their capital was not only an impregnable fortress, but a rich and populous city, which in times of stress could furnish valuable support. Furthermore, their Asiatic and Egyptian provinces had wholly escaped the ravages of the barbarians, and were still prosperous and densely populated. Only a series of able rulers was needed to restore the Eastern Empire to strength and stability.

In the reign of Theodosius II, however, the government at Constantinople reached the depths of inefficiency and degradation. The Emperor was an amiable and well-intentioned weakling, who was dominated by his pious and strong-willed sister Pulcheria, his wife Eudocia, and a clique of eunuchs and barbarian generals. Their intrigues disturbed the peace of an otherwise respectable court, until Pulcheria finally drove Eudocia into an honorable exile at Jerusalem. Tribute to the Huns kept the treasury almost empty. During Theodosius' later years, an Alan named Aspar, who was Master of the Soldiers, exercised a preponderant influence over the government. Yet Theodosius founded a famous school at Constantinople, and, in 438, issued the law code which bears his name. The Theodosian Code is still a mine of information on religious, political, social, and economic affairs in the century and a quarter of Roman history, from Constantine to the time of its completion.

### *Attila Attacks the Western Empire*

It was under these conditions that Attila suddenly shifted his attention from the East to the West, and in 451, began his famous invasion of Gaul. The provinces of the Eastern Empire which he had previously ravaged were nearing exhaustion, and Marcian, the successor of Theodosius II, firmly refused to continue the tribute paid by his predecessor. At the same time Gaiseric, who was on bad terms with the Visigothic king Theodoric, encouraged Attila as a means of diverting the attention of his enemy from himself. With a host swollen by contingents from his Germanic vassals, the Hunnish king crossed the Rhine and laid city after city in ashes. At length, he undertook the siege of Orleans, which resisted bravely. For the moment, however, it appeared that the sovereignty of the West, which the Germanic tribes were gradually wresting from Rome, was to be taken from them in turn by these savage newcomers from the plains of eastern Europe.

In this crisis, Aetius displayed leadership of the first order. Hastily collecting all the forces at his disposal, he hurried to Gaul, where he enrolled under his standards Franks, Alans, and Burgundians. He then patched up his current quarrel with the Visigoths and induced them to send their whole army to his aid. As the allies approached, Attila raised the siege of Orleans and retreated eastward. At a spot called the Catalaunian Plains, near the modern city of Troyes, Aetius and Theodoric came up with him, and the two hosts joined battle. The struggle lasted two days, and was fierce and bloody. Theodoric was killed, but the Huns were forced back to the circle formed by their baggage-wagons. At this point Aetius, who was afraid to increase further the prestige of the Visigoths, broke off the engagement, and Attila recrossed the Rhine without opposition. The Battle of the Catalaunian Plains has been acclaimed one of the "decisive" battles of the world's history on the ground that it saved the West from domination by Asiatic Mongoloids, but its real significance is hard to determine. Certainly, although it did not crush Attila, it helped to hold him in check.

In 452, Attila with a fresh host invaded Italy. Aquilea and many other cities were leveled to the ground, and the Huns appeared bent upon nothing short of the conquest of the peninsula and the destruction of Rome. Aetius, who, in this case, could not count upon Gothic aid, hung upon the rear of the Hunnish host with a small force, cutting off stragglers and fighting skirmishes. For a time it seemed that he was accomplishing little, and Valentinian III at last sent an embassy headed by Leo I, Bishop of Rome, to intercede with the invader. By this time, the plague had broken out among the Huns, provisions were scarce, and troops sent by Marcian from Constantinople were approaching. Attila agreed to retrace his steps, and medieval legend gave to the Pope full credit for the deliverance. A year later, the Hunnish king died, and his kingdom fell to pieces.

Aetius did not long survive the deliverance of which he had been the chief cause. Galla Placidia was now dead, but her jealous and incapable son hated the domineering Master of the Soldiers as intensely as his mother had. In 454, he slew Aetius with his own hands. A few months later two Huns who had served on the bodyguard of the murdered general avenged him by assassinating his murderer. In the West as in the East, the house of Theodosius was extinct.

## The End of the Western Empire

### *The Vandals and Ricimer*

The end of the Theodosian line had very different results in the two halves of the Empire. In the East, it made possible the rise of a series of able emperors — Marcian, Leo I, and Zeno — who gradually reorganized the army with a preponderance of native troops, eliminated the barbarian generals, and restored order. But in the West, the exact opposite was true. The death of Valentinian III was the beginning of even greater calamities than those of the past, culminating in the complete occupation of Italy and the provinces by the barbarians and the extinction of the western line of emperors.

The first person to profit by the political confusion in Italy was Gaiseric. Valentinian's widow was compelled to marry his successor, and in her indignation she appealed to the Vandal king for help. Gaiseric's response was prompt. In June, 455, his fleet anchored in the Tiber. Pope Leo I again interceded for the threatened city, but this time all that he could secure was the promise that it would not be destroyed or its inhabitants massacred. For two weeks, the invaders systematically sacked Rome, taking everything of value. Among the loot were the objects taken by Titus from the temple at Jerusalem. When Gaiseric at last set sail, he had aboard his fleet Eudoxia, the widow of Valentinian III, and her two daughters, together with thirty thousand Romans who were being carried off as slaves.

But the Western Empire, weakened as it was, had still a few more years of life left to it. In 456, Ricimer, a German of mixed Suevian and Gothic blood, became Master of the Soldiers and Patrician, and until his death, in 472, was the real ruler of the state. As the people would not submit to an Arian and barbarian emperor, Ricimer did not assume the title himself, but set up a series of puppets to hold it. Of these, only Majorian (457–461) was a man of any ability, and Ricimer killed him. The others were mere ciphers, who left the power of government entirely in his hands.

### *The Foederati Become Independent*

It was in these years that the barbarian tribes of Gaul, Spain, and the Danubian provinces asserted their independence, assumed control over the Roman provincials among whom they were settled, and founded territorial states. The Visigothic king Euric (466–484) threw off the Roman suzerainty, conquered most of Spain, and shortly after Ricimer's death, extended his kingdom along the Mediterranean coast of Gaul to the Rhone. Fugitives from Britain (then in the process of conquest by the Angles, Saxons, and Jutes) seized the western promontory of Gaul and founded a state aptly named Brittany. The Burgundians spread both westward and northward from their original settlement in Savoy, so that their state came to include Lyons and Vienne on the west, and the land later named Burgundy on the north. The Ripuarian Franks spread westward from the Rhine to the valleys of the Meuse and the Moselle, and the Salian Franks

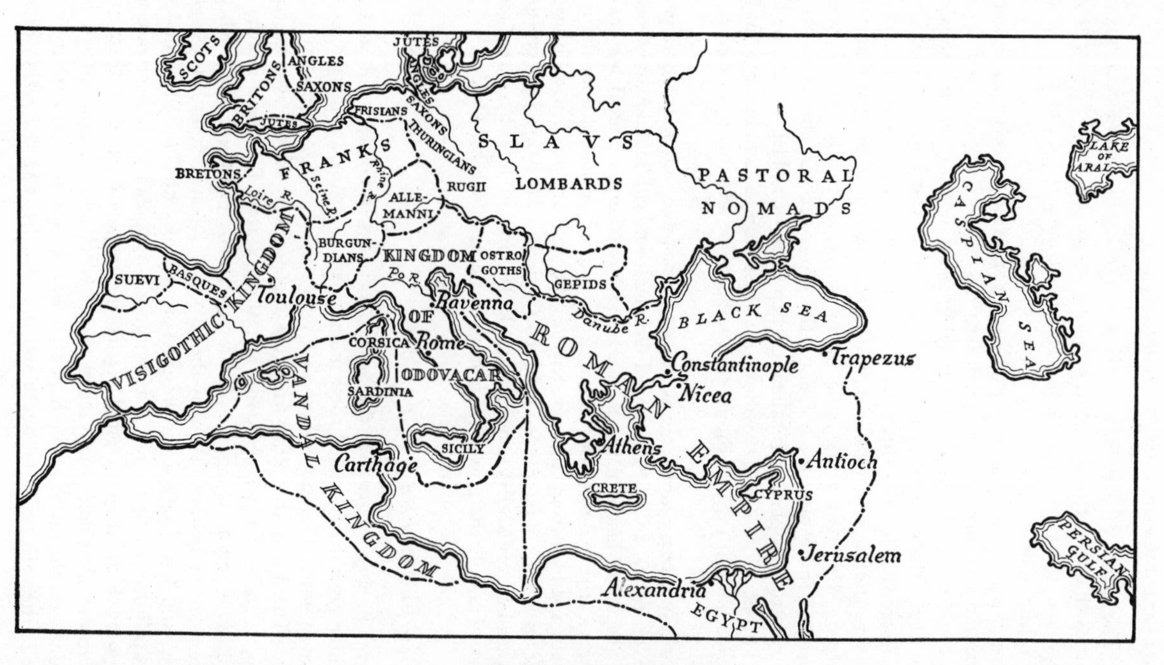


THE BARBARIAN KINGDOMS

*Fifth Century A.D.*

conquered the lands southward from their original Gallic home to the Somme River. Only between the Somme and the Loire rivers did the Roman Count Aegidius preserve a fragment of Gaul for his master, and he was completely shut off from communication with Italy. After his death, his son Syagrius continued to rule this district until conquered and killed by Clovis the Frank in 486. On the other side, the Ostrogoths and other German tribes were settled in Pannonia in a state of practical independence. In fact, as early as 472, when Ricimer died, the government which he and his puppet emperors maintained, controlled only Italy, Rhaetia, Noricum, and a corner of Dalmatia.

*Orestes, Romulus Augustus, and Odovacar: the Fall of Rome*

At Ricimer's death his nephew, the Burgundian Gundobad, tried to continue the system established by his uncle, but he soon returned home to accept the kingship of his tribe. It then fell to Orestes, a Roman provincial from Pannonia, who had formerly been the private secretary of Attila the Hun. The Emperor of the moment was Julius Nepos, appointed by the Eastern Emperor Leo, but Orestes lost no time in driving him from Italy. Nepos took refuge in Dalmatia, where he reigned until 480. In his place, Orestes appointed his own son, a small boy to whom he gave the high-sounding name of Romulus Augustus. The public generally called him by the contemptuous title of *Augustulus*, or the "Little Augustus."

The "Little Augustus" reigned for less than a year. The army was, by this time, wholly composed of barbarians who felt that they, like the Germans in the provinces, were entitled to land-grants. However, when they demanded that one third of Italy be set aside for them, Orestes' Roman pride would not permit him to assent. The soldiers were in no mood to be put off. Odovacar, one of Orestes' officers and a member of a minor German tribe called Scirians, headed a revolt in which Orestes was killed. "Then," says a contemporary historian, "Odovacar entered Ravenna and deposed Augustulus, but spared his life because he pitied his infancy and because he was comely. He gave him an annual income of six thousand solidi, and sent him to live in Campania with his relatives." [1] Having done this, Odovacar induced the Roman Senate to send the imperial insignia to Constantinople, with the statement that there was no longer any need for two emperors, but that the Eastern Emperor Zeno should govern the West also, with Odovacar as his deputy with the title of Patrician.

[1] *Anonymous Valesiani*, p. 716.

Such was the so-called "Fall of Rome," or "End of the Western Empire." Legally, there could be no such thing, for the Roman Empire was, by law, an indivisible unit, administered by one or more emperors. Furthermore, Romulus Augustus had never been recognized at Constantinople, while Julius Nepos was still considered the legitimate ruler. But, in a broader sense, the year 476 has a profound importance. It signalized the possession by barbarians of the last considerable section of that part of the Empire given to Honorius by the partition of 395. The Latin cultural area was now almost completely in the hands of the Germanic invaders. There was, it is true, still a Roman Empire, but it was fast becoming a Graeco-Oriental state, with little trace of its Roman background. Whatever the legal theory, the year 476 represents an excellent conventional date for the end of the ancient world.

*The Anglo-Saxons in Britain*

It will be noticed that little has been said about the fortunes of Britain during the fifth century. After the withdrawal of Constantine from the island, in 407, it must have been completely lost to the Empire, and thereafter little is known about it for nearly two centuries. Apparently, the natives, who were Christianized but had never generally adopted the Latin language, found themselves exposed to attack by their Celtic kinsmen the Picts and Scots from the north and west, and by Germanic pirates on the east and south. They defended themselves stoutly, but before the middle of the fifth century the Germanic tribes of Angles, Saxons, and Jutes had obtained footholds along the coasts, and were slowly pushing their conquests inland. These tribes had never been in close contact with Rome, and were not only pagans, but far less civilized than the Goths, Vandals, Franks, and other tribes who conquered the continental provinces of the Empire. Roman civilization and Christianity disappeared from the lands which they conquered; the natives were killed, driven back, or enslaved; and a new, totally Germanic society arose there. In the north and west the Britons still maintained their independence, and became the ancestors of the modern Welsh, Cornish, and west-country Scotch. The struggle between the Celts and Anglo-Saxons went on until long after the end of the fifth century.

## The Recovery of the Eastern Empire

We have noted that in the Eastern Empire, the disappearance of the House of Theodosius cleared the way for a series of able emperors who stabilized the government and gave to the state a new lease on life. The process of regeneration was a long one, occupying the whole second half of the fifth century and the first years of the sixth. The Emperors to whom it was due were Marcian (450–457), Leo I (457–474), Zeno (474–491), and Anastasius (491–518). Only a brief outline of the process will be sketched here.

### *Sources of Weakness of the Eastern Empire*

The sad plight of the Eastern Empire about 450 was brought about by deep-seated causes which contemporaries did not recognize and which are still not thoroughly understood. The storm of barbarian invasion, which had brought the state to the brink of ruin, was beginning to abate, although its waves continued to pound the Danubian frontier for a long time, and the damage which it had done to the European provinces was never repaired. There remained four glaring evils which were concrete enough to attract the attention of rulers — the barbarian mercenaries, official corruption, oppressive taxation, and religious discord. The first three need no explanation. The fourth centered about the *Monophysite* heresy, which had sprung into prominence in the reign of Theodosius II.

The theological aspects of the Monophysite creed centered about a highly abstruse question regarding the human and divine natures of Christ. The question had been considered at three Church Councils, two of which had been held at Ephesus (431 and 449) and the third at Chalcedon (451). The issue was complicated by a three-cornered struggle for precedence among the Bishops of Rome, Alexandria, and Constantinople, by the interference of the imperial government, and by the reappearance of national consciousness among the subject populations of Syria, Palestine, and Egypt. The first Council condemned both Nestorius, the Monophysite Bishop of Constantinople, and his chief antagonist, Cyril of Alexandria. Cyril was soon restored, and, in 433, a compromise creed was adopted which kept the peace for eleven years. But, in 444, the quarrel was reopened, with Cyril's successor supporting the Monophysite cause. By this time, Leo I was Bishop of Rome, and he prepared to take an active part. He insisted that the Bishops of Rome had the right to settle all doctrinal questions, and prepared an encyclical letter called the *Tome* condemning the Monophysite views. Theodosius II disregarded Leo's claims, and called another Council at Ephesus. Leo's *Tome* was ignored, the Monophysite cause was upheld, and its opponents were condemned. Leo was obdurate, denounced the

Second Council of Ephesus as a "Robber Council," and secured the support of the Western Emperor, Valentinian III. In the second year of Marcian's reign (451) he called a Third Council to meet at Chalcedon to consider the matter. The Monophysites were condemned, and the *Tome* formed the basis of the Council's decision. Rome and Constantinople had beaten Alexandria, but only with the aid of open coercion by the government.

The quarrel had unexpected consequences. In an age when theological disputes often masked many secular issues, the beaten party was almost certain to gain the support of groups who opposed the government for other reasons. The Monophysites soon secured the allegiance of the Egyptians, Syrians, and other depressed eastern peoples, and their creed became a rallying point for a revival of nationality among these groups. After the Council of Chalcedon, the disorders to which this mixture of religious and political causes gave rise, grew steadily in Syria and Egypt in spite of the efforts of the government to conciliate or suppress the heretics. The Greeks in these lands usually supported religious orthodoxy and governmental authority, and were popularly known as *Melchites*, from a Semitic root meaning "king" or "government."

### *Imperial Reformers and Reforms*

The other problems of the government at Constantinople were treated more wisely and successfully. Marcian attempted to lighten the taxes of his harassed subjects by a drastic reduction of expenditure and elimination of graft. We have seen how he stopped the payment of tribute to Attila, and he probably eliminated a major source of corruption by executing Chrysaphius, the former chamberlain of Theodosius II. In later times, his reign was remembered as the "Golden Age."

Marcian had remained on good terms with Aspar, the general of the mercenaries, but Leo I took the first steps toward the creation of a native military force to neutralize the influence of these turbulent hirelings. To do this he had recourse to the *Isaurians*, wild and lawless mountaineers from southern Asia Minor. Leo first enlisted the aid of an Isaurian who took the name of Zeno, married his daughter, and ultimately became his successor. Together they formed a palace guard of Isaurians and other native troops, and added to it combat units of similar materials. In 471, Aspar and one of his sons were treacherously murdered, and the command of the army passed completely into the hands of the Isaurians.

But even after the fall of Aspar, order was not restored for many years.

The reign of Zeno was beset with perils arising from dissensions within the imperial family, the ambitions of his Isaurian supporters, and the turbulence of the Ostrogoths. Soon after his accession, Zeno was dethroned by his mother-in-law Verina and her brother Basiliscus, and was not restored for nearly two years. Later, he fought a long civil war with an Isaurian named Illus, who was not suppressed until 488.

In his dealings with the Ostrogoths, Zeno was compelled, by the insecurity of his position, to adopt an inglorious policy of bribery, duplicity, and cunning. When Attila the Hun died, these barbarians were settled in northern Pannonia. A few years later, under two chiefs both of whom bore the name of Theodoric, we find them in the Balkan provinces, where a section of the tribe was enlisted in the imperial army as *foederati*, while the remainder ravaged the provinces and exacted blackmail from the government. Zeno continued his devious policy throughout the 480's, trusting to time for a solution of his problems. The older Theodoric was accidentally killed in 481, but his namesake continued to be a problem until 488, when, with Zeno's consent, he led his tribe to Italy to attack Odovacar whom he defeated and slew. Thereafter, the Balkan lands were free from Germanic intruders, although they soon had to resist new tribes of nomads from the Steppes.

Neither Leo I nor Zeno was heroic, but they had accomplished much. In the face of difficulties which seemed insuperable, they had freed the state from German domination, and had started it on the road to economic recovery. Both had done what they could to ease the lot of the taxpayer. The lawless violence of the great landlords had been checked by a law prohibiting them from equipping and maintaining private armies. Even in the Church, Zeno had striven to effect a compromise creed (the *Henotikon*) which would satisfy moderates of all parties. But, although the document placated the moderate Monophysites, it was rejected by the orthodox Christians, who hated Zeno for his part in issuing it.

Anastasius, an emperor of far more pleasing personality than either Leo I or Zeno, was able to build upon the foundations which they had laid. He found the army largely composed of Isaurians and commanded by Isaurian officers. By a series of shrewd and energetic moves, he broke their hold upon the government, without returning to German control. A new wall forty-one miles long was built to protect the suburbs of Constantinople. His tolerance toward the Monophysites, although it caused discontent in the capital, helped to keep Syria and Egypt quiet. But his greatest service to his people was in the field of finance. The *Chrysargyrum*, which weighed so heavily upon the lower and middle classes, was abolished, and the *curiales* were relieved of many of their financial responsibilities. Rigid economy kept the government solvent in spite of these losses of revenue.

When Anastasius died, the regeneration of the Eastern Empire was accomplished. The army was once more controlled by native soldiers; the evils of official corruption and taxation had been greatly lightened; and, for the moment, a *modus vivendi* was in effect between the government and the heretics. The Eastern Empire had entered upon a new and independent career, which was to last without a break until the capture of Constantinople by the Crusaders, in 1204.

# 28

****************************************

# *The Civilization of the Later Roman Empire*

## The Spirit of the Age

In the calamitous fourth and fifth centuries, the culture of the Graeco-Roman world underwent a series of profound changes which brought the "ancient" phase of Occidental civilization to a close and launched European man upon a new stage of his career. One may regard these changes as the decay of an old civilization or as the birth of a new one, according to his personal viewpoint. In fact, they combined both processes; for since human history never stands still, a new order is always coming to birth as an old one passes from the scene. These two centuries everywhere witnessed the overthrow of the classical pagan religions, and in the Latin culture area brought with them the destruction of the orderly imperial government, polished city life, money economy, art, literature, and philosophy which had been outstanding features of Latin classical culture. In their place came primitive tribal governments, a manorialized rural economy, an almost complete cessation of artistic activity, and the Christian religion. In the Eastern Empire no such drastic break was apparent between the old order and the new one. There the most obvious changes were to be found in the substitution of Christianity for paganism, and in the increasing prevalence of Oriental artistic and literary influence, with a corresponding decline in the importance of Occidental classicism.

## The Spread of the Latin Language

### *Area and Degree of Latinization*

The last two centuries of Roman rule in the West marked the completion of one important part of Rome's historic mission — the conquest of Gaul, Spain, and parts of northern Africa and the Balkan peninsula by the Latin language. As the Romans made no effort to force their tongue upon un-

*Bettmann*

PROVINCIAL ROMAN AMPHITHEATERS

*Arles* *Verona*

willing provincials, the process was slow and gradual. Its progress is often hard to trace, for Greek and Roman writers were but little interested in the life of the provincials. The discovery of Latin inscriptions in a provincial area is helpful, but it is easy to draw false conclusions from them. Sometimes they were carved by officials and army personnel, who were not natives of the region in which they are found, and again they may have been the work of a small Latinized minority, living among an overwhelming majority of persons speaking other languages. It is certain that the Celtic tongue was never displaced in Britain, that it lasted until the fourth century in Gaul, and that the pre-Roman tongue known as Basque has always been spoken in the Pyrenees Mountains. In North Africa, the Phoenician and Moorish languages were never entirely displaced, although Latin gained wide acceptance in the more progressive communities.

*Literary Latin in the Provinces*

Latin made its way into the provinces by two means: formal teaching, and diffusion by Latin-speaking soldiers, traders, and settlers. For young men of wealth and position there were, in every town, schools where

Latin grammar and rhetoric formed a large part of the curriculum. Their graduates might speak their Latin with a foreign accent, but it was good grammatical Latin, taught largely by the reading and discussion of the classical authors. By the time that Christianity spread into the western provinces, there were in them many educated Latin-speaking men, some of whom became Christian clergymen, while others remained literary *dilettanti* striving vainly to imitate Cicero or the great Roman poets.

### *Vulgar Latin*

These schools, however, had little influence upon the common people. The Latin which they learned to speak was the everyday language of the Romans and Italians of their own class, further vulgarized in the mouths of provincial soldiers and traders. The grammar of this *vulgar* (common) Latin differed widely from that used in the literary dialect. The elaborate declension of nouns and adjectives familiar to the modern student of Latin was almost entirely lacking, while the conjugation of verbs followed an entirely different pattern. Classical Latin used highly inflected single words for the future and perfect tense-forms, and for most of the passive voice. Vulgar Latin, on the other hand, constructed its future tense by combining *habere* ("have") with the infinitive, made up the perfect tenses from forms of *habere* and the past participle, and for the passive voice used variations of *esse* ("to be") with the past participle. Whereas classical Latin had neither definite nor indefinite articles, in vulgar Latin *ille* ("that") was used for the definite article and *unus* ("one") for the indefinite article. Vulgar Latin vocabulary was equally at variance with that of its classical counterpart. Thus, for "house" it had *casa* (literally "hovel" or "cottage") in place of the conventional *domus*, and for "horse," *caballus* (literally "a horse of poor quality," "nag," or "plug") instead of the literary form *equus*. Its importance lies in the fact that from it, rather than from classical Latin, the later Romance languages were to spring.

## The Fine Arts

### *Decline and Change*

Architecture, sculpture, painting, and mosaic all suffered a sharp decline and underwent profound changes. The decadence of ancient city life destroyed the most potent source of encouragement for all the fine arts. In the harassed and regimented urban environment of the fourth and fifth

*University Prints*

RELIEFS FROM THE ARCH OF CONSTANTINE [1]

centuries, there was no longer sufficient wealth to support ambitious programs of building and beautification, while artistic creativity could find no place in communities continually menaced with destruction by invaders, and dragooned by rapacious soldiers and officials. Even the technical skill of the painter and the stonecutter declined amid these unfriendly surroundings. A glaring example of this decadence is to be found in the sculptures which adorn the triumphal arch built to commemorate the victory of Constantine over Maxentius. It was decorated in part with old reliefs stolen from the Arch of Trajan, which were supplemented by new ones. The former display the sure workmanship and realistic touch characteristic of the early second century, but they merely throw into glaring prominence the crudity and ineptitude of the Constantinian work. Portrait sculpture likewise declined from the level of the early Empire in both

[1] Note the difference in quality between the medallions above, which were originally taken from the Arch of Trajan, and the scene below, carved in Constantine's reign.

technical perfection and ability to portray character. Painting and mosaic maintained their standard of artistry longer, but both underwent sharp decline and change. Secular art fell considerably below the level of the first- and second-century work. Fifth-century mosaics from North Africa display the same effort to portray scenes from everyday life that is apparent in the productions of previous ages, but they are heavy and lifeless. In short, classical art in all its forms reflected the deterioration of the old order of things.

Architecture, usually the first of the fine arts to be practiced by a people emerging from barbarism, was the last to succumb. Diocletian and Constantine each erected splendid baths in Rome, of which the former was about equal in size to those of Caracalla and accommodated three thousand bathers at once. Maxentius began, and Constantine finished the famous Basilica of Constantine, a monumental structure of brick and concrete with a vaulted roof. But with the removal of the seat of government from Rome and the foundation of Constantinople, whatever building took place in the later fourth and fifth centuries was done in the "New Rome," or in Milan, Ravenna, and other imperial residence cities. Except in Ravenna, little or none of this has survived. In the provinces, the increasing calamities of the times brought new secular building practically to a standstill.

### *Christian Art*

Christian art, on the other hand, reflected the vitality and seriousness of purpose of the institution which, in this age, was completing its conquest of the Roman Empire. It produced architectural types suited to its purposes and began to adorn them with reliefs, paintings, and mosaics. As a rule, Christian art drew heavily upon pagan or secular models, but it transformed what it borrowed. From a technical viewpoint, much of this work was crude, but at least it was the expression of a real contemporary interest, and not a relic of the past.

Church architecture was principally dominated by an attempt to find suitable meeting places for congregational worship. The pagan temple, which usually did no more than house the cult statue of the deity, with even the altar out-of-doors, was obviously unsuited to the purpose. A few of these structures like the Roman Pantheon or the Athenian Parthenon proved to be adaptable to the purpose of the new religion, and the domed churches of Ravenna and Constantinople were very similar in construction to the Pantheon. But in general, the Church, in planning its places of

*Brown Brothers*

BASILICA OF SANT' APOLLINARE NUOVO [1]
*Ravenna*

worship, imitated the Graeco-Roman basilica. As we have seen, this type of building had been designed to accommodate large crowds of shoppers or litigants, and its clerestory windows provided adequate lighting for the interior. Some of the secular basilicas, such as the one which is known today as the Church of St. John Lateran, were given to the Christians by Constantine or his successors, and transformed into churches. Many more were built upon this plan, from which, centuries later, the Romanesque and Gothic styles were to be developed.

Painting and mosaic were pressed into service to adorn the interiors of these structures. Naturally, the Christian artist used the technical processes employed by his colleagues who treated secular themes, and his

[1] While this church was not built until 500 A.D., it follows closely the floor plan and structural features of Roman basilica churches, and its interior has suffered little change at the hands of later builders. Its fresco and mosaic decorations are sixth-century work, and so fall outside the scope of the present discussion.

work had many of the same features as theirs. But he had a message to deliver, and he concentrated his attention upon it. Symbolism abounded. The evangelists were sometimes represented by animals and birds: the ox stood for Matthew, the lion for Mark, and the eagle for John. Sheep, doves, and fish, each had a conventional meaning understood by the congregation. Christ on the cross reminded the worshiper of the central theme of his religion. Occasionally, the artist pictured heaven with the saints enjoying their eternal reward in the company of the angels and the Virgin Mary. All levels of artistic merit are to be found in these works, but all are full of the enthusiasm of the new faith.

## Education, Science, and Literature

### *The Schools of the Late Empire*

Formal education certainly did not suffer for want of attention or recognition. Never had the emperors or the local governments made greater efforts to encourage or reward teachers. Especially in Gaul, a number of schools were founded which might almost be called colleges or universities, and members of their teaching staffs had a highly privileged position. They were freed from the *munera*, and imperial legislation guaranteed them high salaries. Successful rhetoricians or grammarians could rise to the highest offices. Thus, in the reign of Diocletian, Eumenius, a teacher in the Gallic city of Augustodunum, became a *magister memoriae* to the Caesar Constantius, with a salary of the highest class, and later when he was sent back to be head of the city's schools, his salary was doubled. Valentinian I called the grammarian Ausonius from the schools of Bordeaux to tutor his son, Gratian, who later made his former teacher Praetorian prefect and consul. Exclusive as was the senatorial aristocracy, its ranks were always open to low-born men of learning. The schools continued to enjoy this high status until Roman authority disappeared from the West.

But in spite of the favor shown to men of learning, the level of intellectual attainment continued to decline. Greek had once been widely known among men of education in the Latin world, but when, in 376, Gratian issued an edict providing for a teacher of this language at Treves, he expressed doubts as to whether a suitable person could be found. Latin education was more and more losing touch with life. In the fourth century, the language of the schools was a highly artificial dialect, so different from the spoken tongue of the masses that they were probably unable to understand it. Those who learned to use it fluently usually spent their leisure time writing prose or verse in a tortured and unpleasant style full of antitheses, comparisons, half-suppressed classical allusions, unusual words, and other tricks of expression designed to stimulate the attention of the reader. Law and medicine, both of which were taught in a few of the schools, were by nature practical subjects, but the times were against them. Except for imperial rescripts, creative interpretation of the law practically ceased at the beginning of the Military Anarchy. But the rescripts of the late Empire which were, of course, written by imperial legal advisers rather than by the emperors themselves, were couched in a verbose, bombastic style which proves that the writers were as steeped in rhetoric as the rest of the educated world. No noticeable advance had been made in medicine since the days of Galen (130–200 A.D.).

The splendid intellectual tradition of the Hellenistic Age was, however, not quite dead; probably it lingered at Alexandria longer than elsewhere. It was there that the mathematician Theon pursued his career as a scholar and teacher in the reign of Theodosius I and Arcadius. His daughter, the famous and ill-fated Hypatia, taught Neoplatonist philosophy brilliantly and successfully until her murder by Christian fanatics, in 415. This atrocious crime was characteristic of the narrow intolerance of the Alexandrian patriarchs, which resulted in the destruction of the schools and libraries of this great center of learning. But not all Christians were so narrow-minded. At Caesarea, in Palestine, Origen had established a school in the third century, and his successors carried on his work for seventy-five years after his death. Most important of these were Pamphilus, and his colleague Eusebius, of whom the latter attained lasting fame as a Christian historian. It would seem that the Caesarean scholars did not scorn a knowledge of pagan learning, and their work suffered from the same faults which afflicted Latin education.

### *Latin Literature*

Literature in both East and West reflected the same tendencies which blighted education. The hackneyed classical themes were treated in Latin by many would-be poets, and by a few who under other conditions might have been great. Decimus Magnus Ausonius (born about 310), whose official career has been mentioned, was a man of considerable natural ability, who could at times display both originality and feeling. While nominally a Christian, he was full of the old pagan spirit, which displayed itself in his eulogies upon deceased relatives and the kindly character sketches of his colleagues in the schools of Bordeaux, as well as in his playful trifle, *The Dream of Cupid*. His *Mosella*, which describes a voyage down the Moselle River, breathes something of the love of nature which appears in the *Pervigilium Veneris*. But these works only partly redeem the feeble rhetorical exercises, and empty but ingenious efforts at versification, which make up the bulk of his writings.

More strictly a product of the dying classical world was Claudius Claudianus (died about 408). He was an Egyptian Greek whose later years were spent in Rome, and who wrote in Latin. He was a protégé of Stilicho, and most of his surviving poems commemorate the deeds of his patron or sing the praises of the worthless Honorius. At least, no one can accuse Claudian of the frigid apathy which was the blight of so much of the verse of the late Empire. He lavishes upon the enemies of Stilicho a prodigal wealth of abuse, and rejoices loudly at their misfortunes. His elegiacs and hexameters also celebrate the successes won against Alaric and the Moor Gildo, as well as the consulates of Honorius, in better verse than they deserve. He was a stubborn and unrepentant pagan, who wrote several poems on mythological themes, and in one of these, the unfinished *Rape of Proserpina*, he did surprisingly well. Like Ausonius, he displayed talents which, in a different environment, might have made him a great poet.

At the same time the Christian Church was also producing versifiers of a sort. Ambrose, the great Bishop of Milan in the days of Theodosius I, wrote a number of excellent hymns. A much more prolific hymnologist was the Spaniard Aulus Prudentius Clemens (born 343). From his pen we have a book of *Hymns for Daily Use*, a martyrology called *Crowns*, and a series of lesser works on theological subjects. They are written in a variety of meters, mostly classical, but they scan poorly if the conventional pronunciation is used. The language is vigorous and at times brilliant, and all display genuine religious feeling. But from the point of view of the modern reader they are marred by serious faults. Chief among them is their insufferable length. A hymn of Prudentius is hardly ever less than one hundred lines long, and even a grace to be sung before meals is dragged out to the length of 205 lines. His *Crowns* has other faults not less damaging. Martyrs and persecutors alike deliver endless, ranting orations, so that a single martyrdom is over a thousand lines in length. The tortures endured by the saints are told with a morbid zest which probably reflects the taste of the average Christian of the day.

Historical prose is represented at its best for this age by the work of Ammianus Marcellinus, a Syrian Greek who like Claudian wrote in Latin. Having spent many years as a soldier under Constantius, Julian, and Valentinian I, he settled in Rome and wrote a history which would continue the narrative of Tacitus to his own day. When completed, it consisted of thirty-one books, and of these the last nineteen, which cover the years 353 to 378, survive. Judged by classical standards, his style is bad, but it is redeemed by many excellent features. He was a man of active and independent mind, who had traveled widely and observed closely the countries which he had seen. Although a pagan, he was tolerant on religious matters, and a general air of objectivity pervades his work. He admired Julian, but was not blind to the faults of his hero, while his abhorrence of the cruelty of Valentinian I does not prevent him from praising his good qualities. If the earlier portion of his work had survived, our knowledge of the Military Anarchy and the reign of Diocletian would no doubt be vastly greater than it is.

Other Latin historians did poor work indeed. At some time in the fourth century there appeared a set of imperial biographies treating the lives of the emperors and pretenders from Hadrian to Carinus, commonly known as the Augustan History. It was modeled after the *Twelve Caesars* of Suetonius, but was far inferior to its prototype in every way. As we have them today, these biographies have suffered considerably from interpolation, but that is only a minor fault. Trivial and childish gossip abounds throughout the collection. The careers of such rulers as Hadrian, Marcus Aurelius, or Septimius Severus are described with substantial truth, and have considerable historical value, but those of the Caesars, pretenders, and the emperors of the Military Anarchy period are treated with a series of apocryphal anecdotes, forged documents, and a scant modicum of sober truth. Indeed the documents are a distinctive feature of the collection. Suetonius had access to the imperial archives, and drew from them interesting and valuable letters, decrees of the Senate, and other historical matter. The authors of the Augustan History (traditionally six in number) present an amazing wealth of allegedly similar material, but very few of their documents are genuine. So baffling are the questions of real authorship, date, purpose, and method in this sorry collection that modern scholars have wasted much ink in efforts to solve them, and even yet can hardly be said to have succeeded.

Brief summaries of Roman history appeared, apparently designed for the use of poorly educated emperors and officials. Of these the chief surviving specimens are the *Historia Tripertita* of Aurelius Victor and the *Breviarium* of Eutropius. The former, as its name indicates, is divided into three parts — the "Origin of the Roman people," the "Illustrious Men of the City of Rome," and the "Caesars." Modern scholars are willing to credit only the last of the three to Victor beyond question. The whole collection is organized on a biographical plan, each unit being the barest summary of the subject's career. But Victor (and the other writer or writers, if there were any) at least sticks to accepted facts, and gives us a useful — if very bald — guide to Roman history up to 360, the apparent date of composition. Eutropius' work justifies its name by recounting the whole history of Rome to 364 A.D. in narrative form in about seventy-five duodecimo pages. Necessarily, he provides one with only the barest outline, but he used good sources when they were available, and occasionally supplies information found nowhere else.

### *Christian Literature*

The Christians also began to write histories, chiefly as media for religious propaganda. Eusebius of Caesarea, whose work as a teacher has been mentioned, wrote in Greek a *Life of Constantine*, a *History of the Church*, and a *Chronicle of the World*. He was a broad-minded scholar, and his indifference to religious controversy makes his *History of the Church* and his *Life of Constantine* valuable sources. But he was an ambitious courtier, prone to smooth over unpleasant facts in the career of the pious Constantine. In the later fourth century, St. Jerome translated the *Chronicle of the World* into Latin, brought it up to date, and amplified its earlier parts with notes taken from Roman historians.

We have seen how Alaric's sack of Rome spurred St. Augustine of Hippo to compose a refutation to the accusations of pagans that the Christianization of the Empire was the cause of its misfortunes. The *City of God*, which embodies his ideas on the subject, is a monumental work in twenty-two books, the importance of which lies in the fact that it is one of the earliest existing expositions of a philosophy of history. The central theme is that there are in the universe two opposing forces, which he terms the "City of God" and the "City of Satan." The former includes all those persons, living or dead, who are in obedience to God, and their true fatherland is Heaven. Those not in obedience to God belong to the City of Satan. On earth, the two groups are inextricably mixed, and they will never be separated until the final judgment. Earthly governments have nothing divine or eternal about them, but are mere practical necessities to regulate human relations. The good man is a stranger and a foreigner in this world, and should always keep his eyes fixed upon his true home in the skies. The influence of the *City of God* was enormous. Throughout the Middle Ages, and indeed far into modern times, its thesis was accepted by almost all educated men.

But the *City of God*, while the most important of Augustine's works, was only one item on a rather extensive list. His *Confessions* recount his spiritual experiences from boyhood until his final conversion and attainment of inner peace. He carried on an active campaign against the Donatists and also against the Pelagians, a sect which denied that the human race is tainted with the original sin of Adam. Against the latter he propounded the doctrine of predestination, which he took from the works of the Apostle Paul. His correspondence was voluminous and throws light upon all phases of contemporary secular and religious life. Although the Church saw fit to reject his doctrine of predestination, he was one of its most influential theologians.

To supplement his *City of God*, Augustine induced Orosius, a Spanish priest who had been driven from his home by the barbarians, to write a propagandist history of the world. The title — *Seven Books of History to Refute the Pagans* — proclaims its purpose. The glimpse of the past which it affords is like a landscape seen through a distorted mirror. Every calamity suffered by the pagan world, and all its vices, are played up, while its virtues, one-time prosperity, and cultural achievements are ignored or belittled. Conversely, the calamities of his own time (from which he had personally suffered) are minimized. This wretched travesty of history would hardly deserve mention if it had not been influential in shaping the concept of the ancient world which prevailed throughout the Middle Ages, and which in some circles still prevails.

Salvian, a Gallic priest who wrote about 450, takes a different view in his *Government of God*. He acknowledges the plight of the Roman world, but blames it upon the failure of the Christians to practice the Christian virtues. He draws a lurid picture of the vices and frivolity of Roman society in the days of the invasions, and paints, by way of contrast, a suspiciously rosy view of the virtues of the barbarians. Some portions of his indictment may be approximately true, but the bulk of it is so much at variance with other evidence that it must be dismissed as an exaggeration.

Lastly, we must not forget St. Jerome's Latin translation of the Bible, made at the order of Pope Damasus (366–384), and known as the *Vulgate*. From the viewpoint of accuracy it was a creditable, though by no means infallible, production, but as a literary classic it ranks very high. In Jerome's hands, the Latin language retained its sonorous dignity, but lost its compressed brevity of expression. Although classical Latin was amply provided with both pronouns and prepositions, the writers of the Augustan and Silver Ages did not use them extensively, but generally relied upon the inflection of verbs or nouns to indicate their mutual relations in a sentence. This practice demanded the constant attention of the hearers or readers, who had to analyze every phrase or clause, and to parse each word mentally in order to extract its meaning. In the Vulgate this was not the case. A liberal use of both pronouns and prepositions made the sentences much easier to understand, and at the same time imparted to the language a melodious cadence akin to that of modern Italian. In this new form, Latin was fitted to appeal to the emotions as well as to the intellect. From the Vulgate were to come the materials for the incomparably impressive Roman Catholic service of the Mass. The greatness of Jerome's accomplishment is measured by the fact that the Catholic Church has never found it necessary to make another translation.

Like Augustine, Jerome was a prolific writer of theological essays and letters. He was a vigorous propagandist for the monastic life, and he urged his friends to abandon their nearest and dearest relatives for it. From his monastic cell at Bethlehem he constantly exhorted both men and women to flee from the temptations of the secular world to the ascetic career which in his eyes was the only sure road to Heaven.

## The Church in the Late Roman Empire

### *The Clergy and the Monks*

Jerome's work was all the more timely because the Christian Church was, in his day, gaining the allegiance of classes of the population previously untouched, and was elaborating both its institutional organization and its doctrines. We have seen how, in the fourth century, it overcame the Arian heresy, and relegated it to the position of a creed for German barbarians. In a similar way, it repelled the efforts of the Donatists to subject the clergy to the unlimited control of the laity, suppressed the Monophysites, and drove from its midst the semi-pagan Gnostics and Manicheans who sought to corrupt its teachings with elements borrowed from transcendental philosophy or Iranian Zoroastrianism. The theology of the fifth-century Church was, of course, not identical with that of the first-century Christians, but it retained the essentials of the earlier system, overlaid with foreign elements which demand consideration.

The first of these extraneous elements was monasticism. The view that one could please the divine powers by ascetic self-denial and withdrawal from the ordinary life of mankind was familiar to other Oriental religions long before Christianity arose. Only in the third century A.D. did the Christians of Egypt begin to flee to the desert as a refuge from persecution, and while there to practice an ascetic manner of life. At first, each person led a solitary existence, working at a simple trade to furnish him with the bare necessities of life, and spending his abundant leisure in prayer, reading, or meditation. But they drew ideas from Oriental paganism, and attempted to please God by living in hunger, dirt, and general discomfort, renouncing all ties with relatives and friends. Before long, however, the gregarious instincts of human nature drew many of them together in colonies, which held their religious services in common and formulated elementary rules of community conduct. One of the earliest of these was the *Rule of St. Pachomius*, drawn up for Egyptian monks before 350.

In the fourth century, the monastic movement spread to other parts of the Christian world. Syria and Palestine received it very early. St. Athanasius, the great opponent of Arianism, brought several Egyptian monks with him when he came to Rome, where their filthy and squalid appearance at first excited derision. But powerful forces were at work in the West to render monasticism popular. Prior to Constantine's time, the danger of persecution had itself demanded of every Christian heroic devotion to the cause; now governmental favor, wealth, and ambition had brought into the Church multitudes of lukewarm converts who cared little for God and much for riches and comfort. He who would excel must now do more than merely profess the dominant religion. The sterner spirits began to forsake the world, and to retire to monastic seclusion in the mountains or desert. Again, the increasing harshness of life produced by governmental exactions and barbarian inroads drove many to the monastic life as a respectable form of bankruptcy. In the fifth century, colonies of these devotees were probably to be found in most provinces, and model "rules" or constitutions for such groups had begun to appear. One of these, written by the Asiatic Greek St. Basil about 375, is still in use in the Greek Orthodox Church. Not until the sixth century was Latin monasticism freed from its Oriental vagaries by the sane and statesmanlike *Rule of St. Benedict*, and made a useful element in the life of both Church and society. The popularity of the monastic life is one sign that men were losing confidence in the human future.

The cult of saints and martyrs was beginning to appear. Although frowned upon by men of strict views, this was playing a very important part in readjusting the masses of new converts, imperfectly weaned from paganism, who were flooding the Church, and who regarded the saints as superhuman patrons to whom they could appeal in time of trouble. Paintings and images representing these worthies had long been popular, and in some places gradually began to receive a homage not far different from worship.

*University Prints*

CHRIST ENTHRONED WITH SAINTS
*Mosaic from the Church of Santa Pudenziana, Rome.
About 400 A.D.*

Among the clergy, a hierarchical organization was growing up, roughly analogous to the bureaucracy of civil officials, and almost as surely, a department of state. We have seen how the offices of priest and bishop developed. In the fourth and fifth centuries, these officers were still elected by the members of the Church, and they consequently enjoyed far more popular support and affection than any secular official. Very frequently, they served as protectors of their flocks against the rapacity of Roman governors or the cruelty of barbarian invaders. Their spheres of duty were standardized. Every municipality was divided into parishes, with one or more priests to serve each of them. The priests and laymen of the municipality were supervised in spiritual matters by a bishop. The bishop of the leading city of the province outranked his colleagues, but did not at this time enjoy any actual authority over them. Later these *metropolitan* bishops became *archbishops*, with supervisory powers over the other bishops of their respective provinces. Pre-eminent over all the rest were the Bishops of Alexandria, Antioch, Jerusalem, Constantinople, and Rome. They came to be called *patriarchs*, and their opinions on matters of faith and discipline were treated with great respect. Of these, only Rome was situated within the Western Empire — a fact which began to enhance its status. In addition, the Roman bishopric was said to have been founded by the Apostle Peter, to whom Christ allegedly granted the headship over his fellow apostles. So desirable had this post become that, in 367, Damasus and Ursinus, both of whom claimed it, fought a miniature civil war to decide who should have it. But it was only after the division of the Empire that the Roman bishops began their phenomenal rise to the headship of the Western Church. Whereas the four eastern patriarchates were kept under close government supervision, in the fifth century the Western Empire weakened and finally disappeared. It was then that strong Roman bishops like Leo I (440–461) began to play an independent rôle. The part played by Leo in the struggle against the Monophysite heresy, and his intercession with Attila and Gaiseric on behalf of the people of Rome, have been described. At his death the Bishops of Rome were still held in strict subordination to the secular government, and were to continue so for a long time to come, but Leo had given to his office a moral pre-eminence and prestige which it never afterward entirely lost.

At Constantinople, in the early fifth century, another strong bishop tried unsuccessfully to assert his independence from secular control in spiritual matters. John Chrysostom ("Golden Mouth"), a priest from Antioch who was bishop from 398 to 404, distinguished himself by the fearless frankness with which he denounced wrongdoing in high places. He thus incurred the enmity of the Empress Eudoxia, and of his brother bishop, Theophilus of Alexandria. This coalition was able to effect the ruin of the bold prelate. Condemned by a synod which had been packed for the purpose, he was deposed, exiled, and treated so badly that he died three years later. Plainly, the eastern churchmen had no opportunity to play an independent rôle like those of their Roman counterparts, but remained mere state functionaries.

### *The Decline of Paganism*

Meanwhile, the Church had hardly ceased to be persecuted when she became a persecutor. Constantine I had proclaimed complete freedom of religion, but withdrew government financial aid from most pagan cults, and prohibited public sacrifices. His son, Constantius, ordered the closing of the temples, but the order was practically a dead letter. Then came a lull which lasted until the reign of Gratian. He renounced the title of *pontifex maximus* (which made him the chief priest of the old state cults), and removed the Altar of Victory from the Roman Senate house. Theodosius I began the destruction of pagan cults everywhere. He either closed the temples, destroyed them, or turned them into churches. In this work, monkish fanatics were even more active than the officials. Theodosius also punished as treason all pagan sacrifices, either public or private. Thereafter, paganism had no legal existence, although it still retained the allegiance of many of the aristocracy, and the bulk of the peasantry.

The aristocratic pagan usually clung to the old religion because it was associated with the glorious past of his family, the state, and civilization. Priesthoods were often hereditary in certain families, and each generation in turn learned the ancient rituals as a sort of family heritage and title to social distinction. Under the protection of the old gods, they said, Rome had conquered the known world, and had ruled it in peace and prosperity. The immortal masterpieces of Graeco-Roman sculpture and painting were inspired by pagan ideals, as were the poems of Virgil, Horace, and Ovid. Hence the old religion typified to them the world of polished intellectual life and manly ideals, and they decried Christianity as a barbarous superstition, the cause of unseemly wrangling over obscure theological catchwords, and the destroyer of refined culture. This group was not aggressive, but with the proud reserve characteristic of their kind, asked only to be allowed to practice their worship without interference. Some of them were on good terms with individual Christians, and in a few cases they even tolerated the conversion of members of their families to Christianity. They protested against the removal of the Altar of Victory from the Senate house, and a few were implicated in the rebellion of Eugenius and Arbogast. We have already seen the part which this intellectual pagan coterie played in provoking Augustine to write the *City of God*. But, in general, they were not dangerous to the Church, and in the course of the fifth century, the group to which they belonged either conformed nominally to Christian forms, or died out.

The middle and lower classes of townspeople offered little opposition to Christian missionary activities. Their power of resistance had been sapped by the grinding exactions of the imperial government, while the poor, especially, found in the bishops both protectors and liberal dispensers of charity. Also, the building of churches in the towns proceeded rapidly, bringing them into constant contact with Christian ideas. Hence, the fifth century almost everywhere witnessed the extinction of urban paganism.

In the rural districts, on the other hand, conversion was slow, and was bitterly resisted. The peasant had little contact with new ideas, and felt no need for spiritual regeneration. His religion, which was often rude and primitive, was designed to meet his daily needs, and his gods were those who gave him rain, sunshine, health, good crops, and increase of flocks and herds. They satisfied his spiritual cravings, and he cared no more for the new state religion than he did for the other innovations introduced by the all-powerful state. Hence, it is not surprising that the progress of Christianity was slower among the peasantry than among any other class of the population. The ancestral cults lingered in remote sections of Italy until far into the sixth century. In 529, St. Benedict found the peasants of Monte Cassino worshiping Apollo, and about 600, Pope Gregory I complained of the presence of pagans in Sardinia. There can be no question that in Gaul, Spain, and other western provinces similar conditions prevailed.

The conversion of the rustic population was accomplished by a mixture of missionary work, adaptation, and force. The first point needs no explanation. But churchmen also adapted the Christian faith to the mental level of the peasant in various ways. Many of his holidays were harmless merrymakings, which needed only to be given a Christian significance in order to be fitted into the new religion. Thus, Christmas replaced the midwinter feast, Easter, the spring equinox festival, and St. John's Day, Midsummer Day. Innocent forms of worship were also transferred from the old faith to the new. The cult of the saints furnished the rustic Christian with supernatural protectors in place of the gods whom he had lost. Lastly, force was used when necessary. Christian landlords founded churches in their villages, while bishops and monks, with the blessing of the government, destroyed temples, sacred trees and sacred springs, and forced the rural populations into outward conformity. A monument to the difficulty of the task is the word *paganus* (literally "peasant"), which came to denote a worshiper of the old gods.

## Social and Economic Life in the Late Empire

### *A Decadent Society*

Meanwhile, in the midst of invasions, political decay, and religious change, the everyday activities of life had to continue. To understand the difficulties under which they were carried on is to go far toward comprehending the reason for the barbarian conquests, for it was Roman weakness and not barbarian strength which made these conquests possible.

Aside from the ambitious and aggressive Christian Church, the general picture of society is one of regimentation, resignation, and stagnation. This unhappy condition was the natural fruit of the new social order whose origins we have previously studied. To end the constant revolutions and to stay the forces of social disintegration, the emperors of the third and fourth centuries had evolved a system of castes, from which escape was theoretically all but impossible, and each caste was to meet a different need of society as a whole. While the fact was never quite so harsh as the theory, the actual rise of individuals was infrequent, hard, and dangerous. The urbanizing trend so prominent in the early Empire was now reversed. The urban middle class was being crushed out of existence, and most cities were but shadows of their former selves. The wealth, leisure, and culture of the late Empire was to be found among the great senatorial landlords, who lived on their estates and had little to do with city life.

### *Industry and Commerce: The Urban Workman*

Industry was conducted in part directly by the state in great government-owned factories, and in part by the *collegia* under strict government supervision. Each craftsman had to belong to one of these organizations, which he could not leave unless he had a son to take his place. Naturally, it meant that, come what might, he must stick to his trade. Government agents commandeered whatever portion of his stock they chose, and paid for it whatever they chose to give. Taxation kept him poor, and, in addition, he was subject to draft for forced labor without pay on government projects.

Practically our only detailed information about the lot of the working man in the late Empire is that furnished by Diocletian's Edict of Prices. The failure of this law and its repeal show that the prices and wages which it quotes were not actual market values, but we may presume that they state the relation between wages and prices with reasonable accuracy. All values are stated in terms of the copper denarius, of which 50,000 equaled a Roman pound of pure gold. This fixes its value at approximately 7³⁄₁₀ mills, or a little less than ¾ of a cent. The daily wage of an unskilled laborer was set at 18¼ cents with food, while skilled workmen usually received twice as much money and their food. On this same scale, a bushel of barley cost $1.27, or about 7 days' money wages for the lowest-paid class. Beans cost 73 cents a bushel, olive oil (the commercial source of fats) 51 cents a quart, and pork over 12 cents a pound. Clothing was equally dear. Peasants' shoes cost 83 cents a pair, or more than 4 days' wages, while an ordinary ready-made tunic cost the preposterous sum of $9.71, or 54 days' wages. However, the working man probably wore no shoes, and for five days' wages he could buy 5 pounds of wool — sufficient for a tunic, which his wife would make into a garment. Meat, fish, cheese, eggs, and poultry were too expensive for the laborer to indulge in, and, no doubt, appeared but seldom on the tables of his skilled fellow workers. Bread, porridge, and vegetables made up his diet, and there would be barely enough of these basic necessities. The services of a barber at a 1½ cents for a haircut and beard-trim would take but 1/12 of a day's wage, but that was more than a laborer could afford. Above all came the capitation tax and the forced labor which he must contribute to the municipality and the state. In short, while his lot was probably no worse than that of the modern Oriental, or perhaps even of a southern European worker, it was a round of stark and hopeless poverty. But in all this there was one sad consolation: if one were only poor enough, he ran no risk of being made a curial.

*The Plight of the Curials*

The lot of these municipal senators had now become a nightmare. In the fourth century, their public duties, which had been growing harder for three generations, became even more burdensome. Among imperial officials, corruption and violence were the order of the day. Great landlords who had influence with imperial bureaucrats defied the tax-collector, who had then to make up out of his own pocket what they should have paid. Financial ruin, abuse, and a harassing round of duties must have been constantly in the thoughts of the average curial. Many gave up the struggle, to become Christian clergymen, or surrendered their lands to senatorial landlords capable of protecting them, and became tenants. The emperors, alarmed by the prevalence of such conditions, made law after law designed to protect the curials and to keep them at their tasks. But the bureaucracy which was responsible for the evil did not readily obey imperial laws which crossed its desires, and they were openly or secretly nullified. If unable to escape, the curial tried to protect himself by extorting more and more from the taxpayers who remained. "Every curial is a tyrant," says Salvian. Thus, the middle class was largely crushed out of existence. A few of its members rose, by desperate exertions and usually by illegal means, to senatorial rank. The rest sank to tenancy and serfdom on lands once owned by themselves or their fathers. City life disappeared over wide areas, and elsewhere sank to a place of minor importance.

### *The Senatorial Aristocracy*

But as the other classes sank, the landed aristocracy rose. Although few of its members ever sat in the Senate of Rome or Constantinople, they held the rank and privileges of the members of these bodies. They were excluded from the military service, but monopolized all the important places in the imperial bureaucracy. Those who secured magistracies at Rome or Constantinople made it a point of honor to spend stupendous sums to feed and amuse the people. Three men who, in the late fourth and fifth centuries, held the Praetorship in Rome, spent respectively $426,000, $656,000, and $1,500,000 (in terms of gold) during their single year of office. Only a great fortune could support such expenditure, and the wealthier senatorial aristocrats had holdings whose value must be rated in tens of millions of dollars. Even the poorer senatorials each owned several estates, totaling thousands of acres. Even the most active and ambitious members of this class usually gave only a few of their years to government service, and then retired to lives of elegant leisure. Luxurious and elaborate villas, fitted with all the comforts known to the time and artistically decorated, were their homes. When the barbarians began to infest the country, such residences could be easily transformed into fortified castles. While some of these men lived vicious or self-indulgent lives, others aspired to be poets or even Christian theologians. Their wealth was drawn from the land, and was created by the labor of their slaves and tenants, whose condition must be considered next.

### *The Decline of Slavery: The Coloni*

In the late Empire, slavery was on the wane. Even war captives were now more often settled in colonies and bound to the soil than sold outright, and there was a tendency among private owners to grant full or partial freedom to slaves engaged in agriculture. Hence, most of the slaves of that period were used as household servants, and farming was done by a new class of *coloni*. It consisted, in part, of ex-slaves, settled on plots of ground for which they paid a fixed rent, keeping the remainder of their income for their own use. Another of its elements was a group who had, until the fourth century, been free tenants. The lot of the free peasant had long been deteriorating, due to heavy taxation, *munera*, disorderly political conditions, and barbarian invasions. They had tried to better their lot by appeals to the Emperor, by flight, and by armed rebellion. These rebellions were fairly frequent throughout the fourth and early fifth centuries, and were naturally suppressed with severity. In the meantime, the government had applied the same process to them as to the urban workmen. To prevent them from fleeing, and to keep them at work, Constantine in 332, bound most of them to the soil, and his successors completed the process. In so doing, the emperors had no more intention of depriving them of the other rights of freemen than they had in the case of the urban classes, but, again, conditions were beyond the control of emperors and peasants alike. Obviously, a peasant could not safely enter suit against a landlord who illegally raised his rent or abused his person when he had, even if successful, to continue living under the landlord's authority. As the officials were from the same class in society as the landlord, they were naturally inclined to favor him, and even if they had not been, the state made him responsible for the peasant's taxes. Hence, it was the part of wisdom to submit, deprecate the landlord's wrath, and recognize him as the real master of one's fate. At least he could protect his dependents against the tax-collectors and other official oppressors.

## The Character of the Barbarian Invasion

### *Previous Contacts of Romans and Barbarians*

Into this decadent and moribund society came the German barbarians. Our previous study has shown us that the collapse of the Western Empire was no sudden catastrophe. The Germans had been in contact with the Romans for almost six centuries before the abdication of Romulus Augustus. Sometimes they had come as invaders, but quite as often in the guise of peaceful settlers, or as loyal and efficient mercenary soldiers. Long experience had shown the Roman soldier that he could usually defeat them in pitched battles, and although they had at times devastated provinces, up to 378 they had never effected a permanent lodgment in the Empire except by consent. Yet German influence had been steadily increasing for a long time before it assumed the character of conquest and domination.

The Germanization of the Western Empire had passed through a number of distinct stages. First came the service of the border tribes like the Batavians in the auxiliary forces, and the settlement of similar groups in the frontier provinces by permission of the Emperor. The process went on for centuries, the settlers sometimes coming in groups of a hundred thousand persons at a time, and replacing the native population in areas devastated by war or pestilence. The second stage was reached when the Germans began, in the days of Diocletian and Constantine, to form the most effective portion of the military forces. Some enlisted as individuals or were drafted in groups from the provincial settlements just mentioned, and the abler ones rose to high offices in the Roman service. The third stage came when it became customary to enlist whole tribes (*foederati*), who fought with their own arms and under their own chiefs. During this period the number of Germanic generals greatly increased. Arbogast, Richomer, Bauto, Stilicho, and Alaric all served under Theodosius I. Of these the first three were Franks, the fourth a Vandal, and the last a Visigoth. Bauto's daughter married the Emperor Arcadius, and Stilicho's daughter became the wife of Honorius. Toward the end of the fourth century, a rage for German styles of dress swept over Rome. The populace began to wear long hair, and to substitute the Germanic breeches and furs for their tunics, cloaks, and togas. The imperial government forbade these customs under heavy penalties, but the fact that the law on the subject, which was first issued in 397, had to be repeated in 399, and again in 416, shows that the emperors failed to secure obedience.

### *The Process of Invasion and Conquest*

When at last the frontiers were broken, it was not by a sustained wave of invasion or by enormous numbers of invaders. We hear of eighty thousand Vandals, the same number of Burgundians, perhaps seventy thousand Visigoths, and smaller tribes like the Salian Franks, who, in 496, had only three thousand warriors. The Roman population of Gaul or Spain numbered millions. The barbarians had no fixed purpose of destroying Rome or conquering her territories. The Visigoths, as we have seen, came first as suppliants, fought for the Empire as often as they fought against it, and gained their first settlement in Gaul by the consent of the Emperor Honorius. The Burgundians, after an initial period of hostility, were more consistently friendly to Rome, and gained their settlement in eastern Gaul by the consent of Aetius. The same may be said of the Ostrogoths and some of the Franks. The Suevi and Vandals were more independent and hostile, but even they at times took service in the Roman army. When offended or when pressing demands upon the imperial government, they all had their moments of rebellion, when they ravaged the lands near them, destroyed property, and killed or enslaved the provincials. But they usually returned to their allegiance as soon as their demands had been granted or the Romans had displayed effective force against them. Only at a relatively late date, when the Western Empire was far gone in decay, did they become completely independent.

We have seen under what circumstances the Visigoths, Burgundians,

Vandals, Franks, and Anglo-Saxons found new homes on Roman soil. An analysis of these cases reveals that the process of settlement followed one of three patterns. Examples of the first were the Visigothic and Burgundian colonies in Gaul, in which the newcomers were at least nominal soldiers of the Empire to whom a third or two thirds of the land was assigned by imperial officials to be worked by provincial peasants. As the strength of the imperial government waned, the barbarians gradually usurped sovereignty over the whole area. A second form of barbarian infiltration was that practiced by the Franks in their earliest acquisition near the Rhine and by the Anglo-Saxons in Britain. In these cases, the land had been swept nearly clear of inhabitants either by the settlers or by earlier invaders, and the Germans simply moved in, took possession of all the land, and established purely Germanic states and social organization. The third type, of which the Vandals furnish the only known example in the fifth century, was that in which the invaders conquered their lands by force, drove all the Roman landlords from their homes, and retained the provincial peasants to do the menial work.

*The Reaction of the Provincials*

The reaction of the provincials to the Germanic occupation also varied. They had little or no hostility to Germans as such, and in some cases they seemed relieved to be freed from the social straitjacket and galling exactions to which they had been accustomed while Roman subjects. In fact, they had never known any lot but that of passive instruments in the hands of government, and it mattered little whose government it was. But religious differences were a fertile source of discord and prejudice. In the fifth century, the bulk of the native population of the Empire were Athanasian Christians, while the Germans were either pagans or Arians. The former, which included the Franks, Angles, Saxons, and a few other tribes, were cruel and destructive, while the latter — Goths, Burgundians, Suevi, and Vandals — were hated as heretics. Of the Arians, only the Vandals actively persecuted the orthodox Romans. Yet religious differences were, in the end, to prove fatal to all of the Arian states, for they prevented the peaceful amalgamation of Roman and German, and the growth of new, homogeneous societies whose support would have rendered the Germanic kingdom permanent. What might have been accomplished had this bone of contention not existed is demonstrated by the case of the Salian Franks, who by embracing orthodox Christianity were enabled to found a state which has lasted to the present day.

*The Destruction of Population and Wealth*

In spite of the lack of hostility toward Rome on the part of the barbarians, the invasions proved terribly destructive to the works of civilization. In the Danubian provinces, along the Rhine, and in Britain, broad tracts of land had been swept almost completely clear of inhabitants. Salvian mentions that in his day (before 450) Treves had been sacked three times, and speaks of ruined cities in which the naked bodies of the inhabitants lay unburied. Public order vanished. Roads, bridges, drainage works, and durable buildings were either destroyed or fell into decay from lack of attention. Had provincial civilization been in a flourishing condition, such damage might have been quickly repaired, but it was too far gone in decadence to recover from the shock. An active commerce in luxuries persisted for a long time after the disappearance of Roman authority in the West, but the far greater trade in necessities, which had once flourished, died out as travel became unsafe and transportation facilities

*University Prints*

ROMAN GATEWAY

*Treves, Germany*

declined. Gradually a purely household economy and local trade by barter grew up, and remained until the eleventh century. The Roman system of education, which had already outlived its usefulness, died out except among the clergy, where its bare essentials were to be preserved for ages. These changes did not occur in a day, or even in a generation. In fact, it was not until the sixth century that their cumulative effects became apparent. But when they were complete, the ancient world was at an end.

It is impossible to survey the story of the decline of the Roman Empire and of the civilization which rendered so much of its career glorious without thinking of the problem of the causes which produced so great a catastrophe. Many attempts have been made to solve the riddle. Slavery, Christianity, malaria, and exhaustion of the soil, each has been advanced by individuals or schools of thought as the sole cause, and each of these theories has been discredited in turn. Politically minded scholars point to unhealthy political conditions, and economists to unfavorable economic conditions such as the adverse trade balance which drained the precious metals from the Empire to the Far East. A prominent social historian has recently propounded the hypothesis of a social revolution which he thinks took place during the Military Anarchy and contributed heavily to bring the Roman Empire to destruction. None of these hypotheses has gained general acceptance, and the theory advanced by Oswald Spengler, that every civilization passes through a cycle of which the inevitable end is death, has had no better fortune than the others. We can trace the process of decline, but the ultimate causes seem to be beyond the reach of the historian. We must confine ourselves to the summarizing of the steps by which it occurred, and here at least the facts are reasonably clear. The preceding chapters, in which we traced the evolution of the Roman imperial government from a principate to a theocratic despotism, of economic life from the regime of relatively free individualism to regimented government control, of society from a system of flexible classes to one of closed castes, and of progressive atrophy in art, literature, science, and philosophy sum up the process, but they do not disclose the basic cause of these developments. It is better to acknowledge ignorance when it exists.

Whatever the cause or causes, the drama of ancient civilization was played out. In the East, it is true, there was no violent break between the old order and the new, while in the Latin West the death of classical culture had occurred amid the turmoil of barbarian invasion. Yet it was as surely (although less obviously) dead in the one region as in the other. The pagan religions which had so long inspired poets, sculptors, and painters, were confined to rude peasants and effete aristocrats. Classical literature had long since ceased to produce masterpieces, and the greatest writers of the fifth century were found inside the Christian Church. Greek philosophy still lingered at Athens and Alexandria, but it was a mere breath from the past, without a creative thought to ennoble it. The free political life which had once flowed with such turbulent vigor through the city-states of Greece and Italy had given way to a crushing despotism, which sapped the inherent ability of the whole Mediterranean world. In short, the Graeco-Roman culture had reached extreme old age, and the barbarian inroads were only one of several possible causes of its death.

But because the stage on which the play of human life is acted is never vacant, a new civilization was coming to birth as the old one faded. Not all of the cultural heritage of Greece and Rome was lost. In the East, Greek culture blended imperceptibly with Oriental elements, and even in the West, the best of Roman literature, the practical arts, some remnants of the fine arts, Roman law, and the Christian religion survived. With the aid of this inheritance and of that contributed by the Germanic peoples, European man was destined, centuries later, to raise himself to new heights of cultural achievement, and to spread the knowledge of Rome's greatness to lands which the Romans never knew.

# SELECTED BIBLIOGRAPHY

# *Selected Bibliography*

THIS BIBLIOGRAPHY has been compiled on the same principle as that appended to the first volume. Foreign language material, periodical articles, obsolete books, and others which in the opinion of the author are not suitable for use by the average student have been omitted. It is, therefore, in no sense exhaustive, but should be a useful guide to supplementary reading.

## GENERAL WORKS

*A. Bibliography*

Dutcher, George M., and others (editors), *A Guide to Historical Literature*. New York, 1931, pp. 351–354, and section E.

Botsford, G. W., *A Syllabus of Roman History*. New York, 1915.

*The Cambridge Ancient History*, extensive bibliographies of sources and secondary works in Vols. II (bibliography for chap. 21), IV (bibliographies for chaps. 12 and 13), and all bibliographies for Vols. VII–XII.

See also the book reviews of *The American Historical Review*, *The American Journal of Philology*, *Classical Philology*, *The Journal of Roman Studies*, and similar periodicals for recent publications.

*B. Geography*

For works dealing with ancient Mediterranean geography in general, see Volume I, p. 601.

For the geography of Italy, see *Encyclopaedia Britannica*, 14th ed., article "*Italy*," Topography.

Baedeker, Carl (ed.), *Italy: A Handbook for Travellers* (3d ed., Leipzig, 1928), second part, pp. xxxiv–xxxviii.

## SOURCES

*Note:* The history of the Hellenistic world and of Rome has to be gleaned from both Greek and Latin sources. The following list includes the principal historical, literary, philosophical, and technical works in both languages for which English translations are available. Some of them have been translated several times. Without prejudice to a number of excellent individual translations found elsewhere, it is suggested that the student will find most of the latest and most exact renderings either in the Loeb Classical Library (alternate pages of text and translation) or in the Oxford Classical Series. Everyman's Library and the Bohn Classical Library also provide inexpensive and serviceable translations of many of the sources listed below. For critical evaluation of both Greek and Roman sources the reader is referred to the appropriate sections of the text of the present volume.

*A. Source-Books and Collections*

Greenidge, A. H. J., and Clay, A. M., *Sources for Roman History, B.C. 133–70.* Oxford, 1903.

Howe, George, and Harrer, G. A., *Roman Literature in Translation.* New York, and London. 1924.

Mattingly, Harold, *Roman Coins from the Earliest Times to the Fall of the Western Empire.* London, 1928.

Munro, D. C., *Source Book of Roman History.* Boston, 1904.

*B. Histories*

1. Ammianus Marcellinus, *Histories* (Latin). In the beginning this was divided into thirty-one books, which covered Roman history from 96 A.D. to 378 A.D. The last nineteen books, covering the years 353–378 A.D., are extant. The style is bad, but the historical quality is excellent.
2. Appianus, *Historia Romana* (Greek). This work, when complete, began with the foundation of Rome, and ended with the death of Trajan (117 A.D.). Of the original twenty-four books, nine survive, the lost sections being known through epitomes. The extant books are devoted to Rome's wars in Spain, Syria, and Asia, and to her civil wars. As each war is narrated separately, no comprehensive survey is given. Both style and method are poor.
3. Aurelius Victor, *Historia Tripertita* (Latin). A work divided, as the name indicates, into three books. The first two, dealing with the foundation of the city, the monarchy, and the Republic, were probably not Victor's work. The third book, entitled *Caesars*, is a series of brief biographical sketches of the Roman emperors from Augustus to Julian. The style is bald and compressed, but its accuracy is fair.
4. Gaius Julius Caesar, *Commentaries on the Gallic War* (Latin). A record in seven books of the author's conquest of Gaul to the fall of Alesia (52 B.C.). Aulus Hirtius, a friend of Caesar's, wrote an eighth book continuing the narrative to 50 B.C. Although Caesar probably wrote to justify his official career, the factual matter which he presents seems reliable.
5. Gaius Julius Caesar, *Commentaries on the Civil War* (Latin). A record, in three books, of the early stages of the war between Caesar and Pompey. The style and purpose resemble those of the *Gallic War*. Anonymous writers added three more books which bring the narrative down to the Battle of Munda (45 B.C.).
6. Cassius Dio, *Roman History* (Greek). A narrative history of Rome from her foundation to 229 A.D. in eighty books. Of these, books XXXVI to LX, together with large fragments of LXXIX and LXXX, survive. The remainder are known through epitomes.
7. Dionysius of Halicarnassus, *Roman Antiquities* (Greek). A history of Rome to 265 B.C., in twenty books. Slightly more than half the work is extant.

8. Eutropius, *Breviarium* (Latin). A very brief narrative summary of Roman history to 364 A.D.
9. Flavius Josephus, *Jewish Antiquities* (Greek). A history of the Jews from the Creation to 66 A.D., in twenty books. Books XII to XX, inclusive, treat the Hellenistic and Roman periods.
10. Flavius Josephus, *The Jewish War* (Greek). A narrative of the Jewish rebellion of 66 to 70 A.D., in seven books.
11. Herodian, *From the Death of the Divine Marcus* (Greek). A narrative history of Rome from 180 to 238 A.D. It is mediocre in style, but reasonably reliable in content.
12. *Historia Augusta* (Latin). A collection of biographies of emperors, Caesars, and pretenders from Hadrian to Numerian inclusive. Six authors are listed, but the real authorship, like the date, is unknown. The style is uniformly bad. Forged letters and documents abound in some parts of the work. Some of the biographies are of value to the modern historian, while others have little or no material value.
13. Orosius, *Seven Books of History Against the Pagans* (Latin). A propagandist history of the world, written from a Christian point of view, by a disciple of St. Augustine. The style and historical accuracy alike are poor.
14. Plutarch, *Parallel Lives of Illustrious Greeks and Romans* (Greek). A series of biographies arranged in pairs — a famous Greek with a Roman, whose career the author deemed similar to that of the Greek. A number of the Greeks lived in the Hellenistic period, while the Romans, with three exceptions, all lived under the Republic.
15. Polybius, *Histories* (Greek). A narrative history originally in forty books, of which the first five survive entire, together with extracts and fragments from some of the others. It contains a brief preliminary sketch of Roman history from 390 to 220 B.C., and a very extensive treatment of both Greek and Roman affairs from 220 to 146 B.C.
16. Gaius Sallustius Crispus, *The Jugurthine War* (Latin). A historical monograph covering the relations of the Romans with the Numidian king Jugurtha (118–106 B.C.).
17. Gaius Sallustius Crispus, *The Conspiracy of Catiline* (Latin). A monograph on the two attempts of L. Sergius Catilina to overthrow the Roman Republic, which carries the story down to the conspirator's defeat and death.
18. Gaius Suetonius Tranquillus, *Lives of the Caesars* (Latin). A series of twelve biographies of Roman emperors, beginning with Julius Caesar and ending with Domitian. The plan of each biography is topical rather than chronological.
19. Gaius Cornelius Tacitus, *Annals* (Latin). A narrative history of Rome from the death of Augustus to the death of Nero, in sixteen books. Portions are lost.
20. Gaius Cornelius Tacitus, *Histories* (Latin). Originally carried the

history of Rome from the death of Nero to that of Domitian. The first four books, and part of the fifth, survive. As a stylist, Tacitus is hard to equal, but his historical judgment is clouded by his violent prejudice against the emperors, especially Tiberius.

21. Velleius Paterculus, *Compendium of Roman History* (Latin). A brief sketch, in two books, of Roman history from the beginning to 30 A.D. The latter part of the first book is lost.
22. Zosimus, *Historia Nova* (Greek). A narrative history of the Roman Empire from the early third century to about 410 A.D., in six books. Most of Book II is lost. Zosimus' work is marked by a strong anti-Christian prejudice.

*C. Non-Historical Sources*

*Note:* Non-didactic poetry is usually listed by author and title, without further description.

1. Apollonius of Rhodes, *Argonautica* (Greek). An epic poem in four books, which tells the story of Jason's search for the golden fleece.
2. Apuleius, Lucius, *Metamorphoses* (Latin). A novel in eleven books, consisting of a mixture of witch stories and risqué tales of adventure, with a fine description of the Isis cult in the last book.
3. St. Augustine of Hippo (Aurelius Augustinus), *The City of God* (Latin). A philosophic exposition of the causes of the decay of the Roman Empire, in twenty-two books.
4. St. Augustine of Hippo, *Confessions* (Latin). An autobiography emphasizing the author's spiritual struggles and conversion to Christianity, in thirteen books.
5. Callimachus, *Hecale* (Greek). A miniature epic recounting the adventures of Theseus.
6. Callimachus, *Aitiai* (Greek). A miscellaneous collection which explains the origin of various customs and religious cults.
7. Cato, Marcus Porcius, *De Agri Cultura* (Latin). A practical treatise on farming and farm management as practiced in Italy.
8. Catullus, Gaius Valerius, *Lyric Poems* (Latin).
9. Cicero, Marcus Tullius, *Orations* (Latin). Fifty-seven complete speeches survive, of which about half deal with political questions, while the remainder were composed for delivery in the law-courts.
10. Cicero, Marcus Tullius, *Rhetorical Works*. Includes the *Brutus* and *Orator* (Latin) in which the author's theory of oratory and criticism of Roman orators are stated.
11. Cicero, Marcus Tullius, *Philosophical Works* (Latin). Essays, in dialogue form, on law, government, religion, ethics, and metaphysics. Includes *Old Age*, *Friendship*, *Duties*, *Boundaries of Good and Evil*, *Republic*, *Laws*, *Nature of the Gods*, *Divination*, and *Tusculan Disputations*.
12. Cicero, Marcus Tullius, *Letters* (Latin). Seven hundred sixty-four of Cicero's letters, and ninety written to him, survive. They are classified as *Letters to his Friends*, *Letters to Atticus*, *Letters to Quintus his Brother*, and *Letters to Brutus*.

13. Columella, Lucius Junius, *De Re Rustica* (Latin). A handbook on agriculture, in ten books.
14. Frontinus, Sextus Julius, *Stratagems* and *Aqueducts* (Latin). The former deals with military tactics, and the latter with the maintenance of Rome's water supply.
15. Fronto, Marcus Cornelius, *Letters* (Latin).
16. Galen (Claudius Galenus), *The Natural Faculties* (Greek). A medical treatise in three books.
17. Horace (Quintus Horatius Flaccus), *Odes*, *Epodes*, *Satires*, and *Epistles* (Latin).
18. Juvenal (Decimus Junius Juvenalis), *Satires* (Latin). Sixteen in number.
19. Lucan (Marcus Annaeus Lucanus), *Pharsalia* (Latin). An epic poem on the civil war of Caesar and Pompey, in ten books.
20. Lucian of Samosata, *Complete Works* (Greek). A series of about fifty essays, letters, and dialogues, satirizing religion, philosophy, and human foibles.
21. Lucretius (Titus Lucretius Carus), *The Nature of Things* (Latin). A didactic poem in six books, which describes the universe from the Epicurean point of view.
22. Martial (Marcus Valerius Martialis), *Epigrams* (Latin).
23. Ovid (Publius Ovidius Naso), *Metamorphoses*, *Fasti*, *Amores*, *Ars Amatoria*, *Heroides*, *Tristia*, and *Ex Ponto* (Latin).
24. Persius, Aulus, *Satires* (Latin). Six in number.
25. Petronius, Gaius, *Satyricon* (Latin). A picaresque novel, of which only fragments survive. The longest of these is the familiar *Dinner of Trimalchio*.
26. Plautus, Titus Maccius, *Comedies* (Latin). Twenty of unquestioned authorship survive.
27. Pliny the Elder (Gaius Plinius Secundus), *Natural History* (Latin). An encyclopedia of universal knowledge in thirty-seven books.
28. Pliny the Younger (Gaius Plinius Caecilius Secundus), *Letters* (Latin). Nine books of private correspondence and one book of letters addressed to Trajan, with fifty-one of the Emperor's replies.
29. Plutarch, *Moral Essays* (Greek). A series of treatises principally devoted to ethical subjects, but including discussions of the Isis cult, music, table etiquette, and other topics of interest to the author.
30. Propertius, Sextus, *Elegies* (Latin). Four books.
31. Ptolemy (Claudius Ptolemaeus), *Syntaxis Mathematica*, commonly called *Almagest* (Greek). A manual of astronomy and cosmology, in thirteen books.
32. Quintilianus, Marcus Fabius, *Institutes of Oratory* (Latin). A treatise in twelve books on education in general and the education of the orator in particular.
33. Salvian, *The Government of God* (Latin). A discussion by a fifth-century clergyman of the causes of Rome's decline, written from a Christian point of view, in eight books.

34. Seneca, Lucius Annaeus, *Moral Letters* (Latin). One hundred and twenty-four essays, setting forth the Stoic philosophy of life and written in the form of letters.
35. Seneca, Lucius Annaeus, *Moral Dialogues* (Latin). A collection of twelve dialogues on such topics as providence, the shortness of life, and self-possession.
36. Seneca, Lucius Annaeus, *Questions about Nature* (Latin). A description of the universe and of natural phenomena, as the author understood them, in seven books.
37. Seneca, Lucius Annaeus, *Benefits* (Latin). In seven books.
38. Seneca, Lucius Annaeus, *Clemency* (Latin). In two books.
39. Seneca, Lucius Annaeus, *Tragedies* (Latin). Nine in number.
40. Theocritus, *Idylls* (Greek). Thirty of the author's poems are conventionally included in this class, but some of them are really mimes or types of poetry closely related to the mime.
41. Theophrastus, *History of Plants* and *Causes of Plants* (Greek). The only scientific textbooks on botany which survive from the ancient world.
42. Terence (Publius Terentius Afer), *Comedies* (Latin). Six are extant.
43. Tibullus, Albius, *Elegies* (Latin). In four books.
44. Varro, Marcus Terentius, *De Re Rustica* (Latin). A handbook of agriculture, in three books.
45. Virgil (Publius Vergilius Maro), *Aeneid*, *Eclogues*, *Georgics*, and *Minor Poems* (Latin).
46. Vitruvius (Marcus Vitruvius Pollio), *Ten Books on Architecture* (Latin). A technical treatise on the art of building.

## Secondary Works: General Histories

Boak, A. E. R., *History of Rome to 565 A.D.* 3d ed., New York, 1944.

Bury, J. B., *History of the Roman Empire from the Foundation to the Death of Marcus Aurelius, 27 B.C.–180 A.D.* London, 1893.

*Cambridge Ancient History*, edited by J. B. Bury, S. A. Cook, and F. E. Adcock. 12 vols. and 4 vols. of plates. Vols. VII–XII, and III–IV of plates on Roman history. Cambridge, England, and New York, 1924–1929.

Chapot, Victor, *The Roman World.* New York, 1928.

Clinton, H. F., *Fasti Romani: the Civil and Literary Chronology of Rome and Constantinople from the Death of Augustus to the Death of Justin II*, 2 vols. Oxford, 1845–1850.

Duruy, V., *History of Rome* (edited by J. P. Mahaffy and translated from the French by M. M. Ripley and W. J. Clarke). 8 vols. in 16, London, 1883–1886.

Ferguson, W. S., *Greek Imperialism.* Boston, 1913.

Ferrero, G., and Barbagallo, C., *Short History of Rome* (translated by G. Crystal from the Italian), 2 vols. New York and London, 1918–1919.

Ferrero, G., *Greatness and Decline of Rome.* London, 1907–1909. 5 vols.

Frank, T., *A History of Rome.* New York, 1923.

Gibbon, E., *Decline and Fall of the Roman Empire*, 7 vols. new ed. by J. B. Bury. London, 1900–1902. Vol. I.
Heitland, W. E., *The Roman Republic*. 3 vols. 2d ed., Cambridge, England, 1923.
Jones, H. S., *Companion to Roman History*. Oxford, 1912.
Jones, H. S., *The Roman Empire, B.C. 29–A.D. 476*. New York, 1908.
Methuen Series, ed. M. Cary.
1. Scullard, H. H., *History of the Roman World from 753 to 146 B.C.* London, 1935.
2. Marsh, F. B., *History of the Roman World from 146 to 30 B.C.* London, 1935.
3. Salmon, Edward T., *History of the Roman World from 30 B.C. to 138 A.D.* New York, 1944.
4. Parker, H. M. D., *History of the Roman World from 138 to 337 A.D.* London, 1935.
Mommsen, Th., *History of Rome* (translated from the German by Dickson). 4 vols. New York, 1911.
Mommsen, Th., *Provinces of the Roman Empire* (2d ed. by F. Haverfield). 2 vols. New York, 1909.
Nilsson, M. P., *Imperial Rome*. London, 1926.
Pelham, H. F., *Outlines of Roman History*. 4th ed., London and New York, 1905.
Rostovtzeff, M. I., *History of the Ancient World*. 2 vols. Vol. II, *Rome*. 2d ed. Oxford, 1930.
Sandys, J. E., *Companion to Latin Studies*. Cambridge, England, 1910.
Schuckburgh, E. S., *History of Rome to the Battle of Actium*. London and New York, 1894.
Stevenson, G. H., *The Roman Empire*. London, 1930.

## Special Lists

### *Rome*

*I. Primitive Italy*

Homo, L., *Primitive Italy and the Beginnings of Roman Imperialism*, pp. 1–54. (Translated from the French by V. Gordon-Childe.) New York, 1926. (History of Civilization Series, edited by C. K. Ogden.)
Pais, Ettore, *Ancient Italy*. (Translated from the Italian.) Chicago, 1908.
Peet, T. E., *The Stone and Bronze Ages in Italy and Sicily*. Oxford, 1909.
Randall-MacIver, D., *The Early Iron Age in Italy*. Oxford, 1927.
Randall-MacIver, D., *Villanovans and Early Etruscans*. Oxford, 1928.
Randall-MacIver, D., *Italy before the Romans*. Oxford, 1928.
Rose, H. J., *Primitive Culture in Italy*. New York, 1926.
Whatmough, J., *Foundations of Roman Italy*, London, 1937.

*II. Etruscans, Greeks, and the Foundation of Rome*

Carter, J. B., *The Evolution of the City of Rome*. (Proceedings of the American Philological Association.) 1909.

Dennis, G., *Cities and Cemeteries of Etruria.* 2 vols. 2d ed., New York, 1878.
Fell, R. A., *Etruria and Rome.* Cambridge, England, 1924.
Homo, L., *Primitive Italy*, pp. 54–128.
Johnstone, M. A., *Etruria Past and Present.* London, 1930.
Pais, E., *Ancient Legends of Roman History.* New York, 1906.
Poulsen, F., *Etruscan Tomb Paintings.* Oxford, 1922.
Randall-MacIver, D., *The Etruscans.* Oxford, 1928.
Randall-MacIver, D., *Greek Cities in Italy and Sicily.* Oxford, 1931.
Taylor, L. R., *Local Cults in Etruria.* Rome, 1925.

*III. The Republic and the Empire: Foreign Relations and Domestic Affairs*

*A. The Republic*

Adcock, F. E., *The Roman Art of War Under the Republic.* Cambridge, Mass., 1940.
Baker, G. P., *Hannibal.* London, 1930.
Boissier, G., *Cicero and his Friends.* New York, 1925.
Buchan, J., *Julius Caesar.* Edinburgh, 1932.
Byrne, A. H., *Titus Pomponius.* Bryn Mawr, 1919.
Cobban, J. H., *Senate and Provinces, 78–44 B.C.* Cambridge, England, 1935.
Cowles, F. H., *Gaius Verres.* Ithaca, 1917.
Cromer, E. B., Earl of, *Ancient and Modern Imperialism.* New York, 1910.
Dodge, T. A., *Hannibal.* 2 vols. 3d ed., Boston, 1896.
Fowler, W. W., *Julius Caesar.* London, 1904.
Frank, T., *Roman Imperialism.* 2d ed. New York, 1925.
Greenidge, A. H., *A History of Rome, 133–104 B.C.* London, 1904.
Hardy, E. C., *Roman Laws and Charters.* Oxford, 1912.
Hardy, E. C., *The Catilinarian Conspiracy.* Oxford, 1924.
Haywood, R. M., *Studies in Scipio Africanus.* Baltimore, 1933.
Holmes, T. Rice, *Caesar's Conquest of Gaul.* 2d ed. Oxford, 1911.
Holmes, T. Rice, *The Roman Republic and the Founder of the Empire.* 3 vols. Oxford, 1923.
Homo, L., *Primitive Italy*, pp. 129–352.
Liddell-Hart, B. H., *A Greater than Napoleon, Scipio Africanus.* London, 1927.
Oman, C. W. C., *Seven Roman Statesmen.* New York, 1902.
Parker, H. M. D., *The Roman Legions.* Oxford, 1928.
Peterssen, T., *Cicero, A Biography.* Berkeley, 1920.
Robinson, F. W., *Marius Sulla, and Glaucia.* London, 1912.
Scullard, H. H., *Scipio Africanus in the Second Punic War.* Cambridge, England, 1930.
Sihler, E. H., *Cicero of Arpinum.* New Haven, 1914.
Strachan-Davidson, J. L., *Cicero.* New York, 1903.
Symes, R., *The Roman Revolution*, pp. 1–312. Oxford, 1939.
Taylor, H., *Cicero, A Study of his Life and Works.* London, 1916.
Torr, C., *Hannibal Crosses the Alps.* 2d ed., Cambridge, England, 1925.
Weigall, A., *Life and Times of Marc Antony.* London, 1931.

*B. The Empire*

Baynes, M. N., *The Byzantine Empire*. London, 1926.
Baynes, M. N., *Constantine the Great and the Christian Church*. London, 1931.
Bryant, E. E., *The Reign of Antoninus Pius*. Cambridge, England, 1895.
Buchan, J., *Augustus*. Boston, 1937.
Bury, J. B., *History of the Later Roman Empire from the Death of Theodosius I to the Death of Justinian*. 2 vols. 2d ed., London and New York, 1924. Vol. I.
Crees, J. H. E., *The Reign of the Emperor Probus*. London, 1911.
Dove, C. C., *Marcus Aurelius Antoninus*. London, 1930.
Firth, J. B., *Augustus Caesar*. London, 1903.
Firth, J. B., *Constantine the Great*. London, 1923.
Freeman, E. A., *Historical Essays*. London, 1889. Vol. II (*The Flavian Caesars*).
Gardner, A., *Julian, Philosopher and Emperor*. New York and London, 1906.
Graves, R., *Claudius the God, and His Wife, Messalina*. New York, 1935.
Henderson, B. W., *Five Roman Emperors*. Cambridge, England, 1927.
Henderson, B. W., *Civil War and Rebellion in the Roman Empire, 68–70 A.D.* London, 1908.
Henderson, B. W., *Life and Principate of the Emperor Nero*. London, 1903.
Henderson, B. W., *Life and Principate of the Emperor Hadrian*. London, 1923.
Holmes, T. R., *The Architect of the Roman Empire, 27 B.C.–14 A.D.* Oxford, 1931.
Hopkins, R. V. N., *Life of Alexander Severus*. Cambridge, England, 1907.
Lot, F., *The End of the Ancient World*. (Translated from the French by Philip and Mariette Leon.) New York, 1931.
Marsh, F. B., *The Reign of Tiberius*. Oxford, 1931.
Matheson, P. E., *Marcus Aurelius and His Task as Emperor*. Oxford, 1922.
Momigliano, A., *Claudius, the Emperor and His Achievements*. Oxford, 1934.
Platnauer, M., *Life and Reign of the Emperor Septimius Severus*. Oxford, 1918.
Ridley, F. A., *Julian the Apostate and the Rise of Christianity*. London, 1937.
Rostovtzeff, M., *Augustus*. Madison, 1922.
Schuckburgh, E. S., *Augustus*. London, 1905.
Scramuzza, V. M., *The Emperor Claudius*. Oxford, 1940.
Sedgwick, H. D., *Marcus Aurelius, A Biography*. New Haven, 1921.
Symes, R., *The Roman Revolution*, pp. 313–524.
Tarver, J. C., *Tiberius the Tyrant*. Westminster, 1902.
Vasilieff, A. A., *History of the Byzantine Empire*. Madison, Wis., 1928. Vol. I.

*IV. Rome: Government and War*

Abbott, F. F., *Society and Politics in Ancient Rome*. New York, 1909.
Abbott, F. F., *Roman Political Institutions*. Boston, 1911.

Abbott, F. F., and Johnson, A. C., *Municipal Administration in the Roman Empire*. Princeton, 1927.
Arnold, W. T., *Roman Provincial Administration*. 3d ed., Oxford, 1914.
Arnold, W. T., *Studies in Roman Expansion*. Manchester, 1906.
Baillie-Reynolds, P. K., *The Vigiles of Imperial Rome*. Oxford, 1926.
Botsford, G. W., *Roman Assemblies*. New York, 1909.
Buckland, W. W., *Textbook of Roman Law from Augustus to Justinian*. 2d ed., Cambridge, England, 1932.
Buckland, W. W., *The Main Institutions of Roman Private Law*. Cambridge, England, 1931.
Cheesman, G. L., *The Auxilia of the Roman Imperial Army*. Oxford, 1914.
Clark, E. C., *History of Roman Private Law*. 4 vols. Cambridge, England, 1906–1919.
Declareuil, J., *Rome the Law-Giver*. New York, 1926.
Fowler, W. W., *The City-State of the Greeks and Romans*. New York, 1893.
Frank, T., *Roman Imperialism*. 2d ed., New York, 1925.
Greenidge, A. H. J., *Roman Public Life*. London and New York, 1911.
Hadley, J., *Introduction to Roman Law*. New Haven, 1931.
Hardy, E. G., *Some Problems in Roman History*. Oxford, 1924.
Hammond, M., *The Augustan Principate*. Cambridge, Mass., 1933.
Homo, Leon, *Roman Political Institutions*. New York, 1929.
Jolliffe, R. O., *Phases of Corruption in Roman Administration in the Last Century of the Roman Republic*. Menasha, Wis., 1919.
Jolowicz, H. F., *Historical Introduction to the Study of Roman Law*. Cambridge, England, 1932.
Jones, A. H. M., *The Cities of the Eastern Roman Provinces*. Oxford, 1937.
Lacy, R. H., *The Equestrian Officials of Trajan and Hadrian*. Princeton, 1917.
Mattingly, H., *The Imperial Civil Service of Rome*. Cambridge, England, 1910.
Parker, H. M. D., *The Roman Legions*. Oxford, 1928.
Reid, J. S., *Municipalities of the Roman Empire*. Cambridge, England, 1913.
Sohm, R., *The Institutes, A Textbook of History and System of Roman Private Law*. 3d ed. (Translated from the German edition of 1884.) Oxford, 1907.
Starr, Chester G., *The Roman Imperial Navy, 31 B.C.–324 A.D.* Ithaca, 1941.
Strachan-Davidson, J. L., *Problems of the Roman Criminal Law*. 2 vols. Oxford, 1912.
Sweet, L. M., *Roman Emperor Worship*. Boston, 1919.

*V. Rome: Provinces and Geographic Areas*

Boissier, G., *Roman Africa*, London, 1899.
Bouchier, E. S., *Spain under the Roman Empire*. Oxford, 1914.
Bouchier, E. S., *Syria as a Roman Province*. Oxford, 1911.
Broughton, T. R. S., *The Romanization of Africa Proconsularis*. Baltimore, 1929.
Chilver, G. E. F., *Cisalpine Gaul*. Oxford, 1914.

Collingwood, R. G., *Roman Britain.* 3d ed., Oxford, 1934.
Collingwood, R. G., and Meyers, J. L., *Roman Britain and the English Settlements.* Oxford, 1936.
Frank, T., (ed.) *An Economic Survey of Ancient Rome.* 5 vols. and Index. Baltimore, 1933–1940.
Volume I. *Rome, and Italy of the Republic.* Frank, T.
Volume II. *Roman Egypt.* Johnson, A. C.
Volume III. *Roman Britain.* Collingwood, R. G.
*Roman Spain.* Van Nostrand, J. J.
*Roman Sicily.* Scramuzza, V. M.
*Roman Gaul.* (in French) Grenier, A.
Volume IV. *Roman Africa.* Haywood, R. M.
*Roman Syria.* Heichelheim, F. M.
*Roman Greece.* Larson, J. A. O.
*Roman Asia.* Broughton, T. R. S.
Volume V. *Rome and Italy of the Empire.* Frank, T.
Graham, A., *Roman Africa.* London, 1902.
Haverfield, F., *The Roman Occupation of Britain.* 3d ed., Oxford, 1923.
Haverfield, F., *The Romanization of Roman Britain.* 4th ed., Oxford, 1923.
Jenison, E. S., *History of the Province of Sicily.* Boston, 1919.
Milne, J. G., *History of Egypt under Roman Rule.* 2d ed., London, 1925.
Paravan, V., *Dacia.* Cambridge, England, 1928.
Sutherland, C. H. V., *The Romans in Spain, 217 B.C.–117 A.D.* London, 1939.
Van Nostrand, J. J., *The Reorganization of Spain by Augustus.* Berkeley, 1916.
West, L. C., *Imperial Roman Spain: The Objects of Trade.* Oxford, 1929.

*VI. Rome: Social and Economic History*

Abbott, F. F., *Society and Politics in Ancient Rome.* New York, 1909.
Abbott, F. F., *The Common People of Ancient Rome.* New York, 1911.
Barrow, R. H., *Slavery in the Roman Empire.* London, 1928.
Carcopino, D., *Daily Life in Ancient Rome.* (Translated from the Italian by E. O. Lorimer, and edited by H. T. Rowell.) New Haven, 1940.
Charlesworth, M. P., *Trade Routes and Commerce of the Roman Empire.* Cambridge, England, 1924.
Church, A. J., *Roman Life in the Days of Cicero.* London, 1916.
Clausing, Roth, *The Roman Colonate.* New York, 1925.
Davies, O., *Roman Mines in Europe.* Oxford, 1935.
Davis, W. S., *A Day in Old Rome: A Picture of Roman Life.* New York, 1925.
Davis, W. S., *The Influence of Wealth in Imperial Rome.* New York, 1910.
Dill, Sir S., *Roman Society from Nero to Marcus Aurelius.* Oxford, 1928.
Dill, Sir S., *Roman Society in the Last Century of the Western Empire.* 2d ed., London, 1899.
Duff, A. M., *Freedmen in the Early Roman Empire.* Oxford, 1928.
Fowler, W. W., *Social Life at Rome in the Age of Cicero.* New York, 1915.
Frank, T., *Economic History of Rome.* Baltimore, 1920.
Frank, T., *An Economic Survey of Ancient Rome.*

Frank, T., *Aspects of Social Behavior in Ancient Rome*. Cambridge, Mass., 1932.
Friedlander, L., *Roman Life and Manners under the Early Empire*. 4 vols. New York, 1909. (Translated from the German.)
Giles, A. F., *Roman Civilization*. London, 1926.
Glover, T. R., *Life and Letters in the Fourth Century*. Cambridge, England, 1901.
Heitland, W. E., *Agricola: A Study of Agriculture and Rustic Life in the Graeco-Roman World*. Cambridge, England, 1921.
Inge, W. R., *Society in Rome under the Caesars*. New York, 1888.
Johnston, H. W., *The Private Life of the Romans*. Chicago, 1903; reprint, 1909.
Launspach, C. W., *State and Family in Early Rome*. London, 1908.
Loan, H. J., *Industry and Commerce in the City of Rome, 50 B.C.–200 A.D.* Baltimore, 1938.
Louis, P., *Ancient Rome at Work*. (Translated from the French by E. B. F. Waring.) New York, 1927.
Mahaffy, Sir J. P., *The Silver Age of the Greek World*. Chicago, 1906.
Mattingly, H., *The Development of Roman Coinage*. Oxford, 1937.
Mattingly, H., and Sydenham, E. A., *Roman Imperial Coinage*. 5 volumes in 7. London, 1933–1938.
Maxey, M., *The Occupations of the Lower Classes in Roman Society*. Chicago, 1938.
Park, M. E., *The Plebs in Cicero's Day*. Cambridge, Mass., 1921.
Pellisson, M., *Roman Life in Pliny's Time*. Philadelphia, 1901.
Preston, H. M., and Dodge, L., *The Private Life of the Romans*. Chicago, 1900.
Radin, M., *The Jews Among the Greeks and Romans*. Philadelphia, 1915.
Rostovtzeff, M., *Social and Economic History of the Roman Empire*. Oxford, 1926.
Thomas, E., *Roman Life under the Caesars*. New York, 1899.
Torr, C., *Ancient Ships*. Cambridge, England, 1894.
Treble, H. A., and King, K. M., *Everyday Life in Rome*. Oxford, 1930.
Toutain, J., *The Economic Life of the Ancient World*. New York, 1930.
Tucker, T. G., *Life in the Roman World of Nero and St. Paul*. London, 1910.
Warmington, E. H., *The Commerce between the Roman Empire and India*. Cambridge, England, 1928.

*VII. Rome: Education, Science, and Philosophy*

Arnold, E. V., *Roman Stoicism*. Cambridge, England, 1911.
Bailey, C. (ed.). *The Mind of Rome*. Oxford, 1926.
Bevan, E. R., *Stoics and Sceptics*. London, 1913.
Davidson, W. L., *The Stoic Creed*. Edinburgh, 1907.
Dobson, J. F., *Ancient Education and its Meaning to us*. New York, 1932.
Gummere, R. M., *Seneca the Philosopher and his Modern Message*. New York, 1922.
Gwynn, A., *Roman Education from Cicero to Quintilian*. Oxford, 1926.

Haarhoff, T., *The Schools of Gaul*. Oxford, 1920.
Hicks, R. D., *Stoic and Epicurean*. London, 1910.
Santayana, G., *Three Philosophic Poets* (Epicurus). Harvard, 1910.
Whittaker, T., *The Neo-Platonists*. 2d ed., Cambridge, England, 1918.
Windleband, W., *History of Ancient Philosophy*. New York, 1925.
Zeller, E., *Stoics, Epicureans, and Sceptics* (English translation). London, 1880.

*VIII. Rome: Literature*

Bouchier, E. S., *Life and Letters in Roman Africa*. Oxford, 1913.
Butler, H. E., *Post-Augustan Poetry*. Oxford, 1909.
Campbell, A. Y., *Horace, A New Interpretation*. London, 1924.
Conway, R. S., *The Making of Latin*. London, 1923.
Cruttwell, C. T., *History of Roman Literature*. 6th ed., London, 1898.
Dimsdale, M. S., *History of Latin Literature*. London, 1915.
Duff, J. W., *A Literary History of Rome*. 3d ed., London, 1927.
Duff, J. W., *A Literary History of Rome in the Silver Age*. New York, 1927.
Duff, J. W., *Roman Satire: Its Outlook on Social Life*. Berkeley, 1936.
Fowler, H. N., *History of Roman Literature*. New York, 1928.
Frank, T., *Life and Literature in the Roman Republic*. Berkeley, 1930.
Frank, T., *Catullus and Horace*. Oxford, 1928.
Frank, T., *Vergil, A biography*. Baltimore, 1922.
Glover, T. R., *Horace, A Return to Allegiance*. Cambridge, England, 1932.
Glover, T. R., *Virgil*. New York, 1912.
Harrington, K. P., *Catullus and His Influence*. London, 1924.
Henry, R. M., *Virgil and the Roman Epic*. Manchester, England, 1938.
Hereford, C. H., *The Poetry of Lucretius*. Manchester, England, 1918.
Laing, G. J., *Masterpieces of Latin Literature*. Boston, 1903.
Mackail, J. W., *Latin Literature*. 2d ed., New York, 1915.
Martin, Sir Theodore, *Horace*. London, 1881.
Masson, J., *Lucretius, Epicurean and Poet*. 2 vols. London, 1907–1908.
Sellar, W. Y., *The Roman Poets of the Republic*. 3d ed., Oxford, 1889.
Sellar, W. Y., *The Roman Poets of the Augustan Age — Virgil*. Oxford, 1897.
Sellar, W. Y., *The Roman Poets of the Augustan Age — Horace*. Oxford, 1892.
Sikes, E. E., *Roman Poetry*. London, 1923.

*IX. Rome: The Practical Arts, the Fine Arts, and Archeology*

Amelung, W., and Holzinger, H., *Museums and Ruins of Rome* (edited and translated from the German by Mrs. S. Arthur). 2 vols. London, 1906; reprinted, 1912.
Anderson, W. J., and Spiers, R. P., *The Architecture of Ancient Rome*. Revised ed., New York, 1927.
Barker, E. R., *Buried Herculaneum*. London, 1908.
Boissier, G., *Rome and Pompeii*. London, 1905.
Boissier, G., *Roman Africa: Archeological Walks in Tunis and Algiers*. (Translated from the French edition of 1895 by A. Ward.) London, 1899.

Brewster, E. H., *Roman Craftsmen and Tradesmen of the Early Empire*. Philadelphia, 1917.

Carpenter, Rhys, *The Humanistic Value of Archeology*. Cambridge, Mass., 1933.

Carrington, R. C., *Pompeii*. Oxford, 1936.

Engelmann, W., *New Guide to Pompeii*. 2d rev. ed., Leipzig, 1931.

Frank, T., *Roman Buildings of the Republic: An Attempt to Date Them from Their Materials*. Rome, 1924.

Frothingham, A. L., *Roman Cities of North Italy and Dalmatia*. London, 1910.

Gusman, P., *Pompeii, the City, Its Life and Art*. London, 1912.

Haight, E. H., *Italy, Old and New*. New York, 1922.

Haverfield, F., *Ancient Town-Planning*. Oxford, 1913.

Heckler, A., *Greek and Roman Portraits*. London, 1912.

Hill, G. F., *Historical Roman Coins*. London, 1909.

Huelsen, C. C. F., *The Forum and the Palatine*. New York, 1928.

Jones, H. S., *Classical Rome*. London, 1910.

Lanciani, R., *Ruins and Excavations of Ancient Rome*. Boston, 1897.

Lanciani, R., *Pagan and Christian Rome*. London, 1893.

Lugli, G., *The Classical Monuments of Rome and its Vicinity*. Rome, 1929.

Magoffin, R. V. D., *The Lure and Lore of Archeology*. Baltimore, 1930.

Mattingly, H., *Roman Coins*. London, 1928.

Mau, A., and Kelsey, F. W., *Pompeii, Its Life and Art*. New York, 1902.

Neuberger, A., *The Technical Arts and Sciences of the Ancients*. London, 1930.

Platner, S. B., and Ashby, T., *Topographical Dictionary of Ancient Rome*. Oxford, 1929.

Ramsay, W., *Studies in the History and Art of the Eastern Provinces of the Roman Empire*. London, 1908.

Richter, G. M. A., *Ancient Furniture*. Oxford, 1926.

Rivoira, G. T., *Roman Architecture* (translated by G. M. Rushforth). Oxford, 1925.

Robertson, D. S., *Greek and Roman Architecture*. Cambridge, England, 1928.

Stannard, H., *Rome and Her Monuments*. London, 1923.

Strong, E. R., *Art in Ancient Rome*. 2 vols. 2d ed., New York, 1930.

Strong, E. R., *Roman Sculpture from Augustus to Constantine*. 2d ed., New York, 1911.

Swindler, M. H., *Ancient Painting from the Earliest Times to the Period of Christian Art*. New Haven, 1929.

Van Buren, A. W., *Ancient Rome as Revealed by Modern Discoveries*. London, 1931.

Waldstein, C., and Shoobridge, L., *Herculaneum: Past, Present, and Future*. London, 1908.

Walters, H. B., *The Art of the Romans*. London, 1911.

Wickhoff, F., *Roman Art*. London, 1900.

*X. Rome: Religion*

Altheim, F., *History of Roman Religion* (translated by H. Mattingly). London, 1938.

Angus, S., *The Mystery Religions and Christianity*. London, 1925.

Bailey, C., *Phases in the Religion of Early Rome*. Berkeley, 1932.

Baker, G. P., *Constantine the Great and the Christian Religion*. New York, 1931.

Carter, J. B., *The Religious Life of Ancient Rome*. Boston, 1911.

Charles, R. H., *Religious Developments between the Old and New Testaments*. London, 1914.

Cumont, F., *Astrology and Religion among the Greeks and Romans* (translated by J. Baker). New York, 1912.

Cumont, F., *Oriental Religions in Roman Paganism* (translated by G. Showerman). London, 1912.

Cumont, F., *The Mysteries of Mithra*. Chicago, 1911.

Deissmann, A., *Paul, A Study in Social and Religious History* (translated by W. E. Wilson). 2d ed., London, 1916.

Dibelius, M., *A Fresh Approach to the New Testament and Early Christian Literature*. New York, 1930.

Dobschütz, E. von, *Christian Life in the Primitive Church* (translated from the German by G. Brenner). London, 1904.

Foakes-Jackson, E., and Lake, K., *The Beginning of Christianity*. 5 vols. London, 1920–1935.

Fowler, W. W., *The Roman Festivals*. London, 1899 and 1908.

Fowler, W. W., *The Religious Experience of the Roman People*. 2d ed., London, 1922.

Fowler, W. W., *Roman Ideas of Deity*. London, 1914.

Glover, T. R., *The Conflict of Religions in the Early Roman Empire*. 9th ed., London, 1930.

Glover, T. R., *Paul of Tarsus*. New York, 1925.

Goguel, M., *The Life of Jesus* (translated by O. Wyon). New York and London, 1933.

Goodenough, E., *The Church in the Roman Empire*. New York, 1931.

Guignebert, C. A. H., *Christianity, Past and Present* (translated from the French). New York, 1927.

Gwatkin, H. M., *Early Church History to A.D. 313*. 2 volumes. London, 1909.

Halliday, W. R., *Lectures on the History of Roman Religion from Numa to Augustus*. 1923.

Halliday, W. R., *The Pagan Background of Christianity*. Liverpool, 1925.

Hardy, E. G., *Christianity and the Roman Government*. New York, 1894.

Harnack, A., *The Expansion of Christianity in the First Three Centuries*. 2 vols. New York, 1904–1905.

Hatch, E., *The Influence of Greek Ideas and Usages upon the Christian Church*. 8th ed., London, 1901.

Hatch, E., *The Organization of the Early Christian Churches*. New York, 1918.

Kennedy, H. A. A., *St. Paul and the Mystery Religions*. London, 1913.

Kidd, B. J., *History of the Church to 461 A.D.* 3 vols. Oxford, 1922.

McCabe, J., *St. Augustine and His Age*. New York and London, 1902.
McGiffert, A. C., *History of Christianity in the Apostolic Age*. Revised ed., New York, 1906.
Moore, G. F., *Judaism in the First Centuries of the Christian Era*. 2 vols. Cambridge, Mass., 1927.
Murray, G., *Five Stages of Greek Religion*, chap. 5. Oxford, 1925.
Rainy, R., *The Ancient Catholic Church from the Accession of Trajan to the Fourth General Council A.D. 98–451*. Edinburgh, 1902.
Ramsey, Sir W. M., *The Church in the Roman Empire before A.D. 170*. 6th ed., London, 1900.
Rostovtzeff, M., *Mystic Italy*. Oxford, 1927.
Showerman, G., *The Great Mother of the Gods*. Madison, Wis., 1901.
Sihler, E. G., *From Augustus to Augustine*. Cambridge, England, 1923.
Strong, H. A., and Garstang, J., *The Syriac Goddess*. London, 1913.
Walker, W. A., *History of the Christian Church*. New York, 1919.

*The Hellenistic World*

*I. History and Politics*

Bevan, E. R., *The House of Seleucus*. New York, 1902.
Bevan, E. R., *A History of Egypt under the Ptolemaic Dynasty*. New York, 1927.
Cary, M., *The Legacy of Alexander: A History of Greece from 323 to 145 B.C.* London, 1932.
Casson, S., *Macedonia, Thrace, and Illyria*. Oxford, 1932.
Ferguson, W. S., *Hellenistic Athens*. New York, 1911.
Ferguson, W. S., *Greek Imperialism*. Boston, 1913.
Freeman, E. A., *A History of Federal Government in Greece and Italy* (edited by J. B. Bury). 2d ed., London, 1893.
Jones, A. H. M., *The Greek City from Alexander to Justinian*. Oxford, 1940.
Jouguet, P., *Macedonian Imperialism and the Hellenization of the East* (translated from the French by M. R. Dobie). New York, 1928.
Mahaffy, Sir J. P., *The Empire of the Ptolemies*. London and New York, 1893.
McEwan, C. W., *The Oriental Origin of Hellenistic Kingship*. Chicago, 1934.
McCurdy, G. H., *Hellenistic Queens*. Baltimore, 1932.
Tarn, W. W., *Antigonus Gonatas*. Oxford, 1913.
Tarn, W. W., *The Greeks in Bactria and India*. Cambridge, England, 1938.
Walbank, F. W., *Philip V of Macedonia*. Cambridge, England, and New York, 1940.

*II. Civilization*

*A. General*

Bury, J. B., and others, *The Hellenistic Age*. London and New York, 1923.
Cary, M., *The Legacy of Alexander*.
Jouguet, P., *Macedonian Imperialism*.

Mahaffy, Sir J. P., *The Progress of Hellenism in Alexander's Empire.* Chicago, 1905.

Mahaffy, Sir J. P., *Greek Life and Thought from the Death of Alexander to the Roman Conquest.* 2d rev. ed., London, 1896.

Tarn, W. W., *Hellenistic Civilization.* New York, 1930.

*B. Economic and Social Conditions*

Grenfell, B. P. (ed. and translator), *The Revenue Laws of Ptolemy II Philadelphus.* Oxford, 1896.

Rostovtzeff, M., *Social and Economic History of the Hellenistic World.* 3 vols. Oxford, 1941.

Rostovtzeff, M., *A Large Estate in Egypt in the Third Century B.C.: A Study in Economic History.* Madison, Wis., 1922.

Tarn, W. W., in Bury, *et al.*, *The Hellenistic Age.* 2d ed., chap. 4. Cambridge, England, 1925.

*C. Art*

Anderson, W. J., and Spiers, R., *The Architecture of Greece and Rome.* 6th ed., London, 1907.

Butler, H. C., *The Architecture of Southern Syria.* London, 1919.

Dickins, G., *Hellenistic Sculpture.* 2d ed., Oxford, 1920.

Haverfield, F., *Ancient Town-Planning.* Oxford, 1913.

Mach, E. R. O. von, *Handbook of Greek and Roman Sculpture.* Boston, 1905.

Pfuhl, E., *Masterpieces of Greek Drawing and Painting* (translated by J. D. Beazley). London, 1926.

Swindler, M. H., *Ancient Painting from the Earliest Times to the Period of Christian Art.* New Haven, 1929.

*D. Science and Philosophy*

Bevan, E. R., *Later Greek Religion.* London, 1927.

Bevan, E. R., *Stoics and Sceptics.* Oxford, 1913.

Bunbury, Sir E. H., *History of Ancient Geography.* Chaps. 14–18. London, 1879.

Cumont, F., *Astrology and Religion among the Greeks and Romans.* New York, 1912.

Davidson, W. L., *The Stoic Creed.* Edinburgh, 1907.

Halliday, W. R., *The Pagan Background of Early Christianity.* Liverpool-London, 1925.

Heath, Sir T. L., *Aristarchos of Samos.* Oxford, 1913.

Heiberg, J. L., *Mathematics and Physical Science in Classical Antiquity.* Oxford, 1922.

More, P. E., *Hellenistic Philosophies.* Princeton, 1928.

Murray, G., *Five Stages of Greek Religion*, chap. 4.

Murray, G., *The Stoic Philosophy.* London, 1915.

Singer, C., *Greek Biology and Greek Medicine.* Oxford, 1922.

Tozer, H. F., *A History of Ancient Geography.* Cambridge, England, 1897.

Zeller, E., *Stoics, Epicureans, and Sceptics* (English translation). London, 1880.

*The Barbarian World*

Ault, N., *Life in Ancient Britain.* Part IV. London, 1920.
Childe, V. G., *The Danube in Prehistory.* Oxford, 1929.
Hitti, Philip, *The Arabs, A Short History.* Chaps. 1–2. Princeton, 1943.
Hubert, H., *The Rise of the Celts* (translated from the French by M. R. Dobie). London, 1934.
Hubert, H., *The Greatness and Decline of the Celts* (translated from the French by M. R. Dobie). London, 1934.
Kendrick, T. D., *The Druids*, London, 1927.
MacCulloch, J. A., *The Religion of the Ancient Celts.* Edinburgh, 1911.
Minns, E. H., *Scythians and Greeks.* Cambridge, England, 1911.
Parker, E., *A Thousand Years of the Tartars.* London and Shanghai, 1895.
Paravan, V., *Dacia.* Cambridge, England, 1928.
Rostovtzeff, M., *Iranians and Greeks in Southern Russia.* Oxford, 1922.
Schütte, G., *Our Forefathers: The Gothonic Nations* (translated from the German by Jean Young). Vols. I and II. Cambridge, England, 1929–1933.

# INDEX

# Index

*Explanatory Note:*

To avoid the confusion which may arise from the identity or close similarity of the names of different persons mentioned in the text, and to facilitate identification of persons in general, the following rules have been observed in this index:

(1) Names of kings are followed by the names of the countries over which they ruled, in parentheses.

(2) When two persons bear identical names, a brief identification is inserted after each if possible.

(3) Names of Roman emperors are followed by the dates of their reigns, in parentheses.

(4) Other Roman names are generally listed in the following order: family name, given name, clan name. However, if a Roman is commonly known to the modern world by his given name, his clan name, or an anglicized form of either, he is listed under the name by which he is commonly known, followed when necessary by his full Roman name in the conventional order. Example: "Horace (Q. Horatius Flaccus)."

The conventional abbreviations are used for Roman given names. A list of these follows: A. for *Aulus*, D. for *Decimus*, G. for *Gaius*, Gn. for *Gnaeus*, L. for *Lucius*, M. for *Marcus*, P. for *Publius*, Q. for *Quintus*, S. for *Sextus*, Sp. for *Spurius*, T. for *Titus*, and Ti. for *Tiberius*.